SOMME 1916

Success and Failure on the First Day of the Battle of the Somme

PAUL KENDALL

Frontline Books

SOMME 1916
Success and Failure on the First Day of the Battle of the Somme

This edition published in 2015 by Frontline Books,
an imprint of Pen & Sword Books Ltd,
47 Church Street, Barnsley, S. Yorkshire, S70 2AS.

ISBN: 978-1-84832-905-8

CIP data records for this title are available from the British Library

Printed and bound by CPI Group (UK) Ltd, Croydon, CR0 4YY
Typeset in 10/12 point Palatino

For more information on our books, please email: info@frontline-books.com,
write to us at the above address, or visit:
www.frontline-books.com

Contents

List of Maps

Acknowledgments

This volume is the result of several years of research. I am indebted to many individuals without whose assistance producing such a work would be impossible. Firstly I would like to thank Yves Fohlen, battlefield guide, Caverne du Dragon Museum, for proof-reading and for his continued friendship and support. I have known him as a friend for the past fifteen years and have spent many interesting times walking the battlefields of the First World War with him. I value his guidance, knowledge and tutelage regarding the Somme and all First World War subjects. Walking the Somme with Yves was an overwhelming experience; to follow in the footsteps of the British soldiers who advanced upon German lines on 1 July 1916 brought home the enormity of their task in the face of odds that were not in their favour. Despite the number of books we have read and the knowledge the two of us have acquired over the years, we both learnt so much by having the official war history maps as a reference as we walked this hallowed ground where so many British soldiers fell in one day.

I am extremely grateful to Paul Reed, author and renowned battlefield guide, for his support for this project and for distributing my appeal for information regarding this book on Facebook and Twitter.

I thank Carol Walker, Director of Somme Heritage Centre, for displaying my poster appealing for information for this volume and for kindly sending to me testimonies which are held in the museum's collection. I would also like to thank the Ibis Hotel, Albert, and the Musée Somme 1916, also in Albert, for displaying this poster which resulted in me establishing contact with several descendants of soldiers who fought on 1 July 1916.

I would like to thank the Trustees of the IWM, London, for their kind permission to use material from the Department of Documents and Sound Collections. Every effort has been made, but if anyone has not been credited the publishers apologise and will correct the omission on reprint. Now that the veterans of the First World War have passed away the documents and the interviews that they hold in their collections are a lasting link to our understanding of the ordeal that these brave soldiers endured nearly a century ago, and they are invaluable to students of the subject.

In addition I would like to thank Sir Bayley Laurie (son of Captain John Laurie), Mary Ann Dearlove (daughter of Lieutenant-Colonel C.E. Moy), Dick Hubbard (Great nephew of Private Hal Russell) and Diana Stockford (granddaughter of Brigadier-General Hubert Rees) for kindly allowing me to quote from their relatives' testimonies that are kept in the archives of the Imperial War Museum Department of Documents.

I thank Beryl Read for allowing me to quote from the testimony of her father Private Albert Andrews. I extend my thanks to Sue Richardson for her permission to quote from her late husband Neil Richardson's book *Orders are Orders*, in which the testimony of Private Andrews was published.

I am grateful to Nicholas Coney and Judy Nokes at the National Archives for advising me on copyright issues relating to the material that they hold. Alison Metcalfe was extremely helpful at the Manuscript and Archive Collections, National Library of Scotland, for her assistance in gaining permission to quote from the diary of Field Marshal Sir Douglas Haig.

I extend my thanks to Helen Jones at the Keep Military Museum, Dorchester; Lesley Frater at the Fusiliers Museum of Northumberland at Alnwick Castle; Morag Mitchell and Bert Innes at the Gordon Highlanders Museum; Matthew Gamble at the Somme Heritage Centre, Bangor, for providing me with material from their museum's archives. Sarah Stevenson, collections officer at the Fusiliers Museum, Bury, Lancashire, was extremely helpful in identifying testimonies from the museum archives relevant to this book.

I would like to thank the British Library Newspaper Archives, Colindale whose collection I was able to view on site. I also thank the following libraries, in particular Mark Breeden at Lichfield Library, Gwilym Games at Swansea Library, Mary Bradley & Angea McCrystal at Ballymena Library, Deborah Gahan at Barnstaple Library, Elaine Hunwick at Colchester Library, Susanne Costa Duquette at Taunton Public Library, Angela Shields at Grantham Library, Kevin Best at Lincoln Central Library, Susan Canton at Bradford Central Library, John Simpson at Accrington Library, Elaine Hunwik at Colchester Library, Sara Basquill at Lincoln Central Library, Martin Hayes at Crawley Library, Deborah Gahan at Barnstaple Library, Jane Nicholas at Derry Central Library; Mohamad Al at Nottingham Library.

The Commonwealth War Graves Commission's website is an essential reference for any student of the First World War One in cross-referencing facts and I thank them for establishing and developing an invaluable reference source.

I would like to thank Robin Schäfer, Military Historian, Dinslaken in Germany, for his translation of a chapter relating to Hawthorn Redoubt from 'Regimental History of Infanterie-Regiment No.119', published in 1920.

I extend my thanks to Martin Mace and John Grehan at Frontline Books for their support and enthusiasm for this project. I also thank my parents David and Sylvia Kendall for the wonderful times spent in the distant past when we toured the battlefields of the First World War. I also thank my partner Tricia Newsome for her continued encouragement and support.

Introduction

Through the chalky valleys of Picardy the River Somme flows from high ground north from Ham towards Peronne, then turns west flowing through Amiens towards the English Channel. The word 'Somme' is a Celtic wording mean 'tranquillity'. There was nothing tranquil about the region during the First World War when the peaceful villages, picturesque landscape and pleasant woods of Picardy were transformed into impregnable fortresses and killing fields.

On 1 July 1916 the British Army suffered its heaviest ever casualties, amounting to 57,470 in one single disastrous morning. This date is mistakenly called the first day of the Battle of the Somme, for the first shots of the campaign were fired on 24 June 1916 when the preliminary artillery bombardment which was intended to destroy the German wire, front-line trenches, artillery batteries and the morale of the German infantry had begun. July 1st, the first day of the infantry assault, is synonymous with failure, and it marked the beginning of a campaign which developed into an immense battle of attrition fought for a further four and a half months. On that fateful day fifteen British divisions left their trenches on an eighteen-mile front to attack trenches occupied by six German divisions from German XIV Reserve Corps.

Much controversy has surrounded the Somme offensive relating to its justification and impact upon the course of the war during 1916. General Sir Douglas Haig's strategies have been the subject of much debate about whether the heavy losses sustained were worth the small gains made. The high casualty rate suffered on 1 July have given cause to many to regard the operation on this day to have been a complete futile failure where approximately half a million soldiers were sent heavily laden with arms and equipment across No Man's Land towards strongly defended German positions to be slaughtered by machine-guns. That was the case on many sectors on this day, where British soldiers could not get across No Man's Land into the German trenches, however in other sectors breaches were made in the German lines, culminating in the successful capture of Leipzig Redoubt, Mametz and Montauban. The book highlights the failures and successes on that day and evaluates the factors that caused some divisions to succeed in capturing their objectives and why others failed.

Another aim of this book is to analyse the planning process for the Somme campaign and look at the pressures of command that befell General Sir Douglas Haig as Commander-in-Chief of the BEF and General Sir Henry Rawlinson, commanding Fourth Army. Commanders enter battles with the intent to succeed and they were searching for a strategy to successfully break the deadlock of trench warfare. The British had failed in several independent ventures into breaking through the German lines during 1915 including actions at Neuve Chapelle and Loos; as well as taking part in savage battles in Belgian Flanders during the Second Ypres campaign. The French had also failed to make a breakthrough during that year in their campaigns in the Artois and Champagne regions. Modern industrial weapons prevented either side from penetrating each other's lines, imposing the stalemate of trench warfare. Britain and France had failed to find a way of breaking this deadlock in 1915 and it was therefore decided that both countries would launch a joint initiative during 1916 to achieve that goal with a successful campaign.

The book provides a detailed narrative of events analysing each British sector from Gommecourt to Montauban and demonstrated that despite the unprecedented losses and failure to secure most objectives in the German lines north of the Albert–Bapaume Road, Rawlinson's Fourth Corps did successfully capture ground in the south, which would become a platform to continue the fight on the Somme during 1916.

Author's Notes

Please note that when referring to the men who took part in the Battle of the Somme on 1 July 1916 I have used the ranks that they held at the time of the battle. For the sake of brevity the following units will be listed as follows:

Princess of Wales's Own Alexandra (Yorkshire Regiment) will be referred to as Yorkshire Regiment (The Green Howards).
Duke of Cambridge's Own Middlesex Regiment will be referred to as the Middlesex Regiment.
Duke of Edinburgh's (Wiltshire Regiment) will be referred to as the Wiltshire Regiment.
1/5th London Regiment (London Rifle Brigade) will be referred to as the 1/5th London Rifle Brigade.
1/9th London (Queen Victoria's Rifles) will be referred to as the 1/9th Queen Victoria's Rifles.
1/13th London Regiment (Kensington Battalion) will be referred to as the 1/13th Kensington's.
1/14th London Regiment (London Scottish) will be referred to as the 1/14th London Scottish.
1/16th London (Queen's Westminster Rifles) will be referred to as 1/16th Queen's Westminster Rifles.
Prince Albert's (Somerset Light Infantry) will be referred to as the Somerset Light Infantry.
Prince of Wales's (North Staffordshire Regiment) will be referred to as the North Staffordshire Regiment.
Prince of Wales's Own (West Yorkshire Regiment) will be referred to as the West Yorkshire Regiment.
Princess Charlotte of Wales's (Royal Berkshire Regiment) will be referred to as the Royal Berkshire Regiment.
Princess Victoria's (Royal Irish Fusiliers) will be referred to as the Royal Irish Fusiliers.
Queen's Own (Royal West Kent Regiment) will be referred to as the Royal West Kent Regiment.

The Prince Consort's Own (Rifle Brigade) will be referred to as the Rifle Brigade.
Ross-Shire Buff's, The Duke of Albany's Seaforth Highlanders will be referred to as the Seaforth Highlanders.
Sherwood Foresters (Nottinghamshire & Derbyshire Regiment) will be referred to as Sherwood Foresters.

When referring to German Reserve Infantry Regiments, the abbreviation RIR will be used.

It was difficult to determine the exact number of casualties sustained and there are various sets of casualty figures relating to 1 July 1916. In some cases I have used figures listed in battalion or brigade war diaries as well as slightly differing figures quoted in Sir James Edmonds, The Official History of the War Military Operations: France & Belgium 1916 Volume 1 in order to give the reader an indication of the extent of the losses on that day.

Part 1

Prelude to 1 July 1916

Chapter 1

The British Army 1914–1915

On 4 August 1914, Great Britain declared war upon Germany in response to her invasion of Belgium. The War Office were aware of the magnitude of the enormous conscripted German Army and realised that the British Army, which did not depend upon conscription and was entirely a volunteer force, did not have sufficient resources to fight a large-scale war. Britain never felt the need to use conscription; being an island nation it relied solely upon the supremacy of the Royal Navy to defend its shores, colonies and trade routes. The British Army had fought the Boer War in South Africa a decade before the First World War and was still absorbing the lessons from that conflict, with the first decade of the new century being devoted to restructuring the army. Comprising of approximately 250,000 soldiers in 1914 it was considered a small army in comparison to the German and French Armies. The French Army consisted of seventy-six infantry divisions and ten cavalry divisions totalling approximately 2,000,000 men. The German Army amounted to an awesome 3,800,000 soldiers. On reaching the age of seventeen German males were obligated to serve between two and three years in the army. After completing their service they returned to civilian life, but joined the reserves and carried out military training annually until they reached middle age. Both the French and German Armies were prepared for war in 1914, but Britain was regarded as a junior partner by their ally France. Half of the British Army was deployed overseas throughout the vast expanse of the British Empire at the time war broke out, and it could only assemble a British Expeditionary Force (BEF) of 100,000 men, comprising of six infantry divisions and a cavalry division, to send to France. This small army, derided by Kaiser Wilhelm II as a 'contemptible little army' would play a role alongside the French and Belgian Armies in stopping the onrush of the German Army swarming west through Belgium and into France. They held up the German advance at Mons and Le Cateau during August 1914.

The 4th Division which assaulted the Heidenkopf on the Somme on 1 July 1916 had crossed the English Channel to France to take part in the action at Le Cateau on 22 August 1914. Along with the other divisions belonging to the BEF they took part in the retreat to the River Marne where these resilient, determined British soldiers supported the French at the Battle of the Marne and they then pursued their adversaries to the River Aisne where, along the steep ridges of the Chemin des Dames, the first trenches were dug and the Western Front was initially established. The BEF would take part in the race to the sea and eventually find themselves resisting the German onslaught at Ypres during October 1914.

As the BEF was fighting in France and Belgium during the autumn of 1914, battalions from the British Army stationed overseas were being rushed back from bases across the British Empire to fight the German Army in Europe. When battalions had arrived in Britain they would be formed into new divisions. The 8th Division, which was to attack Ovillers-la-Boisselle on 1 July 1916, was initially comprised of regular army battalions which at the outbreak of war were serving in India, Egypt, South Africa and Malta. This division joined the BEF in Belgium during 6 and 7 November 1914.

The 7th Division, which was to attack German positions south of Fricourt and at Mametz on 1 July 1916, was formed in the New Forest between 31 August and 4 October containing three battalions of regulars based in Britain and nine others which had returned from colonial bases overseas. They arrived at the Belgian port of Ostend with the Royal Naval Division and attempted to march to Antwerp, but the German forces had captured the port before they arrived and they had to march south to Ypres where they took part in the defence of this medieval Belgian cloth town.

To strengthen its forces, the British Army had to rely upon reservists and Territorial units which amounted to 140,000 men in 1914. Reservists were former regular soldiers who had completed their service in the British Army and had returned to civilian life, but were expected to return to their regiments during times of national crisis. These men would be assimilated within their former units and were able to mobilise in the event of war at a moment's notice.

The Territorial Army soldiers received orders to mobilise on 5 August 1914. These men formed a part-time Territorial Force, informally known as 'Saturday night soldiers', whose primary role was to defend Britain while the regular army, supported by reservists, fought overseas.

Field Marshal Lord Kitchener, who had been appointed Secretary of State for War, did not think too highly of the Territorials, disdainfully regarding them as 'a town clerk's army'; his opinion was primarily based on his experience decades before when he saw them as disorganised, ill-equipped, lacking musketry training and drill practice. He was not aware that the Territorial Army of 1914 had developed into a well-trained, disciplined, reliable fighting force. The reforms implemented by Minister of War Lord Richard Haldane during 1908 had restructured it into fourteen infantry divisions and fourteen cavalry brigades. They were publicly-spirited volunteers of high calibre and, despite Kitchener's reservations, could be relied upon in times of national emergency. Being a homeland force the men were not obliged to serve abroad, but could do so if they signed a General Service Obligation. In 1914 soldiers from the Territorial Army could not be transferred to other units.

In September 1914 the war took a critical turn as it descended into the stalemate of trench warfare. After sustaining substantial casualties during the course of Mons, the retreat to the Marne and the Aisne campaign, the BEF was in dire need of further reinforcements to supplant the losses that it had sustained. The Territorial Army was called to assist and asked to join the regulars of the BEF in France. The majority of the Territorial soldiers signed up for service abroad and twenty-two battalions from the Territorial Army were in Europe by the end of December 1914.

The 46th (North Midland) Division was the first Territorial division to be considered completely trained for active service on the Western Front. They lost heavily at Gommecourt on 1 July 1916. Before that disastrous day it had arrived in Belgium during early February 1915 where, for several months, it occupied trenches opposite Messines and around the Ypres Salient. It sustained significant losses at the Battle of Loos during the assault upon the Hohenzollern Redoubt on 13 October 1915.

During the first weeks of the conflict, there existed a common but naive perception throughout Britain and amongst cabinet ministers that this war would be a short conflict estimated to end by Christmas 1914. Kitchener believed otherwise and he could foresee that it would potentially take three years to defeat Germany. He predicted that with the BEF already sent to France, there were not sufficient numbers within the regular British Army to sustain a war of that length and magnitude. Kitchener remained resolute in his low opinion of the Territorial Army and, devoid of confidence in their soldierly abilities, he called for civilians to enlist to form what would be known as the 'New Army' to support the regular army. He wanted raw recruits who had little military experience who could be trained and moulded into an effective fighting force. The BEF would need to fight the enemy for two years while this New Army was being trained. On 7 August 1914, while the BEF was preparing to embark for France, Kitchener issued his appeal for 100,000 volunteers. Within the following eighteen months 2,467,000 British men stepped forward to enlist and many would take part in the action on the Somme on 1 July 1916.

Patriotism, peer pressure, the need to escape poverty and the desire to seek adventure, were among the multitude of reasons why many men enlisted. Throughout the nation men were anxious to play their role and 'do their bit' for their country especially during the early months when newspapers reported significant losses as the BEF retreated to the River Marne.

Following Kitchener's call to arms the recruiting offices of the densely populated industrial towns of the northern counties were overwhelmed by recruits. Northumberland raised nineteen battalions, Yorkshire forty-eight, Lancashire fifty-six and Durham eleven. Enlisting with family, friends and neighbours, from the same streets, villages and workplace, these men joined what became known as Pals Battalions. They were unique because prior to the war these men lived and worked together in their own communities. In 1914 they had enlisted together and on 1 July 1916 many of them would die together.

Some of the less densely-populated regions experienced difficulty in enlisting recruits. For example the county of Devonshire would resort to recruiting soldiers for the ranks in other locations such as London and Lancashire. The 9th Devonshire Regiment which fought at Mametz on 1 July 1916 would be informally known as the 9th London and Lancs.

James Glenn was an office boy employed at the general office within Sheffield Council. He was on holiday in Saltburn on the day that war was declared. He saw mobilised soldiers from the Territorial Army going to the station en route to their barracks, but never thought that the war would have a direct impact upon his life. When he returned to work it was peer pressure combined with the opportunity to escape from a mundane occupation that influenced his decision to enlist. He recalled:

> The first thing I knew about it was from my friend at the office. I got back to the office my pal said they were forming Sheffield Pals battalion, my friend came to me and said shall we enlist? I said yes, let's go at dinner time. He said no, let's go now. So we both put on our caps and walked down and joined up. Fed up with office work and wanting a change. It was not for king and country, it was excitement and chance to travel. Certain amount of patriotism to make us join.[1]

The minimum age limit to enlist was nineteen and some lads, too young to enlist, saw the opportunity to join the British Army as a means to escape the boredom and monotony of their current jobs. Many boys left education at the age of thirteen to work in industry, in the coal mines or in offices working for up to sixty hours a week for poor wages. Enlisting, they believed, offered the chance of slightly more money and the possibility of adventure, without considering the reality that they could see action, and might be killed or maimed.

George Grunwell had previously worked as a yarn scaler in a wool mill, but was working as an office boy in a Coal Merchant's office when war broke out in August 1914. Despite being only sixteen he decided to enlist:

> It was thought that the job I was in, wasn't what I wished, it was different from the yarn scaling, but still isolated in a coal merchant's

> office it was rather boring. The change in the Army life opened out a little bit more, more interesting ... My number was 1042 which was when you think of it just over a thousand men form a battalion, so I was getting in at the back end.[2]

Some employers had serious resource problems when they lost their entire staff as they responded to the national call to arms. Sidney Steele worked in a Liverpool office and enlisted together with his colleagues: 'Everyone was joining up, Kitchener's poster was everywhere, the country was in a bad state and the Army badly needed men as quick as possible. The whole office staff walked out.'[3]

Kitchener's appeal resonated across the Atlantic Ocean to Newfoundland, England's oldest colony. At the outbreak of the First World War the colony created the Newfoundland Regiment with the intention of recruiting 500 men to send to Europe. By 1 September, it had exceeded its target and had recruited 800 men. Lacking uniforms they had to wear civilian clothes during their initial training, however there was an abundance of blue puttees which they wore and they would be informally known as the 'Blue Puttee Boys'. They also lacked rifles and 500 rifles were ordered from a Canadian source. It took a month to establish the 1st Battalion Newfoundland Regiment and with only limited training they boarded the passenger liner SS *Florizel* at St Johns on 4 October bound for England. The Newfoudlanders first saw action at Gallipoli, before being transferred to the Western Front. Even distant Bermuda raised its own force, comprising eighty men which they called the Bermuda Volunteer Rifles Corps. On arriving in Britain they were assigned to the 1st Lincolnshire Regiment whose 2nd Battalion was stationed in Bermuda. The Bermuda Rifles would later take part in the assault upon Fricourt on 1 July 1916. British citizens working overseas also returned home to Britain to join up. Alexander Collie, for example, travelled from Honolulu, Hawaii, to enlist with the 1/14th London Regiment (London Scottish).

Just eight weeks after Kitchener made his appeal, 761,000 men had answered the call. It was an enormous challenge to equip this New Army with uniforms and arms; the unprecedented demand for khaki meant that it was unobtainable during the first months of the war. Those recruits from Kitchener's New Army were issued with greatcoats, tunics and trousers made of navy blue serge cloth as a substitute for khaki and much to the consternation of the recruits for they looked like postmen! With a lack of arms these New Army battalions were forced to drill with broomsticks. Training these men also posed a problem, as most experienced soldiers were already deployed to France. This meant that the New Army was trained by elderly, retired soldiers. Accommodating these men also proved a challenge, and most recruits were either ordered to live at home or were accommodated in tents until huts could be built.

While the New Army was being organised and trained in Britain during 1915, the BEF was launching small scale offensives upon the German lines in France. Some of the divisions involved would take part in the operation on the Somme on 1 July 1916. These included the 8th Division which played a part in breaching the German lines at Neuve Chapelle on 10 March 1915. The 2nd Seaforth Highlanders, a battalion of regulars belonging to 4th Division, sustained heavy casualties while serving on the Ypres Salient during the German gas attacks of April and May 1915.

The 29th Division had been formed during early 1915 from the last eleven regular battalions that had returned from overseas deployments, together with the 1/5th Royal Scots, a Territorial battalion from Edinburgh. It was sent to Gallipoli and landed on Helles Beach on 25 April 1915. After the withdrawal from Gallipoli in December 1915, the division was transferred to France.

Divisions from Kitchener's New Army began to arrive in France from August 1915. The 36th (Ulster) Division arrived on the Somme front during November 1915 and had to adapt to life in the muddy trenches during the harsh winter months of bitterly cold temperatures. Entering the unhygienic world of trench warfare was a shock to the system for all as they had to share their trenches with rats. R.T. Grange recalled:

> The mud at the Somme was often up to my knees. I saw wounded men drowning in the mud. The trenches at first were in an awful state with no duck boards or drainage and weren't too wide. The winter of 1915 was very bad and we were not prepared for it. Later we were given boots that came up to your knees which helped. We were also given goat's skin coats but they attracted vermin. The sleeping quarters were very rough, infested by millions of rats. We had to hang things from the ceiling or put food between two helmets and wired round to stop the rats getting at it. In the forward dug outs you were just like rats, some of the dug outs were 30 feet deep with 3 flights of stairs with landings, these were to stop bombs going all the way down into the dugout.[4]

By 1 July 1916, the British force in France had changed considerably since the BEF arrived there in August 1914. That army comprised of regulars, reservists and Territorials. The army that launched the opening of the Somme offensive two years later would be joined by Kitchener's New Army divisions. The 4th Division would be the only division that entered battle on that day which contained exclusively regular soldiers.

Chapter 2

The Plan for the Somme Offensive

As the second year of the war drew to a close the Allies had yet to mount a substantial successful offensive. At the Chantilly Conference held on 6–8 December 1915, attended by General Joseph Joffre, Field Marshal Sir John French and the representatives from other Allied armies, it was agreed that co-ordinated offensives would be launched against German forces in all theatres during 1916. France, Britain, Belgium, Russia and Italy would attack Germany simultaneously in an effort to wear down its strength and resolve. French agreed with Joffre that Britain and France would launch a joint offensive on the Western Front. When General Douglas Haig succeeded French as Commander-in-Chief of the BEF on 19 December, he considered with Joffre how best to implement this plan and the location of this Anglo-French initiative.

The British Army was continually expanding as divisions from Kitchener's New Army, comprising of volunteers from 1914, started to arrive in France. As the new commander of the BEF, Haig had to alter the structure of command to accommodate these extra divisions and corps which necessitated the creation of new armies within the BEF. He had to appoint suitable officers to command these vast numbers of soldiers; and to ensure that these men were accommodated, fed, trained and used effectively.

Haig had little time to adjust to his new role, and he also had to deal with political pressures from above. There were high expectations from the Prime Minister, Herbert Asquith, and his cabinet, for Haig to achieve results and deliver a decisive victory to defeat Germany. His subordinate generals and the men that he commanded sought leadership and wanted someone who would find a way of breaking the deadlock of trench warfare. Haig would calmly embrace these pressures, being confident in his own ability and that of the men under his command.

Haig was supported by General Sir William Robertson, who had been appointed Chief of Imperial General Staff on 23 December 1915. The size of the BEF far exceeded the army commanded by Wellington during the

Napoleonic Wars a century earlier, it was the largest British force employed to date and Haig was in command of it. Although he was familiar with the problems that faced the Allies in breaking the stalemate of trench warfare, Haig insisted that a full review of the situation be carried out so that he could examine the problems once again.

There were further pressures upon Haig for his remit was not solely confined to being a battlefield commander. As well as being responsible for administration, logistics, training and development of his army into an effective fighting force, together with the general welfare of the men under his vast command, he had also to be a politician who had to foster a relationship with his French ally, General Joseph Joffre, who was pressing for a major British offensive in 1916. Kitchener had instructed Haig that he was to support and co-operate with the French and Belgian armies in their efforts to drive their common enemy, Germany, from French and Belgian soil.

Haig's first meeting with Joffre took place at Chantilly on 29 December 1915. Although the planned offensive for the coming year was prominent on the agenda, they also discussed the possibility of German offensives in the direction of Roye-Montdidier and south of Arras. Thoughts of offensive action later in 1916 were replaced with defensive measures on how to confront this probable German initiative. Joffre requested the BEF to relieve the French Tenth Army on the Somme sector. With German forces massing in these regions Haig thought it imperative to form a significant-sized reserve, which would form the Fourth Army.

Between January and July 1916 large numbers of troops from the New Armies recruited by Kitchener during autumn 1914 began to arrive in France to bolster the British Army from 450,000 to 660,000 troops. Many of these soldiers had still to complete their training and it was Haig's view that the longer the offensive could be deferred the more effective these men would become, thus increasing the chances of a successful offensive.

During January 1916 Haig settled in his general Headquarters at Château de Beaurepaire at Montreuil. This Picardy town, positioned on the Canche River, was close to Etaples and it was here that the new Commander-in-Chief concentrated on reorganising the BEF, and made efforts to improve communication. On 8 January 1916, he convened his first meeting with his three army commanders and stated his intention to hold these meetings every week at the HQ of each Army in rotation, with the purpose of developing 'mutual understanding and closer touch'[1] with the commanders and between their staffs. It was during this meeting that Haig briefed them about the planned offensive operations for the forthcoming year and ordered them to devise schemes for:

a.) preliminary operations to wear out the enemy and exhaust his reserves and

> b.) for a decisive attack made with the object of piercing the enemy's line of defence.[2]

Haig had played a prominent role in writing the Field Service Regulations several years before the war and he reminded his subordinates of 'the importance of good staff work and the need for adhering to the principles of FSR [Field Service Regulations] Part II'.[3]

On 18 January 1916, Haig discussed with Lieutenant-General Sir Launcelot Kiggell, his Chief of Staff, the forthcoming strategy and principals for the offensive planned for that year. It was decided that the two aims were to wear down German forces and make a breakthrough that would lead to ultimate victory. It was important that all Allies attacked German forces in all sectors in a simultaneous attack on their respective fronts. Concerns were expressed about the Eastern Front, as Russia might not be in a position to launch an offensive until mid-summer 1916, during which time Germany might defeat her and negotiate a peace settlement.

Haig had to consider the state of his army, their abilities, strengths and weaknesses before committing to a date for the assault. He also had to contemplate the agendas of politicians at home and of their Allies, as well as consider the readiness of the French, Russian and Italian armies in order to launch a co-ordinated attack. This was an extremely difficult and complex situation that increased the pressure upon the newly appointed Commander-in-Chief.

During January 1916, Haig appointed General Sir Henry Rawlinson as commander of the newly-created Fourth Army and ordered him to take up his appointment on 1 March. Haig had already asked General Sir Edmund Allenby, commanding Third Army, to investigate the possibility of launching an offensive on the sector that they were holding on the Somme. However Haig preferred to launch this campaign on the Ypres sector in order to secure the Belgian coast, and capture the submarine base at Bruges whose submarines from the Flanders Flotilla were threatening British merchant vessels. So he and Rawlinson began assessing the situation in Belgian Flanders to devise a plan.

Haig's strategic preferences were compromised by his loyalty to Joffre, who had different ideas about the future strategy of the war. Haig received a letter from Joffre on 26 January proposing that the British should launch two preliminary attacks in April and May 1916 to wear down German reserves before the main offensive. Haig was reluctant to embark on this strategy fearing that he would exhaust his own army in the process and that the enterprise would fail, resulting in damage to the reputation and prestige of the British Army. In his diary on 28 January Haig wrote:

> I decide that we must let Joffre know at once my views, namely that such attacks as he proposes will be of the nature of attacks in detail, will

> wear us out almost more than the enemy, will appear to the enemy, to our troops and to neutrals, like the French and our own previous attacks which could not breakthrough and be classed as 'failures', thereby affecting our 'credit' in the world which is of vital importance as money in England is becoming scarcer.[4]

David Lloyd George, Minister of Munitions, paid his first visit to Haig's Headquarters at Montreuil on 30 January 1916. The personalities of these two men were different and they failed to form a cordial relationship. Brigadier-General John Charteris, Haig's Chief of Intelligence, recalled their inauspicious meeting: 'Although Haig appreciated Mr Lloyd George's vitality, there was nothing in common between the outlook of the two men, and the seeds of a deep and mutual distrust were already sown.'[5]

At a conference at Chantilly held on 14 February, Joffre continued to persuade Haig to launch an attack upon the German's towards the end of April in an effort to wear them down requesting that the BEF take over the sector currently being held by the French Tenth Army on the Somme. Joffre favoured a joint operation astride the Somme, not for strategic purposes, but simply because the French Army would be adjacent to the British on this sector. There was no tactical advantage to be gained advancing thirty miles into the German lines at the Somme and it would not end the war. Haig resisted Joffre's requests but conceded that the British Army would be ready to relieve the French Tenth Army by winter 1916.

A spirit of goodwill and co-operation prevailed between Haig and Joffre. Haig had succeeded in developing and strengthening their relationship, something which his predecessor French had failed to do. Rawlinson wrote to a friend about the improvement in the Entente Cordiale between the two commanders:

> You need have no anxiety as to D.H. getting on well with our Allies. He went down to Chantilly the other day and had a most cordial meeting with Pére Joffre. He has since gone down again to be present at the meeting of army group commanders and talk over future plans. So I think our co-operation in the future will be much closer than it has been.[6]

Haig's and Joffre's intentions to initiate offensive operations in 1916 were seriously undermined by General Erich von Falkenhayn, German Chief of General Staff, who would dictate and determine proceedings from February to the summer of 1916, by launching a German assault at Verdun.

On 19 February Haig was informed by French General de Castelnau, that it was feared that German forces were about to launch an assault upon Verdun. Haig pledged to Joffre that if Verdun were attacked then he would endeavour to relieve the French Tenth Army on the Somme sector much sooner. Haig chaired an Army Commander's conference on that day and it were agreed that reconnaissance of the Somme sector would be made in anticipation that Verdun would be attacked.

As anticipated, German forces assaulted Verdun on 21 February, putting an enormous strain upon the French Army. Verdun possessed tremendous national symbolism to the French and they were determined to defend it at all costs. The Germans had captured the northern sector of the Verdun salient and penetrated 2,000 yards into French lines, gaining a great observation position that overlooked Verdun. A battle of attrition developed causing heavy losses to the French. The fighting at Verdun could jeopardise the joint Anglo-Franco operation planned for later that year, more importantly a French defeat at Verdun could result in losing the war.

Haig was concerned that German forces might attack on the British sector and he was mindful that his army consisted of inexperienced, untrained troops with no substantial artillery or stores of munitions available to support them. He lacked confidence in their ability to resist a German offensive at that time. The strength of the British Army in France and Flanders amounted to 1,047,000 men by 13 February 1916. Haig wanted more men in order to fight the war effectively. He wanted a further 81,159 men before considering launching a new offensive.[7]

Fearing a German attack on the British sector, Haig was conscious that the BEF might being overrun and if the Channel ports were lost then they risked being cut off from Britain. Haig raised these concerns with Joffre at Chantilly on 24 February 1916:

> I called his attention to the possibility of the enemy attacking on the front Bethune–Arras … the railways towards Lille were very numerous and favoured a rapid concentration on that front. Moreover by breaking our line in that area, and then striking northwards, first, the enemy might destroy two thirds of the British Army, which is not yet fully trained or armed with artillery, the Belgians and also gain the ports between Boulogne and Dunkirk, thus cutting our communications with England.[8]

Haig returned to London on 25 February to meet Kitchener at the War Office where they discussed the possible scenarios that the BEF could face if the situation at Verdun deteriorated. Haig wrote:

> I told him that I thought we ought to be prepared for one of three situations arising as a result of the fighting at Verdun:
> 1. A kind of stalemate. Both sides having lost very heavily, and the French (owing to the lack of reserves of men and ammunition) unable and unwilling to carry out a vigorous offensive again.
> In my opinion, our action should then be to ask the French to take over some of the front from us so as to set free as many troops of ours as

> possible for a large offensive. In this case, or attack should be on the front from Ypres to Armentieres in the direction of the Dutch frontier north of the Lys.
>
> If, however, the French have sufficient troops left for the general attack, then we should make our attack alongside of theirs, say, astride the Somme (as already proposed by Joffre).
>
> 2. In the case of success. We must attack at once on the front of the Third Army. The enemy will probably have had to reduce the numbers of his troops holding the front if he has suffered a check at Verdun.
>
> 3. In the case of disaster. We must counter-attack at once close to where the French have broken. I do not think an attack on the front of our Third Army in such case would do any good. This attack cannot be ready to start at once because there must be delay in preparing for it, which people would attribute to a determination to do nothing! Also the German line would not have been weakened, as would most likely be the case in the event of the Germans receiving a check.[9]

This precarious, uncertain situation would intensify the strain upon Haig. The Allied coalition was in danger of collapse, with the French desperately clinging onto Verdun. Haig had no choice but to act quickly to relieve the pressure placed upon the French army and keep France in the war. As the French were committed to defending Verdun it meant that Joffre was unable to commit vast numbers of troops to the British/French operation that they were planning to launch during 1916. Before the German army attacked Verdun, Joffre was going to deploy thirty-nine French divisions. Now, though, French resources were extremely stretched and Joffre could only offer five French divisions to support the proposed Anglo-French offensive.

The British Army would now be expected to launch this operation with limited French support and sooner rather than later. Haig's predicament was that he knew he needed to deploy his forces early to assist France, but was only too aware that his troops were not ready for engagement in an offensive during spring 1916. Future planning of the Anglo-French offensive would be transformed into a reactionary measure to divert German troops from Verdun.

Rawlinson took up his appointment as Fourth Army commander on 1 March. Six days later Fourth Army was ordered to launch an assault during 1916 and it was left to him to formulate a strategy for an attack on the Somme in a joint offensive with the French Army. This was to take place in either June or July, but before that could happen, another offensive might have to be launched earlier in April to relieve the pressure upon the French at Verdun.

Haig had reassured Rawlinson by advising him that Fourth Army would be reinforced with another Corps. Rawlinson would be also supported with heavy artillery with one howitzer per 100 yards of front to be assaulted. Rawlinson directed his Corps commanders to commence with the preliminary preparations, directing them to focus upon selecting locations for ammunition dumps, batteries, establishing observation posts and the lying of cables for communication.

As British divisions arrived in France, Haig was still not confident of the capabilities of the British army in its ability to fight without further training. Haig expressed his concerns to Kitchener on 29 March:

> I said that I had never had any intention of attacking with all available troops except in an emergency to save the French, and Paris perhaps, from capture. Meantime, I am strengthening the long line which I have recently taken over, and training the troops. I have not got an Army in France really, but a collection of Divisions untrained for the field. The actual fighting Army will be evolved from them.[10]

This diary entry reveals his awareness of his force's weaknesses and that he advocated thorough preparation and training of his army before embarking on any offensive. The battle for Verdun was, of course, sapping the strength of the German army as much as the French, and if Haig could delay the British offensive for as long as possible not only would this and so give him more time to train the New Army, but also the German army would be so weakened that there would be a greater chance of a successful British offensive in July.

Rawlinson established his headquarters at Château de Querrieu, close to Amiens, twelve miles behind the front line where he set about making plans for his Somme offensive. Rawlinson's planning was interrupted when he caught influenza during March and was compelled to take two weeks' leave to recover in the south of France. Brigadier-General Archie Montgomery, his Chief General Staff Officer, was left to continue with a draft plan.

Rawlinson returned to complete the plan which favoured his 'bite and hold' strategy, and submitted the proposal to Haig on 4 April 1916. Rawlinson highlighted the risk of committing untrained and ill-prepared troops into a campaign too soon. With an uncertain date and limited time to prepare these inexperienced troops, he commented:

> It would be in, my opinion, a mistake to have a plan for the 31 May which would need any important modification should it have to be undertaken at an earlier date, as it might lead to confusion and delay in the preparations just at a time when speed would be of the greatest importance.[11]

Rawlinson's plan, with the objectives that he believed could be realistically gained, were based on the limited number of soldiers and howitzers allotted for Fourth Army's use. Seventeen infantry divisions and one cavalry division were made available, excluding reserves. The offensive was expected to last for no more than two weeks. Rawlinson was anticipating the use of 200 heavy howitzers of 6in, 8in and 9.2in calibre. It was Rawlinson's view that the infantry and artillery resources available to him were not sufficient to attack a front larger than 20,000 yards or a depth greater than 4,000 to 5,000 yards. Fourth Army would make the attack with a further Corps held in reserve. He also proposed an assault on Gommecourt to protect the northern flank of Fourth Army.

Rawlinson was confident that the field guns and trench mortars made available to him would destroy the enemy wire and that heavy howitzers and heavy trench mortars were capable of pulverising a large proportion of the first German trench system. If they were to strive for a deeper thrust into the German lines then the number of targets behind the German lines would be increased, which would require more ammunition and would potentially diminish the intensity of the overall bombardment and softening up of the German defences. Rawlinson held reservations about successfully assaulting the German second line at Pozières. He wrote:

> When, however we come to the second line, considerable difficulty arises. South of the Albert–Bapaume Road near Pozières this line is over 4,000 yards from our front line trenches and being on the reverse slope is almost entirely unobserved from our line. It will be difficult to deal with this part of the second line, and especially with the wire, until we have advanced a considerable distance beyond our present line. I do not therefore propose to include the second line south of Pozières in the objective allotted to the Corps.[12]

He presented two options for artillery bombardment; either an intensive bombardment using every available howitzer to pound the German front line five to six hours prior to the assault; or a less intensive barrage, targeting enemy strong points forty-eight to seventy-two hours before the assault. The infantry would either aim to rush the entire German defences in one thrust as they did at Loos in 1915, or advance in two stages. The first stage was the capture of the front line trenches before taking the reserve lines in stage two. Choice of strategy depended upon the strength of the German first and second lines and number of reserves the enemy had in support. Rawlinson considered:

> If the enemy's supports and reserves are in sufficient numbers and near enough to man the rear defences before our leading lines reach them the chances are against our first rush getting through, especially if the wire in front of this line cannot be destroyed.'[13]

On the other hand, he conceded, 'there may be, as has happened in the past, a panic and loss of morale, due to surprise and the severity of the bombardment, which it is of the highest importance to take immediate advantage of.'[14]

However, Rawlinson was concerned that the German machine-guns would survive the bombardment and thwart the operation. He considered the implications if German machine-gunners were able to defend their position and was worried that his inexperienced troops would become disorganised as they advanced across shell-cratered ground fired upon by Maxim machine-guns which could hold them up. At the planning stage Rawlinson was mindful of the destructive capabilities of even a small number of well-positioned machine-guns:

> Unless very well disciplined indeed, it is hard to reorganise them to meet a counter-attack. This is important, as it must be remembered that neither our new formations nor the Old Divisions have the same discipline that obtained in our Army of a year ago.[15]

The assault was scheduled to begin on 31 May and it was stated that no modification was required if the date was brought forward to 1 May, but Rawlinson emphasised that if heavy losses were sustained during the first phase of the attack, then they would be unable to proceed to the second phase in its entirety. If the initial attack failed then it would be hard to reassemble the remnants of the attacking force to launch a second attack. In conclusion, Rawlinson recognised that whatever strategy they followed would be a gamble and doubted that any benefit would be gained by sacrificing Fourth Army as a means of diverting German forces from Verdun. He wrote:

> To sum up, an attempt to rush the whole of the enemy's defences in one rush will, under the conditions that obtain, involve very serious risks and will be in the nature a gamble. Speaking with only a limited knowledge of the general situation it us open to question whether the gamble is worth the risks involved.
> It does not appear to me that the gain of 2 or 3 kilometres of ground is of much consequence, or that the existing situation is so urgent as to demand that we should incur heavy losses in order to draw a large number of German reserves against this portion of our front.[16]

Rawlinson considered that if an attack was to be launched on the Somme it would be with the intent to kill as many opposing soldiers as possible with minimal losses, capture their front-line trenches and invite the enemy to try to regain it. Rawlinson wrote:

> Our forward object rather seems to be to kill as many Germans as possible with the least loss to ourselves, and the best way to do this

> appears to me to be to seize points of tactical importance which will provide us with good observation and which we may feel quite certain the Germans will counter-attack. These points to be, not only ones of special tactical importance with a view to further advance, but to be such that the Germans will be compelled to counter-attack them under disadvantages likely to conduce heavy losses; which we can only ensure if these tactical points are not too far distant from our gun positions.[17]

Rawlinson therefore opted for the plan to capture the front line trenches before taking the reserve lines. Instead of an intensive bombardment lasting few hours before the assault, Rawlinson thought that it would be best if there was a prolonged bombardment that would, if not kill the enemy, wear down his resolve, shatter his nerves and make him hungry and thirsty and in poor physical condition to resist the British attack

> The moral effect of a prolonged bombardment with an effective back barrage to prevent food and ammunition being brought forward to the front line is no doubt very great indeed, as was proved … at Loos. [18]

It was at Loos during September 1915 that the British Army employed gas as a weapon for the first time and it failed because the wind blew in the direction of their own troops instead of the German positions. Rawlinson decided not to use gas on the Somme because of the unreliability of the wind direction, and that German soldiers were issued with gas masks which countered this threat. Instead he opted to use gas on the defensive flanks and smoke to conceal the movement of troops as they advanced towards the German lines. This was to deceive the enemy into thinking that the British would be using gas, which would induce them to put on their cumbersome and uncomfortable gas masks, hindering their ability to resist the British troops as they reached their trenches.

> As regards gas, generally speaking, now that the enemy is provided with efficient masks, it appears to me that the disadvantages of using gas outweigh the advantages on account of its dependence on a suitable wind, its danger to our own troops, and the handicap to our men of masks when assaulting.
>
> The last two objections, however, do not apply to the use of gas on fronts not to be assaulted, when the wind is favourable. I propose, therefore, to employ gas to the fullest extent of the two defensive fronts at Maricourt and Hébuterne and to employ just sufficient gas mixed with smoke along the fronts to be attacked, to compel the enemy to put on his masks and thus place him at a disadvantage to our men who will not be wearing masks.[19]

Rawlinson wanted to launch an attack with the intention of capturing the first German trenches falling short of the German second line that ran across Pozières. Here the advance would pause for three days where they could resist German counter-attacks, while British artillery could be brought forward, before proceeding to capture the second line.

Haig's aims for the Somme offensive were different to Rawlinson's. The latter preferred the cautious approach where limited objectives would be captured and then defended against the predicted German counter-attack, while Haig preferred rapid deep penetration through German lines to break the stalemate of trench warfare and resume the war of movement. Haig wrote in his diary on 5 April:

> I studied Sir H. Rawlinson's proposals for attack. His intention is merely to take the enemy's first and second system of trenches and 'kill Germans'. He looks upon the gaining of three or four kilometres more or less of ground immaterial. I think we can do better than this by aiming or getting as large a combined force of French and British across the Somme and fighting the enemy in the open.[20]

Haig summoned Rawlinson and Major-General Archie Montgomery to his HQ at Querrieu to discuss the offensive. He thought that Rawlinson's plan to capture the first and second trenches too cautious and the long preparatory bombardment, lasting several days, would alert the enemy to an attack, thus losing the element of surprise. Haig wanted to catch the enemy off-guard with an intensive bombardment shortly before the moment of attack, lasting for five to six hours and to drive deeper into the German lines. Rawlinson made no provision for the use of cavalry and insisted that they should be held in reserve until the tactical situation was conducive to their deployment.

Haig rejected Rawlinson's initial proposal. Rawlinson had to revise the plan to accommodate Haig's desire to drive deeper into the German lines, capturing the first and second German trench systems in the first phase of the attack. He also had to revise the plan for the southern sector of the assault, aligning it to the French attack on the British right flank. This placed Rawlinson and Montgomery in a difficult position. They had devised the initial plan based on infantry and artillery allotted to Fourth Army, as confirmed by CIGS Robertson. If they were to extend the depth of the advance where would they obtain the extra troops and guns in order to carry out Haig's orders? Only limited resources were available and the more ambitious Haig's expectations became the chances of a successful outcome diminished.

Haig had overlooked the fact that although he could surprise the enemy with a hurricane bombardment, such a barrage over the course of several hours would not be sufficient to cut the wire across the entire British sector within a short space of time. The sector to be attacked was much larger than the line attacked at Neuve Chapelle during 1915. In order to cut the wire, at least four days would be required. His intention to capture the second German line did not make provision for the fact while British infantry advanced across No Man's Land and across the first German trench system, German reinforcements would be brought forward to the second line to meet them. They would be strong, not having been under bombardment, and the British infantry advancing toward this line would be weakened by loss of casualties. If the British troops did reach the second German line then they would be out range of the British guns and would be unsupported. By stretching the level of penetration into the German lines, Haig was diluting the intensity of the British barrage over a wider area, which could undermine the effectiveness of the bombardment upon the first German trench system. Haig's plan to send in cavalry in the event of a breakthrough was flawed in the sense that the terrain, the labyrinth of German trenches and shell-cratered ground, made a cavalry advance difficult. Rawlinson reluctantly went away to revise the plan.

There were still 1,300,000 soldiers stationed in Britain, but the government could not agree on how or where they should be deployed, and these would be very welcome on the Western Front. On 14 April, Haig was back at the War Office in Whitehall, London. During a meeting with Lord Kitchener and General Sir William Robertson he sought reassurance that British Government supported the joint French / British offensive. Haig wrote of the response he received:

> I saw Lord Kitchener at the War Office … Sir William Robertson was present at the first part of my interview. I asked them definitely, 'Did His Majesty's Government approve of my combining with the French in a general offensive during the summer?' They both agreed that all the Cabinet had come to the conclusion that the war could only be ended by fighting, and several were most anxious for a definite victory over German arms.[21]

While at the War Office, Haig met Colonel Swinton regarding the use of tanks. At that stage of the war, the tank was a top-secret weapon under development. Haig was conscious that his soldiers would be confronted by barbed wire, trenches, shell fire and German machine-guns. Haig wanted to give these soldiers every chance to get across No Man's Land and achieve their objectives, and so Haig placed pressure upon Swinton to get the Tanks ready for the Somme offensive. Haig wrote:

> I … saw Colonel Swinton with Generals Butler and Whigham (the Deputy CIGS) regarding the 'tanks'. I was told that 150 would be provided by 31 July. I said that was too late. 50 were urgently required

> for 1 June. Swinton is to see what can be done, and will also practise and train 'tanks' and crews over obstacles and wire similar to the ground over which the attack will be made. I gave him a trench map as a guide and impressed on him the necessity for thinking over the system of leadership and control of a group of 'tanks' with a view to manoeuvring into a position of readiness.[22]

The tanks would not be ready for the opening of the Somme offensive, but this diary entry demonstrates Haig's ability to consider new methods of fighting the war and one can sense the urgency of the situation. He was under pressure to launch this offensive with untrained men with no experience of combat and was ready to embrace any innovative ideas that give his troops some assistance.

On 19 April, Rawlinson submitted his revised plan to GHQ for Haig's consideration. Montgomery drafted most of the revisions and Rawlinson refined the draft. Rawlinson was aware of the importance of this plan declaring in his diary, 'On it may possibly depend the tactics of one of the greatest battles the British Army has ever fought and I fully recognise the responsibility.'[23]

Rawlinson opened the revised plan with examining the options open to them – Haig's ambitious strategy to push further deeper into the German lines, juxtaposed with his own cautious plan to bite and hold smaller gains. Although he tried to be positive about Haig's strategy, which he refers to as an 'alluring' plan to widen the depth and objectives of the assault, he reaffirms his own plan for a restricted offensive with limited objectives on the first day. Rawlinson wrote:

> I came to the conclusion that two courses were open to me. The first, and most alluring one, was to attempt to capture the whole of the enemy's lines of defences as far south as the Albert–Bapaume Road in one attack. The second, less ambitious but in my opinion more certain, to divide the attack into two phases, the first of which would give us possession of the enemy's front system and all the important tactical points between the front system and the second line. The second phase to follow as soon as possible after the first, so as to give the enemy as little time as possible to construct new defences and bring up guns and reserves.[24]

Rawlinson repeated the concerns made in the initial proposal, that if troops belonging to the Fourth Army got to the second German trench system, German reserves would have enough time to get to this line to repel the attack. Pozières and Contalmaison had been fortified and would be difficult to capture if heavy casualties were sustained in securing the first trench system. If they reached the second trench system, these men would be out of range of the British guns and would have no artillery support, plus the strong belts of wire would be untouched. Also raw troops with no experience in battle could become disorganised and lack the discipline to sustain the attack.

Although Rawlinson maintained his reservations about a deeper advance into the German lines, he had to obey his Commander-in-Chief:

> It seems to me that an attempt to obtain more distant objectives, that is to say, the enemy's second line system, under the conditions above described, involves considerable risks. I however realise that it may be necessary to incur these risks. This will, no doubt, be decided by the Commander-in-Chief and definite instructions sent to me in due course.[25]

In the revised proposal Rawlinson appears to be demonstrating that he is complying with his commander's orders, but he knew that there was a strong possibility that the attempt to capture the first and second lines on the first day might not succeed. He wrote that: 'Should it be found impossible to capture the enemy's second line in the first attack, and should the troops making the attack fail to gain their objective, I consider that the whole operation may be retarded to a greater extent than would occur should the attack be made in two phases as originally planned.'[26]

Rawlinson was resolute, however, in resisting Haig's preference for a short, intensive bombardment. Firstly, there was insufficient artillery to cause a 'hurricane' bombardment on such a wide front and, secondly, there was the possibility that the Germans garrisons could shelter untouched in their deep dug-outs for the duration of a short bombardment. Rawlinson wrote:

> Bearing in mind the existence of numerous dug outs and cellars in the enemy's lines, I do not think that the moral effect of a six hours' intense bombardment will be so great as that of one extended over several days. The effect on moral[e] of a long, accurate bombardment, which will pulverize strong points one by one, gradually knocked in communication trenches, prevent reliefs being carried out, and systematically beat down the enemy's defences, will, in my mind, be much greater, especially as with many new detachments we cannot expect very accurate shooting in a hurricane bombardment.
>
> A long bombardment gives the enemy no chance of sleep, food, and ammunition are difficult to bring up, and the enemy is kept in a constant state of doubt, as to when the infantry assault will take place. His troops in the front line must be relieved every 48 hours, or they will break down under the strain, and it will be our business to so regulate our fire as to inflict heavy losses, even at night, on any relieving detachments he may endeavour to bring forward.[27]

Haig did not respond to Rawlinson's revised proposal which tended towards a deeper thrust into German lines, but reiterated the risk of failure and he repeated statements suggested in the initial plan which Rawlinson favoured. Rawlinson would have to wait a further three weeks before he received a response from Haig. During that period, Rawlinson learnt from Royal Flying Corps reconnaissance reports of existing lines being strengthened and new formidable German defences constructed. Worryingly, there were indications that a third trench system was in the process of being built and on 25 April he was presented with photographic evidence of this extra German defensive line under construction. Rawlinson ordered further reconnaissance sorties to take more photos of this German trench system and he was even flown across the German lines to see the defences with his own eyes – dispelling the myth that British Army generals during the First World War remained within the safety of their HQ normally based in chateaux far to the rear. Despite the inherent danger of such a mission, Rawlinson safely returned to base to report the development of further defences behind the German front lines to Haig, giving the Commander-in-Chief another problem to consider.

British, Belgian and French generals were not the only commanders learning lessons from past offensives. Whilst the Allied commanders were figuring out how they were going to break through the enemy lines, the German commanders themselves were learning how to combat the assaults upon their defences. They had lost heavily in gaining the territory they occupied and were determined not relinquish any ground. The British penetration of the German line and the capture of Neuve Chapelle during March 1915 shocked German commanders to the extent that they could no longer place reliance upon a single line of defence. Going forward, in order to hold onto the ground that they had conquered, the Germans knew that second and even third defensive lines had to be constructed and this policy was adopted on the Somme.

If Rawlinson was fretting about the use of unexperienced troops in a hastily brought-forward offensive, so was the Commander-in-Chief. In a meeting with Monsieur Clemenceau, the Chef du Comité Militaire du Senat on 4 May 1916, Haig remained adamant that he was not going to send untrained troops into battle and reiterated that he would be accountable for any failures.

> My Divisions, I told him want much careful training before we could hope of success. He asked me was I under Joffre's orders? I said certainly not. At the same time, it must be realised that there was only one man responsible for the plans. These Joffre and his Staff worked out for France, and I did my best to co-operate with them, but I was responsible for the method of employment of the British Forces, so that

> if anything unfortunate happened, I am responsible and must bear the blame, not General Joffre.[28]

On 16 May Haig informed Rawlinson in writing that the 'Serre-Mira[u]mont spur; Pozières: Contalmaison, and Montauban [must] be the objectives obtained during the first day's operations.'[29]

Haig knew that Rawlinson did not favour this strategy of pushing further into German lines, but he was asserting his position as Commander-in-Chief and that Rawlinson had to comply with his orders. Haig imposed a plan upon which the Fourth Army commander totally disagreed. Haig also did not agree that a longer sustained bombardment of German lines would break enemy morale, for he wrote in blue in the margins of Rawlinson's revised plan: 'I do not agree that the moral[e] effect of a "long and slow" fire is comparable to the same amount of shell fired upon the same spots in say a tenth of the time.'[30]

Both Haig and Rawlinson were drawing different conclusions from their experiences at Loos and applying them to their completely different strategies for the forthcoming Somme operation. By fixing objectives to the first line Haig was worried that the chance of exploiting a major breakthrough might be lost. At Loos some of the advancing waves went beyond the German first line trenches and Haig thought that if this could be achieved on the Somme then the infantry may be able to advance further and capture German artillery before they were withdrawn. If he sanctioned Rawlinson's bite-and-hold strategy then he would be restraining his infantry at a time when there might be panic amongst the enemy with the potential that the German line could collapse. Furthermore, Haig did not consider that the wire between the first and second German trench systems had to be destroyed.

Rawlinson remembered at Loos that the failure to exploit the breakthrough there was due to the fact that the infantry had gone beyond the range of British artillery support. It was Rawlinson's view, as well as many of the officers under his command, that on the Somme the same mistake would be made in that if British infantry reached the second German trench system then they would be out of reach of artillery support. It remained to be seen who would be correct.

There was also a lack of shells and guns to mount the kind of bombardment Haig proposed on such an extensive front. Major-General J.F.N. Birch, Artillery Adviser at GHQ, told the Commander-in-Chief that the artillery would be unable to conduct such a short barrage effectively with the resources then available and Haig backed down. He therefore delegated the decision as to the length of bombardment to the officers on the ground, allowing them to decide when all obstacles had been totally destroyed before launching a ground assault. Though a prolonged bombardment would take away the element of surprise that Haig had hoped for, he still wanted the Fourth Army to penetrate deeper into the German lines. Both Haig and Rawlinson were embarking on a campaign where their plans were compromised. The operation was destined for disaster.

The date of the impending offensive was still a contentious issue and remained undecided. Haig's intention not to commit ill-trained troops into a large scale offensive would be compromised towards the end of May 1916, with France becoming ever more desperate for Britain to launch an offensive on the Western Front. General Sir William Robertson visited Haig at General HQ at Château de Beaurepaire at Montreuil on 25 May 1916, and discussed Joffre's precarious situation. Despite the BEF being ill-prepared to carry out such an attack, both men agreed that it was necessary in order to keep France in the war. Haig wrote:

> After dinner, we discussed whether the British Army should comply with the French Generalissmo's request to attack in the month of July, or wait till August 15 when we would be much stronger.
>
> I had gone fully into the various aspects of the question and what might be the results if we did not support the French. I came to the conclusion that we *must* march to the support of the French. Robertson entirely agreed.[31]

The following day Haig met Joffre who described the plight of the French Army, which was on the verge of collapse as a result of defending Verdun for three months.

> General Joffre explained the general situation … The French had supported for three months alone the whole weight of the German attacks at Verdun. Their losses had been very heavy. By the end of the month they would reach 200,000. If this went on, the French Army would be ruined! He therefore was of the opinion that 1 July was the latest date for the combined offensive of the British and French.[32]

Haig was aware of the desperate situation that the French faced at Verdun and he knew that although the British Army were not ready to launch a large scale campaign, in order to manage the expectations of his coalition partners, he had to bend to their demands, at the expense of compromise. Haig had already decided that he would deploy the BEF on 1 July, but before making that commitment he wanted to emphasise to Joffre that he was doing so, even though the BEF would not be ready. Initially at that meeting, Joffre thought that Haig was not going to launch the offensive in July and immediately the 75-year-old Field Marshal exploded out of frustration and concern that the French Army and France as a nation would be destroyed and defeated if the British did not launch an assault upon the

German lines imminently. By that stage Joffre was physically and mentally worn out. The French Government, deputies and other high-ranking officers reproached Joffre for not being proactive in strengthening the defences of Verdun and reinforcing the sector despite knowing, along with his staff, that the Germans were going to launch an offensive at Verdun. The people of France rebuked Joffre for allowing the German Army to achieve the gains they had. Haig reported in his diary:

> I said that before fixing the date I would like to indicate the state of preparedness of the British Army on certain dates and compare its conditions. I took 1 and 15 July, and 1 and 15 August. The moment I mentioned 15 August Joffre at once got very excited and shouted that 'The French Army would cease to exist, if we did nothing till then!' The rest of us looked on at this burst of excitement, and then I pointed out that, in spite of the 15 August being the most favourable date for the British Army to take action, yet, in view of what he had said regarding the unfortunate condition of the French Army, I was prepared to commence operations on 1 July or thereabouts. This calmed the old man, but I saw that he had come to the meeting prepared to combat a refusal on my part, and was prepared to be very nasty.[33]

Being Commander-in-Chief of the BEF was no easy task. Not only did he have to consider the needs of his officers and men, Haig had to ensure that they were trained, fed, equipped in order to fight and win the war. He also had to satisfy the expectations of politicians, at the same time working in unison with Allied generals. Relationships with French commanders were frustrated and tested when they changed their minds, which was one major problem of the coalition. Haig therefore agreed for the BEF to attack during July, as he later wrote:

> Finally, I asked them, once the date was fixed, not to postpone it at the last moment as had happened 3 times last year with Foch!! We agreed on having 3 weeks' notice of the exact date of the attack … They are, indeed, difficult Allies to deal with! But there is no doubt that the nearest way to the hearts of many of them, including that of the 'Generalissimo' is down their throats, and some 1840 brandy had a surprising soothing effect.[34]

By 26 May 1916, General Haig agreed with General Joffre that the planned Franco-British offensive on the Somme could not be postponed and that they should launch this operation by the end of June. There were three objectives for launching the Somme campaign. To relieve the German pressure that was brought to bear upon Verdun, to aid the Russian and Italians by keeping German forces on the Western Front and preventing them being transferred to their fronts, and finally to wear down the German forces that opposed the British and French armies on the Western Front. While helping Britain's Allies, Haig considered this to be an opportunity to improve their position on the Western Front in an effort to destroy Germany's resolve to hold on to France and Belgium.

However, at that time it was doubtful that the French army could launch a joint offensive with the British army on the Somme. They were suffering heavily at Verdun and could scarcely hang on. It was a desperate situation. General Rawlinson was warned by GHQ on 27 May that there was great uncertainty whether the Fourth Army's attack on the Somme would take place or not. With French resources severely drained they had to reduce their commitment to support the British assault. Haig advised Rawlinson on 29 May that if French participation in the impending offensive was reduced then his first objective would be to wear down the enemy and improve the line, so that the BEF would be in a more favourable position when it resumed operations during 1917.

In order to carry out the great attack Rawlinson needed to gather as much ammunition and as many guns as possible. During the spring of 1915 the War Office had placed orders for the mass production of artillery shells within the UK, involving over 2,500 manufacturers. David Lloyd George as Minister of Munitions had established two national filling factories at Aintree and Coventry during July 1915 and ten more followed during the following two months, where shell casings would be filled with fuzes and explosives. The success of Kitchener's recruitment drive during the autumn of 1914 took away many highly skilled workers from the munition's factories and there was a significant skills shortage which seriously hindered the production of shells for the campaigns that were fought in 1915. The ramifications of the so-called 'Shell Scandal' were still being felt in 1916 and would have a serious impact upon the Somme campaign. Orders were being placed, munitions factories were being established, but the necessary workers required to fulfil those orders had joined Kitchener's New Army and were training to be soldiers. This meant that fulfilment of these orders fell significantly behind. Since a large proportion of the male population were serving in the armed services fighting the war, women were employed in these factories to carry out this important but rather dangerous work.

Throughout 1915, commanders had to monitor expenditure of ammunition as it would take ten months for the initial orders for shells made by the Ministry of Munitions to be fulfilled – which meant delivery in April 1916. Even so, the quantity of shells arriving in France and Belgium was still not enough and it would not be until 1917 that the problems of supplying a sufficient supply of ammunition were resolved.

In the run-up to the Somme offensive in 1916 there was actually a distinct decrease in the amount of munitions produced over the Easter period due to two Bank Holidays. At home, Minister of Munitions David

Lloyd George had appealed to employers and employees at munition factories to postpone the early June Whitsuntide Bank Holiday to ensure that productivity was not disrupted and that the British army was well supplied with ammunition for the impending operation. On 31 May 1916, Prime Minister Herbert Asquith announced to the House of Commons the suspension of all holidays relating to munition factories and shipyards until the end of July in the national interest. This announcement in the Houses of Parliament would severely compromise the security of the operation as German observers came to the conclusion that an offensive would take place between June and July 1916.

It was not only stocks of ammunition that had to be built up for the new offensive. The entire Fourth Army holding the Somme sector had to be fed and accommodated. Equipment, food, tools had to be brought to this sector. This meant roads and light railways had to be hastily built in order to bring assets into the region that would sustain the Fourth Army. Finally many of the soldiers designated to take part in this offensive had to be trained in the specifics of their tasks. Haig had less than five weeks to achieve this.

A conference attended by Haig's army commanders was held at Third Army HQ at St Pol on 27 May. Haig reviewed the current situation and impressed upon his commanders that however confident of success he was in the forthcoming campaign on the Somme, he held realistic expectations in that he did not expect to defeat Germany in a single offensive before the winter 1916. Lieutenant-General Butler, Chief of General Staff was present at that meeting and recorded Haig's directive to his army commanders:

> It was necessary to look ahead:
> Our object must be:
> To train our divisions, to continue to build-up a large reserve of ammunition and other military resources, and to wear out the enemy as much as possible.
> We must be prepared to support the French (who are losing severely at Verdun) by a resolute attack. While, however, we attack and make preparations to exploit any success gained, we must nevertheless clearly keep in view the necessity for putting our troops in favourable positions for commencing a spring campaign in 1917 so as to make certain success next year.[35]

Haig held high expectations for the impending offensive. British intelligence had estimated that they would be confronting thirty-two German battalions on the front line supported by another sixty-five held in reserve. Haig was buoyant with confidence in knowing that attacking the German sector on the Somme with 164 battalions with sixty-four in reserve; he held the numerical advantage in soldiers and that the chances of a successful breakthrough were very good, despite knowing that many of those battalions required further training. He believed that there was a role for cavalry in this operation. General Sir Hubert Gough had been appointed commander of the Reserve Army during early May 1916. This army would soon become known as Fifth Army and included GHQ Cavalry Reserve. Kiggell had written to Gough intimating Haig's intention to use the cavalry to advance on Miraumont and assist in the assault upon Pozières ridge. By the middle of June Haig's plan was expanding and becoming more ambitious as he wanted to extend the objectives on the initial phase to drive northwards from Pozières to capture Bapaume which was ten miles from Rawlinson's front line. Gough would send three cavalry and two infantry divisions through a breach made by Fourth Army in the German line in order to capture Bapaume. Once Bapaume was secured Haig would be in a good position to join up with the Arras salient, which was a key feature of the Allied defensive line.

Haig convened a conference with Rawlinson and Allenby on 15 June at St Pol at which he outlined his objectives:

> Firstly, to gain the line of the Pozières heights, organise good observation posts, and consolidate a strong point. Then, secondly, (a) If enemy's defence breaks down, to occupy enemy's third line (on line Flers-Miraumont), push detachment of cavalry to hold Bapaume and work northwards with bulk of cavalry and other arms so as to widen the breach in the enemy's line, and capture the enemy's forces in the re-entrant south of Arras. The hill at Monchy le Preux (5 miles S.E. of Arras) with intermediate posts between it and Bapaume, seems a suitable line for the cavalry to hold facing East as a flank guard for covering the operations of the other arms.
>
> (b) If Enemy's defence is strong and fighting continues for many days, as soon as Pozières heights are gained, the position should be consolidated, and improved, while arrangements will be made to start an attack on the Second Army Front.[36]

This change of plan necessitated Rawlinson issuing a further order which incorporated the revised objectives that would now include Bapaume. He also had to convene a conference to discuss with his corps commanders how they would implement Haig's plan. This meeting was scheduled to take place on 22 June.

Joffre asked Haig on 11 June if the day of the assault could be brought forward to 25 June which meant that the bombardment would need to start on 20 June. Not all the heavy artillery batteries had arrived on the Somme nor had five of the Divisions that were meant to participate in the assault. The last artillery pieces were due to arrive on 16 June and the last Division was expected to arrive on 19 June.

Meanwhile, Joffre visited Haig on 17 June and they agreed that the date for the attack should be planned for 29 June. Haig was concerned that the later the date for the start, the greater the risk of the enemy becoming alerted to the attack. Although designated 29 June as the date for the attack, both Haig and Joffre agreed to empower Rawlinson and Foch to postpone this date at their discretion if the weather was bad.

Although the date had been fixed the time of the beginning of the assault had still to be discussed. General Foch favoured 09:00 hours, while Rawlinson wanted 07:00 hours as a start time. Haig decided 07:30 hours as a compromise.

As the day of the assault drew nearer, Haig was becoming uneasy about the initial bombardment and the lack of resources to sustain such a barrage for a week over such a large front. Haig wrote to Rawlinson on 20 June requesting that the preliminary bombardment be shortened to three days on account that there was not enough guns and ammunition to sustain such a long barrage of the German lines on such a wide front, but this request was not pressed further.

Haig met Gough on 21 June and discussed the forthcoming operation. He confirmed that the overall objective would be Bapaume and that the cavalry would play an important part in driving through the German lines. Haig wrote:

> Thus once the Pozières ridge is taken, an effort should be made to push the cavalry through, covered with advanced guards and supported by as many divisions as Rawlinson can collect. The objective will be Bapaume. As soon as that place is secured the front of the Fourth Army will be published forward to the Bapaume-Peronne road.[37]

Rawlinson remained unconvinced that the stretched objectives could be achieved with the resources available. He was under obligation to convey the Commander-in-Chief's orders to his Corps Commanders at a conference held on 22 June, but before discussing the plan, he emphasised his apathy towards the use of cavalry.

> An opportunity may occur to push the cavalry through … and in this connection I will read you the orders I have received on the subject from the Commander-in-Chief … But before I read them I had better make it quite clear that it may not be possible to break the enemy's line and push the cavalry through at the first rush.[38]

Rawlinson affirmed that the decision to deploy cavalry would rest with him if the opportunity arose.

Intelligence briefings had instilled the Commander-in-Chief with confidence. He had received reports of trench raids into the German lines, the capture of prisoners and successful bombardments. It was also reported that the earlier estimates of the strength of German forces opposite the sector to be attacked were reasonably accurate.[39] The British troops would simply overwhelm the enemy; it would be a memorable victory to rank with the great battles in the long history of the British Army.

Chapter 3

Working Out the Details

With the general objectives of the offensive decided upon, the plan for the attack had to be worked out in detail. Allenby's Third Army would launch a diversionary operation to capture Gommecourt, with the five corps of Rawlinson's Fourth Army being given the task of assaulting the German lines from Serre in the north to Montauban in the south. Lieutenant-General Aylmer Hunter-Weston, commanding VIII Corps, allocated the capture of Serre to the 31st Division, of Redan Ridge to the 4th Division and of Beaumont Hamel to the 29th Division. On their adjacent right flank the 36th (Ulster) Division and the 32nd Division, belonging to Lieutenant-General Sir T.L.N. Morland's X Corps, were ordered to capture Schwaben Redoubt and Thiepval with 49th Division held in reserve. Further south Lieutenant-General Sir William Pulteney's III Corps would use the 8th Division to take Ovillers-la-Boisselle and the 34th Division to tackle La Boisselle, with the 19th Division held in reserve. Lieutenant-General Henry Horne's XV Corps comprising of 21st, 17th and 7th Divisions would assault Fricourt and Mametz. Lieutenant-General Walter Congreve's XIII Corps containing the 18th and 30th Divisions with the 9th Division in reserve would advance on the Fourth Army's southern flank to capture Montauban.

The plan to smash through the German lines on the Somme sector after a week-long preliminary bombardment convinced some officers, but not everyone was optimistic of its successful implementation. Captain John Laurie, Adjutant, 2nd Seaforth Highlanders, recalled the reaction of fellow officers when, towards the end of June, General the Hon. Bill Lambton talked through the plan:

> The picture he painted was an extended German army with few reserves and liable to complete disruption once the first trench system was broken. I think that most of us young officers believed this although the C.O. Lt. Col. J.O. Hopkinson ('Hoppy') didn't.[1]

Nine months had elapsed since the Battle of Loos in September 1915. Lessons from this action and other battles that year influenced strategy for the coming offensive on the Somme. Instructions for the Battle of Loos amounted to two pages. Detailed orders had been produced for the Somme campaign with precise instructions in a memorandum consisting of thirty-two sections on fifty-seven pages. Learning the experience at Loos, Haig ensured that each of his corps had a reserve division close to the front line on standby in the event that a breakthrough was made and could be exploited. Trench mortar batteries were formed, and Lewis Guns were assigned to each battalion to provide covering fire. Smoke candles were to be carried by the men to be lit when they reached their objectives to denote success and identify their position to commanders on the British line.

Detailed, comprehensive plans had been devised by staff officers but these were so detailed that they simply overwhelmed the commanders who had to implement them. When Brigadier-General Hubert Rees took over temporary command of the 94th Brigade he had to familiarise himself with the details of the impending attack upon Serre. He had the unenviable task of converting 'the mass of corps instructions into attack orders'.[2]

Rees recalled to the Official Historian Edmonds the nature of the orders which had to be implemented:

> I only arrived at VIII Corps HQ a fortnight before the attack took place. Therefore as a complete stranger to the scheme I was faced with this terrible document 'Scheme for the Offensive' of 76 pages and I found that my division had issued 365 supplementary instructions. It took me three days on reaching my brigade to reduce this enormous mass of instructions to some 8 pages and 5 maps of Brigade orders.[3]

When these orders were communicated to the infantry soldier, the mass of documentation given to officers amounted to very little to the men who were about to go over the top. Private James Snailham recalled: 'They were told nothing to do, but walk over.'[4]

> The plans were rigid and precise, but did not take into consideration if any part of the plan failed. There were no contingencies factored into the plans for failure when things went wrong. Rees was concerned that 'the first principles of war were overwhelmed by a mass of detail which dispensed with individual initiative and any elasticity.[5]

Rees had reservations regarding the time given for the capture of objectives and contested the plans with VIII Corps Commander, Hunter-Weston:

> One of my criticisms of the general plan of operations was that the time allowed for the capture of each objective was too short. I had a severe

> argument with Hunter-Weston before I induced him to give me an extra ten minutes for the capture of an orchard, 300 yards beyond the village of Serre. I was looked upon as something of a heretic for saying that everything had been arranged for except for the unexpected, which usually occurs in war.[6]

Artillery was to co-operate with the infantry advance, lifting at various times ahead of the advancing infantry in the hope of pulverising the enemy that had survived the intensive week-long bombardment and clear a path before they arrived. 18-pounder field guns would fire a shield of shrapnel ahead of the advancing infantry at regulated times. It was the first time that the British Army would attempt a barrage of this nature. If the troops could advance close behind this barrage then they might reach the German lines before any surviving occupants could reach their parapets. Rawlinson learnt from Loos that a covering fire of shrapnel offered best protection for advancing troops. Rawlinson would implement this policy on a large scale on 1 July 1916. Major R.A. Wolfe-Murray recalled:

> During this great fight we were to try the new system of following an artillery barrage, this mode of artillery support had been perfected by the French but had never been tried in our Army on a large scale. It was simply this, the Artillery supporting the Infantry attacking a certain front, maintained their fire on each successive line of enemy trench for a certain fixed time to enable the Infantry to approach that trench and rush in the second the fire lifted. Future operations proved to us that the success of this plan entirely rested on the Infantry keeping right close up to their barrage and the distance and time between the lifts being not too great.[7]

There were inherent dangers in following a barrage of shrapnel. If the infantry advanced too swiftly they could become casualties of their own fire, while they did not maintain a steady pace behind the shrapnel blasts then they were in danger of finding themselves with the barrage falling behind the German lines and German occupants in their parapets firing at the advancing troops. Rawlinson stressed to his Corps Commanders at a conference held on 16 April 1916 that the artillery barrage timetable must be co-ordinated with the infantry advances. However on 1 July in some instances the troops were held up by heavy machine-gun fire and the barrages went over the German lines, proving ineffective. This policy would later be developed and evolve during the Somme campaign in August 1916 into what would be later known as the 'creeping barrage'.

At Loos, attacking waves went forward into the smoke and observers from the British lines could not distinguish between friend and foe and as a consequence many British soldiers were killed by their own artillery. The assaulting infantry would wear tin triangles on their backs so that artillery observers could identify them as friendly forces and not direct fire upon them. Private George Grunwell remembered attaching to his haversack a 'triangular piece of tin so that our artillery would know just where we were so that instead of shelling us they knew we were not the Germans'.[8]

Although smoke was part of the plan, as mentioned before, it was left to Corps and Divisional commanders whether or not to use it. Many of these commanders had no experience of using smoke in battle. On the sector between Mametz and Montauban artillery commanders advised against using smoke because it would obstruct their view of the German positions which they could clearly see and target with some accuracy.

Fearful of suffering heavy casualties, for the first time during the war the second-in-command and some officers, NCOs and men were kept in reserve to reorganise and form a new battalion. Captain John Laurie, Adjutant, 2nd Seaforth Highlanders commented: 'One fortunate decision was taken – namely – to leave out of the attack a strong body of Officers and O.R's to act as first reinforcements.'[9] During battles of 1915, in particular at Loos in September 1915, officers led from the front and many were killed as a consequence. It was decided to keep a proportion of officers in the rear lines so that in the event of losing heavy casualties, they would be able to reform and rebuild the battalion. Canon Ernest Crosse, chaplain to the 8th and 9th Devonshire Regiment wrote:

> The old method of officers going into battle at the head of their men undoubtedly meant that the officer's chance of survival was very small. The battle of Loos showed this quite plainly. Of all the battalion those who were most likely to be hit were our Company Commanders, and as heavy was the loss of these that, after 1916, it became the rule for only one in two to go into the first attack. I can quite remember being asked to spin the coin between company officers as to which should go into a given battle. The men were spinning for their lives and they knew it.[10]

Those men who advanced with the attacking waves had to carry lots of equipment that would be of great use to them once they got to the German lines, therefore they had heavy loads to transport across No Man's Land. To ensure that the attacking infantry had everything they needed to consolidate captured trenches they were made to carry much ammunition, equipment, tools and rations with them as they advanced:

> Each man will carry waterproof sheet, pack (without great coat), equipment, rifle and bayonet, 170 rounds of S.A.A., 2 Mills grenades (one in each pocket), iron rations, also the unexpended portion of two days' rations. The following (bombers, Lewis Gunners, stretcher bearers

> and throwers), 50 rounds S.A.A. (except Lewis Gunners who will carry 170 rounds), waterproof sheet, rations as above. Bombers will, in addition, carry 10 Mills grenades each. All men will carry a filled oil bottle, pull through and flannelette. All men excepting the first wave and bombers, runners and stretcher bearers, will carry a pick and shovel in the proportion of one pick to three shovels.[11]

Brodie Helmets were the first steel helmets issued to British soldiers during early 1916 and would be used for the first time on the Somme. It would be an additional weight to carry, but essential to protect the individual soldier. Although they could not prevent a direct hit from a bullet killing a man, they could afford protection from shrapnel which was the common cause of death amongst many casualties in the first years of the war. However, these steel helmets initially proved heavy and cumbersome, some soldiers complaining of headaches while wearing them. Corporal George Ashurst of the 1st Lancashire Fusiliers recalled:

> We were issued with the new steel helmets before the battle, I didn't like them. They were damned heavy things to put on your head; they were uncomfortable, they only just fit on your head, they were round. I wore it. I had to. But you got quite used to them in a short time.[12]

Brigadier-General Rees expressed concerns about security and maintaining secrecy. The fact that assembly trenches stopped on the left flank of the 94th Brigade front meant that any German reconnaissance aeroplane would immediately know that there would be no attack between Serre and Gommecourt, and German machine-gunners in Serre knew where the British attack would originate from. Rees recalled:

> Surprise was non-existent. Worse than that there was no effort to mislead the enemy at all. For instance a few days before the attack I pointed out to General Hunter-Weston that the assembly trenches stopped dead at the left of the 94th Brigade, and that not a spade had been put into the ground between me and the subsidiary attack at Gommecourt, worse still no effort at wire cutting was made on that stretch either. A child could see where the flank of our attack lay to within 10 yards.[13]

There was no security regarding the handling of sensitive operational information, for when Rees was informed of the postponement of the attack he remembered 'my first news of the postponement of the first attack to the 1 July was hearing it shouted down our village street.'[14]

Rees was aware that each division's ability to succeed on 1 July was reliant upon adjacent divisions achieving their objectives. Each village and strongpoint between Gommecourt and Montauban had been fortified and German forces defending these fortresses could see each other's positions and were able to provide fire to support each other. Rees knew that the 4th Division's capture of the Heidenkopf was dependent upon 31st Division capturing Serre. Rees realised that 'the 4th Division hadn't a hope unless the 31st [Division] took Serre.'[15]

Other officers questioned the plan. Captain C.W. Martin belonged to the 1/8th Royal Warwickshire Regiment which was to assault the Heidenkopf. After reading the orders given to him, Martin was not confident that the plan would succeed and challenged his commanding officer who, although he did not encourage disobedience, concurred with his opinion:

> A very grave misapprehension undoubtedly existed in the minds of the General Staff that enemy machine-guns would largely be out of action and the official Orders constrained the attacking force to advance in broad daylight at a steady walk which in the face of intense Machine-Gun Fire is simply suicide ... On reading through these orders I came to the conclusion that we were all going to commit suicide. In placing my point of view informally before Lt. Col. E.A. Innes CMG, who commanded the battalion, I said that I was quite prepared to be superseded in the command of my Company, but that if left in command, thereof, I proposed to be guided by actual events and take action, if necessary, which amounted to direct, if not disobedience, disregard of the method of attack. Col. Innes replied that he was most unwilling to make any change in regard to command of the Company, as far as he was concerned I could take any action I considered advisable if I was prepared to shoulder the responsibility and that he thought my forecast was probably correct.[16]

Martin read the orders to his company and told them before the assault that they were not going to follow these orders but assess the situation as they advanced across No Man's Land:

> I asked for the use of the Town Hall in which to address my Company. When the whole Company were assembled I read over the material parts of the Orders to them and then said 'You have now heard the orders issued by Headquarters, I have read these Orders to you so that if I happen to sprain my ankle, or anything of that sort, you all know exactly what has to be done by this Company on the day of the attack. What I really intend to do is quite different to these official Orders. First I want you to try and realise what the conditions will be like, you have already had some experience of Artillery barrages, machine-gunning and so on and most of you will grasp that you won't be able to hear anything, so I am going to issue my Orders here and now. If no accident

> happens to me all I want you to do is to imitate my actions, when you see me double up, you follow at the double, when I stop or lay down for a breather, you do the same, when I get up and resume the attack you get up and come along too.'[17]

Although Haig and Rawlinson had tried to learn from the BEF's experience during the campaigns in 1915 and mitigate the risk of failure, their subordinate officers could see that there were flaws in those plans when they began to be considered in detail. Officers found the mass of instructions they had been given difficult to digest or relay to the ranks. The element of surprise would not only be lost during the week-long preparatory bombardment, but as Rees highlighted, stopping the excavation of assembly trenches and the failure to make any attempts to cut the wire in No Man's Land on his brigade's front at Serre was a dead giveaway to where the flank of the British attack would end. The advancing ranks were told no more than to walk over to the German lines and occupy their trenches. Haig and Rawlinson were assuming that the British artillery would pulverise German strongpoints, artillery batteries and machine-gun positions, with no provision for failure or delay. There was certainly a highly-detailed Plan A, but there was no Plan B.

Chapter 4

Preparations

The BEF had been transferred to the Somme sector to relieve French divisions during the summer of 1915. The sector had been quiet since 1914, and the British army did not have the supplies of munitions to mount any large offensives and so they continued with the 'live and let live' approach which had been adopted by their French predecessors. The BEF's inactivity on the Somme allowed the German defenders positioned on the high ridges to fortify their positions with barbed wire, redoubts, deep dugouts, establish machine-gun positions with interlinking fields of fire and construct further lines of trenches behind their front line. A second system of defensive trenches was built a mile beyond the front line higher on the ridge.

All the soldiers that were deployed on the Somme had to pass through the town of Albert. The town contained 1,105 houses with 6,742 inhabitants. As British Tommies marched through the town centre they passed the Basilique Notre-Dame de Brebieres and they would look up at the golden statue of the Virgin Mary holding out the baby Jesus, which was precariously fixed perpendicular from the base. A German shell had exploded beneath the dome which formed the base of the statue during January 1915 causing the statue to fall to an angle of forty-five degrees. French engineers had secured the statue to this position. The statue became the subject of superstition on both sides for it was thought that the war would come to an end when it was shot down. When German forces pushed through the Somme valley during March 1918 they used the tower as an observation post. British Artillery brought it down during April 1918.

While commanders concentrated on converting detailed instructions into orders, the troops on the front line and munitions workers at home ensured that those plans would be implemented. On the Western Front roads and railways to the Somme front had to be either improved or created so that troops, equipment, artillery and munitions could get to the theatre of operations. There was a distinct lack of railway lines that would carry the resources and assets necessary to launch an offensive into the Somme region. One railway line was in operation between Amiens, Abbeville and Calais which crossed the Somme. Another line twenty miles behind the front line ran Amiens–Doullens–St. Pol–Bethune. Fifty trains a day used these lines to carry coal from northern France to munitions factories and to provide power for the city of Paris. It was estimated that Fourth Army required fourteen trains to carry ammunition, eleven trains to transport supplies and six trains to transfer troops on a daily basis, but the existing railway lines did not pass close enough to the front line.

On 1 April 1916, it was decided to construct a new line, seventeen miles long, from Candas branching from the railway line four miles south of Doullens towards Acheux. This new line would create five new railheads into the area of operations. On the Amiens–Albert line another branch was formed which ran north to Contay, eight miles west of Albert and the location of a massive ammunition dump. This new railway line provided three further railheads into the battle front.

Once it was decided that the BEF would launch an offensive on the Somme sector its soldiers found themselves busier out of the line than when they were in the trenches defending the line. The Somme region had to accommodate approximately 500,000 soldiers and 100,000 horses for a period of seven weeks as well as dumps to store the necessary munitions and supplies to sustain the troops. Billets had to be established and pipes to bring in water for drinking and sanitation had to be laid, as did signal cables for communications. Troops in the front line worked laboriously to carry out these preparations for the operation. Work that was originally the sole remit of the Royal Engineers became the day-to-day work of the infantryman. Haig could only offer Rawlinson 5,000 men from five labour battalions to support the preparatory efforts for the battle, this number falling well short of requirements. Rawlinson was therefore compelled to use men who were about to take part in the offensive and in the days when they were meant to be resting or training behind the lines, they found themselves hard at work. This meant that the soldiers who were expected to assault the German lines on 1 July 1916 were undertrained and exhausted by the physical labour they performed prior to the attack.

Major Austin Girdwood, GSO2 at 32nd Division HQ, was aware of this problem. His superior Major-General Rycroft, commanding the division was a cavalry officer and another named Gosset was a Royal Artillery officer and they had little understanding of the function of the infantry and the affect that working the men too hard would have on the operation as a whole. Girdwood wrote:

> General Rycroft was a cavalry man and Gosset a gunner and neither of them knew anything at all about the P.B.I. [Poor Bloody Infantry] or how to treat them. I was too junior to have much influence on either of them though I did protest to General Rycroft that he was not treating

> the infantry fairly and I said so often to Gosset. Naturally I got myself disliked and the proof is in the fact that after the disaster which I had foretold had occurred I was given command of a battalion to get me out of the Staff Office. The real cause of the failure of the 32nd Division is that the wretched infantry were literally exhausted long before the day of the attack. Units were kept in trenches far too long at one time without relief and there was far too much digging and most of it was quite useless and haphazard. The G.1 considered that if the strength of a battalion on paper was 500 men at least 450 should turn out for working parties. Units, after 10 days in the line under heavy fire most of the time and digging day and night, would be relieved and get back to billets after a long and muddy march at daylight the next morning and then had to go back the same night to dig or repair trenches. This went on for many weeks in succession and the men and officers lost heart physically and morally. The plan of attack was doomed to failure from the start as I pointed out to General Rycroft, as it involved a change in direction from which the hostile fire is coming. At that point I was told to mind my own business.[1]

Some battalions did get the opportunity to train for the oncoming offensive interspersed between spells on the front line and periods of heavy labour. There were no regular hours and they had to train when and where they could. The 8th Somerset Light Infantry had arrived on the Somme during April 1916 and was taken to a place behind the enemy lines where a superficial model of the German trench system, laid out using white tapes, was used to train and practise the assault. Private Maurice Symes who belonged to this battalion was trained as a company bomber:

> We went up to the line into chalky trenches ... we were there for ten days, and then out for ten days and then in that working for ten days and then out for ten days, supposed to be rest and instead of resting we were rehearsing for the offensive ... They had a place marked out with the German front trenches, second trenches and communication trenches, that was this and that ... you will not get any resistance here and all that sort of thing for we rehearsed that and where the bombers had to go and all that was rehearsed, that took a bit a time, still did not work according to plan because the Germans were still there.[2]

German units were proactive in engaging their British enemy on the Somme. On 21 February 1916 they assaulted a salient close to Fricourt, known as the Tambour. Their motivation for launching an assault upon this position was that the British and German lines were within close proximity of each other. Each were digging and exploding mines continually which resulted in No Man's Land being transformed into a moonscape of craters.

German artillery shelled this position throughout 21 February day causing tremendous damage, though there were only a dozen British casualties.

The arrival of new divisions along the Somme sector alerted German Supreme Headquarters that a British offensive on this region was inevitable. Regular German incursions into the British lines, capturing prisoners for the purpose of identifying opposing units during mid-April 1916, revealed that some units such as 29th Division which had fought at Gallipoli during 1915 were now in the area.

It became apparent to German Intelligence that British forces were about to launch an attack upon their lines. On 25 May 1916 General Fritz von Below, commander of German Second Army, had proposed a plan to interrupt British preparations on the Somme. He planned for an offensive on a twelve-mile front between Foucaucourt and St Pierre Divion. He wanted to drive his forces twenty-five miles into British lines, hoping to disrupt the preparations for the expected offensive. Von Below did not receive a response to his initial plan from General Erich von Falkenhayn, the Chief of the General Staff. Yet, with British forces massing in the Somme valley, he was fearful of this threat to the Second Army and, on 2 June, he put forward a second plan. This was a limited thrust into the British lines between St Pierre Divion and Ovillers-la-Boisselle. Falkenhayn, though, was still not persuaded to launch a pre-emptive strike upon the British. Reserves were limited and Falkenhayn could only offer von Below one regiment of artillery in support. The German Army was immersed in the struggle for Verdun and on 4 June Russia launched the Brusilov Offensive in the East. There was no chance that extra reserves could be summoned to undertake a limited offensive on the Somme. Von Below had no choice but to drop his scheme. Falkenhayn faced a number of difficult choices. But devoting his resources to the Verdun and the Eastern Front meant that he may have under estimated the threat the British posed on the Somme.

Unable to generate support for a pre-emptive Somme offensive, von Below concentrated on his defensive arrangements. The French were so heavily engaged in and weakened by the struggle for Verdun that it was thought they would not have the resources to support the British on the Somme. Von Below therefore decided to focus his defence north of the River Somme opposite the British positions. In mid-June the 10th Bavarian Infantry Division was transferred from the south of the Somme valley opposite the French lines to the north to face the British. The division was split up, with its three regiments, 6th Regiment, 8th Reserve Regiment and 16th Regiment being deployed in different positions which were thought to be at risk of attack. The 8th Reserve Regiment, for instance, was used to bolster the defences along Thiepval Ridge, south of the River Ancre.

The BEF became increasingly active as the start of the offensive drew closer. Regular patrols were sent out into No Man's Land to assess the impact of the British barrages upon the wire, trench raids were being carried out at night to gather vital intelligence about the extent of the German trenches defences and to identify which German units were occupying them, and to test their levels of alertness and ability to defend those trenches.

In the days preceding the opening day of the 'Great Push' German forces holding the high ground across the Somme could observe the BEF assembling men, munitions and equipment down below. German observers in observation balloons could clearly see the British front lines and beyond, and could direct artillery fire to disrupt the British preparations. Major D.W. Palithorpe recalled the moment when the 8th Devonshire's attracted the attention of German observers and the deadly consequences when that battalion moved in full view of the enemy when they were being relieved by the 2nd Gordon Highlanders at Mametz in early June:

> We were ordered into the trenches opposite Mametz so that the Promised Land could be viewed and the ground over which the battalion were due to attack on July 1st speculated upon. We relieved the Xshires – 8th Devon's, I think, in daylight and before the relief was completed many of their men thoughtlessly took a short cut by going over the top about 400 yards and then re-entering the winding trench further down – the last platoon of the Gordon's, D Company, together with some signallers, stretcher bearers and myself, did the same thing and the Bosche who had a 'sausage' up in the air opened fire on us whilst we were in the open – we hurled ourselves upon the ground as the scream of his shells was heard – high bursting black shrapnel which whistled past us – up again and with two more short bursts reached our trenches with only one man hit in the wrist – a useful lesson as to the folly of exposing oneself entirely unnecessarily. Worse was soon to come as the Bosche seeing kilts now knew that the relief had taken place and to greet us battered our front line and communication trenches still full of men making their way up to their positions – we had 20 casualties including 5 killed in this half hour of shelling. Colonel B.G.R. Gordon standing outside Battalion headquarters dug-out, shook his fist at the Xshires now retiring over the sky line and wished a 5.9 amongst them – it was hard to lose fine men so uselessly.[3]

German forces could see into the British trenches at Mametz and their snipers were able to pick off British soldiers in those trenches. The Gordon Highlanders occupied these trenches and were vulnerable to this obtrusive sniper activity. The battalion medical officer Major Palithorpe, who had to deal with sniper casualties on a daily basis, recalled:

> The Bosche had much better observation than ours at Mametz as he was on higher ground and in places could look right into our trenches

> – a point that was not fully appreciated until Mametz had been taken and we looked back – it was not to be wondered at that we lost a good many men by sniping and the daily journey around the front line with Corporal Smith was by no means dull … Often we had men hit through the head – a rifle bullet at 200 yards, the average distance of the Bosche from us here, shattering the skull and pouring out brain matter, leaves no chance. At first I used to go up and try and get the unfortunate man hauled down the narrow trench – he might be breathing stertorously and to his friends appear to have a chance if got away – but this usually meant involving the exposure of stretcher bearers or others in passing bad corners and the likelihood of further casualties. When we found out that the man seldom lived more than an hour we abandoned this and had him placed quietly out of sight until his body could be brought back more safely at night.[4]

An enormous logistical task was undertaken in the weeks prior to the beginning of the Somme campaign as munitions were brought to the front line directly from railheads by lorries. Shells were deposited in ammunition dumps and at batteries in preparation for the impending weeklong preparatory barrage. Approximately 1,100 rounds were brought forward for each 18-pounder, 1,010 for each 4.5in howitzer, 500 per 2in trench mortar and 300 per Stokes mortar.[5]

These lorries could only operate under the cover of darkness, and being summer with short nights, the time they had to move the munitions was limited. Staff Captain G.R. Codrington recalled:

> The ordinary nightly supply work – rations and R.E. stores – was worked in with lorries delivering stores for the offensive, on a regular time table, and all lorries had to be clear by daylight. Moreover the nights at this time of year were short, and the convoys could not start work until dark. This system went on night after night, nor was there a single hitch.[6]

With all this activity occurring behind the British lines, the soldiers who were about to take part in this impending offensive were fearful that their German opponents could see what was happening, with no possibility of taking the enemy by surprise. Major R.A. Wolfe-Murray recalled in his diary.

> Sometime in May or June we were billeted in Bray and from there went up into the trenches facing Mametz. The activity on this front was terrific, everywhere big gun emplacements were being dug in the white chalk and huge dumps of white boxes of ammunition etc. were being formed. All this must have only too well known to the enemy and had

> any one of us paused to think whether we would effect a surprise we would have uncomfortable thoughts.[7]

Precise arrangements were made for the processing of captured German prisoners. The 108th Brigade file contains details of these plans relating to prisoners captured at Schwaben Redoubt. All prisoners were to be taken to a Divisional Prisoner Collecting Post close to the Albert–Hamel railway. Escorts no less than 15 per cent of the number of captives were to ensure that prisoners did not destroy documents. They were to march their prisoners in silence to ensure that they did not collude with other prisoners or talk to their escorts. Captured officers and NCOs were to be separated and placed under different escorts. A German-speaking officer and NCO would be in position at each Divisional Prisoner Collecting Post who would interview the prisoners.

Orders issued to the 8th Norfolk Regiment stated that prisoners should be grouped together and given an escort comprising 10% of the captured group to rear lines only when there was a lull in the fighting. The escort party was ordered to return to the battlefield. The orders also contained definite instructions for handling difficult prisoners. 'It must be clearly understood that time cannot be wasted with prisoners who give us trouble. Once a man has surrendered if he attempts to escape or offer any more resistance he must be shot.'[8]

There were concerns raised about the distance across No Man's Land between the British and German trenches. There was a distance of 500 yards to cross on the 46th (Midlands) Division front and the 56th (London) Division was 800 yards from the German trenches. In order to shorten the distance and reduce the number of casualties it was decided to dig trenches in front of the existing British trenches. At Gommecourt advanced trenches had been dug in No Man's Land on the 46th (Midlands) Division front. There were no attempts to conceal these operations and were done to deliberately attract the attention of the enemy.

During the night of 26 / 27 May a sap was pushed forward into No Man's Land from the 56th Division's front trench. From there a shallow trench was dug, some four feet deep, and approximately 2,900 yards long, in front of the German lines. This was completed, along with wire defences by 02:30 hours. Eight men were killed and fifty-five wounded during this daring operation.

Major-General Hull went into No Man's Land to assess the newly-dug trenches during the morning of 27 May. The white chalk spoil could be easily seen from above so Hull ordered the Royal Flying Corps to maintain a presence over this sector to ensure that German reconnaissance planes did not discover the previous night's work. It is believed that initial German reports confirmed no change on the sector on that night, but at dawn they could see the chalk spoil in No Man's Land. That a negative report was submitted possibly indicates that the German commanding officer may have been too embarrassed to report to superior officers that new British trenches had been dug so close to their lines, under their very noses. During the following night the 197th Brigade ventured into No Man's Land to increase the depth of the new front line trench and adjoining communication trenches to six feet.

Private Hal Russell from the 1/5th London Rifle Brigade was convinced that their German opponents could see that they were digging trenches towards there lines. He wrote:

> We had moved into a position in front of Gommecourt Wood and, while we were there, we had to edge forward at night digging advanced trenches nearer and nearer the Germans. They could well have observed during the day the result of our activities when the trenches were in full view, but they apparently made no serious attempt to interfere with us apart from sending over devastating mines at irregular intervals, a practice we also followed in retaliation.[9]

Bad weather prevented further trenches being dug closer to the German lines. The 46th Division were closer to the German front line trenches in comparison to the 56th Division's front line and it was a feasible distance for the North Midland Division battalions to advance behind an artillery barrage, however between the British and German trenches were thick lines of barbed-wire defences which had been laid by the French.

The activity of 46th and 56th Divisions was a successful deception without any attack taking place for it aroused German attention and caused alarmed German commanders to divert an entire division with six heavy batteries to the Gommecourt Salient. The Prussian 2nd Guard Reserve Division was brought forward from reserve to bolster the line held at Gommecourt by the German 11th and 52nd Divisions. This division was committed to defending this section of the front and it was too late to divert them to the sector where the main attack was to take place.

Chapter 5

The Preliminary Artillery Bombardment

The programme for the preliminary artillery bombardment was issued on 5 June 1916 and was scheduled to take place over five days before the infantry assault, beginning on 24 June. The first two days would focus upon wire cutting while the three remaining days would continue this work as well as concentrating upon German-held trenches, dugouts, villages and batteries.

The programme for each artillery detachment was divided into two-hour periods which allowed rest for the crews and time for the guns to cool down. Subject to availability of munitions there would be a continuous barrage upon the German lines. Some of the heavy Howitzers were late arriving on the Somme and their crews had little time to become accustomed to the region.

Despite low cloud and rain, the opening shots of the preparatory barrage began on 24 June marking the first day of the Somme campaign. Launched on a grand scale along the entire Somme front, and lasting for eight days, this was the largest bombardment carried out by British artillery to date during the war. Three times the number of field guns and heavy guns were used during this bombardment in comparison to the Loos campaign nine months earlier. The objectives of the preliminary bombardment were to destroy the enemy trench system, to cut breaches through the German wire, to cause casualties and to demoralise their adversaries. An unprecedented number of artillery pieces were at Rawlinson's disposal for this task, including 1,000 field guns, 233 howitzers and 180 counter-battery guns.[1] Brigadier-General Trevor Ternan, commanding 102nd Brigade, recalled:

> The preliminary bombardment began with a roar which seemed to shake the earth. The air was split with the combined detonations of hundreds of guns of all calibres. From the trench outside one heard with the utmost satisfaction the rushing through the air of vast numbers of projectiles of all sizes flying over our heads on their way to the Boche

> lines … It was almost impossible to realise that any human being in any of these places could possibly survive.[2]

The 29th Division War Diary reported:

> The intensity of this bombardment was quite exceptional in the annals of the Field Artillery. Some 1,500 rounds per 18-pounder gun were fired during the seven days. And 400 rounds per gun were expended on the day of the attack, a total of 1,900 rounds per gun in eight days.[3]

The first day of the preparatory barrage focused upon the wire-cutting operation, but counter-battery work was restricted because reconnaissance aeroplanes from the Royal Flying Corps were unable to operate until the weather improved in the early evening. Much of the cloud still lingered and these aeroplanes had to fly at low altitude in order to locate German battery positions. Nevertheless, they successfully directed artillery barrages upon forty targets. Shelling of rear German lines began that night and their artillery offered a weak response. If a German battery fired into the British lines, the British guns responded with four times as many shells.

A favourable wind blowing from the west and southwest were forecast for the evening of 24 June and orders were issued for a discharge of gas at the local discretion of officers. Most divisions refrained from using gas that evening except for the 4th Division opposite the Heidenkopf. The gas was released at 22:00 hours by Special Brigade led by Lieutenant Jones and it drifted slowly towards the Heidenkopf. Fearful of a British infantry attack, German artillery responded with a very heavy barrage thirty minutes later targeting the first trench and support lines occupied by the 4th Division causing heavy casualties amongst the soldiers from the 1st Royal Warwickshire Regiment. German machine-gunners, who were on heightened alert, opened fire believing a British assault was imminent. The wind direction soon changed and blew from the east causing the gas to drift back towards the British line, and the men of the Royal Warwicks had to done their smoke helmets. The situation was made worse when a piece of shell hit one of the gas cylinders causing a leak in the British trench, which overwhelmed Lieutenant Jones' party who were releasing the gas. At 23:00 hours the discharge of gas was stopped.

The weather improved on 25 June, becoming brighter and providing clear observation of the German positions. British artillery continued to pound the wire and trenches, as well as batteries and ammunition dumps further behind the German line. Explosions set ammunition dumps ablaze at Longueval, Montauban, Mametz Wood and Pozières during the day.

As German artillery responded to these direct hits, observers belonging to IV Brigade, Royal Flying Corps identified the locations of 102 enemy batteries operating opposite the sector occupied by VIII and X Corps. These aeroplanes operated in the skies above the Somme overtly and unchallenged by the German Air Force. During that afternoon efforts were made to restrict German observers from looking into the British lines and three observation balloons were successfully shot down. All attempts by German aircraft to interrupt the Royal Flying Corps in carrying out its work to support British artillery on the ground were thwarted. They had complete control of the air. This was evident when a German Fokker E III monoplane flying above Courcelette was intercepted and shot down by a De Havilland pilot belonging to No.24 Squadron.

As the bombardment continued, German troops holding the front line found themselves cut off as roads and communication trenches leading to their positions were targeted. Rawlinson's plan to isolate those men in the front lines cutting off their food, water and munitions supplies succeeded. Leutnant der Reserve F.L. Cassel, 99th RIR, holding the line at Thiepval described conditions the Germans had to endure during the barrage:

> The second day goes on in the same way. Again no hot food comes and the order is given to break the Iron Ration. Now we become aware of the usage of the special Iron Ration kept in the platoon commanders' dugout. The bread of course was not exactly fresh, and the rumour had it that not all the meat rations could be found. But at least it gave something for the stomach. When the fire went on through the third day we began to look at the situation as critical. It appeared they wanted first to starve us and then to shoot us out of our positions. Luckily we could still obtain water from the wells in the position in Thiepval, the use of which had been prohibited for drinking as they were suspected to be contaminated. Now it was help in an emergency. On the evening of the third day a message came: food will arrive. The organisation began to work. On detours around all the villages and visible roads which were all under heavy fire food had been brought, first with motorcars from a distance and then on foot, in large containers. Now we could watch the development for a while longer. We could not leave our holes anyway.[4]

Cassel found life in front-line trenches dangerous and difficult. He and his men had very little sleep; they were surviving off meagre food rations and were hungry. The persistent shelling had a powerful effect upon their minds and their senses. The demoralisation process began to kick in as their nerves became shattered and their stomachs quickly became empty:

> It became obvious that the fire was being directed on to the first and second line trenches and it began to become very uncomfortable. It was not very pleasant in the trench, too much hardware flying about. We were tired too and slept as much as one could. The noise of the barrage

> [*Das Trommelfeuer*] was too monotonous and so prevented sleep for overtired people. Could one rely on the sentries? They stood on the top steps of the dugout and had to watch lest the fire was changed to the rear and had to look in quieter moments across the ramparts whether the enemy was not coming across. Day long, night long, for 10 full days! And not all men are heroes, so from time to time one had to go up to see whether the sentries did their duty.[5]

The long line of observation balloons along the British lines of the Somme sector, together with the intensive bombardment, was a strong indication to the German soldiers that the British would soon attack. Twelve observation balloons could be seen close to Montauban from Longueval where soldiers and French civilians had to resort to sheltering in underground cellars as the shells descended upon the village, tearing down houses.

On the night of 25/26 June four trench raids were carried out to assess the impact of the preparatory barrage upon the German lines. At Ovillers-la-Boisselle the 8th Division reported that the trenches were strongly occupied by hostile troops, but managed to capture a prisoner for interrogation. A raiding party belonging to the 34th Division was repulsed by a strong German defence and was unable a make a breakthrough into the trench system.

The raid carried out by 30th Division, north of Maricourt, had found the trenches to be lightly held and were able to capture one prisoner. The 18th Division's raid on trenches northeast of Carnoy confirmed that the trenches were unoccupied and badly damaged.

Gas and smoke were discharged throughout the morning on 26 June. At 2:00 hours the 4th Division launched gas on the VIII Corps sector opposite Redan Ridge and the Heidenkopf. Smoke was launched by III Corps at 10:00 hours. Fifteen minutes later gas was launched by the 29th Division on VIII Corps sector. Nine gas clouds were launched upon German trenches north of Beaumont Hamel giving the impression that a British infantry attack was about to take place. Howitzers then lifted their barrages to target German support lines at 12:54 hours in order to give further credence to the notion that an infantry attack was imminent. It was hoped to trick German occupiers to move forward into the front line trench to meet an anticipated British assault, then two minutes later those howitzers would revert back to bombarding those front-line trenches and all those soldiers standing within.

X Corps released gas along their sector at 14:30 hours. It was difficult to estimate the effect of the gas upon the German lines at Thiepval:

> The result of the gas cloud on the enemy has not been ascertained, but it seemed to rise too high before reaching his lines, though its path

across No Man's Land was marked by decolourisation of the grass. It was noticed, however, that the enemy sent up reinforcements to the D Line during the gas attack, and these were engaged by our 60-prs.[6]

At 15:30 hours the release of gas and the artillery barrage were temporarily suspended to allow reconnaissance aircraft from the RFC to take photographs of the German lines to assess the impact of the bombardment upon the wire and enemy defences. Although the aerial photos showed satisfactory results it was considered that more attention should be given to cutting the wire and 18-pounders were ordered onto that target.

As the prolonged bombardment continued the combination of nerve-shattering shelling and gas attacks tormented the German occupiers of Thiepval Ridge. Leutnant Cassel wondered when the British would launch their attack:

Won't the scoundrels ever come to end this terrible game of waiting? No, they did not! One evening there was a gas alarm. Everyone into the trenches with gas masks! In front of us, all along the line, a greenish-yellow cloud rolled slowly towards us. She was hesitating, she did not want to go uphill, it resisted, its nature! One could not remain in the dugouts. There the danger of being choked to death was greatest. Luckily the fire on to the trenches was not too bad, and we got away with a few slight wounded. After an hour the poisonous cloud had disappeared, either blowing away over us or moving and thinning out sidewards. No damage had been done. During the night the same thing was repeated once more with the same result.[7]

The policy of a short bombardment followed by the release of gas was continued throughout the day on 26 June. This tactic would keep German defenders on their toes. They would be forced to post guards in the trenches and compelled to wear cumbersome and uncomfortable gas masks in the hot summer weather. This would unsettle the nerves of the German soldiers and make them irritable. The British guns would be wearing down their resolve before the infantry attack. They would become psychologically and physically drained. When gas was discharged in the 8th Division's sector, jittery troops from the German 180th Infantry Regiment holding trenches immediately opened fire into the smoke in anticipation of a British infantry assault. The 8th Division War Diary reported:

The results of the discharge appeared to be satisfactory. Nearly 20 tons of gas was discharged, and at each discharge the enemy opened fire with rifles and machine-guns but on each occasion the fire only lasted a few minutes.[8]

As British artillery pounded the German lines at Beaumont Hamel on 26 June, patrols from the 29th Division went into No Man's Land to assess the damage done to the wire. It may seem remarkable that these patrols would go out in broad daylight but the 29th Division War Diary reported that German forces in this sector evacuated their front-line trenches during the day and reinforced them during the night:

> The enemy appears to be making no attempt to repair the wire across his front. The patrols established the fact that while the enemy may evacuate the front line by day, it is fairly thickly held by night by sentry posts and machine-guns.[9]

The 2nd Royal Fusiliers also found sections of the German wire opposite Beaumont Hamel unaffected by the bombardment with little damage having been done made. 1st Lancashire Fusiliers also conducted a raid on German trenches at Beaumont Hamel days before the main attack and gathered intelligence about the strength of the dugouts. Disturbingly, they discovered that these entrenchments were so strong they could not be destroyed by the bombardment. This critical assessment was reported to VIII Corps staff but no action was taken. Their infantry would be advancing under the presumption that all the defences on the Beaumont Hamel sector would be obliterated; their occupants either killed or wounded, the survivors so nerve-stricken they would be unable to offer resistance. VIII Corps could have implemented actions to try and destroy these bomb proof bunkers, alter the plan or postpone the attack. Instead they allowed the bombardment to continue with accurate intelligence information supporting the fact that deep shelters were untouched by the bombardment and that the German occupants sheltering below could offer resistance when the infantry troops went forward. Deluded by their own optimism they were knowingly sacrificing their troops to an attack which was destined to fail. Captain Ian Grant, 86th Brigade, recalled:

> We had been in the German front line with a successful raid [1st Lancashire Fusiliers] and knew the dugout and tunnels that existed were more or less bombardment proof. The VIII Corps Staff reflecting the Commander's personality were saturated with optimism, particularly as to the effect of the preliminary bombardment.[10]

Life was extremely difficult for the British soldiers in the trenches as the artillery bombarded the German lines. The thunderous noise of the British barrage disrupted their sleep and any attempts at rest. Likewise, the German retaliatory bombardment was equally disturbing and caused many casualties. They were in no fit state to embark on an offensive. An anonymous soldier from Ballymena serving with the 36th (Ulster) Division at Thiepval wrote in a letter home, commenting on his lack of sleep and shortage of food:

> It was a trying time, as our battalion was in the front line trench all this time, and I got little food and less sleep, the awful roar of our guns making sleep impossible – not to speak of the German retaliation. The bursting of shells caused us a good deal of discomfort and the loss of over a hundred men from wounds and shell shock.[11]

The horrendous noise would resonate for miles across the Somme and the concussions and tremors caused by the explosions at impact could be felt throughout the region. With British guns firing upon German lines along the Somme front for approximately twenty miles throughout the day and night, the sound was so loud that on southerly winds it could be heard along the southern coast of England.

On the German side, a dugout was not a safe place to be. Although German units were sheltering in dugouts beneath the German front-line trenches, they were in a vulnerable situation for if the entrances to their dugouts were blocked they would become trapped underground with little prospect of being rescued. Leutnant Cassel was sheltering in a dugout beneath Thiepval. He became anxious when a British shell exploded directly above his dugout. For his own salvation he made the decision to get up above ground into the trench despite the persistent shelling.

> By and by we now become the target of the heaviest calibre to our cost. The English were damned cautious. They wanted to be sure of overkill. Nobody should be alive when their infantry left their trenches. One afternoon, while I was on my wire bedstead, I heard the dump boom of a heavy gun, the awesome whiz and swish of a rising heavy missile, then the earth was quaking, and while dirt was falling through the boards I saw the beams above me bend and slowly descend by about 10 cm. My heart seemed to stop, now comes the end. But the catastrophe did not come. After the momentary paralysis was gone I left my bed and went into the trench. Rather die in the open air than be crushed between the boards. In the evening I went and inspected the rampart above my dugout and found a crater with a diameter of several metres, made by a 21 cm grenade [*sic*], a dud! Had it exploded whoever was in the dugout would have seen the daylight not before the day of resurrection.[12]

The British soldiers waiting in the front-line and support trenches could observe this mass barrage as it pounded intensely upon the German lines. At night time the flashes of the guns and the sight of star shells floating gracefully in the air provided an unforgettable spectacle for observers on the British side of No Man's Land.

The bombardment of the German lines gave some infantry soldiers confidence that their enemies' resolve had been smashed and that they would walk into the German lines. Private Fred Campling, 8th Norfolk Regiment, was positioned in dugouts close to Carnoy where he could observe the shelling of Montauban:

> Having left billets and taken up quarters in specially constructed dugouts in rear of our lines, we settled down to an enjoyment of the persistent and deadly fusillade of metal and high explosive hurled by our guns into the enemy's lines and occupied villages night and day for close upon a week. The effect, from a spectacular point of view was magnificent, and made a great impression upon us as to the important part taken by our artillery, incidentally giving us confidence that no effort would be spared to minimise the difficulties of the task before us. At no time did the response to this onslaught give us cause for anxiety, although occasionally well-timed shrapnel shells caused loss in our front trenches. During this period of suspense, an atmosphere of quiet confidence and determination prevailed amongst all ranks, giving evidence that we possessed that greatest of all assets – sound morale.[13]

Ten raids were carried out on the night of 26/27 June to assess the effects of three days of bombardment. 13th Royal Irish Rifles carried out a successful raid upon the first German trench and a support trench near the Schwaben Redoubt, capturing one officer, one sergeant major and eleven other ranks in these trenches. A positive assessment of the bombardment along the Thiepval sector was made as a result of this raid. 'The wire was found to be well cut and the trenches were so knocked about as to be unrecognisable in places.'[14]

The bombardment of the German wire proved successful along the Mametz sector of the front. Night patrols confirmed that some breaches were made in the wire; however, the shrapnel bombardment proved ineffective against German knife rests. These defences were also reported to exist in No Man's Land by 1st Lancashire Regiment at Beaumont Hamel. Also known as 'Spanish riders', these were solidly-constructed, steel and barbed-wire boxes that could only be destroyed by high explosive shells.

Most sectors of wire along the Somme front were unaffected, however, by the British bombardment. Lance Corporal James Glenn testified: 'Only afterwards we saw that the bullets out of shrapnel were made of lead and saw the German wire which was made of steel we could see that lead bullets could not cut steel wire.'[15]

The preliminary bombardment of German lines did not achieve the expected results. Many shells missed their targets, while others were duds and did not explode on impact. Indeed, a third of all shells fired were classified as duds. Fuzes for 9.2in howitzer shells in particular detached as they was being projected towards their target and the shells failed to explode as a consequence. An officer belonging to V Corps who advanced towards German lines at Mametz reported 'a dud shell every two or three yards over several acres of ground'.[16] At the same time, fuzes in some shells went off prematurely, causing shells to destroy guns and their crews before leaving the muzzle. This was a common problem amongst 18-pounders, 60-pounders and 4.5in howitzers. The skill shortages in the munitions factories, coupled with long hours in the bid to supply the needs of the army, led to errors and failings – failings that materially affected the success of the Somme offensive.

There were also cases of mechanical failure with the guns themselves. The continuous bombardment caused the recuperator mechanisms of the guns which were designed to return the barrel to the initial position after firing to become worn. This altered the calibration of the barrel's position which meant that the subsequent rounds would be wayward. The 4.7in guns which were used for counter-battery fire also became worn through days of unrelenting use.

There were, though, efforts at improving the accuracy of target location. Trigonometry was used to identify German targets in relation to the positions of the enemy batteries; however, inaccurate maps made it difficult to reconcile the results with aerial photographs taken by the RFC. The only reliable method of ensuring that British artillery fired accurately was for Forward Observation Officers near the front line or in the air in captive observation balloons to relay information back to the batteries. However visual observation was severely restricted on the ground and from the air by persistent low mist and rain.

There was also the problem of compromising the element of surprise which Haig feared in Rawlinson's plan for a longer sustained bombardment before the big push. Focusing all its artillery resources in one area was a clear indication to German commanders that an attack would be launched on that front. Rawlinson did not have sufficient guns or supplies of ammunition to bombard other areas of the German line to help deceive the enemy.

Despite the mass of guns firing upon the German lines, many German batteries remained concealed and were untouched by the British bombardment. German commanders had also brought up further guns in anticipation of a British offensive. It was estimated that 598 German field guns and 246 heavier guns survived the British bombardment and were waiting, ready to be used for when the infantry advanced on 1 July.[17]

On 27 June the day began with thick mists which descended into heavy rain, severely hindering the work of the Royal Flying Corps. Although accurate fire could not be attained, the guns still blasted in the direction of the German lines, denying the occupants sheltering underground no respite. As the guns were hurling shells into the German lines, the infantry was preparing for the assault, with many units able to rehearse their advance across No Man's Land. Although they were not told when they would be going over the top, senior officers instilled in the men the belief that British artillery would destroy the German front line, eliminating any resistance. Such confidence was placed upon the success of the British artillery obliterating the German positions, that they believed the infantry would simply walk into the enemy trenches. However the infantrymen who were to make the advance were only too aware that, although things went well during the training, they had no enemy to confront during these exercises. It has been highlighted that many British units did not receive adequate training before the offensive because they were too preoccupied with manual labour in preparation for the attack. However Lance Corporal Sidney Appleyard confirmed that the 1/9th Queen Victoria's Rifles did carry out training and that their last session was carried out in front of all senior officers from the 56th Division:

> After several preliminary attacks we finally made our last 'dress rehearsal' on 26 June which was witnessed by the General of the Army Corps, the 56th Divisional General and all the Brigadier-Generals, so there was plenty of red tape around. The smoke bombs were sent over just before commencement, and the attack was carried out quite satisfactorily, and all the positions carried quite easily, but of course we had no opponents on this occasion. However, we were informed by all Officers from the Colonel downwards that after our tremendous artillery bombardment there would be few Germans left to show fight, and they all fully expected us to carry the lines with very little resistance. Everybody was quite convinced by this time that this attack was really coming off, and was not going to fall through as similar affairs had in the past. So we all decided to make the most of our few days which remained and we thoroughly enjoyed ourselves. The distant rumble of artillery was distinctly heard during these days, and we heard very fine reports of the damage caused by our shells. According to one report, Gommecourt Wood had been knocked to the ground and the Germans had evacuated the whole position.[18]

Further patrols were sent out into No Man's Land and into the German first line during the night of 27/28 June. Two raids were carried out on 30th Division's front but they returned with conflicting reports. One party entered the German lines without opposition, while another team reported the trench further along the line contained many enemy troops.

During the night of 27/28 June, Captain Bertram Butler led a party of specially-trained men from the 1st Newfoundland Regiment in a raid upon the both ends of Y-Ravine at Beaumont Hamel with the purpose of clearing the German wire ahead of them. The operation failed because their wire cutters were unable to sever the thick wire which had been recently erected. Their presence was soon detected by soldiers from the 2nd, 10th and 11th Companies, 119th RIR in the German line and Butler got his men out hastily.

Butler repeated the raid on 28 June. They succeeded in making several gaps in the wire and gained access to the German front line. Here they were met by heavy machine-gun fire and bombs. They held onto a section of trench until they exhausted all their bombs. Private T.M. O'Neil acted quickly when a German bomb fell amongst him and his comrades, quickly picking it up and throwing it in the direction of the soldier who had thrown it. As it left his hand the bomb exploded, severely wounding him. His actions, though, saved his comrades. The raiding party had to retire when all the officers were wounded. They lost six killed and thirteen wounded. All the wounded were brought back to their own lines, but Butler was captured, later being awarded the Military Cross. However, a German patrol was sent forward in a counter-raid on the British line in which they took some British prisoners who were interrogated and revealed useful information. German forces were on high alert and the trench raids that took place at Beaumont Hamel would make them more vigilant.

The date fixed for the assault was 29 June, though, for security reasons, this remained a closely-guarded secret. During the early morning of 28 June the infantrymen were ordered to stack their packs and collect extra munitions and supplies. The men knew this meant the day of the 'Big Push' was at hand, as Lance Corporal Sidney Appleyard recalled:

> Orders were issued on the Wednesday morning for us to stack our packs, which was carried out without delay, and at the same time each man drew extra bandoliers of ammunition and three bombs. By these actions one could only draw the conclusion that we were destined to go over the top the following morning.[19]

General von Below was reaching a similar conclusion and he requested for further reinforcements and artillery. All he received were a further eight batteries, and his guns were still outnumbered by the British artillery. His anxieties were further heightened by the capture of British prisoners in the last few days before the attack, who during interrogations had revealed details about the time and date of the attack. Those prisoners captured prior to 28 June had been told that the attack would take place five days after intensive bombardment. One prisoner in particular, Private Victor Wheat, belonging to 1/5th North Staffordshire Regiment, 46th Division, had been captured during the night 23/24 June while on a wiring party at Gommecourt. They were discovered by a German machine-gun crew and as the British party dispersed Private Wheat was left behind, badly wounded. Wheat become lost in the darkness and tried to make his own way back to the British line. Instead he ventured towards the German wire where he was captured. After his wounds had been dressed he was interrogated, although he was severely weakened due to loss of blood. Wheat suffering badly from shock and gave details of when the attack would take place and that it would be on a thirty-mile front. [20] Captain Bertram Butler had been wounded and captured with Privates Barrows and Coones from the 1st Royal Newfoundlanders during a failed attempt to raid the German trenches at Beaumont Hamel on 27/28 June. It was reported that during the interrogation the two privates had confirmed that after four or five days of bombardment the main attack would take place.[21] Another similar confirmation came from Private Josef Lipmann, 2nd Royal Fusiliers. Lippman, of Russian descent, had volunteered during 1914 and saw action during the Gallipoli campaign in 1915. Disillusioned by the war and aware that he was about to be thrown into another futile campaign, this time on the Somme, he decided to desert. He told his interrogator that he had volunteered to go on a night patrol of No Man's Land on 27/28 June in the hope to find an opportunity to desert, which he did. On reaching the German trenches, he used his limited German to let them know that he was surrendering. Lipmann furnished his German interrogators with details of unit composition, strategies and colours of smoke signals.[22] The prisoner testimonies were credible and the information gathered was verified by the fact that the British guns had been blasting the trenches and villages that the Germans occupied for five days. The announcement of the postponement of the Whitsun Bank Holiday for munitions workers until the end of July also reached Germany. It is not surprising that German commanders were certain towards the end of June that the offensive was imminent.

As it transpired, the weather intervened. Poor conditions meant that observers on the ground could not identify their targets and the aircraft of the RFC were grounded. Furthermore, the ground was extremely wet and trench mortar emplacements were flooded with water. Due to the persistent rain that fell upon the Somme valley the beginning of the offensive was postponed for forty-eight hours. The order to stand down was issued early evening.

Some of these British soldiers had been marched to the assembly trenches and now they were either sent back to their billets or told to remain in waterlogged trenches until the operation began. After being 'pumped up' for the assault, the men now had to wait, and with time on their hands, the men began to contemplate their fate. Inevitably rumours began to circulate over the cause of the postponement, as Lance Corporal Sidney Appleyard wrote:

> Much to everybody's surprise an order came out at 6 o'clock cancelling all movements and stating that the attack had been postponed for 48 hours, and packs were to be withdrawn. This order gave the rumour

> mongers a fine chance to invent something startling and before the day was out various reports were spread amongst the troops, stating the reason for the postponement. The best of these was that an ultimatum to Germany stating that if she didn't give in unconditionally within 48 hours we should at once set about bringing her to her knees by force. Of course this was ridiculous, and the only reason for delay seemed to be on account of the weather.[23]

The 48-hour postponement of the operation did have the advantage of allowing the artillery to focus upon sectors of wire which had not been cut. It was particularly welcomed by British commanders for it was opportunity for their soldiers to get some rest. Lieutenant-Colonel R. Shoolbred, commanding the 1/16th Queen's Westminster Rifles wrote:

> To our Brigade, at any rate, this postponement was a godsend. The men were quite worn out, and they mostly slept solid for the two days in billets in St. Amand. There was a highly successful concert on the evening of the 29th, and after the Battalion did 'come up dancing' when it went in, in the evening of the 30th.[24]

However, some men complained of being hungry and were about to go into battle with empty stomachs. Lance Corporal Appleyard voiced his thoughts on the meagre rations supplied to the 1/9th Queen Victoria's Rifles who were about to attack Gommecourt. 'Our rations were also poor and the bread issued consisted of one loaf per platoon (about 24 men), which was really disgraceful seeing that the next few days would in all probability find us existing on our emergency rations and one usually expects a fattening before the killing.'[25]

The British bombardment had, of course, caused casualties amongst German soldiers holding the line. German casualties amongst the 121st RIR holding Redan Ridge between 24 and 30 June amounted to twenty-four dead, 122 wounded and one man missing. The 119th RIR defending Beaumont Hamel suffered twenty killed and eighty-three wounded. Although these regiments had suffered casualties and had to endure the hardship of living in deep dugouts while British shells exploded above ground, they would still be able to mount a formidable defence of their positions.

Haig had relocated his staff on 27 June to advance headquarters at Chateau Valvion at Beauquesnes. This chateau was positioned twelve miles northeast of Albert and ten miles north of Rawlinson's Fourth Army Headquarter at Querrieu, close to the area of operation. In between Beauquesnes and Querrieu was General Gough's Headquarters at Toutencourt. On 28 June Haig visited Hunter-Weston's VIII Corps HQ at Marieux where he learnt that recent incursions carried out on this sector on 26/27 June had failed to enter the German trenches during night time raids and that the wire had not been cut. Haig wrote that 'Fourth Army report that VIII Corps made raids by all 4 divisions last night. *Not one entered enemy trenches!*'[26] Haig reported this bad news, which could have a disastrous impact upon the operation, to Rawlinson over the telephone: 'Although raids had been ordered to be made, and had been organised, not one had yet entered the enemy's lines! Unless successful raids are made, troops cannot be depended on in the general attack. They said they failed because the wire was not cut.'[27]

The British Army was about to launch the largest operation in its history, and these reports did not bode well. The enormity and scale of the impending attack meant that the plan could not be reversed. However Haig was receiving numerous conflicting reports from various sectors of the front. On 29 June Haig received reports of successful bombardment of the German lines at Mametz. A German deserter from the 109th RIR told of the state of hunger felt by the fact that food could not be brought to the German front indicating that the bombardment was succeeding in breaking the enemy's resolve. Haig recorded in his diary:

> Prisoner of 109th Reserve Regiment surrendered south of Mametz. States no food has reached his regiment for 3 days and that their first line trenches are nothing but shell holes. The want of food shows the value of night firing on enemy's back communications.[28]

Haig had received mixed positive and negative reports of raids that had been carried out across the entire Fourth Army front. With all the preparations that had been carried out, the transportation of troops, munitions and equipment to the Somme and with their French allies bleeding to extinction at Verdun, Haig had little choice but to proceed with the onslaught upon German positions and hope for the best.

Chapter 6

The Day Before – 30 June 1916

Highly optimistic Generals paid visits to the men in the field to boost their morale on 30 June 1916, the day before the infantry assault. Private James Glenn, 1st Royal Inniskilling Fusiliers, recalled: 'Our General told us the battle which was to open on July 1st was to be the greatest ever attempted by British troops, and so it was, and there is no longer, any doubt about who is going to win. We are superior to the Huns now in big guns, men, etc.'[1]

Major-General Wanless O'Gowan, the 31st Division commander, visited his troops in the field to give them words of support and encouragement. Lance Corporal James Glenn listened to O'Gowan's address to the 12th York & Lancaster's (Sheffield City Battalion) and was among those who believed the General that the proposed operation would succeed: 'General told us all the wire would be cut, there would be no opposition. It would be a straight walk through … the thousands of shells that poured in, we believed him.'[2]

Other officers sent messages of encouragement in writing to be read to the troops. Major-General Sir Henry de Lisle, commanding the 29th Division sent a message to the 1st Lancashire Fusiliers and 2nd Royal Fusiliers who were at Mailly Maillet before their attack at Beaumont Hamel. It was meant to have been read to these soldiers and in the message he referred to their experience during the Gallipoli campaign in 1915 to spur them on:

> Please tell 2nd Royal Fusiliers and 1st Lancashire Fusiliers that I intended to come and wish them good luck before they enter this most important battle in which British troops have ever fought.
>
> I was more anxious to see them, as it is the anniversary of our fight at Gully-Ravine last year, where these two battalions did so well and reached their final objective.
>
> I am completely confident that the men of these battalions will do as successfully tomorrow, and I send them my best wishes and good luck.[3]

Considering that most battalions on the 29th Division's sector had failed to make a successful raid upon the German trenches, how could De Lisle have complete confidence in his division in achieving their objectives? He must have known that the odds of success were very slim? After writing this message De Lisle changed his mind and decided to deliver the message in person. The 1st Lancashire Fusiliers were mustered at Mailly Maillet and he addressed them on horseback. Some of the soldiers who had seen active service at Gallipoli bore resentment towards their commander as he delivered his message. Corporal George Ashurst was among those from the battalion who paraded before him:

> Our battalion was formed into a three sided square outside our village – and up came the general. He was on horseback, with one or two lagging on behind him, and he started to make a speech; he said that we were going to make this attack. And he knew that we would do our duty, as we always had done before. He knew our record of the Dardanelles, he knew he could trust us. You can imagine what all the lads were saying, they were cursing during the speech. 'Shut up, yer bastard!' and things like that. Our officer would turn round and whisper 'Shut up your mouths!' but it made no difference they all kept cursing and swearing 'I wish the bloody horse would kick him to death!'[4]

The 1st Lancashire Fusiliers had landed at Gallipoli on 25 April 1915 and six men from the battalion were awarded Victoria Crosses for acts of valour on that day. They bore witness to sacrifices made throughout the bloody campaign on the Gallipoli peninsular. The only success from that campaign was the manner in which it evacuated the region. So when De Lisle gave the false impression that the British guns were to blast the Germans from the front-line trenches and they were to just walk over No Man's Land and enter them, it was quite understandable that they had little faith in the words of their commanders. George Ashurst continued:

> He said that there would be no Germans left to combat us when we got over there. The barrage and the shelling would be so terrific, the guns would blaze day and night for a whole week, big ones and little ones; and to give you an idea of how many guns used, he said if you placed them side by side, wheel to wheel they would stretch from the English Channel to the Alps. We swallowed it all, we had to. We did not believe him. It was a walkover, the way he was talking. We had nothing to do but to trot over and take the trenches.[5]

Haig was highly confident and it is likely that some Corps Commanders displayed undue optimism in order to please their Commander-in-Chief. It could be possible that they told Haig what they believed he wanted to hear in order to protect their own careers and reputations. Despite receiving reports of uncut wire, Haig wrote in his diary on 30 June:

> Preparations were never so thorough, nor troops better trained. Wire very well cut, and ammunition adequate …The weather report is favourable for tomorrow. With God's help, I feel hopeful. The men are in splendid spirits: several have said that they have never before been so instructed and informed of the nature of the operation before them. The wire has never been so well cut, nor the artillery preparation so thorough. I have seen personally all the Corps Commanders and one and all are full of confidence.[6]

It is interesting to note that Haig now considered his men had been thoroughly trained after his earlier concerns. However, he revealed concern for Hunter-Weston's VIII Corps' front: 'The only doubt I have is regarding the VIII Corps (Hunter-Weston) which had no experience of fighting in France and has not carried out one successful raid.'[7]

Some officers had little confidence in the plan and were pessimistic about their chances of surviving the opening day. Brigadier-General John Charteris, Chief of Intelligence, someone who worked closely with Haig, did not share Haig's expectation of a significant breakthrough. He saw the impending operation as a process of wearing down the enemy, but he was pessimistic about the casualties that would be suffered. Charteris wrote in his diary on 30 June 1916: 'We do not expect any great advance, or any great place or arms to fall to us now. We are fighting primarily to wear down the German armies and the German nation. The casualty list will be big.'[8]

Not everyone was doubtful of success, such as Private W.J. Senescall, belonging to the 11th Suffolk Regiment:

> I suppose the Staff knew what they were doing. Anyway this finished with talks from a 'Brass Hat' as to what was going to happen.
>
> Everything on the German side was going to be obliterated. All we had to do was to advance for three quarters of a mile from La Boisselle to near Contalmaison and there consolidate ourselves while later troops passed over us in their advance. That was what we were told and, with the discipline and belief that 'Brass Hats' were demi-gods, we believed it.[9]

Irrespective of the generals' view of the outcome of the opening phase of the infantry campaign, it was left to battalion commanders to raise the spirits of the men under their command. Lieutenant-Colonel Arthur Rickman wished his men of the Accrington Pals 'Good luck' and commented 'we will soon be on our way to Berlin' before dismissing them.[10] Rickman's address to his men succeeded in maintaining the morale of some of his men. Private Jack Hindle wrote of the jovial banter and high spirits that were displayed by the Accrington Pals that evening:

> On Friday, the last day of June, we were told that we were going in the trenches that night to start the attack in the morning. We did not worry, as we expected it, and you may judge how cheerful we were when I tell you that as we were going to the trenches that night there were a lot of the R.F.A. on the wayside and one of our chaps would say to some of them, 'What do you want bringing back – a German helmet or an officer's wrist watch!' and this was not the only joke, as all were promising to have a drink with each other at a village we had to take.'[11]

By the time the Accrington Pals reached their jumping-off trenches opposite Serre their jovial spirits would have been soured once they saw the abysmal state of these muddy, waterlogged trenches. Hindle recalled:

> Well, at last we got to the trenches, through which we had to walk three miles to get to our position, and it was no joke as the trenches were deep in mud and water, and by the time we got to our post (about 11pm) we were wet through.[12]

The night before the assault was an anxious time for the soldiers waiting for Zero Hour. They had witnessed the tremendous bombardment of the German lines, but they inevitably wondered if the guns had succeeded in cutting the wire and if they would encounter strong resistance despite the barrage. More importantly they reflected upon their own mortality and their minds questioned whether or not they would survive the impending battle. While some men played cards to relieve the anxieties of what lay ahead, others looked to the stars in the night sky and reflected on their loved ones at home. One young officer from Colchester, who would not survive the attack, wrote the following letter on 30 June to his parents:

> I am writing this letter just before going into action tomorrow morning at about dawn. I am about to take part in the biggest battle that has yet been fought in France, and one which ought to help end the war very quickly. I never fought more confident or cheerful in my life before, and I would not miss the attack for anything on earth. The men are in splendid form and every officer and man is more than happy and cheerful than I ever seen them. I have just been playing a rag game of football in which the umpire had a revolver and whistle. My idea in writing this letter is in case I am one of the 'costs' and get killed. I do not expect to be, but such things have happened and are always possible. It is impossible to fear death out here when one is no longer an

> individual, but a member of a regiment and of an army. To be killed means nothing to me, and it is only you who suffer it. You really pay the cost.
>
> I have been looking at the stars and thinking what an immense distance they are away. What an insignificant thing the loss of say 40 years of life is compared with them. It seems scarcely worth talking about.
>
> Well, good bye, you darlings; try not to worry about it, and remember that we shall meet again really quite soon.
>
> This letter will be posted if I get it in the neck.
>
> Lots of love.
>
> From your loving son.[13]

Many soldiers resorted to religion to ease their anxieties. Those who had experienced battle knew what to expect and would be fearful of what was to come. The inexperienced soldiers could only imagine on what horrors they would encounter. They attended services that evening to give them spiritual comfort to get them through the impending ordeal. A padre was present in Foncquevillers to offer prayers to those soldiers who were entering the front line trenches that night in readiness for their assault upon Gommecourt, as Lieutenant C.W. Good recalled:

> Presently came the Padre asking permission to say a few short prayers preparatory to proceeding to the trenches. Just two simple prayers, one of which began 'Lord God of Battles,' the Lord's Prayer, said very humbly, very earnestly, and very reverently by all, and last the voice of the Padre half drowned by the din of the guns 'Blessing … Almighty … upon you … now and forever more'.[14]

Corporal Alfred Kettle, 24th Northumberland Fusiliers (1st Tyneside Irish) was feeling homesick, missing his wife and children. Kettle wrote to Bridget, his wife, on 27 June of his fears for his family if he were not to survive the imminent battle:

> Well dear I was at Church last night and after Benediction I went to Confession and I received Communion after, it is a Soldiers privilege to receive before going into battle, and in battle we will be in a few days' time, and by the time you get this I will be in the thick of it, so Dear I will want all the prayers I can get from you all at home, no doubt there will be a lot of us going into our last fight, but I can tell you Dear I am going into it with plenty of confidence and I have good hopes of coming out of it all right, and if it had not been for you and the little ones I would not care a rap what happened to me, but as I am always thinking of you it makes it all the harder for I know how you will go on if

> anything happens to me, so just cheer up dear, and if the worst happens it cannot be helped and it will just be good as God wills it.[15]

Kettle was killed in the assault upon La Boisselle three days later and would become one of the names listed on the Thiepval Memorial – one of the missing.

One soldier from Sheffield wrote the following last letter to his sweetheart on the night before he died:

> Should you get this letter you will know that I have died for my King and country, and I hope whoever picks me up will forward it to you as we are going into action now and make a charge in the morning. It is to be the biggest battle that has taken place, and I am sure we will win it easily, only someone has to pay the death price. I hope you will look after yourself if you are very ill, and this may upset you. But look on the bright side as I shall await you in Heaven where there is everlasting peace. It's a glorious death dear. Never man looked forward to a better death. I wish you to remember me in years to come, as I die with your name deep in my heart.[16]

Weeks later his sweetheart received this bloodstained letter with the words 'Passed away 1 July'.

Some men were not prepared to go through the ordeal of facing the German machine-guns and decided to self-inflict wounds to get them out of the line in order to avoid the attack and, hopefully, return home to their families. Private Albert Hurst recalled one such incident in the 17th Manchester Regiment before the attack upon Montauban:

> One of my friends shot himself through the hand while we were waiting to go over the top. He put a sandbag over his rifle. He was a very brave man – the last man I'd ever expect to do that. He said, 'I'm not going over!' He asked where the clean sandbags were, he was right by me. He took himself off to the dressing station. I was astounded he was such a brave man. We all saw him do it, but no one reported him.[17]

The soldiers who were about go into battle were given instructions in operational orders that would sober their thoughts 'no man is to fall out to attend to the wounded'. There was a fear amongst the generals that if soldiers stopped to attend to wounded comrades then the advance would be seriously hindered. This, though, was not an uncommon instruction during an attack.

The Germans did know that something significant was about to take place on the Somme sector. As mentioned before, some British prisoners had given information confirming an impending offensive. However, hours before the commencement of the attack, the strongest confirmation came at 22:17 hours on 30 June when Fourth Army HQ released a message of encouragement to the Corps which was to be cascaded to divisional and battalion HQs in order to reach the soldiers waiting in the assembly trenches. The message was broadcast over the radio:

> In wishing all ranks good luck the Army commander desires to impress on all infantry units the supreme importance of helping one another and holding on tight to every yard of ground gained. The accurate and sustained fire of the artillery during the bombardment should greatly assist the task of the infantry.[18]

This was extremely careless because the 'Moritz 28 North' listening station positioned at the southern apex of La Boisselle intercepted a fragment of this message which was sent to 34th Division HQ over the radio. This station was below the ground in a tunnel beneath the Glory Hole and could receive electronic impulses through the chalk including radio messages. This listening post overheard the section of the message which after translation into German said: 'The infantry must hold on obstinately in every yard of ground that is gained. Behind it is an excellent artillery.'[19] This intercept was sent back to 56th Reserve Brigade battle HQ at Contalmaison and was rapidly distributed along the entire Somme sector, placing all German units on alert.

Some troops received breakfast as they waited for Zero Hour. The 10th Essex Regiment, in assembly trenches near to Carnoy, were served with hot tea and rum with bacon and bully beef before they went into battle. Rum had been served to some soldiers in their tea, including those in the 11th Suffolk Regiment, and a few soldiers were totally incapacitated by the alcohol. Private Senescall recalled:

> Now the first of many silly things happened. They had laced the tea with rum – the rum out there was the goods – real thick treacle stuff – I had one sip and whoa! I was not going to make myself for the job we were going on. Some chaps drank and then had some more and they were tiddly. Two of them lay on the floor completely out. A S/M [Sergeant Major] was kicking them both as they lay there to bring them round although to no purpose.[20]

By 06:30 hours the morning sun had risen and the birds were singing, as the British soldiers patiently and quietly waited in their assembly trenches for Zero Hour. At that precise time, exactly one hour before Zero, British artillery disturbed the peace and opened up in unison against the German lines along a 24-mile front. The roar and deafening sounds of this awesome barrage were heard nearly 100 miles away along the Sussex and Kent coast. Civilians along this stretch of coastline thought that a massive naval engagement was taking place in the English Channel. Even along the North Kent Downs the firing of these guns could be faintly heard. High-explosive shells caused earth to be propelled into the sky and shrapnel to disburse in all directions. The Battle of the Somme had begun.

Part 2

VII Corps Sector

Gommecourt had been occupied by German forces since October 1914 and held the distinction of being the most westerly point of the Western Front that they occupied. A tree known as 'The Kaiser's Oak' at Gommecourt denoted this point. Haig's motivation for launching an assault upon Gommecourt was merely 'to assist in the operations of the Fourth Army by diverting against itself the fire of the artillery and infantry which might otherwise be directed against the left flank of the main attack near Serre'.[1] General Sir Edmund Allenby's Third Army was responsible for orchestrating this diversion upon the Gommecourt salient. The 46th (North Midland) Division and 56th (London) Division, both Territorial Divisions belonging to VII Corps commanded by Lieutenant-General T. D'Oyly Snow, were given the task of carrying out the attack. This was a brave and daring venture for both these divisions were two miles north from the main British assault at Serre. There were not enough troops or resources to carry out an assault upon enemy lines between Gommecourt and Serre, which meant that the soldiers ordered to attack Gommecourt were exposed to enemy fire north and south of the village. The overall plan to assault Gommecourt involved launching a pincer movement upon the rear of the village. Both advances would drive into the main German defensive trench system where the two divisions would converge behind Gommecourt, cutting off its apex which protruded into No Man's Land, and isolating the village and its occupants. The 46th Division would advance from the northwest, while the 56th Division would strike Gommecourt from the southwest. Once they had met behind the village they would then proceed to reach the second objective thirty minutes after Zero Hour. No offensive action was ordered to take place on the 2,000 yards of front which directly faced the village and park. The assault upon the village was scheduled to take place three hours after Zero Hour. During those three hours heavy howitzers would bombard the village and its defences.

The attack on Gommecourt was, in reality, a diversionary measure, and so no further objectives were set for VII Corps. Nevertheless, Lieutenant-General Snow's men had already achieved what was required, having drawn the elite 2nd Guard Reserve Division with its supporting artillery batteries to Gommecourt to support the German 11th and 52nd Divisions holding the line. When Haig asked about progress at Gommecourt four days before the assault Snow confirmed: 'They know we are coming alright.'[2]

The German forces holding Gommecourt had an added advantage in that 1,000 yards behind the village there was a ridge that gave them commanding views of the British lines. Those lines consisted of poor communication trenches which in many places were visible to German snipers positioned in Gommecourt Wood. In some sectors the frontline could only be approached at night time because enemy machine-gunners could clearly see British soldiers passing through them during daylight.

Private Arthur Schuman, belonging to 1/5th London Rifle Brigade, wrote of the danger of being in the village of Hébuterne: 'It appeared that the Germans were emplaced on much higher ground, were able to watch all our movements and their shelling was most accurate. Our casualties were considerale.'[3]

The British assault was further disadvantaged by having to face German positions which had been strongly fortified. French forces had made an unsuccessful attempt to attack Gommecourt during 1915, which motivated the Germans to strengthen their defences. Over the intervening months Gommecourt had been transformed into an impregnable fortress with an estimated 120 machine-guns in position pointing towards the British lines. A dense wood formed Gommecourt Park and a sharp salient that protruded into the British sector west of the village. There were three lines of German trenches connected by a labyrinth of interconnecting communication trenches and dugouts. The British gave names beginning with F to the front line fire trenches, and the letter E to the connecting communication trenches. A distance of 100 yards separated the first and second German lines.

The Germans also had fortified Gommecourt Cemetery which was situated midway between the first and second trench lines south of the village. The Germans had strengthened their position along the ridge 250 yards east of the village into a formidable defensive system known by the British as the Maze, known as the Kernwerk or Kern Redoubt to the Germans. The 91st RIR held the northwest sector of Gommecourt facing the 46th Division's front; 55th RIR held the centre of the village and 170th Infantry Regiment was in the trenches southwest of Gommecourt facing the 56th Division.

German engineers had constructed three trench lines known as the First and Second Switch Lines and the Intermediate Line which were crossed by various communication trenches. If the British broke through any of the lines at Gommecourt, these switch lines would be used to block or surround any enemy incursions. Gommecourt Park to the west of the village was heavily defended. It protruded into the British lines creating a salient within fifty yards of the British trenches at Fonquevillers. The Gommecourt salient was a dangerous place to be for the German defenders, because they could be directly enfiladed from British fire from Foncquevillers and Hébuterne. As a consequence German commanders ordered the construction of deep dugouts where their soldiers could shelter. Any attacking force would require heavy artillery to destroy the barbed-wire defences and the labyrinth of entrenchments. Some of these German dugouts were forty feet below ground and were fitted with electric lights and beds. Their accommodation was considerably more comfortable than the muddy trenches being occupied by their British opponents. It was within these deep dugouts that the German soldiers sheltered while the British pounded

Gommecourt with shells. Tunnels linked these dugouts to the front and rear lines. Losses were slight on the German side as a result of these deep shelters.

Although 46th and 56th Divisions were ordered to capture Gommecourt, there was no further instructions as to what they were to do if they achieved their objective. There was no forward planning on how they would exploit such a success. There was no initiative to advance southwards behind the German lines to assist the Fourth Army in their sectors. The only advantage gained from the capture of Gommecourt would be to remove the salient that protruded into the British line and shorten that line.

2nd Guard Reserve Division were fully aware that their position at Gommecourt was going to be attacked. They observed the preparations being made during the previous two months and the week-long bombardment heightened that notion. Expecting an attack at Gommecourt, German artillery were ready to pound the British front line trenches. At 04:00 hours on 1 July German artillery opened fire upon British lines opposite Gommecourt in anticipation of an attack using 4.2in and 5.9in howitzers. Lance Corporal Sidney Appleyard was waiting intently in the trenches.

> The next few hours proved to be the most trying of all, for all we could do was to sit tight in the trench with pieces of shells falling all round, and trust to providence that one did not burst in the traverse.[4]

The German bombardment subsided by 05:30 hours, having caused some damage to the trenches held by the 1/13th Kensington. At 06:30 hours British guns opened fire. The ground exploded along the line as shells turned the region into a scene of carnage, levelling trenches, uprooting trees and destroying any ruins that had survived the week-long bombardment. A smoke screen was released from 4in trench mortars and smoke candles at 07:25 hours. German reports indicate that they were fooled into believing that gas was being released.

As British artillery lifted its barrage to aim at the rear German lines, German guns responded with their own bombardment. As soldiers from the 56th Division stood in their jumping-off trenches many casualties were incurred as they waited for the whistles to blow signifying the beginning of the attack. The German response meant that the British had failed to destroy all the German batteries and gun emplacements close to the front line and that German commanders had moved much of their artillery further back in anticipation of the assault upon Gommecourt

Chapter 7

Gommecourt – 46th (North Midland) Division

The 46th (North Midland) Division commanded by Major-General the Honourable Edward Stuart-Wortley was ordered to assault Gommecourt from the northwest attacking German trenches held by 91st RIR. They were meant to establish a defensive flank in German trenches north of Gommecourt and to establish contact with the 56th Division behind the village. It was estimated that it would take three hours to achieve this. Once they had linked up with the 56th Division at 10:30 hours they were to clear, capture and consolidate Gommecourt.

The 46th Division comprised 137th, 138th and 139th Brigades. The 139th Brigade commanded by Brigadier-General C.T. Shipley was to carry the left flank and the 137th Brigade led by Brigadier-General H.B. Williams was to take the right flank. The 138th Brigade, composed of the 4th and 5th Lincolnshires and the 4th and 5th Leicesters, was to provide support to the other two brigades. The 1/5th and 1/7th Sherwood Foresters of 139th Brigade were to lead the attack upon Fool, Foul and Food Trenches in the German front line. They were supported by the 1/6th Sherwood Foresters. The 137th Brigade comprising the 1/5th and 1/6th South Staffordshire Regiments and the 1/5th and 1/6th North Staffordshire Regiment, was to assault the German front line trenches Foolery, Fount and Folly. They were supported by the 1/5th Lincolnshire Regiment, from 138th Brigade, which was held in reserve.

German forces at Gommecourt learnt precise details about the 46th Division's attack upon this sector from Private Victor Wheat, belonging to the 1/5th North Staffordshire Regiment who had been captured days before the assault. Despite the wire being broken and their trenches being flattened much of their complement had survived as they sheltered in deep dugouts whilst the inferno enraged above them. So when the 46th Division arrived, the 91st RIR defending the northwestern sector of Gommecourt was waiting for them.

The trenches on the 46th Division front were in a bad state. The wet weather had flooded the trenches, which were without duckboards, and

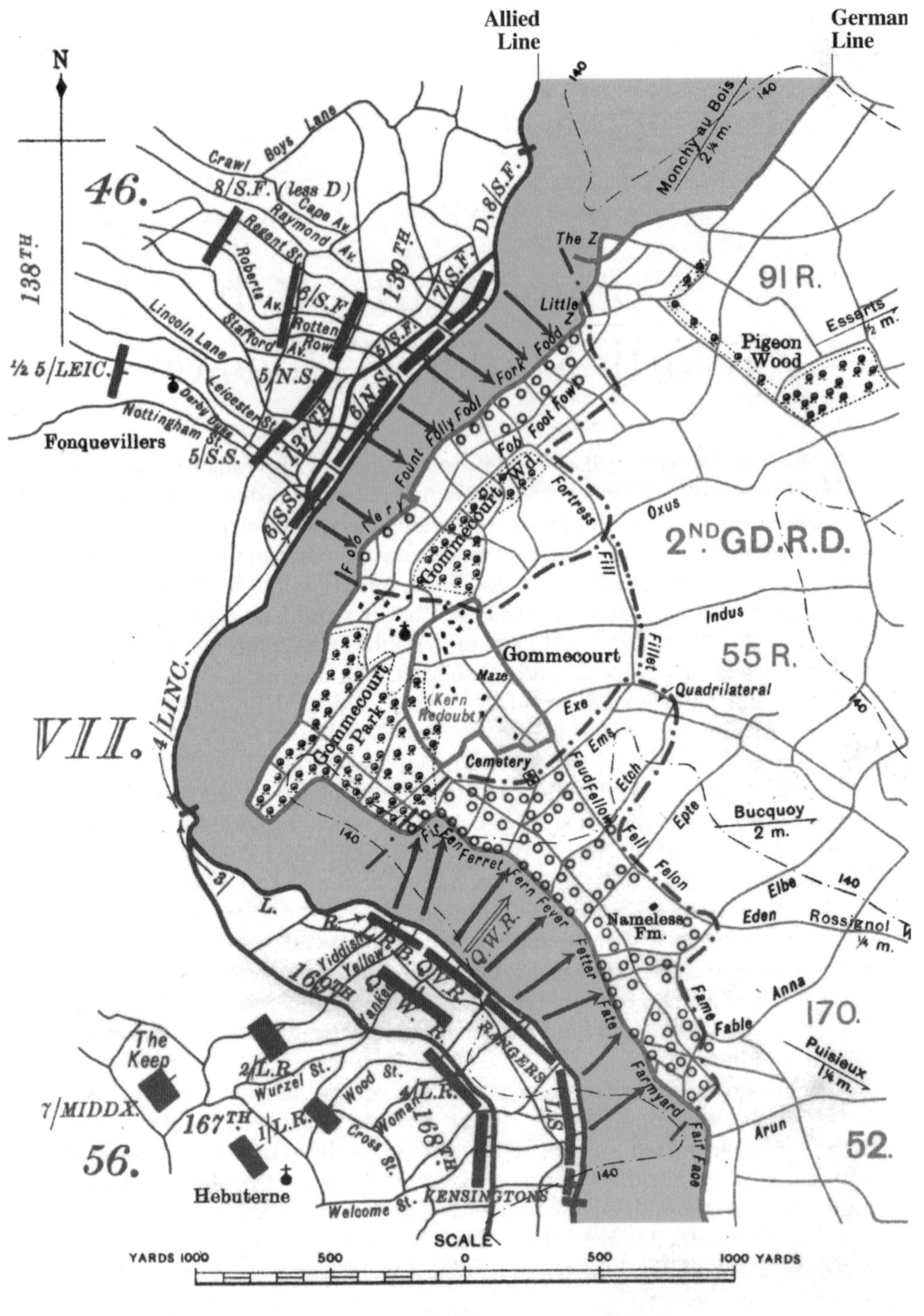

Positions before the assault ....
The Attacks at zero (7.30 a.m.) ....
Advance of reinforcing battalion .... Q.W.R.

First Objective ....
Second Objective ....
Temporary Lodgments .... o o o o o

British names for German trenches (in black) **Fen, Ferret, etc.**

turned them into a muddy quagmire, making passage through them extremely difficult. Lieutenant C.W. Good, the Sherwood Foresters Brigade Intelligence Officer, recalled the dire state of these trenches:

> The weather had completely changed the condition of the trenches; in the Communication and Fire Trenches it was difficult to find a place where the muddy water came below the knees, and for long stretches it was up to the thighs. The effects of this disastrous weather were far reaching; they were in fact, a deciding factor in the attack. Large sections of trenches collapsed altogether. Their sides were simply sliding in, being undermined by the water. Bomb shelters, ammunition dumps, ration stores fared likewise, add to this the damage done by hostile shelling, and the necessary drainage of the trenches to make them even passable with difficulty, and the reader will understand something of the problem confronting the staff, as to how to get the sector ready for the attack.[1]

The men from the 1/7th Sherwood Foresters trudged through the muddy communication trenches, laden with heavy equipment with great difficulty during the night before the assault. The water in these trenches was so deep that they dare not put anything down for a rest break in fear of soaking their equipment or losing it.

The men were packed in so tight within these waterlogged trenches, that when casualties were sustained due to German shelling it was impossible to evacuate them. These wounded men had to rely on being tended to by their neighbours in the trench they occupied, while others sunk and drowned in the mud. Lieutenant C. Ashford recalled:

> Casualties in our own trenches were very heavy owing to the intensity of the bombardment and the congestion and owing to the fact that many men who fell disappeared beneath the mud, it was difficult to help the wounded. I stumbled over many bodies which were out of sight beneath the mud.
>
> The congestion in the jumping off trenches caused still greater congestion in the rear. Men pressing forward, found themselves held up by congestion in front and made a vulnerable target. This caused heavy casualties.[2]

The 137th Brigade advanced on 46th Division's right flank. The first three waves belonging to 1/5th North Staffordshires commanded by Lieutenant-Colonel William Burnett DSO got into No Man's Land with few casualties, but as soon as it was the turn of the fourth wave to leave the British front line a machine-gun, positioned at the south-western end of the German Ford Trench, opened fire and a German artillery barrage descended upon this battalion's sector. Communication trenches leading to the front line became blocked as shells exploded and the fifth wave dropped all their equipment. When the fifth wave reached the British front line trench they found the fourth wave still there, reluctant to enter No Man's Land. The fifth wave passed the fourth wave and went over the top. All the officers belonging to this wave became casualties and when the remnants arrived at the German wire, they found it to be uncut and an unidentified officer gave the order to retire.

Further casualties were incurred as survivors from the battalion withdrew to the British front line. Lieutenant-Colonel Burnett went forward to assess the situation and tried to motivate his men to move forward with Lieutenant Eli Robinson and 2nd Lieutenant Read. Robinson went forward with one party, but Read and the majority of his men were killed. Burnett was discovered lying severely wounded in the abdomen in a communication trench leading to the front line and died from those wounds two days later. Chaos reigned and despite efforts to reorganise the battalion and launch a fresh assault, the battalion remained in the front line and communication trenches during the rest of that day.

The 1/6th North Staffordshire Regiment did not fare much better in their attack. Four waves left the trenches in quick succession, but the advance across No Man's Land faltered when they got bogged down in the muddy ground. The smoke screen which was meant to conceal their movements was so thick that it caused its soldiers to loose direction and when they reached the German wire they found it to be intact. Once German machine-gun crews became aware of an assault they immediately ascended from their deep dugouts, got their weapons into position in shell holes and fired into the smoke. German artillery opened fire as the Staffordshires got caught in the wire. They also targeted the British lines making it difficult for supporting waves to get into formation, causing casualties before they even entered the battle.

When the 1/6th South Staffordshires and the 1/6th North Staffordshires reached the German wire they were met by German bombs and rifle fire. Those few men who got through the wire and entered the German first trench were unable to hold the position and were hastily driven from this trench. The second and third waves that followed them were caught in the wire and mown down by the German machine-guns. Within half an hour of the commencement of the attack the wind changed direction and blew in the direction of the British lines. This meant that the smoke cleared from No Man's Land and German machine-gunners could see the British coming. The assault of the 137th Brigade was brought to a halt.

The 139th Brigade carried the extreme left flank of the 46th Division's assault upon Gommecourt. The first three advancing waves lost heavily as they crossed No Man's Land under the partial cover of smoke but they were able to enter the first German trench. The 1/7th Sherwood Foresters on the left flank of the 46th Division's front and the 1/5th Sherwood Foresters on their immediate right led the brigade upon Fool, Foul and Food Trenches.

The 1/5th Sherwood Foresters experienced difficulty leaving their trenches. Lieutenant Downman's platoon had been reduced from thirty-five men because fifteen were taken for duties as runners, bombers and carriers and the other five had been wounded. Therefore Downman went over the top with fifteen men, but as he led them into the smoke he lost direction and contact with his entire platoon. Linking up with the remnants of another platoon he was one of the few who got into the German trench system on the northwestern perimeter of Gommecourt, as he later recorded:

> Smoke bombs had been thrown out about 7.20 am and did nothing but make a thick fog of evil smelling and tasting smoke on our own parapet, making it difficult to find the way out and calculated to lose one's sense of direction. When beyond the smoke I looked for my platoon which should have been lined up in the prone position in front of our own wire, but I could see no one, either to right, left or ahead. Looking back I saw a party coming out carrying tremendous burdens, offering a good target and moving very slowly. This was No. 4 platoon, supposed to bring up wire, steel poles, bombs, flares etc for 'A' Coy. Without waiting I proceeded towards the German lines alone, taking a direction towards the left, according to instructions. I passed the advanced line, a very shallow and narrow trench and came to a very large shell hole, here I came up with 2 of my platoon who had evidently gone on without waiting for me. They gave me the direction further to the left and followed me. I was not aware of shells, bullets or other missiles whilst in the open. On reaching the German wire I found it well cut and smashed up and had no difficulty getting through. On reaching the German front line I found a trench nearly eight foot deep, very wide and totally blocked at one end and partially blocked at the other. It was quite empty. I jumped in and climbed out the other side, still followed by the two men I met in the open, but I do not remember seeing them after this.[3]

The 1/7th Sherwood Foresters, commanded by Lieutenant-Colonel Lawrence Hind MC, entered the battle with twenty-seven officers and approximately 600 other ranks. Their waves lost direction in the thick smoke as soon as they left their trenches. Captain T.H. Leman with 'A' Company advanced from the new front line trench in No Man's Land. Lieutenant Macpherson and 'B' Company started from the old British front line. As soon as the third and fourth waves entered into the old British line, they came under a torrent of machine-gun and shell fire which decimated their ranks. As the dead and wounded lay in the muddy waterlogged trenches, Captain Round tried to bring 'D' Company forward and found it difficult to pass through the communication trench and did not reach No Man's Land until 20:00 hours.

Hind advanced with the first wave with the battalion adjutant, Captain Roby Gotch. They got to within fifty yards of the German trenches where they had to take refuge in a shell hole. As Hind raised his head to look for a gap in the German wire he was shot in the forehead and killed. Gotch too was killed. Private Bernard Stevenson who advanced with 'A' Company recalled:

> We go over the top. Lieutenant Wilkins leads five platoon. 'Come on Robins'. Out of the smoke come bullets. Someone falls dead. On we go. Thro' the German wire and into their front line trench. Our artillery has not stopped and is dropping shells near us. A red light is burned to try and stop them. Wilkins wounded in arm. Sgt Buckley slightly wounded, also Berry. Captain Leman sees Germans emerging from the smoke between their first and second lines. Shoots at them with his revolver. Is shot in arm and face. Germans advance with bombs from right and left. Everyone attends to himself. I tumble out of trench and see small trench just behind their wire, about 6 yards away. Get in this. Germans throw a bomb into it and the dirt half buries me. Lie doggo. Cpl Small (of 6 Platoon) and a C company private with me. Take subdued counsel, and decide to wait 15 hours. British bombarding German trench all day with heavies, whizz-bangs, rifle grenades and trench mortars. Earth keeps falling on us. Can hear Germans talking and firing.[4]

As the remnants of the 1/7th Sherwood Foresters pressed forward the smoke screen was clearing across No Man's Land exposing them to German machine-gunners. Only twelve men from the leading waves reached the first and second German line and once the smoke had cleared they realised that they were on their own. Isolated and with only small numbers they decided to withdraw to the German front line. Here they linked up with twenty-five men from following waves who were making a spirited attempt to consolidate this position.

Lieutenant Cyril Burton got a small bombing party close to the third German line. Burton was badly wounded, but he and his party took refuge in a shell hole where they fired rifle grenades into the third line. Burton died in this shell hole. Those who were not wounded retired to the German front line trench where they established contact with Captain T.H. Leman, who had been wounded twice, but persisted to organise a defence of the German trench, which was attacked by bombers from both flanks. The Sherwood Foresters were unable to resist because many of their rifles had been dropped in the muddy water of the trenches and would not fire. Their supply of bombs quickly diminished and unable to use their rifles they were left impotent, unable to continue the fight. Those that survived leapt up to the parapet of the old German front line in a bid to escape from the oncoming German infantry and darted for cover in nearby shell holes in No Man's Land. Captain Leman was killed, but later that night under the cover of darkness six men crawled back to the British lines.

The mopping-up and carrying parties from the 1/7th Sherwood Foresters and the attacking waves from the 1/6th Sherwood Foresters were unable to follow the first three waves who became isolated in the German trenches. This was because the men in the rear waves had real difficulty climbing out of their mud-filled trenches and, as the smoke screen cleared, German machine-gunners were sweeping No Man's Land and shells were falling all around. It was a scene of chaos and mayhem.

Those parties who were holding out in the German lines at Gommecourt were running out of bombs and were in desperate need of reinforcements. They soon found themselves cut off and were eventually killed or captured. As the morning progressed German soldiers in the front lines were bombing and firing machine-guns upon the remnants of the 46th Division holding on to their isolated positions in shell holes in No Man's Land.

Lieutenant-General Snow at VII Corps HQ wanted the 46th Division to attack again, to the dismay of Major-General Edward Stuart-Wortley, commanding 46th Division, who knew that to send his troops back into the fray would be a hopeless and forlorn effort with no chance of success. Stuart-Wortley eventually relented and during that afternoon ordered rear waves from the 1/5th South Staffords and 1/5th North Staffords from 137th Brigade and 1/5th Leicesters from the 138th Brigade to attack

The unpopular order to launch another attack filtered down to brigade level. Brigadier-General C.T. Shipley commanding the 139th Brigade ordered another assault upon the German trenches, and Lieutenant-Colonel Goodman received the order at 12:30 hours to attack with two companies from the 1/6th Sherwood Foresters under the cover of another smoke screen at 13:15 hours. It was difficult for carrying parties to bring smoke bombs through the muddy communication trenches to get to the front. With no smoke, Goodman held his men back. Another attack was ordered to take place at 14:30 hours, but still no smoke was available. Goodman received assurances that smoke would arrive at 15.25 hours and that he was to launch his attack five minutes later. The smoke bombs being carried by the 1/6th Sherwood Foresters never arrived, due to the carrying parties being stuck in the mud. Some smoke was discharged by the Staffordshires on their right flank, but this thin smoke drifted back towards the British front line and provided inadequate cover. Goodman realised the consequences if he allowed his men to carry out the order to launch a second assault. His men would be wiped out and with great courage he made the decision not to send them into No Man's Land. He reported:

> About 3.30 pm a small film of smoke appeared but in no way interfered with the view of the enemy trenches. I accordingly at 3.35 pm ordered

> the men not to go over the parapet. There was a heavy and extremely accurate barrage and also considerable rifle fire. I was, and am, quite satisfied that there was no possible chance of reaching the objective and no result could have been achieved. As a matter of fact, owing to a mistake, a party of 20 did leave the trench, most of them were struck down at once.[5]

Those battalions that did attack were easy targets for the German machine-gunners. The situation was so grim that Captain Scott, the 1/7th Sherwood Foresters Medical Officer, assumed command in the absence of a combative officer. He managed to get his party of men seventy yards into No Man's Land. Most of them were hit so Scott decided to withdraw back to the British lines. As well as tending to the wounded Scott organised the defence of this trench for most of the day and was awarded the Military Cross. Some survivors from the assault managed to crawl back to the old British start line. One such was Private Alfred Bennett who was wounded in the German first line:

> I was just getting ready for mounting the German trench when I got my wound, and what made it worse was that I had to get back to my own lines across 'No Man's Land'. I kept creeping in one hole and then another and expecting every minute to be blown to be bits. As I laid in the holes, the earth rocked like a cradle. At last I came to a dressing post. They had just dressed one of our officers and the doctor dressed me next.[6]

The overall failure of the 46th Division to break the German line at Gommecourt meant that the German defenders could concentrate their energies to confronting the 56th Division's assault south of the village. Lieutenant C. Ashford MC cited the following reasons for the failed attack upon Gommecourt:

> Extensive advertising, weather conditions, uncut wire, interval between zero hour and attack, smoke which hid gaps in the wire, overloading the men especially leading waves, congestion in the trenches, exhaustion of men.[7]

The 46th Division's assault upon Gommecourt was a tragic disaster, resulting in 2,455 casualties. Among the battalions belonging to 137th Brigade that lost heavily were the 1/6th South Staffordshires with fourteen officers and 205 out of 500 ranks lost; 1/6th North Staffordshires lost thirteen out of twenty-three officers and 292 out of 740 men. The 139th fared no better, with the 1/5th Sherwood Foresters losing twenty-four officers and 395 men and the 1/7th Sherwood Foresters, eighteen officers and 391 out of 536 men that took part in the operation.

Lieutenant-General Snow, commanding VII Corps, came to the conclusion that 'the 46th Division … showed a lack of offensive spirit. I can only attribute this to the fact that its commander, Major-General the Hon. E.J. Montagu Stuart-Wortley, is not of an age, neither has he the constitution, to allow him to be as much among his men in the front lines as is necessary to imbue all ranks with confidence and spirit.' This was an unjust comment directed at a commander for someone who had lost 2,455 casualties in his division attacking the most heavily fortified position on the Western Front, in which was only supposed to be a diversionary attack. Stuart-Wortley was relieved of his command before a court of enquiry was convened; and was the only commander to be removed as a result of the 1 July attack.

Chapter 8

Gommecourt – 56th Division

The 56th Division commanded by Major-General C.P.A. Hull was assigned the task of launching a diversionary assault upon the village of Gommecourt on a 900-yard front from the southwest. The German 170th Infantry Regiment was holding the south-western section of Gommecourt and was waiting for them to cross No Man's Land. The attack was to be made by the 168th and 169th brigades, their ranks being augmented by the 1/8th Middlesex Regiment and half of the 1/3rd London Regiment who occupied the first British line where they could provide carrying parties to support the attacking brigades. These two battalions belonged to 167th Brigade the rest of which was held in reserve at Hébuterne.

168th BRIGADE

The 168th Brigade, commanded by Brigadier-General G.G. Loch, comprised 1/14th London (Scottish), 1/12th London Regiment (The Rangers), 1/13th Kensington and 1/4th London Regiment, was ordered to assault the German lines between Nameless Farm and Rossignol Wood. 'C' Company, 1/5th Cheshire Regiment (Pioneers) were attached to this brigade to erect barbed-wire to consolidate captured positions. Carrying the 56th Division's right flank, the 168th Brigade had to cross an average 750 yards of No Man's Land to reach the German first line. Their overall objective was to secure the third German trench line named Fame–Felon and to consolidate positions on the flanks including Nameless Farm.

The 1/14th London Scottish was on the right flank, supported by the 1/13th Kensington which was to assault Farmyard Trench in the German first line and then proceed to Farm Trench in the second line. The 1/12th London (The Rangers) on the left flank, supported by the 1/4th London Regiment, was to assault Fetter and Fate Trench in the German frontline and then attack Nameless Farm where together they could continue to the third German lines of Fell and Felon Trench.

The 1/14th London Scottish entered the line during the previous night at 22:00 hours. An hour later scouts from the battalion ventured into No Man's Land to assess the state of the German barbed- wire and discovered that much of it had been untouched by the British barrage. Lieutenant Calder led a party of scouts and two sappers from the Royal Engineers into No Man's Land with two Bangalore Torpedoes measuring twenty feet in length. These were pushed in the uncut wire and detonated, causing a breach in the wire. The sound of this operation was smothered by the British artillery carrying out preparatory barrages.

Major Cedric Dickens (grandson of the novelist Charles Dickens) commanding 'A' Company 1/13th Kensington was ordered to consolidate the trenches captured by the 1/14th London Scottish and to dig a fire trench across No Man's Land to the captured trenches, which would provide a means to link up with the London Scottish in the German trenches and would be used to defend the 56th Division's southern flank from German counter-attacks. His role was an important one and his company was strengthened with trench pioneers and thirty men from 1/5th Cheshires. Snipers were present to provide covering fire and a platoon from the 1/5th Cheshires was on hand to erect barbed-wire defences when the trench had been dug.

Smoke was released on the left flank of the 56th Division's line at 07:20 hours which shrouded the entire line within five minutes, providing cover for the assault waves to covertly assemble in No Man's Land. As they left their trenches German shells began falling upon the British front line and communication trenches. The soldiers from the London battalions lined up along the jump-off tapes and lay on the ground as the shells exploded behind them. At 07:30 hours they rose from their position and advanced towards the German lines.

On the 168th Brigade's front the 1/12th London and the 1/14th London Scottish led the advance followed by the 1/13th Kensington and 1/4th London Regiment. A section from the 1st London Field Company, Royal Engineers, was attached to the brigade to assist in clearance of obstacles and the consolidation of captured trenches.

The 1/14th London Scottish dashed into the dense smoke across 300 yards of No Man's Land. The smoke emitted from the British line was meant to conceal their advance; however it proved to be more of a hindrance than a help, as it caused great confusion. The dense smoke made it difficult for the men to maintain the planned direction of the advance and many became disorientated and lost. High explosive German shells exploded around them and they suffered heavy losses. The left company moved towards Nameless Farm and across the line of advance of the 1/12th London such that the two battalions became interspersed. On the London Scottish right flank No. 2 Platoon of 'A' Company commanded by Captain Sparks became totally lost in the smoke and only two or three men joined the remainder of the battalion in the German lines. No. 3 Platoon deviated from the planned line of advance and was engulfed in shellfire. Only Lieutenant Petrie and a small party reached the German line. The wire on the other platoons' front was uncut but by great fortune they found a path through the wire used by German patrols. They penetrated the German lines at the junction of Fair and Farmyard Trenches on the right flank. Here they met little resistance because the German trenches were severely damaged by the British bombardment and its defenders, who had anticipated the attack, had been withdrawn to support trenches, where they could escape the British barrage. It was here in the support trenches, where they were better equipped and positioned to offer a more effective defence, the Germans had chosen to meet their enemy.

Advancing on the 1/14th London Scottish's centre, Major Francis Lindsay's 'B' Company pushed forward across No Man's Land through the smoke. They found the wire in front of them completely destroyed and the first German trench, named Fate, severely damaged and unoccupied. Encountering no resistance they swept over the second trench called Fall Trench to their final objective Fame Trench, which they found abandoned. Lindsay immediately set about the work of consolidation in the third German line. Although they came under considerable German fire from a second trench line further along a slope, he extended his line left along the trench. On his right flank, Captain Sparks from 'A' Company had blocked the approaches to Fair and Fancy Trenches. German snipers and bombers launched successive counter-attacks in frantic efforts to force 1/14th London Scottish to withdraw from their trenches.

'C' Company, 1/14th London Scottish, commanded by Major Claud Low DSO advanced with Nos. 11 and 12 platoons across destroyed barbed-wire defences and entered the German lines unopposed. However they were unaware that they were passing over many German soldiers sheltering underground in deep dugouts. When Lieutenant Lamb brought forward two further platoons following behind Low's platoons they were stopped by a group of German soldiers who had just ascended from these dugouts. This enemy resistance was subdued by bombs and 'C' Company went further into the network of the German trench system. They dashed across Farmyard and Farmer trenches. Lamb found the remaining elements of 'C' Company in the third trench line. German heavy artillery was targeting their guns on this position and Lamb found Major Low severely wounded and unable to continue leading the company. Command passed to Lamb:

> Our bombardment has been so severe that it was impossible to distinguish any of the Hun trenches, which were all linked up by shell holes outside. I asked Major Low if he knew what trench we were in. He was not certain, but thought it was Farm. As the smoke was still thick it was not possible to see many yards in front.[1]

Lamb was unaware that he was in Fable Trench, the third German line and 'C' Company had deviated towards the right flank of the 1/14th London Scottish line in between 'B' Company on the left and 'A' Company on the right. Lamb took control of the situation sending the wounded Major Low back to the British lines and ordered half of 'C' Company to consolidate and hold Fable Trench. Lamb led two platoons forward a further 120 yards expecting to reach Fable Trench. When the smoke cleared he realised that he had surpassed his orders and had gone deeper into German lines. They were coming under increased German fire as the enemy spotted them on the exposed slope between Fable Trench and the Gommecourt-Puisieux Road. Lamb returned to Fable Trench where at 07:55 hours he found that there were no other officers or NCOs left. With the sixty-nine men that remained, Lamb consolidated the trench he had gained

'D' Company, led by Lieutenant John Brown-Constable, was on the left flank of the 1/14th London Scottish and suffered heavy casualties from the outset. No. 16 Platoon was nearly annihilated by shell fire as it assembled in the jump-off trenches prior to Zero Hour. No. 13 Platoon advanced towards Farmyard Trench but was stopped by the German wire which had not been cut by the British barrage. Unable to make a breach through this wire, the men became vulnerable and exposed to German snipers and bombers holding Farmyard Trench. When Brown-Constable came forward with No. 14 Platoon to support No. 13 Platoon they found a way through the wire and into the German first trench.

The occupiers were driven out and when No. 15 Platoon came forward they established contact with a party from the London Rangers on their left flank. Brown-Constable continued with the assault leading his company along a communication trench but was killed after securing the first German trench. Passing through two German trenches the remnants from these platoons came under fire from a German rifleman and were vulnerable to German bombers. A hole in the traverse of the trench caused some casualties and it was Sergeant Edward Gurney who went over the top and killed the German riflemen. He was killed in this effort to make a breakthrough, but his comrades overwhelmed the traverse and the remnants of the company were able to continue the fight towards the third German trench line.

'D' Company had suffered many casualties but the survivors persisted with great determination to reach the fourth German trench where they were repelled by German bombers. Some got into the trench but were unable to hold their ground and were forced to retire to the third trench line. Here they were overwhelmed by the enemy with bombs and rifles from the front and their exposed left flank.

The remnants of Captain Sparks' 'A' Company, 1/14th London Scottish, worked on consolidating the communication trench that linked Fair and Fancy Trench as a fire trench on the right flank facing south and east. They defended this position with a Lewis Gun, rifles and bombs, bravely repelling German counter-attacks. Lance Corporal Aitken with a bombing party drove back a German assault along Fair Trench, enabling the London Field Company, Royal Engineers, to enter the trench and secure it. As high explosive shells exploded above them and snipers fired upon them, these sappers succeeded in barricading Fair Trench against further German attempts to recapture the position. Knocking down four traverses they blocked each end of the trench occupied by the 1/14th London Scottish and strengthened their defence with barbed-wire at both ends.

Although 'A' Company had consolidated a section of Fair Trench, it was in a precarious position. German artillery was targeting its position vehemently as well as firing shells into No Man's Land. This meant that 1/14th London Scottish could not receive reinforcements and desperately-needed supplies of munitions which were hastily depleting. If they were to hold the position they would need more troops and ammunition.

Two platoons from 'B' Company 1/13th Kensington followed 100 yards behind the rear waves of the 1/14th London Scottish led by Lieutenant Penn and 2nd Lieutenant Pike, accompanied by two squads of bombers from Headquarters to clear and consolidate captured German trenches. 'C' and 'D' Companies from the 1/13th Kensington led by Captain Ware and Taggart occupied the first British trench vacated by the 1/14th London Scottish at 07:50 hours. The clearing parties from the battalion went across No Man's Land to support the 1/14th London Scottish but they too were unable to see through the thick smoke. Major Young, commanding the 1/13th Kensington, recalled:

> Owing to the smoke it was impossible to see from our trenches what progress the London Scottish had made, and as no message was received from them Lieut. Beggs went out with a patrol to ascertain whether they had been successful in occupying the German first line trench. The patrol became separated in the smoke and Lieut. Beggs went on by himself. He got into the German trench and found that the London Scottish were in the first line and then returned to our lines.[2]

Major Cedric Dickens anxiously waited for reports confirming that the 1/14th London Scottish had captured the first German lines, but no news was forthcoming. Dickens' 'A' Company 1/13th Kensington had been ordered not to start digging a fire trench across No Man's Land until the 1/14th London Scottish had secured their objectives. The 1/13th Kensington were in an uncomfortable position as they occupied the British front line trench. German artillery deluged this position with heavy calibre shells. These front line trenches did not have dugouts or bomb proof shelters because they were dug in haste which meant that the battalion experienced heavy casualties. Even if it received word that the London

Scottish had captured its objectives, the 1/13th Kensington were unable to dig a fire trench due to enemy machine-gun fire that was sweeping across No Man's Land. Despite some messages coming from the London Scottish in the German trenches desperately appealing for ammunition and reinforcements they found it extremely difficult to get supplies across. Major Young remembered:

> Owing however to the heavy barrage which the enemy kept up over 'No Man's Land' and to machine-gun fire it was found impossible to dig the trench. At intervals during the morning messages were received from the London Scottish asking for reinforcements and grenades. Every effort was made to comply. A certain number of men were got over but I had been unable to ascertain how many. Some boxes of grenades were got over at intervals during the morning. Capt. Ware displayed great gallantry in getting a carrying party over.[3]

Unable to begin digging across No Man's Land, Dickens focused upon supplying the London Scottish with bombs and ammunition. As German artillery and machine-gun fire intensified as the morning progressed this task became more difficult. 'C' Company which was holding the first British line was called to assist, but its commander Captain Francis Ware, was killed while leading a party in an attempt to cross No Man's Land with supplies.

168th Brigade's position in the German trenches was extremely precarious. Although it occupied the German front line trench, it was engaged in a savage close-quarter battle within the complex German support trench system and the 169th Brigade on their left flank was experiencing problems in getting into the German front trench.

By 08:00 hours it was apparent that the 46th Division had failed to make a breakthrough north of Gommecourt, which meant that the 56th Division was attacking a heavily fortified position with virtually no support. German soldiers that had been sheltering in deep dugouts beneath Gommecourt Park emerged unscathed from the bombardment and were able to launch devastating machine-gun fire upon 168th Brigade. The assault upon this strongpoint was now becoming an isolated operation with enfilade fire hammering at the stranded men from three directions. Some of the trenches were badly damaged and in places lacked adequate cover and were clearly visible to German soldiers holding higher ground. No reinforcements or supplies were forthcoming and efforts to take forward supplies of bombs and small arms ammunition made by carrying parties failed due to No Man's Land being heavily shelled.

The 1/12th London advanced on the left flank of 168th Brigade's front. They had to attack Fett and Felt Trenches before reaching Nameless Farm. They got into Fetch and moved along the communication line named Epte

Trench where they were seen from 168th Brigade's observation post to consolidate the junction of Felon Trench and Epte Trench. The right company had reached the front line where they linked up with the 1/14th London Scottish, but they suffered heavily from machine-gun fire as they advanced to the second German line, Fall Trench when the company was reduced to less than twenty men.

German soldiers belonging to 170th Infantry Regiment occupying Nameless Farm held onto their position. Nameless Farm was derelict and in ruins, but its cellars provided adequate shelter and offered an ideal defensive position. They still held on to Felon Trench behind them although 1/12th London were holding the junction of this trench with Epte Trench. As they held onto this position, the British attackers became exhausted and their supplies of bombs and munitions gradually depleted causing their assault to fizzle out.

The situation was becoming desperate for the battalions still holding on to trenches in the German lines. By 09:00 hours the 1/12th London was compelled to abandon its position and withdraw to the first German trench line. While a small party of 1/12th London was still entrenched close to Nameless Farm, the 1/14th London Scottish line in Fame Trench was left exposed. German counter-attacks converged upon Fame Trench and within fifteen minutes the position became untenable. Major Francis Lindsay ordered the remnants of the two companies under his command to retire to Farm and Fall Trenches. Here they consolidated their new position, established a place to fire their Lewis Gun, set up blocks and made an effort to establish communication with Farmer Trench.

For the rest of the morning the process of consolidating the captured German lines continued. Three hundred German prisoners had been captured. When they were sent across No Man's Land eighty of these captives were killed by their own shellfire. Unable to get to British lines they were then sent down under guard into their own dugouts while the barrage continued.

Between 09:00 hours and 10:00 hours a party of fifty-nine belonging to 1/14th London Scottish still in the British line were formed into three carrying parties with bombs, small-arms ammunition and three machine-guns. They were separated into three parties in the hope that at least one party would get across No Man's Land. Only three men out of the fifty-nine managed to reach their comrades in the German trenches; the rest were either killed or wounded by shellfire as they dashed across No Man's Land. During that morning Lieutenant Frederick Stanley Thomson leading the 1/14th London Scottish section from the 168th Brigade machine-gun Company managed to get a Vickers machine-gun to 'A' Company.

At 09:50 hours the 1/13th Kensington received orders from 168th Brigade HQ to send a company to Fate, Farm and Fall trenches to close a gap between the 1/14th London Scottish and the 1/12th London lines. This message came too late for the 1/12th London as their hold in the German trenches had already been broken. Major Young, commanding 1/13th Kensington, was unaware that the 1/12th London's line had collapsed and he instructed Captain Taggart to lead 'D' Company across No Man's Land. At 10:05 hours Young received a report that Taggart had been wounded and most of his company had not got beyond their first line. Captain Harris, from 'B' Company was ordered to take command of the survivors and lead them across No Man's Land. Harris reported that 'D' Company numbered just twenty men, the rest being casualties, and that it was impossible to cross No Man's Land. Major Young also received a message at the same time from Major Dickens who reported that he too had suffered heavy casualties in the first line and that the combined strength of 'A' and 'C' companies amounted to just fifty men.

Towards noon the situation in the German trenches at Gommecourt deteriorated further. German artillery still targeted No Man's Land and the 1/12th London Rangers and 1/14th London Scottish were unable to hold the trenches that they had captured. The situation in the British front line occupied by 1/13th Kensington was just as bad. At 13:10 hours Major Dickens reported: 'Shelling fearful … Trench practically untenable, full of dead and wounded. Very few men indeed left. Must have instructions and assistance.'[4]

There were no reserves in the British front line that could reinforce the 1/14th London Scottish position even if they could have got across No Man's Land. As snipers pinned them down, a party of German bombers made an effort to get behind them. The London Scottish were isolated and there was no hope of reinforcements and supplies getting through to them.

By 13:30 hours the situation was so desperate for the 1/13th Kensington that all available men around were gathered and sent to bolster Captain Harris's force of twenty men from 'D' Company holding the first British line. Major Young wrote: 'Collected 32 men (Signallers, runners, servants and shell shock cases) and sent them under Capt. Harris to trenches W.47.R.'[5] German shells rained down upon the British lines. Major Young reported: 'The bombardment continued with unabated violence. The trenches in front of the reserve line were now practically destroyed'.[6]

Major Dickens sent the following report regarding the situation in the British trench at 13:48 hours to Major Young. In this report he mentions his search for Captain Ware, but at that time he was unaware that he had been killed:

> Sap absolutely impassable owing to shell fire. Every party that enters it knocked out at once. Captain Ware had been wounded somewhere there. I have just crawled to the end of it with Scottish machine-gun party. Could not find him. One of the Scottish had his hand blown off. Our front line in an awful state. Two more men killed and 1 wounded.

> Estimate casualties 25 killed and 50 wounded. Impossible to man large lengths of our front line. Digging quite out of the question and position of the Scottish serious.[7]

Within fifteen minutes of sending this message the British had lost control of this section of their own front line. Dickens sent the following dismal message at 14:04 hours:

> I have as far as I can find only thirteen left besides myself. Trenches unrecognisable. Quite impossible to hold. Bombardment fearful for last two hours. I am the only officer left. Please send instructions.[8]

Despite the problems in the British front-line trench, the 168th and 169th Brigades were still holding onto parts of the first and second German lines. German artillery continued to target No Man's Land and reinforcements and carrying parties with much needed supplies were unable to get through to the London battalions desperately holding the trenches captured that morning. They were trapped and as they suffered mounting casualties, and their supplies of bombs and munitions became exhausted, the German fought to recover the ground that they had lost. At 14:00 hours the London Scottish was joined by remnants from the Rangers, Victoria's Rifles and 1/13th Kensington whose lines had collapsed on the left flank. This mixed group managed to offer a stout defence of Fate Trench despite their ever-decreasing stock of ammunition.

Captain Sparks, 1/14th London Scottish, returned to Gommecourt after the German withdrawal to the Hindenburg Line in March 1917 and recalled finding boxes of bombs in No Man's Land, together with the remains of the men from the carrier parties who were killed in vain efforts to replenish the stock of munitions of the stranded Londoners:

> The position we had held was most precarious. We were exposed to enfilade fire from the high ground on our right, on our right front, and to fire from our immediate front. The enemy had observation from all these points and could place their shells exactly where they pleased. It was the want of counter-battery work on the part of our artillery; coupled with the impossible position which we held, that rendered the position untenable. I had never been able to appreciate the large number of attempts which had been made to get through bombs and ammunition to us, but I appreciated something of what had been done, during this visit, finding a number of boxes still in No Man's Land with the remains of our fellows who had tried to bring them over.[9]

When Major Francis Lindsay was killed by a sniper, Captain Sparks assumed command. He moved from one trench to the next giving orders and direction to his men. Miraculously he was not hit. When they got to firing their last rounds, they resorted to searching the dead and wounded that lay around them for ammunition. As the British rate of fire decreased, their enemy realised that they were running short of ammunition and that their line was close to being broken. By 16:00 hours Sparks made the decision to retire. He sent the following message to battalion headquarters:

> I am faced with this position.
> I have collected all bombs and S.A.A. from casualties. Everyone has been used. I am faced with three alternatives:
> To stay here with such of my men as are alive and be killed.
> To surrender to the enemy.
> To withdraw such of my men as I can.
> Either of these first two alternatives is distasteful to me. I propose to adopt the latter.[10]

Captain Sparks ensured that as many of the wounded who could be moved would be evacuated back to British lines. He ordered Farm Trench and the eastern section of Fall Trench to be evacuated via the communication trench leading into Farmer Trench. They then proceeded into Farmyard Trench and used a German sap that penetrated into No Man's Land. Here they were able to make the frantic and desperate dash back to their own lines. All available cartridges were given to five men who stayed behind to cover their retirement. Captain Sparks, Sergeant Carl Latham, Sergeant Leggatt, supported by Corporals Fairman and Weston covered the remnants of the London Scottish who ran the gauntlet of machine-gun and shellfire to reach the British line, though some men of the 1/14th London Scottish did not make it.

Sergeants Carl Latham and Leggatt who were covering the withdrawal died in the same shell hole. Battalion Headquarters had received an inaccurate report that Captain Sparks had also been killed by shell fire, but he, like so many others, sought refuge in a shell hole and waited until darkness to crawl back to the British line. Lieutenant-Colonel B.C. Green was astounded and amazed to see that contrary to reports of his demise that Sparks was alive and well, when he later walked into Battalion Headquarters.

Lieutenant Frederick Thomson continued to fire his Vickers machine-gun from Fancy Trench. With the majority of his crew killed he was unable to carry this cumbersome weapon back to the British lines. Before evacuating Fancy Trench he disabled his gun before abandoning it. He requisitioned a German rifle and as he dashed across No Man's Land he turned round to fire at the enemy when he was killed.

By 15:00 hours the remnants from 1/12th London had been pushed out of the German front line. At that same time 'A' Company 1/13th Kensington was having difficulty holding onto the British trench as they had borne the brunt of heavy German artillery throughout the day. Major Dickens had sent a runner to battalion headquarters seeking instructions and an hour later Major Young ordered him to retire to the reserve trench and hold it. At 15:45 hours Dickens reported to Young in person that he had brought back his party of thirteen men together with survivors from the Brigade covering party.

At 16:00 hours German troops had retaken their trenches and, by 15:30 hours, the German bombardment ceased. During that night survivors who were either wounded or trapped in No Man's Land used the cover of darkness to crawl back to the British lines.

169th BRIGADE

The 169th Brigade, led by Brigadier-General E.S.D'E. Coke, consisted of the 1/9th Queen Victoria's Rifles, 1/5th London Rifle Brigade, 1/16th Queen's Westminster Rifles and 1/2nd London Regiment. They were ordered to advance across No Man's Land on the left flank of the 168th Brigade. Their first objective was to assault the first German trench lines named Fern, Ferret and Fen. They were ordered to capture strongpoints at the cemetery, the south-western portion of the Maze and the southern corner of Gommecourt Park. On clearing Ems and Etch communication trenches they were to assault and capture the German occupied garrison named the Quadrilateral. This was an exceedingly tough and ambitious objective. If they reached this stage their third objective was to clear and capture Fill and Fillet Trench. Finally they were ordered to assault a large garrison east of the Maze beyond the first switch line and establish contact with the 46th Division and then both divisions would attack and systematically clear the village of Gommecourt and Gommecourt Park from the east. They were given three hours to complete this operation.

The 1/9th Queen Victoria's Rifles carried the right flank, while the 1/5th London Rifle Brigade assaulted on the left. The 1/5th London Rifle Brigade would be greatly exposed to German machine-guns positioned in Gommecourt Park as they advanced right across their field of fire. The 1/16th Queen's Westminster Rifles were to follow behind these two battalions in support, with 'A' Company, 1/5th Cheshire (Pioneers) and the 2/2nd London Field Company, Royal Engineers.

At 07:18 hours a curtain of smoke was discharged from the south-eastern corner of 'Z' Hedge and within six minutes smoke was covering the entire front. At 07:27 hours the leading assault waves from the 1/9th Queen Victoria's Rifles and 1/5th London Rifle Brigade moved forward 150 yards as the smoke continued to drift across their line of advance. As they continued to move towards the enemy lines, German guns targeted the British trenches along this sector. Captain C.E. Moy was one of the officers left in reserve watching the scene that unfolded before him:

> Looking forward towards the trenches I saw shrapnel bursting in the air, forming fleecy puffs; from the ground rose earth fountains, mingled with the yellow and black smoke of high explosive shell. Soon there was nothing to be seen but smoke … and always the thunder and rattle of guns grew more deafening; always the scream of their flying shells grew louder across the sky. The enemy had now started replying; the din grew heavier and the smoke denser. I was able to discern a few running figures which looked like ants – they were the infantry going over. Immediately from the enemy trenches came the tap-tap and rattle of machine-guns to add to the noise. Above all this the sun shone brilliantly. How many men had already looked upon it today for the last time? [11]

The 1/2nd London Regiment followed the 1/9th Queen Victoria's Rifles. Private F. Inglefield described the ordeal of crossing No Man's Land:

> As 7.30 approached we get the order to stand by, and almost immediately, we knew that the Queen Victoria Rifles had gone over, by the rat, tat, tat, of the machine-guns, their part of the work being to capture the first two lines. Then our Platoon Officer shouted out 'over lads', and we scrambled out on top, without anymore ado, and what a hearty reception we got too, shells of every description, were whistling through the air, machine-guns rattling out, and snipers very busy, and what with the aircraft overhead, the roar was something deafening. Of course we paid no attention to this whatever, and went on, until we reached their barbed wire which proved to be about twenty yards in thickness, but our artillery had made a mess of it, and it was pretty easy to get through. It was here that we lost men, they were being bowled over like skittles.[12]

The first wave of the 1/5th London Rifle Brigade was advancing at right angles to German machine-guns positioned on the southern perimeter of Gommecourt Wood and soon came under fire from this flank, as Arthur Schuman, of 'A' Company, 1/5th London Rifle Brigade, recalled:

> The whole battalion of four companies, were in the front line trench at Hébuterne, awaiting the order to 'Fix bayonets' then 'Over'. Whistles blew. At 7.30 am – up the scaling ladders under the cover of a smoke screen – the advance started towards the German lines. The smoke screen began to lift. Officers led the way, most of whom dropped immediately. machine-guns seemed to crackle from every direction, I kept my head down as low as possible, helmet tilted to protect my eyes, but I could still see men dropping all around me. One on my left clutched his stomach and just collapsed. Another, a yard to my right, slumped onto his knees. The din was terrific, stifling any screams.[13]

Those that got as far as the wire found it cut in most places along the 169th Brigade sector. However the cut wire was still an obstacle, as Schuman explained:

> Entangled wire had to be negotiated. Just one opening – on which the German fire was rapid and most accurate. Not many of us got through. The journey seemed endless, but at last a number of us fell into a German trench.[14]

It was apparent that some gaps in the wire had been blocked with concertina wire by the Germans. The wire opposite Fern and Fever trench was found to be uncut by the British shells and held up a party from 1/16th Queen's Westminster Rifles led by Lieutenant J.J. Westmoreland. However his men were able to inflict considerable casualties upon the enemy using rifles from their position within No Man's Land.

The German front-line trenches had been so badly damaged by the British guns that they had been transformed into nothing but a series of shell holes. A number of trenches were completely levelled and some of the entrances to dugouts had been blocked by displaced earth from the shell explosions. There were also reports of seeing large 9.2in shells which had not exploded. As soon as they got into the German lines sign boards were erected in the captured trenches.

On reaching the German first trench Private Arthur Schuman described the scene as he took breath and looked around to see who else from the 1/5th London Rifle Brigade made it into the enemy trench:

> It was deep and well built, but had been badly knocked about. A few dead lay there. I sat on the firing platform to regain my breath. I felt something very soft. Looking under a ground sheet I saw the body of a German officer. As well as very heavy loads we all had three bombs, but sometime later a party of battalion bombers got through and dropped bombs in every dugout. A few of my company had made it with me, notably Sgt (Bunny) Austin, a great pal of mine at Tadworth, Sgt Olorenshaw, and twin brothers Ebbetts (both Cpls). None of them returned.[15]

Captain G.H. Cholmeley, belonging to the 1/5th London Rifle Brigade, led the first wave from 'A' Company on the extreme left flank towards Firm Trench. Despite being wounded in the shoulder after leaving the British trench, he carried on. Covered by Lewis machine-gunners, Cholmeley got his company into Firm Trench and sent a report to his commander, Lieutenant-Colonel Arthur Bates, reporting that everything was going well. Some of the German occupants were taken by surprise as they ascended from the shelter of the dugouts and immediately threw up their hands indicating their intention to surrender. Other German soldiers offered stouter resistance, but were soon overwhelmed. 2nd Lieutenant Charles Doust got into the German front line but was shot by a German officer, who, in turn, was immediately killed. Three waves followed and they set about securing the German line from Firm to Fir Trenches. Once the first German line had been consolidated they then proceeded through Eel Trench into Feast Trench. At the junction of Fen and Fir Trenches a Lewis Gun was set up which fired upon the left flank. This sole Lewis Gun kept the heads down of the German soldiers from 170th Infantry Regiment defending the southern sector of Gommecourt Park. Sergeant W.M. Lilley recalled that:

> Throughout the day the enemy continually strove to force us out by means of bombers covered by snipers. Their forces steadily increased as time went on. We protected our flank by means of a Lewis Gun mounted at the point where Fen meets Fir. This gun traversed our left front and kept the enemy down. Our supply of grenades gave out and we had to search the trench for the German grenade stores.[16]

Some men from 'C' Company, 1/5th London Rifle Brigade, got into the Maze behind Gommecourt very quickly. Lance Corporal J.H. Foaden wrote:

> On leaving our trenches with the 5th wave we encountered a barrage of shell fire and M.G.s. The smoke was fairly dense, but after advancing 50 yards it was comparatively clear and the M.G. fire very heavy. The enemy was found in his dugouts in Feast. I saw two taken prisoner and others shot or bombed. On reaching the Maze, which was little more than large shell holes, I bore to the left and took up a position in a large shell hole. I was rather uncertain whether my position was correct, but Capt. Harvey arrived and confirmed it as being so. There were about ten men at this point, which we hold and commenced to consolidate at once. Snipers were very busy and killed one and wounded two during the first two minutes. We were filling sandbags whilst lying down, until there was sufficient cover to work our Lewis Gun.[17]

'D' Company, 1/5th London Rifle Brigade got across No Man's Land and managed to secure its objectives within the German trench system within twenty minutes. Corporal Roland Ebbetts reported:

> At 7.27 am the 1st and 2nd waves advanced, the former went 150 yards and got down for a moment and then advanced again, cutting the German wire where necessary. In most places it was blown to pieces and the advance was straight forward. The enemy first line was reached without opposition and a party of company bombers, seven in all, under Lce.-Cpl. H.G.F. Dennis entered the German front line S.E. of Ems

> in Fern and bombed along Ferry to the base of Exe. This party encountered two hostile parties of about six each, all of whom were killed. All dugouts were bombed. This party then proceeded along Exe and, finding no Germans in their second line, occupied Eck, which they proceeded to consolidate. Sentries were posted. Our wiring party put up five rolls of concertina and three strands of barbed wire. A German M.G. in the wood was put out of action, as were several snipers. By 7.50 am all D Company was in Eck as per schedule and were busy consolidating the position.[18]

The 1/9th Queen Victoria's Rifles quickly advanced 400 yards across No Man's Land upon Ferret and Fern Trenches surprising its German occupants and then charged towards the second German line. The German barrage was not heavy and they made this advance with very few casualties. During the advance they discovered that the British bombardment had little effect on some sections of the German wire in front of Fern and Fever Trench. As they proceeded towards Feed and Feint Trenches, in the second German line, the wire was undamaged in some places. German resistance was found to be strong. The 1/9th Queen Victoria's Rifles, and the 1/16th Queen's Westminster Rifles who were following in support, were held up in some places as they tried to find gaps through the wire and by unrelenting machine-gun fire coming from Nameless Farm on their right flank and from Etch trench close to the German front line.

German artillery then began to shell No Man's Land, inflicting casualties upon the supporting waves and began to fire upon the path in front of them. Bridging equipment that was intended to be thrown across the trenches to enable the attacking waves to cross the enemy trench lines had been destroyed in No Man's Land and none reached the German lines. This meant that they had to jump into the German first trench and then climb out on the other side in order to proceed to the second trench line.

The 1/9th Queen Victoria's Rifles and the 1/16th Queen's Westminster Rifles suffered heavy casualties very quickly as they approached the first German trench line. These battalions came under increased rifle fire from Fellow Trench where some soldiers from the 2nd Guard Reserve Division had ascended from their dugouts and immediately set up a strong defence of their position.

Some German soldiers were taken completely by surprise as they emerged from their dugouts. According to reports from the 55th RIR, the first notion that an infantry assault were happening was when the attacking British soldiers appeared from the smoke and were on their parapet. Unable to get into the fight they threw up their hands in surrender. Shells were falling upon No Man's Land continuously and it was impossible to escort the captured prisoners back towards British lines. British casualties were mounting, there was no other option but to send these captives back into the dugouts where they had come from. Many of these German prisoners got back into the fight when the British passed further into German lines and attacked them from the rear.

The British had succeeded in severing telephone cables buried two metres deep, denying the German defenders telephone communication throughout that day. They had to rely upon runners to relay messages from the front to rear lines. Some German soldiers were buried alive within these deep dugouts. With only one entrance into a dugout, there was remote chance of escape and German commanders learnt from that first day of the Somme that it was necessary to construct dugouts with two exits to ensure that occupants could use one to escape if the other was blocked. A report from the 55th RIR noted:

> Even the tunnelled dugouts, which were six metres deep, could not keep out the heavy 15in shells; they were blown in. It was again proved that dugouts should have at least two exits. This is the only way of preserving the occupants from being buried.[19]

The remnants of the 1/2nd London Regiment got across No Man's Land and into the German trenches. Private F. Inglefield described the scenes of carnage and confusion that reigned in these lines and battalions became intermingled as they chased German soldiers fleeing along communication trenches.

> The Germans all this time were beating a hurried retirement, down their communication trenches, very few coming to grips with us. Well on and on, we went, until we reached their third line, and we finally settled ourselves down in it. There were a great many dead, in all three lines, and in the dugout of the first line, a great many were ousted out, by bombs. We then commenced to consolidate our position, of course we were all mixed up, we did not know who was who, an officer and about two N.C.Os remained and eventually these were bowled over. A great many of our wounded that were able, crawled into the trenches with us, and were made as comfortable as possible.[20]

Despite being isolated and lacking reinforcements, the amalgamated battalions of the 1/9th and the 1/16th Queen's Westminster Rifles battled on as they pressed forward from the second line. Parties from the 1/16th Queen's Westminster Rifles got held up at the German wire in between the second and third German trench lines. Company Sergeant Major Donald Hawker advanced with 'C' Company under Captain Hugh Mott:

> We advanced about 7.30 am and progressed steadily, under heavy smoke cloud, over the first and second German lines, which had then

> fallen into our hands. Between the second and third lines we were delayed for some moments by uncut wire, and from this point considerable numbers of enemy troops could be clearly seen, evacuating their support positions and retiring hastily to their rear. They presented an irresistible target to our men who got down behind the wire and opened a strong fire. We now under a heavy shrapnel fire, and the noise was terrific, rendering fire control difficult. Captain Mott, having found and enlarged a gap in the wire, gave the order to cease fire and push on. It was at this juncture, I believe that he became a casualty. It was for some moments difficult to communicate the order and to control the fire.[21]

On reaching the Nameless Farm–Gommecourt Road they formed up behind a steep bank, four and a half feet high, which lined the road. They lined this bank, which provided reasonable cover, to shelter from the heavy machine-gun fire that was been directed from a position ahead of them. They soon became exposed to German machine-gun fire positioned in Gommecourt Wood from their rear left flank. Company Sergeant Major Donald Hawker belonging to the 1/16th Queen's Westminster Rifles recalled:

> I collected a party and advanced as far as a slight bank or raised road, which afforded some cover from a withering machine-gun fire, which now enfiladed us from Gommecourt Wood. We had many casualties here; and while I was walking to a flank to determine our next move, I was put out of action by a shot through the neck and wind pipe.[22]

Hawker tried to get back to the British lines but first he had to leave the embankment at Nameless Farm Road and pass over through the second and first German trench lines at the same time avoiding shell and machine-gun fire from both sides. He wrote:

> Sergeant Courteney of the 2/2nd Londons took over the party, and I made my way towards the rear, hoping to get some medical aid to stop the severe bleeding from my mouth and nose. On my way back I received two more bullet wounds, and on reaching the original enemy front line I lost consciousness.[23]

Back at the embankment along the Nameless Farm–Gommecourt Road they were attracting German fire on their right flank as well as from Gommecourt Wood, but a Lewis gunner from 1/16th Queen's Westminster Rifles kept their heads down. This unidentified Lewis gunner was aided by Corporal L. Ratcliffe MM from the 1/5th Cheshire Regiment and this gunner kept firing his Lewis Gun for twenty minutes until he was shot and killed. They were effectively pinned down by the overwhelming German firepower. Anyone who attempted to ascend this bank along the Nameless Farm–Gommecourt Road was killed. Sergeant G.F. Telfer from the 1/9th Queen Victoria's Rifles was among those men lining the bank:

> The second as well as the first German line was taken with very little resistance, and it was getting to their third that we first caught it really badly. About 20 yards from our objective was a sunken road, about 6 feet deep, at which we were held up for sometime, say ten minutes or a quarter of an hour, owing to the Boche fire being too heavy to climb up the bank and go forward. We were also subjected to heavy cross fire from our right flank as the Rangers had not come up. It was here that poor old Captain Cunningham was bowled over and I am of the opinion he was killed, but of course one did not have the chance of testing his pulse – this is only my opinion, and really I hold out very little hope for our poor skipper, for so many poor chaps were killed instantaneously with bullet wounds through the head when lying up on the bank pouring lead into the Hun.[24]

At 08:20 hours Rifleman J.H. Orchard a signaller from the 1/16th Queen's Westminster Rifles, who had got into the German trench line, braved No Man's Land to take back the only message that battalion Headquarters received that day confirming that Fellow Trench in the German third line was still occupied by the enemy and that both the Queen's Westminster Rifles battalions were suffering heavy casualties. Lieutenant-Colonel R. Shoolbred commanding 1/16th Queen's Westminster Rifles received this message late that evening, after the battle was over, because Orchard found it difficult to pass back across No Man's Land.

Eventually, though, the risk was taken, and the men stormed forwards to the third German line. The majority of officers from 1/16th Queen's Westminster Rifles who had reached the Nameless Farm–Gommecourt Road had become casualties and only one sergeant survived. This breakout was made possible by the actions of a brave junior NCO named Packer, as Sergeant Telfer explained:

> Quite on his own initiative Lce Cpl. Packer, the bombing corporal of No.1 Platoon, who led on our trek up to the trenches, although wounded in the ear, rushed forward and bombed the Germans, followed instantaneously by several others, causing the occupants of the German third line to slacken their fire for a few seconds, and with the help of the QWR, the third line was rushed and taken.[25]

By 08:30 hours some elements from 'B' Company arrived and joined the survivors from 'C' Company of the 1/16th Queen's Westminster Rifles. They fought towards the cemetery then made their way along Ems communication trench in the direction of the Quadrilateral. They established contact with another bombing party which was working on their right flank and together they were able to secure the complete section of the German second line along Feud and Fellow trenches.

An officer from the 1/5th Cheshire Regiment, believed to be 2nd Lieutenant George Arthur, took command of a bombing party from the 1/16th Queen's Westminster Rifles led by Sergeant W.G. Nicholls and pushed further forward up Ems Communication Trench. They reached the Quadrilateral but were stopped by German bombers. They could not advance any further and continued to fight until all their bombs were depleted. By 09:00 hours Arthur realised that they could not hold onto their position without bombs, decided to withdraw. He was killed as he covered the retirement of his party.

At 09:00 hours the London Rangers on the right flank were in control of Felt Trench, the second German trench system. The 1/9th Queen Victoria's Rifles were in Fell Trench, the third line, with elements of the 1/9th and 1/16th Queen's Westminster Rifles were holding Fellow and Feud trenches and Gommecourt Cemetery. On the left flank, parties from the 1/5th London Rifle Brigade were holding Fen and Feast Trench and a position in Gommecourt Park.

The British bombardment had proved to have been effective in some areas. Much of the first line of the German trench network had been levelled or reduced to lines of irregular shell holes. Corporal Roland Ebbetts, 'D' Company 1/5th London Rifle Brigade wrote:

> From 8.00 to 11.30 am the consolidation of Eck proceeded without interruption from the enemy with the exception of a sniper in the wood on the left and one on the right. Our right was in touch with the Q.V.R. until this time. Eck was in such a condition that the Company were in isolated groups in holes with heaps of earth between them. These heaps were very large, but communication was maintained between them by shouting and men crawling over the top. [26]

By 09:48 hours the 1/9th Queen Victoria's Rifles and the 1/16th Queen's Westminster Rifles had secured the third line which comprised of Feud, Fellow and Fell Trenches. However they were on their own for the London Rangers on their right flank and the 1/5th London Rifle Brigade on their left were nowhere near to reaching their objectives. The battalion War Diary reported 'The Germans were pressing hard at this time and the shortage of bombs began to be felt'.[27]

Efforts were being made to get vital supplies to them. Lieutenant-Colonel V. Dickins commanding 1/9th Queen Victoria's Rifles ordered 2nd Lieutenant Ord MacKenzie to lead the reserve company across No Man's Land with supplies of bombs at 09:30 hours but due to congestion in the

British trench lines reinforcements were unable to make an attempt to reach their comrades in the German lines. Once they ascended their trench at 10.30 am they were mown down by enemy fire losing heavily. The War Diary recorded: 'As soon as the party left the trench they came under heavy machine-gun fire and half the party became casualties immediately. This party was unable to get across No Man's Land the enemy's barrage by this time being intense.'[28]

Lance Corporal Sidney Appleyard was among the party who made a courageous but futile attempt to bring vital bomb supplies to the British battalions holding on to their fragile foothold in the German lines: He remembered.

> Orders were then issued that the Company bombers would have to go over with a fresh supply of bombs and render assistance. At 10'o clock we started off under Mr Mackenzie with twenty-four bombs per man, and as soon as we advanced over 'No Man's Land' the Germans opened a very deadly machine-gun fire, which laid a good number out. On we went and it seemed marvellous how the pieces missed us, for the air appeared to be alive with missiles. At last advancing about 30 yards, I was struck in the thigh by a bullet, the force of which knocked me over. The only thing to do was to crawl back.[29]

German counter-attacks with bombing parties were moving down Ems Trench towards Feud Trench. They regrouped north of Gommecourt Cemetery and attacked positions held by the 1/16th Queen's Westminster Rifles and the 1/5th London Rifle Brigade in Gommecourt Park. By 10:50 hours the counter-attacks had reached the cemetery. It was here that a party from 'C' Company, 1/16th Queen's Westminster Rifles held back a German attack behind a barricade for ninety minutes.

At 11:00 hours two platoons from 'D' Company, 1/16th Queen's Westminster Rifles made an attempt to cross what its unit history described as 'the zone of death'[30] in an effort to bring reinforcements and supplies of bombs to the German lines. The only remaining officer from 'D' Company had been hit and it is was left to Sergeant W.H. Couper to organise this new initiative but as soon as each man went over the top they were hit by German fire.

The shortage of bombs became a critical issue for the parties from the 1/9th Queen Victoria's Rifles holding the third line. At 11:35 hours bombers from the reserve company tried to reach them but they could not get across No Man's Land.

Indications that German forces were about to launch a counter-attack to drive out the British from their trenches were becoming apparent on the sector held by the 1/5th London Rifle Brigade, with German snipers operating in numbers close to its position. Lance Corporal Roland Ebbetts noted:

> By 11.30 am the enemy were observed creeping to the edge of the trees in front and on the left, but only singly. From this time the snipers became more and more numerous, and began to fire along Eck.[31]

According to Brigade Major Captain L.A. Newnham, 169th Brigade Headquarters received at 11:40 hours positive news from RFC observers who had flown over Gommecourt, that British troops were strongly occupying the third German line at Feud, Fellow and Fell Trenches and that no forces were occupying the Quadrilateral. This report was received by Brigadier-General Coke:

> At 11.50 am I asked Division for confirmation of the Quadrilateral being unoccupied as I desired to push on to it as soon as possible and at 12.06 pm I received a report from RFC that the Quadrilateral was still unoccupied by either side.[32]

The RFC report arrived before midday and probably related to what its observers had seen earlier that morning. By the time the report had reached 169th Brigade's headquarters the British had lost control of the third line of trenches. Brigadier-General Coke at Brigade HQ did not know that the report was out of date and that the British battalions were barely holding onto the first and second German trench lines, and that German forces were in control of the Quadrilateral and the third line. Consequently, Coke wanted his men to push on and to try and take what he believed was an unoccupied strongpoint.

He therefore ordered that a message be taken to British parties holding out in the German lines. At 12:35 hours six special runners from the 1/2nd London Regiment volunteered to run the gauntlet of shells and bullets to take the following message across No Man's Land:

> R.F.C. observers repeatedly report Ems, Etch, and the Quadrilateral empty of Germans. Push on bombing parties at once and occupy Quadrilateral. Barrage on Quadrilateral lifts at 1.30 pm.[33]

Out of the six runners only one got through and was able to deliver the message which was addressed to 'any officer' in the German trenches. Company Sergeant Major Donald Hawker who was lying wounded in the first German trench line reckoned he received this message around 16.00 hours. By that time those who were able to continue the fight had been driven back to the front German trench line.

At 12:30 hours parties from the 1/16th Queen's Westminster Rifles tried to consolidate Feud and Fellow trenches but exhausted their own supplies of bombs and the supplies that they scavenged from German trenches. Unable to hold the third German trenches of Feud and Fellow, 2nd

Lieutenant J.A. Horne ordered a withdrawal to Feed Trench, the German second line. Horne took hold of the Lewis Gun and provided covering fire as his men withdrew. He died at his gun protecting his men. His commanding officer Lieutenant-Colonel Shoolbred had these words for him:

> His leadership, after the deaths of all his seniors, of the heroic band of Queen's Westminsters and Queen Victorias and Cheshires, who fought for nearly five hours against determined enemy counter-attacks had more to do than it is possible to attempt to set out in detail, with the gallant stand made in these enemy trenches after the failure of the attack. The honour of the Victoria Cross would not have been more than his bravery and leadership merited. The few survivors spoke of him and his conduct throughout the day in terms of glowing admiration, but indeed there were many also with him, N.C.O.s and private riflemen, between whom it is impossible to *differentiate* in the summing up of a day of deeds whereby a glorious page was added to the records of the Regiment.[34]

Determined German counter-attacks continued to assault their fragile line from 12:30 hours, with gas shells reported to have been used by the Germans fifteen minutes later. German forces then launched a concerted effort to drive the British from their trenches from Gommecourt to Nameless Farm. Wave after wave of troops from the 11th and 12th Companies of the 55th RIR, 2nd Guard Reserve Division, fought a brutal close-quarter battle to regain their lost trenches.

The 1/5th London Rifle Brigade was holding its ground close to Gommecourt Park, but German bombers, protected by snipers, steadily reclaimed trenches that they had lost during the morning. There were also indications that German forces were about to launch a counter-attack on the sector held by the 1/5th London Rifle Brigade. Corporal Roland Ebbetts in 'D' Company could see enemy bombers advancing upon positions held by them and the 1/9th Queen Victoria's Rifles:

> At 12.30 pm an enemy bombing party was seen advancing along Ems. A bombing party of ours and the QVR went down Exe and along Female. This party came up against the hostile bombers at the junction of Feed and Female and held it up. Another German bombing party was then seen coming down Emden. At 1.00 pm another enemy bombing party was seen in the maze advancing towards Eck. Owing to lack of bombs our bombing party on the right was forced to withdraw along Female.[35]

Large supplies of German grenades were found in dugouts within Fen and Fir Trenches by 'A' Company, 1/5th London Rifle Brigade, which helped them resist the German assault. 'D' Company, by comparison, was having a tough time on the battalion's right flank and 'A' Company sent over some of these grenades. During that afternoon it was reported that 'D' Company used 300 hand grenades. Their German opponents soon realised that these British soldiers had resorted to using German grenades because they were running out of their own supplies, which gave them the confidence to continue their counter-attacks. When there were no German or British grenades available some individuals took great risks in a desperate bid to keep the enemy at bay. Private Arthur Schuman was so anxious that he returned a German grenade back to the person who threw it into his trench. He later recalled:

> By this time it became obvious that the Germans were in the same trench slinging over stick bombs from both flanks. I must have been really mad, for in the heat of the moment; I quickly picked up a stick bomb, certain that I had sufficient time to throw it back. But the trench being so high, it hit the top and fell back. With two or three others who were near me, we had to nip into the next bay very smartly.[36]

By 13:30 hours the 1/5th London Rifle Brigade could not hold on to their position in Eck Trench and Captain Somers-Smith on the left flank passed down the order to withdraw to the German front line to Captain de Cologan on the right flank. They filtered through Exe Trench into the first German trenches of Fen and Ferret. The battalion sustained heavy casualties as it withdrew being vulnerable to German snipers.

The 1/9th Queen Victoria's Rifles was also sustaining heavy casualties and, with its grenades and bullets almost all expended, it pulled back to the second German line at 13:30 hours. Within thirty minutes they were overwhelmed by the enemy and forced to withdraw further back to the first German trench line. Sergeant Gilbert Telfer recalled:

> For several hours we held our own, getting into touch with 'C' Company and the RE blowing up traverses etc. The Rangers had not got up. The counter-attack then set in by means of bombing parties both from the front and on our right, and we held our own for quite a long time, but owing to a shortage of bombs and ammunition we found it necessary to fight our way down the communication trench leading to their original second line, where we made a stand for sometime with the help of a machine-gun and German hand grenades. It was found that the Boches had got into their second line trench between us and 'C' Company, who were also retiring, and it was not a long time before we were in their first line.[37]

Telfer's party made the decision to abandon the German first line around mid-afternoon and ran back to the British lines. Telfer was wounded:

> By this time our numbers were very small, for reinforcements, bombs, etc., could not be obtained owing to the heavy curtain of fire put up between the old front lines, and after a consultation I had with the C.S.M. we decided it was a case for every man to do his best to get home, for there were not enough men to get to work with the bayonet in the open. Everybody hung on as long as possible, then small parties began to evacuate, but none got far before they were bowled over by machine-gun fire. It was when I tried to get home that I got one from the left through my thigh and, in getting up, one across my back from the right, just taking the skin off my spine and ripping a nice lump out of my left side in the small of the back. I was able to get up and rush into a shell hole where I remained until about 11 pm, having been there for about ten hours – it seemed ten weeks.[38]

However, some parties from the 1/9th Queen Victoria's Rifles continued to hold on to their precarious position in Ferret and Fern Trenches in the German first line. They resisted unwavering German efforts to regain their front line trenches.

The Queen Westminster Rifles made a similar decision to evacuate the second line trench and withdraw to the German first line. 2nd Lieutenants Upton and Bovill were the only officers remaining from those who went over the top that morning. The 1/16th Queen's Westminster Rifles continued to hold their ground, but at 13:45 hours, they made the decision to pull back to the first German trench Ferret, in the hope that reinforcements would reach them by evening.

By 14.00 hours some wounded men from the 1/9th Queen Victoria's Rifles managed to get back to the British trenches bringing with them first-hand reports of the catastrophe that was occurring on the other side of No Man's Land which filtered through to Lieutenant-Colonel Dickins. These were the first reports he received and the news was not good. Captain Harold Leys Cox had tried to send several messages back to Dickins since early that morning, but all the runners were either killed or fell wounded in No Man's Land. His orderly, Rifleman Armitage, then volunteered to take a message to Dickins at Battalion HQ. He too was wounded, but managed to get across No Man's Land to reach Dickins. Armitage was awarded the Military Medal for this action. Rifleman Collins was another runner who eventually got to the British lines that day to deliver a message to Dickins and he was also awarded the Military Medal. Alarmed at the reports and fearful that German forces may exploit the dire situation that the 56th Division was in and push into the British lines, Dickins ordered that all stragglers be gathered and at 16:30 hours he ordered them to hold the first British trench line.

2nd Lieutenant R. Petley's party from 'D' Company, 1/5th London Rifle Brigade were defending Eck Trench and were unaware that his battalion had withdrawn to the German front line trench earlier that afternoon. They were separated from the battalion and were surrounded by the enemy in Eck. He had not received any orders or responses to his messages and was concerned that his supply of grenades were depleting. At 16:00 hours Petley wrote:

> I sent a message to you about two hours ago to the effect that I am holding on to Eck with about 40 men, including a dozen QVR and one QWR, and that I wanted more bombs. Quite out of touch to right and left. Have held off Germans on our right with barricade. It is quite absurd to lay here at night as we are.[39]

It was not until Sergeant F. S. Robinson appeared with verbal orders to withdraw that Petley became aware that the battalion had retired to the German first line. They had to fight their way through to Fen and Ferret trenches, as Petley recalled:

> Sergt. Austin, Cpl (F) Thorpe and myself brought up the rear. Our idea was to try and bring one at least of the wounded back; as soon, however, as the party started we were bombed rather heavily from Female, and, of course, I had to order all wounded to be left alone. We managed to account for two or three of the Huns in Female and kept them down until the rear of our party had passed the top of Exe. We worked our way round to about the junction of Maze and Fibre, Austin and I bringing up the rear.
>
> We had no less than four different bombing parties to keep off, and the whole of my party got to the German second trench with only two or three casualties. It was in the independent rushes across the open, of course, that the casualties occurred, but even then, most of us, I believe got to the German front trench, where apparently were remnants of 'C' and 'D' Companies and a lot of Q.V.R.s [40]

By 19:00 hours there were approximately a hundred British troops from the 1/5th London Rifle Brigade, 1/16th Queen's Westminster Rifles and 1/9th Queen Victoria's Rifles still holding on to the German front line trenches, Fern, Ferret and Fen, maintaining a strong resolute defence, but they were being attacked from three sides. With their numbers dwindling and the supplies of bombs and ammunition exhausted, their defence of the first German line was unsustainable.

It was becoming apparent that they could not hold on any longer and parties were beginning to withdraw across No Man's Land to the British line. It was impractical and impossible to transport the severely wounded who could not make it under their own power and they had to be left in German dugouts. German prisoners who had been captured in these trenches had to be abandoned. The 1/9th Queen Victoria's Rifles and the

1/16th Queen's Westminster Rifles were slowly being driven northwards from Fern into Ferret Trenches. By 20:00 hours they were forced back into Fen Trench which were being held by the 1/5th London Rifle Brigade. Sergeant H. Frost from 'A' Company, 1/5th London Rifle Brigade, reported:

> We could see the other end of the line being gradually driven towards our L.R.B. bit of trench. Twice we had seen parties leave the trenches and cut across the open. Finally about 8.00 pm the remainder (possibly 100 of various regiments) came rushing along to 'A' Company trench followed by Germans who were showering bombs on them. There was no hope of holding on any longer and our party of 'A' Company joined in the rush.[41]

Sergeant Frost sustained a bullet wound to his face as he made a dash for the British line. His body was badly bruised and he was suffering from concussion. Corporal Roland Ebbetts, 'D' Company, 1/5th London Rifle Brigade, reported:

> About 8.30 pm the grenades were quite exhausted and an order was received from the right to close up. The men closed up and overflowing the trench started to crawl or run towards our own lines. Every man who was unwounded then left the German lines. The enemy were in force in the Park on the left before our men started and opened a very heavy fire on them as they crossed the open.[42]

Rifleman Harold Morgan, of 'C' Company, recalled:

> Germans appeared 30 yards in front of us and an officer I believe named Lt Benns said 'Make a stand boys' but saw it was hopeless ... so gave the 'Every man for himself' order ... I started to bolt back to our trench but got hooked up with barbed wire. I got free and by running and falling down several times managed to reach our lines.[43]

As the remnants dashed across No Man's Land they were met with heavy machine-gun fire and shell fire. Some men ran for their lives across this ground dodging the savage enemy fire. Others darted from shell hole to shell hole, while the more prudent crawled on their bellies towards the British front line. Private Arthur Schuman was one of a few who succeeded in getting across No Man's Land. He recalled the terrible ordeal:

> By now I was petrified. I knew that if I stayed in the trench I would have most certainly been killed. I hardly waited for the order, but it came, 'Everyman for himself!' I did not wait to argue – over the top I went like greased lightning – surviving a hail of bullets. I immediately

> fell flat. Then trying to imagine I was part of the earth, I wriggled along on my belly. Dead, dying and wounded, feigning death – who knows? The ground was covered with them. I sped from shell hole to shell hole. Never had I run faster. It was snipers, machine-guns and shrapnel all the way. About halfway across, I rolled into a shell hole and fell on top of a badly wounded German in a pitiable state – probably an abandoned prisoner. All he said was. 'Schlecht! Schlecht!' – which means bad! I don't know what made me do it but I gripped his hand and sped on. I often think that someone above was looking over me through that act of kindness. When I finally scrambled into our front-line trench I was greeted by our Adjutant Captain Wallis and Regimental Sergeant Major MacVeigh who both solemnly shook my hand. I was told that only twenty had returned so far.[44]

It was almost suicidal to cross No Man's Land to the British lines, but they had no choice if they wanted to evade being captured or killed in the German trenches. Many men fell during the attempt. 2nd Lieutenant Edward Bovill was the last man from the 1/16th Queen's Westminster Rifles to leave the German trench. He succeeded in crossing No Man's Land but was killed as he was approaching the British parapet.

Captain C.E. Moy and the reserve company from the 1/16th Queen's Westminster Rifles were summoned forward to the front line at Hébuterne to assist the remnants of the battalion. Here in the first trench they found their comrades exhausted and covered in blood. They spent the night in reconstructing damaged trenches and recovering the wounded from No Man's Land under the cover of darkness. Moy recalled:

> We got into a communication trench and started up to the front line. The trenches had been none too good before, but now they were battered out of all recognition. Soon we came upon two stooping men supporting a third between them – an officer. His uniform was tattered and blood splashed; his face was covered in blood; he was unconscious …
>
> On we went until we came to the old front line. Here we found the 150 men remaining to us. They were dog tired and filthy, but their blazing eyes told us that they were still game. We didn't attempt to sort them out, but just told them to lie down and sleep where they were – an instant after they were all snoring hard. Having left a small party of our batmen and one officer to watch over them, we went on into the newly dug assembly trenches.
>
> The same sight met our gaze on every side; dead men and blood. On until we came out into No Man's Land. Here the sight was indescribably. Dead and dying Englishmen and Germans were lying in heaps, some writhing, some moaning and screaming, some lying still. We spent the remainder of that night getting in the ones who were still alive.[45]

The 56th Division's attempt to hold on to the German lines south of Gommecourt was over by early evening. It was a remarkable feat for the 56th Division to have assaulted a heavily defended position, penetrated its defences and held onto its gains for several hours, but without reinforcements and supplies its position became untenable and it had no choice but to withdraw.

Brigadier-General Coke wrote a report explaining the difficulties that the 169th Brigade encountered in their assault upon Gommecourt. The two primary difficulties were the 400 yards distance across No Man's Land and the intensive German artillery barrage that was maintained throughout the day. As a consequence it was impossible to replenish the assault troops in the German lines with grenades, trench mortar bombs and smalls arms ammunition in order to consolidate their gains. Communications were another problem. The heavy German barrage prevented the establishment of telephonic communications across No Man's Land as well as stopping runners getting messages across. This problem had not been factored in the planning.

The 1/14th London Scottish entered the battle with twenty-three officers and 811 other ranks, supported by one medical officer and twenty-one stretcher bearers. All that remained from the battalion were nine officers, 266 men and twenty-one stretcher bearers. It had been reduced, in total, from 856 to 296 losing 65 per cent of its strength. The men had fought to the last round, held onto a position against an enemy with superior numbers and awesome firepower. They did this without support. It is a wonder that there were any survivors by the end of the day.

The 1/13th Kensington lost sixteen officers and 300 men out of twenty-three officers and approximately 592 men. Major W.H.W. Young commented 'when it is remembered that for the greater part of the time the battalion consisted almost entirely of inexperienced officers and practically untrained recruits, I think that it acquitted itself remarkably well.'[46]

The 1/5th London Rifle Brigade numbered twenty-three officers and 803 other ranks. They lost 83 per cent of its officers and 70 per cent of its NCOs and men.

The 1/9th Queen Victoria's Rifles lost six officers and fifty-one other ranks killed, with five officers and 290 other ranks wounded, as well as five officers and 188 men missing. In total they had lost 545 of all ranks.

The 1/16th Queen's Westminster Rifles lost 600 out of the 750 officers and men that entered the battle.

It was also an awful day for the 1/12th London Rangers who lost heavily. Twenty-three officers and 780 other ranks entered the battle. Only six officers and 280 men answered the roll call that evening.[47] The battalion unit history's comment was:

> So far as the Battalion itself was concerned, July 1st 1916, marked the end of its days as a regiment composed exclusively of actual 'Rangers'.

> So far as the individual members of the Battalion were concerned, it came as the end and abrupt finish of a comradeship which they will never forget during their lifetime.[48]

The 2nd Guard Reserve Division defending Gommecourt lost thirteen officers and 578 men. The combined losses of 55th and 91st RIRs amounted to three officers and 182 men.[49] According to one authority, the 170th Infantry Regiment lost 650, 55th RIR sustained 455 losses and 91st RIR suffered 150 casualties.[50]

Part 3

VIII Corps Sector

Chapter 9

Serre

The 31st Division, commanded by Major-General Robert Wanless O'Gowan, was ordered to capture the village of Serre, which was defended by 169th Infantry Regiment, belonging to the German 52nd Division. Two miles south from the diversionary assault launched by VII Corps at Gommecourt, they would pivot at John Copse and extend a defensive flank along the northern extremity of the main assault that would stretch into Serre itself. The 31st Division was to attack on VIII Corps' left flank and since there was a significant gap between 31st and 56th Division's lines of attack, they could not depend upon each other for support. After the bitter battle with the French in June 1915, Serre had been transformed into a formidable fortress with the German line running west of the village. being perched on top of a ridge, it afforded its German occupants good observation of the British lines.

The 94th Brigade was given the task of capturing Serre, but Brigadier-General G.T.C. Carter DSO had been taken ill and Brigadier-General Hubert Rees took over command prior to the attack. Rees had been recently promoted to Brigadier-General on 13 June 1916. He had seen considerable action and proved to be a capable and efficient officer in the field during the retreat from Mons, the Battle of the Aisne and at Gheluvelt during the 1914 campaign. Rees reported to Lieutenant-General Hunter-Weston, VIII Corps commander, during the following day on 14 June and was briefed on the planned attack upon Serre. Rees met the commanders of his battalions on 15 June and it was left to Lieutenant-Colonel Arthur Rickman, commander of 11th East Lancashire Regiment (Accrington Pals) to take him on a tour of the British trenches opposite Serre. He could clearly see the ruins of the village and several of the German trenches from the British lines:

> The British and German front line trenches were at the bottom of a broad rolling valley, which run down from a water shed, S.W. of Serre, past Beaumont Hamel and Thiepval. Serre village was on the summit of a decided rise and was obviously a point of observation over the

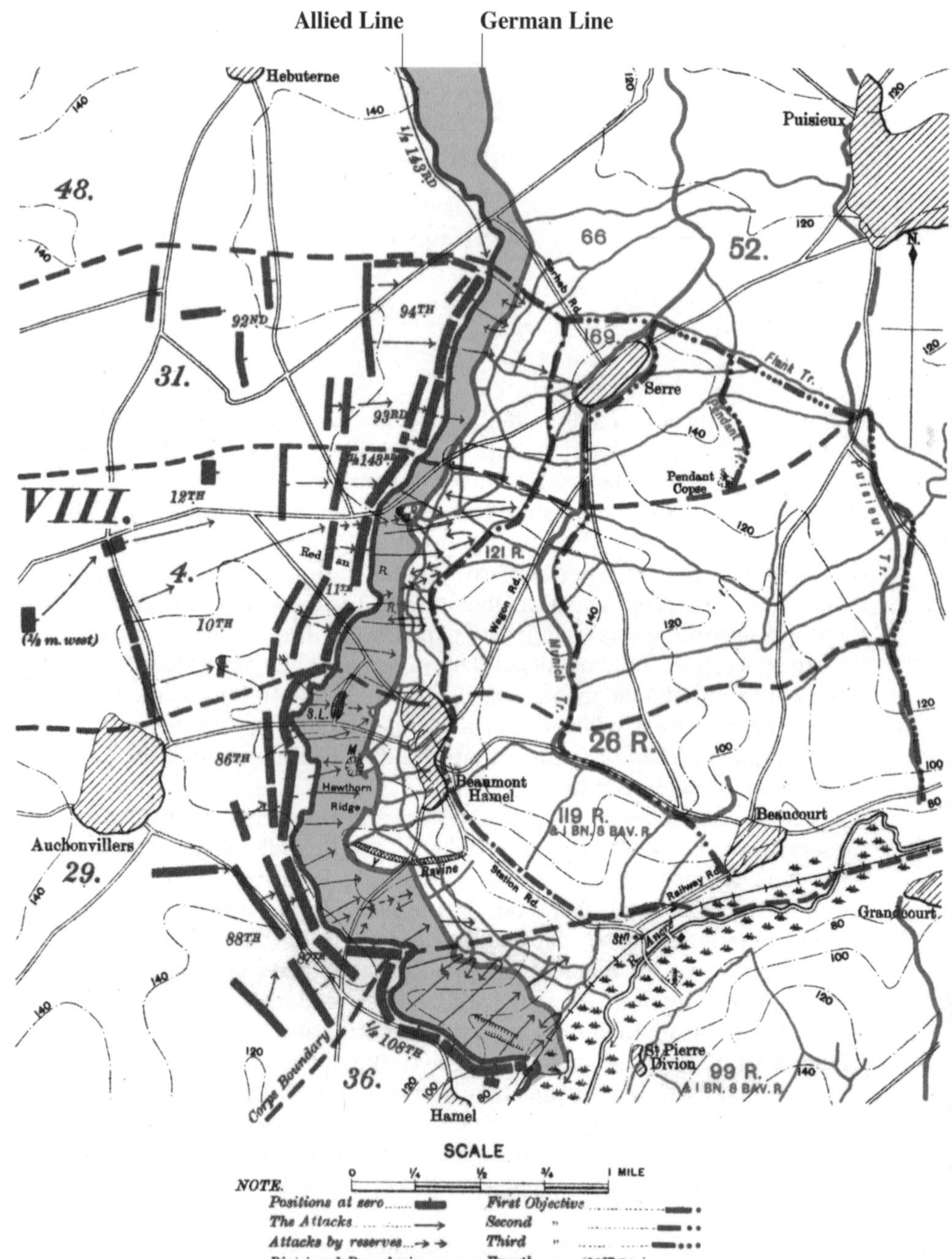
Allied Line
German Line
Hebuterne
Puisieux
48.
½ 143RD
66
52.
94TH
92ND
169
Serre
Flank Tr.
Pendant Tr.
31.
93RD
½ 143RD
Pendant Copse
VIII.
12TH
Red an
R
121 R.
Wagon Rd.
Munich Tr.
4.
11TH
10TH
(½ m. west)
Puisieux Tr.
26 R.
S.L.
M
86TH
Hawthorn Ridge
Beaumont Hamel
119 R.
& I BN. 8 BAV. R.
Beaucourt
Auchonvillers
29.
Ravine
Station Rd.
Railway Rd.
Grandcourt
88TH
87TH
R. Ancre
St Pierre Divion
99 R.
& I BN. 8 BAV. R.
½ 108TH
Corps Boundary
36.
Hamel
N.
SCALE
0 ¼ ½ ¾ 1 MILE
NOTE.
Positions at zero
The Attacks
Attacks by reserves
Divisional Boundaries
First Objective
Second "
Third "
Fourth " (31ST Div)
Lodgments (1ST July)
CORPS. VIII; Divisions. 29; 4; Brigades. 88TH, 10TH; 92ND
M. = Mine Crater, S.L. = Sunken Lane, R. = Redan; Q. = Quadrilateral.

> Boche lines of great value. From our front trenches to the edge of the village no less than four main fire trenches were visible. The distance being 700 yards. The village itself, although good deal knocked about, was quite recognisable as such, roofs of houses being visible amongst the trees with which it was thickly planted. Our advance up the slope to the village was in full view from the north, from the German salient of Gommecourt.[1]

Rees was ordered to capture four lines of German trenches in front of Serre within twenty minutes. They would have to cross 700 yards up a slight gradient to reach the first German trenches. After being allowed a further twenty minutes to consolidate these lines the 94th Brigade were expected to drive forward 800 yards to capture the village of Serre within forty minutes. Twenty minutes later they were then tasked with capturing an orchard positioned on a knoll 300 yards behind the village.

Serre had taken a pounding from the British barrage, but the German soldiers belonging to 169th Infantry Regiment defending this village were still on the ridge and could look down upon the British positions. The British trench system opposite Serre was in such an abysmally muddy state that both 93rd and 94th Brigades experienced difficulty in getting their battalions in their allotted assembly positions.

As a consequence the communication trenches became congested as soldiers heavily laden with arms, munitions and equipment were bogged down. They were behind schedule and to ensure that they reached their assembly positions for the impending attack on time, shortly after midnight on the 30th Lieutenant-Colonel Arthur Rickman ordered the platoons that were to form the second wave of the 11th East Lancashire's attack to leave the communication trenches and head towards the front line above ground under the cover of darkness. Rickman and the head of the column reached the front line at 02:40 hours. These men were totally exhausted by the strenuous efforts to reach the front. They had little time for rest and were expected to launch a large scale offensive within a few hours.

White tape had been laid in No Man's Land to denote the starting line for the assault. Captain Clarke of the 12th York and Lancaster Regiment had ensured that white tapes were laid by 00:30 hours and confirmed that the wire in front of the British line had been cut. However, wire patrols were meant to have ventured over to the other side of No Man's Land to assess the German wire and to cut the wire more completely where necessary, but they were unable to do so because German flares illuminated the sky and German machine-gunners were alert and firing towards the British lines throughout the night. German patrols from the 169th Infantry Regiment ventured into No Man's Land during the night of 30 June/1 July had discovered some of the white tapes and quickly removed them in order to disrupt the inevitable British advance.

German guns began to shell John Copse at 04:05 hours, where the frontline and assembly trenches were occupied by the 12th York and Lancaster (Sheffield City Battalion) – the Sheffield Pals. British batteries in the rear lines were also targeted. It was not until 05:00 hours that both the 93rd and 94th Brigades were in position.

The 93rd Brigade, commanded by Brigadier-General J.D. Ingles, attacked on the 31st Division's right flank in a direct assault upon German positions south of the ruined village of Serre. The brigade comprised of the 15th West Yorkshire Regiment (Leeds Pals), 16th West Yorkshire Regiment (1st Bradford Pals), 18th West Yorkshire Regiment (2nd Bradford Pals) and the 18th Durham Light Infantry (Durham Pals).

The 94th Brigade, led by Brigadier-General Hubert Rees, would carry the left flank and was ordered to capture Serre. This brigade was composed of the 11th East Lancashire Regiment (Accrington Pals), 12th York and Lancaster Regiment, 13th York and Lancaster Regiment (1st Barnsley Pals) and the 14th York and Lancaster Regiment (2nd Barnsley Pals). Two key officers from the brigade were unable to take part in the operation due to illness. As already mentioned, Brigadier-General Rees had been temporarily appointed commander as replacement for Brigadier-General G.T.C. Carter, whilst Lieutenant-Colonel Crosthwaite, commanding 12th York and Lancaster was suffering from exhaustion and stress and, on the morning of 30 June, he was admitted to hospital and command devolved to Major A. Plackett.

At 06:20 hours, both Ingles and Rees confirmed to 31st Divisional Commander Major-General O'Gowan that they were confident that the enemy wire had been cut, despite wiring patrols being unable to access No Man's Land to confirm this. However the artillery bombardment upon the enemy wire was not a complete success. Where the barrage had cut some sections, there was a heap of mangled wire which would severely obstruct the advancing troops. Two tunnels had been dug from the British frontline into No Man's Land, ten feet below the surface. The shafts were opened during that night and Stokes mortar teams positioned in both so that they could propel shells into the German lines at Zero Hour.

The British artillery began its bombardment of German positions at Serre from 05:00 am. The gunners found difficulty in locating their targets due to thick mist that enveloped the surrounding fields and when they did open fire German artillery immediately responded.

It was immediately evident that the British guns had not destroyed the German batteries during the week-long preliminary bombardment. Also some British shells were falling short upon British lines, with the 12th York and Lancaster taking casualties as they waited close to John Copse. Telephonic communications were severed when the wire was cut by either British or German shells. A runner was therefore sent back to Brigadier-General Rees at 94th Brigade HQ with a message to tell artillery officers that they were firing at their own men. The battalion War Diary recorded that at 06:00 hours: 'C Coy reported Bays 31 and 38 heavily shelled. 8 killed & 6 wounded – principally No.12 Platoon. Reply sent, "Report again at 7.00 am. Nothing can be done at present".'[2]

There was poor communication between the battalions waiting to go over the top in the front line and Brigade HQ, and this diary entry reveals that there was also a breakdown in communications between Brigade HQ and artillery commanders in the rear. The fact that Brigade could do nothing to stop its own artillery firing upon its own men demonstrates their impotency and inability to react when required. An hour later British shells were still falling upon the Sheffield Pals as they waited for Zero Hour at John Copse.

Brigadier-General Hubert Rees was standing above 94th Brigade headquarters at 07:20 hours, which was constructed of steel and had two exits. It was positioned in front of Observation Wood, 500 yards behind the front line trench, ten feet underground and could accommodate fifteen men. From here he could see the British guns shelling Serre.

Ten minutes prior to Zero Hour the first assault waves went through breaches in the British wire and laid down in No Man's Land to wait for the whistle to blow signalling the start of the attack. As these Pals battalions assembled in No Man's Land they could be clearly seen by German machine-gunners nestled amongst the ruins of Serre who opened fire upon them. Casualties were being incurred before the advance had begun. Observers were able to relay the positions of the oncoming British infantry to German heavy artillery batteries that were positioned in a hollow close to Puisieux and to field guns positioned near Serre. German shells were falling upon the Pals. German artillery responded by bombarding the British lines opposite Serre with shrapnel and high explosive shells, which caused damage to the fire bays, communication and assembly trenches.

The 11th East Lancashire's advanced between Matthew and Mark Copse. Captain Arnold Tough led the first wave of the Accrington Pals from a position between Warley Avenue and Mark Copse at 07:20 hours. This first wave advanced in extended order as close to the German wire as the British barrage permitted and then laid on the ground where they waited for Zero Hour. Two minutes later, Captain Harry Livesey led 'W' Company behind the first wave from Copse Trench up the gentle incline towards Serre. As soon as these waves came forward red flares were immediately fired into the sky from the German trenches requesting further German artillery support. Machine-gunners and riflemen were already manning their parapets and opened fire, cutting down the advancing waves. Some German troops remained concealed in their frontline trench waiting for the British troops to get within range so that they could throw their bombs at them. The Pals continued to sustain casualties before Zero Hour, as the 94th Infantry Brigade War Diary reported:

> Second wave crossed our front line, and lay fifty yards in rear of first wave. At this time the German front line was seen to be manned, (about one man per yard), by men who had either been lying behind the parados of fire trench during the bombardment, or who had emerged from shelters. These men, despite our artillery and trench mortar barrage, opened a heavy rifle and machine-gun fire, and threw bombs on our first two waves, causing many casualties.[3]

At 07:29 hours, 2nd Lieutenant Williams brought the third wave forward from Campion Trench and Captain Riley led the fourth wave from Monk Trench. By this time German artillery was targeting No Man's Land, the British front line and communication trenches with high explosive and shrapnel shells. Some of this fire was falling 200 yards behind the first line and caused considerable casualties amongst the rear waves.

Hunter-Weston had assured Rees that the British artillery had dealt with the fifty-five German batteries within this area, but they had no knowledge until 3 July that the actual strength of the German batteries had been underestimated and that there were sixty-six batteries that were carefully concealed from the eyes of RFC observers. It is probable that German commanders were aware that there would be a definite attack on Serre and the ranges of their guns were already set upon the British lines, so as soon as they were seen to go over the top the thunderous barrage descended upon them. Rees recalled the horrific spectacle:

> The Germans were determined to protect Serre with a barrage from most of their guns and relied more on M.G's to stop the 4th Division. This barrage which fell at Zero was one of the most consistent and severe I have seen. When it fell it gave me the impression of a thick belt of poplar trees from the cones of the explosions.[4]

On seeing the intensity of this barrage and realising that his men from the 94th Brigade were in danger, Rees tried to stop the attack: 'As soon as I saw it I ordered every man within reach to halt and lie down but only managed to stop about 2 companies, because all troops had to move at once in order to capture their objectives in time.'[5]

Rees observed the remainder of the brigade advance forward into the storm of German shell and machine-gun fire. He also witnessed acts of courage from the German side from his position close to Observation Wood. He recalled:

> At the time this barrage really became intense, the last waves of the attack were crossing the trench I was in. I have never seen a finer display of individual and collective bravery than the advance of that brigade. I never saw a man waiver from the exact line prescribed for him. Each line

> disappeared in the thick cloud of dust and smoke which rapidly blotted out the whole area. I can safely pay a tribute to the bravery of the enemy, whom I saw standing up in their trenches to fire their rifles in a storm of fire. They actually ran a machine-gun out into No Man's Land to help repel the attack. I saw a few groups of men through gaps in the smoke cloud, but I knew that no troops could hope to get through such fire. My two staff officers, Piggott and Stirling were considerably surprised when I stopped the advance of the rest of the machine-gun Company and certain other small bodies now passing my Hqtrs. It was their first experience of a great battle and all that morning, they obviously found it impossible to believe that the whole brigade had been destroyed as a fighting unit.[6]

Private James Snailham was waiting to go over the top with the rear waves from the 11th East Lancaster in a crowded trench and witnessed the destruction of the first waves: 'The lads were slaughtered, fearful, as we got out of the trench; they were knocking them over as fast as they got out.'[7]

A 2nd Lieutenant was meant to have led Snailham's platoon into No Man's Land but he stood at the back of the trench encouraging his men to climb the parapet, as Snailham recalled:

> We were all crushed together. They were all stood there in our trench. The officer said, 'As soon as I blow my whistle you must get over the top through that gulley' I cut a gulley out to slide through under wire, and he stood there, he did not lead his men; there were three of us left in trench. I started to get back I turned and the officer was still there, under cover and those lads were slaughtered out in front. I said 'what about these lads?' he said 'you get out or I'll shoot you' and I had to get out, there were three of us left in the trench.[8]

According to Snailham the 2nd Lieutenant did not leave the trench. When Snailham got above the parapet a shell exploded in a communication trench to the rear. The front line trenches were jagged and could absorb the blast of a direct hit concentrating the casualties along a small section of trench. However, communication trenches were straight lines which led from support trenches to the front line trenches, so when a shell fell directly upon a communication trench the blast would resonate through the straight line causing many casualties. Snailham continued to cross No Man's Land, but it was a scene of carnage, with dead and wounded lying close to the British line. Very soon he too would become a casualty.

> The moment I had to get out over the top there were three men lying dead in the trench … I got over the top, men were lying all over the damn show. I hadn't run far before a shell burst above me. I could see a six inch piece of shrapnel sticking through my leg. That made me take

> cover and the only cover was a shell hole. I got almost to the German wire. I could hear them in front of me and lads that had gone over were lying all over the place shouting for help but no one could get to them at all. The men in shell holes as I was crawling past them were all suffering from wounds caused by shell fire.[9]

Snailham lay in a shell hole from 07:30 hours throughout the day until 19:00 hours. He was suffering considerable pain with the shrapnel sticking out of his leg and he had also suffered a dislocated shoulder as he fell into the shell hole to take cover.

At 07:30 hours the British artillery barrage moved forwards and the surviving Accrington Pals from 11th East Lancaster lying in No Man's Land stood up and were immediately shot down by German machine-guns. Captain Arnold Tough blew the whistle to signal the advance and as soon as he moved forward he received a wound, but continued to lead the first wave. German riflemen were seen to be standing brazenly on their parapets of their front line trench firing at them. Some German soldiers dashed into shell craters in front of their trenches and established a good firing position from No Man's Land. The attackers that survived managed to advance just 100 yards. As soon as the British Artillery lifted their barrage onto the fourth German line, German artillery immediately intensified their barrage with shrapnel and HE shells as they could see the decimated ranks of the Pals battalions approaching their front line.

Adjacent to the 11th East Lancaster on their left flank, was 12th York and Lancaster Regiment advancing between John Copse and Luke Copse. 'A' and 'C' Company entered No Man's Land and laid down 100 yards from the British front trench at 07:20 hours, being covered by an intensive artillery barrage and Stokes mortar bombardment. Casualties were few at this point. The second wave moved forward at 07:27 hours and laid down in No Man's Land thirty yards behind 'A' and 'C' Company. The third and fourth waves followed from Campion and Monk trenches. German artillery began to shell Monk Trench and then rolled backwards towards the front line British trench.

The 12th York and Lancaster experienced difficulty in advancing on the extreme left flank of the 31st Division's sector. 'A' and 'C' Companies went forward first. Artillery barrages, heavy machine-gun and rifle fire greeted them as they advanced towards Serre. The left half of 'C' Company was completely wiped out before it reached the German wire, and those on the right were unable to find a breach in the enemy wire. Both companies carried a Bangalore Torpedo to be used to form breaches in sections of uncut wire. The rear waves carried more Bangalore Torpedoes. The first two waves only carried one each because it was expected that the enemy wire would have been well cut by the British bombardment. The men who were trained to operate these Bangalore Torpedoes were either killed or wounded, and those men that reached the German wire were unable to use them. Here they were within range of German hand grenades thrown from the German line. The battalion War Diary reported:

> As soon as our barrage lifted from their front line, the Germans, who had been sheltering in their dugouts immediately came out and opened rapid fire with their machine-guns. Some were seen to retire to their second and third lines. The enemy fought very well throwing hand grenades into his own wire.[10]

The first wave of the 12th York & Lancaster did not stand a chance against this formidable opposition. Lance Corporal James Glenn a signaller who belonged to the second wave and he would see the devastated ranks of the first waves lying across their line of advance. He remembered:

> The signal to attack was a whistle. Our officers were the first to jump up and blew their whistle and ran forward, they only had revolvers. The first line went and they were walking slowly. They all laid down. I thought that they had different orders, because we had all been told to walk. They laid down because they were shot, killed or wounded. They were mown down just like corn. Our line simply went forward and the same thing happened with our party. We were just trying to find your way in amongst the shell holes, and when we got to the wire you saw the first line a lot of them were stuck on the wire trying to get through.[11]

The majority of troops belonging to 'A' and 'C' Company did not get through the British wire. They were meant to open gaps but were unable to do so due to overwhelming German machine-gun fire upon the wire. The third and fourth waves suffered the same fate. They lost half their strength before they reached No Man's Land. The 12th York and Lancaster assault upon Serre was a disaster. Fire was coming from Serre opposite them and from Gommecourt Wood to the north. Glenn with 'C' Company laid down on the ground to take cover. With so many officer and NCO casualties the structure of command broke down. There was nobody around to give any orders. Two signallers went forward, but were told to return to Battalion HQ. Word got around to the survivors that everybody should get back to their own lines. The source of this order is not known, but the message passed from mouth to mouth and the troops returned to their support line.

Many officers and NCOs from the 11th East Lancs were knocked out of the battle as they assembled in their trench or within moments of going over the top. Private Jack Hindle remembered:

> I myself felt more at ease when we got over than I did in the trench simply because I had the chance of firing back. At 7.30 the bombardment lifted to the German second line, and we looked for someone to lead us, but all the officers and NCOs seemed to have been put out of action, and while we were waiting (which was only a matter of seconds) the Germans came out. Three of them came in front of me and my Corporal (and although the Corporal was wounded he was still firing his rifle) and one of the Germans said 'come on Lancashires, we are the Württembergs, we'll give you beans!' Well the Corporal got one and I got one of them, and the other chap got my Corporal right in the middle of the forehead. He died instantly poor chap. Shortly after my Corporal was hit, I got hit in the foot.[12]

Such was the intensity of the machine-gun fire that Corporal Bridge Greenwood, another Accrington Pal, received several wounds. He later recalled in a letter from his hospital bed:

> I have a piece of shrapnel just in the bend of my knee of the right leg. I fairly got a peppering while I was on the battlefield. I only got hit in five places, two in the left arm, one in the right arm, one in the left hip ... I never thought I should ever see life again after I went on the battlefield – they were being killed on the left and right of me. I saw some awful, ghastly sights ... I got wounded while I was dressing a man's neck. There was a hole right through it, and blood was coming out like a tap. He was praying to God to let him live. There I left him and went on with it, until I got to the German trenches. Then I got a large piece right through the left arm. It finished me did that, and I crept back all under shell fire until I got to the dressing station to have my wounds dressed. I prayed to see my mother and father whilst I was fighting, and I think God must have answered my prayers.[13]

Unteroffizer Otto Lais belonged to a machine-gun crew from 169th Infantry Regiment defending Serre. His rank was the equivalent to the rank of Corporal in the British Army. He recalled the experience on firing upon the Pals battalions that were advancing towards his machine-gun position at Serre:

> machine-gun fire wildly lashed into the masses of the enemy. Around us was the hissing and roar of a storm, like a hurricane as the British shells targeted our artillery which was firing courageously and our reserves and rear. Through this noise, the rumble and the bursts of rifle fire could be heard the hard regular Tack Tack of our machine-guns ... That one firing slower, the other [referring to machine-gun fire] faster in rhythm! It was the precision in material and skill, which played a

> grim tune to the enemy's ranks, at the same time providing high level of security and reassurance for their own comrades firing rifles ... Belt after belt was fired 250 shots – 1,000 shots – 3,000 shots. machine-gun commander orders 'pass up the spare barrels'. The barrels are changed and another 5,000 rounds are fired. The barrel must be changed again. The barrel is red hot and the cooling water is boiling. The hands of the machine-gunners were scorched and scalded. 'Keep firing!' ordered the machine-gun commander. The cooling water in the gun mantle boiled and evaporated due to the continuous firing. The over flow hose slips out of the water jacket. Hissing a fountain of steam shoots upwards, providing a wonderful target for the enemy. Fortunately for us the sun shines in their faces and we have it on our backs. The enemy comes in closer and we continue to shoot incessantly. The steam is weaker. Another barrel change is urgent. The cooling water is almost evaporated. 'Where is the water?' shouted the gunner 'get the emergency rations from the dugout.' 'Nothing there Unteroffizer!' all iron rations were consumed during the eight day bombardment. The English still run forward, despite hundreds being shot, new waves storm forward from start position. We have got to shoot. A gunner takes a kettle and jumps into the trench. A second gunner urinates in the kettle, filling it fast. The English were within grenade throwing range. Hand grenades flying over and over. The barrel change complete, the water jacket filled. Hand and rifle grenades explode close to the gun. 'Just keep calm and unjam the gun'. Clearly say to yourself 'Forward, Down, Back ... Belt on throw safety catch back. Press', raging fire tack – tack – tack ... High vapours of steam are emitted from all machine-guns Most of the steam hoses had been destroyed or shot away. The skin hangs in shreds from the fingers of the scalded hands of the gunners. Constant pressing of their left thumbs on the trigger turned them into shapeless bundles of flesh ... Eighteen thousand rounds fired. The other gun jams. Gunner Schwartz is shot through the head as he feeds belt. The belt is dislodged and feeds rounds into gun diagonally and it jams. The next gunner runs forward and removes the dead man. The gunner takes out the feeder, removes the cartridge and loads again. England's youth bled to death before Serre.[14]

Only a few parties from the 12th York and Lancaster – the Sheffield Pals – got through the wire and into the German trenches on their right flank. Here they met up with the remnants belonging to 11th East Lancashire Regiment, the Accrington Pals. As the Accrington and Sheffield Pals advanced towards the village of Serre, there were no British forces attacking on their left flank and they were met by a torrent of German machine-gun fire from the northeast.

Captain Arnold Tough and Captain Harry Livesey from the 11th East

Lancashires managed to get the remnants of their waves across No Man's Land and there are claims that they fought their way into the German trench system at Serre. Livesey allegedly gathered together those that remained to fortify their position within the village. He sent a runner to Battalion Headquarters requesting reinforcements but Lieutenant-Colonel Arthur Rickman did not receive that message, indicating that the runner had become a casualty. Rickman wrote to Livesey's parents:

> I saw him go forward gallantly leading his men at 7.25 am on the morning of 1st July. I heard subsequently that at the right time, and with Captain Tough, he charged the German front line and got in with what remained of his men. He charged under a hail of bullets from both rifle and machine-guns and nothing could have been finer. Had he have lived I should have brought his name forward for immediate reward.[15]

Private Clarence Glover was Livesey's orderly and he was with him when they were confronted by five German soldiers from around a corner in the first German trench. One of them hurled a bomb in their direction. The explosion grazed Livesey's face but he immediately shot all five with his revolver. As further German reinforcements came forward, Glover and Livesey took refuge in a nearby shell hole. A shell landed close by, and Glover lost consciousness. When Glover came to that night he could find no trace of Livesey.[16] Most of the soldiers from these battalions who were stuck in No Man's Land were either pinned down by enemy fire or lying dead or wounded. Many were caught in the German wire entanglements and were left dangling.

The 13th and 14th York and Lancaster, the 1st and 2nd Barnsley Pals, were the next battalions to go over the top. The 2nd Barnsley Pals was to follow the Sheffield Pals and their starting position was from the support lines. They had suffered significant casualties as they waited in the assembly trenches during the German barrage. The left flank lost thirty percent of its assault and carrying force before it ascended the parapet. Military police were at the back of these trenches to ensure that every soldier went over the top. Private Charles Swales remembered: 'Whistle went; I went over from trench to trench fully clad. But at back there were military police, seeing that I did not miss a turn to go over'.[17]

The 2nd Barnsley Pals did not reach No Man's Land for many officers and NCOs in the first waves were shot down by the machine-gun fire that had previously stopped the 12th Battalion, the Sheffield Pals. Those that survived dived into the first British line to take cover. Private Charles Swales remembered: 'The Sheffielders were in first line of trenches, they had been wiped out by then ... dropped into first British trench. Could not see no officers or NCOs to co-ordinate us.'[18] After their first waves were decimated the orders for the 2nd Barnsley Pals were cancelled.

On the 93rd Brigade's front the leading waves went forward into No Man's Land at 07:21 hours and laid there until Zero Hour. Despite the German wire being cut in several places by the bombardment, the 15th West Yorkshires (Leeds Pals) were mown down in No Man's Land, after leaving Matthew Copse. The awesome resistance offered by German machine-gunners defending Serre was a shock to many of the British soldiers for they were confident that their artillery had destroyed everything in the first German trench. There was no expectation that the German artillery would be able to return fire or that German rifleman would appear, firing with their upper torsos clearly visible, from the first trench line. Private Arthur Hollings of the Leeds Pals did not expect to come under such devastating fire:

> The honour of being first 'over the lid' of our brigade fell to my own platoon (13) and No. 10. Not a man hesitated. In broad daylight last Saturday morning our lads had the order to advance. No sooner had the first lot got over the parapet than the Germans opened up a terrific bombardment, big shells and shrapnel, and their parapet was packed with Germans exposing themselves over the top to their waist and opened rapid fire.
>
> They had machine-guns every few yards, and it seemed impossible for a square inch of space to be left free from flying metal. Our guns had kept up a hot bombardment for seven days and for over an hour just preceding our platoon going over the lid it seemed to us as if nothing could live in their first trench line: individual shells could not be heard however big they were. It was one continuous scream overhead, and roaring and ripping of bursting shells just 'across the way', but at the moment of our advance the Germans seemed to be giving us shell for shell.[19]

Lieutenant-Colonel R.B. Neill, commanding officer of the Leeds Pals, together with all his officers from the battalion had become casualties within the first minutes of the attack. Neill was wounded early during the assault. He had taken command of the battalion ten days previously after Lieutenant-Colonel S.C. Taylor had been wounded. Neill was wounded twice in that short time, but despite his wounds he continued to advance into the storm of bullets:

> On getting out of our front line trench I was hit in the arm by three bits of H.E. [High Explosives] and had scarcely gone 80 yards when I was knocked over by a bullet in the left thigh. The attack was held up and I went with 2 L.guns (Battn. reserve) to try and deal with German M.guns holding up our advance. These like the leading waves were quickly obliterated.[20]

Neill hit the ground and sought shelter in the nearest shell crater where he could appraise the situation to avoid the machine-gun fire:

> I crawled to a shell hole and from there searched No Man's Land and the German defences with my glasses. I saw on the German front line parapet three machine-guns still operating. Five or six men standing up with fixed bayonets on either side of the guns. They were all shot down. They were very gallant.[21]

Neill was certain that no one from his battalion got to the German first trench. The Leeds Pals were all but annihilated, being completely overwhelmed by enemy fire from Serre and from the Heidenkopf (Quadrilateral) on their right flank. Neill continued:

> I did not see a single man of 15/W. Yorks cross the German front line, and I am practically certain that none of them got that far. The German barrage on our front line was very effective and machine-gun fire in No Man's Land most intense. [22]

The survivors lay in lines on the ground or in shell holes in No Man's Land as they sheltered from the devastating machine-gun fire. Lance Corporal James Thomson was among them and wrote about it in his diary:

> Went over at 7.30 am as company bomber-corporal. Just got a few yards in front of our barbed wire entanglements when a huge shell burst just behind. Large piece struck my left shoulder, turning me half right and making my left arm temporarily useless. Another shell, which failed to explode, dropped immediately in front, throwing earth up twenty feet; eyes, mouth, ears and nostrils filled with debris. A wounded comrade lying in a shell hole calling out. Went forward beside him; whilst doing so another huge shell (explosive) burst in front, and a piece half and inch square went right through my left hand. At one time there were eight of us lying in this same shell hole. Several bled badly, and after a helping off with their equipment and a little first aid, they were forced through weakness and loss of blood to crawl back for the doctor's attention. Most of them received other wounds on the way, as the enemy were assiduously attending to every moving object, and particularly were the wounded game for machine-guns and explosive bullets. It was devilish work, in keeping with Hunnish ideas and conduct towards the helpless.[23]

At 07:35 hours the 1st Bradford Pals and a company from the Durham Pals were ordered to capture Pendant Copse on the right flank to the southeast of Serre. They became exposed as they left support trenches to get into the frontline trenches and many fell. Lieutenant-Colonel George Guyon, who was appointed commanding officer of the 1st Bradford Pals just forty-eight hours before the attack was among those killed.

Despite incurring heavy casualties, small parties from the Durham Pals crossed No Man's Land, passing the German occupied garrison at Serre on their left flank, and reached Pendant Copse. The 2nd Bradford Pals, commanded by Lieutenant-Colonel Maurice Kennard followed behind these two battalions in support but could not get across No Man's Land.

As soon as the 18th West Yorkshire's left their position and advanced towards the German lines they were met by heavy machine-gun and shell fire. Sergeant William Moran spoke of the ordeal encountered by the 2nd Bradford Pals as they headed towards Serre:

> It was a glorious, cloudless sky, and the sun shining brilliantly. But the beauties of the day were mocked by the roar of huge shells which fell in front of us and behind us, and the appalling shriek of the shrapnel shells, which burst over our heads, and the everlasting rattle of the machine-guns, which mowed our men down like grass before a scythe. There will be many sad homes and broken hearts in Yorkshire today. The flower of our young men went down on that terrible day.
>
> My platoon and I went through it all, first one dropping, and then two or three together, some of them blown to pieces. It was miraculous how they missed me. We had dwindled to about a dozen, and when we were held up by the exceptionally heavy fire, we sought refuge in a large shell hole.[24]

As the survivors dropped to the ground on their stomachs Lieutenant-Colonel Maurice Kennard remained on his feet, with walking stick in hand and he calmly said, 'Come on boys, up you get', turned and walked towards the German lines. As they moved forward they were fired upon by German machine-gunners in the Heidenkopf. Kennard was soon killed by a shell that burst close to him.

The 18th West Yorkshire Regiment was pinned down in shell holes in No Man's Land. To peer above the lip of their refuge meant certain death or wounding. As shells and bullets descended upon their position they also had to contend with the hot summer sun which caused them to feel dehydrated when their water bottles became empty. Sergeant William Moran recalled:

> We had been there perhaps a good half hour when an immense shell burst on the edge of the shell hole. Then I was hit. I thought all my arm had gone. The blood absolutely poured down inside my sleeve; it was just like pouring it out of a bucket. It was lucky that there was someone there who could bandage it for me, or I should have bled to death.

> Well after a little while all the others had to move forward, and I was left on my own. I kept fainting away, and coming round again. I was laid on my back, with nothing on but my trousers, absolutely helpless and the shells kept dropping within a yard or two of me, and smothering me with dust and dirt.
>
> After a long time I began to pull myself together. I thought I'd better get away if I possibly could, so I got on my hands and knees and crawled slowly and painfully away, dragging my tunic after me. Everything else I left. I crawled along to a shallow trench, over dead men, in all sorts of positions, heaped one on top of each other. Every wounded man I crawled over cursed me for hurting him.
>
> At last I managed to land in a large hollow, and I lay on some sandbags, face up. The heat was awful, and I thought I should die of thirst. There was about a dozen other poor chaps. Most of them as bad as myself, and some of them worse. One had his right foot blown off. The moans and groans were fearful to hear.[25]

On 94th Brigade's sector, a company from the 1st Barnsley Pals left Copse Trench at 08:10 hours and after advancing over the British front line and entering No Man's Land their ranks were decimated by German high explosive shells, and only a few remnants were seen entering the first German line. Once the German barrage subsided Brigadier-General Hubert Rees decided to send further companies to try to breakthrough into Serre:

> It was obviously necessary to attempt to get a footing in the German first trenches ... The hostile barrage had eased off by now and was no longer formidable, so I ordered two companies of the 13th York & Lancaster to make the attempt. I did not know that the German barrage was an observed barrage, but thought it was probably mechanical. As soon as this fresh attack was launched down came the barrage again. One company was badly mauled, whilst the other wisely halted short of it.[26]

Around 08:00 hours, Lieutenant-Colonel R.B. Neill, the wounded CO of the Leeds Pals, sheltering in a shell hole could see through his field glasses parties entering Serre:

> I did see in Serre village about half hour after zero two weak platoons, eleven in one party and about 15 or so in the other. About the same time I saw a few men (25 or 26) of the 4th Division in the Quadrilateral [Heidenkopf]. These were the only British troops I saw in the German defences. The ground between the Quadrilateral and Serre being low limited the view. [27]

Communications had broken down within the 11th East Lancs and Lieutenant-Colonel Arthur Rickman lost contact with his men who had advanced towards Serre. All he could see were many of his men lying wounded in No Man's Land. He reported at 08:10 hours: 'I could see odd groups in my front believed to be wounded. Also that I could not see any of my waves. No further report from waves.'[28]

Private H. Wilkinson was amongst the wounded of the 11th East Lancs:

> We knew we were going to certain death, but not one man faltered. It was simply marvellous. But the Germans gave us a gruelling, shrapnel, universal and high explosive shells simply rained down on us. Every two or three yards of the German lines seemed to hold a machine-gun, and the bullets simply rained across No Man's Land. But on we went until we got dropped. I was dropped just against the German wire, but I did my little bit. The Germans can shoot with their artillery. Heads and legs blown off was a common sight.[29]

It was a confusing time for the British commanders because of the conflicting reports they received. Divisional observation posts reported at 08:25 hours, 'Small party of our men in Serre. Saw sun shining on their triangles'.[30] Three minutes later Major-General O'Gowan at 31st Division Headquarters received a message from the Forward Observation Officer of 165th Brigade Royal Field Artillery reporting 'our infantry advancing through Serre'.[31] Within this short space of time O'Gowan was receiving contradictory information for a message was received at 08:37 hours from 171st Brigade, RFA indicating that Brigadier-General Ingle's 93rd Brigade was in trouble, reporting 'considerable number of our infantry lying down in between trenches north of the Quadrilateral. They are being heavily shelled by enemy 77 mm guns.'[32] At that same time another message was received from 169th Brigade, RFA, confirming 'that German front line which is now held by us opposite John and Matthew Copses is being enfiladed from batteries near Rossignol Wood.'[33]

At 08:40 hours Brigadier-General Rees knew that his men from the 94th Brigade had penetrated the German line and that they were coming under heavy enemy artillery barrages, but had no further information. O'Gowan stated that he received the following telephone message reporting 'that his line got across German front trenches but it is very difficult to see what is going on. He has no definite information, but they are being heavily fired on. He proposed to send forward another Company up to the front line to back them up.'[34]

The only information that Lieutenant-Colonel Arthur Rickman received about the progress of the 11th East Lancs was from vague reports from the wounded that were crawling back to the British line. He ordered reinforcements from 94th Brigade HQ to enter the fray. At 08:45 hours two companies from the 1st Barnsley Pals were ordered to go forward and hold the German first and second line trenches. Two waves from this battalion advanced forward, but they were stopped by the deadly barrage that was descending upon No Man's Land. Unable to proceed beyond the British front trench they were recalled and ordered to reassemble in Monk Trench. The German barrage was fired to cause maximum devastation upon the British lines and prevent reinforcements from crossing No Man's Land. German observers could clearly see into the British trenches opposite Serre and direct accurate fire as and when required.

At 09:00 hours Lieutenant-Colonel Arthur Rickman had received a report on the 11th East Lancs sector from the wounded Corporal Rigby, belonging to the first wave, who stated 'that 7 of his platoon got into 1st line. They held it for about 20 minutes and bombing Germans back till bombs were exhausted.'[35]

The 93rd Brigade assault on the right flank had also faltered. It was coming under heavy machine-gun fire from the direction of the German occupied Heidenkopf redoubt southeast of their position. Brigadier-General Ingles knew that 4th Division should have captured the Heidenkopf and beyond that the German strongpoint Munich Trench. At 08:55 hours Ingles sent a contingent from the 2nd Bradford Pals forward to the front line trench to ascertain the situation.

Also at 9:00 hours Rees reported to O'Gowan that the 11th East Lancs were in the second German line but had suffered heavily. He confirmed that he had sent two companies from the 1st Barnsley Pals to support them. Rees questioned whether it was advisable to send in the 2nd Barnsley. O'Gowan promptly replied stating that 'he did not propose to use reserves until situation is cleared up.'[36]

At the same time German forces were seen massing in Serre and appeared to be preparing to launch a counter-attack. Guns from the 170th Brigade, RFA fired a barrage upon their position to break their lines.

Six platoons from the 2nd Barnsley Pals were reportedly seen going forward and were holding their ground in the German second trench line at 09:00 hours, but by 10:35 hours there was none left to continue the battle. Major-General O'Gowan at 31st Division Headquarters was still unaware of the situation in Serre by 09:45 hours although troops from the 4th Division were seen close to Pendant Copse.

When the wounded Lieutenant-Colonel Neill left his shell hole in No Man's Land around 10.00 hours he could see a mass of dead from his battalion, the Leeds Pals, lying before him:

> There was no life visible in No Man's Land, nor could I see a soul in the enemy lines. I left it with the impression that if a fresh attack could be at once delivered it would be successful, but I quickly altered my mind

> on reaching our own front line to find it filled with troops whose morale was nil.[37]

The Leeds Pals lost heavily and were unable to make any further attempts to reach the German lines. Of the twenty-four officers and 650 men that went into action, according to the battalion War Diary, eleven officers were killed, thirteen wounded and 504 men were either killed or wounded.

Communications had broken down at divisional, brigade and battalion level, with scant information coming from Serre. Brigadier-General Ingles relayed the following message at 10:13 hours to 31st Division HQ which was based on information that had taken ninety minutes to reach his headquarters from each Battalion HQ between John Copse and Luke Copse:

> Message from 12th York & Lancaster timed 8.45 am states no information from waves. From East Lancaster all four waves went on but no reports received from waves. From 13th York & Lancaster 3 companies moved forward, remainder in Monk [trench], amounting to about 70 men at present. 14th York & Lancaster had 1 ½ Companies in Campion and Monk remainder digging Russian sap. 3rd and 4th waves came under very heavy shell fire, just behind our front line trench. Fear casualties very heavy.[38]

Brigadier-General Rees received confirmation at around 10:00 hours that he had lost the commanding officers from the Leeds and 1st Bradford Pals and most of their other officers. Rees reported this bad news to O'Gowan who received it at 10:27 hours. Rees retained his support battalions in the front line on the 94th Brigade sector. Brigadier-General Ingles kept the 2nd Bradford Pals and the 18th Durham Light Infantry holding the British lines. Both Rees and Ingles were afraid that if they sent their reserve battalions into the battle there would be no units remaining to oppose an expected German counter-attack, and there would be a critical undefended gap in the British line.

The German artillery barrage fell on the German second line at 09.18 hours supporting their troops in trying to clear the small parties of British soldiers that had managed to enter their trench system at Serre. An hour later this barrage lifted and German bombing parties were observed bombing their way through communication trenches towards the German first line. By 10:45 hours German forces were in control of their front line trench and were firing upon the dead and wounded lying in No Man's Land on the slope leading to Serre. The 94th Brigade war dairy reported:

> At odd intervals, and for the rest of the day, small groups of Germans were seen in the first line, standing up on the fire step sniping at any of

> our men in No Man's Land who showed any sign of life, and making target practise of dead bodies. Our machine-guns were turned on these groups, apparently with some effect.[39]

Reports of the enormity of losses sustained reached Brigadier-General Rees who reported the disaster to O'Gowan at 10:50 hours. 'Estimated casualties at 10.00 am 15th West Yorks Regt 400 all ranks. 16th West Yorks Regt 300 all ranks.'[40] More precise information was conveyed to O'Gowan at 31st Division HQ at 11:07 hours:

> 93rd Bde reports 15th and 16th West Yorks practically non-existent. Adjutant 16th West Yorks reports he has only one officer and hardly any NCOs. Cannot get into touch with any officer of 15th West Yorks. Remains of both regiments are in front line. Adjutant 18th West Yorks was ordered to sort them out. 18th West Yorks should be holding front line with 18th Durh. L.I. in reserve.[41]

It must have been difficult for O'Gowan at 31st Division HQ, Rees and Ingles at brigade level to make appropriate decisions without reliable information as to the situation at Serre especially after receiving reports of the enormous casualties incurred by 31st Division. At 11:15 hours German soldiers were seen on their front line parapet opposite John and Luke Copses. Despite reports of heavy casualties and the visual confirmations of German soldiers occupying their front line trenches there was still false hope that a breakthrough had been made at Serre. 31st Division reported 'Germans visible on their own front line parapet … Possibly they might want to surrender.'[42]

Ten minutes later Rees confirmed to O'Gowan that no movement could be seen in any of the four lines of German trenches. However he reported that his Brigade Observer had seen the discs on the back of British soldiers in the fourth German line at Serre. These conflicting reports could not hide the fact that the attack was a disaster on an enormous scale with the trenches filled with casualties. A desperate need for stretchers meant that those who were in urgent need of medical attention could not be evacuated.

By midday German guns fell silent at Serre except for the snipers who appeared from their parapet shooting at random those British soldiers wounded or trapped in No Man's Land. British machine-gunners soon stopped them from operating in order to give those lying in No Man's Land a chance of survival. Rumours that British troops were in Serre and had secured the village were inaccurate and unfounded. At 12:15 hours O'Gowan ordered the rest of 94th Brigade to advance across No Man's Land in an effort to enter Serre and confirm whether a foothold had been established within the village.

Those soldiers who had already gone over the top that day and survived, found themselves being ordered to repeat the ordeal. Only twenty unwounded men from 'C' Company, Sheffield Pals who advanced, had returned for roll call. They received the message from 31st Division HQ which wanted them to do it again and launch another attack about noon. They were traumatised after the initial attempt and unable to launch an effective assault. Lance Corporal James Glenn recalled: 'We were shocked, like sheep didn't know what we doing or where we were going. Nobody knew what to do'.[43] Rees, wisely, recommended that any further attack to be postponed until more definite reports about the situation at Serre were received. There were also alarming reports that German forces had counter-attacked from Serre and were in the British lines. Rees recalled the confusion in the British lines.

> The wildest reports were rife at divisional headquarters at this time. I was ordered to send a company to bomb the Germans out of the front trench of the 93rd Bde. I expostulated and said that no front trenches existed, but to no purpose. I therefore ordered seventy men near Bde Hdqtrs to draw bombs from the dump and take their time about it. A little later, I was talking to General O'Gowan and told him that I didn't believe the Germans were in the 93rd trench at all. He said to my considerable astonishment, 'Nor do I.' 'In that case,' said I, 'I will stop the attack which you have just ordered me to make' and rushed out of the dugout to cancel the order. Baumgartner told me afterwards that he had a circumstantial report that the Germans were in possession of my Bde Hdqtrs. When people had recovered from the unbalancing effect of this disaster, I was asked whether I recommended making an attack with the 92 Bde. I said 'No' very decidedly.[44]

During the afternoon the Sheffield Pals HQ was moved further south to Luke Copse because the previous location in a dugout in John Copse was destroyed. It was moved again later to Observation Wood. With their ranks decimated, there was no one left from the Sheffield Pals to eat the hot food that had been cooked and was about to be brought forward to the front line. Lance Corporal James Glenn was detailed with two others to go behind lines to prevent these rations from being brought forward, but they were mistaken for deserters by personnel belonging to the military police which they encountered. Glenn recalled:

> My company officer gave me a message to go back to the transport lines to tell them not to send any rations up because there was nobody to eat them. A friend of mine and another signaller and we set off. We got just outside the trench system. The Military Police put us into a cage, which was really erected for prisoners when they got them. They took us for

stragglers. They gave us a meal. While they were doing something else we slipped out and took our message to transport lines and then we went back where we come.[45]

Lieutenant-General Hunter-Weston at VIII Corps HQ was anxious for results and at 15:05 hours ordered the consolidation and defence of the British front line and then to send all available men to Brigadier-General Rees to assist 94th Brigade for another assault against the German lines opposite John Copse during that evening. There still remained the mistaken belief that parties belonging to the 31st Division were in control of sections in Serre and Pendant Copse and the hope that they would be able to establish contact with them.

By 15:50 hours German artillery was pounding the British positions opposite Serre. Much of this fire was thought to have originated from Rossignol. Lieutenant-Colonel Rickman was desperate for reinforcements for he had only fifty-five men from the 11th East Lancs in the British front line and most of them were wounded. There were two Lewis Guns with only two men to operate them, one of whom was also wounded. The situation was so fraught that ammunition rounds for these Lewis Guns were put into position by officers' servants.

A report received at 16:07 hours from an observer from the RFC stated that no part of Serre was occupied by British troops. All they could see were small parties of British soldiers in No Man's Land occupying trenches between Serre and the German front line.

Major-General O'Gowan received Hunter-Weston's orders to launch a further assault upon Serre with the intention of bombing the Germans from their first trench and linking up with British held pockets that were thought to be in Serre. O'Gowan promised Rees two battalions from 92nd Brigade and reported that the 48th Division would allocate an entire brigade to support the renewed attack. Rees knew that the remnants from 94th Brigade were in no fit state to go over the top again. Around 18:00 hours O'Gowan consulted with his brigade commanders, Ingles and Rees, and he decided that their men had taken such heavy losses that they were not in a position to conduct further attacks. O'Gowan expressed this opinion to Hunter-Weston at VIII Corps Headquarters:

I have had a long talk with General Rees, who has a consultation with General Ingles and they are both of the opinion that neither of the Brigades are in a fit state to make any further effort. General Rees says that he watched his attack today, and that the first 3 lines went over excellently, and then they got it rather stiff. He also says that at present it is his opinion that there are very few, if any, men left on the other side of the enemy's line, and that the men who got over are probably killed or captured by now. He thinks that in Serre they are either killed or

> captured, and he is very strong on the point, and I have had my signalling people trying to get into communication but cannot get any sign at all. They have got a very good view now – neither of the Brigades are fit to fight and I should like to put it up that the 92nd Brigade should hold the line.[46]

Hunter-Weston immediately ordered that the front line at Serre be reorganised and two battalions from the 92nd Brigade be brought forward to launch a night attack at 02.00 hours on 2 July in an effort to link up with British held pockets still thought to be in Serre.

If fresh troops were available to launch another assault they would need to reach the British front line which was full of dead and wounded from the 93rd & 94th Brigades. These trenches would have to be cleared first before any attack could be launched. The major problem at this time was defence of the British front line, as there were scarcely any men to hold the trenches. This is exemplified by Rees' report of 21:00 hours:

> 11th East Lancaster. Regt. about 30 all ranks. 12th York & Lancaster. 3 officers and 6 other ranks. 13th York & Lancaster. About 250 all ranks. 14th York & Lancaster. About 350 all ranks.[47]

When this disastrous information was relayed up to VIII Corps HQ, Hunter-Weston reconsidered and at 21:50 hours he decided to abandon any further assaults and that 92nd Brigade would be brought forward to defend the British line.

During that evening two German soldiers were seen removing the British wounded close to their lines from No Man's Land. At 21:20 hours Lieutenant-Colonel Arthur Rickman confirmed that approximately fifty men were all that remained from the 11th East Lancs with no Lewis or machine-guns in their line. He reported 'the men are a good deal rattled and have very few NCOs.'[48]

Private John Valentine Chapman was among the few survivors from the 2nd Bradford Pals to get back to the British lines. Badly wounded from shrapnel wounds he wrote the following letter to his father in Shipley:

> I am indeed lucky to be alive after our terrible experience. I fear very very many of both Bradford Battalions are no more, and the same applies to the Leeds Battalion. I walked over our dead in scores both in the open and in the trenches when working my way back. I possess nothing but what was in my pockets, as I had to discard everything to give myself a sporting chance of escape. My left hand is almost useless yet, but I expect to have an operation soon. July 1st will never fade from my memory. I thank God that I am left to live, yet it is miraculous.'[49]

From the few men who returned to the British lines some intelligence was gathered about the German trench system at Serre. The following report was written on 5 July 1916 and stated:

> Owing to the very small number of men who returned to our lines after having penetrated the German System, considerable difficulty has been experienced in collecting the following information. –
>
> Most of the earth appeared to be on the parados; the trenches were very deep, and all our men who jumped into them were entirely lost to view. The support line was fire-stepped.
>
> Only one dug-out has been described by men returning from the German line. This was 20 ft deep, under the parapet of the front line. This particular one was smashed in at the opening.
>
> Two pieces of information about machine-guns appear to be fairly well corroborated.
>
> machine-guns were emplaced in deltas at the junction of communication and fire trenches.
>
> machine-guns were used very considerably from our left flank to enfilade our advancing waves.
>
> It appears that considerable numbers of the enemy lay down between the trenches during the bombardment or were hidden in dug-outs. It is certain that the front line filled up with Germans very rapidly, and after our barrage had passed over it – both from the flanks and down the communication trenches.[50]

Despite being in the advantageous position of possessing the high ground, the German 169th Infantry Regiment lost 141 killed, 219 wounded and had two missing during the defence of Serre. The 31st Division lost heavily during 1 July 1916. Ingles' 93rd Brigade had lost ninety-four officers and 1,730 men while Rees 94th Brigade had lost fifty-five officers and 1,544 men.[51] Many of the Pals battalions that were formed in 1914 were all but destroyed on the battlefield at Serre on 1 July 1916. The 2nd Barnsley Pals had fifteen officer casualties, together with 468 casualties amongst the men.[52]

Many of those who died on 1 July 1916 remained where they fell. German forces held onto Serre for the remainder of 1916 and it was impossible to recover the dead and the wounded due to the dangers of entering No Man's Land. It is quite possible that many of the wounded, who slowly died in No Man's Land, might have lived if they had received medical attention.

On 23 February 1917, British intelligence reports indicated that German forces were in the process of evacuating Serre. This signalled the beginning of the German withdrawal to the Hindenburg Line. When the 2nd

Honourable Artillery Company eventually entered Serre, they found that the village had been pulverised by British artillery. More disturbing was the sight of the decomposed skeletal remains of the soldiers from 31st Division who had been caught in barbed wire six months previously during the catastrophic first day of the Battle of the Somme. Private William Parry-Morris belonging to 2nd Honourable Artillery Company recalled the gruesome sights as he passed across the battlefield towards Serre:

> Around the village of Serre were rows and rows of barbed wire, German barbed wire, which had been put up there in 1915 and 1916 and was where one of the places which the British Army attacked on July 1st 1916 and they never even got to the wire. There was so many men killed trying to get to the wire and when we went through the village of Serre in March 1917, their bodies were still hanging on the barbed wire, 30 or 40 of them.[53]

Parry-Morris recalled that the men were disturbed to see their dead comrades left hanging there without dignity, and that they had to leave them without burying them as they pursued the German Army that was withdrawing to the Hindenburg Line.

Lack of secrecy, inability to cut the German wire and failure of British guns to destroy all of the German gun batteries in the vicinity, were key reasons why 31st Division failed to capture Serre on 1 July 1916. Major A. Plackett, commanding the Sheffield Pals, gave a detailed appraisal of why the Yorkshiremen failed in their attack:

> The failure of the attack was undoubtedly due to the wire not being sufficiently cut. Had this been cut the enemy's machine-guns could have been dealt with by the men who managed to reach the front line. As it was, they could not be reached and there was no means of stopping their fire. Bombers attempted to silence them with grenades but could not reach them – consequently succeeding waves were wiped out and did not arrive at the German wire in any strength.[54]

Plackett then went on to list suggestions and criticisms of the tactics that failed with fatal consequences for the troops:

> (A) The wait in the assembly trenches were too long.
> (B) The first wave should not have occupied the front line. Owing to the Trench Mortars being in position in the front line, it became a death trap when the enemy retaliated against them.
> (C) More bombardment slits should have been dug. It was found that men occupying these suffered very slightly compared with those in Assembly trenches; those that were dug should have been dug deeper.

(D) More men should have been trained in in the use of the Bangalore torpedo. It was found that all trained men had become casualties by the time the torpedoes were actually required.
(E) Smoke bombs would have been useful to conceal our efforts to cut the enemy's wire. As it was, anyone attempting to cut the wire was immediately sniped.

Tactics (i.) The assault should have been made at dawn or soon after. As it was the enemy had 4 1/2 hours to prepare for an attack, as our intention was undoubtedly given away by the gaps cut in our wire and tapes laid out in front. Men who reached the German wire state that on looking towards our own lines, they could see almost every movement. This being so any attack by day was scarcely likely to succeed.
(ii) The attack should have been in double time.
(iii) The waves were too far apart, the distance between them allowing the enemy to pay attention to each wave before the next came up.
The general opinion was that Officers, NCO's and machine-gunners were marked men.[55]

Chapter 10

Redan Ridge and the Heidenkopf

South of Serre, the 4th Division commanded by Major-General the Honourable General William Lambton, together with two battalions from Major-General R. Fanshawe's 48th Division were ordered to capture Redan Ridge and the German-held strongpoint called the Heidenkopf. Named after a German officer who served on this sector, it was also known as the Quadrilateral to British commanders because of its shape. Serre Road Cemetery No. 2 now stands on the position of the Heidenkopf. This redoubt protruded into the British lines and was positioned beneath Redan Ridge, between Serre and Beaumont Hamel. It originally lay along the German front line which stretched northwards through Matthew Copse and Touvant Farm, but the line was pushed back towards Serre by the French during June 1915. German forces held onto the Heidenkopf and a salient subsequently developed. 121st RIR from Württemberg, belonging to Generalleutnant von Wundt's 51st Reserve Brigade defended Redan Ridge from Beaumont Hamel to the Serre–Mailley Road.

British observers confirmed that the wire had been cut along this sector and that British artillery had also destroyed the German trenches. However these reports conflicted with patrols that were sent to assess the wire two nights prior to the attack which stated that there were no gaps in the wire on 4th Division's sector. Although much of the wire had not been cut British artillery and mortar attacks upon the Heidenkopf were so strong that most of the garrison of the 121st RIR was evacuated from the position. A single machine-gun was positioned in the Heidenkopf together with a small contingent of German engineers commanded by Leutnant der Reserve Eitel were stationed within this salient. As British shells targeted the Heidenkopf these German engineers dug four mines and filled their chambers packed with explosives. Anticipating that this vulnerable salient would be swarmed by British Tommies and fearful that they were unable to hold the position, they planned to detonate these mines and inflict as many casualties as possible when they appeared.

The 1/6th and 1/8th Royal Warwickshire Regiment, two Territorial battalions belonging to the 48th Division, assaulted the left flank upon the northern portion of the Heidenkopf and the trenches that ran from this garrison northwards. The 1/8th battalion led the assault followed by the 1/6th. The 4th Division was wholly comprised of regular army battalions. The 11th Brigade, commanded by Brigadier-General Charles Prowse, advanced in the centre with the 1st Rifle Brigade leading, supported by the 1st Somerset Light infantry and they were deployed opposite the southern perimeter of the Heidenkopf. On the 4th Division's right flank was the 1st East Lancashire Regiment, followed by 1st Hampshire Regiment also from 11th Brigade. These units were tasked with securing the first German trench and the second trench line known as Munich Trench. Once this ground had been captured 10th Brigade, commanded by Brigadier-General C.A. Wilding, and 12th Brigade led by Brigadier-General J.D. Crosbie, would pass through these lines and secure the third German line along Redan Ridge which stretched between Serre and Beaumont Hamel.

As British artillery pounded the German trenches that connected to the Heidenkopf and along Redan Ridge obstinate German machine-gunners, who were anticipating a British attack, fired intermittently into the British lines from the directions of Beaumont Hamel, Ridge Redoubt and from a position north of Ten Tree Alley. German machine-guns were massed on high ground on Beaucourt Ridge above the Heidenkopf in the first, second and third German lines.

Hawthorn Crater exploded close to Beaumont Hamel at 19:20 hours and as the British barrage lifted further into German lines the German machine-gun fire intensified, since the barrage passed over German dugouts enabling machine-gun crews to come out of the dugouts and set up their positions. German gun batteries also laid down their own barrage across No Man's Land at that same time, which promptly lifted onto the first British trench line, pre-empting the British offensive.

The soldiers of the 1st East Lancs were feeling tense and apprehensive as they waited in their trenches for Zero Hour. The tension was palpable as they waited for the whistles to blow to signal the assault. Some men were so anxious they went over their parapets into No Man's Land prematurely. Lance Corporal C.E. Grime, belonging to the 1st East Lancs explained this:

> On July 1st we were all anxiously waiting the arrival of half past seven. At six o'clock in the morning an officer came down … and set all watches at the correct time so that there would be no mistake. The moments crept on slowly and we were getting ourselves ready to spring over the parapets. At 7.20 the order was given to remove the sandbags and make footholds on the parapets. In the anxiety to get their grips some men went over the parapet after doing this but the adjutant called them back.[1]

No doubt German observers in the opposing trenches would have seen these men venturing out into No Man's Land then being called back. They would have sensed that an attack was imminent and were on a heightened increased state of alert. When Zero Hour did arrive German machine-gunners were poised and waiting to ascend from their trenches.

Further north, German machine-gunners positioned in Serre opened fire on the left company of 1/8th Royal Warwickshire Regiment as the battalion advanced, as Captain D.R. Adams remembered:

> The left of the 8th/Warwick during their advance across No Man's Land found that there was no touch with the right of the 31st Division and that consequently their left flank was exposed to an increasingly severe infilade fire from machine-guns on the ridge in front of 93rd Bde. This machine-gun barrage was at first too high and the front line was reached with comparatively few casualties. Thence onwards, however, the German machine-gunners shortened their range and casualties became so heavy that by the time that isolated parties had reached the support trench (about 200 yards behind the front line) further advance was impossible. I was with the left company, but one and was wounded near the support trench about 7.50 am. At that time there were the remnants of D Coy (The left Coy) still advancing on my left.[2]

The 1/6th Warwick followed behind at 07:40 hours and had suffered eighty casualties before reaching the British front line and they were able to join the 1/8th Battalion in the German lines. The right company of 1/8thWarwick got across No Man's Land and entered the first German trench. Captain C.W. Martin held reservations about the plan and had already told his men that he was not going to follow the plan, but instead to judge the situation at the time. He thought from the start that the advance upon heavily-defended positions was suicide. He could see on his right flank the 1st Rifle Brigade suffer heavy casualties as they went over:

> A second or two before Zero on 1 July 1916, I climbed out of the 4th line of our trenches and saw the left Coy. of the Rifle Brigade which had been put up by their O.C. according to his promise to me, extending in good order to their left, which movement cost at least 25% of their strength in casualties. At once I realised that my anticipations were proving only too correct, there seemed to me only one place where comparative safety could be found and that was in the enemy trenches, so I ran through the three waves and put myself at the head of the leading one and got them to run like hares for the first enemy line.[3]

Captain Martin rallied his men and overwhelmed the occupants of the first trench before proceeding to Point 92 with few losses. Lieutenant-Colonel

Innes commanding 1/8th Warwick was killed between the second and third German lines and Major Alfred Caddick stepped on a man-trap in the first German trench line.

The 1st Rifle Brigade advancing directly upon the Heidenkopf suffered heavy casualties from German machine-guns as soon as they advanced. 2nd Lieutenant G.W. Glover recalled:

> We started out as arranged, and things seemed going quite well till we, or rather our first wave, reached the German front line, they slowed and we bunched rather and the most fearsome hail of rifle and machine-gun fire with continuous shelling, opened on us. Most of us seemed to be knocked out.[4]

The 1st Rifle Brigade came under fire from German machine-gunners positioned at Ridge Redoubt and stopped them from reaching the German trenches. The company advancing on the left flank with supporting waves veered to the north to avoid this enemy machine-gun fire and captured the German trench known as Trench 77–92 and a small semi-circular trench further east. Lieutenant Glover was among those that got into the German trench system where they experienced difficulty consolidating their position. They were joined by Colour Sergeant Major Selway and Sergeant Hunt, but with no contact with the 1st East Lancs on the right flank, and hostile machine-gun fire coming from that direction, they were unable to press forward. Instead of attempting to move forward they made efforts to fortify their position. Reinforcements belonging to the 1/6th Warwick were able to get across No Man's Land to join the 1st Rifle Brigade. Glover was in a better position to proceed forwards. He recalled:

> We were enfiladed too from the left but some Warwicks came up, and apart from shelling we were fairly comfortable. Trevor turned up and Greetham of the Somersets and we decided to carry on, stretch out our right as far as we could with the battalion bombers, about half a dozen, on our right flank.[5]

German reinforcements armed with bombs kept coming forward and tried to outflank Glover's position on its right flank. A Lewis Gun was positioned upon the parapet of a communication trench and that seemed to keep these bombers out of range for the time being. Captain Martin of the 1/8th Warwick joined Glover and the mixed units of the 1st Rifle Brigade and 1st Somerset Light Infantry and was able to bolster their position on the left flank.

Captain Martin organised stragglers and they erected blocks in the sector of German trench that they held. Another officer from 1/8th Warwick joined them and Martin sent him with a bombing party along a communication trench that connected with Serre. This party carried a yellow flag waving above the trench and Martin could see them reach the village. This party was cut off and did not return. Martin was unable to send support in the direction of Serre because his party was resisting German counter-attacks and they too became isolated:

> At this time I was busy with the other flank and before I could send along support we were attacked and had to be content with trying to hold what we had. Bombing stops were made and things were quite comfortable except that we had no communications in any direction and consequently could obtain no replenishment of the fast disappearing bombs, as a constant pressure was kept up on both our flanks and the only help of beating off these enemy attacks was to be able to throw bomb for bomb.[6]

As they continued the fight a few officers, all wounded, arrived with some NCOs and fragmented parties from other units including the 1st Rifle Brigade. When reinforcements from 1/6th Warwick arrived the 1st Rifle Brigade advanced deeper into the German trench system and three parties occupied Trench 59 to 05. A bombing party held onto a position at a junction of trenches for several hours before being overwhelmed by German bombing parties advancing from Ridge Redoubt.

The leading waves from the 1st East Lancs left their trench, followed at 100-yard intervals by the other waves. They came under heavy fire from machine-gun crews at Ridge Redoubt and Beaumont Hamel. Lance Corporal C.E. Grime watched the first waves go forward:

> Six minutes later our officers and NCO's were on the parapets calling to the men: 'Come on boys, we've got 'em'. Over they went but did not go a couple of yards before they were shot down. As soon as we got into the open the Germans opened up a 'triple barrage' – artillery, rifle and machine-gun fire. It was terrible to see our boys drop down like sheep. But, undaunted, the rest struggled through this curtain of fire towards the 1st line of the Germans.
>
> When we – Col. Green, DSO, Capt. Heath MM, the Adjutant, some signallers and myself and two runners reached the first line trenches bullets were whistling and shells bursting all round us, and God only knows how we were missed.[7]

Only three platoons from the company advancing on the 1st East Lancs left flank reached the German trenches. The remainder of the battalion never got beyond the wire which was found in tact in many places. Lieutenant-Colonel Green was wounded close to the wire and sought refuge in a nearby shell crater. Lance Corporal Grimes took shelter in the same shell hole:

> We came to a shell hole wherein we found some wounded men and our Adjutant sent the runners back to our lines with a message. At this time there was only the Colonel, the Adjutant and myself left, and the Colonel asked me to go to the German front line and see how our fellows were getting on. In accordance with orders I went from shell hole to shell hole, several of which were full of wounded soldiers.
> I looked to my right … and it was a splendid sight to see a long line of our soldiers advancing towards the German trenches … I reached the wire entanglements when I was shot through the knee and I crept into a shell hole where I roughly dressed my wound, but found I could not move. I hadn't been there long when I was joined by one of the 'Hants' who fell into the hole, wounded in the leg. I dressed his wound and we lay there beside a dead man, whose water bottle we took and shared its contents. We lay there from eight in the morning till eleven at night, and when darkness came on I had to crawl back to our own lines on one knee – 200 yards away, and had then to walk, three miles to a dressing station.[8]

Soldiers from the 1st East Lancs advancing on the left flank found breaches in the wire and were able to reach the German trench, where they were met by hostile rifleman in large numbers. Here they engaged in close-quarter battles with the German occupants. Some managed to fight their way into the German support trench system. Thirty minutes after advancing three Very lights were observed in this direction that indicated to commanders watching intently in the British line that they had reached their objective in the German line. The position could not be consolidated for those that valiantly fought their way into the German trenches at Redan Ridge were surrounded and were either killed or captured. Only two men who reached Redan Ridge returned to the British line that day.

The German plan to detonate a mine beneath the Heidenkopf as soon as British infantry entered the position was an abysmal failure. As soon as British waves were seen advancing towards them, the only German machine-gun defending the position had jammed, and the engineers detonated the mines too soon, before the first waves arrived. The engineers blew themselves up together with the machine-gun crew. This proved advantageous for the British battalions because the earth displaced from the ground thrown into the air fell upon the entrances to German dugouts within the nearby trench system. With the dugouts blocked many of the German defenders of the 121st RIR occupying this position were trapped underground. British battalions were therefore able to overrun the German line and the Heidenkopf.

Ten minutes after the first waves from the 1st Rifle Brigade and 1st East Lancs went forward towards Redan Ridge, the 1st Somerset Light Infantry and 1st Hampshire Regiment followed them across the shell-cratered No

Man's Land. The 1st Hampshire Regiment suffered heavily as enemy machine-gunners fired upon them as they left their trenches as they tried to follow the 1st East Lancs. Lieutenant-Colonel the Honourable Lawrence Palk DSO commanding the 1st Hampshire was among those killed. Remnants from the battalion continued with the advance, but the German machine-gun fire from the heights of Redan Ridge was so strong that many of these supporting waves were forced to take cover in shell holes. No-one from the 1st Hampshire reached the German trenches. The battalion War Diary confirmed:

> As soon as our troops left their trenches heavy machine-gun fire was brought to bear on them from all directions and it was impossible even to reach the German front line. Our casualties in officers amounted to 100% and was also very heavy in other ranks. After lying about in shell holes all day the men came back to their original front line.[9]

Pinned down by this relentless fire in No Man's Land some of these men from the 1st Hampshire had to wait until dark to withdraw to their own lines.

The 1st Somerset Light Infantry suffered the same fate as they followed the 1st Rifles Brigade. Lieutenant-Colonel John Thicknesse, commanding the 1st Somerset Light Infantry, had been killed as soon as he left the British trenches. German machine-guns decimated their ranks and many never reached the German trenches. Sergeant Holley belonged to the first wave:

> At 7.30 am the fire was lifted and the order was sent down the line, 'Up and at 'em!' and we met such a storm of machine-gun and shell fire that you would think impossible to ever live in. But I will say that for our boys – they never flinched. Our boys and the Rifle Brigade took the lead, but I don't think many of us reached the trench before we were cut down. But if we did not reach it, we opened the door for the others to do so, and by the look of things it was a proud success. But would you believe that fritz new as well as we did what time the attack was coming off, secret as it was supposed to be kept.
>
> I did not last very long. We got up within 20 yards of their front line, when my officer collected the platoon together to make a charge. He asked me if we were all ready, and I said 'Yes'. We got up to charge, but if you ever saw the vanishing trick put on about sixty men it was when he said 'Charge!' They were waiting, and we went down like sheep. They gave me mine in the left thigh, right in the bone, and there it stopped. It was not being hit that I worried about; it was having to stay out there all day, but I suppose I must think myself lucky that I am in the land of the living.[10]

The 1st Somerset could see on the right flank that the 1st Hampshire and 1st East Lancs were being held up by the wire. They were also coming under heavy German machine-gun fire and were forced to deviate from their intended line of advance and head north-eastwards towards the Heidenkopf.

The 1st Somerset managed to get into the German front trench and was met by a scene of utter carnage as they could see the results of the British bombardment and the German mines. Lance Corporal E.F.M. Lewis recounted:

> When we reached their trenches we could see heaps of their dead killed by our shells. A lot of the Germans who were left took refuge in their dugouts and these had to be bombed out. All of us were carrying one or two bombs as well as our rifles in case of emergency. I had one narrow escape after I had lost my own rifle. A German suddenly came for me with a bayonet and I did the first thing that came to my head, I managed to dodge the first thrust of the bayonet and then gave the German a terrible kick in the stomach which put him out completely. It was the only chance I had not having any weapons on me at the time, but I managed to pick up another rifle soon afterwards.[11]

The Germans were so desperate to regain control of the front-line trench that they began shooting the wounded that lay in the trenches. Lance Corporal Lewis recalled:

> Our fellows were maddened by one thing which happened and the Germans got no mercy for sometime afterwards. We had taken a line of trenches and were searching about the communication trenches to see if they were clear of the enemy when a body of Germans made an unexpected raid on a part of the captured trench and killed some of our defenceless wounded. We had our revenge afterwards.[12]

The 1st Somerset experienced difficulty as some sections became entangled in German wire in between the first and second lines, as Lewis explained:

> We were hung up for a bit by what remained of their barbed wire entanglements, but were making for the second line as soon as possible. We had a good deal of trouble with some of the German dugouts which had not been destroyed by the bombardment and we were attacked by the occupants in some unexpected quarters, but our bombers soon encountered them. Several Germans came out yelling for mercy and some of them were absolute wrecks. At one point there was fierce hand to hand and those who had lost their rifles and bayonets and who could not use them properly fought with their fists. At any rate the first line

> was taken quite comfortably, but when we were approaching their second line, they made a better show of resistance. machine-guns appeared and did a good deal of damage checking us for a short time. The Germans concentrated for a counter-attack, but we obtained reinforcements and succeeded in capturing their second line. Our carriers did fine work in bringing up ammunition, but they suffered heavily from shell fire.[13]

As they were going forward some soldiers of the 1st Somerset were searching for souvenirs. Lewis recalled: 'Even during the advance our fellows were hunting for souvenirs, and several could be seen wearing German helmets.'[14]

Meanwhile, parties from 1st Rifle Brigade were trying to secure a footing in the German Trench 94–49 and were joined by elements from the 1st Somerset, but the German opposition was strong and they were unable to consolidate the position.

The survivors from the 1st Hampshire and 1st Somerset were able to reinforce the 1st Rifle Brigade and the two Warwickshire battalions, who were fighting a determined battle to keep control of the Heidenkopf. These battalions held on to trench 59 to 05, but they were under attack from bombing parties coming from communication trenches leading from Munich Trench. Lance Corporal Lewis was wounded as he headed for the third German trench line, as he recalled:

> I got hit myself between the second and third German lines. I was going across to help the Warwicks bomb some Germans out of a dugout when a shrapnel shell burst, killing two of the Warwicks. One of the shrapnel bullets caught me in the chest near the shoulder and I knew no more for a time. When I came round I had to make my way back as best I could. I had lost a lot of blood, and the journey back was worse than the advance for the German shells were then falling thickly, but I surely reached some R.A.M.C. men and was carried on a stretcher back to the dressing station.[15]

Lewis' two brothers, Private Jesse Lewis and Private Harry Lewis, were also wounded in the assault upon the Heidenkopf during that day. Although there were British soldiers trying to gain control of the Heidenkopf, No Man's Land was a field of deadly fire. Many soldiers from the 4th Division lay dead or wounded, many were trapped in the numerous shell holes.

The brigade commanders from the 4th Division were positioned in headquarters 400 yards behind the front line. Here they had a panoramic view of the entire front from Serre in the north, Redan Ridge, directly opposite them and Beaumont Hamel in the south. They could see the 29th

Division's failure to secure Beaumont Hamel from their vantage point. However they could not decipher the progress of the 4th Division. The signal for 'stopped by uncut wire' was one white flare and three white flares to signify 'objective gained' were too alike and when white flares were released the brigade commanders could not determine progress along their front.

By 08:45 hours no messages about the progress of the 11th Brigade had been received and commanders in the British line were left in total ignorance as to what was happening in the German lines. Two RFC reconnaissance aeroplanes made brave attempts to assess the situation from above the Heidenkopf. They flew so low they were within range of enemy small-arms fire from the ground. Captain D.R. Adams, of 1/8th Royal Warwickshire commented on the bravery of the RFC pilots from his position in the German lines:

> RFC on 11th Bdg front the two contact patrol aeroplanes displayed amazing daring, often flying at the height of about 50 feet under a heavy small arms fire along the whole front of the advance in order to maintain touch with our progress.[16]

A report from one of these Royal Flying Corps aircraft reached 4th Division Headquarters confirming that soldiers from 1st Somerset Light Infantry had reached their objective and were in Munich Trench.

Despite being fired upon from German machine-guns in Redan Redoubt, elements from the 1st Rifle Brigade and the 1/8th Royal Warwickshire managed to get onto Redan Ridge and from their positions were able to penetrate the defences of the Heidenkopf. They secured the support trench that led into the German bastion from the east occupying 600 yards. The left flank of the 1/8th Royal Warwickshire entered the German first trench, but it became exposed from German machine-guns being fired from Serre, as well as a number that were well-concealed beneath burnt hay stacks. Only a small number of men of the 1/8th Royal Warwickshire reached the German support line.

Some messages filtered back to the British line from the 11th Brigade urging the support brigades not to leave the British line. These were sent at 08:35 hours. These instruction did not reach 11th Brigade Headquarters until 09:00 hours when an order to suspend the attack was immediately dispatched. The runner delivering this vital message got to the rear waves who were held back, but he was unable to get to the front waves of the 10th and 12th Brigade before they were to leave the British parapets.

The 2nd Essex Regiment, the 1st King's Own Lancaster Regiment, and the 2nd Lancashire Fusiliers of the 12th Brigade, moved forward behind the 1/8th Royal Warwickshire on the left flank towards the Heidenkopf. These battalions came under fire as they assembled before going over the top, with many from the 1st King's Own being cut down before they reached the British front line. Despite their heavy losses the men continued to advance across No Man's Land towards the Heidenkopf but only a small proportion of men from the King's Own got into the German lines.

Battalions of the 10th Brigade were scheduled to advance towards Redan Ridge at 09:00 hours on a 1,500 yard front. The 2nd Royal Dublin Fusiliers, 1st Royal Irish Fusiliers together with the 1st Royal Warwickshire Regiment advancing on the right flank, surged towards the Heidenkopf and Redan Ridge, but heavy German machine-gun fire stopped them.

The 2nd Royal Dublin Fusiliers went over the top but their ranks were quickly cut down by machine-gun fire from Beaumont Hamel and Ridge Redoubt. Only a few men reached the German front line. When battalion commanders realised that remnants from the 1st Hampshire and 1st East Lancs were pinned down in shell holes immediately in front of their line of advance in No Man's Land, they aborted the assault and held their rear waves back in the British frontline trench.

The message to stop the advance came too late for the 2nd Royal Dublin Fusiliers which had left its assembly trench at 09:00 hours. Before they reached the British front line they came under heavy fire from German machine-guns positioned at Beaumont Hamel. Five minutes later the order 'Stand Fast' was received followed by the message 'Your Battalion not to go beyond English front line trenches till further orders'.[17] Runners were immediately dispatched to stop the attack, but it was too late. Most of the battalion were in No Man's Land being slaughtered. The battalion CO managed to stop the rear ranks of 'A' Company from entering No Man's Land when he relayed the message verbally to a Sergeant. Twenty-three officers and 480 men advanced towards the German lines, but within minutes fourteen officers and 311 men had become casualties.[18]

By 08:45 hours the 2nd Seaforth Highlanders, commanded by Lieutenant-Colonel J.O. Hopkinson, had not received any information from 11th Brigade or from their own 10th Brigade Headquarters. Telephone wires had been severed by enemy shellfire. 2nd Lieutenant Harrison led a patrol into No Man's Land and came under heavy fire. Harrison was fatally wounded, dying five days later at Doullens. Hopkinson sent two orderlies to 10th Brigade HQ for information, but they did not arrive before 09:00 hours and so he ordered the advance to begin as scheduled.

As soon as the 2nd Seaforth Highlanders accompanied by two companies of the 2nd Lancashire Fusiliers ascended their parapets they were met by machine-gun fire principally coming from the direction of Beaumont Hamel. A German machine-gun directly opposite them perched on Redan Ridge did proved particularly deadly, but a Lewis Gun from the rear knocked this out. As they crossed No Man's Land south of the Heidenkopf they were afforded some protection from hostile fire by a rise in the ground. These soldiers managed to join the men defending their position in the Heidenkopf. Some of these soldiers from the 10th Brigade managed to breakout from the Heidenkopf 500 yards eastwards towards Munich Trench which led towards the German garrison at Serre. They moved forward in defiance of the German guns. Captain John Laurie, adjutant 2nd Seaforth Highlanders recalled: 'As soon as we crossed over our front line we came under withering machine-gun fire and the advance became a rush forward – and finally came to a halt in the shell pitted ground between the 1st and 3rd German lines. The whole area was covered by the remnants of the 11th Bde. who had suffered terrible casualties (all four C.O.s and the Bde. commander were killed). Movement of any sort became impossible and we could not get further than the 3rd line of German trenches.'[19]

The 1st King's Own and 2nd Essex Regiment from 12th Brigade, followed the path of the 1st Rifle Brigade and 1/8th Royal Warwickshire. The 31st Division had failed to capture and secure Serre, which meant that German machine-gunners in that village were able to pour fire in the division's direction as it crossed No Man's Land. The men were also being targeted by German artillery and as they advanced on 4th Division's left flank they sustained heavy casualties.

Two small mines were detonated as the 1st King's Own approached the Heidenkopf, causing more casualties. These might have been some of those laid by German engineers that failed to explode earlier that morning. Despite its losses the 1st King's Own got into the Heidenkopf along with the 2nd Essex. Both Major J.N. Bromilow commanding the 1st King's Own was fatally wounded while Lieutenant-Colonel Sir George Stirling, commanding the 2nd Essex was also wounded.

Undeterred, both battalions continued towards Munich Trench and fought their way northwards in the direction of Serre. Remarkably they got as far as the western edge of Pendant Copse, but persistent and determined German attacks from Serre prevented them from consolidating their gains. Private J. Stanley, 1st King's Own recalled:

> When we got to the second line the scrapping began in real earnest and when we had finished there the corporal and officer and myself were the only ones left of the section – one dead and three wounded we left in the trench. We then attached ourselves to another section and went forward to the next line, and with us were a bombing section from the Duke's, who are in our Division, and when we got there, there was what the Yanks call 'some' fighting, for when we had finished we had to wait for reinforcements, which arrived in about half an hour.[20]

When their bomb supplies were exhausted they had to rely upon rifles to continue the fight. Eventually they were forced to withdraw back to the

Heidenkopf. By mid-morning fragmented parties from the 4th Division holding this redoubt doubted that they could hold on to their position. The War Diary of the 2nd Essex recorded:

> At about 9.30 am the 10th Brigade were holding a line about 50 yards short of the German 2nd line and some parties had forced their way through and got so far as Pendant Copse. The main line tried to consolidate themselves in the line of craters but this work was practically impossible owing to the intense machine-gun fire brought to bear on them from the direction of Serre on the left flank and Beaumont Hamel on the right.[21]

A desperate message from 2nd Essex in the German lines was sent to Major-General William Lambton at 4th Division Headquarters during that morning 'For goodness sake send reinforcements'.[22] Lambton did not receive this message until 13:00 hours.

Continued efforts were made by the RFC to track the progress of the 4th Division. Flying fifty feet above the German front line trenches they were unable to see what was occurring below due to the smoke. The 4th Division had broken through at the Heidenkopf and Redan Ridge, but the failure of 31st Division to capture Serre in the north and 29th Division to secure Beaumont Hamel meant that German forces from these villages were able to descend upon the parties from the 4th Division occupying sections of their trenches in and around the Heidenkopf.

By 11:00 hours the 1st Rifle Brigade was holding a line of the trench 92 – 56 within the Heidenkopf together with remnants from the Seaforth Highlanders, Royal Warwickshire and 1st Somerset Light Infantry. This trench was getting full of wounded and stragglers belonging to 10th and 12th Brigades. 2nd Lieutenant W.C. Glover, 1st Rifle Brigade, tried to extend the line of 11th Brigade to the right, while Captain Martin from 1/8th Royal Warwickshire made efforts to extend the line of the 10th and 12th Brigades to the left, but they were unable to because the trench was too blocked due to the large numbers sheltering within it. Also they were coming under attack from another German bombing party on their right flank.

The situation was becoming desperate as their Lewis Guns had become inoperable and supplies of bombs and ammunition were depleting fast. The small amounts of supplies that remained in the left sector of the trench were passed down so that 2nd Lieutenant Glover and his party from 1st Rifle Brigade could hold their section of the line against attacks on the right flank. Lieutenant Glover recalled:

> About 11.00 am to 12 noon, we were short of bombs, and the Lewis Guns were more or less out of action. All the bombs we had and could spare from the left were passed up and with the help of a Corpl. I

> managed to get together about four throwers who absolutely kept the trench for us for hours. They were a magnificent lot, splendid fellows, they deserve any praise or reward. There was another even finer, the runner of the Colonel of the 8th Warwicks, I believe … This runner made the trip between that trench and our own at least 20 times, bringing bombs and l.G. ammunition. He did more than any single individual to keep things going.[23]

At that same time the last two remaining companies from 2nd Duke of Wellington's and 2nd Lancashire Fusiliers were ordered to cross No Man's Land and they were able to reinforce the men in the Heidenkopf. As the morning progressed those soldiers from the 4th Division were sustaining further casualties and their supplies of bombs and ammunition were fast becoming exhausted as repeated German counter-attacks were delivered against their position. Drummer Walter Ritchie from Seaforth Highlanders stood upon the German parapet and sounded the advance on his bugle to encourage stragglers who were making their way back towards the British line to come forward and support them. His courageous act resulted in the award of the Victoria Cross.

Captain C.W. Martin continued to hold onto his sector of German trench until the early afternoon, as he explained:

> At 1.00 pm as our supply of bombs was exhausted and the material under my command was much too valuable to lose in an obstinate effort to remain where we were without much hope of accomplishing anything useful. I decided to get back and try to hold a more rearward trench from which I could communicate and obtain supplies. The retirement was carried out in good order and the two enemy machine-guns that were trained on our position refrained from firing, possibly in the fear that we might get annoyed and return, so the casualties were practically nil.[24]

Martin's party withdrew to the German second line where they joined Lieutenant-Colonel Hopkinson and his party from the Seaforth Highlanders.

Meanwhile, back in the British lines, at 13:00 hours the 1st Royal Warwickshire, together with a company from 1st Royal Irish Fusiliers were ordered to lead a fresh assault upon the German lines, but the enemy fire was so strong they could not proceed across No Man's Land. At 13:05 hours Lieutenant-Colonel G.M.B. Forster commanding the 1st Royal Warwickshire received the order to send a patrol across No Man's Land to make another attempt to reach the German front line. Forty minutes later Forster received an order to stop any attempt at entering the German lines. This was bad timing because Forster had already ordered a party forward from 'A' Company led by Lieutenant Reginald Waters and this had already set off. The enemy machine-gun fire coming from the direction of Beaumont Hamel was overwhelming and they were unable to make any progress towards the German lines. Waters and the remnants of his patrol were back in the British trenches by 14:15 hours.

Likewise, Major-General Lambton recognised that it was impossible to make a breakthrough at Redan Ridge and at 14.55 hours he reported to Hunter-Weston at VIII Corps Headquarters that he had lost so many men, particularly officers, that he was unable to launch further assaults. The 11th Brigade had lost its commanding officer, Brigadier-General Charles Prowse, together with several of its battalion commanders. Lambton ordered that the remnants of 11th Brigade to be regrouped and reformed as a divisional reserve with 10th and 12th Brigades defending the line.

Lieutenant-Colonel J.O. Hopkinson commanding the Seaforth Highlanders continued to hold onto the Heidenkopf during that afternoon, with remnants from 11th Brigade. Regimental Sergeant Major E. Paul MC led a carrying party across No Man's Land to bring badly needed supplies of grenades to the men of the Somerset Light Infantry who were holding on to their precarious position. He found that Captain A.J. Harington MC and Lieutenant G. Greatham were the only officers from the battalion left to lead the defence of their section of the Heidenkopf. When these two officers were wounded at 13:30 hours, it was left to Company Sergeant Major Chappell to take control of the remnants of the battalion. Supplies of grenades were becoming exhausted once again and Sergeant Imber and Private Hodges made valiant efforts while exposed to enemy fire to signal from the German position for further more grenades to be brought forward.

Around 14:00 hours Lieutenant Glover received a written message from Lieutenant-Colonel Hopkinson to hold his position and that he was shortly going to send more ammunition to the 1st Rifle Brigade. The question was, could they last until then? Glover wrote:

> The throwers were dog tired and the Germans full of energy; by persuasion we managed to get a team of about half a dozen who carried on manfully, also carriers and men to keep the fire step just there. Some others would have done so had they not been wounded. By way of precaution we built a barricade, leaving about 35 yards of straight trench with a L.G. on top of a traverse commanding it, but held on in our original position till we were suddenly rushed and retired behind the barricade about 4.30 pm.[25]

By 15:00 hours the remnants of the 1st Rifle Brigade, the Seaforth Highlanders, and the Somerset Light Infantry decided that their position had become untenable and they retired to the first German trench line. A message was received at 15:35 hours from Major Townsend, who reported that he and a small party of men from 1/8th Royal Warwickshire were still holding out in the German third line, but soon they too had to withdraw to the first German trench line.

What was left of the 4th Division was cut off from the British lines, and unable to replenish their ammunition. But, despite being isolated, they defended this position throughout the day. At 16:00 hours men from 2nd Essex Regiment holding a position close to Pendant Copse were overwhelmed by German bombers and they were forced to retire to the German front-line trench.

Lieutenant Glover's party of the 1st Rifle Brigade held off German attacks from behind the barricade, but at 16:30 hours they were compelled to retreat, and they gradually withdrew to the first trench of the Heidenkopf where they established contact with Lieutenant-Colonel Hopkinson of the Seaforth Highlanders who was in overall command of the British units in the Heidenkopf. As the survivors from the 4th Division were preparing to withdraw from the German lines at 19:00 hours, they received reinforcements in the form of 'D' company from the 1st Royal Irish Fusiliers led by Captain Barefoot.

The battle for the Heidenkopf continued with the remnants from the 2nd Essex, the Seaforth Highlanders and 1st Royal Warwickshire fighting off repeated German efforts to recapture the position. They were precariously placed as they repelled German counter-attacks. Occasionally, they also came under fire from British guns. 2nd Essex War Diary noted:

> The fighting in the Quadrilateral was entirely by bombing and our men were hampered by an inadequate supply of bombs although they used the bombs found in the German trenches. At one time our heavy artillery also began to shell the Quadrilateral, but was stopped before doing any harm by means of an electric lamp found by a signaller. Communications was also kept with our front line by means of visual signalling and in this way bombs were asked for but the difficulty of getting them across 'No Man's Land' though the fire was very great.[26]

The Seaforth Highlanders continued to hold onto a section of German trench in the Heidenkopf during the evening. Captain John Laurie recalled:

> The C.O. and Adjutant (myself) and two other wounded Officers and about eighty men were all that could be collected by the end of the day and we were the only unit in 8th Corps still in the German lines by night fall. The Germans on our flanks in the same trench began to try to bomb us out but were rejected by their own medicine I, having collected a sandbag full of Mills bombs for some such eventuality.[27]

Captain A.G. de-la-Mare and 2nd Lieutenant L.J. Ward held on to a section of the Heidenkopf until 03:00 hours on 2 July with a small party belonging to 2nd Essex along with a mixed band of men from the Seaforths and Royal Warwickshire.

At 21:00 hours Hopkinson received two untimed messages giving contradictory orders from 10th Brigade HQ brought by Drummer Ritchie. The battalion War Diary recorded: 'The first contained orders to hold at all costs and the other had contained orders to return to our own lines. These messages were not timed, but both were brought by the same orderly.'[28] Captain John Laurie recalled the confused communications:

> Drummer Ritchie came through with two messages from Bde. HQ – one written by the Brigadier, one by the Brigade Major – neither timed or numbered as it was impossible to know in which order they had been written. One told us to return to our own lines, the other to hold on until we were relieved by a Company of the 87th R.I.F. at about 2.00 am, on 2 July.[29]

Despite these reinforcements Hopkinson could not hold on for much longer, he therefore decided to withdraw. German attacks upon the British battalions in the Heidenkopf and surrounding trenches subsided later that night enabling Hopkinson to withdraw during the early hours of 2 July.

Only the small party from 1st Royal Irish Fusiliers led by Captain Barefoot did not receive the order to retire and it defended its section in the German front line trench throughout that night and during the following morning. It eventually received the order to withdraw at 11:30 hours and they successfully retired to the British line, evacuating all their wounded together with three German prisoners. Captain Martin wrote:

> Just prior to relief my party consisted of 1 Corporal and 23 men of the 6th R. War. And 16 men of the 1/8th. Early that same morning the two Battns. had been of a strength approximately 50 officer and 1700 NCO's and men.[30]

The 4th Division committed 5,752 officers and men into securing Redan Ridge. They lost 1,883 killed, 3,563 wounded, 218 missing and eighty-eight prisoners.

The 11th Brigade suffered heavily, losing 145 officers and 3,034 men, including Brigadier-General C.B. Prowse. This brigade lost six battalion commanders with lieutenant colonels Hon. L.C.W. Palk (1st Hampshire), J.A. Thicknesse (1st Somerset Light Infantry), D. Wood (1st Rifle Brigade) and E.A. Innes (1/8th Royal Warwickshire killed, whilst Lieutenant J.E. Green (1st East Lancashire) and H. Frankin (1/6th Royal Warwickshire) were wounded. The 1st Somerset Light Infantry lost twenty-six officers and 438 men.[31]

With most of their officers either killed or wounded, there was no one left to write the 1st Rifle Brigade War Diary.

The 10th Brigade suffered casualties amounting to fifty-five officers and 908 men.[32] The 2nd Royal Dublin Fusiliers lost 325 men.

12th Brigade lost sixty-five officers and 1,479 men. Twenty-four officers and 606 men from the 2nd Essex entered the battle. By the evening their numbers had been reduced to two officers and 192 men. Approximately 150 German soldiers were found dead amongst the damaged trenches of the Heidenkopf.

Those survivors who had held onto the Heidenkopf for most of the day, losing many comrades in the process, felt despondent at having to withdraw and questioned why they were unable to consolidate the position. Lieutenant Glover had strong views on why he believed the attack on the Heidenkopf had failed:

> The whole day was hopeless, both flanks in the air, continuous bombardment from the Germans, and our guns doing nothing. When we saw aeroplanes we burnt flares but it made no difference. The German counter-attacking party sent up Very lights at short intervals and their artillery changed to a nicety. Why couldn't ours have held our right flank and put a barrage beyond? We should have held out then. Why didn't they go for the German guns? They were silent all day instead I think the Germans managed their M.G. fire by putting up mounds of earth between the third and fourth trenches so as to shoot over their own parapets and sweep the whole surface of the ground. They did it wonderfully but it was the cruellest slaughter.[33]

It was a remarkable feat for 4th Division to enter the Heidenkopf and penetrate further eastwards into Pendant Copse and hold these positions throughout the whole day. As well as a lack of support from the artillery, and an inability to reinforce or resupply the forward units, it was the failure of the 31st Division to capture Serre to the north and 29th Division to secure Beaumont Hamel to the south that exposed both of the 4th Division's flanks which, ultimately, rendered its position untenable.

Chapter 11

Beaumont Hamel

Major-General Sir Henry de Beauvoir De Lisle's 29th Division, of VIII Corps was ordered to capture Beaumont Hamel, Hawthorn Ridge and its surrounding trenches. This sector was strongly held by the 119th RIR of the 52nd Reserve Brigade, which defended the line from Beaumont Hamel south towards the River Ancre. The soldiers of this regiment spent June 1916 strengthening their defences. Beaumont Hamel comprised of 162 houses and there existed a labyrinth of caves beneath the village which were utilised as underground shelters, storage spaces for ammunition and field kitchens. The village was positioned between the front German line to the west and the second line, Munich Trench, to the east. German commanders had incorporated the contours of the slopes and ridges within their defences. There was a redoubt known as the Bergwerk north of the village.

The 121st RIR held the line north of Beaumont Hamel and Hawthorn Redoubt positioned west of village. Y-Ravine to the south of Beaumont Hamel was also a potential problem. This stronghold was so called because of its Y shape which punctured the southern slope of Hawthorn Ridge. Known to its German occupiers as Leiling Schlucht, the ravine pierced towards the British line from the southern extremity of Hawthorn Ridge. Tunnels were dug into the ravine to gain access to the front line trenches, which meant that German troops could reach these trenches without being seen from the British lines.

The 86th Brigade, commanded by Brigadier-General W. de L. Williams was ordered to initiate a direct assault upon the village of Beaumont Hamel. Of the other two brigades of the 29th Division, the 87th Brigade was to assault on the left flank, and the 88th Brigade the right flank.

The 29th Division had been holding the sector opposite Beaumont Hamel for many months and had exploited the cover provided by a ridge north of the Auchonvillers–Beaumont Hamel Road to established dugouts, battalion HQs and aid stations on its reverse western slope which could not be seen by German observers. This ridge was called White City, due to the chalky terrain.

A major threat to the advance of the 29th Division was Hawthorn Redoubt. It held commanding views over the line held by men of the 86th Brigade. This strongpoint had the potential to stop their assault upon the village with machine-gun fire. To neutralise this danger a mine was laid beneath the redoubt consisting of 40,000 pounds of ammonal. The arduous task of digging this mine was undertaken by the 252nd Tunnelling Company, Royal Engineers, commanded by Major Rex Trower. It had taken them two months to dig a tunnel 1,000 feet long to reach under the Redoubt. Pioneers from 119th RIR were also aware that mining activity were being undertaken by British tunnellers but were unable to detect where the mine was being dug.

Lieutenant-General Sir Aylmer Hunter-Weston, commanding VIII Corps, requested permission to detonate this mine at 03:00 hours on the day of the assault. He wanted to destroy the redoubt then capture and consolidate the crater before the main attack. Rawlinson consulted with Major-General R. Harvey, the Inspector of Mines, who was conscious that during the first two years of the war the British Army had not successfully captured a crater and that German forces were quicker at seizing such opportunities.

Harvey therefore decided that Zero Hour was the appropriate time to detonate this mine. Haig and Rawlinson settled upon a compromise with Hunter-Weston allowing him to detonate the mine at 07:20 hours. They thought that if this mine was detonated ten minutes before the assault it might divert the enemy's attention from the attack upon German positions south of the Ancre Valley. No one had ever exploded a mine of such magnitude and there were concerns amongst staff officers at VIII Corps HQ that troops waiting in assembly trenches would become casualties due to falling debris; exploding of the mine ten minutes before Zero Hour would prevent this from happening. Major Rex Trowers recalled:

> VIII Corps were of the opinion that the falling debris would kill a great many of our own men, and not having fired any mine as big, I was not willing to swear that some of our men might not be hit by falling stuff. That is, I think, the point that VIII Corps insist on 0-10 as the hour. The mine being fired by battery as well as fuse, no defects had there been any, could possibly have been remedied and most certainly I needed no ten minutes grace.[1]

The 86th Brigade comprised the 1st Lancashire Fusiliers, 16th Middlesex (Public Schools Battalion), 2nd Royal Fusiliers and 1st Royal Dublin Fusiliers. They were to launch a direct assault upon the village of Beaumont Hamel, with the 1st Lancashire Fusiliers on north of the Auchonvillers–Beaumont Hamel Road and the 2nd Royal Fusiliers south of the road. 16th Middlesex and 1st Royal Dublin Fusiliers supported these two battalions. The 86th Brigade reached its allotted positions by midnight on 30 June.

Two tunnels were excavated beneath No Man's Land to within thirty yards of the first German trench line, which were used as Stokes mortar emplacements. These tunnels were opened at 02:00 hours on the morning of 1 July.

Another tunnel was dug from the British line occupied by 1st Lancashire Fusiliers to a Sunken Lane which was positioned north of the Auchonvillers–Beaumont Road, half way across No Man's Land. Failed attempts had been made in both British and German raids to secure this tactically important position. British commanders realised the potential of using the Sunken Lane as a safe starting position for the initial waves for the assault upon Beaumont Hamel. It would also provide some cover for when Hawthorn mine was exploded. The Royal Engineers had therefore dug a tunnel from Sap 7 close to the British front line towards the Sunken Lane. Captain E.W. Sheppard, who was Battalion Intelligence Officer for 1st Lancashire Fusiliers recorded:

> The road from Auchonvillers to Beaumont Hamel ran up a shallow trough, from which the ground rose on the south to Hawthorn Ridge (on the crest of which the big mine was blown) and on the north to another more distant crest on which was situated the Redoubt. Half way across No Man's Land (here about 400 yards wide) a sunken lane ran due north from this road, gradually flattening out to ground level on the northern ridge. Half way again between this and the German line lay a small bank or linchet giving some shelter from enemy fire. Apart from these features No Man's Land was open and bare of cover. Control of No Man's Land rested and had rested for sometime with us and in the few days before the attack the RE had pierced a tunnel a few feet below the ground from our front line to the sunken lane, opening up the exit on the last night.
>
> Unfortunately this exit came out a few yards too far north, at a point where it was exposed to enemy fire in part, and that one had to use it on hands and knees. Its purpose was to serve as a sort of covered communication trench for the sunken lane … Through this tunnel our two front companies, B and D, were passed to the lane, which was to be the jumping off line for the first wave.[2]

At 03:00 hours on 1 July 'B' and 'D' Companies from the 1st Lancashire Fusiliers, together with a special bombing company amounting to 100 men with four stokes mortars used this tunnel to reach the Sunken Lane. Despite the exit of the tunnel being exposed to the German lines during daylight hours, they could use this access into the Sunken Lane where they could assemble without being seen by the enemy. At 07:00 hours Lieutenant-Colonel Meredith Magniac commanding 1st Lancashire Fusiliers, moved Battalion Headquarters from White City in the British line to the Sunken

Lane, half way across No Man's Land. German forces had no knowledge that the 1st Lancashire Fusiliers was so close to their lines until around 07:00 hours their presence was discovered when German observers spotted some men at the southern end of the Sunken Lane close to the Auchonvillers–Beaumont Hamel Road. As a consequence German 77mm guns began to shell the Sunken Lane causing approximately twenty casualties. Despite this setback Captain Sheppard recorded that 'the morale of all was astonishingly high and confidence universal'.[3]

The officers belonging to 86th Brigade wore khaki like their men to prevent them from being targeted by German snipers and machine-gunners, though when the attack was launched the officers led from the front, with correspondingly high casualties.[4]

The British artillery was ordered to revert to bombarding the second and third German lines ten minutes before Zero Hour to allow for the detonation of the mine beneath Hawthorn Redoubt. As the barrage lifted, it is thought that this policy enabled German soldiers sheltering within the deep dugouts at Beaumont Hamel to reach the surface and prepare themselves for the British assault. These soldiers were on a high state of alert as they waited in their deep dugouts. Despite depriving the soldiers of the 119th RIR of sleep, food, water and straining their nerves, the intensive bombardment heightened their preparation for an oncoming attack. The German unit history for 119th RIR reported:

> Our regimental positions were ready to be stormed, but everyone was in cheerful spirits even if the preliminary bombardment, which had lasted 7 days, had left its mark on the nerves of the men. Many weeks of hard labour strengthening and reinforcing our positions had paid off. 7 days of constant shelling had cost the regiment only 20 dead and 83 wounded. A couple of days' earlier 10th company had taken a prisoner who had told us about an impending attack that was going to start on the 1st of July.[5]

As well as the captured British prisoner, intelligence received from an intercepted partial message from the British confirming that an attack was imminent at Moritz Station 28 at La Boisselle had reached most of the German line on the Somme, so the soldiers belonging to 119th RIR at Beaumont Hamel carried extra ammunition and had their rifles and machine-guns to hand, ready to ascend from their dugouts and confront the attack immediately.

When the mine was exploded at 07:20 hours, it propelled tons of earth, debris and human remains into the sky. Once this debris fell to the ground, smoke lingered ominously in the air. It must have been a terrifying ordeal for the soldiers of the 1st Lancashire Fusiliers who were sheltering in the Sunken Lane for they were close to the explosion and felt the ground shake.[6] No. 9 Company, 119th RIR bore the brunt of this almighty explosion, as its regimental account reported:

> During the intense bombardment there was a terrific explosion which for the moment completely drowned the thunder of the artillery. A great cloud of smoke rose up from the trenches of No. 9 Company, followed by a tremendous shower of stones, which seemed to fall from the sky over all our position. More than three sections of No. 9 Company were blown into the air, and the numbering dugouts were broken in and blocked. The ground all round was white with the debris of chalk as if it had been snowing, and a gigantic crater, over fifty yards in diameter and some sixty feet deep gaped like an open wound in the side of the hill.[7]

A significant proportion of No. 9 Company, 119th RIR had been wiped out by the explosion beneath Hawthorn Ridge. Most of 1st Platoon, commanded by Leutnant Renz, and some of 2nd Platoon led by Leutnant Böhm, were destroyed by the explosion. The remainder of Böhm's Platoon and Leutnant Breitmeyer's 3rd Platoon were trapped within their dugouts from falling rocks which blocked the entrances. Some men were killed outright by explosion their bodies blown to unidentifiable pieces. Others were crushed to death as tunnels collapsed upon them. Those that were trapped within their dugouts slowly suffocated to death as their oxygen supply ran out.

The explosion signalled that the British were about to attack so survivors that were able to leave their dugouts established a firing position. Sections from the left and right flank of the crater ascended from their dugouts and got their machine-guns into position. Some soldiers trapped in their dugouts were able to extricate themselves by digging themselves out. The result was that around two sections were in a position to defend the crater before British troops arrived.[8]

As soon as Hawthorn Mine exploded the Stokes mortars positioned in the Sunken Lane in No Man's Land fired into the German first line and provided some cover for the infantry dashing across No Man's Land, but this was limited, as only twenty rounds per mortar were available with no further replenishment due to the ammunition carriers being killed in attempting to reach their position.

The battalions from 86th Brigade left there trenches and began to assemble in No Man's Land under the cover of the mortar fire. Two platoons from 'D' Company, 2nd Royal Fusiliers, armed with four Lewis Guns and four Stokes Mortars rushed forward to occupy the crater and the German first line on the right flank, while 1st Lancashire Fusiliers advanced on their left towards the village. The Fusiliers suffered casualties as they dashed towards the western lip of the crater as they were fired upon by machine-gunners from the left and right flanks.

Approximately 120 men, of the 2nd Royal Fusiliers avoided the guns of the 119th RIR and reached the crater where they briefly held their ground. They had reached a sector in the German line which had been occupied by 9th Company, 119th RIR, but the Germans had been obliterated by the explosion. Some parties from the 2nd Royal Fusiliers got into the German trench on the left sector of the crater which was meant to be defended by 3rd Platoon of the 9th Company 119th RIR. Here they reached the entrance of a partially blocked dugout where Leutnant Breitmeyer and company commander, Reserve Oberleutnant Mühlbayer were making frantic efforts to escape. Three of the four entrances had been blocked by tons of falling debris. There was a small hole in the fourth entrance which a sentry was trying to enlarge so that he, Breitmeyer and Mühlbayer could escape into the trench. The sentry was bayoneted by a soldier from the 2nd Royal Fusiliers and fell dead down the stairs of the dugout. Another German soldier named Vizefeldwebel Davidsohn standing next to the sentry fired a flare through the hole and in the face of the British soldier holding the bayonet. This action brought swift retribution as they threw Mills bombs through the same hole forcing Oberleutnant Mühlbayer and his party to withdraw deeper into the dugout to escape the oncoming blast. Vizefeldwebel Davidsohn recalled:

> The English had managed to break into our trench. We had only just opened the exit of the dugout when they were upon us. A bayonet thrust killed the man who was holding the shovel, his body fell down the stairs of the dugout tearing the men that were just in the process of getting out down again. I had no rifle with me but managed to fire a signal flare into the face of one of the attackers. The English answered by throwing some hand grenades which forced us to withdraw.[9]

The 2nd Royal Fusiliers called for their surrender but they stayed where they were in the hope that German reinforcements above ground would clear the British from their trenches. Moments later, help did arrive when Unteroffizer Aicheler, of the 2nd machine-gun Company launched an attack with two light machine-guns upon the party of the 2nd Royal Fusiliers, who responded with hand grenades. Aicheler's machine-guns held their ground and repelled the assault, for which he was awarded the Iron Cross Second Class.

Within five minutes of the explosion of the mine at Hawthorn Redoubt German batteries, which had seen red flares fired into the sky requesting artillery support, unleashed a hurricane bombardment of the British lines and No Man's Land as British infantry waves advanced slowly towards them. Because the British artillery had lifted to concentrate on the German second and third lines, the machine-gunners in the first line were able to occupy the eastern lip of the crater, sweeping No Man's Land with their deadly fire, whilst German rifleman were brazenly standing on their parapets firing towards the British waves. The regimental history of the 119th RIR reported:

> This explosion was a signal for the infantry attack, and everyone got ready and stood on the lower steps of the dugouts rifle in hand, waiting for the bombardment to lift. In a few minutes the shelling ceased, and we rushed up the steps and out into the Crater positions. Ahead of us wave after wave of British troops were crawling out of their trenches, and coming forward towards us at a walk, their bayonets glistening in the sun.[10]

The 2nd Royal Fusiliers advancing directly upon Beaumont Hamel sustained heavy casualties and only a few men reached the undamaged wire. The battalion lost 490 men including twenty-seven officers. Deardon and Baldwin, both company commanders, were the only officers who came out of the ordeal unscathed.

The 1st Lancashire Fusiliers advanced on their left flank. 'B' and 'D' Companies advanced from the Sunken Lane while 'C' Company, forming the second wave, and 'A' Company the third wave, launched their assault further back, from British front line trenches west of the Sunken Lane and south of the Auchonvillers–Beaumont Hamel Road.

'B' and 'D' Companies were accompanied by a bombing party, a hundred strong, two Lewis machine-guns and four Stokes mortars. As soon as these companies debouched from the Sunken Lane and dashed forward into No Man's Land in extended order, German machine-guns and rifles opened fire. The Fusiliers had no chance of reaching the German trenches. Captain E.W. Sheppard recalled the appalling carnage that befell the Fusiliers as they left the Sunken Lane:

> A few minutes (not as much, I should have said, as five) after the mine went up we had seen the battalion on our right, the Royal Fusiliers, start off across No Man's Land, the first wave went forward. The east bank of the lane lay in a slight dip which concealed men getting out of it from the enemy view and fire, but two steps brought them into exposure and the bulk of the first wave got no further than the edge of this dip where they were swept over in swither, and those who were still alive crawled or were dragged down into the lane which was now full of wounded.[11]

The third and fourth waves were completely wiped out by the machine-gun fire as they left the Sunken Lane. Both company commanders Captain Nunneley and Captain Wells were among the wounded and managed to crawl back to the shelter of the Sunken Lane. Only a few men in the first and second waves from 'B' and 'D' companies got as far as a bank of earth which was close to the wire referred to by Sheppard as a lynchet. The German machine-gun fire was so intense they could not get beyond this position and they had to take cover by this dip in No Man's Land. Sheppard recalled:

> A party of about fifty men and two officers, got as far the lynchet, where they stayed till night to give them a chance to re-join the unit in safety: from where they could not even see the enemy front, and would have been quite unable to defend themselves against a counter-attack. No men worth mentioning ever reached the enemy wire as far as I know.[12]

Sheppard may have been referring to the depression that leads to the part in No Man's Land where Beaumont Hamel British Cemetery is now located. Germans placed a wire by this lynchet so that when the Lancashire Fusiliers dropped down the depression they were trapped by the bank of earth behind them and the wire in front, making them easy targets for German machine-gunners and snipers if they were standing up.

Some 150 yards west of the Sunken Lane, 'A' Company, 1st Lancashire Fusiliers, was preparing to leave the British front line. They had to first reach the Sunken Lane and then go on seventy-five yards to the German lines. With the Fusiliers was Corporal George Ashurst:

> Before the attack, you couldn't move in those trenches it was that packed with men. They were grumbling and grousing, some were trying to be brave and joking. There were all sorts. Then it goes quiet and then it is time to go over.[13]

German machine-guns opened fire as soon as 'A' and 'C' Companies left their trench. Captain Dawson and Company Sergeant Nelson were hit as they stood on the parapet ordering their men to advance. George Ashurst continued:

> When I stepped on top of our trench, over the top, it was badly blown down and there was a corporal lying there and all his shoulder was gone, blown away. Hit by a whizz bang. He looks up at me, and he said, 'Go on Corporal! Get the bastards'. I daren't stop, I just said 'OK' and buggered off as fast as I could and run.[14]

Despite the hostile fire Lieutenant Caseby and about sixty men reached the Sunken Lane. However, one platoon led by Lieutenant Jones got blocked in the communication trench by wounded comrades. Caseby later gathered seventy-five stragglers and moved forward towards the northern road leading into Beaumont Hamel. Corporal Ashurst, was among the few from 'A' Company that reached the Sunken Lane:

> There was gun smoke, you can hear when a bullet hits somebody against them and you would hear him groan and go down. machine-guns cut us up. There seemed to be bullets everywhere I was zig zagging I seemed to be dodging in between them, holding my head down so a bullet would hit my tin hat, I kept going, I kept running about 150 yards, that was the only way to get there. I dove into the sunken road when I got there.[15]

Captain E.W. Sheppard, who could see from the southern edge of the Sunken Lane, concurred: 'None of the second wave got even as far as the lane, and when Colonel Magniac, the CO, sent me out to bring forward any I could find, I saw no one moving at all, and was hit in the head whilst still searching round.'[16]

Sergeant Caulfield, a battalion machine-gunner, identified a German machine-gun position in the ruins of Beaumont Hamel. Pointing this position out to Lieutenant-Colonel Magniac, CO 1st Lancashire Fusiliers, two Lewis Guns were detailed to aim at this from the northern section of the Sunken Lane. German artillery observers saw these two machine-guns and very quickly delivered a barrage of German 77mm shells on this section of the Sunken Lane and knocked out one of the Lewis Guns. This German machine-gun continued to operate unabated.

The Sunken Lane was a scene of chaos and devastation as the survivors from 'A' and 'C' Companies sought cover. Here they joined the wounded from 'B' and 'D' Companies. The momentum of the assault had clearly been lost, as the battalion War Diary revealed:

> The bank into the sunken road is a steep drop of about 15 feet, and men encumbered with coils of wire, mauls etc. rolled down this to the bottom. There now ensued some delay whilst C Coy & remainder of A Coy who had entered down the steep bank were collected and sorted from the 100 wounded who had now collected in the sunken road, preparatory to further advance.[17]

Incorrect reports of success on the 87th Brigade's sector at Y-Ravine were received, which were believed, embellished and overstated by staff at 29th Division Headquarters. Captain Ian Grant, Brigade Major, 86th Brigade recalled:

> I cannot understand how the success of the 87th Brigade elements got on was so exaggerated at divisional headquarters, immediately before I went forward I spoke on phone to the B.M.87 Brigade (Capt. J.C. Brand), and my recollection is that he definitely stated 'their attack had broken down and our right supporting battalion didn't appear to have left their trenches'.[18]

The 1st Royal Dublin Fusiliers and 16th Middlesex Regiment were meant to follow the 1st Lancashire Fusiliers and 2nd Royal Fusiliers but were delayed as they tried to reach the front line via the network of communication trenches which became heavily congested by stretcher bearers carrying wounded and the walking wounded filtering back in the opposite direction. Dead and wounded who could not walk also blocked their passage through to the British front trench. Captain Ian Grant had to get above the parapet in order to rally the 1st Royal Dublin Fusiliers to go forward. As he did so he was shot by enemy machine-gun fire:

> We had an advance headquarters about the support line, and I went up to No Man's Land over the open, and was endeavouring with two brigade headquarter orderlies to get the 1st Dublin Fusiliers going until I was filled up with m.g. bullets, the Staff Captain, Capt. Gee VC.MC was shot too somewhere on my right (i.e. south) I think, rallying another company, so I came personally under this fire, there was however intense M.G. fire mainly from Beaumont Ridge.[19]

The 1st Royal Dublin Fusiliers eventually reached the British front line and its commander Lieutenant-Colonel H. Nelson DSO was faced with a desperate situation, finding that most of the battalion that he was to have supported was still in the front line and the wire in No Man's Land remained intact. Nelson recalled:

> Eventually most of the battalion did manage to reach the front trench to find that parties of the R.Fusiliers were still in it. Utter chaos prevailed. Looking over the parapet one could see the wire entanglement uncut, and the various passages through it choked with the bodies of the dead and wounded.[20]

Just before 08:00 hours the 1st Royal Dublin Fusiliers and 16th Middlesex Regiment were then sent forward to force a breakthrough into the German lines at Beaumont Hamel. It is worth mentioning that the 16th Middlesex Regiment was comprised of men drawn from Public Schools and was largely officer material. Many men did leave the battalion to take up commissions, but some men who would have made potentially good officers decided to remain in the ranks and would distinguish themselves at Beaumont Hamel.

Both the 1st Royal Dublin Fusiliers and 16th Middlesex Regiment found the British wire was cut at forty-yard intervals. As soldiers massed around these few gaps in the wire German machine-guns from the Bergwerk positioned on Beaucourt Ridge, east of Beaumont Hamel, trained on these positions and caused heavy casualties.

The 1st Royal Dublin Fusiliers were meant to have gone through the 2nd Royal Fusiliers lines to capture the German front line, then to assemble in Y-Ravine before moving on to their second objective. Nelson lost approximately 300 men during the opening phase of the assault and could not achieve their objectives. Not many men from these battalions got beyond the British wire. Those few that did get through managed to advance between 50 and 60 yards before being shot. Lieutenant-Colonel Nelson peered into No Man's Land and could see that the 1st Royal Dublin Fusiliers were either on the ground dead or wounded and could see that advances on both flanks had faltered:

> I climbed up and looked over the edge. The German wire was close to the front, but I saw no sign of life on our side of it, and very few bodies near it to the right, which were the area allotted to the 87th Brigade, or to the left where the Royal Fusiliers were supposed to be. It was obvious that the attack had failed and of no use going further.
>
> Reports that reached me made it clear that progress forward was impossible. The confusion in the front line trench was terrible, and control was out of the question. Stretcher cases and the slightly wounded of both battalions made communication by trench almost impossible, and very few reports reached me as to the progress of my left leading company.[21]

No one from the 16th Middlesex got into the German trenches. A party of twenty men of 'D' Company did reach the western perimeter of the crater led by Captain Frederick Sidney Cockram, adjutant, who had been wounded three times. Each time he got back on his feet to continue the fight, however on the fourth time he was unable to go any further. He had sustained eight bullet wounds during that morning and was recommended for the Victoria Cross, but instead received the DSO. Cockram was captured and spent the rest of the war in a German PoW camp.

Despite the German machine-gun fire, 200 men of the 86th Brigade held pockets close to Hawthorn Crater but the remaining elements of the brigade were unable to capture the German first line. Lieutenant-Colonel J. Hamilton Hall, 16th Middlesex Regiment, recalled:

> I arrived at the near lip of the Crater about 8.00 am and found about 200 dotted about in small parties of two's and three's, the greater proportion being on the right half of the Crater. These 200 appeared to consist of about 30 to 40 of the Royal Fusiliers, two sections of the Bde. machine-gun Coy, and 3 Stokes mortar guns, the balance about 120 from my battalion, there were 7 Lewis Guns also. Our machine-guns were firing, and most of our Lewis Guns; the Stokes mortar guns soon ran out of ammunition after my arrival. About half the men were firing and some were endeavouring to creep round both lips of Crater. On the further lip of the Crater I believe there were either 2 or 3 enemy machine-guns, which were

> firing over the lip of the Crater …fire from these guns was sweeping the top edge of the Crater in the centre and on both flanks. From the trench running N.E. from the crater there appeared to be a machine-gun firing W.N.W. from about point Y: this trench was according to accounts fairly well held by infantry; and reinforcements were seen pushing up in parties of 7 or 8 up a communication trench from the East. In the trench running S from the Crater there was another machine-gun sweeping N.W. from about a point Z. The enemy's shell fire (shrapnel and light percussion) which was directed on this part of the attack all appeared to fall well clear of the near lip about 80 to 100 yards to the West; but the whole surface of the ground above the undulations caused by the mine was swept by machine-gun fire and especially so on both flanks of the Crater. This broken ground about 2 to 2 ½ foot high gave cover from view, but was by no means bullet proof for the top 12 inches and 18 inches. Luckily the enemy did not realise this.[22]

It was difficult for Hamilton Hall to organise the scattered men in the crater because it was impossible to get messages across to them. He could not call upon a British artillery barrage upon the troublesome German machine-gun positions for fear of firing upon these men. Hamilton Hall recalled:

> Movement was extremely difficult, and it took me sometime to ascertain the state of affairs at the Crater. Owing to the close proximity of the two forces it was apparent that our artillery could give us no assistance (i.e. directly in front). Carriers were sent back to bring up more ammunition for the Stokes guns, but they never returned.[23]

Hamilton Hall was powerless to consolidate the crater without getting further reinforcements and more ammunition. Realising that it was impossible to get men and munitions across No Man's Land he tried to get messages to his men to dig in and hold what little ground they occupied. If they could hold on until nightfall then maybe reinforcements could reach them under the cover of darkness and they could resume the attack later. Throughout the morning, the amalgamated ranks from the 2nd Royal Fusiliers and 16th Middlesex holding the crater continued to defend their precarious position against determined German counter-attacks.

Meanwhile, back in the Sunken Lane it took half an hour to reorganise the decimated ranks of the 1st Lancashire Fusiliers, with 2nd Lieutenant Caseby assembling seventy-five men for this renewed attack. At 08:15 hours the battalion's Stokes mortars launched a rapid burst of covering fire as Caseby led these men from the 1st Lancashire Fusiliers from the northern section of the Sunken Lane towards some high ground north of Beaumont Hamel. If they could reach this position they might be able to reach Hawthorn Crater from the north, but their valiant attempt was curtailed by machine-gun fire from Beaumont Hamel. Fifteen minutes later Captain R. Gee, Staff Captain, and later Captain Ian Grant, Brigade Major, with the 86th Brigade, were sent forward to organise another attempt to get reinforcements to the crater. There were thirty men who were unable to join the assault waves initially due to communication trenches being blocked by the wounded. These men were reorganised, but efforts to resume the assault ended when both officers were wounded. Twenty-five German soldiers led by one officer were seen trying to capture the lip of the crater. As soon as a machine-gun opened fire upon them, German artillery unleashed another covering barrage.

Lieutenant-Colonel Hamilton Hall, 16th Middlesex Regiment, could see the disaster that befell the Lancashire Fusiliers at the Sunken Lane from Hawthorn Crater:

> From my position at the lip of the Crater I saw at about 8.30 am what appeared to be about 200 in the sunken road NE of point W, with some 50 to 60 bodies on the rise just E of that road; about that time or slightly later I saw a party of about 20 to 30 make an advance from the sunken road, but they only were able to push forward about 30 to 40 yards. I searched the front lines of the enemy opposite to their position with my field glasses, but could find no further trace of any.[24]

Eventually at 10:00 hours the 2nd Royal Fusiliers and 16th Middlesex came under heavy trench mortar fire and lost control of their fragmented positions close to the crater, forcing them to withdraw. Hamilton Hall, 16th Middlesex, described the moment when German forces overwhelmed the scattered parties from his battalion and the 2nd Royal Fusiliers:

> About 10.00 am an explosion occurred about point V; this I personally put down at the time to a small trench mortar of the enemy: some who were near there state that it was due to the enemy's hand grenades thrown by men who had crept round near the south edge of the Crater: in my opinion the explosion was too loud for that: there were grenades being thrown on that flank. About six men got up and retired about 10 yards from the point V. Two to three minutes after that there was another similar explosion near point V, but a few yards further west; about a dozen men got up and began to withdraw in an orderly fashion evidently with the object of taking up a fresh position near at hand, but before they had got down again a third explosion took place still a few yards further west of the second explosion and about another 20 men got up and before one could realise it the whole of the right of the force got up and began to fall back.
>
> This example was contagious; the few officers remaining and one or two others endeavoured to stop this withdrawal, but without effect.[25]

The sight of the remnants from the 2nd Royal Fusiliers and 16th Middlesex withdrawing from Hawthorn Crater caused panic and concern amongst the men of the 1st Lancashire Fusiliers in the Sunken Lane. Some were fearful of a German counter-attack and those who were able to, made an effort to evacuate the Sunken Lane via the tunnel leading into Sap 7. Lieutenant-Colonel Meredith Magniac DSO had to restore order by threatening his soldiers with his revolver to prevent them from retreating through the tunnel, as Captain Sheppard testified:

> Sometime later, I should say about 10.30 am, the enemy apparently counter-attacked and drove out the Royal Fusilier elements still holding out in the Crater, and at the sight of these coming back there was an incipient panic among the wounded and unwounded but badly shaken men in the lane. A number of them tried to escape through the tunnel and swarmed round the entrance, but the CO drew his revolver and threatened to use it, and the officers and NCO's managed to restore order, and quieten the men, and organise the line of defence. The enemy counter-attack, a rumour of which had caused the alarm, apparently stopped after the recovery of the front line.[26]

Some soldiers went over the top twice that day. Corporal George Ashurst was one of them:

> Colonel Magniac said 'Every fit man – over the top again, come with me - over the top!' Right enough, I ran up the ground, whether a lot more did I don't know or whether they disobeyed him, but he went over. I ran on and there was nobody with me I am by myself, I got a bit frightened then. When I came across this shell hole I dropped in it and I could lie there in it and look back over our lines, I could see our frontline, I could see our wounded, they would get up and try to go on and then they'd drop, they'd been shot again. While I am lying there I had a drink from my water bottle. Looking back I noticed the Royal Fusiliers on the left were running back to their trenches. I didn't know what they were doing, but I thought, Jerry's counter-attacking, what about me, if he comes over the top here, I'm for it all right, there's nothing for me!. So I made my mind up that I'd got to move and move very quick. I got up and dashed down this slope again and dived into the Sunken Road once more. Safe again – they'd missed again![27]

Lieutenant-Colonel Hamilton Hall accepted that Hawthorn Crater could not be held, but his main concern was for the vulnerability of the British line. The 16th Middlesex held ten percent of their reserves in support lines and only a handful of military police occupied the front line, insufficient numbers to prevent a German counter-attack. If German infantry suddenly decided to attack, they would be able to enter the first British trench virtually unopposed. Defending the British line became the priority.

Hamilton Hall dashed to a position called Cripps Cut to detail the men of the reserve to occupy the British front trench and prepare for a German counter-attack. Major Utterson, second-in-command of 1st Lancashire Fusiliers made a similar decision and had brought forward his battalion reserve. Yet instead of defensive action they received orders from Brigade Headquarters to renew the attack at 12:30 hours! But there was simply not enough men for this, and Captain Sheppard commented that 'it was quite clear that the renewal of the attack, was, as far as we were concerned, an impossibility'.[28]

The 2nd Royal Fusiliers suffered a further setback when their CO, Lieutenant-Colonel Johnson, became the victim of friendly fire when he was wounded by a British high explosive shell in the British front line trench at 13:00 hours. The men were reported to have been 'severely shaken' by this incident. Johnson vowed to carry on, but was taken off the line. Major G.V. Goodliffe reported:

> Lieut.-Colonel A.V. Johnson, the C.O. was buried on the front line trench, which was blown in by one of our 6" batteries. I helped to dig him out, and found the fuze lying against his cheek. I later took it back to Gunner HQ who told me that it was fired by the South African 6" battery. Lieut.-Colonel Johnson insisted on remaining on, but owing to shock, was really quite incapable of commanding, and was evacuated that same night.[29]

Goodliffe, now in command of the 2nd Royal Fusiliers, also received orders to make another attack upon the German lines, but this was simply not possible, as he explained:

> During the day I was given an order, emanating from General Williams, for the attack to be resumed. But it was not possible to carry out the order. No one knew, who, owing to casualties, was actually commanding. Further the trenches were full of troops including the Dublin Fusiliers; they were blocked by dead and wounded and in many cases blown in by enemy artillery fire, so that communication of orders were practically impossible.[30]

By the time that Major Utterson, 1st Lancashire Fusiliers, had reached the Sunken Lane, Brigadier-General W. de L. Williams, commanding 86th Brigade, had realised the futility of ordering further assaults upon Beaumont Hamel. Williams reported:

> At 12.30 I realised that further attack could only mean needless loss of life. I had heard that the Brigade on my right had failed and I had seen

> the Brigade on my left could not advance. I instructed Lancs Fusiliers to hold the Sunken Road and with the remainder of the troops took up defence of our own line.[31]

By 13:00 hours Lieutenant-Colonel Meredith Magniac began the process of evacuating the wounded men of the 1st Lancashire Fusiliers from the Sunken Lane, via the tunnel to the British first line where they could be transferred to a casualty clearing station. Captain Sheppard, who had sustained a head wound, recalled:

> The wounded who could walk, of whom I was one, were ordered to make their way back through the tunnel ... The tunnel made by the RE was of great value; without it we certainly could not have held and probably should have not tried to hold the line as first line.[32]

Magniac was ordered to hold the Sunken Lane and detailed one officer, an NCO and twenty-five men to remain in this position. Corporal George Ashurst was the NCO in question. They made sure the southern and northern entrances to the Sunken Lane were blocked and guarded and a detachment was deployed to the centre to ensure that German units did not gain control of this tactically-important lane. Ashurst recalled:

> Later on in the day a message came across, 'one officer, one NCO and twenty five men only to man the Sunken Road.' That meant we'd got to stop there all night and all next day. There was only this officer knocking about. He said, 'That means me and that means you, Corporal!' We got twenty five men and we put about eight men at the bottom end of the road and about eight at the top of the road and about eight or nine in the middle of the road under the oldest soldier because there were no more NCOs. The thing quietened down, the quiet after the storm; we were practically sleeping all night, just lying there.[33]

A number of wounded men attempted to crawl back to the British lines throughout the day. There were reports of some suffering from severe shell shock, such to the extent that in one instance a soldier became confused and fired into the own friendly lines, as Major Goodliffe reported:

> Throughout the day wounded were returning from No Man's Land. Many crawled in; many badly wounded, others shell shocked. Two of the latter were quite mad (one had taken off all his clothing), and fired at their own trenches when anyone showed himself.[34]

A Red Cross flag was reported to have been placed by German soldiers at

Hawthorn Crater during that afternoon. Captain Eric Hall, 16th Middlesex, was among the wounded lying in No Man's Land:

> I was taken prisoner about 5.00 pm on the evening of July, 1916. I had been lying out all day since 7.45 am in the morning and unable to move as I was wounded in the knee. About 5 the Germans put up a white flag with a red cross on it and sent Three Red Cross men out to collect the wounded. These men were armed with revolvers. All this took place about 80 yards in front of the German first line trench at Beaumont Hamel. After being carried in by four of our men, I was taken on a stretcher by two German Red Cross men to a dressing station in the village where after an hour or two I was attended to by a doctor, who dressed my wound and gave me a glass of wine.[35]

Lieutenant-Colonel Hamilton Hall, commanding 16th Middlesex, saw a white flag of truce being flown from the German lines earlier that afternoon:

> About 2.30 pm the enemy raised a white flag on his front line, and sent over stretcher bearers to No Man's Land: in addition to helping our wounded, he no doubt was helping himself to the machine-guns, Lewis Guns, rifles etc. lying about close to his front line. (These in any case he would have had no difficulty in collecting at night). This was reported to the brigade by telephone, and permission requested to send out our stretcher bearers to bring in our wounded. Permission was refused (I believe from higher authority), and instead instructions were issued to fire on the enemy's stretcher bearers. These instructions were not acted on with any enthusiasm by our riflemen in the front line.[36]

This testimony shows that some soldiers were prepared to disobey orders in situations where their own natural humanity was compromised. To fire upon enemy stretcher bearers who were tending to their own comrades in the field was morally wrong and these men from the 16th Middlesex, knew that right thing to do was to allow them to continue with their work unmolested. Unfortunately, British artillery then shelled the front and support lines held by the 16th Middlesex in error and it took Hamilton Hall twenty minutes to get Brigade HQ to call off the barrage. Throughout the afternoon German riflemen shot at the British wounded lying in No Man's Land at Beaumont Hamel.[37]

Stretcher bearers made courageous efforts to remove the wounded from the Sunken Lane throughout the night, but the recovery operation was made difficult, due to the large number of casualties, and after dark German artillery focused its fire on the junction of the front line trenches and communication trenches. Remnants from the 16th Middlesex were among the volunteers to go into No Man's Land to search for wounded comrades, as Major Goodliffe observed:

> I remember seeing many men of a Middlesex Regiment helping to evacuate our wounded. They told me that they had volunteered for this job. I was particularly struck by the fact that most of these men were gentlemen.[38]

The assault upon Beaumont Hamel was a disaster for the 86th Brigade. The 16th Middlesex, 2nd Royal Fusiliers and 1st Lancashire Fusiliers could not get beyond the German wire and lost heavily. Of the twenty-three officers and 689 men of the 16th Middlesex Regiment who entered the battle, only one officer and 196 men could later be mustered. In the days that followed 549 casualties were listed for Colonel Hall's regiment.

The 1st Lancashire Fusiliers had eight officers killed and ten wounded, with 186 men being killed, 298 wounded and 11 missing. The Sunken Lane had to be evacuated during the following day.

The 2nd Royal Fusiliers had six officers killed, fifteen wounded and two listed as missing. They also lost 158 men killed, 334 wounded and forty-six were missing. The 1st Dublin Fusiliers had six officers killed and ten wounded; the other ranks had seventy killed and 219 wounded.[39]

The failed assault upon Beaumont Hamel was disastrous for the 29th Division and the reasons for failure to breakthrough there were numerous. German forces were prepared for an assault on this sector and they had reinforced the line around Hawthorn Redoubt. They had brought up additional machine-guns which were stored in the deep underground caves and dugouts beneath the village. Beaumont Hamel had been transformed into a fortress. The dugouts could be entered from front and support lines and being thirty-feet deep in the chalk they were large enough to accommodate two battalions. So as soon as the attack began reinforcements did not have far to go to repel the attackers. The element of surprise had been lost when Hawthorn Mine was exploded ten minutes before the start of the attack thus alerting the enemy. There was a ten minute lapse between the explosion of the mine and the advance of British troops. During that period the British barrage moved beyond the German front line to support lines, so that it would not interfere with the explosion of the mine. This allowed German soldiers sheltering in dugouts in the front line to rise to the surface and prepare for the oncoming British assault.

Chapter 12

Beaumont Hamel: Y-Ravine

The 87th Brigade, commanded by Brigadier-General C.H.T. Lucas, was tasked with securing Y-Ravine and capturing Beaucourt Ridge. The brigade comprised 1st Royal Inniskilling Fusiliers, 2nd South Wales Borderers, 1st King's Own Scottish Borderers and 1st Border Regiment. The German first trench followed the gradient of Beaumont Hamel Valley and along the edge of Y-Ravine which ran east and west approximately 900 yards south of Beaumont Hamel, from Station Road to the German front line. It was a deep ravine with steep sides, lined with dugouts, with two extending protruding arms at the west end that pointed towards the British trenches. The nature of the terrain meant that this German strongpoint known as Leiling Schlucht and occupied by soldiers of 119th RIR had been untouched by the British bombardment. These German soldiers were able to enter and leave the underground complex freely without being seen by the British.

The British trenches looked down a gradual slope towards the ravine. They were unable to see the German wire from this position and much of the wire had remained uncut. As they advanced down this descent, they would become exposed to enemy fire. The German defenders could see them and fire at them with ease. The British forces were unable to see their enemy for they were sheltered in the deep dugouts in the side of Y-Ravine.

At 23:00 hours on the night of 30 June, 1st Royal Inniskilling Fusiliers and 2nd South Wales Borderers were in their designated position in the firing line known as Regent Street. The support battalions from 1st King's Own Scottish Borderers and 1st Border Regiment were in position shortly after midnight in rear line trenches.

The Inniskilling Fusiliers on the right and the South Wales Borderers on the left flank were the leading battalions. The first wave was accompanied by wire cutters and bridge carriers. Bombers formed the second wave and they were designated with the task of clearing the second and third German lines. Consolidating parties formed the fourth wave. Two machine-guns also accompanied each of these battalions to provide covering fire.

At 07:30 hours the Inniskilling Fusiliers advanced upon the German positions south of Y-Ravine to capture the first three enemy trenches. Immediately as they ascended their parapets they attracted German machine-gun fire. They found the German wire had not been cut and they could not breakthrough. They sustained heavy casualties as they advanced down the slope, among them was their commanding officer Lieutenant-Colonel R.C. Pierce who was killed. Major J. Hardress-Lloyd who assumed command of the battalion, recalled:

> My impression at the time was that the first attacking wave of Innis. Fus: carrying short ladders reached the front line of the German trenches which they crossed and were then hidden from my view by the contour of the ground. The ladders were carried with a view to facilitating the crossing of the trench system. I then saw the Germans standing up in the front line trench, the parapet of which had been practically obliterated by our shell fire.
>
> In a standing position they fired at the advancing waves of the attack. I do not think that any men of these waves reached the German front line – few even reached the German wire.[1]

Major-General De Lisle at 29th Division HQ received vague, incorrect information that a breakthrough had been made at Y-Ravine. Royal Artillery observers also claimed to have seen a bombing party in Y-Ravine and to have observed infantry reaching Station Road who were bombing dugouts. Very Lights had been seen fired from the 87th Brigade's leading battalions. By 08:15 hours De Lisle and staff officers at 29th Division HQ were uncertain of the progress made in the assault at Y-Ravine:

> It appears that portions of the enemy's 3rd line must have been captured between Y-Ravine and the River Ancre and possibly some of our troops actually reached the Station Road, but from this time onwards no more was heard of any such success except from unreliable statements of wounded men who say our men got into the 2nd and 3rd German line of trenches. The Inniskilling Fusiliers completely disappeared and no news has been heard of them.[2]

Those men from the Inniskilling Fusiliers that had survived the fusillade of machine-gun and shell fire in No Man's Land were held up by the uncut wire and many became entangled and ensnared like flies in a spider's web as machine-gun bullets tore into their torsos. Some parties managed to penetrate the German wire and pass over the German trenches. A small number of bridge carriers were seen positioning their bridges over the first German trench line on the right flank. There was not enough of them to achieve their objectives. As forward parties went further into the German trench system, there were no units following behind to consolidate captured trenches, which meant that German machine-gun crews were able to appear from their deep dugouts underground, set up their Maxim Guns and fire upon these parties from behind. Failure to mop up the first line trenches meant that these men were either killed or captured. The Inniskilling Fusiliers began the battle with thirty-six officers and 916 men, and had four officers killed, four missing and eleven wounded. In the ranks fifty were killed, 225 missing and 265 wounded. By 07:35 hours the battalion had lost over half its strength.

The South Wales Borderers, commanded by Lieutenant-Colonel John Going, on the left flank advanced opposite Y-Ravine, with the target of capturing the first two German trench lines. Major Wilfred Raikes, the second-in-command, wrote:

> The order was that the Battn was to leave their front trenches in sufficient time before Zero to enable them to reach a position 100 yards from the German front trench by Zero. This meant leaving our trenches 6 minutes before Zero on the right and about 3 minutes before on the left. It was of course broad daylight. Warned partly by the mine at the Hawthorn redoubt and partly by direct observation, the German machine-gun and rifle opened on the leading companies while they were advancing before Zero.[3]

Most of the battalion got entangled within the British wire and were mown down by three machine-guns positioned in the German trenches. Private J. Tucker was among the battalion's wounded:

> Directly the signal to advance was given we mounted the parapet. We met with a terrible fire from artillery, but it was the machine-gun fire which did the most damage in our ranks. But we continued to make good progress. Our officers displayed the greatest gallantry. One Lieutenant, an attached officer, urged us on in the most gallant fashion, and was himself twice shot, first in the leg and the second time in the body. It was just about this time that I myself was shot in the right arm and while I lay on the ground I could see the Germans turning their machine-guns on our wounded, whilst in some cases I actually saw the Germans bandaging our wounded. I determined myself to lay quiet until it was dark, and then attempt to crawl out of danger, and in this effort I succeeded.[4]

Lieutenant-Colonel Going had returned to the Western Front from sick leave a few days before the attack to resume command of battalion. He was adamant that the explosion of the Hawthorn Crater ten minutes before Zero Hour had compromised the success of the attack:

> It is quite accurate and undoubtedly the explosion of the mine too soon spoilt what little chance there was if taking even the first German line, the wire in front of the latter being in places untouched. This fact was told to division before the 1st July. Many men of C, the left company, were hanging on the wire after the attack, and very few men, if any, of that company came back.[5]

Few men from the South Wales Borderers got to within 100 yards of the German front line trench. The attack failed and all that remained of the battalion were isolated pockets sheltering in shell holes in No Man's Land. Lieutenant Fowkes was wounded five times during the advance. His life was saved when Private Perkins picked the wounded officer up from the ground in full view of the German machine-guns and courageously brought him to safety. Major Wilfred Raikes, second-in-command 2nd South Wales Borderers went over the top with the battalion and sought shelter in a shell hole until 23:00 hours that day. He recalled:

> Some men and an officer (Lieut. Dulton) reached the German wire but the right company was practically mown down before it reached its position 100 yards from the German trench, the enemy machine-guns could be plainly seen on the parapet. By 7.35 am all that was left of the battalion were scattered individuals lying out some 10 to 100 yards from the German trench.[6]

The battalion adjutant and orderly, who was with Raikes was wounded and he brought them both back to British lines that night. Raikes reported that, 'the Battn. strength going over the top was 21 officers and 578 other ranks'. Casualties were 15 officers and 384 other ranks. It is practically certain that all 'missing' were killed.[7]

German field batteries were positioned behind Beaucourt Ridge and, together with heavy artillery further back, were able to smother No Man's Land and the British trench system with shells. British communication trenches leading to the front line were within range of these guns and they were able to inflict casualties amongst the support battalions – 1st King's Own Scottish Borderers and 1st Border Regiment – that were moving forward into No Man's Land.

These two battalions represented the second wave that were scheduled to advance at 08:05 hours.

The 1st Border Regiment was tasked with capturing Beaucourt Redoubt. However, it was apparent that the German guns had not been silenced indicating that the first waves had not secured the German front line. Officers thought it prudent to delay their advance until a further bombardment could subdue the German guns. It had been planned that white flares would be fired by the first waves once they had secured the first objective, but white flares fired by the enemy misled Major-General De Lisle at 29th Division HQ into thinking that the operation was going well and he ordered the Scottish Borderers and Border Regiment to go forward.

At the designated time the Scottish Borderers led the attack on the right flank, supported by the Border Regiment on the left. The Scottish Borderers were cut down by German machine-guns and could only get as far as forty yards from the German front trench. Tin triangles were worn on the backs of the advancing troops of the 29th Division. Sewn into their haversacks this had proved helpful to Forward Observation Officers during the Gallipoli campaign in 1915 to identify the advancing units, but on 1 July at Beaumont Hamel they revealed their position to German machine-gunners as the sun reflected upon the triangles. Those that were trying to withdraw into craters to seek refuge were particularly vulnerable as their backs were facing the Germans and the sun's rays glistened upon the tin triangles. Captain G.E. Malcolm wrote:

> The 29th Division carried the following distinguishing mark: a triangle cut from a biscuit tin, worn on the outside of the haversack, which was carried on the man's back in the then fighting order. This triangle was much used in Gallipoli, and helped F.O.O.s to spot the leading troops in an advance. It was adopted as the Divisional sign, carried out in red. Actually on 1 July 1916 the sun shining on the tin helped to show up any men trying to take cover from enemy M.Gs and increased casualties. As far as I know it was never used again.[8]

The 1st Border Regiment had to climb over the parapets in the support lines because the communication trenches and the front British trench were blocked by casualties from the South Wales Borderers. Many of these men were killed before reaching No Man's Land. Bridges were placed over the first British trench line and these had been spotted by the German machine-gunners who concentrated their fire upon these points. The men then became bunched as they tried to filter through the narrow gaps in the wire. The German machine-guns had the range of these positions and brought devastating fire upon the attackers. Heaps of dead bodies lay by these gaps in the wire and those that survived made futile attempts to continue the assault but were unable to get into the German line. The battalion War Diary recorded:

> The 1st Btn. The Border Regt. then went over the top from our support line and over the first line, the bridges over the front trench having being ranged by the German machine-gunners the day previously. We met with heavy losses while crossing these bridges and passing through the lanes cut in our wire. The men were absolutely magnificent and

> formed up as ordered outside our wire, made a right incline, and advanced into 'no man's land' at a slow walk also as ordered. The advance was continued until only little groups of half a dozen men were left here and there, and then, finding that no reinforcements were in sight, took cover in shell holes or wherever they could.[9]

The advance of the Border Regiment had been brought to a complete halt. Lieutenant-Colonel A.J. Ellis had been wounded and was brought back to the British line by Private Newcombe. Major Meiklejohn with the reserve 10 per cent of the battalion was brought forward to take charge and re-organise the survivors of this disastrous assault in a support trench. The Border Regiment entered the battle with twenty-three officers and 809 men. During their attempt to enter No Man's Land they lost all but three officers and 619 men – slightly more than 75 per cent of its strength.

Communication within 87th Brigade had completely broken down. There was no telephone communication between Brigade HQ and the frontline. It was impossible to use visual communications due to the intensity of the smoke and dust caused by the artillery barrages, and the only means that the brigade could communicate was by runners.

The 88th Brigade, commanded by Brigadier-General D.E. Cayley, was meant to provide the third wave that would pass through the German front line trenches and Y-Ravine which should have been secured by the other battalions and capture Beaucourt Ridge. The brigade comprised the 2nd Hampshire Regiment, 1st Essex Regiment, 1st Newfoundland Regiment and 4th Worcestershire Regiment. Given that South Wales Borderers and the Scottish Borderers had failed to secure the German front line, this third wave now had to try to succeed where they had failed.

Telephone orders to move forward and take the German first and second line trenches and proceed as far as Station Road in conjunction with 1st Essex were received by the Newfoundland Regiment at 08:45 hours. Lieutenant-Colonel A.D. Hadow, commanding the Newfoundland Regiment, asked Brigade HQ if these trenches had been taken but this could not be confirmed. Hadow was about to send his soldiers across No Man's Land without knowing if the German line had been taken. They were put in a situation where they did not know if they had to take the objectives of the first waves or go on to secure their own objectives further into the German lines.

At 09:15 hours the Newfoundland Regiment began its advance upon the German lines without the support of the Essex Regiment because its move to the front was impeded by casualties lying in the communication trenches. Before they could leave their trench, the men had to pile up the bodies and move aside the wounded. This can hardly an encouraging start to their impending assault. In the end the Newfoundland Regiment had to launch its attack from support trenches in the rear. This meant that the men had to pass 250 yards, up a slight slope, over two support trenches and the front line trench before reaching No Man's Land.

Inevitably, the Newfoundland Regiment sustained many casualties as it moved forward to the first British trench line. Once the men arrived at the front line trench they were on the summit of the slope and could see a gentle decline towards the German trenches and Y-Ravine. At this point, they had no cover and became visible to German machine-gunners. The Newfoundland Regiment suffered the same fate as the other battalions as they became entangled in the British wire or mown down trying to pass through the gaps. The battalion War Diary confirmed:

> The advance was made direct over the open from the rear trenches known as St John's Road and Clonmel Avenue. As soon as the signal for advance was given the regiment left the trenches and moved steadily forward, machine-gun fire from our right front was at once opened over us and then artillery fire also. The distance to our objective varied from 650 to 900 yards. The enemy's fire was effective from the outset but the heaviest casualties occurred on passing through the gaps in our own front wire where the men were mown down in heaps.[10]

Some managed to get through the wire and their line of advance was from where the Newfoundland Caribou statue now stands, towards the direction of where Y-Ravine Cemetery is positioned. As the Newfoundlanders crossed this valley of death they congregated by a grove which they called the 'Danger Tree'. They were easy targets for the machine-guns ahead of them at Y-Ravine and on their right and left flanks. A sole tree still stands and possibly could have grown from the original tree of that grove. Only a few reached the German first trench where they were either shot or captured. The War Diary recorded:

> In spite of losses the survivors steadily advanced until close to the enemy's wire by which time very few remained. A few men are believed to have actually succeeded in throwing bombs into the enemy's trench.[11]

Within ten minutes of launching their advance upon Y-Ravine the Newfoundland Regiment had lost 710 men.

Meanwhile, on the right flank, the Essex Regiment assembled in support trenches. Initial reports received indicated that the Scottish Borderers' assault was proceeding well and that they were in the German lines. A wounded soldier from that battalion who had been wounded in the wire had seen soldiers from the Scottish Borderers' in the German trenches and confirmed this fact to Captain G.A.M. Paxton commanding 'Z' Company. Around 09:30 hours Paxton received orders from battalion headquarters ordering him to stand to and wait for further instructions. Five minutes later Paxton received orders to move 'Z' Company to the front line where he met Lieutenant-Colonel A.C. Halahan, CO 1st Essex Regiment. Paxton recalled:

> Just as I was going over the top myself, my CO came up and told me to hold up my advance, as the German front line was still intact, and the wire uncut. He further said our artillery was shelling the German front line. I told my CO that I had already begun my advance, and that it would be difficult to collect the company and stop the advance at this stage. He told me to collect what I could of all coys and form up in St James Trench. I collected about half of my own company and together with men assembled from other companies, I had about 120 men and an officer.[12]

It was too late to prevent the remainder of the Essex Regiment from leaving their trenches and they advanced towards German lines to almost certain death. Their ranks were devastated so quickly that the fourth company was ordered not to leave the trench.

Private J. Elsden, of the Essex Regiment was wounded as he advanced towards Y-Ravine and saw his platoon officer Lieutenant Ronald Horwood fall. Elsden wrote the following account from his hospital bed in Woolwich:

> It was July 1st, a bright sunshine morning, about half past-seven, when we were waiting for orders to go over the top. My platoon officer was Lieut. R.B. Horwood, a very nice officer. He always thought a lot of his platoon. At last orders came down the line to get ready. The shells were bursting all around us, but we were quickly over the top. We continued going a little distance at a time, then all of a sudden over would come half-a-dozen shells. Down we should get, then up again, and go forward. My platoon officer was in front, and when he got within 20 or 30 yards of the German trenches he was hit. It was just before that I was hit with shrapnel in the left leg, which means a slight fracture and three wounds, but I am pleased to say that I am getting on all right now. I must say Lieut. Horwood did his duty like a soldier and he died a hero.[13]

At 10:05 hours Major-General De Lisle received bad news that the 29th Division had failed to make a breakthrough at Beaumont Hamel and that heavy casualties had been sustained. He immediately ordered that no more units be sent forward and that the artillery barrage be brought back to assist his faltering battalions. Not knowing the positions of those men who had advanced earlier that morning the barrage had no effect. After abandoning the attack he sought to form a defensive line, fearing a German counter-attack would take place. At 10:30 hours the division's ten per cent reserves were brought forward to defend the British front line.

At 11:30 hours De Lisle sent forward the 4th Worcestershire Regiment and 2nd Hampshire Regiment to bolster the front line. German artillery was targeting the communication trenches that were leading to the British front line and as a consequence the Worcestershire Regiment suffered the loss of five officers and ninety-six men. The bombardment also severed telephone lines which meant that Brigade Headquarters had to communicate through runners. There was no possibility of these two fresh battalions launching a further attack. At 14:30 hours they were ordered to consolidate the British line. British dead and wounded caused massive congestion and it was a herculean task clearing the trenches and re-constructing the battered parapets.

The 10 per cent battalion reserve from the Newfoundland Regiment was also brought forward and it formed the nucleus of a new battalion that would later be reformed. In the afternoon and evening together with the survivors from the Newfoundland Regiment they went forward into No Man's Land to look for wounded comrades, despite being fired upon enemy machine-gun crews and snipers. Private J. Cox and Private Stewart Dewling defied the German guns to reach those wounded lying in pain in No Man's Land in a valiant effort to bring them back to their lines. Both these men were awarded the Military Medal. Many of the wounded lay helplessly in No Man's Land under the intense heat of the summer sun. They were losing blood, thirsty and lacking water they were seriously dehydrated. The longer they lay there unattended lessened their chance of survival. There were other men sheltering in the shell craters in No Man's Land. German machine-guns and snipers targeted these positions and to raise their heads above these shell craters would mean certain death. These men were in effect trapped and had to wait until nightfall before they could crawl back to the British line.

The casualties sustained by 87th and 88th Brigades were shocking. In the 88th Brigade the South Wales Borderers lost 372 men, the Scottish Borderers lost 552 men, the Inniskilling Fusiliers lost 568 men, and the Border Regiment 575.[14] The 88th Brigade lost heavily too, with the Essex Regiment losing 229 men and the Newfoundland Regiment lost 710.[15] The German casualties sustained by 119th RIR included 8 officers, 93 men killed and 191 wounded as they fought off attacks from all three brigades belonging to the 29th Division from the Sunken Lane to Y-Ravine.

Despite the British Army incurring the heaviest casualties in its history, especially north of the Albert–Bapaume Road, Haig saw those losses, in particular those suffered by the 1st Newfoundland Regiment, has aiding the successes made on the southern sector of the attack. Haig wrote to Sir E.P. Morris, the Newfoundland Prime Minister:

> As it was the action of the Newfoundland Battalion and the other units of the British left contributed largely to the victory achieved by the

> British and French farther south pinning to their ground the best of the German troops and by occupying the best of their artillery, both heavy and field. The gallantry and devotion of this battalion, therefore was not in vain, and the credit of victory belongs to them as much as to those troops farther south who actually succeeded in breaking the German line. An attacking army is like a football team; there is but one who kicks the goal, yet the credit of success belongs not alone to that individual but to the whole team whose concerted action led to the desired result.[16]

The 1st Newfoundland Regiment was all but destroyed at Beaumont Hamel on 1 July 1916. This battalion (together with the 10th West Yorkshire which assaulted Fricourt) suffered the highest number of casualties that day. The battalion was so badly depleted that it was withdrawn from the line for three months so that it could be rebuilt with drafts from England.

Y-Ravine at Beaumont Hamel was a formidable position to capture on 1 July 1916. The troops from the 87th and 88th Brigades were disadvantaged by the fact that the underground dugouts were bombardment-proof and dug into Y-Ravine, and the enemy was alerted by the explosion of the Hawthorn Mine. The heavily laden troops never had a chance. It was not until 13 November 1916, nearly four and a half months after the initial attempt, that Beaumont Hamel was finally captured by infantry from the 51st (Highland) Division.

Part 4

X Corps Sector

Chapter 13

Schwaben Redoubt

The 36th (Ulster) Division commanded by Major-General O.S.W. Nugent, was in Lieutenant-General Sir T.L.N. Morland's X Corps. The division was raised in Ulster and comprised the 107th, 108th and 109th Brigades. Their objective on 1 July 1916 were for the 109th Brigade supported by battalions from the other two brigades to capture the four lines of German trenches, including the heavily-fortified strongpoint called the Schwaben Redoubt (Schwaben Feste), and the village of St Pierre Divion in between the southern bank of the River Ancre and Thiepval and then proceed towards Grandcourt. Brigadier-General C.R.J. Griffith commanding the 108th Brigade had to separate his forces with 9th and 12th Royal Irish Rifles attacking north of the River Ancre and 11th and 13th Royal Irish Rifles (County Down) advancing parallel to the southern bank.

Situated on the north-western edge of Thiepval Ridge the redoubt had commanding views towards St. Pierre Divion and across the valley towards Beaucourt-Sur-Ancre and Beaumont Hamel. The capture of the Schwaben Redoubt by the 36th Division was therefore absolutely necessary if Thiepval was to be captured by the 32nd Division on its right flank and Beaumont Hamel secured by 29th Division on its left

This sector was defended by the 99th RIR together with 8th Bavarian RIR, both belonging to the 26th Reserve Division. The 99th RIR had been defending Thiepval since March 1916 and had plenty of time to familiarise itself with the terrain and fortify the positions. In shellproof dugouts and shelters excavated thirty feet into the chalk with a labyrinth of tunnels and connecting command posts. With hundreds of men ensconced within its deep chambers, the Schwaben Redoubt had been turned into a veritable fortress.

The redoubt was also protected by other redoubts in the area. Guns in St. Pierre Divion, the Stuff and Goat Redoubts could fire upon any attack upon the Schwaben Redoubt. Two battalions from 107th and 108th Brigades were therefore designated to attack German lines west of the Ancre to prevent German machine-gun fire interfering with the 36th Division's main assault upon the Schwaben Redoubt on the opposite bank as well as securing the

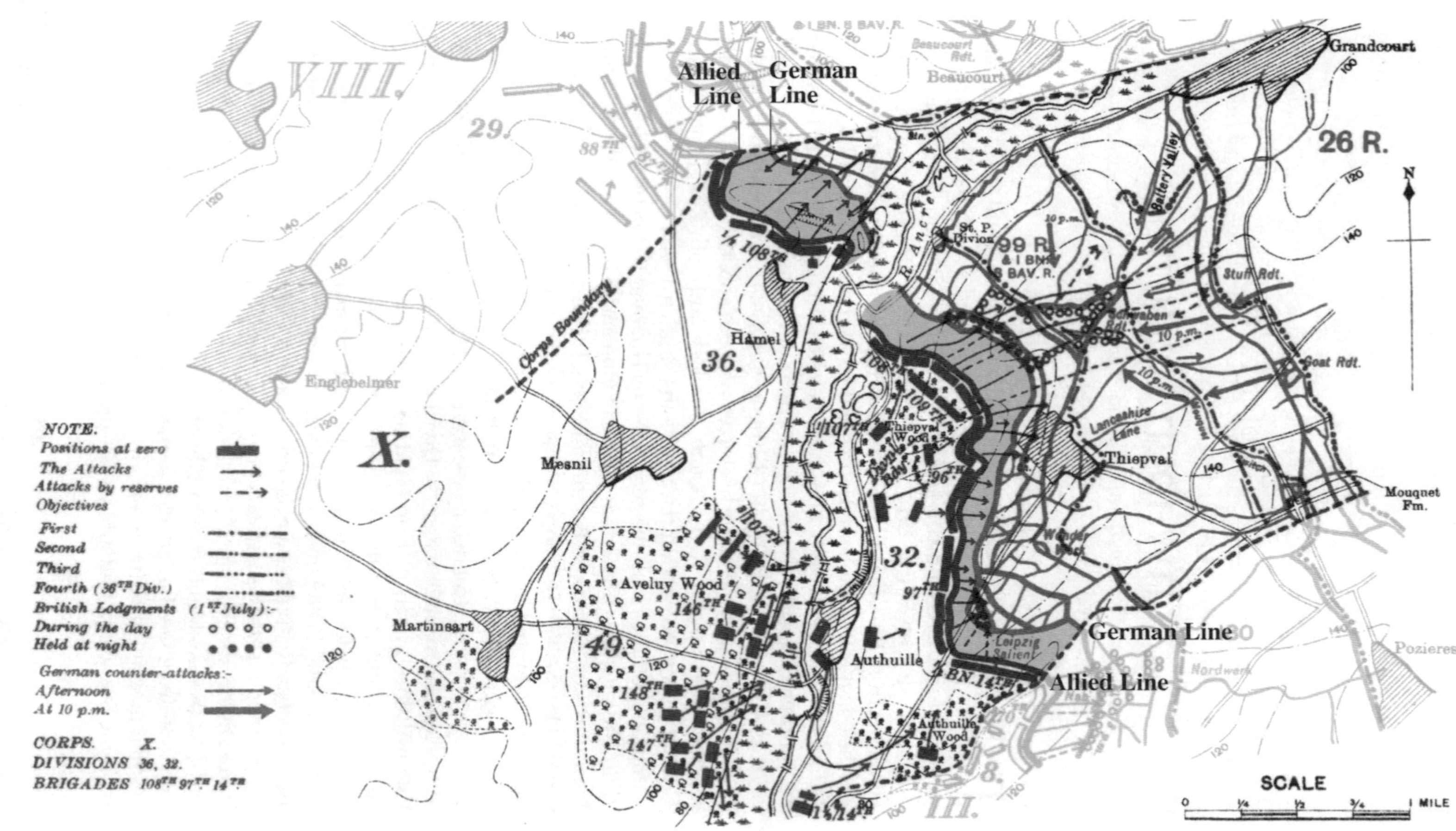
Allied Line
German Line
German Line
Allied Line
Grandcourt
Beaucourt
26 R.
99 R.
VIII.
29.
X.
36.
32.
49.
III.
Hamel
Mesnil
Englebelmer
Martinsart
Thiepval
Thiepval Wood
Aveluy Wood
Authuille
Authuille Wood
Mouquet Fm.
Pozieres
Nordwerk
R. Ancre
Battery Valley
Stuff Rdt.
Schwaben Rdt.
Goat Rdt.
Lancashire Lane
Leipzig Salient
Corps Boundary
St. P. Divion
NOTE.
Positions at zero
The Attacks
Attacks by reserves
Objectives
First
Second
Third
Fourth (36TH Div.)
British Lodgments (1ST July):-
During the day
Held at night
German counter-attacks:-
Afternoon
At 10 p.m.
CORPS. X.
DIVISIONS 36, 32.
BRIGADES 108TH 97TH 14TH
SCALE
0 1/4 1/2 3/4 1 MILE

right flank of the 29th Division in their assault on Beaumont Hamel to the north. The limit of their objectives were to secure Beaucourt Station.

Since the fortress was located on a ridge the 36th Division was further disadvantaged in that it was attacking from Thiepval Wood up a slope. As they were moving in an easterly direction a rising sun in the East would dazzle the eyes of the men as they advanced towards the enemy trenches.

Despite the difficulties that faced them, the Ulstermen did have a psychological advantage, for the start date of the Somme infantry offensive fell on 1 July, the anniversary of the Battle of the Boyne in 1690. This was the day when King William III appointed the Inniskilling Regiment as his guard and the Boyne was the first engagement they fought as regular soldiers, so in some way the attack in 1916 was symbolic. It was also the first engagement of the 9th, 10th and 11th Royal Inniskilling Fusiliers and they were keen to prove themselves in battle on this significant anniversary.

108th BRIGADE – ADVANCE NORTH OF THE RIVER ANCRE

The 108th Brigade was split into two groups. The group assaulting German positions north of the River Ancre comprised the 9th Royal Irish Fusiliers (Co. Armagh, Monaghan AND Cavan) and the 12th Royal Irish Rifles (Central Antrim). Here the German lines were defended by 119th RIR, north of the 36th Division's main line of advance. Their objectives were to capture three lines of enemy trenches, Beaucourt station and the trench immediately to the north.

Three companies from the 12th Royal Irish Rifles commanded by Lieutenant-Colonel G. Bull on the left flank was to deliver a direct assault upon the German occupied positions whilst the 9th Royal Irish Fusiliers advanced as central column. One company belonging to 12th Royal Irish Rifles was on Bull's right with one platoon detailed to clear the marshland by the river.

Prior to Zero Hour, the first wave of the 9th Royal Irish Fusiliers left their parapet and crawled towards a ravine in No Man's Land with few casualties. This ravine was within 150 yards of the German first line and was around seventy yards wide with banks fifteen to twenty feet high.

At 07:30 hours, as soon as the first wave had left the ravine, they were met by heavy machine-gun fire. The British artillery barrage upon the German front line had been ineffective, so as soon as the barrage lifted, the Germans in the front line were quickly into position and able to fire upon the oncoming British infantry.

The second wave suffered even more casualties, as by the time it began its advance the German trenches were fully manned. German artillery had also been alerted and began dropping shells on the rear ranks between the British line and the ravine. The battalion War Diary states that the third and fourth waves were 'practically annihilated'.[1]

Major A.H. Burne DSO, of the 3/154th Royal Field Artillery gave his views on the ineffectiveness of the British guns:

> There is an impression that the failure N. of the river was because the wire was not cut as well as it was south. This is incorrect. I don't consider the wire was as well cut behind the front line as S. of the river (owing to more difficult observation), but the failure became before ever our infantry reached the wire. Our barrage on the front line was too thin. The fastest rate I fired was only 3 rounds per gun per minute, and it did not prevent their M.Gs opening on our people going through our own wire before ever our barrage lifted. Considering we had been in position for months and knew every inch of the ground, we could have supported our infantry better by observed fire than by a fixed timetable of lifts'.[2]

The plan had gone disastrously wrong, the barrage continued to fall deeper into German lines, but it was of no use to the Royal Irish Rifles who were trying to get through the wire. Burne recognised the problem they endured and tried to react to the changing situation by asking his superiors to bring the barrage back to deal with the hostile fire coming from the German front line. Burne continued: 'As it was our successive lifts left our infantry miles behind, and when I asked for leave to bring my fire back it was refused (so I then did it without permission!!)'[3]

Despite sustaining heavy casualties, remnants of the two companies advancing on the left flank and the company on the right flank were able to reach the German wire and enter the first German trench. In some sectors of this trench the occupants immediately threw up their hands to surrender. However when they realised that they outnumbered their attackers they resumed the fight for the trench. The centre right company was observed to have penetrated through three German trench lines and reached its objective at Beaucourt Station.

The German machine-gun fire was intensive and unrelenting. Only one runner from the left company returned from the German lines with the message 'Cannot advance without support'.[4] Half a company from the 12th Royal Irish Rifles was the only available reserve, but it came under heavy fire as it tried to cross No Man's Land to support the 9th Royal Irish Fusiliers. The men unable to get to the German first line.

The defenders of St. Pierre Divion and the Beaucourt Redoubt were firing upon them. One machine-gun emplacement that was responsible for inflicting heavy casualties on the advancing Ulstermen was concealed in an emplacement on top of a shaft, which was accessed by a tunnel from the railway embankment. Only a small party from the 108th Brigade reached Beaucourt Station, where most of them became casualties.

The assault upon German lines north of the River Ancre dissolved into failure with the four companies of the 9th Royal Irish Fusiliers sustaining heavy casualties. No further news reached the British line until late that evening when two wounded men had crawled back across No Man's Land from the third German line. This battalion incurred 244 casualties. Every officer became a casualty and only eighty men returned to the British line unwounded. Efforts to clear those left lying wounded from No Man's Land were made by the second-in-command, adjutant, stretcher bearers and men from the Royal Engineers under the cover of darkness.

The 12th Royal Irish Rifles suffered the same fate as the 9th Royal Irish Fusiliers. It advanced on the Irish Fusiliers left flank, the focus of its assault being a small salient. Three companies were detailed for this assault and one was left in reserve. On the right flank of 9th Royal Irish Rifles, one platoon from 'B' Company, 12th Royal Irish Rifles, was ordered to seize the railway sap and another platoon was ordered to patrol the marsh between the River Ancre and the railway line. The three companies were in position to launch their assault at 07:30 hours on 1 July. Private Robert Letters who advanced with the 12th Royal Irish Rifles wrote:

> I was through it all on Saturday when the Division attacked the German trenches at Thiepval on July 1. Where I was fighting was severe, but we advanced into their third lines, and inflicted very heavy losses on them and captured a great many prisoners. We suffered some losses, and I have to mourn for a few of my comrades who have fallen. Lieutenant T. Haughton is amongst those from Cullybuckey who have fallen, but they died doing their duty – upholding the honour of the 36th (Ulster) Division. The 1st of July will be a day never forgotten in Ulster; it will live in my memory for ever, and the sights that I have seen … You will be glad to know that I and a chum captured 15 Germans ourselves – two in one of their own dugouts. I brought them out at the point of a bayonet, and ran them across 'No Man's Land' into our lines. When I was going across with them a German machine-gun opened fire on us and a bullet from it struck my rifle and smashed it. I have the bullet as a souvenir, and also a German cap and pipe and a small book which one of the prisoners gave me.[5]

There were only two small gaps in the wire which were covered by German machine-gunners positioned directly opposite in the front trench line. Many men were brought down by these guns but some got through and entered the German first trench. Captain John Griffiths saw these men gain a footing in the enemy line, and so he gathered other men that got through the wire and charged in their direction to reinforce them, but Griffiths was killed. Further attempts to enter the German line on this sector were thwarted. The remnants of the right company withdrew to a sunken road close to the British line with the exception of three NCOs who remained to continue the fight. Their names were Sergeant Cunningham, Corporal Herbison and

Lance Corporal Jackson. Lance Corporal Hervey rallied some men and tried to break through the wire but was forced to withdraw.

The two left companies of the Irish Rifles, 'A' and 'D', launched a direct assault upon the German salient under intensive machine-gun fire. Despite sustaining significant casualties they entered the German front line trench which was strongly held by their opponents. They came under attack from German bombing parties on both flanks and from a communication trench. Several machine-guns also fired upon them at close quarters. As their ranks were diminishing some officers and men fought their way into a communication trench where they were killed. The remnants of these companies reformed and launched two successive attacks which also failed.

'A' Company attacked the salient on the extreme left flank and was in touch with parties from the 29th Division advancing to the north upon Y-Ravine, Beaumont Hamel. They reached the German front line in small numbers, amongst them was Lieutenant McCluggagn, but they were forced to retire. This was partly because some German soldiers realised that there were no supporting troops so they resumed the fight after they had initially surrendered.

Elements of the Irish Fusiliers and Irish Rifles captured three German lines. The first line was easily entered with little resistance from the enemy, however, the strongly defended second line was difficult to capture. Here the defenders stood on their parapets and threw bombs into the front line, while steady fire was concentrated upon advancing elements of the Irish Fusiliers which suffered heavily. An order to retire was heard amidst the chaos and confusion of battle, but 2nd Lieutenant Sir Harry Macnaghten, commanding 'D' Company, motivated his men to continue the fight:

> Sir Harry got out of the trench to order the men not to retire but to come on and just as he got out he was shot in the legs by a machine-gun only a few yards away, and fell back into the trench. Rifleman Kane who was quite close to Sir Harry bayoneted the German who was firing the MG.[6]

'D' Company fell back after Macnaghten was killed, but 2nd Lieutenant Dickson rallied the remnants who were reinforced by survivors from 'A' Company. Dickson then led another charge upon the German lines. They came under heavy fire from the German-occupied salient and were forced to retire with Dickson being wounded. Sergeant McFall assumed command and led another failed attempt.

The platoon, of 'B' Company, 12th Royal Irish Rifles, that was ordered to clear the marshland and the railway sap on the right flank of the Irish Fusiliers was obliterated by shrapnel and machine-gun fire. Despite suffering heavy casualties a party did enter the railway sap and was able to cut communication leads there and kill two German officers. They were met by a significant German force and the platoon was reduced to two men who managed to escape back to the British line.

As we have seen, the 29th Division's attack on Beaumont Hamel to the north had faltered, however, it was going to re-new its attack and the 12th Royal Irish Rifles were ordered to assemble as many men as possible to attack again on its front to coincide with that against Beaumont Hamel. About 100 men were gathered, but when they went forward they were stopped by machine-gun fire. At 12:30 hours a message was received that the 29th Division was going to launch a further attack and the order for the 12th Royal Irish Rifles to attack was repeated, but this time they could only muster forty-six men. They went forward in compliance with orders, but 29th Division's attack did not materialise and these men were brought back. The assault upon German trenches north of the River Ancre had failed.

108th BRIGADE – ADVANCE SOUTH OF THE RIVER ANCRE

Half of the 108th Brigade was ordered to assault trenches south of the River Ancre. The 13th Royal Irish Rifles (County Down) advanced on the left and the 11th Royal Irish Rifles (South Antrim) on the right flank. They were supported by 15th Royal Irish Rifles (North Belfast) from the 107th Brigade.

The 13th Royal Irish Rifles were able to advance from Thiepval Wood to the starting tape that had been laid in No Man's Land from 07:15 hours without casualties. They crawled to within 150 yards of the first German trench, but as soon as they leapt to their feet at Zero Hour German machine-guns opened fire from the ridge in Thiepval village on their right flank and from German machine-gun posts along the banks of the River Ancre on their left.

By 08:05 hours German machine-gunners had dispersed the 32nd Division's battalions in the south and were now firing northwards towards the line of advance of the 13th Royal Irish Rifles which tore through its ranks. Their losses were so heavy that they were unable to carry out their designated task of forming a defensive flank of the 36th Division's line of advance south of the River Ancre. Captain G.W. Matthews led 'A' Company on the right flank into the first German line but could not go any further without covering fire. At 08:06 hours Matthews sent a message to battalion HQ requesting a Vickers Gun. Two reserve machine-guns from 108th machine-gun Company were brought forward to the first German line by Captain J.S. Davidson, suffering casualties as they entered No Man's Land.

Two companies from 15th Royal Irish Rifles of the 107th Brigade followed the 13th Royal Irish Rifles. They reached the first German line by 07:50 hours where they encountered numerous German soldiers that just emerged from their dugouts. These enemy soldiers were either killed or wounded and the 15th Royal Irish Rifles was able to consolidate the first German line. It came under heavy machine-gun fire from the northern bank of the Ancre, sustaining heavy casualties as their supplies of ammunition and bombs began to run out.

By 09:20 hours, Lieutenant-Colonel W.H. Savage commanding 13th Royal Irish Rifles was unable to discover what had happened to his battalion. It was difficult to see the operation in progress from the observation post at the bottom of Thiepval Wood. No messages were coming through because all the messengers became casualties. As it happened, only two platoons from the 13th Royal Irish Rifles reached the second German line.

The first message from the German lines were received an hour later, timed at 10:20 hours from Captain Davidson who had reached the second line. The message read: 'Am in B Line and have got two Vickers guns, am consolidating both. Cannot say how many infantry are in line, but as this part there are only about 30 men of 13th and 15th R.Ir.Rif. We cannot possibly advance, and reinforcements, bombs and ammunition most urgently needed.'[7]

Lieutenant Marriott-Watson, battalion intelligence officer was sent forward to assess the situation. He had been a scout officer and led reconnaissance parties into this area in the weeks prior to the start of the offensive and so knew the terrain, but he was wounded before he could gain any information about the 11th Royal Irish Rifles position within the German lines on their right flank. Heavy artillery and machine-gun fire prevented carriers bringing forward any supplies of bombs and small arms munitions to Captain Davidson. Lieutenant-Colonel Savage resorted to sending two officer's servants and the three remaining N.C.O.s at Battalion HQ to carry the necessary supplies to Davidson but all became casualties. Davidson continued the fight until he was wounded. The 13th Royal Irish Rifles' assault had failed and it was not until nightfall that any attempt was made to recover the wounded by stretcher bearers and volunteers.

At 07:15 hours, the 11th Royal Irish Rifles advancing on the right flank suffered casualties from German shell-fire as they moved forward from assembly trenches in Thiepval Wood to the front line. Two platoons were completely wiped out before they reached No Man's Land. The remnants from the battalion lined up along white tapes of the start line by 07:25 hours and five minutes later they advanced towards the German lines. By 07:32 hours, within two minutes of beginning the attack, they were in the German first trench sustaining very few casualties. They then continued to the objective known as A Line. The only resistance they encountered were two isolated German riflemen shooting from their parapet. There was no organised resistance and mopping-up parties were left to clear the dugouts and consolidate the line. A number of Germans were captured sheltering in their bunkers, one group was even caught while in the process of shaving.[8]

Two companies from 15th Royal Irish Rifles from the 107th Brigade followed in support of the 11th Royal Irish Rifles. Both these companies arrived in A Line at 07:45 hours but by 07:50 hours they had sustained sixty casualties as they crossed No Man's Land. Nevertheless, five minutes later one of these companies got to the German B Line.

A number of men from the 11th Royal Irish got to within fifty yards of the next objective, B Line, by 07:48 hours where they had to halt and wait for the barrage to lift. Two minutes later they charged upon B Line. Bombing parties were left to clear the line of any remaining enemy while the advance continued. At this moment they moved in conjunction with the 109th Brigade on their right flank which was progressing well and they advanced in one continuous line. The 11th Royal Irish Rifles however had lost contact with the 13th Royal Irish Rifles on their left flank. As the battalion advanced upon the C Line it came too close to the artillery barrage and, at 08:05 hours, had to briefly retire 100 yards. They caught up with the barrage again at 08:18 hours and had to retire once more.

The 11th Royal Irish Rifles reached C Line by 09:20 hours without encountering strong resistance and without sustaining casualties. As the men went deeper into the German positions, however, they found the enemy better organised and the battalion came under machine-gun fire from both flanks.

Consolidation of the ground they had taken was begun immediately put in hand in conjunction with the 10th Royal Inniskilling Fusiliers of the 109th Brigade who had advanced on the right flank. The work of consolidation was restricted in C Line because of the lack of men and materials available. Two carrying parties had ceased to exist before leaving Thiepval Wood. Six machine-guns and Lewis Guns were brought forward to this line and put in key positions. The 108th and 109th Brigades were becoming intermingled and the 108th was ordered to move to the left and the 109th to move towards the right.

Support from the 15th Royal Irish Rifles, 107th Brigade, arrived at 11:00 hours at C Line and the men attempted to advance upon the German D Line but failed. They retired to form a defensive flank between B and C Lines. At 14:00 hours German artillery began to shell the 36th Division's lines with high explosives and shrapnel. This bombardment was the precursor to a German infantry counter- attack upon the C Line. The attack was repulsed by British artillery and machine-guns positioned in C Line.

German bombing parties got close to the C Line and 11th Royal Irish Rifles, enabling them to pin-point the attackers' position and relay this position to the German artillery batteries. Between 16:30 and 17:00 hours German guns opened fire on C Line causing many casualties. Most of the officers were either killed or wounded and the remaining men were exhausted and thirsty. The 11th Royal Irish Rifles were eventually forced to retire to B Line.

Another German counter-attack was made upon B Line at 20:30 hours. Unable to resist this attack the remnants of 11th Royal Irish Rifles withdrew to A Line which was defended by battalions from the 49th Division. An ammunition dump was established in one of the dugouts in A Line. Attempts were made to attempt to replenish this dump with ammunition throughout the day but the carrying parties became casualties and by 15:00 hours there was no one left to bring supplies to the first captured line. Water was also brought up in bags but there were few men left to drink it. The wounded lying in A Line could be rescued but the men left in B and C Lines had to be left where they laid and hoped that German medics would tend to their wounds.

Remnants from the 107th and 108th Brigades began to filter back to the start line at Thiepval Wood as soon as it got dark. A party of one officer and eighteen men held out in a section of C Line throughout that night and withdrew to A Line at 03:00 hours on 2 July.

109th AND 107th BRIGADE – ASSAULT UPON SCHWABEN REDOUBT

The 109th Brigade, commanded by Brigadier-General R.G. Shuter, attacked on the 36th Division's right flank directly upon the Schwaben Redoubt. Its battalions left their trenches on the edge of Thiepval Wood and advanced up the slope towards the German fortress. The 9th Royal Inniskilling Fusiliers (County Tyrone) were on the right flank supported by the 11th Royal Inniskilling Fusiliers (Donegal & Fermanagh). On the left flank was the 10th Royal Inniskilling Fusiliers (County Derry) supported by 14th Royal Irish Rifles (Belfast Young Citizens). Both columns advanced on a 250 yard front and were ordered to capture four German defence lines including Schwaben Redoubt. The 109th Brigade were supported by the 107th Brigade, which was assembled in Thiepval Wood. The 107th Brigade contained the 8th Royal Irish Rifles (East Belfast), 9th Royal Irish Rifles (West Belfast), 10th Royal Irish Rifles (South Belfast) and 15th Royal Irish Rifles (North Belfast). Their objective was to pass through the positions captured by the 109th Brigade and push forward towards Grandcourt.

German observers knew the ranges of the crossings over the River Ancre and Lieutenant-Colonel Ross, Smyth commanding the 10th Royal Inniskilling Fusiliers, became a casualty of the German bombardment when he was thrown from his horse when a shell exploded as he was crossing a pontoon bridge. Major Macrory then took command of the battalion, which included Corporal Jim Donaghy: 'As we entered the trenches everything was in commotion. The first thing my Platoon had to do was to move to the side to allow the stretcher-bearers to pass. They were carrying boys down to the first aid post. They were screaming in pain from shell shock.'[9]

The 9th Royal Inniskilling Fusiliers was commanded by Lieutenant-Colonel Ricardo and its objective was to capture Schwaben Redoubt and a position in the third German line called Lisnaskea Line (named after the Ulster town). While the battalion was assembling in Thiepval Wood the Allied guns began firing at 06:25 hours prior to the infantry assault. The awesome barrage clearly affected the morale of German soldiers occupying Schwaben Redoubt for one German soldier approached the lines of the 9th Inniskilling Fusiliers prior to Zero Hour with the intention of surrendering Private Thomas Ervine was reluctant to shoot him, despite being encouraged by his comrades to do so. Ervine later recalled:

> Before the Battle of the Somme started I captured a German, well, I didn't capture him as much as he came up to me with his hands up. And some of the men – like all you could see was the tops of their heads looking up over the trench – well – anyway, they were shouting at me 'Shoot him, Tommy, shoot him". But I didn't like to shoot the man in cold blood, it wouldn't have been right anyway. So I took him down the hill and searched him at the bottom, but he had nothing on him – we got word at that time that the Germans had been using daggers. I don't believe it though because I don't think the Germans were really bad people or wicked in any way, as far as I could see. So I walked him along to where the reserves were coming up and I told him to go down there, and he walked down the hill with his hands up, and that was the last I saw of him.[10]

During the early hours of the 1 July sections of the British barbed-wire were cut to enable easy access into No Man's Land. At around 06:00 hours narrow openings were cut through the parapets of the front-line trenches so that the attacking Ulstermen could walk out of the trenches instead of climbing their parapets and going over the top. Bridges and ladders were placed over assembly trenches in the rear to allow troops in the following waves to cross as they moved forwards. Rum had been issued at 06:00 hours to calm the nerves of the men.

The 109th Brigade did have an advantage since the British front line was positioned along the edge of the tree stumps of Thiepval Wood which meant that assembly positions within the shell-shattered wood were hidden. Also a quarter of the way across No Man's Land there was a bank which skirted along the north side of the St Pierre Divion–Thiepval Road which would provide the men with some cover from hostile fire from the Schwaben Redoubt.

As they waited for Zero Hour the Ulstermen observed the sun rising in the east over the enemy lines. Private Leslie Bell of the 10th Inniskilling Fusiliers noted that it was 'a very red colour. Someone said it was blood on the sun. Someone else said there would be a lot more on it before it went down.'[11]

At 07:00 hours Stokes mortars of the 10th Inniskilling Fusiliers opened fire upon the German frontline trenches. The purpose of this final barrage was to weaken German frontline defences prior to the main assault and serve as cover for units crawling into No Man's Land. German artillery responded to the British guns five minutes later with a barrage upon communication trenches within Thiepval Wood. It was during the German bombardment that Private Billy McFadzean was distributing grenades to his fellow comrades of the 14th Royal Irish Rifles. They were to support the 10th Inniskilling Fusiliers at Zero Hour. As a shell exploded nearby, a box of grenades slipped and fell to the ground of McFadzean's trench. Two bombs fell out, together with their pins. Within four seconds there would be an explosion and without hesitation or concern for his own safety, he threw himself on the grenades in order to shield his comrades from the blast. In saving the lives of his mates he lost his own and was killed instantly. Only Private George Gillespie was injured which resulted in the amputation of a leg. For his ultimate sacrifice at the young age of eighteen, Billy received a posthumous Victoria Cross. This was the first Victoria Cross to be awarded for the Somme campaign.

The men of the 36th Division were of the Orange Order and as Zero Hour approached prayers were said and hymns sung while the final phase of the bombardment was taking place. Corporal Jim Donaghy, 10th Inniskillings, remembered the final moments before the attack:

> The noise was terrific and the Germans now opened up with a heavy bombardment in retaliation, in fact the noise was unbelievable. We had spent most of the night on our knees, with our faces towards the parapet to protect it from shrapnel, our backs getting some protection from our steel helmets and back packs. The noise was terrible. No one was talking. You couldn't even hear yourself speak. Men had their wee bibles out and were reading them. Others had taken photographs of their mothers, wives and children out of their tunic pockets and were looking at them. Some were making their wills in the back page of their pay books. Just before the first units went out into no-man's-land, my Platoon was one of them, we all said it again. We sang hymns even though we could hardly hear our own voices.[12]

At 07:15 hours the first wave carefully passed through gaps in their own wire to reach No Man's Land where they crawled towards the first German line, stopping 150 yards from the line. Here they waited flat upon the ground three yards apart. The second and third waves followed behind and there was a distance of fifty yards separating each wave. Jim Donaghy was one of those waiting in No Man's Land:

> As I was lying there I got a feeling of loneliness as I couldn't see anyone else. I looked back over my shoulder and spotted four or five of my Platoon lying behind me to my left. All of a sudden a big six inch shell landed in between them. It ploughed through the ground and came up through the soil, just like a salmon coming out of the water. It lay there

> with its shiny silver nose pointing upward. We cringed, but it didn't explode![13]

Commanding officers were ordered not to participate in the assault; their role was to plan and co-ordinate the attack from the British lines. Lieutenant-Colonel F.P. Crozier commanding the 9th Royal Irish Fusiliers later wrote of his anger at this decision, 'The whole idea was repulsive. It cut right across the foundations of mutual trust, emphasized in training, between private soldier and officer.'[14]

Crozier and Lieutenant-Colonel Herbert Bernard, commanding 10th Royal Irish Rifles, expressed their grievances against this order. Those Crozier regarded as 'the higher hierarchy' dismissed their protests and concerns, but Crozier and Bernard decided to disobey the order. They agreed that they could not lead from a dugout, where they could not respond to developments. Crozier recalled their 'plan was to meet in No Man's Land, if alive. There we would supervise the deployment and make any necessary alterations in the plan over which we had little control.'[15]

At 07:30 hours the British bombardment stopped and the bugle sounded to signal the advance along 109th Brigade's front. At that moment platoon leaders blew whistles and the first waves left their starting positions and marched at a steady pace towards the enemy lines. Private Lindsay Hall also advanced with the 10th Inniskilling Fusiliers recalled: 'We shall never forget the morning of the 1st July when we got the word "You go up and the best of luck". Crossing over the German lines we were as cool as though we were on parade. We went steadily over line after line. A machine-gun on the left in a strong German position swept our advancing lines and I saw the boys falling on my right and left. We did not stop on we went.'[16] Some of the leading waves of the 10th Inniskilling Fusiliers followed too close to the artillery barrage just before it lifted and casualties were incurred as they charged into it. One company drifted slightly to the left and overlapped the 11th Royal Irish Rifles line of advance.

The 9th Inniskilling Fusiliers left its trenches and in parade-like fashion with great discipline proceeded towards the Sunken Road in No Man's Land. Here they sustained many casualties from machine-gun fire from Thiepval positioned on the high ridge, perpendicular to the 36th Division's line of advance. The Sunken Road was a scene of carnage and slaughter would become known as 'Bloody Road'. The 11th Inniskilling Fusiliers following behind the 9th Battalion suffered a similar fate as they assembled in the Sunken Road. Many of the battalion's officers and NCOs had become casualties before reaching the Sunken Road.

German snipers were also targeting soldiers from the Inniskilling Fusiliers as they advanced across No Man's Land. Private Thomas Ervine was wounded by a sniper, but managed to fire back and kill him. Ervine recalled: 'I didn't get very far until somebody fired a gun and hit me in the leg. I fired back at him and hit him in the face, and I could see the blood shooting out of his face, in gushes like, coming out of his cheek. He was a nice looking young man but he was a sniper, and if I hadn't got him God knows how many people he would have killed before we would have got him'.[17]

Despite a bullet wound in the leg Private Ervine continued to advance up the slope towards German lines but a shell explosion knocked him unconscious:

> Anyway I was still able to walk and I went down into the trench. I only got a few yards when a shell burst above my head and there was all shrapnel in my shoulders and my back; my arms had pieces of shrapnel everywhere, so I went out for the count right there. When I wakened up again on the 4th July I was in Colchester Hospital. I don't remember how I got from France to England. When I wakened up I saw two nurses looking at me and they laughed and one of them says 'there's a wee souvenir for you' – it was two wee bags made out of pieces of lint and they were filled with wee pieces of shrapnel and a bullet was taken out of me'.[18]

As the Ulsters advanced they discovered that some sections of the German wire had not been cut by the British barrage and the deep German dugouts had not been affected. Jack Christie, a stretcher bearer remembered:

> The dugouts were so good and strong only the surface was being ploughed up and it did not do what it was supposed to do. They knew we were coming and they held their fire and waited for us to come. There were over 5000 casualties. In parts they got forward where the wire had been cut but where the wire had not been cut they were caught in machine-gun fire and they did not get through. That meant the line had not moved forward uniformly so that meant the men who had got through and reached their objective were able to be attacked on the flanks[19]

In other sections of No Man's Land it was evident that the artillery had succeeded in destroying some sections of the enemy wire. The 10th Inniskilling Fusiliers War Diary reported that not one man needed his wire cutters to get through the wire. Private Lindsay Hall testified:

> When we reached the German front line we were not troubled with cutting their wire, for the simple reason that there was none there to cut. It had been completely blown away. All that could be seen were a few twisted iron spikes and bits of wire lying in the bottom of shell holes and all over the place. Their front was barely recognisable. It was blown up in every direction. There were a few dugouts with Germans

> in them. In these we threw bombs and the Germans came up with their hands in the air, crying 'Mercy Kamerade!'[20]

Despite sustaining heavy casualties, the three Inniskilling battalions charged towards the first German trench reaching it very quickly, finding these trenches to be levelled and its occupants demoralised and confused. This line was captured without a fight and with few casualties. German soldiers belonging to the 99th RIR were slow in surfacing from their deep dugouts 'dazed and bewildered'[21] and were keen to surrender.

Those that surrendered were sent back towards Thiepval Wood under escort, sixteen German prisoners to one British soldier. German shells descended upon No Man's Land and some of these German prisoners dashed forward ahead of their escort and were killed by supporting waves who were not aware that they had surrendered and had inadvertently mistaken them for a German counter-attack and fired at them. The sight of German prisoners being escorted towards the British lines caused misleading reports to be sent to the German 26th Divisional HQ stating that a German advance was in progress from the Schwaben Redoubt towards Authuille.

The leading waves of the 10th Inniskilling Fusiliers went determinedly towards the German second line, known as the Crucifix Line. Again they followed too close behind the barrage and had to withdraw temporarily. Once the barrage lifted further they reached the German second line by 07:50 hours where they met only slight opposition. Those who resisted were either shot or bayoneted.

General der Infanterie Freiherr von Soden at 26th Division HQ received reports at 08:05 hours from an observation post positioned along the northern bank of the River Ancre that British soldiers were in the Schwaben Redoubt and immediately ordered the 2nd Battalion, 8th Bavarian RIR, his only divisional reserve, to launch a counter-attack with a machine-gun company and a platoon from a rifle company. There was a delay in organising this attack due to telephone wires being successfully cut by the British artillery. It was not until 08:55 hours that Major Roesch commanding 2nd Battalion, 8th Bavarian Infantry Reserve Regiment, received this message, ordering him to launch a counter-attack from Stuff Redoubt to regain the position.

Roesch and his battalion were five miles away, at Irles. They had been waiting to be deployed since 05:30 hours that morning. Due to the severity of the British barrages that fell on the rear lines they did not reach Grandcourt until 14:00 hours. Within that time it was too late for German forces to react and the Ulstermen were able to continue to hold Schwaben Redoubt. However, the situation was precarious for the 36th Division since Thiepval was still under German control.

The first waves of the 36th Division had incurred few casualties but the supporting waves suffered from heavy machine-gun fire coming from the direction of Thiepval village, and by 08:00 hours it had to be accepted that the Division had failed in its objective to capture Thiepval Ridge. Lieutenant-Colonel F.P. Crozier, commanding the 9th Royal Irish Rifles witnessed the fate of the 32nd Division on his right flank and realised that they were behind schedule before he himself led his battalion across No Man's Land:

> Then I glance to the right through a gap in the trees. I see the 10th Rifles plodding on and then my eyes are riveted on a sight I shall never see again. It is the 32nd Division at its best. I see rows upon rows of British soldiers lying dead, dying or wounded in no man's land. Here and there I see an officer urging his followers. Occasionally I can see the hands thrown up and then a body flops to the ground. The bursting shells and smoke make visibility poor, but I see enough to convince me Thiepval village is still held, for it is now 8 a.m. and by 7.45 a.m. it should have fallen to allow of our passage forward on its flank… Again I looked southward from a different angle and perceive heaped up masses of British corpses suspended on the German wire in front of the Thiepval stronghold, while live men rush forward in orderly procession to swell the weight of numbers in the spiders web.[22]

Extra German machine-guns were in operation within the ruins of Thiepval and after they had repulsed the advances of the 32nd Division, they then redirected their awesome firepower to bear upon the Ulstermen. The divisional history records, 'The 11th Inniskillings and 14th Rifles, as they emerged from the wood, were literally mown down, and "No Man's Land" became a ghastly spectacle of dead and wounded'.[23]

With so many of his soldiers falling as they charged towards Schwaben Redoubt. Major-General Nugent at 36th Division HQ was reluctant to order 107th Brigade into the fray. Crozier wrote:

> Nugent was 'rigid' in so far as the obedience to his orders was concerned, although I see *he* asked Morland definitely if 107th Brigade should go forward *as the situation had altered*. Bernard predicted this situation and he and I made arrangements to meet probably altered situation. But Nugent had laid down that no C.O. should go further than his battle HQ. Had this been acted upon I do not think 9th or 10th Rifles would ever have deployed or got going.'[24]

Lieutenant-Colonel Herbert Bernard, who disobeyed the order not to participate in the attack, was killed by a trench mortar shell as he left Battalion HQ in Thiepval Wood. The adjutant of the 10th Royal Irish Rifles informed Lieutenant-Colonel Crozier of the death of Bernard. 'The colonel and half his men walked into the barrage of death during the advance. All died behind him as he resolutely faced the edge of the wood in an impossible effort to walk through a wall of raining iron and lead.'[25]

Crozier, who also disobeyed the order to remain at his Battalion HQ during the attack, justified his insubordinate behaviour.

> Observing what was happening to Bernard 500 yards away on my right, I was driven to alter, by word of mouth above the din, the mode of my deployment. The deployment was accomplished – but, of course, had I been obeying orders in my dugout no such alteration could have been ordered. The four company commanders would have thought and acted in four different ways. The alteration meant that instead of losing everybody in the first five minutes, we lost only about fifty men.[26]

Private Davy Starrett was at Crozier's side when they witnessed the slaughter of the advancing waves. 'On past Gordon Castle – into inferno of screaming shells and machine-gun bullets. Crouching, we slowly moved across No Man's Land. The colonel stood giving last orders to his company commanders, and I beside him, Bullets cutting up the ground at his feet he watched the advance through his glasses. Then he went off the deep end, and I danced everywhere at his rear. Something had gone wrong. When the fumes lifted we saw what it was – a couple of battalions wiped out. Masses of dead and dying instead of ranks moving steadily forward.'[27]

Crozier was anxious to salvage the situation and attempt to lead his own battalion and the remnants of the 10th Royal Irish Rifles against the Schwaben Redoubt. Private Davy Starrett followed Crozier as he dashed into the sunken lane to organise an advance:

> Between the bursts Crozier doubled to the sunken road, his batman making a bad second in the race. 'The Tenth Rifles are wiped out!' he shouted. We reached our men. They had taken what cover the place afforded. Bernard had been killed. Crozier rallied what was left of the Tenth. 'Sound the advance!' he yelled. 'Sound: Damn you: Sound the advance!' The bugler's lips were dry. He had been wounded. His lungs were gone. A second later he fell dead at the colonel's feet.[28]

Crozier was in a position to take command of Bernard's battalion, but some of the survivors were reluctant to go forward after seeing their comrades mown down by machine-gun fire. Crozier recalled:

> Withdrawing my revolver from its holster, I called upon Bernard's remnants to follow me to the front line, a distance of about 300 yards. Not a man moved. I told them I would shoot … had I been unarmed, and told those men to go forward, I very much doubt if any notice would have been taken of me. The disobeying of an order, at the wise suggestion of Colonel Bernard, who paid for it with his life, surmounted

> by the fact that his men got there, enabled the Ulster Division to claim justly that it had carried all before it and fulfilled its task.[29]

Crozier's presence on the battlefield leading his battalion motivated his men, but it was because he disobeyed an order to remain at his battalion HQ that his valiant efforts were not rewarded with a Victoria Cross. Starrett witnessed his attempts to rally the men. 'Crozier was signalling the men on. He walked into bursts, he fell into holes, his clothing was torn by bullets, but he himself was all right. Moving about as if on the parade ground he again and again rallied his men. He was, I believe, recommended for the V.C. for that day's fighting, and should have got it, for without him not a man would have passed the Schwaben Redoubt, let alone reach the final objective.'[30]

Crozier was in fact recommended for the DSO for the courage he showed at Thiepval, but because he disobeyed Major-General Nugent's order not to leave battalion HQ, and because a fellow commanding officer who also acted against those orders was killed as a consequence, Nugent overruled the recommendation to award Crozier. Crozier wrote:

> Yet Nugent, owing to Bernard's death, kicked up such a fuss about 'disobedience' that I, for personal post battle safety, draw a very heavy veil over events. I saw the original recommendation for a DSO for me, made out by Withycombe scratched across in red ink by Nugent (a great friend of mine) 'Rank disobedience of orders, should be court martialled!!!'[31]

Before advancing Crozier ordered Private Davy Starrett to return to battalion HQ in the front line trench and bring forward ammunition supplies. So many casualties were lying in the trenches and on the parapets that it was difficult to reach his destination, as Starrett recalled:

> Trenches and tops were blocked with the dead, but on days like that there's no sympathy in your heart. Over them you go. I found the signals, and the office staff, McKinney and Bowers were always exactly in the right place. The dugout was being used as a clearing station. Twas hard passing without a word men in terrible pain – men you knew. The fierce shelling continued, and the place seemed taped to an inch. Stretcher bearers fell every minute. Most that reached Doncaster Dumo were wounded carrying wounded.[32]

Major George Gaffiken of the 9th Royal Irish Rifles took off his Orange sash, held it above his head for his men to see and shouted the war cry of 'Come on boys! No surrender!' which motivated his men to cross No Man's Land. On breaking out there was a charge against the third German line, where unfortunately casualties were sustained from friendly fire from their own guns.

Some men disobeyed the order to walk at a steady pace and charged the German machine-guns with bayonets, which were being fired, from the parapets of their front-line trenches. As a result of this deviation from orders the 36th Division reached and actually surpassed its objectives. The 13th Royal Irish Rifles went over the top at 07:30 hours. On capturing the German first line by 07:35 hours they then charged onto the second line known as the Crucifix line, though still taking casualties. Many casualties were caused by British guns, since they had ignored the order to approach the enemy at a steady pace under a lifting barrage. By 07:48 hours the first and second German lines had been captured. Some German machine-gun crews had become casualties during the bombardment and those remaining could only fire for a short while before they were overrun.

As they continued to the third line, German machine-gun fire from Thiepval became more intense and from the third line itself. Despite the heavy fire a small party led by 2nd Lieutenant McKinley of the 9th Inniskilling Fusiliers reached the third line objective called Lisnaskea. They held this position for an hour resisting superior German numbers anxious to reclaim the lost ground. The 8th Royal Irish Rifles and 9th Royal Irish Fusiliers of the 107th Brigade, following the 109th Brigade, moved through the three German lines and charged towards the German fourth line they were bolstered by the sight of enemy soldiers holding their hands up to surrender in the third German line. Some German troops were slow to surface from their deep dugouts and were firing in small pockets from the first line and shooting the advancing Ulstermen in the back as they advanced to the second and third German Lines.

At 09:00 hours, reinforcements from the 14th Royal Irish Rifles, the 11th Inniskilling Fusiliers and later elements from the 107th Brigade joined the 9th and 10th Inniskilling Fusiliers in their consolidation of the trenches around the Crucifix, which was at the southern apex of the Schwaben Redoubt. Many Officers and NCOs were killed before they reached the Sunken Road. Major William Sewell of the 11th Inniskilling Fusiliers had led his men to the first line of trenches but was mortally wounded in the charge to the second line. Lieutenant Henry Gallaugher was the only unwounded officer from the battalion who survived to lead his men to the German second line, which he immediately secured by organising a barricade across the communication trench. Gallaugher returned to the first line to bring men and stores to this newly-captured position. As he was doing this C.S.M. Bullock led remnants of the 11th Inniskilling Fusiliers onto the third line, dealing with several parties of German soldiers on the way. Gallaugher, back in the front German line first, established a barricade across communication trenches leading to the Crucifix then he ordered the construction of a fire step on the reverse side of the trench to establish a firing position, before returning to the A Line to bring forward reinforcements and equipment. Some sections of the A Line had not being secured and he found that German soldiers occupying the position. Gallaugher then organised a bomb assault upon the position. On securing A Line he organised a barricade to block the right flank of the trench and left a Lance Corporal and six men to defend the trench. Gallaugher gathered all the men he could and took them to the Crucifix to defend the position with the other battalions for the remainder of the day.

The 15th Royal Irish Rifles were briefly held up in the first German trench by a party of German soldiers missed during the consolidation, or who had worked its way along a communication trench from St Pierre Divion. This party was soon overwhelmed, its complement either killed or captured. As the 11th Inniskilling Fusiliers followed behind the 9th and 10th Inniskilling Fusiliers to the Crucifix Line they too suffered casualties from machine-gun fire from Thiepval village. The capture of three lines of enemy trenches and some parts of the fourth line was the limit of their success. They had made the most significant gains north of the Albert–Bapaume Road, but Ulster Division could not consolidate and hold the ground that it had captured.

A large number of German prisoners had been secured and were being processed within Thiepval Wood. The 109th Brigade reported:

> Prisoners were now coming in very fast, and in a reply to a message sent to our Brigade Prisoners collecting Post which was situated in a very large open dugout just east of Brigade HQrs, we received word at 9.30 am that 200 prisoners had passed through, and that their shoulder straps denoted men of three different regiments.[33]

Although the Ulstermen were taking casualties, they still held positions in and around the Schwaben Redoubt and this would cause great anxiety to German commanders. News that Schwaben Redoubt was under British control reached General Leutnant von Stein at XIV Reserve Corps Headquarters at 09:45 hours. He immediately ordered that the bastion be recaptured at all costs. Von Stein was not prepared to wait for the arrival for the 2nd Battalion, 8th Bavarian RIR which was on its way, but immediately sent 1st Battalion, 8th Bavarian RIR, commanded by Major Prager, to recapture the redoubt.

This unit was accompanied by 1st machine-gun Company belonging to the 119th RIR and 89th Sharp Shooter Troop. At 10:00 hours these units left from the German second line and approached the Ulster-occupied Schwaben Redoubt from the northeast behind St Pierre Divion. Major Beyerköhler commanding 3rd Battalion, 8th Bavarian RIR, was ordered to assault the redoubt from Hill 153. These German units took time in receiving these orders and did not reach Schwaben Redoubt until the afternoon.

In the meantime, surviving parties from 26th Reserve Division continued close-quarters fighting in the Schwaben Redoubt and connecting trenches. Since the 32nd Division on their right was not successful in capturing its objectives German machine-gunners continued to exploit the 9th Inniskilling Fusilier's exposed flank. Attempts were made by the Germans to cut off this party, which forced it to withdraw to the Crucifix line, where the 11th Inniskilling Fusilier was consolidating its positions. Here they fought off successive counter-attacks and suffered continuous machine-gun fire from Thiepval for most of the day. Heavy casualties were endured and as the day progressed supplies of water, ammunition and bombs rapidly diminished. Many men were isolated from their units and fought off German attacks independently. Lance Corporal Lyttle ('D' Company) with a Lewis Gun and a Vickers inflicting many casualties upon the enemy until the ammunition was consumed. Lyttle destroyed both the guns then made his way back to positions held along the Crucifix. Those who were wounded in the initial attack and who had crawled back to the safety of their own trenches could not be transferred back to dressing stations, because of heavy German selling which continued throughout the day. Many men sought refuge in the Sunken Road in No Man's Land.

When it was certain that the second German line was secured, efforts were made to move supplies of ammunition and bombs across No Man's Land to the first German trench. Sergeant Gillen from the 10th Inniskilling Fusiliers led a party from brigade dump using the handcarts, but because many of the trees in Thiepval Wood had fallen down across communication trenches during the German bombardment they had to dispense with the handcarts and move the munitions to the front by hand carriers. Gillen got some supplies to a point in the German first line but was wounded during a second journey. A significant amount was transferred across No Man's Land on the 10th Inniskilling Fusiliers sector, but none got across on the 9th Inniskilling Fusiliers front. The right flank was in direct line of fire from machine-guns firing in Thiepval.

This machine-gun fire made it virtually impossible to get stores across No Man's Land and replenish units holding the Crucifix. It also prevented messengers getting across which meant that little communication took place between advanced party and battalion commanders. Ninety minutes after the assault began 109th Brigade War Diary reported:

> Very few reports were now coming in from the front line on account of the fact that machine-guns in Thiepval were enfilading No Man's Land, and men who attempted to get back with information were killed. About 9.00 am Lt. Colonel Ricardo, D.S.O., commanding 9th R. Innis. Fus. that Major Peacocks, who had got as far as one of our saps, reported that there was enfilade machine-gun sweeping the Sunken

> Road running from Thiepval to Hamel making it impassable. This was confirmed by one of their signallers who had just come in wounded.[34]

But the momentum of the attack was lost as the War Diary records, 'Owing to the intensity of the fire only 1 runner got through, with the message "Cannot advance without support"'.[35] A platoon from the supporting 12th Royal Irish Rifles was sent to assist, but was completely wiped out. By 10:00 hours most of the officers were casualties and it was left to the surviving NCOs to organise counter-attacks later that day.

As the morning progressed some parties of the brigade were fighting desperate battles for control of the third German line but communication between these advanced parties and brigade HQ in Thiepval Wood were lost because of the machine-gun fire coming from Thiepval. By 10:25 hours No Man's Land remained impassable and 109th Brigade was also coming under fire from German machine-guns at Beaumont Hamel.

The intermingled units of the 109th Brigade holding out in the German first and second lines were on their own. Beaumont Hamel and Thiepval were still under German control which meant that both their flanks were exposed and vulnerable. The parties who had entered the fourth German line were unable to consolidate the position and gradually had to relinquish control back to the enemy as they withdrew to the third line around 11:00 hours. A further message was received at the 109th Brigade Headquarters at 11:25 hours from 2nd Lieutenant Wheeler requesting reinforcements and confirming that the 11th, 13th and 15th Royal Irish Rifles were mixed.

By noon many of the officers had been either killed or wounded and the attack was being co-ordinated by a small number of remaining officers and NCOs. From noon onwards there was considerable confusion especially as the battalions were intermingled. At one point around midday, units from the 10th Inniskillings and the 107th Brigade advanced and captured the fourth line of German trenches, holding these positions for a short time until they were bombarded by German artillery, which caused many casualties, forcing a withdrawal to the third line.

German artillery also bombarded the 14th Royal Irish Rifles occupying the second line at noon. With the Ulstermen isolated in the German lines unable to move forward or backwards, the 109th Brigade HQ was asked by Division HQ by wire at 12:10 hours to detail pioneers to dig a communication trench across No Man's Land from Thiepval Wood to the German first trench line to re-establish contact and to send reinforcements and supplies. Division replied at 12:15 hours confirming that pioneers from 16th Royal Irish Rifles (Pioneers) had been sent up to the front line to dig this communication trench.

Despite the German machine-gun fire sweeping No Man's Land, fragmentary pieces of information were filtering through to the British line. A message was received at 12:46 hours from 11th Inniskilling Fusiliers holding the second German line, requesting ammunition, and that it had no men it could to send back to help do this.

At 13:00 hours a message timed at 10:40 hours was received from 10th Inniskilling Fusiliers holding the German line confirming that it was consolidating this line, but that there was a barrage on the fourth line. The message also confirmed that Captains Robertson and Proctor had become casualties. During the two hours and twenty minutes it took to receive this message some elements from this battalion had gone further and had reached the fourth German line. Private Lindsay Hall belonged to a party from the 10th Inniskilling Fusiliers who broke through into the German fourth line:

> When we reached our objective we were under enfilade fire from both sides and in front. The position was on the slope of a small hill but we got there at a cost. We gathered all our bombs together for the Germans were coming on our left flank along the trench and we bombed them out. I was in a shell hole at the side of the trench, and when I was hit another piece of shrapnel struck the back of my equipment, cut the belt, and glanced off the entrenching tool. That saved me. I tied up my leg with the field bandage when a lot of wounded were going back and joined them, and after a trying time we got back to our lines.[36]

The 109th Brigade's headquarters felt helpless as it knew that its soldiers were left in German lines unsupported and exposed to machine-gun fire from Thiepval. There was some hope from 36th Division HQ when a message was received at 15:50 hours stating that a barrage of German first and second lines at Thiepval would commence at 15:30 hours until 16:00 hours and then the 49th Division would launch an attack upon Thiepval. This message was received, of course, as the barrage was taking place.

Major Peacock from 9th Inniskilling Fusiliers Battalion HQ led a party across No Man's Land and reached the Crucifix. Since 10:00 hours Peacock had organised the remnants of the 9th, 10th and 11th Inniskillings into holding the second line of German trenches throughout the day. Around 15:00 hours they came under heavy HE and shrapnel fire, at the same time being attacked by German infantry. Despite exhausting their own supply of bombs they held on to that section of trench throughout the afternoon and during the evening. The 9th Inniskilling Battalion War Diary described Major Peacock's conduct:

> He fought hand to hand with the enemy, repeatedly leading his men to repulse their bombing attacks. He was the life and soul of the defence and it was entirely due to his example of coolness and gallantry that our unsupported troops held on to this position for the length of time they did.[37]

At 15:55 hours a message was received from Peacock, as recorded in the 109th Brigade War Diary: 'He stated that he believed No.1 Company 9th R. Innis. Fus was at Lisnaskea, but he was unable to get to them owing to the machine-guns at Thiepval. About 300 11th R. Innis. Fus were at Omagh. He had some of the 9th with him and was holding just N.E. of Crucifix. All Brigades were mixed up and could do no more attacking, but were holding all the ground from B.15 to Crucifix.'[38]

The next message at 16:55 hours from Peacock was more urgent: 'Please do all you can to send up Vickers machine-gun Belts, Bombs and S.A.A. I think we shall hold on only men are rather done up.'[39] As their supplies of ammunition became exhausted Peacock's men resorted to hand-to-hand combat. Private T.G. Gibson saw three Germans manning a machine-gun from their parapet and killed all three with the butt of his rifle. Lieutenant R.W. McKinley led a small band of men to the 9th Inniskilling's final objective, Lisnaskea, where they held on for as long as they could, before being overwhelmed by a determined German assault. McKinley withdrew his men to the Crucifix line and assisted Major Peacock in the defence of the second line. Despite depleted stores of ammunition they held on till 22:00 hours, when the intermingled ranks of the 9th, 10th & 11th Royal Inniskilling Fusiliers were forced to withdraw to the first captured lines then back to the British start line. By midnight they were back at their start point and had not managed to consolidate and hold their gains taken that day.

Meanwhile, Major Beyerköhler, commanding 3rd Battalion, 8th Bavarian RIR west of Stuff Redoubt, was ordered to launch a counter-attack upon Schwaben Redoubt at 15:00 hours. At 14:40 hours, the 2nd Recruit Company received orders from Major Prager to attack the same target. Beyerköhler saw Prager's men go forward with fixed bayonets through gaps in the wire and thought that was the signal for his battalion to attack as well, earlier than he was ordered to do so. They were met by machine-gun and mortar fire from the Ulsters in the Hansa Line, northeast of the Schwaben Redoubt. The 2nd Recruit Company had twenty-three men killed and 100 wounded as they advanced, but despite these casualties they penetrated the defences of the Hansa Line, taking twenty prisoners and two Lewis Guns. At the same time a party of four men led by Unteroffizier Stumpf assaulted a shell hole defended by twenty British soldiers. Most of the British defenders were killed, with three officers and two men being captured.

A party of Bavarians belonging to Major Beyerköhler's 3rd Company 8th Bavarian RIR assaulted another British-occupied strong point, clearing the junction of Stuff Trench with Loch Weg along the Thiepval–Grandcourt Road. It was here that Captain Clarence Craig MP for South Antrim, of the 11th Royal Irish Rifles was wounded and captured together with a sergeant. Craig was a well-built Irishman and was so heavy that his captors had to

Above: A still from the film *The Battle of the Somme*. Whilst this image is part of a sequence purportedly showing British soldiers moving forward on 1 July 1916, it is now generally considered to have been staged for the camera, possibly at a Trench Mortar School well behind the lines, and filmed prior to the start of the battle. (Courtesy of Pen & Sword Books)

Right: The Commander-in-Chief of the British Expeditionary Force during the Battle of the Somme – Field Marshal Douglas Haig. (Historic Military Press)

Above: Gunners of a siege battery of the Royal Garrison Artillery loading a 9.2-inch howitzer. The Ordnance BL 9.2-inch howitzer was the principal counter-battery equipment of British forces in France in the First World War. (Historic Military Press)

Left: Lance Bombardier Henry Rundle (standing) and Corporal Harrington. (Courtesy Diana Smith, grand-daughter of Henry Rundle)

Above: The day before the offensive. Though this picture purports to show soldiers of 'C' Company, 1st Battalion Lancashire Fusiliers fixing their bayonets prior to the attack on Beaumont Hamel on 1 July 1916, research by the historians Alastair Fraser, Andrew Robertshaw and Steve Roberts (detailed in their book *Ghosts on the Somme*) suggests that it was in fact taken the day before. One 'C' Company veteran, Corporal George Ashby, recalls that the men were given "a tot of rum and a packet of cigarettes" in return for posing for the photographer. Company Sergeant-Major Edward Nelson can be seen front right – he would be wounded in opening day of the Battle of the Somme. (Courtesy of Pen & Sword Books)

Right: The calm before the storm. Troops pictured waiting, some still asleep, in a support trench shortly before zero hour near Beaumont Hamel. (Historic Military Press)

Above: The explosion of the mine under Hawthorn Ridge Redoubt – a moment that Lieutenant Geoffrey Malins captured on film. The film footage that Malins took of this eruption lasted about twenty-three seconds with a slight pause as the cloud of dust and debris expanded. (Historic Military Press)

Below: Two minutes before zero hour on 1 July 1916, the largest mine exploded on the Western Front in the First World War, the Lochnagar mine, tore through the German lines south-east of La Boisselle. This is the resulting crater pictured as it is today. The buildings of the rebuilt village of La Boisselle can be seen in the background. (Historic Military Press)

Above: At about 06.30 hours on 1 July 1916, these men from the 1st Battalion Lancashire Fusiliers were filmed by Lieutenant Geoffrey Malins waiting to go 'over the top' in the sunken lane in front of Beaumont Hamel. (Critical Past)

Below: Men of the 103rd (Tyneside Irish) Brigade, part of the 34th Division, pictured advancing from the Tara-Usna Line to attack the village of La Boisselle on the morning of 1 July 1916. The 34th Division suffered heavier losses than any other British division that day. (Historic Military Press)

Above: British troops, believed to be the 2nd Battalion, Gordon Highlanders, crossing No Man's Land near Mametz on 1 July 1916. The trench lines are clearly marked by the white chalk excavated during their construction. (Historic Military Press)

Below: Gommecourt Park viewed from the rear wall of Gommecourt British Cemetery No.2. A clear view of the 56th Division's line of advance on 1 July can be seen from this spot. (Author)

Above:German Trenches at Serre 1916. (Author)

Right: An artist's impression of Drummer Walter Ritchie's Victoria Cross action at Redan Ridge. Serving in the Seaforth Highlanders, Ritchie, notes the original caption, 'stood on the parapet of an enemy trench and, under heavy machine-gun fire and bomb attacks, repeatedly sounded the "Charge", thereby rallying many men of various units who, having lost their leaders, were wavering and beginning to retire. Throughout the day Drummer Ritchie carried messages over fire-swept ground and showed the greatest devotion to duty.' (Historic Military Press)

Left: This is the sunken lane in front of Beaumont Hamel from where 'B' and 'D' companies, 1st Lancashire Fusiliers began their advance across No Man's Lands on 1 July – and where Lieutenant Malins filmed them as they waited for Zero Hour. (Author)

Below: A view of the Newfoundland Memorial Park at Beaumont Hamel. The 51st (Highland) Division Memorial can be seen on the left, the Y-Ravine Cemetery on the right. The German lines ran between these two positions. The battalions belonging to the 29th Division were mown down on this hallowed ground on 1 July 1916. (Author)

Right: The 'Danger Tree' the Newfoundland Memorial Park at Beaumont Hamel. This solitary tree stands in what was No Man's Land on 1 July – a grove of plum trees once stood here. This spot was known to the soldiers who crossed this ground as the 'Danger Tree' because this was where they became most vulnerable to enemy fire. (Author)

Below: Y-Ravine at Beaumont Hamel provided a secure position for the German occupants of their forward line. Dugouts were constructed into the banks of the ravine, providing effective shelter from the British bombardment before the assault on 1 July 1916. (Author)

Above: A depiction of the British barrage falling upon the Schwaben Redoubt and German retaliatory bombardment upon Thiepval Wood before the assault on 1 July. (Author)

Below: An illustration showing British troops storming the Schwaben Redoubt on the Somme. First assaulted on 1 July 1916, a permanent Allied lodgment in this German defensive position was not achieved until the attacks of 26 to 28 September 1916. The Schwaben Redoubt consisted of a mass of gun emplacements, trenches and tunnels, a warren of defensive works which helped anchor the German line on the Somme until late 1916. (Author)

Below: A drawing depicting the moment that Private William 'Billy' McFadzean, 14th Battalion Royal Irish Rifles, was killed on 1 July 1916. His Victoria Cross is displayed at The Royal Ulster Rifles Museum, Belfast, Northern Ireland. (Author)

Below: Looking along Thiepval Road which leads from Thiepval in the direction of Beaumont Hamel. Thiepval Wood, which is on the left of the picture, was the starting position of the 36th (Ulster) Division which advanced eastwards up the slope towards Schwaben Redoubt (where the trees are seen on the horizon right of picture). Ulster Tower can be seen in the centre. The road that crosses this battlefield was once called Bloody Road. It was here on 1 July 1916 that soldiers from 36th (Ulster) Division were shot down by machine-gun fire from both the Schwaben Redoubt and Thiepval itself, forcing them to withdraw to this position, sheltering by the bank in this picture. (Author)

Above: A German trench amongst the ruins of Thiepval in 1916. (Author)

Above: Soldiers of 'A' Company, 11th Battalion, the Cheshire Regiment, occupy a captured German trench at Ovillers-la-Boisselle on the Somme during July 1916. (National Archives of the Netherlands)

Below: This image shows the ground over which the men of the 7th Queens (Royal West Surrey Regiment) and 8th East Surrey Regiment advanced on 1 July 1916. (Author)

Above: An example of the work of the RFC during the Battle of the Somme. This aerial photograph of Mouquet Farm and its defences (north at top) was taken in June 1916 (North at top). The battered farmhouse buildings are the rectangular area at lower centre. The trench across the top right is the western end of 'Fabeck Graben', whilst the trench at top left, heading NNW, is 'Zollern Redoubt'. (Historic Military Press)

Below: Images such as this were vital to the men fighting on the ground. It was taken not from an aircraft, but a balloon of the RFC's No.1 Kite Balloon Squadron on 1 July 1916. (Historic Military Press)

Above: German prisoners captured during the opening day of the Battle of the Somme. (Author)

Below: Another still from the footage shot by Lieutenant Geoffrey Malins that was used in the film *The Battle of the Somme*. The image is part of a sequence introduced by a caption stating 'British Tommies rescuing a comrade under shell fire'. In spite of considerable research, the identity of the rescuer remains unconfirmed. The casualty, who died some thirty minutes after reaching the British line, appears to be wearing the shoulder flash of 29th Division. He is the same person pictured by Ernest Brooks being carried over the New Beaumont Road. (Critical Past)

Above: For eighty-two years, Private George James Nugent, serving with the 22nd (Service) Battalion (3rd Tyneside Scottish) Northumberland Fusiliers, was one of the many missing from the fighting on 1 July 1916. Then, in 1998, his remains were found at this spot near the edge of Lochnagar crater, final confirmation came when DNA tests were undertaken with his descendents. George Nugent was subsequently reburied with full military honours in Ovillers Military Cemetery on 1 July 2000. (Historic Military Press)

Below: One of the most iconic of the Commonwealth War Graves Commission's cemeteries or memorials linked to the fighting of 1916 is undoubtedly the Thiepval Memorial, the Memorial to the Missing of the Somme. Towering over the landscape of the Somme battlefield, it bears the names of more than 72,000 officers and men of the United Kingdom and South African forces who died in the Somme sector before 20 March 1918 and have no known grave. However, over 90% of those commemorated died between July and November 1916. (Courtesy of Aero Photo Studio)

evacuate him to the rear on a wheelbarrow. The Bavarian attack, however, was beginning to falter as casualties mounted.

General der Infanterie Freiherr von Soden at 26th Division HQ was becoming concerned that the Schwaben Redoubt was still under enemy control. He instructed Oberleutenant Grabinger, adjutant of 3rd Battalion, 8th Bavarian RIR to detail two parties to assault and capture the Schwaben Redoubt and relieve the remnants of 99th RIR. Major Beyerköhler's, 3rd Battalion, 8th Bavarian RIR, was engaged in a struggle for a British-held trench at 16:00 hours. According to Hauptmann Herbert von Wurmb, a British soldier appeared near Beyerköhler and a member of his staff called out to him, 'Herr Major, A British soldier'. Beyerköhle ordered 'Pass me a rifle'. As he took aim with the rifle the British soldier shot and killed the Major. Beyerköhler's batmen took the bloodstained rifle that and avenged his commander's death by killing the British soldier.[40] Wurmb took command of the battalion and the 89th machine-gun Sharp Shooter Troop. By 18:00 hours Wurmb's party had been reduced to approximately forty soldiers. Nevertheless Wurmb continued to press forward his attack westwards south of the Thiepval–Grandcourt Road in order to gain entry into Schwaben Redoubt, but the Germans were stopped by a machine-gun defending the eastern face of the strongpoint.[41]

Meanwhile Offizierstellvertreter Lunau was ordered to assess how far the enemy had penetrated into German lines. He led a patrol from the 14th Company, 99th RIR, southwest of Wurmb's line of advance. Lunau's party encountered another British machine-gun position and, acting on his own initiative, led an assault upon it. After overwhelming this position he advanced from the south-east of Schwaben Redoubt and cleared the Ulstermen from Loch Weg, Martinspfad, and entered the accommodation trench of Schwaben Redoubt. It was here that Lunau subdued three Ulster machine-guns including the position that was causing Wurmb's party problems.[42]

At the same time – around 18:00 hours – Leutnant Arnold, 1st Recruit Company, 180th Infantry Regiment, belonging to Prager's group launched a counter-attack upon Ulstermen holding sections of the Hansa Line in an effort to enter Schwaben Redoubt from the northeast. The Ulstermen could see the first wave led by Arnold appear from over the heights southeast of Grandcourt and immediately opened fire with machine-guns and rifles. British artillery soon fired upon the ridge held by Arnold's men, causing further casualties. Arnold was wounded and the remnants were unable to continue their attack upon the Hansa Line.

By 18:30 hours the Ulstermen were entrenched in the Schwaben Redoubt, holding the eastern perimeter along the Thiepval-Grandcourt Road and the Hansa line to the northeast. Their position was vulnerable, because they were unable to receive reinforcements and supplies of ammunition, because they could not get into the Schwaben Redoubt due to

German shelf fire and machine-gun fire sweeping No Man's Land. 11th Royal Irish Rifles holding the second line resisted a German counter-attack from St Pierre Divion at 8.30 pm however repeated bombing attacks later that evening wore down their resistance and they withdrew to the first German line. The 13th Royal Irish Rifles had consolidated another section of the captured second line trench. They repelled an enemy counter-attack at 8.30 pm from Thiepval direction, but could only hold the position until 9.45 pm when German artillery began to shell the Schwaben Redoubt.

Captain McCallam was still holding out in the German third line with a small party from the 8th Royal Irish Rifles. After fighting off repeated German bombing attacks he withdrew his men to the second line. Finding no one in the second line he took them further back to the first line where he set up a defensive position with a party belonging to 107th Brigade machine-gun Company led by Lieutenant Stewart.

Fortunately the German soldiers were just as exhausted which meant that the 36th Division could withdraw unmolested. Hauptmann Wurmb's small party continue to fight its way into Schwaben Redoubt as German shells supported them. This party tried to deceive the Ulstermen with their battle cries giving the false impression that it was a larger force. Eventually Wurmb's party established contact with Lunau's party and they bombed their way into the fortress.

At 22:05 hours another German bomb attack was launched on the left flank. The attack was driven off at some points. The 8th Royal Irish Rifles stock had been reduced to twelve bombs and they used these effectively to repel this assault for a time until they could hold on no longer. The 36th Division War Diary noted:

> The exhaustion of some of our men at this point was so acute that they were scarcely able to move. The two officers who had taken command of our remaining troops and who had by their gallantry and devotion prolonged their resistance, Major Peacock of the 9th R. Innis. Fus. and Captain Montgomery of the 9th R. Ir. Rif., made a last attempt to rally the men. They succeeded in holding together a certain number, but these men were in a state of fatigue which rendered them unfit to continue resistance. They were in imminent danger of being surrounded in the dark. They therefore fell back to our lines. Captain Montgomery reported to his commanding officer at 10.30 pm in a state of collapse.[43]

German forces hastily established defensive positions in the Schwaben Redoubt, which was littered with many dead soldiers from both sides. They also captured 100 men. Wurmb who had played a major role in the capture of this position was awarded the Knight's Cross of the Royal Bavarian Military.

By midnight the remnants of the 36th Division were back at the start point, their own front-line trenches. After the battle the dead, the dying and the wounded were still lying out in No Man's Land. Crozier recalled, 'the wounded try to crawl back to our line. Some are hit again in doing so, but the majority lie out all day, sun-baked, parched, uncared for, often delirious and at any rate in great pain.'[44]

Those who could not move waited for assistance. For some it was too late, dying from loss of too much blood. Others died from their wounds, shock, or lack of water. Efforts to rescue wounded casualties were made during the following three nights. Jack Christie was a stretcher bearer at Thiepval. He recalled:

> Our people were cut down and at the end of the day they all had to come back to where they started except the thousands that had been lost. I had a picture of it all because we were carrying stretchers for hours up and down for many hours without stopping, to a first aid post and then they got taken on down to ambulances which took them to the first Field Dressing Station then to the Casualty Clearing Station, then to the coast and on to England. We were doing it in our sleep only half conscious of what was going on. It was a terrible shambles.[45]

From 19:00 hours till midnight on the 1 July the adjutant of the 9th Royal Irish Fusiliers Lieutenant Geoffrey St George Shillington Cather went out into No Man's Land under German heavy fire to search for wounded men and bring them to safety. By midnight he had rescued three. On the following day he made further attempts to rescue wounded men lying in No Man's Land. He brought in a further man, and he gave comfort and water to those he had left behind, promising that they would be later rescued. At 10:30 hours while taking water to another man 'in full view of the enemy and under direct machine-gun fire' he was killed. For this self-sacrificing act of bravery he was awarded the Victoria Cross. Likewise, during the evening of 1 July, Private Robert Quigg ventured out into No Man's Land to search for his platoon commander Sir Harry Macnaghten, who was reported missing. After several attempts he failed to find him but instead he brought seven other men to safety. For this action he too was awarded the Victoria Cross.

During the night of 1/2 July the men of the Royal Inniskillings that were lying exposed in No Man's Land were subjected to persistent enemy shelling. Captain Moore and Lt. H. Gallaugher (9th Battalion) led twenty volunteers into No Man's Land to search for wounded. They rescued twenty-eight of their wounded colleagues and brought them to the safety of their lines.

The 36th Division succeeded in surpassing their objectives and took approximately 600 prisoners, but unfortunately as a result of not being able to consolidate their gains, they were forced to their own front line by the day's end. Their brave deeds were a credit to their country, but the division had 2,000 men killed, 2,700 wounded and 165 taken prisoner. At battalion level, the 9th Royal Inniskilling Fusiliers lost sixteen officers and 461 other ranks – half their original unit strength. The 10th Royal Inniskilling Fusiliers entered the battle with twenty-two officers and 742 other ranks and returned with ten officers and 336 other ranks. The 11th Royal Inniskilling Fusiliers suffered lost fifteen officers and 577 other ranks. The casualties of the 9th Royal Irish Fusiliers were nine officers and 235 men.

An undisclosed staff officer was reported in the *Londonderry Sentinel* to have written the following letter to Lieutenant F.H. Crawford.

> The Division has been through an ordeal by fire, gas and poison. It has behaved marvellously, and has got through all the German lines ... Our gallant fellows marched into a narrow valley of death shouting 'No Surrender' and 'Remember the Boyne." I wish I had been born an Ulsterman, but I am proud to have been associated with these wonderful men – the most gallant in the world. I fully realise how you feel where you are ... Many a family in Ulster will have lost a son a father out here. I do not believe men ever passed to another world in so glorious a light. After the day before yesterday I hope I may be allowed for the rest of my life to maintain my association with the Ulster provinces.[46]

On 1 July 1916 the 36th (Ulster) Division were the only division, north of the Albert–Bapaume Road to penetrate deep into the German lines and make significant gains despite the fact that the opening day of the battle of the Somme being regarded as a total disaster. By charging across No Man's Land within ninety minutes they had overwhelmed and captured five lines of enemy trenches, including the fortress of the Schwaben Redoubt. They had succeeded in achieving their objectives; however their success was not sustained as a result of the failure of the right and left flanks in failing to achieve their objectives and the failure to bring up ammunition and reinforcements. By the evening of 1 July, 36th (Ulster) Division had been driven back to their starting line.

Chapter 14

Thiepval

The 32nd Division, commanded by Major-General W.H. Rycroft, was ordered to capture Thiepval, which was positioned on a high spur, and comprised sixty-five houses, a church and a chateau forming part of the German defensive line. Thiepval Chateau faced west and its large cellars were utilised as living accommodation for the German 99th RIR holding this sector and could accommodate an estimated 1,500 soldiers underground. Thiepval Farm further behind the line was used as a grenade store.[1]

The British bombardment prior to the 1 July had reduced the village to a pile of rubble but beneath the ruins of the village existed a network of underground cellars, linked together by a warren of tunnels. The bricks and rubble that lay above ground protected these chambers from British shells. The ruins had been transformed into a formidable fortress and well-concealed German machine-gun crews nestled within the fallen masonry, were untouched by the bombardment. There was also a concentration of machine-guns within the ruins of Thiepval Chateau that could provide sweeping fire along the western slope of Thiepval ridge, the line of advance that the attackers would have to take.

The 96th Brigade, commanded by Brigadier-General C. Yatman DSO, was given the task of capturing Thiepval on a 1,000-yard front. The brigade comprised the 15th Lancashire Fusiliers (1st Salford Pals), 16th Lancashire Fusiliers (2nd Salford Pals), 16th Northumberland Fusiliers (Newcastle Commercials) and 2nd Royal Inniskilling Fusiliers.

Once Thiepval had been secured they were to link up with the 97th Brigade on their right flank and advance eastwards across Nab Valley. Thiepval was a tough nut to crack because these battalions were expected to leave their trenches east of Thiepval Wood and advance up the steep western face of Thiepval ridge where they would be vulnerable to German fire directly ahead of them from the fortified position at Thiepval, from their left flank at Schwaben Redoubt and on their right flank from Leipzig Redoubt.

Without sanction from his superiors, Yatman had covertly arranged a trip in an RFC reconnaissance aeroplane to see the battlefield from the air:

> Air reconnaissance carried out by a number of officers from my brigade and myself previously was very useful. I changed the site chosen for my battle headquarters after a long look at things from the air. Absurd as it may now seem I sneaked up without asking permission as probably it would not have been granted and I failed to persuade adjoining brigadiers to go up.[2]

The battalions of the 96th Brigade assembled below Thiepval Ridge during the night of 30 June /1 July. German guns tried to find the range of the roads leading to the communication trenches in the valley below Thiepval and inflicted many casualties amongst soldiers from the 16th Northumberland Fusiliers once they entered the trench system.

The 1st Salford Pals on the left flank assembled in the front line from where Union Street on the 36th (Ulster) Division's sector met the front line to Maison Grise Sap. The 16th Northumberland Fusiliers were next, on the Fusiliers' right from Maison Grise Sap to Skinner Street. The 2nd Salford Pals were holding trenches in the reserve line close to Johnstone's Post where they were split in half and were ordered to follow the leading battalions in support. The attack was supported by Vickers guns and Stokes mortars. 2nd Inniskilling Fusiliers was held in reserve south of Caterpillar Wood. Providing the 96th Brigade succeeded in capturing Thiepval, the 14th Brigade, commanded by Brigadier-General C.W. Compton, would move forward to capture the second German trench line. They were held in dugouts behind the steep slopes south of Authuille.

As the British artillery bombardment intensified the 96th Brigade came under shell, sniper and machine-gun fire from Thiepval Ridge. The 16th Northumberland Fusiliers arrived at their assembly trenches at 02:30 hours and stood in the crowded trenches for five hours waiting for Zero Hour. As the men waited, enemy fire descended upon them causing many casualties.

The 2nd Saford Pals, commanded by Lieutenant-Colonel C.M. Abercombie, suffered casualties as they were passing through communication trenches in Thiepval Wood as German shells brought down several trees. An anonymous member of the battalion wrote:

> At last we entered the communication trench leading to the assembly trench. This lay through a thick wood, and enemy shell fire had brought down heavy trees, which partially blocked the way and made progress slow. We were almost at our rendezvous when a crash in front warned those behind that things were not well. The party halted and the order was rapidly passed down: 'Officer wanted in front at once.' An officer

> started off crushing past the crouching men, and then whizz crash, a whizz bang fired enfilade along the trench fell amongst us, followed by others. We were trapped in a deep trench and the enemy had a perfect range. Sergt. W. Taylor one of the best of the NCO's and nicest of fellows, only 12 hours back from leave, and four men, were killed immediately. Others were wounded, including 2nd Lieutenant Powell, platoon commander of No.8.[3]

The 2nd Salford Pals were unable to pass through the communication trench to reach their designated assembly position. As the shells descended upon their line and further trees crashed upon them Captain Thomas Tweed, decided that it was necessary that 'B' Company should leave the communication trench and go above ground through the shattered wood in order to get to their starting positions. 'Then the Captain's order: "Leave the trench, over the top, boys!" and a wild scramble out of the trench, through the foliage and fallen trees, and finally the reaching of our place of assembly in the early hours of July 1.'[4]

Leutnant der Reserve F.L. Cassel of the German 99th RIR was aware that the British were coming thirty minutes prior to Zero Hour and he was met by a most gruesome sight as he darted up the stairs from his dugout into the German trench:

> On July 1st, at 7 a.m. exactly 10 days after the start of the barrage, the shout of our sentry: they are a coming! Tore me out of the apathy. Helmet, belt, rifle and up the steps. On the steps something white and bloody, in the trench, a headless body. The sentry had lost his life by a last grenade, before the fire was directed to the rear, and had paid for his vigilance with his life. It had torn his head and his brain was lying on the steps.[5]

Once the alarm was sounded the German soldiers left their underground shelters and manned their parapets. Many were only partially clothed, such was the urgency to prepare themselves for the coming infantry assault. Some wore their soft caps, called Feldmütze, for comfort instead of the Pickelhaube, which was uncomfortable to wear and the spike provided an ideal target for a British rifleman or sniper. With the weather being hot some German soldiers dispensed with their heavy tunics in favour of shirtsleeves, A German observer reported that the 96th Brigade advanced in 'solid lines without gaps, in faultless order, led by its officers carrying little flags and sticks. Wave after wave was shot down by well aimed fire … a wall of dead British was piled up on the front.'[6]

On the 96th Brigade's right flank a football was kicked into No Man's Land and the men of the Newcastle Commericals, commanded by Lieutenant-Colonel Ritson, were expected to follow it. 'A' and 'B' Companies had been waiting in No Man's Land since 04:00 hours and were

100 yards behind the British artillery barrage. At 07:30 hours these companies advanced forward. As soon as they left their trenches they were immediately attacked by German snipers and machine-gunners as they left their trenches. Some German riflemen holding the high ground at Thiepval were seen taunting these soldiers from Newcastle as they stood or knelt upon their parapets beckoning them to 'Come on' as they picked them off with accurate fire.[7]

'A' Company was led by Captain Arthur Young and was one of the Newcastle Commericals' leading companies together with 'B' Company commanded by Captain Percy Graham. Graham was among the first killed as he went over the top. Newcastle Commericals' War Diary reported:

> When the barrage lifted 'A' and 'B' Coys moved forward in waves and were instantly fired upon by enemy's M.G. and snipers. The enemy stood upon their parapet and waved to our men to come on and picked them off with rifle fire. The enemy's fire was so intense that the advance was checked and the waves, or what was left of them, were forced to lie down.[8]

Due to the intensity of the enemy fire that was pouring into their direction they suffered many casualties and those that survived became pinned down in No Man's Land not far from the British front line. These German machine-guns, had held off the British advance and when the British barrage lifted German rifleman had sufficient time to ascend from the shelter of the underground cellars and dugouts and fire upon the British infantry trying to advance from the bottom of the slope.

Private Ernest Watson, of 'A' Company, Newcastle Commericals, saw the first waves go over the top:

> At 7.30 word came along for No.1 Platoon to go over. It was a grand sight to see them go over, but at the same time sad. Not one of them hesitated. At intervals of a few minutes 2 and 3 Platoons followed, and then word came along for No.4 Platoon to go over. I had just turned to get hold of my rifle which was standing against the parados when something burst above me and a piece of shrapnel hit me in the mouth, and dust and earth nearly blinding me for the time being. I later found the roof of my mouth was also slightly damaged. Jimmy [His brother-in-law] dragged me to a dug-out close at hand and then he went over the top. There were already two other wounded in this dug out, one hit in the arm and the other in the leg – both shrapnel wounds.[9]

Within minutes the advance of the 16th Northumberland Fusiliers had been stopped. These men were advancing eastwards up a slope, the sun shining in their eyes, dazzling their vision. Unable to overcome the awesome fire power being fired downwards in their direction, the only option for them was to take shelter in the shell holes. The survivors of 'A' and 'B' companies lay on the ground or dived into nearby craters for shelter from the overwhelming enemy fire. 'C' and 'D' companies were brought forward together with Newcastle Commericals Battalion HQ to the front line. 'C' Company, followed 'A' and 'B' companies and suffered the same fate. The first platoon could not get beyond the parapet and was immediately mown down. The remainder were stopped from going over the top and ordered to man the fire steps in the British line where they could provide covering rifle fire aiming for the German soldiers that were clearly visible firing from the top of their parapet. The 96th Brigade War Diary reported that soldiers of the Newcastle Commericals 'hung on in No Man's Land under heavy shell fire in addition to M.G. fire by getting into shell holes and improvising cover with entrenching tools they remained there suffering from shell and machine-gun fire. The few that remained there were withdrawn at dusk.'[10] Captain Arthur Young returned to the British trench in order to report that the advance of 'A' Company had faltered. He then returned to the remnants of his company in No Man's Land to rally them but he too was killed.

Leutnant Cassel could easily see the British waves as they moved towards them:

> We rushed to the ramparts, there they come, the khaki-yellows, they are not more than 20 metres in front of our trench. They advance fully equipped slowly to march across our bodies into open country. But no boys, we are still alive, the moles come out of their holes. machine-gun fire tear holes in their rows. They discover our presence, throw themselves on the ground, in front of our trenches, once these were trenches, now a mass of craters, welcomed by hand grenades and gun fire, and have now to sell their lives themselves.[11]

The German machine-gun fire was so overwhelming that the Newcastle Commericals could not get beyond the British wire. Private Ernest Watson, lying in a dugout in the first British line, heard a report from a runner who had been sent back to confirm that the battalion had suffered many casualties:

> One of our runners brought in word that the boys had not been able to get much further than our own barbed wire. The Germans had been quite prepared and expecting us, for no sooner had our first wave appeared over the parapet than they mounted their own parapet and absolutely mowed our men down.[12]

At 07:40 hours the 16th Northumberland Fusiliers Battalion HQ was moved forward to the front-line trench. Realising the severity of the situation and seeing that the attack of the three companies that had already advanced had faltered in No Man's Land, 'D' Company was ordered to go forward. The first platoon from this reserve company was decimated and the remainder was ordered to secure the British line. German high explosive shells and shrapnel soon poured upon the British trench occupied by the Newcastle Commericals. The heavy casualties sustained meant they had little strength to defend the British front line, let alone capture Thiepval. During the first ten minutes of the attack, the Newcastle Commericals lost approximately 400 men. Of the twenty-one officers who entered the battle six were killed and thirteen were wounded.[13]

Adjacent to the 16th Northumberland Fusiliers position, on their left flank the 1st Salford Pals advanced. Captain Alfred Lee-Wood led 'A' Company on the right, while Lieutenant Clarence Wright led 'C' Company on the left but was shot as he went over the parapet at Hammerhead Sap. Private A. Walsh was with Wright:

> I was one of a small section that jumped over the parapet along with Lieutenant Wright who was in command of C Company. We had advanced to about 100 yards of the enemy's first line under a heavy shower of shrapnel and machine-gun fire when I saw Lieutenant Wright drop on his knees with a bullet through the forehead, the last word I heard him say before he dropped that being 'Go on boys!'[14]

The 1st Salford Pals suffered heavily and many were held up by the barbed wire in No Man's Land, as Sergeant Major A.K. Brown testified:

> The wires were unbroken opposite our position and none of my party even reached the German trenches. Only two men from C Company arrived back unwounded. I myself was wounded just as we reached the wires. None of my officers reached that point and I had to take the remains of C and D companies on. I was afterwards partly buried for two days and two nights only getting back to our own lines about 3.00 am on Monday morning.[15]

Private Walsh continued across despite the enemy fire, but he also reported that he could not get beyond the German wire:

> We carried on until we got to Fritz's barbed wire, which had not been touched by our artillery in this particular part, so that all we could do was to fling our bombs into the trench. At the finish I got hit on the left thigh and left elbow, so I dropped into a shell hole ten yards from the German barbed wire.[16]

Walsh remained in that shell hole for four days, unconscious for two of them. As he fell wounded into the hole other elements from his battalion continued to find breaches in the wire. Private Harold Beard was tasked with erecting barbed-wire defences as part of the process of consolidating the first German line trenches, but he was wounded before reaching that objective:

> We did get a warm reception from the Prussians. When we advanced on their first line of trenches coal-boxes, whiz-bangs and aerial torpedoes were sent amongst us. There was also a terrific hail of bullets from their machine-guns. I was one of a wiring party. When the German first lines of defence had been captured we had to put up barbed wire in front of the new ground, but I was wounded long before I got to that objective. I had some narrow escapes from death. Once I was lifted two feet in the air by a high explosive shell. Then I lay on the ground stunned and smothered with slush for at least 15 minutes, but otherwise I was none the worse for the experience. When I got my wound the shock of it put me in a 'talking position with the earth,' and I lay there some considerable time.[17]

It was a dangerous enterprise for the wounded Beard in trying to get back to the safety of his own lines with machine-gun bullets whizzing around him and getting entangled in barbed-wire:

> I then got up and set off back for our first line of trenches. This was a slow process for all the time the enemy's fire was murderous. However, I stumbled on through it all, and just before I arrived at our first trench I got entangled in a lot of barbed wire. I was a long time extricating myself from – altogether it took me over two hours before I arrived at our dressing stations.[18]

Communication was maintained between 15th Battalion HQ and their parties in No Man's Land by a chain of runners, but this lasted for only fifteen minutes. By 07:45 hours German machine-gunners at Thiepval and on the flanks had shot down some of these messengers and the line of communication was broken.

Private J. Roberts later reported that he could see from Hammerhead Sap around 200 men of the 1st Salford Pals fighting in Thiepval. Reinforcements were unable to reach them and they became isolated and cut off. Mopping-up parties tried to cross No Man's Land but were stopped by the German bullets. 1st Salford Pals War Diary recorded that:

> After a leading line or two had got into the front line trench, leaving mopping up parties, the Germans reoccupied the front line, coming in from our right and overcame the mopping up parties. It is probable that one or two of our mopping up parties had been wiped out on the way

> over. When the later lines followed on it was found that the German front line was occupied. It was known that the earlier lines had penetrated. All attempts by the later lines resulted in the instant killing or wounding of the party moving forward. It was obvious by 9.00 am that further efforts in this direction were only useless waste of life.[19]

Those men from the 1st Salford Pals who got into the German lines and were unable to head back to the British line, later moved north where they established contact with elements from the 36th (Ulster) Division south of the Schwaben Redoubt. By 09:00 hours the CO, the adjutant and the machine-gun officer together with between thirty and forty men were all that remained of the 1st Salford Pals in the British trench at the bottom of the slope that led up to Thiepval.

As the leading battalions were being slaughtered in No Man's Land, the 2nd Salford Pals, commanded by Lieutenant-Colonel C. M. Abercombie, was assembled in support trenches. At 08:20 hours Abercombie, was ordered into the front line trenches to secure the sector and support the Newcastle Commericals. It was supposed to take up material obtained from the Royal Engineers for the purpose of consolidating the ground they intended to capture on the heights of Thiepval. This was now superfluous, its role would not be of consolidation, they were to abandon the equipment and try to succeed where the Newcastle Commericals had failed in its assault upon Thiepval.

Two companies, 'A' and 'C', were sent up to support the beleaguered Newcastle Commericals. 2nd Lieutenant Charles Marriot led his men into the British front line which had been obliterated by German high explosive shells. He was met by a scene of appalling carnage:

> After all these years I still clearly see certain gruesome sights, burnt into the memory, as we struggled up to the front line. Hands, feet and shin bones were protruding from the raw earth stinking of high explosive. A smallish soldier sitting in a shell hole, elbows on knees, a sandbag over his shoulders: I lifted it to see if he were alive, and he had no head. Further on, a corporal lying doubled up and bloody; just in case anything could be done for him I bent down to raise him a little, and his head was only attached by a bit of skin. The front trench was so blown up and gouged by H.E. that only bits of it remained, and it took sometime to deploy out along it.[20]

It was evident that many of the Newcastle Commericals had fallen as soon as they left their trench, either by machine-gun, rifle or shell fire:

> I was told that a badly wounded officer was lying in it [referring to the British front line trench] about twenty yards along. I got to him over a

> great blown-in block, bullets whizzing like wasps, and found a tall young Northumberland Fusilier Lieutenant, shot through both knees, one wrist and one shoulder: the moment he got up onto the parapet the impact of the bullets had flung him backwards into the trench. I tried to bandage him up a bit (his courage was so superb I think I was weeping as I did so, which wasn't really much help) and sent an urgent call for stretcher bearers. But there was too much to see, I had to leave him, and never knew what happened to him. We found others like him shot straight back off the parapet, one, a sergeant, drilled through the forehead, his brains spread like hair over the back of his neck.[21]

Exposed to the pitiful sights of the wounded and dead men from the Newcastle Commericals, Lieutenant Marriot was expected to lead his platoon into another suicidal assault upon Thiepval, only too aware that he and his men would certainly suffer the same fate. To his great relief they were held back and the attack abandoned:

> At last we were ready, and I was bracing myself for the hideous decision to go over the top when we were saved from further massacre in the nick of time by a sweating runner with a message from the C.O. to stay put. My God, what a moment! No Man's Land, covered with bodies, was a sight I can never forget: the whole of the 16th Northumberland Fusiliers seemed to be lying out there.[22]

Captain Thomas Tweed, commanding 'B' Company, also assumed command of 'D' Company and as they advanced upon Thiepval they sustained casualties as soon as their ascended their parapet. Tweed had raised the Eccles Company during August 1914 and he knew the men very well, for many had worked for him in civilian life. Now he was about to lead them into a torrent of shellfire and machine-guns. One of his soldiers recalled:

> Then the captain's voice 'Fix bayonets', a few pregnant minutes, and a further order, '5 and 6 over the top, and good luck, boys'. Like hounds from a leash the men sprang over the parapet, followed by 7 and 8 platoons. A few minutes later 'B' Co. were leading the battalion to the attack. Then it was the machine-gun opened up again. Some, like young Grindley, were killed getting over, and rolled back into the trench, but through the perfect storm of lead the company went on.[23]

Those who were not hit persevered across the open ground. When they reached a road the enemy fire intensified and they had to move forward by darting from each shell hole. Some of this fire came from concealed machine-gun positions. Such was the ferocity of the German fire that the remnants of the 2nd Salford Pals became trapped in shell holes in No Man's

Land. Captain Tweed brought forward two platoons who had lost all their officers and NCOs and encouraged those in the shell holes to advance. As they followed Tweed many more casualties fell. They only got as far as fifty yards before the few that remained sought refuge behind a high bank in No Man's Land. They stayed there for two hours. 'Ignoring the rain of death that whistled about them, they kept running from shell hole to shell hole, on and on. Pals of years' association dropped, others fell riddled with bullets, never to rise again.'[24]

Sergeant E. Wild was among Tweed's party who sheltered behind this high bank and he confirmed that most of the casualties incurred fell within 100 yards from the British trench. It happened very quickly. Wild felt exposed behind this bank and sought refuge in a nearby shell hole which was sheltering four other wounded British soldiers. They were joined by a sole Prussian Guardsman, who surrendered. One of the wounded British soldiers raised his head above the shell hole to see if there were more German soldiers, but he was shot in the head by a machine-gun bullet. It was perilous for anyone to raise their head from this shell hole. When German shells fell upon No Man's Land, Wild made a dash for the British line where he walked into a dressing station. His eyes were blackened due to shrapnel and a fragment of bullet was embedded above his eye, but he survived to return to the UK.

Corporal Stephen Sharples, 2nd Salford Pals, together with Privates Howell and Jones tried to go forward beyond the bank, but as they crawled along they were killed by machine-gun fire. Captain Tweed was anxious that his company could not advance and made an attempt to get a message back to battalion headquarters to inform them of the dire situation. As the messenger left the cover of the bank towards the British line he was immediately cut down. Tweed tried to write another message, but his notebook was hit by a bullet and was hurled out of his hands. Eventually a message got through and Tweed obtained the required orders to initiate a withdrawal.

Unable to make any headway in securing Thiepval ridge between the village and Leipzig Redoubt Major-General Rycroft ordered the 32nd Division to launch a further assault at 09:10 hours. This decision could have been based on vague reports that divisional troops were seen in Thiepval. The 32nd Division War Diary reported:

> At 9.10 am the leading troops of the 15th Lancs. Fus. were seen East of Thiepval by an observing officer in Coniston Street. On hearing this I urged Brig. Gen Yatman to push supports round the northern edge of Thiepval pointing out that as a Brigade of 49th Division was available to support either 32nd or 36th (Ulster) Divisions, he could use his reserve battalion, 2nd Innis. Fus. For this purpose.[25]

The 2nd Royal Inniskilling Fusiliers and two companies from the 2nd Salford Pals had been held in reserve at Johnstone's Post, on the eastern corner of Thiepval Wood. Unable to launch a direct onslaught upon Thiepval, Rycroft recognised that a different policy was necessary in order to capture Thiepval. The revised plan would mean getting these reserves into Leipzig Redoubt where they could launch an attack along the German first line and enter the fortress of Thiepval from the southwest and reinforce surviving elements from the 1st Salford Pals who were allegedly holding out within the village. At 09:10 hours they were ordered to launch an attack upon Thiepval to support the 1st Salford Pals and to link up with the 36th (Ulster) Division which had gained a foothold in the Schwaben Redoubt.

By 10:00 hours the 2nd Royal Inniskilling Fusiliers had reached Johnstone's Post to assemble for a further attempt on Thiepval. Such was the situation, instead of attacking the enemy the men spent their time recovering the wounded from No Man's Land. Major-General Rycroft received a further report of sightings of British troops in Thiepval from artillery observers at 10:55 hours. Forty-five minutes later he informed Corps that another attempt was being undertaken to establish contact with parties of the 1st Salford Pals who were seen near to Thiepval and suggested that the Corps reserve be deployed to support this. Brigadier-General Yatman reported to Rycroft at 11:57 hours that the two companies from the 2nd Salford Pals which had failed to reinforce the 1st Salford Pals earlier that morning had been strengthened by three companies from 2nd Royal Inniskillings with Stokes mortars and that they were ready to launch another effort against Thiepval. This attack was delivered at 13:50 hours. It failed.

At 15:00 hours two companies of the 2nd Royal Inniskilling Fusiliers, two companies from the 2nd Salford Pals and two companies from 1/6th West Yorkshire Regiment from the 49th Division were ordered to launch another attack north of Thiepval in an effort to link up with elements from the 36th Division on the left flank who were thought to be holding onto positions in the Schwaben Redoubt and close the gap in the line.

'C' and 'D' companies of the 1/6th West Yorkshire Regiment led this effort to capture Thiepval when the British artillery barrage lifted at 16:00 hours. Uncut wire and intense German machine-gun fire from Thiepval made it impossible to achieve their goal and they were forced to withdraw to their trenches. The 1/5th West Yorkshire Regiment arrived when the 1/6th West Yorkshire Regiment had failed. It was ordered to attack Thiepval but the order was countermanded with the battalion being instructed instead to occupy the British front. The battalion later received the order to occupy Schwaben Redoubt. Lieutenant-Colonel Wood commanding the battalion led a small party that reached the redoubt while the remainder of the battalion was moved to Johnstone's Post.

Throughout the day, as the wounded lay exposed in No Man's Land they were targeted by German machine-gunners. Hundreds of men lay dead along the slope that descended from Thiepval. An attempt to search and recover wounded cost the lives of ten men from Captain Tweed's company. No wounded were recovered. The 2nd Salford Pals lost nine officers and 217 men, the Newcastle Commericals eighteen officers and 362 men. The 1st Salford Pals entered the battle with twenty-four officers and approximately 600 men; by evening only three officers and 150 men remained. The Salford community would learn within days that it had lost many fathers, sons and brothers.[26]

Captain Tweed wrote on 4 July, 'I am the only officer in the company who came out unhurt by some wonderful miracle. The men fought and died with a wonderful bravery which brings tears to my eyes at the recollection.'[27]

In another letter dated 10 July, Tweed wrote of the effect of the annihilation of B Company:

> I feel that the wiping out of the Eccles Company must have given Eccles a great shock. I think that a good proportion of the wounded will recover, and there are still nearly 100 men of the original company left here. There are the men temporarily in hospital, those away on special duties and those attached to battalion headquarters, transport, signallers etc. who did not fight and have much less risk. Of the 140 officers, NCOs and men I led over the top – to be crumpled up by German machine-guns, I am the only officer left, and when the company was relieved that night it was composed of myself, three lance corporals and 19 men. These have been augmented by stragglers and reinforcements and we are ready to fight again. I feel the loss of my NCOs and men very keenly, and it is only by a great effort that I can throw off great depression. Proud of them as I was when the company was in its prime, earning an unrivalled reputation for smartness and courage my heart is prouder than ever when I recall the way they fought and died. We had bad luck. Our brigade was given a task which turned out to be one of the toughest places in the attack, bristling with machine-guns and as B Company led the battalion to the attack they suffered thrice as heavily as other companies. The enemy's line crumpled up before the chief advance, but here and there hidden forts suddenly sprung into being and it was our bad luck to meet one of these.[28]

Lancashire Fusilier Harold Beard was one of the lucky ones who survived the slaughter at Thiepval. 'It was worse than hell itself. Such a row I have never heard before in my life, and it was terrible to see the men lying in the field of battle. I can tell you anybody who came out of that scrap on that first morning was lucky.'[29]

The attack failed because the German machine-gun positions and underground barracks at Thiepval had not been destroyed by the British artillery. It was a strongly fortified position on the ridge which made it impregnable. It was a remarkable feat for those small parties to enter Thiepval, but they were unable to capture the village because fresh supplies of ammunition and reinforcements could not reach them. One major failing was the inaccurate reports received at 32nd Division HQ. Incorrect reports that the 32nd Division had occupied Thiepval meant that British artillery stopped targeting the village and allowed the Germans to sweep their machine-guns across No Man's Land. Command on the Thiepval sector had failed to assist the 32nd Division with artillery plus the 49th Division was not deployed in full to support the attack against Thiepval, though whether sending more battalions against Thiepval would have made much difference is debatable.

In 1930, fourteen years later, Brigadier-General C. Yatman reflected upon the failure to capture Thiepval on 1 July 1916:

> Prolonged study of this position before and since the attack of 1 July only confirms my opinion that in the circumstances only bullet proof soldiers could have taken it. Whether holding attack until you could put the pincers on would have been a better plan is not for me to say. A direct attack having been ordered I do not see even now with added knowledge that it could have been done differently.[30]

Chapter 15

Leipzig Salient

Major-General W.H. Rycroft's 32nd Division was also designated the objective of securing Leipzig Salient which was positioned across Thiepval Spur overlooking Authuille Wood and was a strongly fortified position. The Granatloch was a fortress at the western tip of the Leipzig Salient defended by machine-guns that were able to sweep No Man's Land to the south and west. The distance between the British and German lines varied from 200 yards to 600 yards and the attacking force would have to ascend a steep slope in order to assail this difficult objective. A trench line named Hindenburg Stellung skirted the eastern perimeter of the Granatloch. Further beyond was a second trench line called Lemberg Stellung and further behind the Hohenzollern Stellung which incorporated another German strongpoint called Wundt Werk (known as Wonder Work to the British).

The defenders of Granatloch, from 3rd Company, 99th RIR, were protected by flanking fire from Thiepval in the north, the Wundt Werk in the rear, the Nordwerk and Ovillers-la-Boisselle due southeast. There was also a quarry in the centre of Leipzig Redoubt where these German troops could take shelter from artillery fire. The German 180th Infantry Regiment, of the 26th Reserve Division defended the sector south of Leipzig Redoubt through Ovillers-la-Boisselle to the Albert–Bapaume Road. This unit had spent the past year strengthening the defences of Serre until June 1916 when it was transferred to this sector.

The 97th Brigade, commanded by Brigadier-General J.B. Jardine DSO was ordered to advance from its lines between Nab Valley and Thiepval Wood on an 800 yard front. This brigade comprising 16th and 17th Highland Light Infantry supported by the 2nd King's Own (Yorkshire Light Infantry) was to lead a direct assault upon Leipzig Redoubt. They were supported by four Vickers guns and a Stokes mortar battery. It was planned that once they had overwhelmed the German defence of the Leipzig Salient, the 11th (Service) Battalion Border Regiment (Lonsdale), which was waiting in Authille Wood opposite the south face of Thiepval Ridge, was to consolidate the German trenches that had been overrun and advance to a position north of Mouquet Farm. This was a highly ambitious plan.

Lieutenant Bogue and two men of the 16th (Service) Battalion (2nd Glasgow) Highland Light Infantry (known as the Glasgow Boys Brigade) patrolled No Man's Land to assess the condition of the German wire and confirmed that it had been broken down with numerous gaps. Bogue concluded to his superiors that he anticipated no problems in getting through the wire.

'A' and 'B' companies of the 17th Highland Light Infantry (Glasgow Commercials) commanded by Lieutenant-Colonel D. Morton carried the right flank and crawled from their starting line at 07:23 hours into No Man's Land. During those seven minutes prior to Zero Hour under the cover of the artillery and Stokes mortar barrage they crept to within forty yards of the German front line. German sentries were unaware that the Highlanders were close by, so when the British bombardment lifted and the whistles blew they leapt to their feet and charged forward, overrunning the front German trench system without encountering resistance, rapidly entering Leipzig Redoubt and the approaches to Hindenburg Stellung. Many of the Germans in the Leipzig Redoubt from 3rd Company, 99th RIR were sheltering in their dugouts in the chalk quarry which was at the epicentre of the garrison. It was here where they put up a strong defence of the position and engaged in bitter hand-to-hand fighting, but they were taken by surprise and swiftly annihilated. By 8.00 am Leipzig Redoubt was taken and in British hands.

Lance Corporal J.L. Jack of the 17th Highland Light Infantry recalled how they swarmed over the German first trench:

> At 7.23 am we climbed out of the trenches and started to move across No Man's Land. We were loaded down with full kit, and in addition, a spade or shovel or pick. We soon reached the enemy front line and the work of the moppers-up began, shouting down dug outs to the Hun to come up. The battalion had started kicking footballs in front of them. Alas almost every Company Officer had been killed. D Company had been almost annihilated.[1]

Lieutenant B. Meadows recalled in his diary how the shiny steel helmets made each man of the 17th Highland Light Infantry an easy target for German snipers and machine-gunners as the sun glistened upon them:

> We wore steel helmets, at that time they were without sandbag coverings, and in strong sunlight reflected almost as brilliantly as polished steel. I noticed on the 1 July, looking back from the advanced line to the German original front line, how the helmets of our reserves holding that line shone up and made their wearers clear targets.[2]

Once in Leipzig Redoubt, the Highlanders continued their advance a further 150 yards across an exposed slope towards the German line behind the redoubt known as the Hindenburg Stellung. By 08:30 hours every company officer was a casualty and their advance was curtailed when they became dangerously exposed to a German machine-gun positioned in the Wundt Werk which forced them to return to Leipzig Redoubt. Some became trapped and could not go forward to the Hindenburg Stellung nor could they return to the Leipzig Redoubt. A desperate close-range bombing battle took place.

Lance Corporal Jack had a lucky escape when a bullet penetrated his steel helmet, but he survived to engage with the enemy at close quarters:

> Advancing the Hun second trench I felt as if a mule had kicked me above the right eye and lying prone I endeavoured to think what had happened. It turned out later that I had been sniped, the bullet piercing the steel helmet (first time we had worn them) in the front and circling inside three times had cut a furrow above my right eye. The other eye had swollen up and having crawled into the trench, almost blinded, I was ordered by Captain Laird, my platoon commander, to proceed to the rear. Looking back I saw him hit by a shell adding another officer casualty to the growing number. Proceeding round a traverse to the Hun communication trench I spied a large Hun officer at the top of the dugout. I immediately gave him three of the best as I peered at him. He did not move and getting closer I found that he had been the victim of one of his own shells, part of the casing having fixed his head to the entrance to the dugout and he had not been missed by the moppers up, as I first thought.[3]

With most of their officers killed or wounded it was left to the NCOs to assume command and continue the defence of the positions they had captured within Leipzig Redoubt. 'B' and 'D' companies on the 17th Highland Infantry's left flank were virtually annihilated by machine-gun fire from Thiepval Chateau. Sergeants Macgregor and Watts organised parties to try and hold together those that remained.

Sergeant James Turnbull was another NCO who took charge of the situation in the absence of officers. It was his courageous efforts and sound leadership that prevented the battalion from being cut off by a German counter-attack. He continued to battle on for sixteen hours that day until he was killed by a sniper. He was awarded the Victoria Cross.

By 09:00 hours the 17th Highland Light Infantry had lost twenty-two officers and 400 men. The assault upon Leipzig Redoubt lost momentum, but the remnants still held on to their perilous position. Observers from 161st Brigade Royal Field Artillery could see the predicament of these Highlanders and reported to their commander Lieutenant-Colonel A.S.

Cotton that they could not keep up with their barrage. Cotton relayed the plight of the 17th Highland Light Infantry to Brigadier-General Jardine. He also confirmed that the barrage was going forward, but no infantry could be seen following it. Jardine therefore ordered Cotton to focus two batteries upon the German rear line, Hohenzollern Stellung and the Wundt Werk, to enable the Highland Light Infantry to get back to the Leipzig Salient.

At 09:00 hours the right flank of the 2nd King's Own (Yorkshire Light Infantry) – 'A' Company with half of 'C' and 'D' companies – had crossed No Man's Land to help the survivors of the 17th HLI to consolidate Leipzig Redoubt. Lieutenant-Colonel Morton commanding the 17th HLI realised that due to the 8th Division's failure to secure its objectives on their right flank at Ovillers-la-Boisselle it was necessary to retain the 2nd King's Own to defend the front line trench because of its exposed right flank. Captain Butler, commanding 'A' Company, joined the 17th HLI in the German support line opposite Hindenburg Stellung which was held in great strength by the Germans. Two machine-guns were also brought forward and were operating from the Leipzig Redoubt together with three Stokes mortars which had been brought forward by the 2nd King's Own. Two of these Stokes mortars were knocked out by German fire but the remaining one continued to shell German positions from inside the quarry of the Leipzig Redoubt. Bombing parties made an attempt to advance to the north and east along Hindenburg and Lemburg Stellung, but they were fought off by determined German defenders.

The 11th Border Regiment was brought forward from the 97th Brigade Reserve at 08:30 hours. It advanced from Authuille Wood according to orders and wrongly believed that the attack was succeeding. The dust and smoke concealed the fact that many casualties had been sustained and that German forces were offering a stubborn resistance. Before they left Authuille Wood in an attempt to reach the British front line trench, Corporal Fred Francis remembered his CO Lieutenant-Colonel Percy Machell DSO giving his final instructions:

> The Colonel gave the command 'When I blow the whistle dash out of the wood and try and get into your own front line trench'. So he blew the whistle and I remember distinctly he patted us all on the back and said 'good luck, but if things don't go well, I will come out and lead you myself". As they did not go well because of German machine-guns focused on us. He came out, got shot through the head and was killed immediately.[4]

After leaving Authuille Wood the men were exposed to German machine-gun fire from the Nordwerk to the southeast incurring heavy casualties with many of the dead and wounded lying behind the British first trench and in front in No Man's Land. Waves of men from the 11th Border

Regiment fell quickly as German machine-guns tore into their ranks. Twenty-eight officers and approximately 800 men left Authuille Wood towards Leipzig Redoubt. Within minutes they had lost twenty-five officers and 500 men. It was a terrible disaster for many did not get beyond the British front trench. The remnants from the 11th Border Regiment reached Leipzig Redoubt and joined the 17th HLI with the task of consolidating the captured German strongpoint.

The 16th Highland Light Infantry advanced on the 97th Brigade's left flank. It was ordered, along with two companies of the 2nd King's Own, to capture the Wundt Werk which provided supporting fire for the Leipzig Redoubt. As the battalion was assembling in No Man's Land prior to Zero Hour they were vulnerable to enemy fire from the German frontline trench and the ruins of the nearby Thiepval Chateau. 'A' Company was spotted by German machine-gunners and shot down in No Man's Land before the attack had begun. German artillery shelled the front line and communication trenches occupied by the 16th HLI with HE, shrapnel and mortars. They were unable to reach the German front line trench, as the battalion War Diary recorded:

> The enemy opened heavy machine-gun and rifle fire as soon as our men jumped over the parapet, and manned their parados with bombers, with two yards interval. Our Platoons advanced in waves of extended order, and were simply mown down by the machine-gun Fire, and very heavy casualties resulted.[5]

Some of these men on the right flank deviated southeast, entered the German trench system and linked up with their counterparts from the 17th HLI holding Leipzig Redoubt. The second wave on the left flank got as far as the German wire but could not get through. The British bombardment had failed to make any breaches in the wire on this sector, and many men became entangled. Survivors held up on the left flank sought whatever cover they could in nearby shell holes from where they could fire upon the enemy when they appeared. One Lewis Gunner fired twenty-four magazines of ammunition until he expended his supplies. He was the only survivor from his crew and crawled back to British lines under the cover of darkness with the gun. The 16th HLI lost nineteen officers and 492 men including Lieutenant-Colonel D. Laidlaw who was among the wounded. The remainder of the 16th HLI became marooned in No Man's Land as they were pinned down by German machine-guns and snipers. During the course of the day these survivors crawled back to Authuille Wood where they regrouped.

The 1st Dorsetshire Regiment left Black Horse Shelters at 07:10 hours and entered the south-western corner of Authuille Wood. As it headed towards the British front line along the Dumbarton Track it was held up by the 11th Border Regiment whose rear columns had not cleared the wood. They were unaware that the operation was not going to plan and they tried to advance across No Man's Land, not knowing that German machine-gun emplacements had not been neutralised. When the first wave left the cover of the wood it attracted hostile fire causing heavy casualties before it reached the British front line. Unperturbed, the men advanced forward in rushes, but Lieutenant-Colonel J.V. Shute commanding the battalion was wounded. The battalion was so badly hit that only six officers and sixty men from the first two companies reached Leipzig Redoubt. They had been mown down by the same machine-guns that had decimated the ranks of the 11th Border Regiment. Some of this fire was coming from the Nordwerk on their right flank. The remaining two companies from the 1st Dorsets were held back in Authuille Wood.

The 19th Lancashire Fusiliers was next to go forward, following the 1st Dorsets. Its commander, Lieutenant-Colonel J.M.A. Graham asked the Brigade trench mortars to produce a veil of smoke to cover their advance and brought forward two Lewis Guns and two Vickers guns to provide covering fire. Protected by the cloud of smoke from the 4in mortars, three companies – 'A', 'B' and 'C' –went forward towards Leipzig Redoubt. Their objective was to capture the third and fourth German lines north of Mouquet Farm. Unfazed by the smoke screen German machine-gun crews fired through the smoke and into their ranks.

Six officers and sixty men of the 1st Dorsetshire Regiment together with two officers and forty men from the 19th Lancashire Fusiliers succeeded in reaching Leipzig Redoubt. Captain G. Hibbert, commanding 'A' Company, 19th Lancashire Fusiliers reported in a letter to Lieutenant-Colonel Graham:

> The Bosch harassed our advance from the gap in the wood [Authuille] at which point I have often wondered how you and Moxey escaped being shot, as you were so exposed to the fire from our right front. My 3rd platoon had gone over from the gap and I should have taken the last platoon, but as no one appeared to be moving in front, you called me forward to ask what my men were doing. I was given orders to go out and get them on the move, but each line I came to were either dead or wounded. Making short rushes to dodge the tantalising machine-guns, I eventually reached the German front line by myself, as I had not found anyone fit to go forward, Mr Middleton having been hit in the arm just outside the gap, Mr Chambers 15 or 20 yards further on, shot through the head and in our own front line trench I found Mr Hewitt, badly wounded in the leg by machine-gun fire. This accounted for my three platoon commanders not being on the move.
>
> When I reached the Bosche trench, I collected what men I could find (about 40). The Borders were engaged further ahead, but as we made in that direction under the impression that we had got all the front line,

> two wounded officers (I think of the Borders) came along the trench from the right and told me the German's were moving along the trench in that direction and throwing bombs. I did not see the officers again, as they were making for a dressing station.
>
> We found the trench blocked. Who blocked it I don't know, but I think it was done by the Borders. We captured a Bosch Major and nine or ten men, whom I sent back to our lines. The bombs we had started with were used by now also some we found lying about, but with such a small party I thought it would be more effective and safer to hold the blocked trench by rifle fire from a position along a traverse and broken ground which commanded the dividing line between us and keep on the defensive. Had the Bosch got any further along the trench, the forward party would have been between two fires.[6]

Hibbert sent a runner back to Battalion HQ recommending that no further reinforcements be sent forward. On receiving this message Major-General Rycroft held back the remaining battalions of the 14th Brigade.

Rycroft established communication with Major-General Morland at X Corps HQ by telephone and briefed him of the dire situation developing at Leipzig Redoubt. He recommended that an attack be made against Thiepval from the north, capturing the Wundt Werk as it went along. He had already ordered the 2nd Royal Inniskilling Fusiliers to carry out this attack, but also suggested that the 49th Division, being held in reserve, should support this initiative. He also requested a supporting artillery barrage from heavy howitzers to focus upon the Wundt Werk, Thiepval Spur and trenches in German trenches in Nab Valley and in the Nordwerk.

By noon Lieutenant B. Meadow's party of the 17th HLI became isolated as it attempted to push forward its attack beyond the Leipzig Redoubt. Without reinforcement the assault would fizzle out. Meadow's recalled:

> It became evident that we, who were working up between two communication trenches, after two or three rushes, that further advancing was impossible without support. We waited for our own reserve waves and the Lonsdales who should have come on behind. But no reserves reach us and we saw our only hope lay in the fact that they had rushed one of the communication trenches and might manage to bomb out the machine-gun. But the bombers were checked out of range of the gun. We began to work towards the communication trench, but owing to the lie of the ground we were badly exposed and I at length found myself the only living occupant of that corner. About twelve o'clock I managed to leap the parapet without being hit. I found my platoon officer, Lieut. MacBrayne, lying shot through the head. Of the others of my platoon I could get no news, except those I saw lying dead or wounded'.[7]

Morland had taken Rycroft's suggestions on board and X Corps artillery began to bombard German positions around Thiepval Ridge from 12:05 hours and continued until 13:30 hours when the renewed infantry assault was about to take place. At that time two companies of the 2nd Royal Inniskilling Fusiliers advanced towards Leipzig Redoubt from Thiepval Wood but were stopped in No Man's Land by machine-gun fire from the ruins of Thiepval Chateau. The 2nd Manchester Regiment was also held in reserve and was ordered to move to Leipzig Redoubt to assemble for a strike upon Thiepval. This battalion succeeded in reaching Leipzig Redoubt at 13:45 hours and was able to reinforce the 97th Brigade with minimal losses. It tried to make a breakthrough from the Leipzig Redoubt by bombing along Hindenburg Stellung and Lemberg Stellung but heavy German fire and trench blocks prevented them going further into the German trench system.

German trench mortars began to shell the Granatloch. The casualties amongst the British battalions holding desperately to the redoubt were mounting as they could be clearly seen from all sides. They were coming under fire from the German 180th Infantry Regiment on their right flank and by mid-afternoon the Germans had regained possession of Hindenburg Stellung.

Lieutenant Meadows, who was alone, eventually made contact with a party from his battalion, 17th HLI:

> An order came up the trench, '17th HLI move to the left and prepare to support the Dorsets'. The communication trench was at this time chiefly manned by KOYLI (who should have supported the 16th HLI who had been held up by the German wire and cut up before able to take the first line of defences. Those left were forced to retire to their own line. A few Lonsdales (11th Borderers had been cut up coming up through Blighty Wood, Colonel and Adjutant killed and all officer casualties) were able to give us no practical support and a Company of Manchesters, sent from Divisional Reserve. An officer suddenly jumped the parapet and shouted 'Come on, the 17th' I followed him along with about twenty others. But we found the barbed wire impossible to cut through and he gave us the order 'Every man for himself'.[8]

The exhausted Meadows tried to get back to the British lines, but had to take cover in a shell hole, sharing it with a wounded soldier where they both fell unconscious.

The 32nd Division continued a desperate battle to hold onto the ground that it had captured in the Leipzig Salient throughout that afternoon. At 16:30 hours Brigadier-General Jardine was told 'that he was at all costs to hold on to and consolidate his gains, and take every opportunity to exploit the same.'[9] Pioneers from 17th Northumberland Fusiliers succeeded in digging a trench from a Russian sap driven from the British line to within forty yards of the German lines by 16:30 hours. A Russian sap was a narrow trench dug similar to a mine shaft so that the surface of the earth above was not disturbed and enabled access to enemy lines without being detected. This particular sap enabled reinforcements and ammunition to reach the British soldiers holding on to Leipzig Redoubt under cover.

Around 17:00 hours Meadows, who lay wounded and unconscious in a shell hole, was roused by the sound of a German counter-attack:

> Their artillery became violent and they attempted to come over the open. We ran for the communication trench and found it disorganised. Orders got mixed and some seemed anxious to retire. Fortunately the 17th HLI bombers who were in the advanced position, held their ground, driving the enemy with their own bombs, and the attack over the open was checked by our brigade machine-guns which had been massed in the German front line.[10]

Brigadier-General Jardine reported to Rycroft that progress was being made and that with the assistance of the 2nd Manchester Regiment the 97th Brigade would be able to capture ground in the direction of the Wundt Werk. The information supplied to Jardine was not accurate and in reality little progress had been made. At 18:50 hours Jardine reported back to Rycroft confirming 'that his holding in the Leipzig Salient was not so extensive as he had been led to believe'.[11] Rycroft then noted: 'At 7.50 pm I saw the Corps Commander who stated it was believed that some of the 15th Lancs. Fus were still in East of Thiepval and that 2 battalions of 49th Division were to be put at Brig. Gen. Yatman's disposal to help him in getting touch with the right of 36th (Ulster) Division about the Crucifix and to open a way into Thiepval.'[12] This plan had to be abandoned when it was discovered that there was no solid presence in or near Thiepval, and that 0the 36th (Ulster) Division had withdrawn to its original front line trenches and the only reinforcements the 49th Division could offer that night were two battalions.

However, as late as 20:00 hours a small contingent of British soldiers was still holding onto Leipzig Salient. A report from 99th RIR reported that there was a British presence in a section of the Hindenburg Stellung. The British were holding the quarry. It also confirmed that the 99th RIR had sustained heavy casualties in trying to recapture the Leipzig Salient. The 9th Company, 8th Bavarian RIR was brought forward with orders to recapture the quarry and Leipzig Salient in a counter-attack scheduled to take place at 03:00 hours during the following morning. When they reached a section of the Hindenburg Stellung they found the remnants of 3rd Company, 99th RIR led by only two officers. It was expected to make contact with parties from the 180th Infantry Regiment, but they were not around.

During the night of 1/2 July, Jardine withdrew the 17th HLI and the remnants of the16th HLI, leaving the 2nd Manchester and two companies from the 2nd King's Own to defend Leipzig Redoubt. Parties from the Royal Engineers came forward to consolidate and secure the redoubt while these battalions repelled a German counter-assault.

The losses in Jardine's 97th Brigade were heavy. The 17th HLI lost twenty-two officers and 447 men. The 16th HLI entered the battle with twenty-five officers and 755 men, and suffered losses amounting to twenty-one officers and 518 men. The 2nd King's Own incurred losses of fourteen officers and 311 men; and the 11th Borders lost twenty-five officers and 519 men. 17th Highland Light Infantry was the only battalion that reached, occupied and held the enemy's trenches north of La Boisselle. Lieutenant B. Meadows recalled the sacrifices made by the battalion:

> During the whole action we lost no ground that had been previously gained. By this time our Battalion had been badly hit. 'B' Company on our left had been caught in the wire and cut to pieces by machine-gun fire. My own company, 'A' was down to low numbers. My Captain and Platoon Officer were both killed, all the Platoon NCO's were killed or wounded, two Sergeants outright and all the L-Corporals dead. We had 17 officers killed and were working the Battalion with two officers.[13]

The 97th Brigade had gained a foothold in the Leipzig Redoubt, despite many of the attackers being held up by uncut wire. Although the adjacent 96th Brigade had failed to secure Thiepval and 8th Division was unable to capture Ovillers-la-Boisselle in the south, the 97th Brigade was able to hold onto its position within the Leipzig Redoubt. It succeeded in capturing the stronghold because some of the wire had been cut and the men were able to reach the redoubt before their occupants could leave their dugouts and respond. Its ability to bring forward reserve battalions and the Royal Engineers being able to go forward and consolidate the position was also a factor in its success, together with flexible artillery support which targeted areas of strong resistance.

Part 5

III Corps Sector

Chapter 16

Nordwerk

The capture of the Nordwerk and Ovillers-la-Boisselle was allocated to Lieutenant-General Sir William Pulteney's III Corps. The 70th Brigade commanded by Brigadier-General H. Gordon was attached to the 8th Division from the 23rd Division and comprised the 11th Sherwood Foresters, 8th King's Own (Yorkshire Light Infantry), 8th and 9th York and Lancaster Regiment. It was ordered to launch its assault upon the first German line north of Ovillers-la-Boisselle, known as the Nab, held by sections of the 180th Infantry Regiment. It was then to continue its advance upon the Nordwerk, a bastion positioned in the second German line where its occupants could fire on the British attacking the southern perimeter of the Leipzig Salient to the northwest and Ovillers-la-Boisselle in the southwest. This was a formidable position and the battalions designated with the task of capturing the Nordwerk came under fire from the Leipzig Salient, Ovillers-la-Boisselle as well as the Nordwerk.

The 8th King's Own (Yorkshire Light Infantry) which was occupying trenches in front of Authuille Wood prior to the assault had lost 10 per cent of its numbers from German retaliatory fire during the British preliminary bombardment. There was no senior officer available and temporary command of the battalion was placed upon the shoulders of Captain Kenneth Poyser, who was a barrister before the war.

The front line trench in Nab Valley, occupied by 8th York and Lancaster led by Lieutenant-Colonel B.L. Maddison, came under heavy shell fire between Chorley Street and the front line. Machine-gun fire swept over the front line parapet from the opposing German line and from Leipzig Salient on its left flank, but few casualties were incurred. The left company bore the brunt of this fire and could only get as far as the first German trench, suffering heavy casualties. A smoke screen was supposed to be discharged to cover their advance across approximately 350 yards of No Man's Land, but because of unfavourable wind direction this was cancelled.

The leading two waves from the 8th York & Lancaster's, on left flank and the 8th King's Own (Yorkshire Light Infantry) on right flank left their

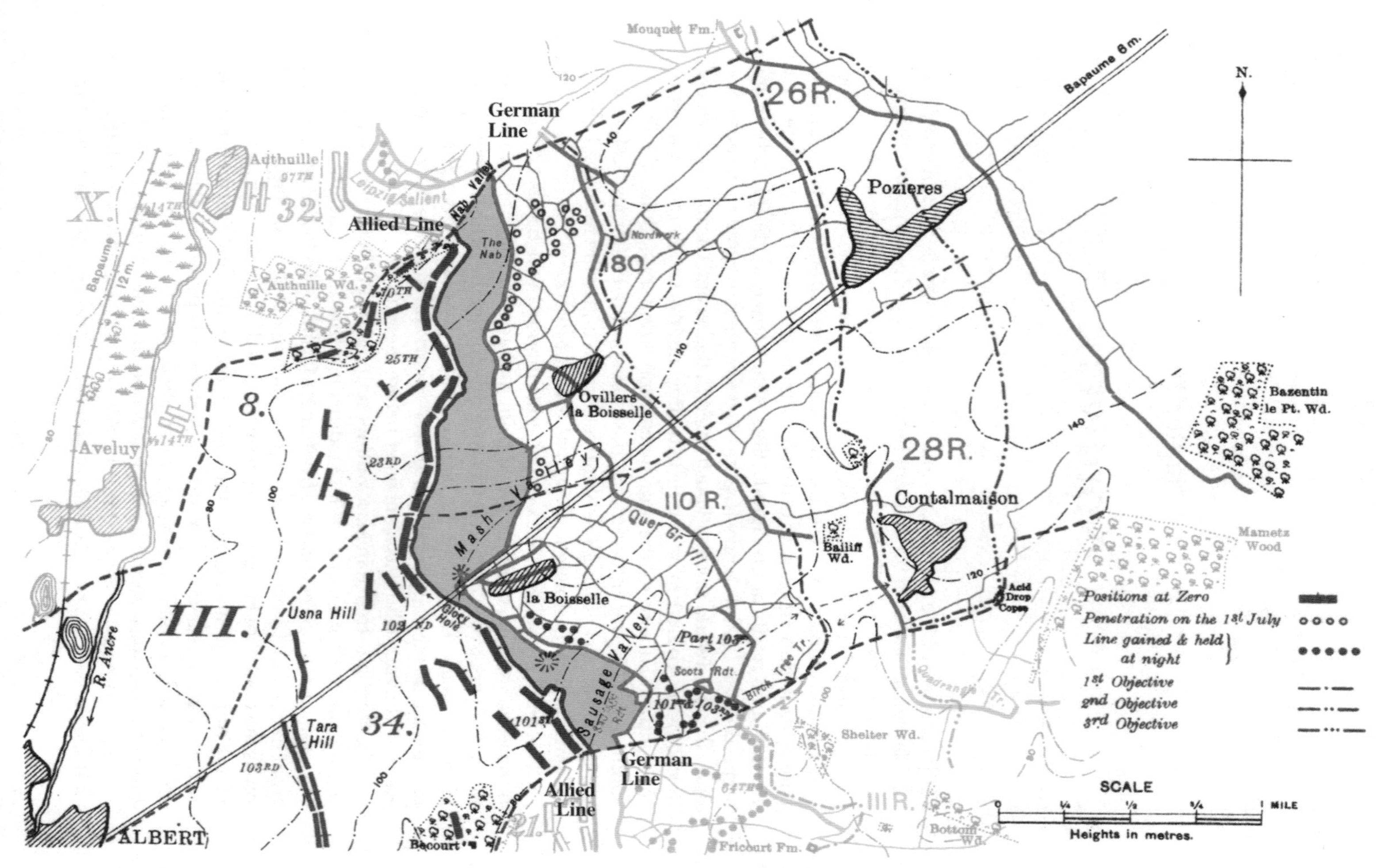

N.
Mouquet Fm.
Bapaume 6 m.
26R.
German Line
Allied Line
Authuille
Leipzig Salient
Nab Valley
The Nab
X.
32.
Authuille Wd.
Bapaume 12 m.
Pozieres
Nordwerk
180
Ovillers la Boisselle
8.
Aveluy
Mash Valley
110 R.
Quer Gr.
28R.
Contalmaison
Bailiff Wd.
Bazentin le Pt. Wd.
Mametz Wood
Acid Drop Copse
la Boisselle
Glory Hole
Usna Hill
III.
R. Ancre
Sausage Valley
Part 103rd
Scots Rdt.
Birch Tree Tr.
101st & 103rd
101st
34.
Tara Hill
ALBERT
German Line
Allied Line
Shelter Wd.
Quadrangle Tr.
III R.
Becourt
Fricourt Fm.
Bottom Wd.
Positions at Zero
Penetration on the 1st July
Line gained & held at night
1st Objective
2nd Objective
3rd Objective
SCALE
0 ¼ ½ ¾ 1 MILE
Heights in metres.

trenches at 07:27 hours and they passed through breaches that had been made in the wire and reached the German front line with minimal losses. As they advanced further the 8th York and Lancaster, in four waves, suffered severely, and Colonel Maddison was among those killed. The remnants got to the German wire to find that it was almost untouched by the British barrage. Further casualties were incurred as the men tried to cut their way through. Despite the enemy fire, the battalion succeeded in breaking through to reach the German first and second line trenches. The battalion War Diary recorded: 'It was reported that an enemy machine-gun was found in the front line with two Germans chained to it. Both were dead, one having been bayoneted and the other apparently killed with the butt of a rifle. The gun was destroyed.'[1] There are several accounts from British soldiers stating that they found German machine-gunners chained to their weapons. It is hard to believe this as they had endured a heavy British bombardment for several days and they were regarded as elite soldiers amongst their peers within the German Army. It is more likely that carrying straps for moving these machine-guns were attached to the German soldiers who may have been killed in the process of relocating their weapons. Some men from the 8th York and Lancaster were reported to have gone beyond the second German line, but they were never seen again.[2]

A section of four guns from the machine-gun Corps was positioned in dugouts close to the Nab. At 07:28 hours this section advanced into No Man's Land behind the 8th York and Lancaster to support it in trying to secure the left flank. Its ranks were decimated by machine-gun fire as it went forward and it was forced to seek shelter in shell holes. The machine-gun Corps report stated:

> As soon as the attack was launched a number of hidden enemy machine-guns unmasked their loopholes and swept our advancing troops from the left. The section did not hesitate, they went forward, and of 25 men and 2 officers all fell except some 8 men and 1 officer, and the skeleton of two teams with two guns, took up position in a shell hole. The officer crawled back and from an advanced signalling station reported for orders. The two remaining guns being in a shell hole would probably be safe for a time, so he was instructed to hold on and advance with the guns when the front line was taken, and give any supporting fire they could, but this was proved unpractical and they lost heavily from shell fire and machine-gun fire and only five men of this section crawled back that night unwounded.[3]

Another section from the machine-gun Corps was positioned in a tunnelled bank which protruded into No Man's Land. The men were able to fire 6,000 rounds over a section of German trench which was not attacked by British troops and succeeded in preventing its occupants from manning the parapets and firing at the advancing waves. However, five men from this section were overcome with cordite fumes within this confined, space and fainted.

The first two waves from the 8th Yorkshire Light Infantry advancing on the right flank towards German positions north of Ovillers-la-Boisselle had reached the first German trench and then continued onto the second trench line. Here they became intermingled with parties belonging to the other battalions. The battle for the second line was severe and parts of this German trench changed hands several times.

The following waves from the 8th Yorkshire Light Infantry suffered heavy casualties as German machine-gunners got their guns into operation and poured fire upon them from both flanks causing 50 per cent casualties before they got to the German first trench. The battalion regimental history recorded: 'Over the flat rising ground the enemy machine-guns acted like so many reapers and wave after wave of men was mown down in this harvest of the manhood of the nation.'[4] Every officer from the 8th Yorkshire Light Infantry became a casualty within the first minutes of the attack. The losses were so immense amongst the battalion's officers, the War Diary was written by Captain G.L. Pyman who interviewed survivors on the ground.

Parties from the 8th York and Lancaster were also fighting for control of the first and second German lines where a savage battle erupted. Such was the desperation of German efforts to regain possession of these trenches that they launched a series of assaults.

> Bombing then continued between parties of the enemy and our men in both second and first line and many of the enemy including several officers were shot who attempted to come over the top of the trenches. Eventually all the men in the second line became casualties. The men in the first line joined up with the Lincoln's on the right and had apparently came too far left.[5]

It is doubtful that the 8th Yorkshire Light Infantry reached the Nordwerk bastion because their bombers became intermingled with parties from the 2nd Lincolnshire Regiment and the 1st Royal Irish Rifles in the German lines. These battalions were advancing to the south directly upon Ovillers-la-Boisselle. This suggests that the machine-gun fire was forcing them to move southwards.

An order to withdraw was issued on the right flank around 08:30 hours. It was thought that this order was instigated by a German soldier who could speak English in order to confuse their enemy. The 2nd Lincolnshire along with approximately twenty to thirty men from the 8th Yorkshire Light Infantry withdrew, returning to the British front line. The 8th York and Lancaster War Diary recorded:

> Word came down from the right to retire and the Lincoln's left the trench. At the time fighting was not so heavy. An officer was seen trying

> to get the men on the right back again, but they were not seen to come back.[6]

During this time the 9th York and Lancaster was moving forward in support and the advance waves from this battalion had reached the British front trench. Remnants from the 2nd Lincolnshire and 8th Yorkshire Light Infantry who had returned to the British front line and reassembled were, ordered to accompany the 9th York and Lancaster back across No Man's Land. These men had already gone over the top once, reached the German lines, withdrawn back to the British line and now they were ordered to run the gauntlet of No Man's Land yet again. German artillery had also increased its intensity upon the British rear lines. One company from the 9th York and Lancaster lost half its strength when a shell exploded upon Bamberidge Street, a communication trench which led to the British parapet, before they even reached No Man's Land. It was extremely difficult for this battalion to get to its starting position. The 70th Brigade War Diary reported that they were 'hampered by the enemy's intense artillery barrage on our support trenches, and streams of wounded who were now returning'.[7]

At 08:40 hours the 9th York and Lancaster advanced across No Man's Land. The waves advancing on the centre reached the German second line, despite suffering severely, and were able to provide support to 8th Yorkshire Light Infantry. The left flank of the 9th York and Lancaster suffered the same fate as the 8th Battalion as they came under heavy machine-gun fire from Leipzig Redoubt, Thiepval Spur and north of Nab Valley. The enemy fire was so strong that they were unable to leave the British front line.

The centre of the attacking waves was still holding a position within the second German trench line an hour after the assault began and were seen to repelling German efforts to evict them. Some units were thought to have infiltrated the third German line, but these men were either killed, wounded or captured.

The 11th Sherwood Foresters in Brigade reserve followed the 9th York and Lancaster. Battalion commander Lieutenant-Colonel H.F. Watson DSO had received a message at 07:45 hours confirming that the first German line had been captured and he was ordered to move forward to the front line trenches which had been vacated by 9th York and Lancaster. The first wave went over No Man's Land and was held up by hostile machine-gun fire in No Man's Land. At 08:56 hours the second wave was about to leave the British parapet, led by Major G.H.W. Bernal DSO, when news came through from the 25th Brigade on the right flank that their assault upon Ovillers-la-Boisselle had failed and it was back in the British line. Survivors of the 11th Sherwood Foresters tried to crawl forward but the men were stuck in No Man's Land.

Colonel Watson was ordered to try and enter the first German line and he walked diagonally across No Man's Land in an effort to rally the men, but the German guns overwhelmed them. By 09:00 hours the British barrage lifted deeper into German lines, which meant that German machine-gunners and riflemen could fire upon the assaulting waves from the 70th Brigade unmolested. Only the first wave had got to the German first line, but the rest of the 11th Sherwood Foresters could not advance across No Man's Land and the attack ground to a halt:

> The Sherwood Foresters suffered severely crossing No Man's Land, being enfiladed on both flanks by M.G. and much hostile shrapnel fire which was now barraging our front line whenever troops attempted to advance.
>
> It was impossible to stand at all in No Man's Land and the battalion crawled forward on hands and knees to help the battalions in front. It is doubtful if any of the second wave ever got further than just outside the German front trench.[8]

Captain C. Hudson with a party of fifty men, including battalion bombers from 11th Sherwood Foresters and a mixture of fragmented parties from the other battalions, tried to enter the German lines through a sunken road on the right flank, but as they came over the crest of a small hill eighty yards into the advance they were confronted by heavy machine-gun fire which stopped them in their tracks.

Machine-gun fire criss-crossing this sector of No Man's Land meant that it was impossible to take reinforcements and supplies to the parties of soldiers who were fighting in the first and second trench lines. A telephone line which had been laid earlier that morning had been cut by the German barrage and attempts to use signals failed. There was no way to communicate with the forward waves that were in the German lines, they were therefore on their own.

The well-positioned German machine-gun crews were carefully placed to support each other along the sector between Thiepval Spur and Ovillers-la-Boisselle and were in control of No Man's Land. The 70th Brigade War Diary noted:

> It was apparent that unless the high ground around Thiepval and R.31. was heavily barraged, and the machine-guns on the high ground about Ovillers-la-Boisselle barraged or captured, that no communication could be effected across No Man's Land until after dark.[9]

By 10:00 hours, with the exception of 100 men from the 9th York and Lancaster on the left flank, the entire 70th Brigade had left its trenches and all communication with those that had entered the German line had been severed. Major-General H. Hudson, 8th Division commander, had no knowledge of what was going on.

At 11:48 hours Brigadier-General H. Gordon reported to Hudson that until these machine-guns were silenced he was unable to communicate with the parties fighting in the German lines close to the Nordwerk.

After midday a second attempt to storm the Nordwerk was ordered to take place at 17:00 hours. It was left to fifty men from the 9th York and Lancaster who were unable to get across No Man's Land on the left flank to clear the British first trench of the dead and wounded. During that afternoon, the isolated parties within the German trench system continued to engage with their opponents who were keen to reclaim the trenches that they had lost. The remnants of the 8th Yorkshire Light Infantry still continued to fight for the sectors of German trenches they held. Without officers, NCOs, and in some instances privates had taken the initiative to rally surviving comrades to defend their position. Others were rallied by officers from the 2nd Lincolnshire. The 70th Brigade War Diary reported:

> There is no possible doubt that during our occupation of the hostile trenches very heavy loss was inflicted on the enemy whose front line trenches were crowded. Up to 2.30 pm various observers report seeing bomb fighting going on in the front German line. Parties of our men were seen standing on the parapet and throwing bombs, doubtless these had been driven back fighting from the 2nd and 3rd trenches. They were eventually overpowered by the enemy who got at them from both flanks which were open.[10]

German forces pressed forward with further counter-attacks during the afternoon. The 8th York and Lancaster held on until it had expended all its ammunition and bombs when they risked death to search the bodies of dead comrades and those lying wounded in No Man's Land for bombs in order to continue the fight:

> The enemy then attacked in stronger force and as ammunition and bombs were exhausted some of our men went out into No Man's Land and searched the casualties. Further heavy fighting continued until only odd parties of two and three men were left. These were eventually driven out of the trenches and retired.[11]

Later that afternoon the fighting on this sector ceased. Reports that the attack upon the Nordwerk had failed were reported to Major-General Hudson at around 15:30 hours and any plans to launch a further assault were abandoned. As the wounded crawled in from No Man's Land, they were repeatedly sniped at by German marksmen. The last man from the 8th Yorkshire Light Infantry reached the British line at 18:00 hours, who reported that no other British personnel were alive in the German trenches.

The 8th King's Own (Yorkshire Light Infantry) entered the battle with twenty-five officers, one medical officer and 659 men. After the failed attempt to capture the Nordwerk, their numbers had been reduced to the single medical officer and 110 men after losing twenty-one officers and 518 men.[12] Twenty-two officers and 680 men from 8th York and Lancaster Regiment went over the top. Only sixty-eight returned including one sergeant, three corporals, ten lance corporals and fifty-four men after losing twenty-one officers and 576 men.[13] Approximately 180 men of the 9th York and Lancaster Regiment answered the roll call that evening out of twenty-five officers and 736 men who took part in the action. The battalion lost fourteen officers and 409 men.[14] The 11th Sherwood Foresters lost seventeen officers and 420 men.[15]

Ineffective artillery bombardment of German positions and in particular machine-gun positions between Nordwerk and Ovillers-la-Boisselle; the failure of adjacent divisions to capture Thiepval and Ovillers-la-Boiselle and the inexperience of New Army troops were reasons for failure to secure the Nordwerk

Chapter 17

Ovillers-La-Boisselle and Mash Valley

The 8th Division, commanded by Major-General H. Hudson, was ordered to advance east through Mash Valley towards Pozières. This sector of German line defended by the 180th Infantry Regiment was regarded as a formidable sector that stretched north of La Boisselle and west of Ovillers-la-Boisselle. German field engineers had utilised the natural features to incorporate well-defended machine-gun emplacements, barbed-wire and deep dugouts to offer an almost impregnable defence. All three brigades of the 8th Division were ordered to assault this section. The 23rd Brigade was on the right flank opposite Ovillers-la-Boisselle and the German lines that crossed Mash Valley. The 25th was to advance directly upon the village in the centre and, as documented in the previous chapter, the 70th Brigade was to attack the Nab and Nordwerk on the left flank.

The 23rd Brigade was ordered to advance through German trenches south of Ovillers-la-Boisselle via Mash Valley towards the second German defence line along Pozières Ridge and capture Pozières. The 2nd Middlesex Regiment, in four waves, formed the right flank, the 2nd Devonshire Regiment was on the left flank followed by 2nd West Yorkshire Regiment in support with the 2nd Cameronians (Scottish Rifles) retained in reserve. 25th Brigade was to advance on the 23rd Brigade's left flank with the 2nd Royal Berkshire Regiment carrying the right flank and 2nd Lincolnshire Regiment, the left. These battalions had assembled in trenches during the previous evening where they waited for Zero Hour.

On the night of 30 June/1 July, Major-General Hudson at 8th Division HQ received reports that the German wire had been sufficiently cut on this sector. A trench was dug into No Man's Land on this sector weeks prior to the assault from which the assault was to be launched. This trench is referred to as 'New Trench' in the 2nd Devonshire's War Diary.

At 07:20 hours 'A' and 'B' companies of the 2nd Devonshire Regiment left New Trench and crawled into No Man's Land. Captain E.G. Roberts, commanding 'A' Company was severely wounded by German shellfire as he left New Trench and 2nd Lieutenant Leonard Carey was killed at the same time. Captain James Andrews commanding 'B' Company had to take charge of both companies.

The British artillery barrage continued for a further ten minutes as Andrews led the two companies in four successive waves without incurring any further casualties. As they assembled in No Man's Land a mist drifted from the German trenches which obscured their view of the enemy lines. 'C' and 'D' companies entered the vacated New Trench. Stokes mortars began their barrage of the German positions eight minutes before Zero Hour.

German soldiers of the 180th Infantry Regiment waited with nervous anticipation in their dugouts for the barrage to lift towards their rear lines. It is probable that the intelligence intercepted by the Moritz listening post at La Boisselle had reached them advising that the British were about to attack. They had their guns and ammunition close to hand. Some wore belts containing grenades and ammunition. Their nerves had been shattered by the shelling and now the adrenalin flowed through their bodies as they waited. They knew that there would be a race to reach their firing positions once the barrage had lifted before the British reached their trenches. One German soldier recalled:

> The intense bombardment was realised by all to be the prelude to an infantry assault sooner or later. The men in the dug outs therefore waited ready, belts full of hand grenades around them, gripping their rifles and listening for the bombardment to lift from the front defence zone on to the rear defences. It was of vital importance to lose not a second in taking up position in the open to meet the British Infantry which would immediately advance behind the artillery barrage.[1]

At 07:30 hours the British artillery barrages lifted onto the second and third German trench lines. At that moment 'A' and 'B' companies received the order to advance from Captain Andrews.

The Germans used periscopes from entrances to their dugouts to peer into No Man's Land and could see British Tommies advancing towards them. Once the barrage lifted they rushed to their parapets and prepared themselves for battle. One of those soldiers wrote:

> Looking towards the British trenches through the long trench periscopes held up out of the dugout entrances there could be seen a mass of steel helmets above the parapet showing that the storm troops were ready for the assault. At 7.30 am the hurricane of shells ceased as suddenly as it had begun. Our men at once clambered up the steep shafts leading from the dug outs to daylight and ran singly or in groups to the nearest shell craters. The machine-guns were pulled out of the dug outs and hurriedly placed in position, their crews dragging the

> heavy ammunition boxes up the steps and out to the guns. A rough firing line was thus rapidly established. As soon as the men were in position, a series of extended lines of infantry were seen moving forward from the British trenches.[2]

This German observer sensed that the British had complete confidence in their artillery bombardment and of the expectation that everything in the German lines had been obliterated.

> They came on at a steady pace as if expecting to find nothing alive in our front trenches. Some appeared to be carrying Kodaks to perpetuate the memory of their triumphal march across the German defences.[3]

The Kodaks that he refers too may not have been cameras but could have been baskets carrying messenger pigeons or other equipment necessary for the consolidation of the trenches. Most of these soldiers never reached the German front line. According to this account, soldiers of the 180th Infantry Regiment let the British Tommies advance to within 100 yards of their position before opening fire. He recalled.

> The front line, preceded by a thin line of skirmishes and bombers, was now half way across No Man's Land. 'Get ready!' was passed along our front from crater to crater, and heads appeared over the crater edge as final positions were taken up for best view, and machine-guns mounted firmly in place. A few moments later, when the leading British line was within a hundred yards, the rattle of machine-gun and rifle fire broke out along the whole line of shell holes. Some fired kneeling so as to get a better target over the broken ground, whilst others in the excitement of the moment, stood up regardless of their own safety, to fire into the crowd of men in front of them.[4]

The four waves advance at a steady pace as they moved forward into heavy German machine-gun fire from the front and both flanks. They advanced towards Ovillers-la-Boisselle in the direction where the Ovillers Military Cemetery is now located. Heavy casualties were taken from machine-gun fire from Ovillers-la-Boisselle in the northeast and La Boisselle in the southeast as the first three waves were mown down. Captain James Andrews was one of the first to fall, struck in the head by a bullet.[5]

Private Cyril Jose was amongst the first wave from the 2nd Devonshire Regiment who advanced upon Ovillers-la-Boisselle. Jose was just seventeen-years-old and recalled:

> We were told that it would be a walk over. Our artillery had their machine-guns and batteries all weighed off and would splash them all

> out in the last few hours of the bombardment. Of course we might expect to be sniped at by a stray German naturally! We would advance, take first line, go on to village of Ovillers-la-Boisselle then on to third and fourth lines to village of Pozières. If we met any opposition here we would dig in and other regiments would come through us. Quite simple.[6]

The German gunfire was awesome, Mash Valley was a death trap with fire coming from ahead in the village at Ovillers-la-Boisselle and in particular from the high ground at La Boisselle on their right flank. Within five minutes of leaving the British front line, Jose realised that the assault upon Ovillers-la-Boisselle would not be an easy task:

> Well, we went over – after all the batteries and machine-guns had been wiped out though somehow those batteries laid our trenches almost flat. Well, as I said we went over with the feeling in us of the song 'Over the top, over the top and never come back again' Some people say you go absolutely mad. You don't! I've never felt so cool and matter of fact in my life. I was surprised. But I was still more surprised at the reception. You know what hailstorm is. Well that's about the chance one stood of dodging the bullets, shrapnel, etc. Of course it must have been that stray sniper!! 'Johnny' [referring to the Germans], always considerate, ordered me to have a rest when I had got about 20 yards from his parapet. That was about 7.35 am July 1st.[7]

Flares were fired from the German trenches at Ovillers-la-Boisselle urgently requesting artillery support, which was promptly given to devastating effect amongst the ranks of the 2nd Devonshire Regiment. A German soldier recalled:

> Red rockets sped up into the blue sky as a signal to the artillery, and immediately afterwards a mass of shell from the German batteries in the rear tore through the air and burst among the advancing lines. Whole sections seemed to fall, and the rear formations, moving in closer order quickly scattered. The advance rapidly crumpled under this hail of shell and bullets. All along the line men could be seen throwing up their arms and collapsing, never to move again. Badly wounded rolled about in their agony, and others, less severely injured, crawled to the nearest shell hole for shelter.[8]

Within a short space of time the 2nd Devonshire Regiment was decimated in No Man's Land with many soldiers from the battalion lying dead and wounded in front of Ovillers-la-Boisselle, Jose recalled:

> There were several dead around me but I saw some wounded a bit too far off to speak to. They were all the result of a few minutes going across. That's where we lost most of our men.[9]

The Devonshire Regiment official history described the pitiful sight of lines of men lying in rows dead in No Man's Land. 'At first it looked as if the waves were lying down intact in No Man's Land, but then it was realised that they were lying still because they had been shot down wholesale and were practically all casualties.'[10]

The remnants from the Devonshire Regiment were unperturbed by their losses and quickly transcended from a steady walking pace to a rapid charge across No Man's Land. Shattered elements from the fourth wave managed to reach the German first line despite the enemy machine-gun fire. A German soldier, respectful of their British adversaries wrote:

> The British soldier, however, has no lack of courage, and once his hand is set to the plough he is not easily turned from his purpose. The extended lines, though badly shaken and with many gaps, now came on all the faster. Instead of a leisurely walk they covered the ground in short rushes at the double. Within a few minutes the leading troops had advanced to within a stone's throw of our front trench, and whilst some of us continued to fire at point blank range, others threw hand grenades among them. The British bombers answered back, whilst the infantry rushed forward with fixed bayonets. The noise of the battle became indescribable. The shouting of orders and the shrill cheers as the British charged forward could be heard above the violent and intense fusillade of machine-guns and rifles and the bursting bombs, and above the deep thunderings of the artillery and shell explosions. With all this were mingled the moans and groans of the wounded, the cries for help and the last screams of death. Again and again the extended lines of British infantry broke against the German defence like waves against a cliff, only to be beaten back. It was an amazing spectacle of unexampled gallantry, courage and bull dog determination on both sides.[11]

'C' and 'D' companies of the Devonshire Regiment followed behind the leading companies despite the heavy casualties they had incurred. The few survivors from the Devonshire Regiment that successfully crossed No Man's Land were able to enter the German front trench, but could not hold the line due to their limited numbers. Germans swarmed to the surface from their dugouts and immediately set about reclaiming their trenches. The small parties of the Devonshire Regiment 'put up a determined fight against enormous odds and were soon killed'.[12]

Some of the Devonshires were lying wounded in No Man's Land and found refuge in nearby shell craters as German snipers and machine-gunners tried to shoot them. Many were trapped in these shell holes all that day, while some took their chances and tried to evade the sights of the snipers to crawl back to their starting lines. Company Sergeant Major Baur and Sergeant Lock, together with two other men, fortified their position within one of these shell holes and used it as a firing position. They were seventy yards from the German front line and continued firing until they had expended all their ammunition. They were unable to leave the protection of the holes and remained stranded all day under the summer sun with only the water they had carried with them. Cyril Jose was one of those stuck in No Man's Land:

> I couldn't get back to our own lines until next morning. I didn't eat anything, but lived on pulling off dead men's water bottles. I was as thirsty as anything at first but got a few water bottles. About 6.00 am July 2nd I began crawling back to our line. Old "Johnny" sniped at me all the way back but I dodged him by getting in shell holes etc. and got back at last. I offered up a prayer of thanks when I dropped in our trench right by a chap on a periscope who had been watching me come in.[13]

The 2nd Middlesex Regiment, commanded by Lieutenant-Colonel Edwin Sandys, was advancing on the right flank of the 2nd Devonshire Regiment. It's first wave also suffered heavy casualties by the same hostile fire that devastated the ranks of the Devonshires. Its line of advance into Mash Valley was in between the high ground on the left where Ovillers Military Cemetery is now located and the garrison of La Boisselle on the right.

As the rear waves advanced forward into No Man's Land, they reached the leading waves lying either dead or wounded. The War Diary of the 2nd Middlesex Regiment reported: 'As soon as the leading waves left our trenches to assault it was caught by heavy machine-gun fire and suffered heavy losses. As soon as the succeeding waves came under this fire, they doubled forward and before anyone reached the German front line, the original wave formation had ceased to exist.'[14]

Many fell soon after they left their parapets. Despite the loss of officers the remnants from the two advanced companies continued to push forward and 200 soldiers from the 2nd Middlesex managed to cross Mash Valley and entered the German front line. After a short skirmish using bayonets they went forward and entered the second German trench line. The 2nd Middlesex had lost half its number by the time its men got into this trench, and they were unable to consolidate their position due to lack of reinforcements and ammunition. This party was reduced to 100 before retiring to the German first trench where Major H.B.W. Savile and the remnants of the regiment began to consolidate the line.

At 08:25 hours three and a half companies from the 2nd West Yorkshire

Regiment made a valiant attempt to cross No Man's Land to support and reinforce the 2nd Devonshire and 2nd Middlesex regiments holding portions of the German first trench but they too suffered heavy casualties and were stopped by German fire as they tried to leave New Trench.

Officers at 23rd Brigade HQ were unaware of the disaster that was enfolding. The morning mist, together with the smoke and dust caused by the shellfire from the opposing artillery barrages had made observation difficult. Runners were sent by companies from the Devonshire Regiment to report the situation, but none returned to Brigade Headquarters, they were either killed or wounded. There was a complete breakdown in communication.

As the mist and dust receded it became apparent that the three battalions had made little progress and those who had reached the German trenches could not sustain their occupation without support. The wounded that had managed to crawl back to New Trench were able to corroborate that the operation had failed.

At 09:15 hours the British artillery was re-directed to concentrate upon Ovillers-la-Boisselle and the 2nd Cameronians (Scottish Rifles) were instructed to assemble in New Trench and be ready to advance when ordered. German artillery retaliated by shelling New Trench, support lines and communication trenches, severely damaging some of the trench walls. Lachrymatory (tear gas) shells were also being fired from German guns and the gas caused great problems to soldiers in New Trench not wearing gas protective goggles. Common sense prevailed at midday when orders were issued detailing that no further advances would take place. The 2nd Cameronians (Scottish Rifles) waiting in reserve were held back and were ordered to secure the British front line trenches and to recover the wounded.

25th Brigade commanders went to 23rd Brigade HQ to discuss the situation and decide on the next move in light of the failure to secure the first objectives. They decided to recommend to the General Staff a fresh assault after a further heavy barrage that would last an hour. The plan was to launch an attack upon Ovillers-la-Boisselle from the north and south instead of a frontal assault.

At midday the 2nd Devonshire Regiment received orders from 23rd Brigade HQ that no more advances would take place until further orders were received. At the same time British artillery opened fire upon the first German trench line in order to give the wounded from the 23rd Brigade a chance to crawl back to the British line at New Trench. Small groups of wounded began to trickle back, and as the afternoon progressed more wounded managed to return. There were problems evacuating these wounded fellows from New Trench to the Regimental Aid Post because the trenches were too narrow to enable stretcher parties to pass and some parts of the trench were so badly knocked down that the stretcher bearers and the wounded that they carried were exposed to shellfire and machine-gun fire.

A medical officer of the Devonshire Regiment ventured into New Trench to help the wounded. Stretcher bearers and regimental pioneers were sent from Brigade Headquarters to evacuate the wounded from No Man's Land carrying them in waterproof sheets on their backs to the Regimental Aid Post in New Trench. Many wounded were left in New Trench because there were insufficient orderlies sent forward to help with the recovery process despite numerous requests for more assistance.

A telephone order was issued at 12:55 hours instructing the 56th Brigade to prepare for an attack upon German positions north of Ovillers-la-Boisselle in an effort to breach the German line and link up with the 70th Brigade on the left flank. The 23rd Brigade would attack Ovillers-la-Boisselle from the south. The 56th and 70th Brigade commanders agreed to launch the assault at 17:00 hours after a preliminary artillery barrage lasting thirty minutes.

However, throughout the late afternoon the true situation was becoming clear to brigade commanders and the prospect of 23rd Brigade launching another attack looked remote. A meeting was convened at 16:00 hours at 23rd Brigade Headquarters which all battalion adjutants were summoned to attend. The Brigade Major decided that the 2nd Cameronians would hold the front line while the remnants of the three other battalions were to be withdrawn to support trenches.

The 56th Brigade remained on standby to launch the next assault upon Ovillers-la-Boisselle throughout that afternoon, however Brigadier-General Stephens became concerned that a preliminary bombardment of the German trench line on the 25th Brigade's sector would fall on some of his parties that may have infiltrated the German line. This concern resulted in the cancelation of the second assault. Lieutenant-General Sir William Pulteney commanding III Corps took into consideration the casualties incurred and, doubting that a foothold had been established in the German lines, decided to call off the attack at 16:15 hours. At 17:17 hours the 8th Division was ordered to withdraw to Albert, with the 56th Brigade being instructed to stand down and hold the front line to cover the withdrawal. At 18:45 hours III Corps ordered 12th Division to relieve the 8th Division in the line opposite Ovillers-la-Boisselle and the 56th Brigade to return to the 19th Division.

At 20:00 hours a patrol from the 2nd Cameronians was sent to assess whether any troops from the 8th Division had entered the German first trench at Ovillers-la-Boisselle. They were met by German machine-gun fire. The officer commanding this patrol was killed and it was reported that the trench was strongly held by the enemy.

During the early hours of 2 July a mere fifty men from the 2nd Middlesex Regiment answered their names at roll call. Second Lieutenant H.C. Hunt was the only officer from twenty-three who returned to the British line unwounded. The battalion lost twenty-two officers and 650 men.[15] Lieutenant-Colonel Sandys was wounded and brought to London to recover from his wounds. Sandys was so dispirited by the loss of so many men within his battalion during that fateful day that he was unable to come to terms with the disaster that befell his battalion and he took his own life on 13 September 1916.

The 2nd Devonshire Regiment suffered heavily, with 431 casualties, including eleven officers and 221 men killed or listed as missing; five officers and 194 men wounded.[16] The 2nd West Yorkshire Regiment lost eight officers and 421 men.[17] Amongst the wounded was Private Robert Conmy who came from Hungate, York and was aged only sixteen. He was evacuated from the battlefield and taken to a Casualty Clearing Station close to Daours where he died from his wounds on 4 July. He was buried at Daours Communal Cemetery Extension.

The 25th Brigade, comprising the 2nd Lincolnshire Regiment on the left flank and the 2nd Royal Berkshire Regiment on the right, was due to assault Ovillers-la-Boisselle from the northwest. The 1st Royal Irish Rifles were held in support at Pendle Hill and Coniston with the 2nd Rifle Brigade in reserve. On 25th Brigade's front, patrols from the 2nd Lincolnshire Regiment commanded by Lieutenant-Colonel Reginald Bastard went into No Man's Land during the early hours of the morning of 1 July to assess the wire. At 02:30 hours they confirmed that it was cut along their sector, but in the process they came under fire. The battalion was in its assembly positions by 03:30 hours. When the British heavy barrage opened up at 06:25 hours German artillery retaliated with shrapnel which fell over the 2nd Lincolnshire Regiment's position. After the 2nd Devonshire Regiment had been spotted entering No Man's Land around 07:15 hours German machine-guns opened fire upon the sector held by the 25th Brigade. British Trench mortars opened fire from concealed positions at 07:022 hours in order to provide covering fire for the leading assault troops. At 07:25 hours the leading two waves of the 2nd Lincolnshire Regiment got into No Man's Land, coming under enemy machine-gun fire.

Once the British barrage had lifted at 07:30 hours, the men of the entire 2nd Lincolnshire Regiment advanced towards the German line. Accurate German rifle fire, which appeared to originate ahead of them from the German second line forced them to advance in rushes and then stop to return fire. They were also being harassed by machine-gun fire coming from their left flank. Despite fire that was sweeping No Man's Land the battalion's left flank reached the German first line where it was stubbornly resisted by its occupiers who showered them with bombs. After a fierce contest, by 07:50 hours the 2nd Lincolnshire Regiment overwhelmed the Germans and secured 200 yards of the German front trench. The right flank of the battalion failed to get to the German line close to the village. Some elements of the 70th Brigade came forward in support. Lieutenant-Colonel Reginald Bastard reported:

> The few officers that were left gallantly led their men over the German trench to attack the second line, but owing to the rifle and machine-gun fire, could not push on. Attempts were made to consolidate and make blocks, but the trench was so badly knocked about that very little cover was obtainable, from the enfilade machine-gun fire and continual bombing attacks which were being made by the enemy the whole time, and one frontal attack from their second line which we repulsed.[18]

The 2nd Royal Berkshire Regiment commanded by Lieutenant-Colonel Arthur Holdsworth advancing to the right of the 2nd Lincolnshire Regiment were thwarted by heavy machine-gun fire. With their ranks cut down in No Man's Land, only a small party reached the German front line. Without support, this party on the left flank was unable to secure a foothold and was forced to withdraw. Within fifteen minutes of beginning of its advance, the 2nd Royal Berkshire Regiment lost 53 per cent of its strength. Lieutenant-Colonel Holdsworth and his second-in-command Major G.H. Sawyer DSO were wounded and it was left to Acting Adjutant 2nd Lieutenant C. Mollet to lead the remnants of the battalion. Severely mauled it was unable to launch a renewed attack, which meant that those units from the 2nd Lincolnshire in the German lines had no support and were extremely vulnerable.

Those men tried in vain to hold onto the section of German first line trench that they had captured but the trench was in poor condition, the sides had collapsed and there was little cover. Nevertheless, they succeeded in repelling a German counter-attack that came from the German second trench line. Eventually by 09:00 hours their position in the section of the German first trench became untenable as they were slowly being overwhelmed by German bombers and enfiladed by German machine-gun fire. Devoid of cover, unable to receive reinforcements of men and replenishment of ammunition, they became isolated. The left flank collapsed and withdrew. All that remained in possession of the 2nd Lincolnshire was 100 yards of trench. Those holding on fought a desperate battle. The wounded also joined the unwounded in the defence of this small section of German trench until they were compelled to retire back across No Man's Land.

Lieutenant-Colonel Bastard returned to the British line where he reassembled the remnants of his battalion, together with elements from the 1st Royal Irish Rifles and organised another assault upon the German line. This was a grim and terrifying prospect for those men who were about to go over the top a second time that day. They were met by intense German machine-gun fire which made it impossible for them to cross No Man's Land and the attack failed. By 10:00 hours Bastard could only muster thirty men. Bastard would cross No Man's Land four times during that day exposed to hostile fire. His courage and determination would be acknowledged with a Distinguished Service Order.

The 25th Brigade War Diary reported:

> The German front was very much damaged by our shell fire, practically obliterated, but the deep dug outs beneath them were undamaged. Several were entered by Officers and men. It was also stated that tunnels connected them with the second line, but this was not verified.
>
> The fact that these trenches were so much damaged did not prevent a heavy rifle and machine-gun fire being brought to bear upon our front 15 minutes before Zero Hour, from both flanks of our advance, and from our front, possibly in the main from the second and other lines, but this is not entirely certain. Our troops were able to use the bayonet with considerable effect in the first line. But after passing over this line they appeared to have been attacked again from the rear, as well as from the front and flanks. It would appear, therefore, unwise to push on until the supporting wave is close at hand.[19]

'A' Company of the 1st Royal Irish Rifles managed to reach the German first line and two platoons succeeded in advancing onto the second line, but they could not consolidate their gains and had to withdraw. The two rear companies suffered from machine-gun fire trying to reach the assembly position in the British front line. Only fifty men reached this line. All that remained of the battalion was three officers and 100 men. The 25th Brigade War Diary reported:

> The progress of this Battalion through our trenches was rendered exceedingly difficult by the wrecked state of the trenches, which were moreover blocked by dead and wounded men, and by men of the assaulting battalions, who had been unable to go forward, or had been driven back.[20]

As the first three battalions of the 25th Brigade went forward, the 2nd Rifle Brigade entered the front-line trench where it was ordered to stand fast. It had already suffered 100 casualties but it was expected that the men would launch a renewed attack with the 1st Royal Irish Rifles. At 11:00 hours the battalion commander received a report stating that the 1st Royal Irish Rifles was unable to carry out an effective assault given the casualties it had sustained. He felt that the 2nd Rifle Brigade could not possibly launch a solo attack as they had also suffered significant casualties. He therefore ordered the battalion to defend the line. They entered the line with twenty-three officers and 727 men and lost 5 officers and 128 men casualties.[21]

The 2nd Lincolnshire Regiment held its line opposite Ovillers-la-Boisselle until it was relieved by the 6th Royal West Kent Regiment at midnight on 1/2 July. It entered the battle with twenty-two officers and 650 men and lost twenty officers and 434 men.[22] The 2nd Royal Berkshire

Regiment assaulted with twenty-four officers and 800 other ranks, but within fifteen minutes lost twenty officers and 414 men.[23] The 1st Royal Irish Rifles strength before the battle was twenty-one officers and 600 other ranks. By the end of that morning they had lost sixteen officers and 381 men. The commanding officer was seriously wounded and the adjutant killed.

Successful efforts were made to recover the wounded on the 25th Brigade's sector. The brigade War Diary reported:

> At dusk every possible effort was made to get in our wounded, with excellent results. The R.E. and Pioneers rendered great assistance. As far as could be ascertained all wounded up to, but exclusion of, the German front line were brought in. Many unwounded also returned. This was accomplished under constant Artillery and M.G. fire.[24]

The 8th Division held the front line until relieved later that night by the 12th Division. The casualties incurred by the 8th Division on the 1 July were so severe that it had to be withdrawn from the line and replaced with a fresh division. The 2nd Devonshire Regiment was all but destroyed on that day. It was transferred to the First Army and were given three months rest after its ordeal on the Somme.

The trenches that crossed Mash Valley were defended by two battalions from 180th Infantry Regiment which lost four officers and seventy-nine men killed, eight officers and 181 men wounded, with thirteen missing. Ovillers-la-Boisselle was eventually captured on 16 July by the 8th Division.

The 8th Division's failure to capture Ovillers-la-Boisselle can be attributed to a strong defence by the Germans, the British artillery's failure to neutralise the opposing batteries or to destroy the enemy's trenches and wire. The failure of the attacks by the two divisions on its flank also meant that the 8th Division came under heavy enemy fire from all sides.

Chapter 18

La Boisselle

The capture of La Boisselle and then Contalmaison and Pozières was allocated to the 34th Division, commanded by Major-General Edward Ingouville-Williams. The 34th Division comprised the 101st, 102nd and 103th Brigades. This would be the division's first combat operation.

La Boisselle was defended by the German 110th RIR, 28th Reserve Division. The village contained thirty-five houses and was part of the mining community which flourished there before the war. It was a key objective on 1 July 1916 and since the village was situated south of the Albert–Bapaume Road its capture was vital for the advance onto Bapaume, located nine miles to the northeast. The village had been under German occupation for two years and during that time they had constructed strong defences and deep dugouts. These were secure and comfortable shelters, many being fitted with electric lighting. Some of these dugouts were thirty feet deep and were connected by a labyrinth of tunnels. All this had been achieved without any interference from the French or the British.

The defences that skirted the perimeter of La Boisselle formed a salient that extended towards the British line with the apex only 100 yards from the British trenches. La Boisselle was positioned on a spur with Mash Valley to the north and Sausage Valley in the south with good observation over these valleys.

The village of La Boisselle was a formidable position with German machine-gunners hidden behind sandbags in the ruins of the devastated village, so any full frontal advance or from the flanks across Mash Valley and Sausage Valley would meet very strong opposition.

The village formed part of a series of mutually-supporting redoubts and strongpoints. These bastions included the fortified village of Ovillers-la-Boisselle north of La Boisselle, Schwaben Höhe, southwest of La Boisselle and then further along the line, there was Sausage Redoubt which was connected to the garrison known as Heligoland Redoubt to its German occupants, which overlooked Sausage Valley. Beyond this was another fortified position called Scots Redoubt which was a series of trenches with shelters linked to one large dugout. They were all joined by a system of trenches built along the contours of a low ridge.

A second line of defence, known as the Kaisergraben, was positioned below the highest point of the ridge at Pozières which ran from Mouquet Farm to Bazentin le Petit. Three miles beyond that the Germans were in the process of constructing a further third defensive line.

Major-General Ingouville-Williams plan to capture the stronghold of La Boisselle involved exploding two mines two minutes before the start of the attack. They were to be detonated at two enemy strong points located at Y Sap, north of the village, and beneath Schwaban Höhe, southwest of La Boisselle. Two brigades would capture German trenches on either side of the village. The 102nd Brigade (Tyneside Scottish) would attack trenches to the north of La Boisselle and advance along Mash Valley. The 101st Brigade and the 103rd Brigade (Tyneside Irish) would attack trenches south of the village and sweep along Sausage Valley. This valley was named Sausage Valley because of the sausage-shaped German observation balloon which was suspended above it. The 101st and 102nd Brigades objective were to capture four lines of German frontline trenches within forty-eight minutes of Zero Hour. They were then expected to capture the intermediate line of trenches known as Kaisergraben located before the villages of Pozières and Contalmaison. Both brigades had designated bombing parties which would attack La Boisselle from the left and right flanks in a pincer movement.

The 103rd Brigade, comprising of four battalions of Tyneside Irish were positioned on the Tara-Usna Line, which ran across the Albert-Bapaume Road between the two hills named Tara and Usna. The role of the 103rd Brigade supporting the other two brigades was to cross the Avoca Valley from this line to the British trenches a mile away, then cross No Man's Land to the captured German trenches and proceed beyond La Boisselle. Its second objective was to capture and hold Contalmaison and Pozières. They would then consolidate a line east of Pozières in preparation for the eventual assault upon another German trench system which lay 800 yards beyond.

German forces at La Boisselle were expecting to be attacked. They had seen lots of activity along the British lines opposite them and the bombardment of their lines was another clear indication that something major was about to occur. Their fears of an attack upon La Boisselle were confirmed after the interception of the British 'good luck' message by the Moritz 28 North listening post which was positioned at the southern apex of the village. At 03:45 hours on 1 July, the headquarters of the German 56th Brigade reported to the 28th Reserve Divisional Headquarters that an attack was imminent.

Y SAP AND LOCHNAGAR MINE

Mine operations had been taking place at La Boisselle in the hard Picardie chalk since early 1915 while the French were holding this sector. French and

German miners were mining and countermining in the area southwest of La Boisselle, known as the Glory Hole. The 185th Tunnelling Company Royal Engineers had been operating at La Boisselle since 24 July 1915 and were involved in offensive mining, driving galleries towards German strongpoints in an effort to destroy them. Some of these tunnels were as deep as thirty feet, with the deepest being 120 feet below the surface. German miners laboured in defensive mining, digging transversal tunnels eighty feet deep parallel to the first of their trench lines.

The 185th Tunnelling Company had begun to dig a tunnel named Lochnagar from the British line towards the Schwaban Höhe Redoubt during November 1915. It was named Lochnagar because the shaft for this tunnel was sunk in the British trench named Lochnagar Street, which was a support trench 300 feet from the front line and 900 feet from the German front line. The tunnel was dug as an incline to a depth ninety-five feet. German engineers became aware of these operations and established a defensive mining system deeper than the British tunnel. The 185th Tunnelling Company left trenches opposite La Boisselle during March/April 1916 and responsibility for this sector and maintenance of the tunnel passed on to the 179th Tunnelling Company of nineteen officers and 384 men, commanded by Major M.H. Hance.

Despite the German counter-measures, it was decided to continue the work on this tunnel in order to reach two strongpoints within the German line at La Boisselle, namely Y Sap (known by the Germans as the Blinddarm) and Schwaben Höhe. The objectives of these mines were to:

> 'destroy the enemy trench and to knock out his machine-guns at this point, where his trench formed a pronounced salient;
> destroy his underground system whatever it might be;
> kill any troops he might have sheltering underground from our bombardment'.[1]

In the Lochnagar tunnel, at a depth of fifty feet, tunnellers began to dig beneath No Man's Land towards the Schwaben Höhe. Candles were used to determine the presence of oxygen. A less intense flame indicated low oxygen levels and would be the signal for its occupants to leave the tunnel.

As the miners got closer to the German lines work slowed down because they had to make as little noise as possible. Despite the great depth of the mine, sound could travel fast and in one tunnel the miners could hear Germans talking in their dugouts or tunnels. Tins containing water were also positioned close to where the tunnel was being excavated as a warning device for enemy tunnellers digging towards their position. Sound travelled through chalk and the sound of digging would reverberate through the chalk and would be picked up by the water in the tin disturbing the surface of the water causing ripples. Major Hance reported:

> Latterly the enemy was heard very plainly working at a slightly lower level than ourselves. Subsequent examination points to his work having been of the nature of a defensive mine system in which it is probable that the sounds we heard were caused by his work on a transversal gallery as they did not seem to come any closer (as would have been the case had he been driving an attack gallery) but rather to cross our front.[2]

Great efforts were made to muffle noise. Tunnels were carpeted with sandbags and miners worked barefoot, without boots. Bayonets were used to dig through the last 150 yards of the tunnel which involved the laborious procedure of a miner digging the chalk with a bayonet and then another man catching the distracted pieces of chalk with his hands before it fell upon the floor. Major Hance described the mining operations:

> The work was carried out by A Section under Capt. W. Young. RE. It was done in silence. A large number of bayonets were fitted with handles. The operator inserted the point in a crack in the face, or alongside a flint, of which there were any number in the chalk, gave it a twist which wrenched loose a piece of stone of varying size which he caught with his other hand and laid on the floor. If, for any reason, he had to use greater force, another man from behind would catch the stone as it fell. The men worked bare-footed, the floor of the gallery was carpeted with sandbags and an officer was always present to preserve silence. As sandbags were filled with chalk they were passed out along a line of men seated on the floor, and stacked against the wall ready for use later as tamping. Air was forced in from bellows through armoured hose and 'exhausted' out through the gallery. The dimensions of this latter length of tunnel were about four feet six inches x two feet six inches. The work was extremely laborious and if we advanced eighteen inches in 24 hours we thought we did well. We could hear the Germans quite plainly in their mining system below us, and in the dug outs in the upper part of such system. All such dug outs, and the men sheltering in them, were destroyed when the mine was blown. At the end of the gallery bifurcated in the form of a 'Y'. The two charges mentioned (60 ft) apart were lain in the chambers roughly excavated for them. Each charge contained the number of detonators for efficient detonation 'in series', the two circuits being simultaneously fired by the same exploder in 'parallel'.[3]

The lumps of displaced chalk would then be passed back through the gallery for disposal above ground. There was another operation to remove this chalk further behind the British lines. If German reconnaissance aeroplanes spotted chalk deposits on the surface close to the tunnel entrance then they would become aware of the location of the tunnel entrance.

Since work became slower as they got closer to the German lines it would have taken a long time to fill one chamber with explosives, so therefore it was decided to excavate two chambers where more explosive charges could be laid at the same time. When they were 100 yards from the German line two tunnels were dug in a Y branch formation leading to two chambers which were close to the Schwaben Höhe sixty feet apart and fifty-two feet deep where the explosive ammonal could be positioned. The chambers were not quite beneath the German strongpoint or the German front line, but they were deliberately packed with sufficient explosives to cause a crater with a fifteen-foot-high rim.

A mine was also dug by 179th Tunnelling Company beneath Y Sap Redoubt positioned northwest of La Boisselle. Y Sap Redoubt was a tactically important strongpoint for the German occupiers where its machine-guns were aimed towards the 200 yards of No Man's Land in Mash Valley and in front of Ovillers-la-Boisselle. British artillery shelled it constantly and as soon as it was damaged, German engineers hastily strengthened its defences with concrete and steel. The 2nd Dorsetshire Regiment conducted raids upon Y Sap Redoubt during January / February 1916 and they discovered that it was protected by a deep mining system. At that time, during early 1916, British artillery only had sufficient munitions to resist German incursions into British trenches; there were not enough large-calibre shells to smash the defences of the Y Sap Redoubt.

Major Hance put forward a plan to place a mine under this redoubt and destroy it. This proposal was at first rejected on the grounds that it would take too long to dig, but Hance knew that the success of any infantry force attacking the German line between La Boisselle and Ovillers-la-Boisselle depended upon the destruction of Y Sap Redoubt. He persevered and permission was granted to proceed with the mining operation. Corporal Fred Francis of the 11th Border Regiment had been employed as a coal miner before the war and when officers from the Royal Engineers asked for volunteers to dig the mine under Y Sap he stepped forward to undertake this dangerous enterprise. He was told that this mine would be of great importance:

> The RE called for anybody who knew anything about mining. As I had a haphazard career, I had been a miner, a stage manager, a performer, I said yes I worked six years in a mine in County Durham, so they said to me would you volunteer to dig a mine under the German front line and I said I am sorry but it calls for a personal risk, actually it was similar to saying I was going to commit suicide. They said well as we were only 15 yards from their line and it would help to bring a war to an end if you could dig a mine underneath. I said well that is a great personal risk to me being 15 yards apart. We can't tell you what it is for, but we feel this mine dug we could practically end the war. So again I

> volunteered to dig this mine under the German front line which is similar to you and me are sitting now … again being the only miner I volunteered to dig this mine.[4]

German soldiers of the 9th Company, 110th RIR, heard from their lines the sound of mining activity being carried out by the 179th Tunnelling Company, but were unable to detect the precise location. Therefore Y Sap was evacuated and a small party of sentries left to patrol and defend this section of the line. Similarly British tunnellers could hear German soldiers digging tunnels underground not far from their own tunnels. Corporal Fred Francis recalled this nerve racking experience:

> When I got half way underneath say 7½ yards I can hear somebody above me namely the German with the same idea. I could hear him hacking away, so I very hurriedly dug my part and got out quick. I am likely to be blown up by the Germans. But however the mine that I dug was filled with hundreds of tons of high explosive.[5]

Major Hance did not have any confidence in the preliminary barrage of the German lines at Ovillers-la-Boisselle and La Boisselle and thought it imperative to destroy Y Sap Redoubt, in order to give the infantry a chance of reaching the enemy trenches. He sought permission to explode the Y Sap mine two days prior to the infantry assault but this request was denied by III Corps Commander Sir William Pulteney, who thought that exploding the mine earlier would alert the enemy that an attack was imminent and compromise the element of surprise.

Lochnagar and Y Sap Mines were exploded at 07:28 hours, two minutes before Zero Hour. The Lochnagar Mine contained 60,000 pounds of ammonal. Y Sap contained 40,600 pounds of ammonal. Captain James Young was the officer from the 179th Tunnelling Company who pressed the switch that detonated the Lochnagar Mine. He had blown the biggest mine of the Great War leaving a crater twenty-two metres deep and eighty meters in diameter. It all but wiped out the entire 5th Company, 110th RIR who were occupying Schwaben Höhe. 102nd Brigade Headquarters was positioned along the Tara-Usna Reserve Line, fifty yards north of the Albert-Bapaume Road where Brigadier-General Trevor Ternan reported that 'the two huge mines on the flanks of La Boisselle simultaneously exploded with a concussion that shook the ground for miles round, and the attack began. The mine on the right had been charged with thirty tons of ammonal, and that on the left with twenty tons, so that the effect of the explosion was terrific.'[6] The shockwaves from these explosions were felt for hundreds of miles. They were so strong that they caused leg fractures to some soldiers in trenches 250 metres away. The explosion sent flames, soil, stones, rocks, broken chalk, human remains and debris high into the air, turning the blue sky black. Second Lieutenant Cecil Lewis, a pilot of No.3 Squadron, RFC, flying a Morane Parasol, witnessed the explosion of the Lochnagar and Y Sap mines from the air:

> At Boisselle the earth heaved and flashed, a tremendous and magnificent column rose up into the sky. There was an ear splitting roar, drowning all the guns, flinging the machine sideways in the repercussing air. The earthy column rose, higher and higher to almost four thousand feet. There it hung, or seemed to hang, for a moment in the air, like the silhouette of some great cypress tree, then fell away a widening cone of dust and debris. A moment later came the second mine. Again the roar, the upflung machine, the strange gaunt silhouette invading the sky. Then the dust cleared and we saw the two white eyes of the craters. The barrage had lifted to the second line trenches, the infantry were over the top and the attack began.[7]

The 10th Lincolnshire Regiment and the 11th Suffolk Regiment were ordered not to move until five minutes after the explosion in order to avoid sustaining casualties from falling debris. Once the sky had cleared, it could be seen that the mine had caused an enormous crater with lips fifteen feet high, as predicted. According to the Official History map of La Boisselle, the Lochnagar Mine was exploded under the south-western perimeter trench line of Schwaben Höhe Redoubt and not beneath the centre of this strongpoint.

As the 10th Lincolnshire (Grimsby Chums) and 11th Suffolk of 101st Brigade waited the prescribed five minutes for the debris to clear, the Germans of the 4th Company, 110th RI,R poured out of their dugouts to secure the western lip of the crater, giving them enough time to prepare their defence. Pulleys and slides had been installed in the dugout shafts to enable the machine-gunners to quickly bring their weapons to the surface to meet the advancing British waves.

OVER THE TOP

In addition to the mines of Y Sap and Lochnagar Crater a smoke barrage was arranged to be launched at 07:26 hours and to be continued five minutes after Zero Hour, from British trenches opposite the Glory Hole, with the intention of deceiving the enemy into thinking that there would be a direct infantry assault across the cratered ground in front of La Boisselle. This was not conducted successfully 'owing to the direction and weakness of the wind'.[8] The wind was blowing at one mile per hour from a southerly direction along the British front line.

At 07:30 hours the 34th Division was ordered to stand-to, fix bayonets and advance. All the men of the Division leapt from their trenches and made the tragic journey at walking pace. The 102nd Brigade (Tyneside Scottish), commanded by Brigadier-General Trevor Ternan advancing on the left flank attacked north of the village along Mash Valley and led a direct assault upon the site of Y Sap which had been destroyed by the mine. The 101st Brigade attacked positions including the Schwaben Höhe south of La Boisselle. The 103rd Brigade Infantry (Tyneside Irish) commanded by Brigadier-General Neville Cameron was located along the Tara-Usna Line in readiness to support the 101st and 102nd Brigades. They ascended their parapets in the reserve line and advanced above ground towards the British front line before reaching No Man's Land. Very soon after the sound of the whistles the harsh reality of the state of the German defences and the effectiveness of the week-long bombardment were soon to be discovered. As the 34th Division advanced towards the German trenches, it became clearly apparent that the bombardment was not effective; it had failed to cut the wire and had not destroyed the German defenders. Broken barbed-wire scattered across No Man's Land became an obstacle which hindered their advance.

During the two-minute period between the explosion of the mines and the scheduled start of the infantry assault German machine-gunners emerged from their deep dug-outs, and made ready their Maxim machine-guns. By the time the British had waited for debris from the mines to fall and commence their advance at walking pace, the machine-gunners from the 4th Company, 110th RIR had their weapons in position along the lip of the mine crater and had established a firing line along Bloater Trench where they were able to unleash devastating fire into the advancing ranks of the 34th Division which had between 200 to 800 yards of No Man's Land to cross. They patiently waited until the British were close to the German front line trench before releasing a torrent of bullets into the advancing and rear waves. Wave after wave was cut down. The Tyneside Irish which started its attack from reserve trenches on the Tara-Usna Line was severely mauled before it arrived at the British front line trenches. It had taken two years to form and train the 34th Division but within ten minutes after the start of the assault it had suffered 80 per cent casualties.

Major-General Ingouville-Williams watched the 34th Division go forward and praised the bravery of his soldiers. 'Never have I seen men go through such a barrage of artillery … they advanced as on parade and never flinched.'[9]

102nd BRIGADE ATTACK UPON LA BOISSELLE & MASH VALLEY

The 102nd Brigade's assault focused upon two sectors. The 21st Northumberland Fusiliers (2nd Tyneside Scottish) attacked the German line between La Boisselle and the Lochnagar Crater. The 20th Northumberland Fusiliers (1st Tyneside Scottish) and the 23rd Northumberland Fusiliers (4th

Tyneside Scottish) advanced north of the village through Mash Valley. They were supported by the 25th Northumberland Fusiliers (2nd Tyneside Irish).

After the mines exploded at Y Sap and Schwaben Höhe, 20th Northumberland Fusiliers, commanded by Lieutenant-Colonel Charles Sillery left its trenches at 07:36 hours to advance up Mash Valley in four waves at 100 yards intervals. They had to advance down into a depression as they advanced through Mash Valley. On their right flank German trenches skirted along the eastern perimeter of La Boisselle with the first line running parallel with the Albert–Bapaume Road and then across Mash Valley towards Ovillers-la-Boisselle. These German trenches looked down upon Mash Valley and provided a perfect field of fire for German machine-guns and snipers.

The intensive bombardment had not succeeded in neutralising German defences and as the Brigade advanced across the exposed fields in Mash Valley, they were cut down by machine-gun fire, from La Boisselle and Ovillers-la-Boisselle to the north. The ranks of the 1st Tyneside Scottish were devastated by this fire. The 8th Division on their left flank had not taken Ovillers-la-Boisselle which meant that the Tynesiders were receiving enfilade fire from this village as well. Few men got through this awesome fire without becoming a casualty. Many were killed, wounded or trapped in the shell holes in No Man's Land in Mash Valley. However some parties did manage to breakthrough into the German lines, as the battalion War Diary recorded:

> It is difficult to discover exactly what happened, but though a few reached the 3rd German line, the remaining survivors fell back to our first line under cover of darkness. Not a single officer who went forward escaped becoming a casualty.[10]

The 1st Tyneside Scottish had ten officers killed, including the CO Lieutenant-Colonel Charles Sillery, ten wounded and seven missing, together with sixty-two men killed, 305 wounded and 267 listed as missing; a total of 661 casualties.

At 07:35 hours the 23rd Northumberland Fusiliers (4th Tyneside Scottish) followed in support of the 20th Battalion, going over the top to the sound of bagpipes. Many of these men did not get beyond their parapet being mown down by German machine-guns. Despite seeing their comrades from the 20th Battalion lying dead and wounded before them in Mash Valley they went forward and those who were not hit carried on relentlessly.

> Each line immediately it advanced to and over the front line parapet came under very heavy fire from the German Artillery and machine-guns firing from the direction of Ovillers and La Boisselle. Heavy casualties were at once incurred many men of our first line even being hit whilst getting over our front line parapet...Each line advanced

> without the least hesitation and through and across No Man's Land the battalion suffered very heavily indeed in all ranks. The losses principally being due to machine-gun Fire.[11]

Major S.H. Mackintosh, commanding 'C' Company, was on the right flank of the 4th Tyneside Scottish line of advance and bore the brunt of the fire coming from La Boisselle. He recalled:

> It was perfectly evident to us in the Front Line that the enemy was very much alive to what was happening and that our only hope of getting across No Man's Land was that the mine would be successful in destroying the machine-gun emplacements.[12]

The Y-Sap mine had not destroyed the enemy machine-guns, however, and the advancing troops stood little chance of getting through Mash Valley. Major Burge of the 4th Tyneside Scottish fell only a few yards from the British trench. Captain Joseph Cubey who led 'A' Company was killed 100 yards after leaving the parapet. Captain John Todd commanding 'B Company was cut down as he reached the British wire.

Lieutenant-Colonel William Lyle, the battalion commander managed to get close to the German front line, as the battalion War Diary described: 'Lieut. Col. W. Lyle, who was last seen alive with walking stick in hand, amongst his men about 200 yds from the German trenches'.[13] An unnamed witness of the 2nd Middlesex Regiment watched the 4th Tyneside Scottish attack:

> The pluckiest thing I ever saw was a piper of the Tyneside Scottish playing his company over the parapet in the attack on the German trenches near Albert. The Tynesiders were on our right, and as their officers gave the signal to advance I saw the piper – I think he was the Pipe Major – jump out of the trench and march straight over No Man's Land towards the German Lines. The tremendous rattle of machine-gun and rifle fire, which the enemy at once opened on us and completely drowned the sound of his pipes. But it was obvious he was playing as though he would burst the bag, and just faintly through the din we heard the mighty shout his comrades gave as they swarmed after him. How he escaped death I can't understand for the ground was literally ploughed up by the hail of bullets. But he seemed to bear a charmed life and the last glimpse I had of him, as we too dashed out, showed him still marching erect, playing furiously and quite regardless of the flying bullets and the men dropping around him.[14]

This eyewitness may have been referring to Piper Major John Wilson of the 1st Tyneside Scottish. Wilson was awarded the Military Medal for 'conspicuous bravery and devotion to duty' on the 1 July. However his uncle Lance Corporal Piper Garnet Wolsley Fyfe was not so fortunate and was killed as he piped the 4th Tyneside Scottish across No Man's Land.

The 1st Tyneside Scottish advanced with the 4th Battalion along Mash Valley, north of the village. It was because this was the widest part of No Man's Land that these two Tyneside Scottish battalions were almost completely annihilated. Some parties did reach the German front line and broke through to the second line, but as their ranks diminished and the casualties increased they soon became overwhelmed and outnumbered by resilient and resolute German defenders. The 4th Tyneside Scottish War Diary reported:

> The German first line was taken and the second line was also reached but owing to the heavy casualties it was impossible to hold on to these lines. A party of our men hung on for a time on to a portion of their front line trench a little north of the Albert-Bapaume Road. The Germans, however, launched a very strong counter-attack against this party who fought gallantly but owing to being greatly outnumbered they were obliged to fall back and take cover in No Man's Land where they lay all day and waited ready to go forward again with the next attacking force.[15]

South of the Albert–Bapaume Road and La Boisselle the 2nd Tyneside Scottish led a direct assault upon Schwaben Höhe. Its commanding officer, Lieutenant-Colonel Dunbar-Stuart, had been invalided prior to the day of the attack and was replaced by Major Frederick Heneker, who was second-in-command of the 1st Tyneside Scottish. The men advanced across No Man's Land at 7:30 hours and although they had suffered many casualties due to the German barrage they got into a section of the German front line. Private Tom Easton, of the 2nd Tyneside Scottish recalled:

> Then Zero Hour came, and the Great Mine was exploded at 7.28 a.m. shaking the very earth on which we stood, and throwing into the air thousands of tons of earth. When this had settled, the whistles blew and we clambered into the open and began our advance, keeping in line and extended order. Men began to fall one by one. One officer said we were O.K. all the machine-guns were firing over our heads. This was until we passed our own front line and started to cross No Man's Land. The trench machine-guns began the slaughter from La Boisselle salient. Men fell on every side, screaming with the severity of their wounds. Those who were unwounded dare not attend to them, we must press on regardless. Hundreds lay on the German barbed wire which was not all destroyed, and their bodies formed a bridge for others to pass over and into the German front line ... When we got to the German trench

> we'd lost all our officers. They were all dead, there was no question of wounded. About twenty five of us made it there.[16]

Major Heneker was among the casualties. Those that got into the trench repelled German counter-attacks coming from La Boisselle.

The 3rd Tyneside Scottish followed the 2nd Tyneside Scottish. Despite heavy casualties they managed to get across No Man's Land to reach the first German line and continue to the second German line. A small party ventured to the third line, but it had to withdraw due to overwhelming enemy fire. Lieutenant-Colonel Arthur Elphinstone commanding the 3rd Tyneside Scottish was killed and Major Acklom assumed command.

The 103rd Brigade supported the advances of the 101st and 102nd Brigades. It advanced between 1,000 and 1,500 yards beyond the British front line trenches from the Tara-Usna Line just after the mines exploded. To avoid congestion in the communication trenches the men moved above ground. Lieutenant-Colonel John Shakespear commanding 18th Northumberland Fusiliers (Pioneers) recalled: 'The mines went off and a few minutes later the 103rd Brigade began coming over the hill in beautifully regular lines, dressing and intervals maintained as well as on ceremonial parade. Everyone felt proud of that lot of Tynesiders.'[17]

This meant, nevertheless, that as they advanced towards the British front line they would be exposed to German machine-gun and shell fire for twenty minutes before they reached the front British trench. As a result the men were decimated before they even left the British lines. The battalion War Diary only records the tragic few moments of their demise:

> Heavy fire from machine-guns and rifles was opened on battalion from the moment the assembly trenches were left, also a considerable artillery barrage at 3 places on the line of the advance. The forward movement was maintained until only a few scattered soldiers were left standing, the discipline and courage of all ranks being remarkable.[18]

Bombardier Edward Dyce wrote home to his brother in Gateshead: 'The scene baffles description. The gates of Hell were opened, and we accepted the invitation. The courage and coolness of the Tyneside Irish were marvellous. Not a man wavered.'[19] Dyce was wounded in the assault along Mash Valley towards La Boisselle. Enemy fire made his efforts to get back to the start line very difficult. He recalled: 'The return to safety was as bad as the charge. We came down a slope which we now had to ascend. machine-guns were rattling and German snipers from the opposite hill were picking off the wounded.'[20]

The 2nd Tyneside Irish began the advance with twenty officers and 730 other ranks. They lost sixteen officers and 610 men. The command structure was in disarray with the loss of so many officers. Temporary command of the battalion deferred upon Captain T.L. Williams.

It was impossible for the brigade commanders to assess the situation in No Man's Land. Brigadier-General Trevor Ternan, commanding 102nd Brigade, found it difficult to ascertain the progress of the attack as a result of poor visibility. 'The bottom of the valley was quickly obliterated from our view by the dust thrown up and the smoke of countless shells, so that one could see little or nothing except the movements of the companies of the reserve Brigade as they went forward. They too were quickly lost in the haze'.[21]

Brigadier-General Cameron, commanding 103rd Brigade, was standing alongside Ternan:

> The enemy, in addition to maintaining a terrific fire on our troops as they advanced , did not overlook our back trenches in order to make it hot for any reserves who might be there, and the trench were occupied was from time to time swept by machine-gun fire, and occasional bits of shell fell into it. While we were trying to make out what was going on, General Cameron was hit by a machine-gun bullet in the arm and thigh. We did what we could for him, and arranged for his removal by stretcher.[22]

Lieutenant-Colonel G.R.V. Stewart DSO, commanding the 4th Tyneside Irish, was summoned to take charge of the 103rd Brigade, before his battalion left the trenches. According to his own account Stewart had advanced with his battalion and was in the German first line trench when he was brought back to command the brigade.

Ternan was totally oblivious of how the advance was developing either side of La Boisselle. He sent runners out into No Man's Land for intelligence and for an indication of the progress of the attack. It was a dangerous task and some runners never returned. It was later learnt that some trenches were captured on the right flank after sustaining heavy casualties. Only small numbers remained on the left flank having suffered severely while crossing the wide Mash Valley. Ternan recalled:

> … it became evident that the attack had been pressed on without avail. Officers and men had been literally mowed down, but in rapidly diminishing numbers they had resolutely pushed on to meet their deaths close to the enemy's wire. No Man's Land was reported to be heaped with dead. It was impossible to estimate at all accurately the extent of our losses, but steps were taken to ascertain from the advanced dressing stations the names of the wounded officers and the numbers of the men dealt with.[23]

During the afternoon Brigadier-General Ternan received a report from an officer sent by Major Acklom, commanding the survivors from the 2nd and 3rd Tyneside Scottish who had captured and were holding a stretch of enemy front trench south of the Lochnagar Crater. The men were exhausted, thirsty and their stock of bombs and ammunition were fast becoming depleted. An early relief of fresh troops, water and supplies were urgently needed.

A party of the 179th Tunnelling Company had dug a passage from one of their tunnels into the Lochnagar Crater. Contact had been established with elements of 102nd Brigade who had consolidated their position in the crater by the afternoon. Communication through the tunnel, though, was very difficult because of the many wounded who kept crawling into the tunnel as a means of escaping from the enemy's fire. Messages did eventually get through and it was later established that Major Acklom and approximately three hundred men from the 2nd and 3rd Tyneside Scottish were holding positions close to the crater. By nightfall Major Acklom still held those positions. A few others managed to hold a stretch of trench north of La Boisselle. Most of the Brigade was lying dead, dying or wounded in No Man's Land. No Officer or sergeant could be found from the 1st Tyneside Scottish. Except for a few men holding onto small positions the 102nd Brigade had been wiped out.

On 3 July Brigadier-General Ternan crossed No Man's Land to visit Major Acklom. Here he witnessed the enormity of the tragedy that occurred two days previously as he 'passed through successive lines of dead Tyneside Scots lying as regular as if on parade.'[24] The 102nd Brigade Tyneside Scottish had, to all intents and purposes, ceased to exist, with 940 killed and 1,500 wounded. Eighty officers went over the top and only ten survived. What remained of the 4th Tyneside Scottish were collected and mustered at 09:00 hours on 2 July behind the Tara-Usna Line for roll call. Only 100 men answered their names. Twenty other men appeared later that day. These men were rested for the day, but that was all the respite that they would get. Despite suffering that terrible ordeal on 1 July during the evening of 2 July the survivors were formed up into parties to carry rations and ammunition in support of battalions on the front line.

101st BRIGADE ATTACK UPON SAUSAGE VALLEY

The 101st Brigade, commanded by Brigadier-General R.C. Gore, was ordered to capture four trenches of the front German trench system south of La Boisselle. The fourth trench, which was 2,000 yards from the start point, was scheduled to be taken at 08:18 hours. It was then to advance upon the second defensive line known as the Kaisergraben which stretched in front of Pozières and Contalmaison and capture this line by 08:58 hours.

Here the 101st Brigade would halt alongside the 102nd Brigade on its left and allow the 103rd Brigade to pass through its lines to capture the villages of Contalmaison and Pozières, reaching a line east of Pozières by 10:10 hours.

Prior to the assault Brigadier-General Gore had given precise orders that the Lieutenant Colonels, second-in-commands and adjutants of all his battalions were not to go forward until ordered by the Brigade HQ. He did not want them being lost at the start of the advance.

The 10th Lincolnshire Regiment, the Grimsby Chums, commanded by Lieutenant-Colonel E. Cordeaux was on the left flank. It was supported by the 11th Suffolk Regiment and was tasked with securing the eastern lip of the Lochnagar Crater and a sector of Bloater Trench, which connected Schwaben Höhe with Sausage Redoubt and Heligoland Redoubt. The 15th Royal Scots (1st Edinburgh City) with the 16th Royal Scots (2nd Edinburgh City) following behind were tasked with the capture of Sausage Redoubt on the right flank. Before they got to the German front line they would need to cross 500 yards of No Man's Land.

The front waves of the Grimsby Chums assembled in reserve trenches because it was too dangerous to occupy the front trench as it was close to the mine that exploded beneath Schwaben Höhe. They were immediately disadvantaged because they would need to cross 150 yards of shell-cratered terrain before they could reach the British first line then proceed to cross 800 yards of No Man's Land towards the crater and Bloater Trench. They had waited for five minutes to allow the debris of chalk, earth and human remains that were propelled into the sky to settle. During that time survivors of the German 110th RIR were able to ascend from their dugouts, occupy the lip of the crater and set up their machine-guns ready for the anticipated attack.

As soon as the Lincolnshire's left their trenches German machine-guns from La Boisselle and Sausage Redoubt tore into the advancing waves and some men were hit many times during the day. Major Walter Vignoles of 'D' Company, later recalled:

> I went over with my Company, the enemy had escaped our tremendous bombardment to a great extent by the use of deep dug outs, and as soon as our barrage lifted, brought out his machine-guns and got them into action. In our sector opposite La Boisselle it was impossible to advance, the m.g. bullets kicking up the dust like a hail storm. Only two Officers escaped being killed or wounded, while about 70 per cent of the other ranks became casualties. I was wounded through the hand, fingers being broken and a small artery cut, and walked back to Albert about three miles away. The trenches were packed with wounded trying to get out. Casualties having been enormous.[25]

A German barrage soon descended upon the British line causing casualties amongst the 11th Suffolk as it was about to follow the Grimsby Chums. The battalion War Diary reported:

> Our advance from the moment it left our assembly trenches was subjected to a very heavy fire from machine-guns from La Boisselle. In spite of the fact that wave after wave were mown down by machine-gun fire, all pushed on without hesitation though very few reached the German lines.[26]

The 11th Suffolk managed to attack Sausage Redoubt only to be stopped by German flamethrowers, with many men being burnt to death:

> One particularly fine effort was directed by a dozen men against a part of the German trenches known as the Heligoland Redoubt. They sprang suddenly, as it seemed, to life, and dashed forward at a sharp pace, only to be burnt to death by a discharge of flamethrowers as they breasted the parapet. The sight of their crumpled figures, staggering back from the tongues of flame and smoke, tearing hopelessly at their burning clothes and then falling one by one was terrible to behold.[27]

The Grimsby Chums and the 11th Suffolk suffered severely, with only small parties reaching the lip of Lochnagar Crater, from where they were able to access the adjoining frontline Bloater Trench. Amongst these was 2nd Lieutenant J.H. Turnball's platoon of the Grimsby Chum's 'D' Company:

> There were 50-100 wounded. We consolidated round the lip of the crater and found the sandbags very useful but of course our parapet was of uncertain thickness and very crumbly. There was a certain amount of cover for all but very shallow. Before evening all three officers seem to have disappeared and I was left only with Colonel Howard, who was badly wounded and who has since died.[28]

During the day, Lieutenant-Colonel Louis Howard, commanding the 1st Tyneside Irish was at one point the only senior officer present at positions held north of the Lochnagar Crater, until he was wounded and taken back to the crater where he died of his wounds.

The advancing waves of the Grimsby Chums and the 11th Suffolk were reduced to small parties of three or four men, such was the deadly impact of the German machine-guns. As these men pushed forward they were joined by fragments from other battalions. 2nd Lieutenant Hendin with a party of three Grimsby Chums was able to advance on the right flank and helped consolidate a sector of trench that protected the 21st Division's left flank.

As the lip of the Lochnagar Crater was being consolidated it was necessary for a communication trench to be dug from the British lines to enable safe passage for reinforcements and supplies. The 18th Northumberland Fusiliers (Pioneers) comprising miners who worked at Northumberland and Durham collieries before the war, were tasked with digging a communication trench from the Nose across No Man's Land to the lip of the Lochnagar Crater.

By evening two communications trenches were dug across No Man's Land into captured German frontline trenches. The Pioneers used these trenches to take supplies of water, bombs, ammunition and stores to their comrades holding the captured front line. However, the process of transporting the supplies into the occupied German lines was slowed down by stretcher parties moving in both directions along the same trench.

As the German machine-gunners concentrated their relentless fire upon the Grimsby Chums and the 11th Suffolk, the 1st and 2nd Edinburgh City battalions were able to cross No Man's Land with few casualties. Lieutenant-Colonel A.G.B. Urmston commanding the 1st Edinburgh City became unwell when he was knocked down by an explosion as he watched the assault. Suffering from a severe headache and feeling sick, command of the battalion passed to Major Arthur Rose, although Urmston remained at Battalion HQ. Under the cover of the final intensive bombardment and mortar fire the first two waves of the 1st Edinburgh City was able to assemble in No Man's Land and was 200 yards from Bloater Trench at Zero Hour.

A Pipe Major of the 1st Edinburgh City had the opportunity to remain with the transport behind the British lines, but chose to lead his comrades across playing the pipes. Brigade Major E.A. Osborne recalled: 'In spite of orders to remain with transport the Pipe Major 15/R.Scots went over the top in front of the 1st wave playing the pipes presented by the City of Edinburgh. Presently the bag was punctured so he threw them away, knocked out a German with his fist and took his rifle. He went on until severely wounded.'[29] However the third and fourth waves were mown down as they left their trenches by enemy machine-guns positioned in south of the village and in Sausage Valley.

The 2nd Edinburgh City left the assembly trenches at 07:35 hours. Captain Lionel Coles, 'C' Company, had removed his tunic and wore the same equipment as the other ranks and carried a rifle to ensure that German snipers did not identify him as an officer. The 2nd Edinburgh City soon caught up with the 1st in No Man's Land. Together the two battalions charged at the first German trench with few casualties and overran the position before the occupants had an opportunity to get into position.

By 07:48 hours the two Edinburgh City battalions had reached the summit of Fricourt spur on their right flank, but because enemy machine-gun fire from La Boisselle forced them to deviate eastwards the German occupied strongpoints Sausage Redoubt and Scots Redoubt had not been captured. Major Harris Stocks had led 'C' Company, 1st Edinburgh City past Scots Redoubt and reached Peake Trench. This error was not realised until 08:20 hours after advancing for a mile and having reached Birch Tree Wood on 21st Division sector.

Major Stocks and Lieutenant Robson were the only remaining officers to lead the remnants from the 1st Edinburgh City along Birch Tree Trench towards Peake Woods while the 2nd Edinburgh City held a firing line in the Sunken Lane which was part of the Fricourt–Pozières Road. Major Harris Stocks' men were attacked by a bombing party from a company from the reserve battalion of the 110th RIR, which came down Birch Tree Trench. They also came under heavy fire from their rear left flank from the German occupants of the third and fourth lines and Scots Redoubt.

Both Edinburgh battalions were taking casualties. Major Harris Stock's party was in an exposed position and was forced to withdraw 300 yards back along Birch Tree Trench to a position in the vicinity of Birch Tree Wood and Shelter Wood. Major Stocks was mortally wounded during the withdrawal and was left in the trench to be taken captive. He would die from those wounds later that day.

Lieutenant Robson was now in command of the mixed battalions that were holding Birch Tree Wood and Round Wood. Elements of the 2nd Edinburgh City led by Lieutenant R.C. Lodge together with fragments from the 4th Tyneside Irish and the 11th Suffolk joined them when they withdrew to Round Wood. The men in Lodge's platoon were surprised that he had survived the assault for he was six feet eight inches tall and was an easily identifiable target for German machine-gunners and snipers. When the slightly wounded Captain Osbert Brown from the 11th Suffolk linked up with them, he assumed command. Overall there were three officers and approximately 100 men from various units. From Birch Wood and Round Wood these mixed units were able to converge on Wood Alley and launch an attack upon Scots Redoubt, capturing the fortress from the southeast. However these valiant men would find that they were isolated and surrounded by the enemy. It was important to hold onto Wood Alley because it secured the left flank of the 21st Division.

Communication between the advancing waves driving through the German lines and the battalion commanders was poor. Captain Lionel Coles sent a message at 08:45 hours confirming that 'C' Company of the 2nd Edinburgh City were 400 yards west of Peake Wood and 'that units were much scattered but that reorganisation was in progress.'[30] Lieutenant-Colonel Sir George Macrae did not receive that message until 11:03 hours.

The two Edinburgh battalions were now in possession of their sector of Fricourt Spur and faced Contalmaison Spur which was 1,000 yards beyond. German accounts report that a party from the 2nd Edinburgh City had entered Contalmaison but all had been killed.

The 24th and 27th Northumberland Fusiliers (1st and 4th Tyneside Irish), of the 103rd Brigade continued to advance in support of the 101st Brigade. The survivors reached the British lines twenty minutes after Zero Hour. They proceeded to cross Sausage Valley under heavy machine-gun and shell fire. Both battalions lost heavily. Instead of passing through the lines of the forward battalions to advance on their own set objectives they had to assist them in securing the first and second lines which were the objectives of the 101st Brigade. Only a few men from the 4th Tyneside Irish led by 2nd Lieutenant Thompson on the left flank in support of the 11th Suffolk and the Grimsby Chums got close to reaching their objective at Contalmaison, but they were overwhelmed by superior German numbers and were forced to withdraw to the second German line trench which they held until reinforcements arrived.

The 4th Tyneside Irish was meant to have followed 2nd Edinburgh City. It was able to cross Avoca Valley with few casualties until it reached Chaps Spur when the advancing waves entered the sights of the German machine-gunners reduced their ranks. Nevertheless, the battalion continued to advance over the British line and across No Man's Land.

By the time it reached the German front line trench, Kipper Trench, which ran south from Heligoland Redoubt, they had suffered 70 per cent casualties, though some parties did reach the Fricourt–Pozières Road. Corporal Robert Kennedy, of the 4th Tyneside Irish recalled the experience of advancing across No Man's Land in a letter to his wife Florence:

> 'Over the top with the best of luck' was the cry. So over we went only to meet a perfect storm of machine-gun fire. Then our lads began to fall, the first of mine to fall was a chum by my left side called Nicholson of Ellison St. Gateshead, then my bosom pal Sergt. Hall. After that my memory was not very clear, I was seeing blood until I was in the thick of it in the German lines.[31]

A small mixed party of the two Tyneside Irish battalions reached the German frontline where it found troops from the 101st Brigade. Despite the option of taking shelter, they fought their way into the German rear. The C.O. of the 4th Tyneside Irish was still leading the attack, however as a result of the Brigade Commander being wounded, he was recalled to Headquarters. At this point, very little of the 103rd Brigade remained.

Corporal Robert Kennedy successfully got across No Man's Land and fought through the first and second German trench lines. There were not many of his party left by the time he got to the second line, but undeterred he led them into the third German line where they fought a close-quarters battle for control of the trench, as he recalled:

> On looking my men up I found that there were only 3 of us left of my platoon, however as I was senior N.C.O. left, I took charge of all the

> men around about which were a mixed lot of all regiments. We advanced and took the German third line with very little trouble, but Fritz started then to bomb without doing much damage, it was here that they nearly got me with a bomb. I was inspecting the line when we almost ran into a strong German bombing party, but as luck would have it we saw them first and made them a present of nearly a dozen which gave them quite a turn, however one of theirs almost got me, seeing it coming I just had time to step back into the next bay when it went off.[32]

Kennedy met his commanding officer, Captain Ralph Pritchard, and together they decided to launch an assault upon the fourth German trench line:

> On returning down the line I met my Captain to whom I reported the work done and the work in hand. However as many more stragglers had come in, the Captain decided to attack the fourth line, so over the top we went again to be met by heavy machine-gun fire, which took a heavy toll, my Captain among many.[33]

Overwhelmed by the German defence and with mounting casualties they were unable to make a breakthrough into the fourth German line. Kennedy and the remainder of his party withdrew to the third German line, but on seeing Captain Pritchard lying wounded and exposed in between the third and fourth trench line he went back to recover him:

> It proved too hot, we were driven back to the third line. My Captain was lying out there between us and the Germans, so two of us went out and carried him into a shell hole where we dressed him, then we crawled back to our chums. After seeing the Captain safe I went along the trenches and it was on returning that a sniper got me.[34]

Brigadier-General Gore at 101st Brigade HQ was unaware of the situation in the German lines. No definite information was forthcoming and he could only make decisions on what was seen from that side of No Man's Land. The 101st Brigade War Diary reported that at 10:00 hours that 'the attack appeared to be progressing'.[35] On this assumption three sections from 297th Field Company Royal Engineers were ordered to move forward from Bécourt Wood, cross No Man's Land and consolidate positions occupied by 101st Brigade in the German lines. They could not get beyond the British front line because of the severity of German fire criss-crossing No Man's Land.

By noon the situation at 101st Brigade HQ was still rather confused. Its battalions had advanced out of sight over the crest of the ridge but German soldiers could be seen in their front lines behind those advancing waves.

Clearly something had gone drastically wrong. The brigade War Diary noted:

> No Man's Land still unpassable owing to machine-gun fire. The situation as far as could be seen, was, that all the assaulting troops of the Brigade had passed out of sight over the hill and there was no sign of life west of Horseshoe line. Very little hostile shelling. At this time it became evident that a large number of Germans had been passed over in the front and support lines.[36]

At 12:45 hours a runner reached Brigadier-General Gore's HQ sent by Major Stocks, who was holding Peake Trench. During the time taken to relay this message Stock had been mortally wounded. Knowing that parties from the 101st Brigade were holding positions behind enemy lines, Gore knew that he had to act to clear the enemy troops in the German front lines at Kipper Trench, Heligoland Redoubt and Bloater Trench. At 13:00 hours one company of the Northumberland Pioneers was placed at the disposal of Gore with the intention of sending them across No Man's Land to clear the German front line trenches. Gore arranged for Kipper and Bloater Trenches to be bombarded until 15:20 hours and then an attempt to recapture these trenches would be made. Two Platoons from the Northumberland Pioneers tried to advance to left of the 21st Division line with the intention of bombing up Kipper Trench towards Heligoland Redoubt. A further two platoons of Pioneers together with thirty men remaining from the carrying company of the Grimsby Chums tried to enter the crater and made an effort to bomb southwards along Bloater Trench and attack Heligoland from the north. As soon as they left the parapet of the old British front line they were showered with machine-gun fire and twenty-three of these men thirty men were either killed or wounded. The assault failed. Those that were left were then detailed to join the two platoons from their battalion who were meant to be attacking Kipper Trench on 21st Division's left flank, but this initiative also faltered under heavy German machine-gun fire that commanded No Man's Land.

During the night of 1/2 July Captain Osbert Brown's party of intermingled battalions struggled to hold onto Wood Alley and were surrounded by the enemy. The Germans still occupied Heligoland Redoubt, which cut off Brown's men from the main force of the 34th Division. Reinforcements and supplies could not get to them. Captain Brown and his mixed band of men from the Suffolk, Royal Scots and Northumberland regiments had to hold on to Wood Alley until 01:00 hours on 3 July.

Brigadier-General Gore at 101st Brigade HQ was unaware that Osbert's party had secured Wood Alley, and were protecting the left flank of the 21st Division, until early evening. Macrae at 2nd Edinburgh City HQ had received a message from Captain Armit, commanding 'B' Company stating that 'he, four of his own men and 150 O.Rs of different units were holding position on German Support Trench and that enemy was present in neighbouring trenches.'[37] It was not until 00:15 hours on 2 July that Gore received a direct message from Osbert Brown confirming that he, together with twenty men from the 11th Suffolk and approximately 200 men from the other units were holding Wood Alley. They were surrounded for German forces had regained control of Bloater Trench, Sausage Redoubt and Heligoland. Brown and his party were isolated. It was doubtful that they could effectively resist a strong German counter-attack.

Gore was conscious that the men holding Wood Alley would be in need of water, ammunition and bombs. He immediately ordered his battalion commanders, Lieutenant-Colonel Urmston and Lieutenant-Colonel Sir George Macrae, to go forward with the remnants of their battalions and establish contact with their units behind German lines. Only Macrae received the orders and at 09:25 hours he led his men forward. However, the German barrage was so intense they were forced to take cover on several occasions. The route taken by Macrae's party to Wood Alley was extremely difficult but eventually it reached a position occupied by Lieutenant Lodge and 2nd Lieutenant Hamilton with 150 men at 03:30 hours. A second party from the 2nd Edinburgh City made an attempt to advance into Scots Redoubt but they were forced to withdraw after encountering the enemy. They eventually joined Macrae's party via the 21st Division sector.

Captain Brown and his party had been defending the trench for the entire day under an intensively hot summer sun. Captain R.C. Greig, of the 1st Edinburgh City, who was brigade Staff Captain volunteered to lead a water carrying party through the German lines to Wood Alley, under the cover of darkness. Major John Ewing recalled:

> In pitch blackness and under heavy shell fire he and his men laboriously forced a way over corpses that now formed the floor of the trenches, and ultimately they clambered on top and proceeded across country in the direction of Scots Redoubt, till they found a trench occupied by a Company of the 21st Division.[38]

Captain Greig began his excursion into German lines with twelve men and when he returned back to British lines he was left with just three men. Although Greig had failed to resupply comrades in Wood Alley, Lieutenant Ash managed to reach them during that night taking bombs and other supplies and assisted to consolidate the trench.

2nd Lieutenant Hamilton reached Lieutenant Lodge who was now in command of 150 men of the 2nd Edinburgh City. 2nd Lieutenant Robson was also in Wood Alley Trench with eighty-six men and there were elements from the Grimsby Chums, the 11th Suffolk and the 4th Tyneside

Irish. When Macrae arrived at daybreak there were eleven officers and 293 men holding the position. There was also another party from 'B' Company, 2nd Edinburgh City led by Captain Armit which was holding another trench beyond Wood Alley Trench. The appearance of Macrae with reinforcements and supplies was an enormous boost to the morale of these men who had used all their ammunition and consumed their emergency rations. After twenty-four hours fighting they were exhausted, hungry and dehydrated. In order to consolidate Wood Alley Trench it was imperative that they capture Scots Redoubt which was positioned in between Wood Alley and the British lines. Before he could initiate an attack on this strongly defended point Macrae ensured that his men were fed, had had water and were armed.

By midday on 2 July Macrae's force was ready. An hour later at 13:00 hours Lieutenant Robson of the 1st Edinburgh City armed with bombs led an assault upon Scots Redoubt. He successfully seized the position and captured three officers and fifty men. 2nd Lieutenant Hamilton led a simultaneous attack upon a trench system which linked with Scots Redoubt named the Horseshoe. Hamilton succeeded in securing 150 yards of this horseshoe-shaped trench but was held up by a barricade which was established by German bombers.

Despite securing Scots Redoubt and the Horseshoe the men were still in a vulnerable position because Heligoland and Sausage Redoubt were occupied by German forces. Conscious that Macrae's rear and left flank was exposed Brigadier-General Gore ordered two companies from the 7th East Lancashire Regiment of the 19th Division to capture Sausage Redoubt and Heligoland before dusk on 2 July. This was achieved, establishing a direct link between the British line and Macrae's force in Scots Redoubt. At 09:00 hours four sections from the Royal Engineers arrived with picks, shovels and several coils of wire to consolidate Scots Redoubt and the captured section of Horseshoe trench.

German commanders were desperate to regain the positions that they had lost and initiated a bombardment throughout that night. Despite the heavy shelling 400 reinforcements from the 101st and 103rd Brigades bolstered Macrae's force. At 23:45 hours rations, water and supplies of small arms ammunition had reached Scots Redoubt. The 2nd Edinburgh City's quartermaster, Lieutenant D. Gray, managed to send cooked meat and grocery rations up the line to ensure that these men got a hot meal, the first since the assault begun. Sir George Macrae was appointed commander of 101st Brigade in these advanced positions. On 3 July this force fought off a German counter-attack.

By holding onto Wood Alley and defending it for two days, the 43th Division ensured that La Boisselle would be captured by the 19th Division on 3 July. It lost heavily. The 15th Royal Scots lost eighteen officers and 610 casualties. The 16th Royal Scots losses amounted to nine officers and 460 men out of twenty officers and 790 men that took part in the attack. These two battalions had been entirely raised from men living in Edinburgh, but so severe were the losses the direct connection with the Scottish capital could not be maintained and the gaps in the ranks had to be filled by men from across Scotland.

AFTERMATH

Major-General Ingouville-Williams had deployed all his battalions in the assault upon trenches north and south of La Boisselle. With no battalions in reserve the old front line was devoid of any reserve troops and became vulnerable to German counter-attacks. It was apparent that the scale of the casualties incurred by the 34th Division was such that Ingouville-Williams was concerned that the British old front line was exposed. He therefore asked the III Corps Commander to send some troops forward to hold and secure this line. One squadron from the Corps Cavalry Regiment and the Corps Cyclist 1st Company were sent forward to occupy the front line and placed under the command Lieutenant-Colonel John Shakespear commanding, 18th Northumberland Fusiliers (Pioneers).

The 34th Division suffered the most casualties of any division on the 1 July 1916, amounting to 6,380 officers and men. All four commanding officers from the 102nd Brigade were killed as well as all second-in-commands and adjutants. At roll call on the 2 July only 100 soldiers of the 4th Tyneside Scottish answered their names. A further twenty men were found alive later that day. Only two officers survived from this battalion.

For this terrible loss the Tyneside Irish and Scottish had captured frontline trenches of the Schwaben Höhe and the Scots Redoubt which amounted to twenty acres. This was tragically the only significant result of a drive on to Bapaume nine miles further up the road. The Tyneside Brigades were so reduced in number that they were detached from the 34th Division and sent to Vimy Ridge, a quiet sector of the Western Front to rest, recover and rebuild their battalions. The 1st and 2nd Edinburgh battalions sustained 513 and 466 casualties respectively, which had a devastating effect upon the city.[39] The Grimsby Chums suffered 502 casualties from a force of 842. Private Harry Baumber survived and described Grimsby as 'a town in mourning after the Somme with almost every street affected in the same way'.[40] The battalion captured the Lochnagar Crater and held the position, though they suffered 502 casualties from a force of 842. The 11th Suffolk Regiment lost 691 men.

The reasons why the 34th Division failed in achieving its objectives and suffered high casualties on 1 July 1916 are numerous. The week-long artillery bombardment failed to destroy German barbed-wire and front line defences. The congestion in the small gaps in the wire as the men tried to pass through presented the Germans with an obvious and inviting target.

The two-minute delay in waiting for debris to fall from the mine explosions and the order for advancing troops to move at a walking pace gave German troops sufficient time to appear from their deep dugouts and prepare their machine-guns for action. The bloody efficiency of the German machine-gunners was another reason for high casualties. As the approaching British infantry advanced at walking pace they were easy prey. The Germans also held the advantage in being positioned on high ground.

The fact that commanding officers advanced with their men, and became casualties, resulted in a breakdown in the command structure, particularly as the day wore on and officer casualties mounted. More importantly many enemy machine-gun emplacements that were hidden in Mash and Sausage Valley were not identified during aerial reconnaissance. This meant that the artillery bombardment only concentrated their barrage upon trenches, artillery positions and strongpoints. They did not fire upon open ground, which was the reason why these secret emplacements were missed. As the barrage went forward and the leading waves followed this barrage, German forces were able to get into the German front line trench system, blocking the path of the support waves and isolating the leading waves.

Finally, Major-General Ingouville-Williams' decision to commit every brigade simultaneously into the attack without leaving reserves was a serious flaw in his plan to capture La Boisselle. The 103rd Brigade was ordered to mount its parapets at the same time as the 101st and 102nd Brigades. The 1st Tyneside Scottish had a distance of 500 yards across Mash Valley before they reached the German lines. The 2nd Tyneside Scottish had a shorter distance of 200 yards to across No Man's Land before they reached the German trenches. However the Tyneside Irish battalions in the 103rd Brigade had to cross between 1,000 and 1,500 yards of the exposed Avoca Valley before reaching the British front line and No Man's Land. The consequence of not using the communication trenches to the front line was that they were exposed to German machine-guns, and a large proportion of this brigade was cut down before it ever got to the battlefield. With so many casualties suffered by all brigades Ingouville-Williams had nothing in reserve to deploy.

By the evening of 1 July 1916 the village of La Boisselle remained under German control. However, the small gains that were made by the 34th Division on 1 July would act as a stepping stone for the 19th Division's subsequent, and successful attack upon La Boisselle.

Part 6

XV Corps Sector

Chapter 19

Fricourt

The 21st Division commanded by Major-General D.G.M. Campbell, of Lieutenant-General Henry Horne's XV Corps was given the objective of capturing Fricourt, where the German line turned eastwards towards Mametz and Montauban. The German 111th Infantry Regiment had occupied Fricourt since March 1916. The village comprised 176 houses and was nestled beneath a ridge, named Fricourt Spur, protected by German front line trenches. There were significant efforts by both sides to dig mines west of the village where three mines had been dug beneath the German-occupied position called the Tambour by Royal Engineers of the 178th Tunnelling Company, commanded by Major E.V.C.W. Wellesley, a relation of the Duke of Wellington. They had been working on mines at the Tambour since 5 August 1915. The Tambour consisted of several craters above ground.

Lieutenant Norman Dillon, 14th Northumberland Fusiliers (Pioneers) had been an apprentice mining engineer at Seaham Colliery before 1914 and prior to the Big Push in 1916 he was seconded to 178th Tunnelling Company as a listener, working on one of the tunnels being dug beneath German positions close to Fricourt. He recalled:

> I was attached to this tunnelling company, all I did with them is to take my turn and listen. That meant sitting down in the bowls of the earth, because the chalk pit mines went very deep and listening for what was going on, in front of the village of Fricourt. We dug a drist mine, you go in at the slope and you went deeper and deeper. You had to listen to what the Germans were doing. You had to outsmart them, that was the difficulty, that is why one had listening posts deep down in the chalk. We had primitive listening instruments, some form of electrified ear phones, and you could easily hear people tapping away long distance through the chalk. If you listened carefully if they were making a chamber to put the explosive charge in you could hear a much more hollow noise of digging then following that the sinister sliding of bags

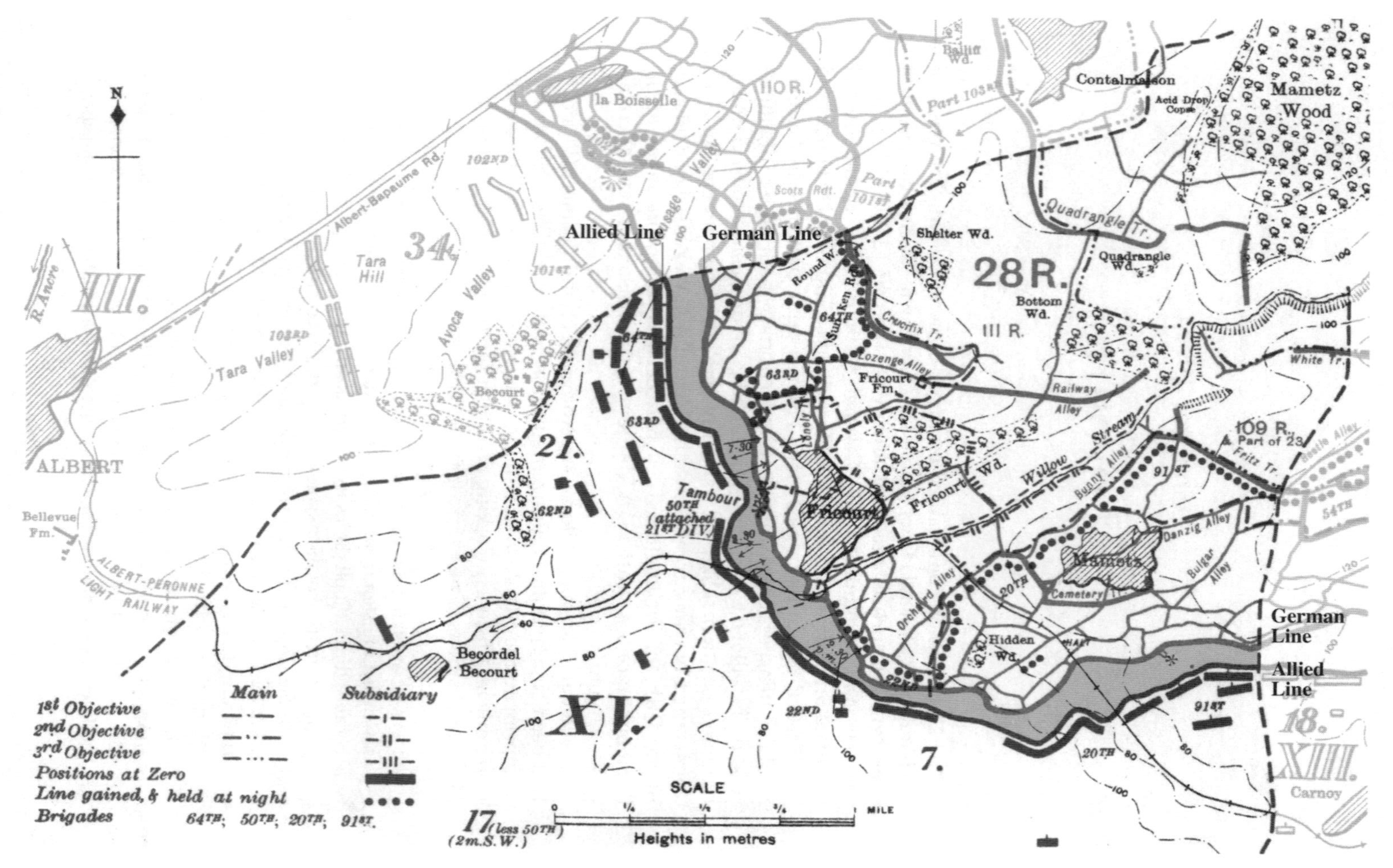

N
R. Ancre
III.
ALBERT
Bellevue Fm.
ALBERT-PERONNE LIGHT RAILWAY
Albert-Bapaume Rd.
Tara Valley
Tara Hill
34.
102ND
103RD
101ST
Avoca Valley
Becourt
la Boisselle
110 R.
Valley
Scots Rdt.
Part 101ST
Part 103RD
Bailiff Wd.
Contalmaison
Acid Drop Copse
Mametz Wood
Allied Line
German Line
Shelter Wd.
28 R.
Quadrangle Tr.
Quadrangle Wd.
Bottom Wd.
III R.
Round W.
Sunken Rd.
64TH
Crucifix Tr.
Lozenge Alley
63RD
Fricourt Fm.
Railway Alley
White Tr.
109 R.
Part of 23
Fritz Tr.
54TH
21.
62ND
Tambour
50TH (attached 21ST DIV.)
7.30
Lonely
Fricourt
Fricourt Wd.
Willow Stream
Bunny Alley
91ST
Danzig Alley
Mametz
Bulgar Alley
Cemetery
20TH
Orchard Alley
Hidden Wd.
2.30 p.m.
22ND
German Line
Allied Line
Becordel Becourt
XV.
7.
18.
XIII.
Carnoy
Main
Subsidiary
1st Objective
2nd Objective
3rd Objective
Positions at Zero
Line gained, & held at night
Brigades 64TH; 50TH; 20TH; 91ST.
17 (less 50TH) (2m.S.W.)
SCALE
0 1/4 1/2 3/4 1 MILE
Heights in metres

> of explosive into the chamber, following that you got out if you could … otherwise there would be no following.
>
> There was someone listening twenty-four hours a day. It was vital to know what the Germans were doing. If you didn't you lost track of the whole operation. It wasn't very pleasant work. Tunnelling companies lost a great number of people with a very high casualty rate. But one was young and took it all in one's stride, in a sense you were under cover, and at least you were out of the range of shell fire for a few hours which was unusual. You had on the surface a rough plan of what you thought the Germans were doing and of course you knew what your mines were doing and you would have several listening posts they were not all in one place so by cross listening you could get a rough idea of where the enemy was.[1]

The 63rd and 64th Brigades of the 21st Division were ordered to penetrate German trenches north and south of Fricourt. They had to advance up the western slope of Fricourt Spur then descend on the other side towards the Sunken Lane before they could reach Crucifix Trench, their first objective. It was not to be a direct assault upon the village but a pincer movement with the intention of each flank meeting with the 7th Division behind Fricourt in Willow Avenue and isolate the German defending the village. The 50th Brigade had been attached to the 21st Division from the 17th Division and was designated with the task of capturing Fricourt, Fricourt Wood to the east of the village and to protect the 21st Division's right flank. The 22nd Brigade from the 7th Division was ordered to capture German positions south of this village on 50th Brigade's right flank.

The intensive bombardment upon the German lines began at 06:25 hours. At 07:22 hours Stokes mortars joined the field guns that were pounding Fricourt and surrounding trenches. At 07:25 hours the British Field artillery lifted its barrage from the German front line trenches towards the support trenches. Simultaneously British infantry left their trenches and crept towards the German lines.

At 07:28 hours two of those small mines beneath the German Tambour exploded with the intention of diverting the enemy's attention and to form craters that would block German machine-gunners' field of fire. However, almost immediately after the mines had been detonated German troops rapidly secured control of the craters.

64th BRIGADE

The 64th Brigade commanded by Brigadier-General H.R. Headlam carried the 21st Division's left flank north of Fricourt. It was ordered to assault South Sausage Trench before pushing forward to a line called Crucifix Trench which connected Round Wood and Lozenge Wood, south of Contalmaison.

The 10th King's Own (Yorkshire Light Infantry) (KOYLI), commanded by Lieutenant-Colonel King, was tasked with the capture of the eastern perimeter of Shelter Wood on the brigades left flank. Once this was secured it was to allow the 1st East Yorkshire Regiment, led by Lieutenant-Colonel M.B. Stow, to pass through its lines and advance forward towards Quadrangle Trench. The 9th KOYLI, led by Lieutenant-Colonel Colmer Lynch, followed by Lieutenant-Colonel Fitzgerald's 15th Durham Light Infantry, were to advance on the right flank towards Shelter Wood.

The 9th and 10th KOYLI, the two leading battalions, were in their allotted assembly trenches after dusk on 30 June. The 1st East Yorkshire and the 15th Durham Light Infantry following behind experienced trouble in reaching their assembly positions for they were severely delayed by the 14th Northumberland Fusiliers (Pioneers), blocking the communication trench leading to the front line, as the 64th Brigade War Diary reported:

> The delay was caused by the condition of the working party of the 14th Northumberland Fusiliers (Pioneers) allotted for work with the Brigade. This party had been ordered to be in position by 11.15 pm, but many of the men and the officer in command were drunk, and blocked Pioneer Avenue. The party got into place at 1.15 am.[2]

The 9th and 10th KOYLI crawled into No Man's Land via a Russian sap five minutes before Zero Hour and waited for the British barrage to lift from the German front line. This strategy meant that they could assemble 180 yards from the German front line and reduce the distance required to cross No Man's Land. However, German machine-gunners ascended from their dugouts while the barrage was still falling close to their line and were able to begin their defence as soon as these two battalions entered No Man's Land, causing significant casualties before the attack had begun. At 07:30 hours the men of the 9th & 10th KOYLI got on their feet and began to dash across No Man's Land in quick time. They came under hostile fire from South Sausage Trench, immediately in front of them, from Fricourt to the southeast and from machine-gun positions at La Boisselle north-east of their position. The 64th Brigade War Diary reported:

> Almost immediately after our men began to show in the open the machine-guns got to work notwithstanding the barrage. As soon as this lifted many Germans also lined their parapets, and opened fire. The majority of the casualties in the Brigade occurred in No Man's Land.[3]

They continued their advance and reached South Sausage Trench where they were within range of stick grenades thrown by the German defendants, as well as riflemen along the parapets of the 4th Company, 111th Infantry Regiment.

Despite being attacked by bombs, the 9th KOYLI overwhelmed this determined German defence and was able to drive its advance deeper into the enemy lines:

> The men, however, never hesitated and went straight on in gallant fashion. They dealt promptly with the Germans on the parapets and once the main German network of trenches were passed, we suffered no damage from hostile rifle or M.G. fire from our immediate rear.[4]

Out of twenty-four officers from the 9th KOYLI who left the trenches only five subalterns reached the German front line. Lieutenant-Colonel Colmer Lynch commanding the battalion was killed.

The two KOYLI battalions were followed by the 15th Durham Light Infantry, 1st East Yorkshire Regiment and pioneers from the 14th Northumberland Fusiliers who reached the German support trench. Their advance into the German lines was rapid. Within ten minutes all four battalions of the 64th Brigade had crossed No Man's Land and were consolidating the ground captured.

Clearing the enemy from South Sausage Trench, they assaulted the support trenches where there was a running fight as the Germans withdrew to rear lines. By 08:00 hours they had reached the Sunken Road where a series of small fights had erupted involving the bomb and bayonet. Once the German defence had been overwhelmed the shelter of the Sunken Road provided a secure place to reorganise the brigade.

The first objective line, Crucifix Trench, together with Round Wood, was secured by 08:15 hours and, despite their reduced numbers, they were able to consolidate the trenches that they had captured and secured a considerable number of German prisoners.

Brigadier-General Headlam sent Captain Yeo forward to appraise the situation at 07:50 hours, but when he did not return by 08:20 hours, Headlam decided to move Brigade Headquarters further forward. When he was 400 yards west of the Sunken Lane he looked north and could see approximately 100 men, of the 34th Division withdrawing just north of the skyline from Round Wood. Headlam immediately detailed twenty men to form a firing line facing north as a precaution against a German counter-attack on their own flank. When he reached the Sunken Road he found remnants from his brigade lined along the eastern embankment with others in Round Wood and lined along Crucifix Trench. They had succeeded in reaching their objective of Crucifix Trench, but Headlam was concerned for he reported:

> Fearing my left flank, I urged parties of men up the road and also directed Captain Bevan of the M.G. Co. to send guns to Round Wood. With other men and Major Bosanquet I then went over the open to

> Crucifix Trench, with idea of passing over it and getting Birch Tree Wood whilst it was possible to do so. Unfortunately a German M.G. was brought up into action at this moment and Major Bosanquet and several others were hit.[5]

Headlam returned down the Sunken Road and found Lieutenant-Colonel Fitzgerald, commanding the 15th Durham Light Infantry, who reported that the right flank was in a state of chaos and that he had sent a Lewis Gun team to the northern perimeter of Lozenge Wood. Knowing that Fitzgerald was proactive in trying to secure the right flank, Headlam became more concerned about protecting the left flank and ordered Captain Willis to consolidate Round Wood which had been captured by 'A' Company, 1st East Yorkshire Regiment at 09:45 hours.

Communication between Headlam and 21st Division HQ was non-existent as the brigade signallers had not reached their advanced position. Fitzgerald was the only commanding officer remaining from the 64th Brigade. Headlam placed Fitzgerald in command of the captured positions as he returned to Brigade Headquarters to establish telephone communication with Divisional Headquarters. Fitzgerald was instructed to await orders before advancing upon Crucifix Trench. Unbeknown to Headlam and Fitzgerald some parties had got as far as Crucifix Trench. The 64th Brigade was in control of German trenches that stretched from Round Wood, along Crucifix Trench and Lozenge Wood, but it was coming under fire from all sides as well as shell fire. This situation would continue throughout the day and would intensify by nightfall. Remnants from the 34th Division began to arrive from the north intermingled with parties of the 64th Brigade at Round Wood, Round Wood Alley and the Sunken Road.

Private J. Kearford, 9th KOYLI, established contact with the 63rd Brigade on the right flank and discovered that there were comrades from the brigade who were in Crucifix Trench. The 9th KOYLI War Diary reported that he:

> Performed a risky and invaluable piece of work by proceeding down the Sunken Road towards Fricourt, not knowing what he might chance, until he found and established communication with the 4th Middlesex Regt, 63rd Brigade. It was also soon discovered that there were a few of our troops right ahead in Crucifix Trench; there were men of each battalion of the Brigade there under 2nd Lt A.E. Day of this battalion, who had continued the advance so far in spite of shrapnel wounds received in the fight while crossing No Man's Land.[6]

The wounded 2nd Lieutenant Day and his party held onto Crucifix Trench throughout that morning. Fitzgerald was ordered by Headlam to wait for orders from Brigade HQ which meant that Day had to remain isolated in this position until early afternoon. The extent of the poor communications was evident when Headlam arrived back at the British line. He wrote:

> I got back to my old Bde H.Q.in our trenches at 10.30 am and reported situation verbally to Div H.Q. To show difficulties of communication I may state that a written situation report sent by me from Sunken Road half an hour before I left there, for transmission to Div reached my H.Q. telephones about an hour after I had returned myself.[7]

Headlam received a message from 21st Division HQ at 11.30 hours that the 1st Lincolnshire Regiment was being sent from the 62nd Brigade to bolster the left flank. An hour later another message was sent by wire confirming that the 34th Division on the left had pushed forward its advance towards Peake Wood and that the 1st Lincolnshire should be deployed on the right flank in an effort to establish contact with the 63rd Brigade.

The 10th Yorkshire Regiment (The Green Howards) and 1st Lincolnshire Regiment, including a contingent of eighty-one men from the Bermuda Volunteer Rifle Corps were brought forward to reinforce 64th Brigade's line. The 1st Lincolnshire was deployed to the Sausage Support system. The 10th Green Howards was ordered to go forward and connect with the 63rd Brigade on its right, but were unable to do so because the 1st Lincolnshire had blocked Aberdeen Avenue and the men could not go forward. The 10th Green Howards did not reach Crucifix Trench until 06:30 hours. The Lincolns also arrived there at the same time.

German forces assembled in Shelter Wood east of Crucifix Trench later that morning launched a bombing attack from Birch Tree Wood Trench. This counter-attack was repelled. At midday Major-General D.G.M. Campbell, C-in-C 21st Division, ordered Headlam to organise an assault upon Shelter Wood. Headlam sent orders to Lieutenant-Colonel Fitzgerald to attack this position at 13:30 hours at which point the artillery barrage was scheduled to lift. The message did not reach Fitzgerald until 13:40 hours. As soon as the message was received the troops waiting in the Sunken Road moved into action and headed towards Crucifix Trench. The 9th KOYLI advanced towards Crucifix Trench in three waves led by the three surviving officers, Lieutenant B.L. Gordon, 2nd Lieutenant G.F. Ellenberger and R.F. Frazer. As soon as they entered the trench they consolidated the position. The wounded 2nd Lieutenant Day had been holding on to the trench since the morning and his condition was getting worse to the extent that he was incapacitated. He refused to go back to get his wounds tended until ordered by Lieutenant Gordon. Pioneers from the 14th Northumberland Fusiliers came forward to consolidate the trench.

At 14:30 hours an initiative to push forward the line was launched from Crucifix Trench when the 10th KOYLI and 15th Durham Light Infantry moved forward to capture Shelter Wood, but this effort failed due to lack of artillery support. At 16:35 hours Headlam ordered the 64th Brigade to consolidate the ground that it had captured. The 62nd Brigade were ordered to relieve the 64th Brigade at 18:45 hours. This was not completed until 06:00 hours the following morning.

64th Brigade had achieved a partial success. The German wire had been cut and its troops were able to swiftly cross No Man's Land and enter the German trenches, however their casualties on 1 July were heavy. The 9th KOYLI lost twenty-one officers and 383 men; 10th KOYLI lost twenty-one officers and 428 men; 15th Durham Light Infantry lost fifteen officers and 373 men and 1st East Yorkshire Regiment lost twenty-one officers and 478 men.[8]

63rd BRIGADE

The 63rd Brigade commanded by Brigadier-General E.R. Hill advanced north of Fricourt on the right flank of the 64th Brigade. The 4th Middlesex Regiment on the right flank was allotted the task of seizing Fricourt Farm and positions between Railway Alley and Copse. The 8th Somerset Light Infantry carried the left flank and was given the task of securing the sector of Crucifix Trench south of Shelter Wood. The second wave comprising the 10th York and Lancaster Regiment on the right and the 8th Lincolnshire Regiment on the left was ordered to take the second objective line Quadrangle Trench to Trench Junction.

The 63rd Brigade began its assault upon German lines north of Fricourt five minutes before Zero Hour and three minutes later two mines were exploded near the Tambour. Two companies, 'A' and 'B', of the 4th Middlesex Regiment tried to crawl into No Man's Land at 07:25 hours but suffered a setback when they were spotted by German machine-gunners who immediately opened fire upon them inflicting substantial casualties forcing them to return to their starting line. The casualties it had suffered were so severe that men were ordered to advance in one single line instead of two. At 07:29 hours this line left its trench a second time to advance in defiance of the German machine-guns. 'C' and 'D' companies followed behind. They came under fire from six machine-guns which were untouched by the British bombardment. The British barrage continued to go forward and the 4th Middlesex could not keep up with the rate of the barrage. Lieutenant-Colonel H.P.F. Bicknell, commanding 4th Middlesex Regiment went forward with Battalion HQ along with 'C' Company, and recalled:

> The chief feature of the attack on 1 July was that our own artillery barrage moved forward much too rapidly. Owing to the severe fighting in and around the German front and support trenches and the heavy losses there, the infantry never got near enough to it again for it to be the slightest use: we saw it getting further and further away, whilst the intervening ground was full of Germans who were as safe as we were.[9]

Two enemy machine-guns were positioned between the German front line named Empress Trench and the support line; and there were four other machine-guns pouring fire onto them from north of Fricourt. Regardless of this 'A' and 'B' companies reached Empress Trench. They had lost most of their officers and the majority of the NCOs were either dead or wounded. Pushing forward without their leaders the two companies passed over Empress Trench to reach the German support line and a party of forty men had advanced as far as the Sunken Road. Here they repelled a German counter-assault. Their numbers were bolstered later that morning by the support battalion, the 8th Battalion Lincolnshire Regiment and they held on to this position for the next two days when they returned to the British line led by Sergeant Millwood.

The two rear companies, 'C' and 'D', could only reach the German front trench because their advance was halted by six enemy machine-guns, two positioned in between Empress Support and Empress Trench and four machine-guns firing from the Tambour and north of Fricourt. Bicknell's party amounted to four officers and 100 men with three Lewis Guns. German troops were seen assembling on their right flank in Fricourt and Bicknell decided to consolidate and remain in Empress Trench. Bicknell ordered a barricade to block the right of Empress Trench and across the communication trenches linking to the Sunken Road in anticipation of a German counter-attack. Here they held on to their position and resisted three German bombing attacks from the south.

The 8th Somerset Light Infantry, commanded by Lieutenant-Colonel J.W. Scott, advanced on the left flank of the 4th Middlesex Regiment. They too were spotted by German machine-gunners as they crawled into No Man's Land five minutes before Zero Hour. Most of the officers became casualties, including Scott who was wounded. Those that survived remained in No Man's Land.

Once the artillery barrage lifted at 07:25 hours the remnants of the battalion charged across No Man's Land. The 8th Somerset Light Infantry War Diary reported:

> Our men advanced in quick time. They were met by very heavy machine-gun fire and although officers and men were falling everywhere the advance went steadily on and was reported to by a Brigade Major who witnessed it to have been magnificent. The leading platoon lost quite 50% going across No Man's Land.[10]

Private Maurice Symes, 8th Somerset Light Infantry, recalled:

> We were told that this place that we were mining under Fricourt, when that went up in the morning that was the signal to go over the top. There was this terrific bang and of course we was ready to go, we got

> out of the trenches and go … it was like a training exercise we were just in extended order, with pack, rifle and bayonet with entrenching tool and everything else, just walked straight towards the German lines in extended order. We were sitting ducks all the way. The German machine-guns and their artillery were still there. That is where the casualties came from there was so many of them. You would run, then lie down and then you would run a bit further. This was walking straight into a death trap, hundreds of us. It was just hopeless. The Germans were ready for us. We thought that everything was going to be destroyed by the bombardment but they were still there. We were in the first wave of the lot. We got out of the trench and walked forward. You could see people going down all around getting shot. It was not a very pleasant feeling. I got hit myself and knocked me out … I was surprised. I wondered what had happened. It felt like someone had kicked me in the stomach. I knew I could not go any further, I just dumped everything except my water bottle and crawled into a shell hole and stayed there for a bit.[11]

As they advanced towards the German lines, German artillery unleashed a barrage upon No Man's Land and the British front-line trench causing further casualties. Symes who was sheltering from machine-gun fire in a shell crater suffered a further wound caused by shrapnel as the German artillery targeted No Man's Land.

After losing most of their officers the remaining NCOs from the 8th Somerset Light Infantry took command of the situation and ensured that the survivors continued the operation. Despite taking heavy casualties the leading waves reached the German front line where their advance was momentarily halted by a machine-gun. As the support waves caught up with them they were able to overwhelm this machine-gun position and clamber into the German front-line trench which was found to have been severely battered by the British bombardment. Only a few enemy machine-gunners were found alive and these were immediately killed.[12]

Bombing parties then bombed their way along the German communication trenches clearing dugouts as they went along. They discovered that the British artillery bombardment prior to the assault had succeeded and that the trenches 'had been battered out of all recognition, and only consisted of a mass of craters.'[13]

A Stokes mortar was brought forward and assisted the advance into German lines, but the team operating it was soon knocked out. A Lewis Gun crew led by 2nd Lieutenant Kellet came forward and provided covering fire as the advance continued. The men moved from crater to crater until they reached Lozenge Alley which had been untouched by the British bombardment. Here they linked up with Lieutenant Hall and the combined strength of their two parties amounted to approximately 100 men. Lozenge Alley was a communication trench and it was necessary to dig fire steps into the sides of the trench. They would hold this position throughout the night and resisted a German counter-attack from Fricourt.

The support battalions – the 10th York and Lancaster Regiment commanded by Lieutenant-Colonel Ridgway and 8th Lincolnshire Regiment led by Lieutenant-Colonel R.H. Johnston – were ordered to leave the British line an hour later at 08:30 hours, and pass through the positions won by the 4th Middlesex and 8th Somerset Light Infantry and then proceed forward towards the second objective line between Bottom Wood and Quadrangle Trench at the southern tip of the Contalmaison Spur. Due to the heavy casualties and the opposition encountered by the 8th Somerset Light Infantry and 4th Middlesex Regiment it was initially decided to abort any efforts in trying to secure the second objective line. Lieutenant-Colonel Johnston received a message at 08:20 hours ordering the 8th Lincolnshire Regiment not to start the advance at 08:30 hours and to wait for further orders. This message came too late as his two leading platoons from 'A' and 'B' Company had already started to advance.

In the meantime, the 50th Brigade was unable to hold on to German trenches in front of Fricourt and was forced to retire. This greatly exposed the right flank of the 4th Middlesex. The situation became critical as German machine-gunners and riflemen were able to work their way forward. Fragmented parties of the 8th Somerset Light Infantry had successfully reached Lozenge Alley and the Sunken Road, but their situation was precarious too. At 08:15 hours Bicknell, commanding 4th Middlesex, sent reports to Brigadier-General E.R. Hill at Brigade HQ that severe losses had been incurred and it was impossible to advance further to the second objective due to the strength of the opposition.

Brigadier-General Hill had received similar reports from the 8th Somerset Light Infantry. The message was clear, they would not be able to hold on to the trenches that they had captured without reinforcements. At 08:40 hours Hill ordered the 10th York and Lancaster and the 8th Lincolnshire to go forward. Both battalions came under heavy enemy fire as they dashed across No Man's Land from Fricourt and Fricourt Wood. Casualties mounted quickly, including many of the officers. Sergeant William Hattersley of the 10th York and Lancaster assumed command when all the company officers fell. Hattersley had already distinguished himself before the start of the offensive when he went over the parapet and brought in his wounded company commander who had been examining the wire in front of the British line. On 1 July he took control of the company, rallied and reorganised it, and led the advance towards Lonely Support Trench. For this action he received the Military Medal. The 10th York and Lancaster secured the position it captured by blocking the trench with sandbags. This battalion passed through the 4th Middlesex Regiment and reached Lozenge Alley. A fierce struggle developed for this trench using bombs. Private Harry Jones risked his life in order to turn the tide of the battle. His citation for the Military Medal stated:

> Devotion to duty and splendid work in bombing the enemy's trenches. At a critical moment he got out of the trench and advanced towards the enemy bombing them from the outside their own trench. This action greatly helped to turn the scale in our favour.[14]

The battalion then went forward towards Dart Lane and beyond where they came under heavy machine-gun fire from Fricourt Wood. The men were in a vulnerable position, because they had to confront three large German bombing parties that were bombing their way along trenches from the south. At the same time the battalion bombers were trying to fight off another bomb attack in Lonely Trench. German bombs had destroyed three of their barricades and their line was in serious danger of collapsing. Lieutenant-Colonel Ridgway then ordered that a barricade be placed across the north end of Lonely Trench close to the junction of Lozenge Alley. He sent a party from 'D' Company with stragglers from other units into Arrow Lane to protect that flank, supported by one gun crew from the machine-gun Corps. This position was in danger of being isolated as German bombing parties made several determined attempts from the south to bomb up Empress Support and the remains of Empress Trench. The remainder of the battalion held Lozenge Alley with 8th Lincolnshire and other units.

As the 10th York and Lancaster and 8th Lincolnshire pushed forward at 11:00 hours, Bicknell was ordered by Hill to protect the right flank. Bicknell had already blocked trenches leading to Fricourt. He reorganised the remnants of his battalion to defend their right flank and their defence was strengthened by Lewis machine-guns which was able to inflict heavy casualties amongst the Germans in Fricourt.

At 17:00 hours Lieutenant-Colonel Ridgway reorganised the 10th York and Lancasters and took the men to secure Dart Lane. He had deployed a party of bombers in Arrow Lane and in the communication trenches between Dart Lane and Arrow Lane The battalion held this trench until 14:00 hours on 2 July.

The 8th Lincolnshire Regiment bolstered the front held by the 8th Somerset Light Infantry. 'B' and 'C' companies led the battalion, supported by 'A' Company. 'D' Company followed behind bringing up vital supplies of bombs, ammunition and desperately needed entrenching tools. The leading platoons suffered 50 per cent casualties as they dashed across No Man's Land. The survivors reached Empress Trench then crossed Empress Support Line. They then proceeded along the communication trenches named Dart Lane and Brandy Trench clearing enemy occupied dugouts as they went along. Their bombers then swept along Lozenge Alley reaching the Sunken Road. They could not proceed any further and were unable to capture the objective at Fricourt Farm. Lieutenant-Colonel Johnston wrote:

> Men were meantime getting forward of Lozenge Alley, up which I advanced trying to find out the situation on the right. I could not see any advance here. It was therefore necessary to watch our right flank. I pushed up men to Lozenge Wood and along Sunken Road, getting touch with 64th Brigade on Sunken Road and in left (north) portion of Crucifix Trench. Those advancing up Lozenge Alley meeting Germans coming from Fricourt Farm. The Germans made 2 bombing attacks up Lonely Trench both of which were repulsed. Though at one time the Germans got a few men into Lozenge Alley here. They used rifle grenades as well as bombs and so could out distance our bombers until we got up our rifle grenades. The Germans left at least 20 dead in Lonely Trench up to Lozenge Alley and some in Lozenge Alley.[15]

Lieutenant-Colonel Johnston, who was an expert on musketry, got involved with the fighting. Captain F. Brown, battalion adjutant reported after the war: 'In the attack of the 8th Lincolnshire's I met one wounded officer, Captain R.G. Cordiner, who remarked "You ought to see the Colonel who is now doing 'kneeling load' for all he's worth"'.[16]

A small party of men from the battalion advanced north along the Sunken Road towards Crucifix Trench. Here it opposed a German counter-attack from Lonely Trench and held its ground. Communication had totally broken down within 8th Lincolnshire which became reliant upon pigeons to send desperate requests for water and ammunition. Captain F. Brown recalled:

> I must however record one particularly memorable piece of communication by pigeon. Supplies of water and ammunition were short and all means of communication seemed cut – numerous ground wire signals were cut as soon as laid. Even the NCO in charge of pigeons was missing. Pigeons only remained. A strand of wool taken from my stocking effectively fastened message to the leg of the pigeon go home and we received ammunition and water, which we so urgently needed.[17]

By midnight the 4th Middlesex was holding Empress Trench from Ball Lane and Empress Support; the 8th Somerset Light Infantry held positions west of Lozenge Wood, Sunken Road and Lozenge Alley; the 10th York and Lancaster was in Dart Lane and the 8th Lincolnshire was holding Dart Alley to Lozenge Wood. The brigade had achieved a definite success in securing these gains but they failed to capture the second objective line and were unable to move through Fricourt Wood and join 7th Division at Willow

Avenue which would have completely isolated Fricourt. This failure could be attributed to the fact that many of the German machine-guns had not been knocked out during the bombardment and that before Zero Hour many of the troops from this brigade were spotted and fired upon causing enormous casualties before they advanced towards the German first line. The 4th Middlesex had lost nineteen officers and 521 men, though the Official History states casualties of nineteen officers and 469 men. 8th Lincoln Regiment lost thirteen officers and 239 men.[18]

50th BRIGADE ASSAULT UPON FRICOURT

The 50th Brigade, commanded by Brigadier-General W.J.T. Glasgow, was transferred from the 17th Division to support the 21st Division in the assault upon Fricourt. Comprising the 10th West Yorkshires Regiment, 7th East Yorkshires Regiment, 7th Yorkshire Regiment (The Green Howards), 6th Dorsetshire Regiment and 7th York and Lancaster (Pioneers), it was given the task of launching a direct assault upon the village.

The 10th West Yorkshire Regiment carried the left flank of the brigade covering the sector from the apex of the salient named Purfleet to the Tambour. It was to capture Konig Trench and then proceed east towards Red Cottage and Lonely Copse. Its role was to cover the flank of the 21st Division advancing north of Fricourt. Once the 21st Division had established contact with the 7th Division behind Fricourt in a pincer movement isolating Fricourt, the 7th Green Howards, together with the 10th West Yorkshire, would move directly upon Fricourt.

The 7th Green Howards were disposed on the brigade's right flank from the Tambour to the Cemetery and were given the task of capturing Fricourt Trench, the first German line that led from the Tambour, and then seize Fricourt. The 7th East Yorkshire Regiment assembled in Bonte Redoubt where they waited for the 10th West Yorkshire to advance and they would enter the line that they vacated. The 6th Dorsetshire Regiment was held in brigade reserve at Méaulte.

At 07:30 hours two companies of the 10th West Yorkshire Regiment attacked on a 600 yard front from Konig Trench towards Red Cottage, which was situated in the north section of Fricourt. They suffered few casualties because the Germans did not have time to get machine-guns set up quickly enough to fire upon these first two companies. By the time the third and fourth companies were advancing across No Man's Land the German machine-guns were in position at the Tambour and within Fricourt and they wreaked a devastating fire upon them. Lieutenant-Colonel Arthur Dickson commanding the 10th West Yorkshire, his second-in-command Major James Knott DSO, and the adjutant were all killed which meant command, control and communication within the battalion had been lost at the start of the attack. Only a few remnants reached the German front line where they remained until nightfall. The War Diary reported that the 10th West Yorkshire Regiment lost twenty-two officers and approximately 750 men.

Information about the 10th West Yorkshire's progress was obscure throughout the morning. Brigadier-General Glasgow at 50th Brigade HQ had no knowledge that the first and second companies had reached their objective until wounded stragglers returned to the British lines. Communication were established with survivors from the third and fourth companies in Konig Trench, but the officers here were junior and were ignorant of the situation with the first and second companies further east. With German machine-guns firing continuously from Fricourt, it was impossible to move freely above the parapet of Konig Trench. Meanwhile, soldiers from the 10th West Yorkshire holding Red Cottage were overwhelmed by a German counter-attack later that morning. Small pockets holding positions further north from Red Cottage were able to link up with elements from the 63rd Brigade.

The 7th Green Howards fared no better than the 10th West Yorkshires. This battalion, commanded by Lieutenant-Colonel R.D. A'Fife, was meant to have launched its direct assault upon Fricourt at 14:30 hours, after the 63rd and 64th brigades had encircled the village. 'A' Company, on orders from its company commander, Major R.E.D. Kent, launched an attack upon one of the strongest points of the Fricourt defences in error at 07:45 hours (although 50th Brigade states time as 08:20 hours). The company was all but wiped out by a sole machine-gun over an area of twenty yards. No explanation was given that explained why Kent advanced seven hours ahead of schedule. The battalion War Diary reported:

> Owing to the unfortunate mistake on the part of the Officer commanding A Coy: his company assaulted at 7.45 am as soon as they began to climb over our parapet terrific machine-gun fire was opened by the enemy and the company was almost at once wiped out. The survivors lay in crump holes some 25 yards in front of our own wire until after dark.[19]

At 13:00 hours Brigadier-General W.J.T. Glasgow received orders from Major-General Campbell at 21st Division HQ that the second phase of the assault on Fricourt, involving the 50th Brigade's direct attack upon the village would take place at 14:30 hours. There was insufficient time to prepare for this attack due to the rapidly changing circumstances with the 10th West Yorkshire struggling to keep control of Konig Trench.

The 7th East Yorkshire Regiment together with three companies from the 7th Green Howards launched a further attack upon German positions at Fricourt. Lewis Guns positioned by the railway embankment covered their advance as they filtered through four gaps in the German wire. During the first fifty yards of its advance across No Man's Land the 7th Green Howards suffered 351 casualties within three minutes. Some of the survivors reached the perimeter of Fricourt but were either killed or captured.

The 7th East Yorkshire Regiment headed towards Red Cottage, advancing over the ground covered by the 10th West Yorkshire earlier that day. 'C' and 'D' companies were unable to reach Konig Trench, the German front line, and 'B' Company was unable to beyond the British front line due to overwhelming machine-gun fire. The battalion lost 155 men during the first steps of the assault. The shambolic attack upon Fricourt was aborted as a result.

The battalions of 50th Brigade lost heavily in their disastrous attempt to capture Fricourt with no evidence of success. The brigade was thwarted by strongly positioned machine-guns which had not been neutralised. The tragic losses were unnecessary as these battalions were able to walk into Fricourt without opposition on 2 July when its German occupants evacuated their trenches during the night.

7th DIVISION AT FRICOURT

The 22nd Brigade, commanded by Brigadier-General J. McC. Steele was ordered to take German positions in a sector of heavily-cratered woodland called the Bois Français, south of Fricourt at 10:30 hours. The intention was to advance through German positions to Willow Avenue where they would meet battalions from the 63rd Brigade and seal off Fricourt. The 20th Manchester Regiment (5th Manchester Pals) covered the right flank and the 1st Royal Welch Fusiliers were to provide support on the left. The 2nd Royal Warwickshire and 2nd Royal Irish Regiment were held back at Divisional Reserve. The assault of 22nd Brigade upon Fricourt was dependent upon the 20th Brigade securing Orchard Alley on its right flank.

At 07:25 hours the 20th Manchester released smoke, but this alerted vigilant machine-gunners and artillery observers and brought an immediate response from German machine-guns and artillery upon their first line trench. At 10:30 hours the 20th Manchester and 1st Royal Welch Fusiliers received orders that their advance was postponed for four hours and instead they were to attack at 14:30 hours. Supported by a preliminary bombardment lasting thirty minutes, the 20th Manchester Regiment launched its assault upon on time. 'A' and 'B' companies advanced towards the Sunken Road which ran between Wing Corner, south of Fricourt to a hill close to Bois Français Wood. 'C' Company advanced over the craters of Bois Français, with 'D' Company in reserve.

The first wave encountered little resistance as it advanced through Bois Français Wood towards Sunken Road Trench. It deviated slightly towards the right from its intended course. One party crossing the craters was confronted with limited German opposition, which was quickly eliminated. As soon as the 20th Manchester reached Bois Français Support Trench they were engaged in a bomb fight with a German party.

Once German forces became aware that an assault was taking place southwest of Fricourt, the supporting waves from the 20th Manchester succumbed to heavy machine-gun fire from Wing Corner and the village of Fricourt. The 7th Green Howards had not captured the village and the German machine-guns operating from their caused havoc amongst the ranks of the 20th Manchester. Lieutenant-Colonel Harold Lewis commanding 20th Manchester was killed within the first fifteen minutes of the attack. Battalion adjutant Captain F. Bryant assumed command.

No British troops were seen advancing upon Fricourt on their left flank. Fricourt was still occupied by German units which meant that they could concentrate their fire upon their left flank from the village. Captain F. Bryant, Lieutenant Denton-Thompson and nine men were all that remained on the battalion left flank as they entered Sunken Road Trench where they established Battalion HQ. Bombers advancing with the support waves were hit by this concentrated fire. These men were meant to have bombed along Sunken Road Trench, Kitchen Trench through to Copper Trench in the direction of Fricourt, but they were lying dead or wounded in No Man's Land. The advance upon the left flank could proceed no further.

As the leading wave of the 20th Manchester passed over Sunken Road Trench they suffered heavy casualties as they were fired upon from strongly-held German positions along Sunken Road Trench, close to Fricourt, Rectangle Support, Zinc Trench and Orchard Alley. Lieutenant H.S. Bagshaw and 2nd Lieutenant A.G.N. Dixey managed to penetrate the strongly-defended German position known as the Rectangle with a few men, but once they were in the German position there was no-one left to command. German bombers made a forceful attempt to evict them from the position. In fear of becoming surrounded and isolated these two officers moved to the right where they collected remnants from their company and they linked with comrades from 'C' Company in Bois Français Support. Here they were able to reorganise these men and order a bombing party to advance down Orchard Alley. They succeeded in reaching the junction of Zinc Trench where they erected a barricade. They continued to go forward towards Papen Trench but here they met heavy resistance. A bomb fight ensued but they could not breakthrough the strongly-held trench and they came under German machine-gun fire from their rear left flank. This attack faltered at Papen Trench because they had exhausted their bomb supplies. They were forced to retire to Bois Français Support. Captain F. Bryant, Lieutenant Denton-Thompson and nine men positioned in Sunken Road Trench, came under German counter-attacks and became isolated. They put up a spirited defence, but Denton-Thomas and four of the nine men were shot.

News reached the British line stating that the 20th Manchester was losing control in the German lines and German bombers soon forced them from the Bois Français Support Trench. At 15:45 hours the two remaining platoons from the Brigade reserve were ordered forward to reoccupy Bois Français Support Trench in support of the 20th Manchester. The 1st Royal Welch Fusiliers were to cross No Man's Land but became a target for a German machine-gunner positioned at Wing Corner. Lieutenant-Colonel Stockwell ordered a bombing party and 'A' Company to cross under the shelter of the craters of the Bois Français. They were ordered to bomb westwards from the captured German trenches along the Sunken Road and Rectangle Trenches.

By 17:25 hours reports were received from Brigade HQ that Bryant, the adjutant of the 20th Manchester and six men were holding a position in Sunken Road Trench. German forces still held onto the Rectangle. Two platoons from 1st Royal Welch Fusiliers were sent to Sunken Road Trench to assist this small party. These platoons took time in reaching the position as they crossed over the craters. As they headed towards Sunken Road Trench, two further platoons were sent forward. These platoons from 1st Royal Welch Fusiliers sent bombing parties along Sunken Road Trench and either side of the Rectangle in the direction of Apple Alley. This action relieved pressure on the 20th Manchester Regiment which held on to its positions. By 18:40 hours the Welch Fusiliers had secured the Rectangle. At that same time elements of the 20th Brigade were seen entering Fricourt Wood from Mametz.

At 07:15 hours a bombing party from the Welsh Fusiliers had established contact with Bryant and his small party in Sunken Lane Trench and had secured the left flank. Bryant moved Battalion HQ to a safer position in Bois Français Support. A German counter-attack regained possession of the Rectangle at 22:10 hours but within an hour the Welsh Fusiliers had recaptured the position.

The 20th Manchester Regiment had eleven officers killed, six officers wounded, 110 men killed, twenty-nine missing and 171 wounded. The 1st Royal Welch Fusiliers had four killed and thirty-five wounded. 200 German prisoners and a large number of heavy trench mortars were captured.

The 22nd Brigade had failed to link up with 63rd Brigade and as a consequence Fricourt was not taken on 1 July 1916. It was an extremely tough position to capture because it was positioned in a valley. British artillery was therefore unable to reach the village. It was well defended by machine-gun and sniper nests in nearby Fricourt Wood and Mametz Wood. However the efforts and partial gains obtained by 7th and 21st Divisions had convinced the German 111th Infantry Regiment occupying the village that their position was vulnerable and they evacuated Fricourt the following day.

Chapter 20

Mametz

The 20th and 91st Brigades of the 7th Division, commanded by Major-General Herbert Watts, were ordered to capture Mametz. This village comprised 120 houses and was defended by 109th RIR, 28th Reserve Division, up to the boundary of the Carnoy–Montauban Road. This German unit had been transferred from the Ovillers-la-Boisselle sector to Mametz on 16 June 1916. The defences at Ovillers-la-Boisselle were securely fortified so when the men of the 109th RIR arrived at Mametz they were dissatisfied with the poor conditions of the trenches and set about strengthening and fortifying this sector.

The line at Mametz was different to other sectors because the deep dugouts were positioned in the front-line trench. There were no dugouts in the second or third lines which, compared to other sectors, meant there was insufficient underground shelter for the troops defending the sector to resist a massive artillery barrage. It also meant that the line at Mametz was extremely vulnerable if the first trench line was captured by the enemy. The defences at Mametz were deficient of switch lines and communication trenches which would enable its occupiers to move quickly within the trench system and entrap any hostile forces who penetrated their defences. There were poor communications with limited telephone lines and there were insufficient barbed-wire defences. They had only a few days from the day of their arrival until the opening bombardment to improve the situation.

The Germans could not live in the trenches whilst the improvements were being made, which meant they had to move into the front line from billets in the rear where the risk of taking casualties during the journey to the front line from enemy artillery fire was great. By the time the British barrage had begun on 24 June some dugouts had been dug, barbed entanglements had been intensified and some switch lines created, but the work could not be continued under such a relentless bombardment. Much work was still required to improve these defences and strengthen them to the same high standard in the north sector.

Regardless of the deficiencies in the defences at Mametz its capture still remained a formidable task because the village was positioned on high ground, protected by tactically-placed machine-gun positions. The 7th Division was to advance northwards from its trenches in a direct assault upon the village and would be exposed to these machine-guns throughout its advance across No Man's Land.

Despite the intensive British barrage the soldiers who were about to assault Mametz knew that they faced a tough task, as Private F. Smyth, 2nd Gordon Highlanders wrote:

> The place where we fought was a beautiful little country place – green meadows covered with poppies. In front of us lay what was once a peaceful and prosperous village, but looking at it then was a sorry spectacle. But within that ruined village there were thousands of Huns with every engine of destruction known to science.[1]

However these British soldiers were unaware that on this sector the preparatory bombardment had succeeded in smashing German artillery close by, as well as cutting most telephone communications within Mametz. Many of the fifteen machine-guns that supported the 109th RIR had also been destroyed. They were also unaware of the deficiencies of the German defences at Mametz.

The 91st Brigade commanded by Lieutenant-Colonel J.R. Minshull-Ford consisting of the 1st South Staffordshire Regiment, 2nd The Queen's (Royal West Surrey Regiment), 21st Manchester Regiment (6th Manchester Pals) and 22nd Manchester Regiment (7th Manchester Pals) was on the 7th Division's right flank and was ordered to take the tip of Mametz Spur and the western sector of the village. The men first had to seize Bulgar Trench, Bulgar Alley and Bucket Trench. On securing these trenches they were to continue to Dantzig Alley, known as Staubwasser Graben, which led into Mametz. They were to advance along Dantzig Alley westwards until they reached the village. The second objective was to secure Fritz Trench and Valley Trench and form a fire line to counter expectant German counter-attacks from the northeast. Their third task involved securing the 7th Division's final objective of the day, the capture of Bunny Alley and the sector northeast of Mametz. It was hoped that they would link up with XIII Corps in Beetle Alley on their right flank.

The 20th Brigade, led by Brigadier-General C.J. Deverell, comprising the 2nd Border Regiment, 2nd Gordon Highlanders, 8th and 9th Devonshire Regiment, was ordered to capture German trenches south and southwest of Mametz, secure the western sector of the village, form a defensive line facing Fricourt and protect the flank of the 91st Brigade's advance. The 2nd Border's and 9th Devon's objective was to secure Orchard Alley which was positioned between Mametz and Fricourt. They were to link up with the 22nd Brigade on their left flank east of Bois Français. The 2nd Gordon Highlanders was expected to drive through the German lines in the western section of Mametz and secure Bunny Alley which ran north of the village. Four Russian saps were dug towards the German lines and would be used as starting points in No Man's Land for the advance.

Six mines were detonated on this sector to assist the 7th Division in its assault upon Mametz and to act as a diversion. A large mine was dug beneath Bulgar Point opposite the 1st South Stafford's start line where 2,000lbs were exploded. Five other mines, which were smaller at 500lbs, were detonated opposite Hidden Wood in between the line held by 2nd Border and the 20th Manchester Regiment of the 22nd Brigade.

German artillery and trench mortars had caused considerable damage to the brigade's front-line trenches and it was not safe for these battalions to assemble there because of the danger caused by enemy artillery and trench mortars. It was therefore necessary to bring forward the start of their advance two minutes before Zero Hour to enable them to leave from the support trenches then to pass over their frontline to get to No Man's Land.

The 22nd Brigade was scheduled to attack positions south of Fricourt later that morning and the success of their operation was dependent upon 20th Brigade securing these trenches. Once this objective had been captured, the 2nd Royal Warwickshire Regiment and 20th Manchester Regiment would sweep through German-occupied trenches southwest of Mametz. Their first objective was to secure Rose Alley and then push on to its second objective which was a line which ran from Willow Avenue to Bunny Wood where they would meet the 21st Division and isolate Fricourt in a pincer movement.

The 109th RIR suffered casualties during the British bombardment. Their nerves were shattered and their bodies exhausted from the heavy labour undertaken in improving the defences. It was decided to withdraw them to rear lines where they could rest and if required act as reserve. It was decided to relieve them with 23rd Infantry Regiment which had previously held this sector. The 109th RIR should have been relieved during the night of 30 June / 1 July but only one and a half companies of the relief had reached Mametz with the remainder still at Montauban. Unbeknown to the soldiers of 7th Division, they were attacking a position held by exhausted German troops who were expecting to be relieved.

91st BRIGADE – MAMETZ

When British guns opened fire at 06:25 hours, German artillery responded with heavy fire directed into the 91st Brigade's frontline trenches, but these men were evacuated to support trenches in the rear and were unaffected by the German barrage.

At 07:29 hours British Stokes mortars began their bombardment of German front-line trenches on this sector and the first waves from the 91st Brigade began to move forward towards the first German line. German machine-gun crews opened fire upon these waves. 1st South Staffordshire on the left and the 7th Manchester Pals on the right flank advanced behind a creeping barrage across No Man's Land which measured between 100 and 200 yards wide between Mansell Copse and the Carnoy–Montauban track. They got into Bulgar Trench, the German frontline trench, within two minutes.

The 7th Manchester Pals was followed by 2nd Queen's starting their advance from a trench that was dug astride the Carnoy–Mametz track at 07:30 hours. They came under German machine-gun fire on the high ridge from Mametz and Dantzig Alley. Some men became casualties but despite this enemy fire the rest swept across No Man's Land, advancing 700 yards. Within the first opening fifteen minutes of the attack the 1st South Staffordshire had reached the south-eastern corner of Mametz and the 7th Manchester Pals had fought its way into Black Trench. They encountered stronger opposition the further they advanced into the German lines.

By 08:00 hours the 7th Manchester Pals had fought its way into Bucket Trench positioned between Mametz and Pommiers Redoubt. As it pressed forward to secure Dantzig Alley at 08:15 hours German opposition intensified. A fierce struggle in one sector ensued between parties from the 7th Manchester Pals and waves from a German counter-attack from Fritz Trench. The 7th Manchester Pals could not hold onto this sector of Dantzig Alley and had to withdraw to Bucket Trench which it then consolidated.

The 1st Staffordshire Regiment on the brigade's left flank advanced through Bulgar Point and Bulgar Trench. According to the War Diary 'the attack was pushed forward very successfully and with very few casualties'.[2] By 07:45 hours it had captured Cemetery Trench and had reached the southern outskirts of Mametz. The men proceeded to enter the ruins in the northeast sector of the village by 08:00 hours. Initially the German defence of Mametz was lacklustre, but eventually they encountered determined German resistance further inside the village. Sporadic bursts of enemy machine-gun fire from the ruined houses the rubble of the village caused heavy casualties amongst the South Staffordshire. There was a concrete machine-gun post with 4in armour-plated loopholes in the south-western portion of the village which put up a stubborn defence. Two companies from the 6th Manchester Pals, and later a third company, were sent forward to support the 1st South Staffordshire. The advance of the 1st South Staffordshire Regiment was held up by enemy opposition from the north and west of Mametz and from Dantzig Alley. The 1st South Staffordshire could not hold onto its position within the village and was forced to retire leaving only a small force there. They withdrew to hedges skirting the southern perimeter of Mametz to Cemetery Trench south of the village.

At 09:00 hours an observer from XXII Brigade Royal Field Artillery saw the problems that the 7th Manchester Pals and 1st South Stafford faced and ordered supporting fire upon Dantzig Alley in anticipation of a further attempt to move forward. The 106th Battery provided assistance to the 1st South Staffordshire by bombarding Bunny Wood. The 104th Battery targeted German artillery guns that were withdrawing from Mametz Wood and was credited for striking a direct hit upon one of those guns killing its crew. Around that same time 7th Manchester Pals captured Bucket Trench to the east of Mametz.

'A' and 'C' Companies from 2nd Queen's advanced towards Dantzig Alley at 09:50 hours. They were initially held up by direct machine-gun fire from east of Mametz. Sustaining heavy casualties they deviated to the right flank eventually arriving at Bucket Trench to support the 7th Manchester Pals. The 2nd Queen's was unable to advance through the Manchester Pal's line to take Dantzig Alley.

The 1st South Staffordshire's position was bolstered by the appearance of the three companies of the 6th Manchester Pals, but they could not get beyond Cemetery Trench. The remaining company of the 6th Manchester Pals was sent to support its sister battalion.

The 91st Brigade was unable to advance from Bucket Trench and Cemetery Trench and the objective of capturing Mametz was looking remote unless the German machine-gunners and snipers positioned northeast of Mametz were cleared. Major-General Watts was aware that 91st Brigade were in dire need of artillery support in order to force a breakthrough into the village, so he ordered an artillery barrage for half an hour which began at 10:00 hours to bombard enemy-occupied positions on the high ground, northeast of Mametz. The bombardment was focused upon a triangle bordered by Dantzig Alley, Bunny Trench and Fritz Trench but was seemingly ineffective as the German resistance was undiminished.

Small parties managed to enter Dantzig Alley but were counter-attacked by the enemy from Mametz. They were unable to consolidate their position and were forced to retire. The 91st Brigade's right flank was greatly improved at 10:15 hours when Pommiers Redoubt was captured by the 54th Brigade, on the 18th Division's sector on their right flank.

The 1st South Staffordshire had reached the north-eastern corner of Mametz by noon. Its situation became precarious as they pushed forward. Fritz Trench was still in German hands and the 1st South Staffordshires had to withdraw to Dantzig Alley, close to Mametz at 15:00 hours.

By midday, Major-General Watts had received favourable reports that XIII Corps on the right flank had captured Montauban and that the enemy was retreating to Bazentin-le-Grand. On receiving this encouraging news he ordered the 91st Brigade to make another effort to capture Dantzig Alley and Fritz Trench in order to drive the Germans from Mametz.

Brigadier-General Minshull-Ford had received reports that hostile troops were assembling opposite their lines and was fearful that a counter-attack would be launched imminently. He therefore ordered an artillery barrage of the triangle area between Fritz Trench, Dantzig Alley and Bunny

Trench which began at 12:25 hours and deployed the two remaining companies of the 2nd Queen's in a pre-emptive assault before the German forces launched their attack.

The barrage, which lasted for thirty minutes, also focused upon German communication trenches that led from Mametz and Montauban as well as Beetle Alley that ran northeast from Dantzig Alley behind Pommiers Redoubt. This bombardment was more successful and when it finished, the 7th Manchester Pals, supported by a company from the 6th, launched a further attack upon another sector of Dantzig Alley which was occupied by the enemy. The German defenders, who had stubbornly held on throughout the morning, withdrew in the direction of Mametz and northwest along Fritz Trench. Bombing parties pursued fleeing German soldiers along Fritz Trench and followed them into Bright Alley. By 14:30 hours they had consolidated Dantzig Alley up to the junction with Fritz Trench.

On the right flank the remaining two companies of the 2nd Queen's, 'A' and 'C', had left the British line and advanced towards the junction of Dantzig Alley and Fritz Trench. They established a firing line as they moved to Bucket Trench and Bulgar Alley at 13:00 hours where they were ideally positioned to launch an assault upon Dantzig Alley and Fritz Trench northeast of Mametz.

Once they captured this section of the trench, bombers moved westwards along Dantzig Alley and then proceeded north along Bright Alley. Bright Alley was captured by 13:40 hours. Their success enabled the South Staffordshire to capture Bunny Trench north of Mametz. Elements from the 2nd Queen's managed to secure a section of Fritz Trench around 13:30 hours from the eastern end of Dantzig Alley and overcome a German strongpoint taking seventy-five German prisoners. A bombing party overwhelmed a party of twenty and another party of twenty-six of the enemy 'who gave themselves up without having much fight'.[3]

This bombing party was only small and when the German officer from one of these parties realised that they had greater numbers, he changed his mind about surrendering. The War Diary recorded: 'The officer on seeing how superior in numbers his party was tried to get at his revolver, but on being shot in the right shoulder he again threw up his hands.'[4]

The 2nd Queen's proceeded from the east section of Dantzig Alley with bombers and had reached the eastern section of Fritz Trench by 16:00 hours. Lieutenant Eric Hobbs, of the 2nd Queen's and Lieutenant Leslie Day from Royal Field Artillery, Trench Mortar Battery reorganised 'B' Company and within the following hour they had cleared Fritz Trench. Both these officers were killed during this operation and only NCOs were left in charge. Corporal Shaw got hold of a German automatic rifle and turned it upon the enemy as they tried to escape from Fritz Trench, which was secured by 16:30 hours.

The 1st South Staffordshire and the 7th Manchester Pals had cleared Bunny Alley and Bright Alley to the north of Mametz and were able to provide bombing support to the 2nd Queen's. By 17:30 hours the 1st South Staffordshire was able to move battalion headquarters into Mametz. The War Diary reported:

> Battalion headquarters moved up into Mametz, and on reaching the village found that the Battalion's final objective had not been captured. Major Morris with great skill, at once reorganised all the troops in the village and allotted each a task, and sent the following message to Brigade at 8.00 pm. 'On reaching Mametz I found 80 men of the 2nd Gordons, two companies of the R. Warwicks and about 1 ½ Coys of Manchesters with 500 South Staffords. The Colonel of the Gordons had not arrived and the general line held by two units was Dantzig Alley from East to West, running through the village. After a short conference I ordered the whole force to reorganise and advance to the final objective and forthwith consolidate – this is now in progress.' The final objectives were taken and held by 7.40 pm. During the operations 150 prisoners and two machine-guns were captured.[5]

The 1st South Staffordshire also captured German automatic rifles, portable telephones and large quantity of stores and supplies. It then moved along Bunny Alley from Mametz at 19:30 hours to where it crossed Fritz Trench. At this point it consolidated the ground which it had captured, and the trench was secured.

At the same time the 1st South Staffordshire, supported by three companies from the 6th Manchester Pals, advanced 200 yards across exposed ground from Cemetery Trench towards Mametz where pockets of German resistance still held out in the north part of the village. They entered the village and occupied derelict houses in the southern sector of the village. They linked up with comrades who had been holding isolated positions since early morning and proceeded to the centre of the village and from the main street entered the western end of Dantzig Alley.

The 91st Brigade had established a line through Fritz Trench–Valley Trench–Bunny Alley– Bunny Trench. It had suffered heavily with the 7th Manchester Pals having approximately 500 casualties, the 1st South Staffordshire around 350, the 2nd Queen's, some 307, and the 6th Manchester Pals, about 250. The success of the brigade can be attributed to a number of factors. Firstly the German defences were weak and not as well prepared as the German trench system between Gommecourt and La Boisselle. The German forces defending Mametz were exhausted in the days leading up to 1 July as they laboured frantically to strengthen the trenches. The British preparatory barrage had succeeded in destroying German batteries, trenches and had reduced much of Mametz to rubble. The brigade moved rapidly across the weak defences and was able to take advantage of the fatigued German occupants. When their strong resistance held up the brigade's advance, Brigadier-General J.R. Minshull-Ford saw where artillery support was required and expediently called for help to subdue enemy strongpoints to enable the infantry to continue its advance. All these factors contributed to the success of 91st Brigade achieving their objectives.

20th BRIGADE – MAMETZ

The 20th Brigade was on the western flank of the 91st Brigade's line of advance. The British line ran across the hill known as Mansell Copse, which was under direct observation from the German lines on higher ground at Mametz. It was continually subjected to German bombardment and could clearly be visible to German snipers and machine-gunners. It was therefore necessary to dig deep, narrow trenches with numerous traverses, a measure which greatly reduced casualties amongst battalions that held the line here during the months preceding the attack.

However, the state of the British line at Mansell Copse seriously deteriorated in the days before the launch of the offensive, as the Germans responded to the British barrage with 5.9in howitzers, field guns and trench mortars concentrating their fire upon the front line and support trenches that crossed Mansell Copse.

The trenches were in such a dire state that it was necessary for an assembly trench to be dug 250 yards behind the front line on this sector at Mansell Copse, out of range of the German mortars and concealed from the sight of German observers so that 20th Brigade could assemble in a relatively safer position before Zero Hour. The wire in front of the British line was cut under the cover of darkness in preparation for the forthcoming operation during the three previous nights. Ladders were put into position, and steps were dug into the parapet to aid the process of going over the top.

The 9th Devonshire, 2nd Border and 2nd Gordon Highlanders formed up in these trenches during the night of 30 June. The 2nd Border was positioned on the brigade's left flank and had orders to advance towards Hidden Wood and the German trench named Apple Alley. The 9th Devonshire Regiment in the centre was to advance from reserve trenches behind Mansell Copse over the crest, descend into No Man's Land and then climb another crest to reach the German frontline before heading towards a German position known as the Halt where they would meet with the 2nd Gordon Highlanders on their right flank. Here both battalions would push forward towards Dantzig Alley and Apple Alley. A railway line and embankment separated the 9th Devonshire and the 2nd Gordon Highlanders. The 2nd Gordon Highlanders were positioned east of the railway embankment and was ordered to assault the Halt and the southwestern sector of Mametz.

Captain R.A. Wolfe-Murray commanding 'D' Company, 2nd Gordon Highlanders, recorded in his diary, 'none can deny that there can be few men who do not feel an unknown black terror gripping at their innards during those minutes before Zero Hour.'[6]

The British guns opened fire upon the German lines at Mametz at 06:25 hours. Ten minutes later the Germans responded by shelling the British frontline. This had no effect upon the 2nd Border Regiment and the 9th Devonshire which were assembled in the newly-dug assembly trench 250 yards behind the front line. Major W.D. Palithorpe described the impact of the retaliatory German barrage falling upon trenches being held by the 2nd Gordon Highlanders:

> The Bosche put down a barrage on part of our front line but not, thank goodness, on our assembly trenches – the sky was lit up with the bursts of high explosive and by Very lights – the acrid stench of Lyddite filled my throat and the din was so tremendous that I could hardly hear myself speak.[7]

At 07:27 hours sixteen Stokes mortars opened fire upon German lines. Three minutes later the barrage lifted, the whistles blew, and the leading waves of the 20th Brigade climbed up trench ladders, entered No Man's Land and advanced upon Mametz Trench.

Their advance was complicated because they had to move up a valley where there existed a light railway embankment that went in the same direction. German machine-gun crews which had not been destroyed during the British preparatory barrage were able to pour fire into this valley. There were several German dugouts built into the eastern side of the railway embankment that also proved troublesome.

The 9th Devonshire Regiment advanced west of the railway embankment from Mansell Copse. 'A' led the battalion across No Man's Land from support trenches followed by 'B' Company which formed the second wave with 'C' Company in support. 'D' Company was left behind as battalion reserve. Bombing parties were detailed to deal with hostile opposition on the flanks and, once in the German lines, to block trenches. 'C' Company was ordered to mop up from the rear.

As previously mentioned their frontline close to Mansell Copse had been destroyed by German artillery fire which meant that they had to start their advance from the newly-built assembly trenches behind their frontline three minutes before Zero Hour. The trees of Mansell Copse had been reduced to stumps and the 9th Devonshire Regiment could be clearly seen by German machine-gunners from opposing lines on the summit of Mansell Copse.

The men suffered heavy casualties as they advanced over the top of Mansell Copse from German machine-guns directly in front of them in

Danube Trench and beyond in Hidden Wood, which were able to pour devastating fire across the track close to Mansell Copse. There was a further machine-gun positioned 800 yards away on high ground to the northwest in the cemetery in a location known as the Shrine or Matratzenweg (Cemetery Trench) to the Germans. Captain Duncan Martin, 'A' Company commander, 9th Devonshire Regiment, who was a professional artist prior to the war, had created a detailed Plasticine model of the terrain while on leave weeks prior to the assault. The prospect of attacking such a position worried Martin. When he returned to the Somme he used this model to brief his fellow officers and he predicted that they would suffer badly from this particular enemy machine-gun fire at the Shrine. Reverend E. C. Crosse, padre to the 8th and 9th Devonshire battalions recalled:

> Having made the model he came to the conclusion that there must be a great concentration of fire just in front of Mansell Copse. This is just what happened. Captain Martin and most of his company fell just here, and when on the following day I started to collect the dead I buried them at Mansell Copse, because I should say more than half the dead of the 9th Devons lay at this point. Nowhere else on the front of the 8th and 9th Devons was there any great concentration of dead. I believe it was this one machine-gun at the Shrine which killed nearly all these.[8]

Martin could foresee that as they reached the summit of Mansell Copse and descended down the slope into No Man's Land, they would become exposed to machine-gun fire from this position which was perched above Shrine Alley. Martin's forecast was accurate for it would cause many casualties amongst 'A' Company of the 9th Devonshire Regiment. As they advanced from Mansell Copse towards Fricourt, the German machine-gun crew was pouring their deadly fire into their right flank. The leading waves lost all the officers. Captain Martin was among the first to fall and the poet Lieutenant William Hodgson MC was also killed.

There were numerous German machine-gun posts and dugouts built into the western bank of the railway line concealed by undergrowth which proved too formidable for the 9th Devonshire's to overcome. The machine-gun fire coming from Shrine Alley was so devastating that the steep sided valley in which the road and the railway passed through could not be entered, which meant that there was a gap between the 9th Devonshire and the 2nd Gordon Highlanders line of advance.

Private William was among those that fell wounded from the Devonshire Regiment and appreciated the Brodie steel helmet that he was wearing:

> I was unlucky enough to get wounded in the charge on Saturday, 1st July receiving injuries to the head by shrapnel. In the same I was lucky

> to escape alive. I expect I have lost a lot of comrades. They kept dropping on each side of me. The Germans were shooting at our wounded as they lay helpless on the ground. I believe that my helmet saved my life.[9]

Those that survived the maelstrom of machine-gun bullets crossed No Man's Land and advanced through Danube Trench, the first German line. Remnants from 9th Devonshire Regiment soon reached the next line, Tirpitz Trench and Shrine Alley, 250 yards beyond, but they could proceed no further. Having lost all their officers and unable to establish contact on either their left and right flanks, they found themselves isolated and pinned down by the troublesome machine-gun in the Shrine, as the 20th Brigade War Diary recorded:

> The battalion moved on steadily at first, but the leading companies losing all their officers soon after entering the hostile trenches, and having to pass over trenches completely wrecked beyond recognition by shell fire, became somewhat disorganized and remained in the vicinity of Tirpitz Trench and Shrine Alley, collected in small parties, and engaging the enemy in front of and behind them wherever met. They undoubtedly did great service in keeping the enemy engaged, and in clearing the trenches, and sent back many prisoners. They did not however succeed in getting into touch with the battalions on their right and left, and failed to carry out the task of clearing the 'dug outs' in the wooded bank west of the railway.[10]

'D' Company, held in reserve, was brought forward to support the assault at 07:40 hours, but it lost all its officers before it reached the German lines and it too became disorganised.

On the 20th Brigade's right flank, the 2nd Gordon Highlanders, commanded by Lieutenant-Colonel Bertrand Gordon DSO, left its trenches on a 400 yard front and advanced east of Mansell Copse along the valley east of the railway embankment towards a position called the Halt. 'C' and 'D' companies advanced on the left and 'A' and 'B' companies on the right flank. As they proceeded through the valley across No Man's Land the 2nd Gordon Highlanders was shielded by a slight ridge on its right flank, but as soon as the men were visible from Mametz they came under heavy fire from the machine-gun positioned in the Shrine within the cemetery on high ground just below the village. This German machine-gun crew had decimated the ranks of the 9th Devonshire Regiment and also could see right across the 2nd Gordon Highlanders path of advance in the valley below. The ranks of the 2nd Gordon Highlanders were cut down by this unrelenting enemy fire, together with the shrapnel being fired in their direction. An NCO from the 2nd Gordon Highlanders recalled:

> It was half past seven to the tick when we scrambled out across our trenches and went across into the shell-swept area. We pressed quickly onward, dodging shells, shell holes and traps of all kinds strewn about for the feet of the unwary. Our losses were light enough until we came abreast of the village of Mametz.[11]

Although the men steadily moved towards the German lines under a hail of bullets 'D' Company were sustaining heavy casualties fast in the low valley. Captain R.A. Wolfe-Murray, who led 'D' Company commented: 'The folly of such tactics were soon too ghastly apparent, we were shot down like balls at a fair before ever we could cover the 200 yards separating us from the enemy's front line.'[12]

Despite their casualties, 'A' and 'B' companies of the 2nd Gordon Highlanders were able to keep pace with the 1st South Staffordshire Regiment on their right and although being exposed to heavy machine-gun fire they swiftly crossed No Man's Land. They were able to move forward because British artillery had successfully cut the wire and the men were shielded by some high ground for some of the distance on their right flank. They reached Mametz Trench, the first German line, where the occupants were in a state of panic as they hastily tried to prepare themselves to defend the trench with bombs. Their assault was so rapid that the German defenders panicked as they threw their bombs without drawing their pins. The ineffectual German resistance was subdued by these courageous Gordon Highlanders. Private F. Smyth, 2nd Gordon Highlanders recalled:

> Well promptly, at 7.30 with the sun smiling down on us we climbed over the parapet, the Huns were dumbfounded at us coming over in daylight, as they expected we would have charged under cover of darkness. Briefly there was some hard bayonet fighting, especially in the second and third lines of trenches, but before getting that distance we lost almost half the regiment. Our objective was the crest of a hill beyond the village, but we suffered heavily before we reached it, as the Huns had some machine-guns covered and protected with steel plate and concrete, which defied our explosives. We stuck it, and soon got a footing. A fierce fight took place at close quarters. It was "hell' for a time. We kept at them with bombs and bayonets, some of them thinking 'Discretion the better part of valour' took to their heels.[13]

By 07:50 hours, and despite heavy casualties, 'A' and 'B' companies had reached the road that ran northeast from the Halt. Within five minutes they had reached the southern approaches to Mametz and had succeeded in securing the Sunken Road north of the cemetery where they assembled and prepared to launch an assault upon the village. Captain A.N. Davidson commanding 'A' Company reported that he had reached the Sunken Road and was trying to reorganise the remnants including 'B' Company for an assault upon Mametz. Here they had to wait for 'C' and 'D' companies to join them. At this time the German machine-gun position at the Shrine was still operational and it was able to fire upon the men of these two companies, many of whom were entangled in the German wire. Meeting strong resistance, these two companies were held up. While these two companies were delayed, 'A' and 'B' companies were holding on to their position in the Sunken Road and were fighting off waves of German counter-attacks.

With no prospect of going forward Wolfe-Murray sent a runner to Captain G.H. Gordon to seek support from 'C' Company, which had broken into the German lines. Wolfe-Murray recalled:

> Another officer who contributed greatly to the success of the day was Captain G.H. Gordon, M.C. who commanded C Coy. in support to D Coy. When I realised how hopeless it was for any advance on my Coy front to succeed I sent back L/Cpl. Garrity of the Drums, who was wounded in the arm, to Captain Gordon to tell him how hopelessly we were held up. This officer who had seen a lot of fighting immediately appreciated the situation and with the understanding of a real fighter, left me severely alone. Filing his men across to the shelter of the German front line and then began clearing the enemy out of the trenches to my front taking them in flank. This eased the situation considerably but it was unfortunately from the cemetery in Mametz and from the reverse slopes of the hill near Hidden Wood, that the main fire came from, where M.G. with telescopic sights were kept in the deep dug outs, these nuts took much longer to crack and it was not until 12.30 p.m. that a man could crawl to tie up a wounded comrade in that valley of death, without bringing a hail of bullets around him as I and my servant Pte Earl knew to our cost, this devoted soldier never left me, 'I'll no leave ye sir.' Was his word when I was first struck and gallant C.S.M. Campbell took on the Coy Headquarters, between us we got hit five times for trying to crawl about the men just bled to death around us, how often has one dreamt of it at night.[14]

At 09:00 hours Captain A.N. Davidson's 'A' Company, was still holding a section of Shrine Alley and some sections of the Mametz–Halt Road. Here the Highlanders made contact with a fifty-strong party from the 1st South Staffordshire Regiment that was without officers or NCOs on their right flank, but they still urgently required further reinforcements in order to carry out an attack upon Mametz. Davidson had no contacts on his left because 'C' and 'D' companies, were still being held up at the German wire on the left flank. Davidson sent runners to search for them while he dealt with serious opposition from machine-gun positions west of the Shrine. They were also coming under intense German sniper and heavy shelling.

Davidson's position was under control by 09:30 hours, but there was still no sign of 'C' and 'D' companies. At that same time 2nd Gordon Highlanders Battalion HQ received the following message from Captain G.H. Gordon, commanding 'C' Company confirming 'I am held up by wire – I am going to try and work round on the left'. This, as Wolfe-Murray related, Gordon was able to do and he managed to capture part of the German trench.[15]

Davidson's company was coming under fire from German machine-gunners ahead of it in dugouts cut into the railway embankment and fire further ahead from Fricourt and Fricourt Wood. They had to flush out the enemy from these dugouts as well as parties of Germans that were still active in Mametz Trench, in the front line. As a consequence the Gordon Highlanders and the 8th Devonshire Regiment, from Brigade reserve, had still not been able to link up with the 9th Devonshire Regiment on their left flank.

The 2nd Border Regiment on the 20th Brigade's left flank steadily advanced adjacent to the 9th Devonshire Regiment in four lines. The first wave of the 2nd Borders advanced towards Danube Trench, the first German trench line taking few casualties. The artillery had successfully cut the German wire on this sector, creating breaches for the men of the 2nd Border Regiment to filter through and swarm into Danube Trench. Their rapid advance meant that they were close to charging into their own barrage, so they had to briefly halt in order to prevent casualties from running into it. They took the front German trenches and secured the western sector of Danube Trench then in accordance with their orders, turned left and advanced towards Hidden Lane. 'During this advance the lines became broken into lines of groups,' noted the brigade War Diary, 'bombing and bayoneting the enemy who were fighting stubbornly holding shell holes and communication trenches.'[16]

The 2nd Border Regiment reached Shrine Alley, its first objective, where it was briefly stopped by enfilade fire from Mametz and indirect fire from Fricourt. Small parties of German infantry launched minor attacks, but they were repelled by bombers who attacked from Kiel Support Trench and by parties who charged across open ground to counter the assault. When reinforcements arrived 2nd Border was able to continue its advance towards Hidden Lane. Its progress was temporarily halted by German machine-gun positions within Hidden Wood and at the junction of Kiel Support Trench and Bois Français Support Trench.

A bombing party worked its way along Kiel Support Trench to overcome the opposition coming from Bois Français Support Trench. German counter-attacks from Kiel Support and Bois Français Support were repelled and then the 2nd Border charged across open exposed ground and into Hidden Wood. The advance lost momentum as the 2nd Border split up into smaller parties, encountering stronger enemy resistance amongst the numerous shells holes in Hidden Wood. The men made slow progress as they fought these small groups of Germans who obstinately defended their ground. Armed with bombs and bayonets, the 2nd Borders launched an assault upon Hidden Wood knocking out German machine-gun positions and at last a breakthrough was made when the leading elements got into Apple Alley on the left flank close to Pear Trench. Only part of this trench system had been taken and 2nd Borders would need more help if the whole position was to be taken.

The failure of the 9th Devonshire Regiment to advance meant that they could not maintain contact with the 2nd Border Regiment who had to establish a defensive position to protect their rear flank. The left flank of the fourth wave were kept as reserve in Kiel Trench to protect the right flank, since there was no contact with the 9th Devonshire's. The right flank from the fourth wave moved into Hidden Wood. The 9th Devonshire had secured a foothold in Shrine Alley and Tirpitz Trench. Prisoners captured in Shrine Alley were arriving at 23rd Brigade HQ by 08:14 hours.

Despite the success of the 2nd Border Regiment, the reserve companies from 9th Devonshire could make no progress due to strong German machine-gun fire which swept across their path. The momentum of the 20th Brigade's attack came to a halt by 10:00 hours. 'D' Company, 9th Devonshire suffered heavy casualties with all their officers mown down in No Man's Land and the survivors were either scattered by the machine-gun bullets or got caught up in the entanglement of German barbed-wire. It was thought that the bombardment of the German wire, rather than cutting it, made it even more of a tangled mess for the men to try and cross. Only a small number of the advancing waves reached the German front line and got to a position east of Hidden Wood. Here the 9th Devonshire was held up, coming under attack from German bombers from Mametz. The 2nd Border Regiment consolidated Hidden Wood, but there was a gap between it and the 9th Devonshire.

20th Brigade Headquarters became aware of this situation from a battalion runner who arrived with his report at 09:30 hours. 'C' Company, 9th Devonshire was sent forward to try to bridge the gap between the 2nd Border and the 9th Devonshire, but this company alone was not strong enough. It was therefore necessary for the brigade's reserve battalion, the 8th Devonshire, to enter the fray.

At 10:30 hours, 'B' Company, commanded by Captain Mahaffy, was ordered to advance from Reserve Trench and support the left flank of the Highlanders and the right flank of the 9th Devonshire Regiment. Mahaffy led his company through Mansell Copse down the slope into the hollow on the Bray–Fricourt Road. 'B' Company suffered heavily from machine-gun fire as it moved past Mansell Copse. Mahaffy was badly wounded and rapidly all its officers became casualties. With all their officers down, Company Sergeant Major Walter Holwill took charge of the remnants of the company which remained in the hollow ground along the Bray–Fricourt

Road throughout that morning, eventually reaching Mametz Trench during the afternoon. Holwill received the Military Cross for his actions that day.

At 10:20 hours Lieutenant-Colonel H. Storey, commanding 9th Devonshire Regiment, ordered 'A' Company, 8th Devonshire Regiment, to advance on the right flank of the 9th. Captain Geoffrey Tregelles led this company in a desperate effort to advance in the direction of the Halt and reach Hidden Wood but was cut down by machine-gun fire as it advanced past Mansell Copse. All four officers from 'A' Company were either killed or wounded. Storey lost contact with 'A' Company for the remainder of the day and it was not until late evening that 2nd Lieutenant Duff reported its fate.

'D' Company, 8th Devonshire was assigned to the 2nd Gordon Highlanders. Two platoons led by 2nd Lieutenant Davidson moved forward to support the Highlanders' assault upon Mametz. When Davidson was wounded Sergeant Tucker took charge and led the platoons forward. As they advanced they engaged with several hostile parties and took several German prisoners.

'C' Company, 8th Devonshire, commanded by Lieutenant Saville, was waiting in Reserve Trench and could see the calamitous situation. By midday it was apparent that the advance of 'A' and 'B' company had stalled Lieutenant-Colonel B.C. James, commanding the 8th Devonshire, ordered Lieutenant Saville to reinforce the line close to Hidden Wood via Mansell Copse. Like the units that tried before them, the first two platoons were shot down in No Man's Land as they passed Mansell Copse. Realising that it was futile to advance in the direction ordered, Saville made the sensible decision for the remainder of the company to deviate on their left flank in an effort to continue to advance but take advantage of the cover provided by the nearby slope which protected them from deadly German machine-gun fire coming from Mametz. Lieutenant Saville's wise decision saved many lives as they advanced on the left flank, crossed No Man's Land and reached Hidden Wood without many casualties. It then advanced towards Orchard Valley where it later established contact with the Border Regiment. This became a mixed group of remnants from the 2nd Border, 8th Devonshire and the remnants from the 9th Devonshire which had been mopping up trenches in the rear.

The 9th Devonshires had not linked up with the 2nd Borders on their left nor with the 2nd Gordon Highlanders on their right. They were embroiled in a dogged battle and were unable to breakdown the German defence which was being supported by effective machine-gun fire coming from Fricourt. The terrain was difficult, and they were fighting their opponents for trenches and shell holes. As the day progressed the casualties amongst the 9th Devonshire were increasing. The 2nd Border had penetrated deep into German lines but it still not had gained complete control of its final objective, Apple Alley. The men consolidated their gains and waited for the 9th Devonshire to come along on their right flank before continuing with its bid to gain complete control of Apple Alley.

Throughout that morning Captain A.N. Davidson's 'A' Company, 2nd Gordon Highlanders, was still holding out, unsupported, in the Sunken Road close to the Shrine. The German machine-gun nestled in the Shrine which caused enormous casualties to the 9th Devonshire was still operational, and without further support, Davidson could not commence the assault upon Mametz. At 11:05 hours battalion headquarters received a report from Davidson, 'Left flank by Shrine still in the air. Patrols cannot find D or C Coys and have met with serious opposition from enemy's machine-guns in the valley W. of Shrine. Am occupying from Shrine to point F.11.a.7.9 along bank of road. Propose advancing to objective when Devons and Gordon on left get into line.'[17]

By early afternoon 'A' Company was in a serious situation as the men fought off repeated German counter-attacks. Davidson sent the following desperate message at 13:45 hours. 'Situation grave, being bombed by large parties at Shrine. Reinforcements absolutely necessary.'[18] It must have taken nearly an hour for battalion HQ to receive this message, for a reply was not sent to Davidson until 14:40 hours confirming: '2 Coys of 2nd Warwicks arrived are coming up to support you at once, hold onto your position at all costs.'[19]

Before this message was sent Brigadier Deverell was informed that 22nd Brigade would launch an assault on his left flank at 14:30 hours and that two companies from the 2nd Royal Warwickshire Regiment would be placed at his disposal to bolster his brigade. He assigned these two companies to support the remnants of 2nd Gordon Highlanders together with two platoons from the 8th Devonshire and displaced men from the morning's attack. They were ordered to launch an attack in conjunction with the 91st Brigade on their right flank upon Mametz to take complete control of the village. The 9th Devonshire was ordered to establish contact with the 2nd Border in Hidden Wood and go forward to secure Apple Alley. The company from 8th Devonshire Regiment lying down in front of Mansell Copse was ordered to move to Plum Lane to link up with the 2nd Gordon Highlanders and support their assault upon Mametz. This company was unable to go direct to Plum Lane because of enemy fire, so it had to move west across the sector crossed by the 2nd Borders, and then once it reached Hidden Wood turn right in order to meet up with the Highlanders.

The two companies of the 2nd Royal Warwickshire arrived at 15:40 hours and five minutes later advanced in four waves without opposition towards the Sunken Road, where Captain Davidson and 'A' Company, of the Highlanders had been holding on. At that same time the 2nd Border had linked up with the 22nd Brigade and parties from the 8th and 9th

Devonshire had been filling the gap in line between the 2nd Border and 2nd Gordon Highlanders.

Davidson and the two Warwickshire companies, as well as two platoons of the 8th Devonshire, advanced upon the north-western sector of Mametz. When they got within close proximity of the village they had to be extremely cautious, for they were exposed on open ground and there was fear amongst the officers of being ambushed by German forces concealed within the ruins of Mametz. But, as the 20th Brigade War Diary recorded, they had an entirely different reception:

> When the advance of the 2nd Royal Warwickshire Regiment began, the enemy appeared to have no stomach for any further fighting, for before the advancing reinforcements had reached the position occupied by leading companies of 2nd Gordon Highlanders in front of Mametz they came out to the number of 400 men approximately and surrendered.[20]

An unidentified NCO from the 2nd Gordon Highlanders reported that the capture of Mametz was not an immediate capitulation and described a different scenario as they went cautiously forward towards Mametz:

> As we approached the village the only sign of life was a thin stream of smoke issuing from a solitary chimney. Still we went warily and in a few minutes our caution was justified. There was a blaze of rifle fire, a sheet of flame, and a perfect din of noise, gradually rising into one prolonged roar, as though a million mountain torrents were set agoing at once. Above the roar could be heard the cries of our officers, 'Steady the Gordons,' 'Not so fast, my men' and other calls all designed to restrain our impetuosity rather than to rally us, for we were eager enough to get into it.[21]

The order to advance was given and as the Highlanders moved forward they were met by enemy fire. They had to dash for their lives across the exposed ground. To hesitate would have meant certain death.

> Finally the order to charge was given and the attacking column dashed forward with a mighty cheer that must have made the souls of the Germans quake. We were met with a fiendish fire, and many a comrade went down, but there was no thought of anything but closing with the foe. It was victory or death with us, and in that spirit we won our way to the outskirts of the village.[22]

Lance Corporal Walker, of the 2nd Gordon Highlanders led a bombing party in the assault upon Mametz. However, because some dugouts were not cleared by supporting waves he was shot in the leg from a concealed German soldier to his rear. He recalled:

> We charged the first three German lines, took them all right and hundreds of prisoners. We then charged the village of Mametz, under a terrible shower of machine-gun bullets and gun shells. As I was kneeling face to face with the Huns firing with my teeth set and my hair on end. I got hit from one behind.[23]

There remained a strong, determined contingent of German soldiers of the 109th RIR who were prepared to defend the village at all costs. Despite being wounded Walker continued to put up a fight before withdrawing to the British line and was able to deal with hostile parties in their rear that had not been cleared:

> My rifle was now red hot, and, being in charge of the bombers, I had two bags of bombs around my neck, so I had to start and crawl back to my own lines. On my way back I found good use for my bombs, as there was a party of Huns shooting at us from behind, after we had passed over their trenches. So I got right close to them and started to pepper them with my bombs. I soon had them lying stiff, as there wasn't a shot fired from that trench after that. Mind you I couldn't stand on my feet at that, and I still had to crawl about 150 yards. When I got to my own lines I had neither kilt nor hat. My hat was torn to pieces with the barbed wire, and so were my knees. But never mind, I was always anxious to get to close quarters with them, and I made short work of a few when I did get the chance.[24]

The rest of the Gordon Highlanders pushed forward their advance into Mametz and a desperate street battle was fought amidst the ruins. Each house, including their cellars had been fortified and machine-guns and snipers were perched in trees. The 2nd Gordon Highlanders would come under hostile fire from the ground, from below and from above. An unidentified NCO from the 2nd Gordon Highlanders recalled:

> Here the enemy had made a fort of every house and from every window, and even from the trees in the gardens, machine-guns and sharpshooters were firing away at us. Our men took no more notice than they would a few raindrops on a summer evening, but set to work systematically to clear the houses out.[25]

A bitter struggle ensued for control of each house. Bombs and bayonets were used and, as the following testimony from an NCO suggests, the

German defenders of Mametz deployed flamethrowers during the battle for the village.

> Bombing parties dashed forward to tackle each house in turn, and very soon they were clear of all but dead Germans. Slowly but irresistibly we won our way through the village for the last tussle that was to fling the Huns headlong from the position they had held so long. It was bayonet work at the last. The order was given, and the men tore forward with a rush that nothing on earth could stop or even delay. Behind their barricades the Huns were strongly posted, and met us with a furious fire. We threw ourselves on the barricades. Barbed wire, galling fire, jets of flame, gas and the rain of bombs were forgotten or only remembered as additional reasons for cleaving our way to victory, and we clambered over the barricades in fine style, flinging ourselves on the now terrified Huns on the other side like an avalanche.
>
> There was, perhaps, half an hour of hard, grim, bayonet fighting, in which we stabbed and thrust at the Huns until we ached with the pain of it all. One desperate rally was made by the enemy in a prepared position just outside the village. Against this we now advanced under a deluge of fire. The whistling of bullets had now grown into a grand chorus and in that fatal advance men seemed to be shaking hands with death at every step of the way. But it didn't matter. For it was the handshake of men certain of victory, and ready to lay down their lives to achieve it. We carried the position with a rush, yelling 'Scotland forever!' at the top of our voices, and beating time to the music of the whistling bullets with our bayonets on the bodies of the Huns who tried to bar our way to victory.[26]

It took less than an hour to clear and consolidate Mametz after systematically searching and clearing every house and derelict building. By 16:45 hours two companies of 2nd Gordon Highlanders, two companies of the 2nd Royal Warwickshire's, two platoons from 8th Devonshire and three machine-gun sections were in possession of Mametz and set about establishing defensive positions in advance of an expect German counter-attack. Contact had also been made with parties of the 1st South Staffordshire Regiment.

While the battle for Mametz was being fought, an operation to capture German trenches southwest of the village was taking place. At 16:00 hours, Lieutenant-Colonel James, commanding 8th Devonshire Regiment sent 2nd Lieutenant Duff forward to find out what remained of 'B' Company, with orders to continue the advance with them and 'C' Company towards Hidden Wood. Twenty minutes later Duff found survivors from 'B' Company in Mametz Trench under the command of Company Sergeant Major Holwill. He organised these men and together with elements from the 2nd Gordon Highlanders, Duff led them in the direction of Dantzig Trench and Hidden Wood to the Halte.

Two platoons from 'D' Company, 8th Devonshire, arrived at 16:00 hours to support the Gordon Highlanders' right flank and they set about assaulting German trenches further west of where 2nd Lieutenant Duff was positioned. With so many officers having fallen, the NCOs, the backbone of the British Army, came to the fore and took control. Sergeant Cater led elements from the 8th Devonshire into advanced German positions at Mametz. Lance Sergeant Clay rallied and steadied his platoon when they lost their platoon commander. As his platoon advanced forward it was held up by the entangled mesh of German barbed-wire. Clay asked for volunteers to cut the wire. Private H. Wadsworth came forward. As he started to cut through the wire he was struck by a bullet. Undaunted by his wounds he continued to cut the wire and made a breach to enable his platoon to go forward. However, the nineteen-year-old Wadsworth was killed outright by a second bullet.

'C' Company, 8th Devonshire Regiment, had pushed forward from Hidden Wood towards Orchard Alley and was able to enter the south-western sector of Mametz where it established contact with men of the 2nd Border Regiment who were gaining ground on their left flank. 'C' Company advance in three groups led by 2nd Lieutenant Barber on the left flank, 2nd Lieutenant Joseph in the centre and Lieutenant Saville on the right. When Saville reached Orchard Alley he led his party on the right where he, Sergeant Paddon, and his batman Private Pitman, encountered and captured 100 German soldiers. The regimental history records that these captives 'had had enough and were only too pleased to find someone to whom they could surrender'.[27]

At 15:10 hours Duff linked up with 2nd Lieutenant Joseph from 'C' Company and with Company Sergeant Major Melhuish from 'A' Company and parties from the 9th Devonshire Regiment. He sent the following report to Lieutenant-Colonel James:

> We have worked under the bank to Halte and beyond, are now working round to Hidden Wood. I have taken and sent back many prisoners from under the bank including four officers.[28]

Company Sergeant Major Melhuish's leadership during this engagement was recognised when he was later awarded the Distinguished Conduct Medal.

2nd Lieutenant Duff also summoned assistance from a party led by CSM Holwill and with his group consisting of the 8th and 9th Devonshire and the 2nd Gordon Highlanders they swarmed across the central sector of 20th Brigade's objective and dashed through Dantzig Trench where they assaulted the dugouts that were built into the western railway embankment and took a significant number of German prisoners, including several officers. After clearing these dugouts they were able to continue along Shrine Alley and attack the machine-guns in this trench that had caused so much trouble for the battalions of the 20th Brigade. After subduing these machine-guns the vast piles of empty cartridges the men discovered was evidence of the carnage and devastation they had caused that morning. The lines of dead and wounded that lay in No Man's Land close to Mansell Copse demonstrated the effectiveness of this machine-gun crew as it worked its guns. Lieutenant-Colonel James reported:

> The nature of the engagement was affected by mopping up parties not clearing the trenches leaving machine-guns and Snipers who caused practically all their casualties. The bank by the Halte was entirely disregarded and all dug outs in Dantzig Trench were found occupied; the enemy using the bank above could concentrate and enfilade fire on troops advancing to Hidden Wood of Mametz. Also the traverses being fire stepped, they could shoot down the valley to our lines. A machine-gun was found at the Halte which had fired a great quantity of rounds. The enemy had taken advantage of this high bank to make it an impregnable position advanced on by a bombing party down to Combe Alley or along the bottom of the bank.[29]

As soon as the 20th Brigade had captured Mametz the men immediately began to consolidate and establish defensive positions. The 95th Field Company, Royal Engineers, supported by a company of pioneers entered the village later that evening and commenced work on strengthening the fortifications under the cover of darkness. Throughout that night they erected barbed-wire defences to the north of the village and established strongpoints and strategically positioned machine-guns in preparation for a German counter assault. They were also able to utilise materials captured from a German dump to assist in the consolidation process.

All the battalions that had taken part in the capture of Mametz were formed into a defensive line. The remnants of 8th and 9th Devonshire Regiment were mixed and were positioned west of Mametz. They had lost heavily during their assault upon enemy trenches at Mametz. The 8th Devonshire casualties included three officers killed with forty-seven men listed as killed or missing. Seven officers and 151 men were wounded. The 9th Devonshire Regiment suffered too. Eighteen company officers had entered the battle and only one, 2nd Lieutenant Porter, survived without injury. The battalion had eight officers killed as well as 141 men were killed, fifty-five listed as missing, and 267 wounded. A total of 775 men from the battalion entered the battle and 463 became casualties. The 2nd Border Regiment's casualties were not as high as the other battalions due to the trench mortars successfully cutting the wire. They had three officers killed and six wounded, one mortally. Seventy-nine men were killed together with 240 wounded, ten of whom subsequently died. Four men were reported missing. The 2nd Gordon Highlanders started the battle with twenty-four officers and 783 men. It had seven officers and 119 men killed, with nine officers and 287 men wounded, and thirty-nine reported missing.[30]

While the battle for Mametz was being fought during that afternoon, Chaplain Ernest Crosse had been searching the front-line trenches for the wounded and to try to identify suitable positions for aid posts. As he ventured towards Mansell Copse he discovered the body of Captain Duncan Martin. He recalled:

> A journey round our front line revealed four badly wounded in a dugout. I helped Hicton drag them out and then went for the stretcher bearers. About 3.30 pm Doc, Gertie and myself walked down the road to Mansell Copse. The road was strewn with dead. Almost the first I looked at being Martin.[31]

The 7th Division suffered significant casualties on 1 July, but it had achieved its objectives, having captured Mametz and trench lines to the north of the village. The men caused heavy casualties amongst the German defenders and compelled them to withdraw from Fricourt. German artillery within the vicinity was also forced to pull back. The German 109th RIR suffered heavy casualties during the period 24 June to 1 July at Mametz, numbering 2,104.[32]

The 7th Division was able to make a breakthrough at Mametz because the village had not been as strongly fortified as other villages on the northern part of the Somme. The dugouts were primarily in the front line trench so once this position was overwhelmed the Germans were unable to bring up reinforcements that would have been occupying the second and third line if sufficient number of dugouts were constructed in these lines. Although well-positioned machine-guns tore into the ranks of the 7th Division, once the remnants moved forward they were able to eventually nullify these German guns and secure the village. The fact that soldiers of the 109th RIR had been exhausted by efforts to strengthening the defences before the assault was another reason why the 7th Division was able to succeed in securing Mametz.

Part 7

XIII Corps Sector

Chapter 21

Pommiers Redoubt

Major-General F.I. Maxse's 18th Division was ordered to capture positions defended by 109th RIR west of Montauban up to Beetle Alley including the German bastion of Pommiers Redoubt (known as Jaminwerk by its defenders).

The 54th Brigade were ordered to launch a direct assault upon Pommiers Redoubt on 18th Division's left flank. On its right the 53rd Brigade was to assault Montauban Alley, a trench which ran between Pommiers Redoubt and Montauban; while the 55th Brigade was designated the sector of Montauban Alley west of Montauban. The Division was to be aided by the explosion of two mines at 07:27 hours. The 183rd Tunnelling Company, Royal Engineers, had dug mines at Casino Point containing 5,000 pounds of ammonal in front of the 6th Royal Berkshire Regiment frontline and another consisting of 500 pounds of ammonal on 11th Royal Fusiliers sector on the western flank.

Russian saps were dug into No Man's Land on this sector, as Lieutenant-Colonel B.G. Clay, 6th Royal Berkshire Regiment, explained:

> As regards to Russian saps to the German front line ... in one case it actually penetrated into a German dug out. The officer came to me very agitated running out our end of the trench to say the whole show was given away as his air gun had pierced through into an officers' dug out and he could hear every word they were saying. He thought that they must know and all was discovered. On enquiry I elicited from him the fact that there had been no interruption in their talk – no dead silence – no raised voices so was able to assure him that according to human nature all was well!! I identified the spot later and it was quite true that he had pierced through in an officers' dugout.[1]

As the 54th Brigade, comprising the 11th Royal Fusiliers, 7th Bedfordshire Regiment, 6th Northamptonshire Regiment and 12th Middlesex Regiment, waited in the assembly trenches it came under German machine-gun fire.

N.
SCALE
YDS1000
500
0
1000 YARDS
1/4
1/2
3/4
1 MILE
Heights in metres
Bazentin le Pt.
Bazentin le Gd.
Longueval
Delville Wood
Mametz Wood
28 R.
2 BNS OF 12 R DIV 12-45 p.m.
Trones Wd.
Willow Stream
Caterpillar Wood
23 (2 BNS.
Triangle Pt.
Bernafay Wd.
62.
White Tr.
Montauban Alley
90TH
55TH
53RD
Montauban
12.
109 R. & Part of 23.
54TH
Pommiers Rdt.
Loop
Briqueterie
Glatz Rdt.
Pommiers Tr.
Train Alley
21ST
1 1/4 BNS. 6 BAV. R.
89TH
Warren
Castle
Dublin Rdt.
German Line
Allied Line
Casino Pt.
Breslau Tr.
Bois Faviere
54TH
53RD
55TH
18.
21ST
German Line
Talus Boisé
XIII
Allied Line
7.
Carnoy
30.
89TH
XV.
90TH
39.
6 BAV. R.
Maricourt
XX.
11.
Franco-British Boundary
Y Wood
British
French
1st Objective
2nd Objective
3rd Objective
Positions at zero
Line gained & held at night
Brigades 21ST, 89TH, 54TH

At 07:30 hours the men of the 11th Royal Fusiliers on the brigade left went over the top 'like bloodhounds let loose from the leash'.[2] They went forward and found that the British guns had succeeded in destroying the German wire. As they reached the German first line, Austrian trench, they found some sectors of these trenches filled with barbed-wire and spiked stakes, but there were no opposition.

The advance of 11th Royal Fusiliers from Austrian Trench to Emden Trench was hindered by a machine-gun in the Triangle and another on its left flank. Both of these were put out of action. Lance Corporal A. Payne, of 'B' Company rushed one of these positions.

Private H. Wheeler became detached from his party of the 11th Royal Fusiliers within Emden Trench. He suddenly encountered seven German soldiers, he shot three of them with his rifle, but the bolt in his rifle jammed. Still outnumbered and in danger he withdrew behind a traverse, mounted the parapet and shot the remaining four German soldiers with a revolver that he had found.

On the right of the Royal Fusiliers, the 7th Bedfordshire Regiment suffered heavy casualties as they dashed forward towards Austrian Trench. The British bombardment had failed to knock out German machine-guns that ripped through its advancing waves. The battalion commander reported:

> As the machine-gun fire, even on cessation of intense bombardment, was still very galling, the waves hurried through the gaps in the wire and doubled down the slope. It was on the gaps and the top of the slope that the machine-gun fire was principally directed. There was practically none at the foot of the slope.[3]

When the 7th Bedfordshire reached Austrian Trench the men also found that some sections were filled with barbed wire and spiked stakes. This front-line trench was occupied by a small defensive force supported by a machine-gun. The barbed wire may have been a means to compensate for limited forces along this sector. Some of the wire was placed across the top of the trench parapets and may also have been placed as a defensive measure against British trench raiders. The spikes had only been recently installed as a measure to counter the numerous raids that occurred in the weeks before the attack. The second line was close behind and contained deep dugouts where the main defenders were garrisoned. As the 7th Bedfordshire advanced from Austrian Trench to Emden Trench, German machine-gun-fire knocked out many of its officers and wrecked the command structure of the battalion, leaving the survivors leaderless.

By 07:40 hours Emden Trench was captured and the 54th Brigade continued to advance towards Bund Trench. The Royal Fusiliers continued to Bund overcoming all resistance. During the advance from Bund Trench to Pommiers Trench, a thirty-strong party of German soldiers launched a counter-attack from Mametz which threatened the Brigade's left flank. The quick-thinking 2nd Lieutenant John Parr-Dudley wheeled his platoon half left and led a charge with rifles, bayonets and bombs directly at the Germans. The platoon overwhelmed this German force with the only casualty being Parr-Dudley who was killed.

The 7th Bedfordshire Regiment's advance was temporarily halted between Bund and Pommiers Trench, particularly because of a machine-gun position in Popoff Lane, a communication trench that connected Pommiers Trench with Bund Trench. As hostile machine-gun fire poured upon it from its right flank, the 7th Bedfordshire was unable to push northwards towards Pommiers Trench because a 500 yard sector of German wire had not been cut by the British bombardment on the sector before Pommiers Trench. A group of men, from the 7th Bedfordshire and the 6th Royal Berkshire Regiment, deviated in a north-westerly direction to cut the wire. The 54th Brigade War Diary reported that 'they proceeded to complete the task under very heavy shell fire in a most methodical and fearless manner.'[4]

Captain Bull, 7th Bedfordshire Regiment reported: 'The ½ hour outside that trench [Pommiers Trench] will be a nightmare for years to come, and this was our expensive time. There were about 20 Berkshires and about that same number of my lot; the way they cut through the wire just as if nothing was doing was splendid.'[5]

At 07:50 hours the British barrage lifted from Pommiers Trench and the 11th Royal Fusiliers were able to advance towards this trench. A small party bombed along Black Alley towards Pommiers Trench. A machine-gun positioned in Pommiers Trench prevented them from going further. Private W.T. Taverner located the position of this machine-gun but was unable to shoot at the gunner. He jumped on top of the emplacement and directed the advancing waves of the Royal Fusiliers left and right of the machine-gun. For his bravery Taverner was awarded the Military Medal. Private J. Nicholson was another individual from the battalion who distinguished himself when he shot six German snipers and subdued another machine-gun position.

The advance had to halt in Pommiers Trench for forty minutes in accordance with the plan of attack. This allowed time to consolidate Pommiers Trench and clear the dugouts which were still occupied by German soldiers in large numbers. Much hand-to-hand fighting took place and many Germans were killed by bombs before they could leave their dugouts. German counter-attacks from Mametz continued to come their way but they were effectively resisted by reserve waves of the Royal Fusiliers.

The Royal Fusiliers was in a vulnerable position as it advanced further into the German lines because its left flank was exposed. At that time the

22nd Manchester Regiment had not captured Dantzig Alley and German forces were still occupying Fritz Trench to the north and were able to fire from this ridge upon their position. In order to protect the left flank two Lewis Guns were hastily set up in Black Alley Trench to fire upon the approaches to Fritz Trench. Two 3in Stokes mortars were brought forward and once they fired shells into Fritz Trench the German soldiers occupying it abandoned this trench and were then mown down by the two Lewis Guns.

Having taken Pommiers Trench and secured the left flank from counter-attacks, the next task for 54th Brigade was to assault and capture Pommiers Redoubt and Maple Trench which led from this strongpoint westwards towards Mametz. This was regarded as the most difficult phase of the assault. A strong contingent of determined German soldiers defended this strongpoint and the wire that surrounded it had not been cut on the eastern perimeter by the British barrage. The defenders greeted the Royal Fusiliers and 7th Bedfordshire with intense machine-gun and rifle fire. Such was the strength of the German resistance these two battalions could not get beyond the wire west of the redoubt. Several attempts were made to rush the wire but many were shot down. Unable to make any progress with a frontal assault upon Pommiers Redoubt, advancing on the right flank, Captain Johnston led a party from 'B' Company, Royal Fusiliers into Black Alley and bombed its way along this trench towards Maple Trench in an effort to enter the German position from the western flank and avoid going through the wire. Sergeant Brisby aided a bombing party which obstructed their path through Black Alley. He was positioned from the left of this trench and as he charged towards it he shot a German soldier who was throwing bombs at him from the fire step. He then jumped into Black Alley and bayoneted the remaining three members of this party.

The last sixty yards of Black Alley was straight and there was a German machine-gun positioned at the end of it which prevented Johnston and his party from going forward. Johnston then decided to get above the parapet and attack Pommiers Redoubt from the rear, but as they charged across open ground they became exposed to German snipers positioned in the southwestern section of Beetle Alley which ran behind Pommiers Redoubt. Johnston ordered 2nd Lieutenant William Savage, who was advancing on his left flank with 'A' Company, to attack these snipers. Savage succeeded in overwhelming them very quickly, enabling Johnston and his party to get close to Pommiers Redoubt without further casualties. Savage was killed as he cleared German snipers from Beetle Alley.

German soldiers could be seen tightly packed in the trenches within Pommiers Redoubt, firing head and shoulders above their parapet supported by a machine-gun which fired along the trench. This stout defence prevented the Royal Fusiliers from entering this stronghold. Johnston therefore deployed his Lewis Guns at the end of Black Alley in order to enfilade the southern line of the redoubt. The occupants of the redoubt were taken by surprise and were wiped out. The Royal Fusiliers and the 7th Bedfordshire Regiment on its right flank were then able to rush the defenders of Pommiers Redoubt. They encountered many dugouts containing German soldiers who were unwilling to surrender but after bitter hand-to-hand fighting the redoubt was taken at 09:30 hours, with Maple Trench being secured later. Both sides suffered heavily in the battle for Pommiers Redoubt. The Royal Fusiliers and the 7th Bedfordshire were able to continue their advance and sent bombing parties northwards towards Beetle Alley and Montauban Alley. At 10:15 hours the British barrage lifted from Beetle Alley and this trench was rushed by these two battalions.

Although 54th Brigade had succeeded in capturing Pommiers Redoubt, it was isolated, because the 91st Brigade on its left flank had not secured its objectives and only got as far as Dantzig Alley. Meanwhile on its right flank, the 53rd Brigade was held up by German resistance along Pommiers Trench and the strongpoint called The Loop. Communication was difficult and signallers had to use shutters and flags in order to send messages. Private Hughes of the Royal Fusiliers had an important message to convey and risked his life by mounting a captured German parapet to wave a white signalling flag as shells were exploding around him.

Supported by reinforcements from the 6th Northamptonshire Regiment, the Royal Fusiliers and 6th Royal Berkshire Regiment were able to capture Beetle Alley. They endeavoured to move eastwards along Beetle Alley and Montauban Alley, but German resistance prevented them from going further. One major problem for the British battalions which had penetrated into German lines was that German machine-gunners who had hidden in dugouts were using tunnels to relocate into better firing positions. Some British soldiers found themselves coming under hostile fire from behind. One sergeant from the 6th Royal Berkshire Regiment commented:

> The Bosche is very cunning with his machine-guns. I don't know how he does it and then he has his tunnels from the first to the second line, so that he can drag his machine-guns about and use them in either. You think you are all right, and then they begin to play on you from behind.[6]

At 14:30 hours a bombing party of the 10th Essex Regiment cleared 400 yards of Montauban Alley, eastwards from Pommiers Redoubt and was able to reach White Trench. By 15:30 hours they were in line with The Loop to the south.

The 12th Middlesex Regiment formed the 54th Brigade's reserve battalion and moved forward to mop up and consolidate the captured German trenches. The battalion War Diary reported: 'The German trenches were very much damaged and in places almost obliterated. There were many German dead in the trenches and prisoners taken appeared dazed and shaken, testifying to the intensity of our bombardment.'[7]

At 16:00 hours the 7th Bedfordshire and the Royal Fusiliers captured White Trench. They met parties from the 6th Royal Berkshire and the 8th Norfolk Regiment at 17:40 hours in Montauban Alley and the process of consolidation began twenty minutes later. After exhaustive fighting throughout the day and achieving their objectives the officers and men from the 54th Brigade had to summon further energy to dig in and consolidate their gains. Those men who were not digging were responsible for keeping a lookout and resisting potential German counter-attacks, but many of these men were so fatigued that they fell asleep. Captain Aley, 11th Royal Fusiliers wrote:

> It was very hard for the diggers, but it was really pitiful to see the others. Everybody was tired out, and I had to keep on constantly waking the men up, for as soon as they touched the ground they automatically succumbed into deep sleep. It is not altogether fun being so tired as we all were in the face of the enemy.[8]

At 22:30 hours a covering party in front of White Trench which ran along the reverse slope of Montauban Ridge, opened fire upon a party of German soldiers advancing towards them. As soon as they opened fire this German party dispersed.

The 11th Royal Fusiliers lost four officers and forty-nine men killed, seventeen listed as missing, 148 men wounded, including four men suffering shell shock. The 7th Bedfordshire lost fifteen officers and 306 men.[9]

THE 53rd BRIGADE'S ATTACK

The 53rd Brigade comprising the 8th Norfolk Regiment, 6th Royal Berkshire, 10th Essex and 8th Suffolk advanced on the right flank of the 54th Brigade. They were given the objective of securing Mine Trench, Bund Trench and Bund Support Trench. They had to overwhelm a German redoubt in between Bund Trench and Bund Support Trench known as the Castle. They were then expected to progress north towards Pommiers Trench and another German bastion called The Loop before going to capture Montauban Alley which extended from Pommiers Redoubt. 6th Royal Berkshire Regiment advanced on the 53rd Brigade's left flank towards Casino Point. The 8th Norfolk advanced on the right flank towards Mine Trench and the Castle. The 10th Essex followed behind these two battalions in support, with the 8th Suffolk as brigade reserve. On this sector, engineers also dug six Russian saps across No Man's Land towards the German lines. A flamethrower supported the 8th Norfolk Regiment's sector close to the cratered area around the Carnoy–Montauban Road.

The 8th Norfolk had assembled in their positions during the night of 30 June and spent a quiet night in the four assembly trenches allotted to them. While waiting for Zero Hour the men laboured to dig small holes into the side of the trench to provide them with some cover. This would prevent casualties later that morning when shells fell upon their positions when German artillery responded to the intensification of the British bombardment as the clocked ticked slowly towards Zero Hour. Officers walked through the trenches speaking to their men to give them words of comfort and reassurance. Private Fred Campling recalled: 'The night passed in comparative quietness; at intervals our officers passed round, giving a word of encouragement here and caution there'.[10] The battalion War Diary also confirmed that it was very quiet on this sector and that at 17:30 hours the usual ration of tea, bread and bacon, together with rum, was brought up from Carnoy and served to the men in their assembly trenches. The intensification of the British bombardment at 07:20 hours, British artillery launched an intense bombardment for the last ten minutes prior to Zero Hour. This ignited a response from the German side and German shells were soon falling upon the fourth assembly trench held by the 8th Norfolk.

At 07:27 hours a series of mines were detonated beneath Casino Point and under two Russian saps with success. However, the mine beneath Casino Point was half a minute late in exploding. The enormity of the explosion took everyone by surprise including the 6th Royal Berkshire and 10th Essex who suffered considerable casualties from chalk and debris as it fell upon the first two assembly trenches. The 18th Division War Diary reported:

> Our mine under Casino Point which should have exploded at 7.27 did not go up until 7.28. It made a much bigger explosion than was expected and a certain number of casualties were caused by falling debris, some of these casualties actually occurring in our trenches. One machine-gun was seen to go up in the air, and was afterwards found in 'No Man's Land' considerable number of dead Huns were also seen lying round the crater.[11]

Some zealous parties of the 6th Royal Berkshire dashed across No Man's Land and got in the German trench before the mine exploded. Private Fred Henwood wrote: 'We was standing on the fire step just as the attack had started and we had orders that we were going to send a mine up before our men took the front line German trench. But our men were so mad to get there they rushed forward under cover of smoke bombs, a slight wind carrying the smoke towards the German line. One of our companies, being well in front, got to the German parapet and was just landing in the trench when the mine went up and blew most of that company up with it. Just as that happened we had orders to go over the top and extend out.'[12]

Lieutenant-Colonel Clay noticed that: 'The mine at Casino Point actually went off after zero hour (possibly 20 seconds) and practically wiped out 2 of my leading platoons with the falling debris ... The Bn stood the shock wonderfully well and realised that the M.G. nest which went up in the explosion would have caused them considerably heavier losses.'[13]

As the mine at Casino Point exploded 'C' and 'D' companies of the 8th Norfolk left the front line to a position thirty yards into No Man's Land where they laid down without incurring any casualties as German shells whistled over their heads into the third and fourth British trench lines behind them. Three minutes after the mines exploded these two companies moved off, followed by 'A' and 'B' companies in four waves. With the German wire completely destroyed by British artillery they had no obstructions in front of them and were able to advance with ease. The War Diary recorded:

> There was no rush or charge, in the usually accepted meaning of the word, the movement being carried out calmly, at a walking pace with methodical precision, rifles slung over right shoulders.[14]

Private Cleveland, from the 8th Norfolk was in a support trench waiting for the order to go over the top. He knew when 'C' and 'D' companies went forward because he heard the sounds of the German guns:

> The shells from our guns were hissing over in a constant stream, when bullets began to crack and we knew the boys of the first line were over. No shouting, no cheering, all bullets and shells as the boys rushed over, scrambling round shell holes, one line catching up the other, until they leapt into what remained of their front lines. It was a mixture of mountains and valleys in miniature, no straight cut trench anywhere.[15]

Mine Trench, the first German trench, and Mine Support were reached without encountering any resistance. Those German soldiers who survived the bombardment were in no state to fight and immediately surrendered. 'C' Company advancing on the right flank took thirty prisoners from the west perimeter of the craters. Private Fred Campling was among those from the 8th Norfolk that advanced towards Mine Trench:

> The assault was immediately precipitated by the explosion of a series of mines which our sappers had laid close up to the German front line, and the shower of debris had hardly fallen when the order came for the first wave to advance...With a thrill of excitement I received the order, shouted down the trench, 'Over 16,' and every man leapt to the parapet at the exact moment of our artillery 'barrage' lifted from the Bosche front line to his first support line. The opposing artillery fire, consisting

> wholly of shrapnel, which had sent the two men on my immediate left hobbling to the first aid post, now practically ceased. Quickly crossing our own front line trench, we reached the Bosche firing trench and there a scene met my gaze which will remain stamped indelibly upon my memory for the rest of my mortal existence. Cowering in the trench, clad in the pale grey uniforms we had longed for twelve months to see, unarmed and minus equipment, with fear written on their faces were a few of these valiant warriors of the Kaiser, whose prowess we were out to dispute. Here let me digress to say that the absence of arms and equipment suggests that the exact moment selected for our attack had taken the Huns by surprise. This view was subsequently confirmed by prisoners who said that they had expected us earlier in the day, and stood down. Many Germans rushed forward with hands in the air, crying for mercy.'[16]

It is apparent from Campling's testimony that the German soldiers in the trenches west of Montauban had been severely affected by the barrage, maybe suffering shell shock, totally unprepared to defend their trenches and resist the British advance. This evidence suggests that on this sector the British artillery barrage had succeeded in breaking the morale and the will of the German soldier to fight back. Mine Support trench was secured ten minutes later and it was found that the wire defences in front of it were completely destroyed by the British bombardment. Remarkably the battalion suffered few casualties.

Private Cleveland from the 8th Norfolk advanced from the British support trenches fifteen minutes after Zero Hour and belonged to the support waves responsible for consolidating captured German trenches.

> We were supposed to go over at a quarter to eight, but we had equipment on, magazines on, bayonets on, and 'one up the spout, and nine in the tin box.' Down in the trench we certainly felt a little windy, but once up, we felt as if we were on a field day. Shells and bullets in the air, great holes, scraps of wire, shells & co., laying everywhere, but we kept on – a little bunch of men, artillery formation. Then we crossed our front line, from one hole to another in case a machine-gun opened, until we slipped into the front trench. Two Huns were running about frantically like mad men. We went into the second trench, and we had a rest, while we found out where we were, and we had to keep our eyes 'skinned' to the corners and our rifles ready.
>
> German names on boards naming the trenches where a German trench mortar gun used to be. The entrances of deep dug outs blown in or otherwise filled up. I wondered how many men were buried in them. They had stood to from midnight till about four, expecting us to attack at dawn, and then entered their dug outs for a very little necessary sleep.[17]

On the 8th Norfolk's left flank, the 6th Royal Berkshire Regiment was able to cross No Man's Land with ease and secure Mine Trench and Mine Support and found many dead German soldiers. Here, the men went forward to Bund and Bund Support Trench without meeting any resistance. As they proceeded forward from Bund Support Trench, their advance was hindered by three German machine-guns positioned in Pommiers Trench. Two assault companies from the 6th Royal Berkshire incurred heavy casualties as a result. A third company was brought forward to support them. A bombing party captured one of these guns by bombing along Popoff Lane, a communication trench which connected Bund Support Trench with Pommiers Trench. The other German machine-gun crews realised that their situation was precarious and withdrew in haste from Pommiers Trench. The 6th Royal Berkshire Regiment entered Pommiers Trench at 07:50 hours

The work of consolidation began in earnest, but the men came under machine-gun fire from The Loop which was linked to Pommiers Trench. Throughout the advance the Royal Berkshire was in contact with the 7th Bedfordshire of the 54th Brigade on its left flank. However the 8th Norfolk's advance on their right flank was held up by machine-gun fire and could not keep up. With the Royal Berkshire's right flank exposed Captain Fenner deployed three bombing parties supported by a Lewis Gun crew to protect their exposed flank.

After securing Bund Trench, the 8th Norfolk encountered the first serious opposition when they reached the German strongpoint known as the Castle and from enfilade fire from Breslau Trench and Back Trench on their right flank, causing many casualties. By 07:53 hours the defenders of the Castle had been overwhelmed, with a platoon from 'B' Company taking many prisoners.

Captain B. Ayre led 'D' Company northwards from the Castle towards Bund Support Trench and The Loop. Captain J. Hall led 'C' Company on the right flank, but the right section was soon held up by machine-gun fire at the junction of Mine Alley and Breslau Alley. 'D' Company, 8th Norfolk would be held up here until the afternoon.

Captain B. Ayre was killed and the majority of officers were wounded. Private Fred Campling commented on the reluctance of the German soldiers to engage in close-quarters combat and how they came under heavy fire from the German fourth line:

> It was obvious that they were past any pretence at fighting, so ignoring them, I leapt the trench – it was occupied by only dead and wounded – and gained the second line. At this stage we began to feel the effect of a deadly German machine-gun fire from their fourth line and our gallant captain was amongst the first to fall, as also my platoon officer. Not a single German did I see attempt to offer the least resistance at close quarters.[18]

With no officers able to continue the assault Company Sergeant Major A.F. Raven took command of 'D' Company. He led the remnants of his company to the first objective, Pommiers Trench. The remainder of 'C' Company advanced with 'D' Company towards Pommiers Trench which they secured by 08:15 hours.

Meanwhile, the 6th Royal Berkshire had consolidated its section of Pommiers Trench and had launched its attack upon Pommiers Redoubt via the communication trench named Pommiers Lane. A bombing party with a Stokes mortar worked along Pommiers Lane. Its path through this trench was delayed by barbed-wire which had been placed in the trench. The left company of the 6th Royal Berkshire went forward at 09:30 hours to assist in the attack upon Pommiers Redoubt. They assembled with the remnants from the other companies in Pommiers Trench and advanced towards Maple Trench which branched westwards from Pommiers Redoubt. Casualties were caused by a German machine-gun positioned south of Pommiers Redoubt, but by 10:20 hours they reached Maple Trench and were able to launch an assault upon Montauban Alley.

About the same time remnants of 'C' Company, 8th Norfolk led by Captain J. Hall, amounting to 100 men, kept pace with the advance and got into Pommiers Trench close to The Loop at 10:20 hours taking sixty German prisoners, however their advance was held up by a German strongpoint positioned at the junction of Back Trench, Bosche Trench and Mine Alley. A machine-gun supported by bombing parties made this a well defended position. Captain J. Hall was wounded in both legs just after leaving Bund Support Trench and responsibility of command of 'C' Company was passed to 2nd Lieutenant Attenborough.

Private Cleveland formed part of the support waves clearing the captured trenches and dug outs. He recalled:

> After a rest we went along a communication trench to the third trench. Half way along we had to stop, so we commenced to make a fire step facing the opposite way, and began to consolidate. We were near two deep dug outs. Down the first one went a bomb, and then came up one Hun, shaking and trembling, hands above his head, shouting as best he could, 'Mercy, Comrade,' with eyes staring. He seemed so utterly scared that the majority could only pity him. His hand was bleeding a good bit, the result of the bomb. Just behind him came another, as mad and shaking as the first. Then another dark one with a handsome beard, staring eyes, a wounded forehead, a red cross on his arm, to which he pointed. There were about five of them. An officer told off an escort, and they were off, and the dugout was set on fire.
>
> Then we went on to the third trench. One of our sergeants was shot through the ankle, another fellow through his side, these were the first

> cases of blood shed we had seen, but I will not speak more of it, than I can help. In the third trench we had to wait. Huns lay about in the most awful conditions, and we had to steel our nerves and look away, but we tried to see the best side. We were winning, we were in the German trenches so we lit up our cigarettes and were happy. All the time we kept on alert, working to make our position defendable.[19]

Both the 8th Norfolk and 6th Royal Berkshire struggled to advance throughout the morning. By 12:15 hours the 6th Royal Berkshire was within eighty yards of the Mametz–Montauban Road with bombing parties advancing to the west of Montauban Alley. At the same time the 8th Norfolk was advancing along Loop Trench towards Montauban Alley. It was behind the 6th Royal Berkshire and was trying to close the gap between them and the 7th East Kent (The Buffs) on their right flank. A German machine-gun positioned to the west of Loop Trench, protected by bombers and a sniper positioned in Loop Trench at the junction of the Mametz–Montauban Road, stopped the advance of the Royal Berkshire and the Norfolk battalions. An effort was made to bomb the sniper out from his lair, but proved unsuccessful. A stokes mortar team led by 2nd Lieutenant Frank Rushton, from the 53rd Trench Mortar Battery, was brought forward. They only had four rounds and once these were fired they withdrew. Unable to dislodge the sniper from Loop Trench the frustrated 2nd Lieutenant Rushton leapt from Loop Trench and tried to shoot the sniper with his rifle, but was killed. 2nd Lieutenant Lancelot Sayer, of the Royal Berkshire took a rifle and made a further attempt to take out this sniper. Sayer fired at the sniper at the same time as the sniper was about to fire at him. Sayer killed the sniper, but was badly wounded and died on 11 July at Etaples. With the sniper dead, bombing parties moved along Loop Trench.

To the southeast of Loop Trench elements of the 8th Norfolk Regiment were being held up by a German machine-gun at the junction of Mine Alley and Breslau Alley. During the afternoon, at 14:00 hours a platoon of reinforcements led by 2nd Lieutenant G.E. Miall-Smith and 2nd Lieutenant Gundry-White together with battalion bombers under Sergeant H.H. West, of the 8th Norfolk, came forward with a Stokes mortar and launched an attack upon this troublesome position. It was difficult to get this mortar into action because some of the party carrying ammunition were hit by enemy fire. Sergeant West's bombers were able to overwhelm this German position via Breslau Alley and Mine Alley supported by Stokes mortars positioned in The Loop and Mine Alley.

A white flag was soon seen hoisted above this position where two officers and 150 men from a Bavarian Regiment offered their surrender. This allowed the 8th Norfolk to assault The Loop which at that time was still occupied by German forces. 'C' Company was then able to advance and capture the eastern sector of Pommiers Trench. 'A' Company in reserve had completed consolidating Mine Support and now proceeded to Bund Support Trench to commence the consolidation of this trench.

'B' Company which had already sent three platoons to support 'C' Company pushed forward to The Loop and beyond to Pommiers Trench. By 15:00 hours 'B' Company, 8th Norfolk Regiment, had captured The Loop and then proceeded to secure the battalion's final objective, Montauban Alley. It was met by German machine-gunners in Montauban Alley ahead of them and from the north-western sector of Montauban. 'D' Company advancing on the left suffered casualties as a result. 2nd Lieutenant J.H. Attenborough led repeated attempts to dislodge the enemy from Montauban Alley but they were repelled. A bombing party led by 2nd Lieutenant L.A. Gundry-White affected a breakthrough in Montauban Alley by fighting its way northwards along Loop Trench. Attenborough and Company Sergeant Major Jeremiah Coe were killed before Montauban Alley was captured.

Private Fred Campling had been forced to take cover amongst the foliage on the ground to avoid the heavy machine-gun fire from the German fourth line linked up with another party of reinforcements who were sent to capture this trench. They could see that Attenborough's party had broken into Montauban Alley.

> Getting down at full length, partly concealed by the vegetation, I got slowly forward, and came upon Sergeant Lewis Colman and a few of his men similarly held up. Peeping out cautiously, we observed that our bombers had gained a footing in the German fourth line trench, and were working their way up to the position of the machine-gun, which was causing the discomfiture of our little band. After taking a few shots at the machine-gunner, we crept in single file to the left, entered the trench, and were delighted to see the survivors of our company.[20]

Campling and his party had yet to reach Montauban Alley which in some sectors was in German hands:

> At the point where machine-guns had caused our delay a considerable number of Germans were still holding out, but our men had secured a foothold on both flanks and the passing of the whole fourth line into our hands was only a matter of time and skilful bombing.
>
> It was now nearly four o'clock in the afternoon and we were still some few hundred yards away from our final objective. On the order to advance we extended in the open, and our appearance was at once greeted with the rattle of the inevitable machine-gun. Profiting by our former ghastly experience, we took cover in numerous shell holes and got forward slowly and in snake like fashion, suffering some few

casualties. Whilst executing this manoeuvre we had the satisfaction of seeing a large number of prisoners taken in the trench we had just left, the resistance there having been finally broken.

It was now apparent that the enemy was in full retreat; our guns had lifted yet further, and were giving him the benefit of a deadly accurate fire. The trench we now sought to capture was only feebly held; by further skilful and daring work by our bombers it fell into our hands.[21]

By 15:20 hours bombers from the 6th Royal Berkshire had pushed forward along Loop Trench to a position fifty yards beyond the Mametz–Montauban Road. The German defenders of Montauban Alley had double-blocked Montauban Alley which slowed down the Berkshire's advance along this trench from the west. Stokes mortars were brought forward into Montauban Alley and once they got into action, the German soldiers defending this trench retired. At 17.20 hours, Stokes mortars were able to target the junction of Loop Trench and Montauban Alley and the position was captured by the Royal Berkshires together with fifteen German prisoners. The Royal Berkshire handed over this section of Montauban Alley to the 8th Norfolk Regiment because this area were one of its objectives. The 8th Norfolk was then able to make contact with the 7th Queen's Regiment from the 18th Division on its right. As the trench was consolidated, patrols from the 8th Norfolk were sent forward as far as Caterpillar Valley.

It was a long day for the men of the 8th Norfolk Regiment who left their trenches at 07:30 hours and spent the entire day fighting their way to Montauban Alley. There was little time for rest and it was important to consolidate their gains in case of counter-attacks. Private Fred Campling recalled:

In the evening encouraged by our success – for we had now reached our objective for the day – we proceeded to consolidate our new position as quickly as possible, and prepared to resist any counter-attack. Fire positions were hastily hacked into the parados, ammunition brought up, sentries posted, and after the hardest and most thrilling day we had ever experienced we sank to the ground to snatch a brief rest.[22]

Campling and soldiers from the 8th Norfolk Regiment were denied time to rest for at 20:00 hours German artillery launched a violent barrage of the lines that they had lost, especially around The Loop and Montauban Alley. Campling wrote:

Our respite was short-lived however, for the worse was yet to come in the shape of a cruel bombardment of our position by a battery of heavy calibre guns firing high explosive shells. Never shall I forget that night.

> Bursting on all sides with an ear splitting roar, these missiles caused us several casualties. This state of affairs continued throughout the following day until evening, when we were relieved to return, exhausted, weary, but triumphant to our new support line, there to discuss our adventures and compare the helmets and other souvenirs we had captured.[23]

The 8th Norfolk Regiment lost eleven officers and 292 men.[24] The 6th Royal Berkshire Regiment lost thirteen officers and 337 men mainly due to lack of support on their right flank.[25]

The success of 53rd and 54th Brigades in the assault upon Pommiers Redoubt and Montauban Ridge was attributed to the fact that the German forces kept their machine-guns in the two front lines in their dugouts while the bombardment took place and only brought them out when the barrage lifted. The success of the British bombardment in destroying the German wire in No Man's Land was another factor that aided the operation. Everyone in the brigade including NCOs and privates had studied the positions of the enemy trenches and strongpoints, so when their officers became casualties, they were able to take over and ensure that the operation was continued until completion. Also, supplies of ammunition and equipment were systematically brought forward behind the advancing troops, which ensured they had what was required to achieve their objectives together with effective supporting waves who searched and cleared dugouts as the leading waves went forward.

Chapter 22

Montauban Ridge

The 55th Brigade, commanded by Brigadier-General Sir T.D. Jackson, formed the eastern flank of the 18th Division's assault, facing a 200 yard-wide front towards Montauban Ridge. It was ordered to secure a trench line 200 yards north of the Mametz–Montauban Road, along Montauban Alley in between Pommiers Redoubt and Montauban. This sector was defended by 6th Bavarian Reserve Regiment which had only been in these trenches for a few hours. The brigade comprised the 7th Queen's (Royal West Surrey Regiment), 8th East Surrey Regiment, supported by two Platoons from the 7th Buffs (East Kent Regiment) and the 7th Royal West Kent Regiment in brigade reserve. Covering fire was provided by the 55th machine-gun Company with four guns positioned along the Peronne Road, and four guns in the front line.

The plan for the 55th Brigade was for 7th Buffs advancing on the brigade's left flank to capture the Carnoy Craters which were the result of earlier French mining operations. The 7th Queen's was to work its way around Carnoy Craters, establish contact with the 8th Norfolk Regiment of the 54th Brigade on the left flank and head northwards to secure a trench line 200 yards north of the Mametz–Montauban Road. The 8th East Surrey Regiment was to advance on the brigade's right flank pushing through Breslau and Breslau Support Trench to reach Mametz and Montauban Road, capturing trenches west of Montauban and extending the line captured by the 7th Queen's.

Lieutenant-Colonel Ransome's 7th Buffs was ordered to clear and occupy the Carnoy Craters. Two platoons of 'B' Company, commanded by Captain Arthur Kenchington, were assigned to this operation and on the day before the assault he arranged for bomb supplies and equipment to be stored at the far end of No. 10 Sap. At the end of each sap and trenches in this sector notice boards were installed to direct runners to the crater area.

The 8th East Surrey Regiment came under shell fire from German artillery at 22:30 hours on the night prior to the attack which targeted the front line and assembly trenches. Several sections of trenches were knocked down and considerable damage was done to some dugouts as well as inflicting thirteen casualties amongst the battalion. By 05:00 hours on 1 July, the German barrage subsided until 06:30 hours when German guns resumed targeting along the 55th Brigade's sector. A German machine-gun positioned in No Man's Land strafed the 7th Queen's and the 7th Royal West Kent on the left flank.

British artillery barrages supported the infantry assault and moved forward in scheduled stages lifting from Breslau Trench at 07:30 hours to Breslau Support Trench at 07:35 hours, lifting off to Back Trench at 07:40 and then to Pommiers Lane at 07:50 hours. The 7th Buffs, led by Kenchington's two platoons, had a tough task ahead of it. The artillery had not destroyed the German machine-gun positions within the Carnoy Craters and they were held by approximately 300 enemy soldiers covered by German machine-guns in Breslau Trench and Back Trench. The area that Kenchington was ordered to secure was vast, the ground was extremely muddy, the crater was filled with barbed wire and they were greatly outnumbered by fresh troops from the 6th Bavarian Reserve Regiment which entered the position on the night before the 7th Buffs made their assault. The Carnoy Craters formed a slight salient and the machine-guns in this position would cause devastation amongst the advancing waves of the 55th Brigade.

Three sections from each platoon advanced on the flanks of the craters, while the remaining two sections, accompanied by snipers advanced towards the centre. Lieutenant Edouard Goss led the platoon that were tasked with securing Mine Trench, the German front line, west of the Carnoy Craters. As soon as they entered this trench Goss was killed by a shell. With their platoon leader killed the men continued to work their way round to the rear section of Carnoy Crater. Here they were opposed by two German bombing parties and between three and four snipers whom they overpowered by 08:15 hours. Reporting that they had cleared their designated sector they were ordered to assist 'R' Platoon that was assaulting Breslau Trench, which linked to the eastern perimeter of Carnoy Craters.

'R' Platoon, commanded by 2nd Lieutenant V.G.H. Tatam, had left No.3 Sap at Zero Hour. As it advanced towards the eastern side of the Carnoy Craters it came under heavy machine-gun fire from the direction of Breslau Trench on the right flank. While crossing No Man's Land 'R' platoon lost 40 per cent of its complement. Tatam led the remnants of his platoon northwest in the direction of the Carnoy Craters where they were able to enter in groups of twos and threes into the German trenches inside the crater. There was one particular machine-gun position that poured fire across the entire 55th Brigade's front. It was protected by three German snipers, and bombing parties who made it difficult for Tatum and the twelve men still with him to overwhelm the position. A fierce struggle lasted for an hour, but at 08:45 hours one of Tatum's marksmen shot and killed the machine-gunners. Although they had knocked out the machine-gun position there were still snipers to be dealt with and enemy reinforcements heading in their direction. Captain Kenchington wrote:

> During this hand to hand fighting the benefit of properly organised parties was seen as our party killed at least 3 to 1. At this stage only 8 or 9 men were left yet they continued fighting in the trenches and bombing dug outs. 2/Lieut. Tatum and Sergt. Upton P.C. jumped into one trench containing 5 Germans. They dispatched these and also 7 more who came out of a side trench one by one to the fight. Afterwards these men (supported by 3 of their men) who had joined them by now, counted for another party of 6.[1]

Kenchington was unaware of the progress being made by his platoons which had penetrated the German lines. He was receiving vague reports from his observer who was watching the battle from the end of a Russian sap. He had sent an additional bombing party and three snipers to support them with orders to outflank the German snipers in the crater.

At the start of the assault, two Livens Flame Projectors had discharged jets of burning oil into the German lines west of Carnoy Crater. This horrific weapon will be discussed in the following chapter, but the first prisoner captured by Captain Kenchington, was a badly-singed man close to Carnoy Crater from whom they were able to deduce that their opponents were the 6th Bavarian Reserve Regiment.[2]

The 7th Queen's (Royal West Surrey) Regiment, commanded by Lieutenant-Colonel M. Kemp-Welch advanced adjacent to the 7th Buffs on its right flank towards Breslau Trench. 'A' and 'D' companies charged across No Man's Land towards the German line where they came under hostile fire from Breslau Support Trench and Back Trench ahead of them. 'D' Company, the left leading company, was practically wiped out by machine-gun fire coming from the eastern lip of the Carnoy Craters. Only twenty men from 'D' Company reached Breslau Support Trench. Two sections were detailed from the 7th Queen's to assist the 7th Buffs by advancing around the western perimeter of the craters with the purpose of keeping in touch with the 8th Norfolk Regiment on its left flank.

Lieutenant D.R. Heaton led 'A' Company on the battalion's right flank into Breslau Trench but was unable to progress beyond the second line, Breslau Support Trench, because it was far outnumbered by the Germans defending this trench, as well as machine-gun fire coming from the third enemy line. Heaton had passed the 7th Buffs in the Carnoy Craters and the plan was to link up with the 8th Norfolk advancing past the western perimeter of the craters. Enemy machine-gun fire prevented the 8th Norfolk and the Queen's from linking up north of the craters. Heaton lost many casualties, but he organised a bombing party and led them along a communication trench into the German third line, where they took 163 German prisoners. Heaton established contact with two platoons from 'D' Company 7th Buffs and together they advanced upon the Montauban–Mametz Road.

At 07:35 hours, after witnessing the leading waves from 'A' and 'D' companies taking heavy casualties, 'B' Company pressed forward towards the German lines. Three platoons advancing on the left flank suffered heavily from German fire coming from the eastern perimeter of the craters and few reached Breslau Support Trench to join the other two companies in wrestling for control of the second German line. 2nd Lieutenant A.B. Marston and a party of twenty men from 'B' Company did manage to get beyond Breslau Support Trench and secured shell holes and a section of unoccupied trench south of Middle Avenue. Here they encountered heavy resistance from a German strongpoint nearby, which they soon overwhelmed.

At 07:50 hours Lieutenant C. Haggard's 'C' Company advanced from the British front line. They incurred few casualties as they began their advance, covered by the craters and a rise in the ground in No Man's Land, but as they drew nearer to the German lines the two platoons on the right suffered heavily. Five minutes after leaving the start line Haggard was wounded in the head which rendered him unconscious for an hour. He later took command of the remnants of the company and led them to the Montauban–Mametz road which they reached at 13:45 hours. Here Haggard's condition deteriorated and he had to be evacuated from the battlefield.

The 8th East Surrey Regiment, on the 55th Brigade's right flank begun its advance three minutes prior to Zero Hour when four footballs supplied by Captain Wilfred Nevill were kicked into No Man's Land in order to spur them forwards as they began their advance towards the German trenches. Prior to the assault Nevill had approached Major Alfred Irwin, battalion command, and proposed using the focus of these footballs to ease the minds of the men as they crossed No Man's Land and to divert their fears of the German guns. The opposing Germans may have thought the idea of kicking football's across No Man's Land as eccentric, but from the British perspective, most lads in Britain played and followed football and Nevill would try anything to raise the spirits of his men as they went across. Irwin granted Nevill permission to use footballs on the day under strict conditions. Irwin recalled:

> Captain Nevill was commanding B Company, one of our two assaulting companies. A few days before the battle, he came to me with a suggestion. He said that he and his men were all equally ignorant of what their conduct would be when they got into action. As he had four hundred yards to go and knew that it would be covered by machine-gun fire, so he thought that it would be helpful if he could furnish each

> platoon with a football, and allow them to kick it forward and follow it. That was the beginning of the idea and I sanctioned that, so long as he and his officers really kept command of the units, and didn't allow it to develop into a rush after the ball. If a man came across the football, he could kick it forward, but he mustn't chase after it.[3]

Nevill had distributed one football to each platoon within his company; the platoon which kicked the ball closest to the German front trench line would be declared the winner. One of the original footballs is on display at Dover Castle inscribed with the words 'The Great European Cup Final – East Surreys vs Bavarians'. The intention was to dribble the footballs across No Man's Land towards the German first line. Four platoon commanders kicked their footballs into No Man's Land and the fatal match began as men dropped rapidly amidst the hailstorm of machine-gun fire. The battalion War Diary reported:

> At 7.27 am, B Company started to move out to their wire, Captain Nevill strolling quietly ahead of them, giving an occasional order to keep the dressing square on to the line of advance. This company took four footballs with them which they were seen to dribble forward into the smoke of our intense bombardment of the Hun front line.[4]

Many soldiers from Nevill's Company fell as soon as the advance had begun. Lance Corporal Harry Taylor was among those that kicked the ball who died. A sergeant from his company wrote:

> He was shot through the head and died at once. He was only a few yards away from me when it happened and he was firing away at the Huns, when he met his death. He was killed ten minutes after going over the parapet. As we went over the top Harry had a football, and he and I, with a few others, kicked the ball towards the German trenches. Four of us kicked the ball. The other three are killed, including our company officer and our platoon officer. Harry died fighting.[5]

As the British barrage lifted, German riflemen and machine-gunners came out of their dugouts and fired upon the 8th East Surrey as it approached them. They inflicted many casualties amongst the officers and men. Much of the hostile fire was coming from the craters and the high ground behind it. Captain Nevill got close to the German line but was among those killed. In a letter home to Nevill's brother dated 15 July 1916, 2nd Lieutenant Charles Alcock described his last moments:

> Five minutes before zero time, he strolled up in his usual calm way, and we shared a last joke before going over. The company went over the

> top very well, with Soames and your brother kicking off with the company footballs. We had to face a very heavy rifle and machine-gun fire, and nearing the front German trench, the lines slackened pace slightly. Seeing this Wilfred dashed in front with a bomb in his hand, and was immediately shot through the head, almost side by side with Soames and Sergeant Major Wells.[6]

Major Irwin thought that the use of footballs helped the battalion to get across despite the casualties. 'I think it did help enormously. It took their minds off it. But they suffered terribly.'[7]

Pommiers Redoubt in the northwest had not been captured by the 53rd Brigade and this caused problems for the 55th Brigade which was engaged in close-quarter fighting in Breslau and Back Trench. The western side of the craters had been taken but their German occupants were still resolutely holding on to the eastern side. A defiant German machine-gun position was causing casualties amongst the 7th Queen's to the extent they did not have sufficient men to cover their own front line. Sweeping across No Man's Land this German position created a gap between the 53rd and 55th Brigades. It was also firing into the support line preventing reinforcements from reaching the front line. 'B' Section from the 55th machine-gun Company tried to advance but suffered heavy casualties due to this machine-gun fire. Another German machine-gun position in the Loop which was behind the craters was causing problems. Runners heading for brigade headquarters were being cut down by the German fire, which severely affected communications with brigade commanders.

At 08:05 hours the 8th East Surrey's bombing section commanded by 2nd Lieutenant P.G. Heath was sent forward with two Stokes mortars into the German trenches and report to the nearest East Surrey officer to find out how best to utilise these weapons. The battalion adjutant twice left battalion HQ to assess the situation from the British front line at 08:05 hours and 08:25 hours. On each occasion he reported heavy casualties and hostile fire coming from the craters and the high ground above on the left flank. Major Alfred Irwin, commanding 8th East Surrey's requested reinforcements from the 7th Buffs for support.

At 08:30 hours Captain Kenchington crossed No Man's Land to appraise the situation in the Carnoy Craters. Kenchington sent an extra bombing party accompanied by three snipers to support the attack by getting behind the northern lip of the craters and clearing the enemy snipers that were operating there. His No 1 Lewis Gun team had mown down a party of German soldiers withdrawing up along the Montauban Road during the first ten minutes of the attack. Kenchington thought it was imperative that his platoons receive supplies of bombs in order to sustain their attack upon the craters so he withdrew this Lewis Gun team and used this extra resource to carry bombs across No Man's Land to replenish their stock.

Kenchington had a rough approximation of the location of the enemy snipers and directed a Stokes mortar team at them, as Kenchington reported:

> This had excellent results. A concerted rush on the part of the men remaining (with 4 more bombers sent by Major Kemp-Welch commanding the 7th Queens) carried the dump and the snipers were bayoneted. They died splendidly with heaps of cartridges round them. The M.G. emplacement was found to be concreted. The gun we kept.[8]

By 08:37 hours it was apparent that Pommiers Redoubt had not been captured. And the 55th Brigade could not push forward until it had secured the craters. Lieutenant-Colonel Ransome of the 7th Buffs was ordered to send two further platoons to support Captain Kenchington in capturing the crater. Once this position had been taken he was ordered to establish contact with Major Kemp-Welch CO of 7th Queen's to see if he needed assistance. If the 7th Queen's did not require support then he was to take the 7th Buffs to the right flank and support the 8th East Surrey Regiment.

The British barrage lifted from Back Trench and Pommiers Trench at 08:45 hours, but the 7th Queen's were unable to go forward without artillery support. The heavy losses suffered by the left flank of the battalion meant that there was a gap in the line which could not be filled until the afternoon. They were unable to get beyond Back Trench. The right flank of the battalion aligned with the 8th East Surrey Regiment, but could not advance with the East Surrey Regiment when it went forward.

At 08:55 hours Lieutenant-Colonel Ransome sent two platoons to support Captain Kenchington in the assault upon the craters and because he received information that the 8th East Surrey required assistance he sent two platoons led by Lieutenant Dyson and two platoons led by Captain Tait to the Surrey's right flank. Dyson had earlier received confirmation that the 8th East Surrey needed support and had already dispatched two platoons to their aid. When he received the order from his CO he went with the remainder of his company.

Around the same time the 21st Brigade had captured Glatz Redoubt to the East, but had taken casualties from enemy fire from the Warren, which was to the east of the 55th Brigade's position. However 2nd Lieutenant Stiason, who had been wounded in the arm, arrived at 8th East Surrey's HQ at 09:00 hours and reported seeing German soldiers in the railway line advancing along Valley Trench and Valley Support Trench, which were southwest of Glatz Redoubt. It was imperative that 8th East Surrey Regiment pushed forward. A message was sent to Lieutenant-Colonel Ransome from the 8th East Surrey Regiment requesting him to send two platoons to move along the Valley and into Train Alley. One platoon was duly despatched but the other was held in reserve.

The 8th East Surrey Regiment was pinned down for half an hour, until the 30th Division had pushed towards Montauban. German forces were afraid that they would become cut off from the advance of the 30th Division and began to feel threatened. This enabled the 8th East Surrey Regiment and two companies from the 7th Buffs to launch a bomb assault into the Warren and towards Train Alley. This created a gap in the line between the 8th East Surrey Regiment and the 7th Queen's. This meant that the 7th Queen's were isolated and fighting alone in Breslau Trench. It was also vulnerable to enemy fire coming from the east side of the Carnoy Craters.

8th East Surrey Battalion HQ intercepted a message at 09:21 hours stating that its units were held up in Back Trench, but at that same time Private Billison, a battalion orderly who had been sent forward to remind companies that they were to wave their artillery flags to signal, had returned to report that the battalion was occupying the Pommiers Line. Minutes later a report was received from a Forward Observation Officer that the 8th East Surrey was in Train Alley.

At 09:30 hours the right flank of the 8th East Surrey had overwhelmed the German defenders of the Warren which were causing problems to the 21st Brigade in the east. The 7th Queen's were still struggling for control of Breslau Trench. Around that time the 7th Buffs had cleared the Germans out of the craters. Kenchington immediately cancelled an order for howitzers to shell the position which the snipers were holding. He later recalled:

> The opposition in the crater area was not overcome until 9.30 am. The crater party was never reinforced. It was reorganised to withdraw men from the centre as and when possible to work round the flank of the M.G. and the Coy.L.G. was utilized in an attempt to neutralise this M.G. In the end a gallant dash by a subaltern and a sergeant into a wire filled sap and thence round the flank of the M.G.'s succeeded and allowed the survivors to clear the area. The crew of the M.G. were clubbed. Heaps of used cases testified to the stout way they had served their guns.[9]

At 09:40 hours Kenchington established his headquarters close to the dump where the machine-gun and snipers were positioned. He led a search party to ensure that there were no enemy present within the crater and they found three German soldiers who were promptly killed. Every dug-out they came across was bombed as they conducted their search.

Kenchington had one officer and eighteen men remaining and he ordered them to clear Breslau Trench on the 7th Queen's and 8th East Surrey's sector. No. 13 Platoon from 'D' Company, 7th Buffs, had come forward to reinforce Kenchington's men and together they were ordered to capture Breslau Support Trench. Both platoons set about clearing dugouts and securing prisoners. Once this was done Kenchington led one officer and twenty men up Mine Alley and reported to the officer commanding 7th East Buffs. Kenchington's party was ordered to consolidate a section of Pommiers Trench: 'We dug a new trench on what remained of an old one for the left face, cut fire steps on the N.W. face, cleared and fire stepped that part of Pommiers Trench and put out some wire.'[10]

At 10:00 hours Major-General Maxse, commanding the 18th Division, was conscious that the 90th Brigade in the east was pressing forward in its assault upon Montauban. He wanted to ensure that his division would maintain its attack and achieve its objectives to prevent the 90th Brigade's flank from being exposed. He therefore deployed the 8th Suffolk Regiment, from the 53rd Brigade reserve, to relieve the 7th Royal West Kent which was holding the British front line. The 7th Royal West Kent was ordered to send one company to relieve the 7th Buffs on the Pommiers Line and the remaining companies to push through this line to reach the final objective. The commander of the 7th Royal West Kent had received a message timed at 09:23 hours reporting that the 8th East Surrey Regiment was held up by strong German resistance and could not proceed along Train Alley. He therefore decided to initiate an attack at 10:10 hours.

'C' Company with Captain Waddington went forward, encountered no opposition, reached the final objective and established contact with parties belonging to the 90th Brigade on their right flank. The remaining two platoons from this company led by Lieutenant Innocent got left behind and did not reach the final objective until 15:00 hours. 'A' Company met strong opposition and its advance was slower than 'C' Company. Its company commander was wounded and the platoons became separated during the advance. Company Sergeant Major Klien collected the remnants of these platoons on the Pommiers Line around midday and led them forward to the junction of Nine Alley and the western side of Montauban where he reported to Captain Waddington.

By 10:00 hours parties from the 7th Queen's had fought along communication trenches, captured the Loop and entered the western sector of Train Alley. German machine-gunners were seen massing in Mill Trench and Mine Alley and were about to converge on the Mill and Mine Alley. An artillery bombardment was called to fire upon these positions which neutralised these positions immediately. The right flank of the 8th East Surrey Regiment was able to advance and occupy Breslau Alley at the junction where it joins Mill Trench by 11:00 hours. The Adjutant of 8th East Surrey Regiment went forward into the third German trench line to establish the Battalion HQ where signallers had laid and telephone communications established. The signallers reported to the adjutant that Major Irwin was in Pommiers Trench and would be returning to this telephone. It was from here that they got a panoramic view of Montauban Ridge and they could clearly see the dispositions of the 8th East Surrey Regiment. The Adjutant reported the new position of 8th East Surrey

Regiment's Battalion HQ and emphasised the urgent need for reinforcements to push the assault forward.

At midday Major Irwin arrived at the 8th East Surrey's new Battalion HQ position and ordered 2nd Lieutenant Wightman to go to Captain Bowen who was engaged on the left flank and ask him to go forward with all the men that he could collect. Irwin then ordered his adjutant to extend the line from Breslau Alley to Mill Trench where he was either to consolidate there or go forward to Montauban, depending on the situation.

The 7th Royal West Kent Regiment was waiting in reserve along the Albert–Peronne Light Railway east of Carnoy. It received orders to assist the 8th East Surrey at 11:00 hours. 'A' and 'C' companies were duly sent forward. 'D' Company was meant to have advanced towards Pommiers Line but the runner carrying the order was killed and the order was not delivered. An hour later the battalion adjutant found that this company was still in reserve in the British lines. At midday the first party of reinforcements from 'A 'and 'C' companies arrived and together with the 8th East Surrey they captured Back Trench. Once this trench had been secured both battalions began to push forward towards Montauban Ridge

The bombardment of the Mill and the Orchard continued as the 8th East Surrey and 7th Royal West Kent went forward towards Breslau Alley and Mill Trench at 12:10 hours. No shots were fired from their immediate front and it was decided to go forward towards Mill Trench and Mine Alley. They had to briefly halt while they waited for the barrage to lift, but once it moved forward the 8th East Surrey went forward to the road west of Montauban, which they reached at 12:22 hours. Their right flank occupied two houses on the western perimeter of Montauban and their left flank rested on a position 100 yards east of the Orchard. There was no sign of any enemy presence close to the Orchard. Sergeant Willis leading a party of six men was ordered to capture the nearby Windmill where they could observe the left flank. Further reinforcements joined them and from here they were able to extend their line from the Windmill, across the Mametz–Montauban Road, and along this road from the copse towards Montauban Alley. When Sergeant Willis reached the Mill he captured one officer and eight men.

The 7th Royal West Kent encountered stubborn resistance from enemy soldiers that still occupied Pommiers Line. 'A' Company on the left flank suffered badly and lost all its officers before it overcame this resistance. 'C' Company led by Captain Waddington fared better on the right flank as he led two platoons into Montauban Alley.

By 12:35 hours the East Surrey and Royal West Kent battalions had reached the Mametz–Montauban Road and began digging a trench along the road. A contact aeroplane from the Royal Flying Corps flew over Montauban Ridge around this time sounding a klaxon and the pilot received the previously agreed signal from a hand mirror reflected on the ground which indicated that British troops had secured this road.

Major Irwin, commanding 8th East Surrey, arrived at 12:55 hours and took command of all troops of the 55th Brigade west of Montauban. Elements from the Buffs and Royal West Kent also came forward and were ordered to consolidate Montauban Alley with the East Surrey in close support. Lance Corporal Brane arrived with a bottle of champagne which was drunk by the remaining officers from the East Surrey Regiment. The plan was to drink this bottle beyond the German lines. Satisfied that he had achieved his objective Major Irwin ordered his Battalion HQ to be brought forward to Mill Trench.

The advance of the 7th Queen's was not going so well. Its commanding officer, Major Kemp-Welch, went forward at 11.45 hours to assess the situation in person. He met up with his battalion at the junction of Breslau Support Trench and Carnoy–Montauban Road. It numbered 100 men and they were occupying sections of Breslau Support Trench and Middle Avenue. They were isolated and were not in touch with other battalions on either flank. On the right, the 8th East Surrey Regiment had moved towards Dug Out Trench, adjacent to the Warren. No reinforcements had filled the gap in between the 7th Queen's and the 8th Norfolk. The advance of the 7th Queen's was held up by the enemy in Back Trench.

The battalions of the 55th Brigade had become intermingled. At 13:00 hours 2nd Lieutenant Marston led a party comprising of fifteen men along Back Lane and reached Mine Alley. Lieutenant D.R. Heaton (7th Queen's) led a bombing party and some members from the 8th Royal Sussex Pioneers along Middle Avenue and they reached the junction of Middle Avenue and Back Trench. At that same time the remainder of the 7th Queen's and Captain Gerald Neame's party from the 8th Buffs launched a direct assault upon Back Trench from Breslau Support Trench while Heaton attacked from within the trench. The Germans were overwhelmed and their position collapsed. One hundred and sixty German soldiers left Back Trench and surrendered, to just 100 men of the 7th Queen's.

At 01:15 hours Lieutenant C.A. Haggard and Lieutenant Heaton reorganised the remnants of the 7th Queen's and led them in a drive upon the final objective which was 200 yards north of the Mametz–Montauban Road. As they headed north they passed Blind Alley which was occupied by the enemy.

2nd Lieutenant H. J. Tortiss brought a bombing party from the 7th Queen's to tackle this position. So many bombs had been used by his party that Tortiss resorted to distributing only one bomb to each man and with this limited weaponry they successfully captured Blind Alley together with twelve German prisoners. In Montauban there was a strongly-held position of three machine-guns which maintained a defence for three hours. Tortiss charged this position with the bayonet, killing several of the enemy and securing the position. By 13:30 hours Lieutenant Heaton had extended the line held towards the 8th East Surrey Regiment. German machine-gunners in Montauban Alley held up the advance but by 14:00 hours the 7th Queen's were in possession of their allotted sector of the Mametz–Montauban Road. It was joined by elements from the 8th East Surrey Regiment and by other stragglers.

In order to secure this final objective they had to link up with the 53rd Brigade on their left flank. Major Kemp-Welch and Lieutenant-Colonel Ransome talked through the situation at 14:30 hours in Mine Alley. Ransome ordered the only two remaining platoons at his disposal to prolong the line along the Mametz–Montauban Road westwards in an effort to establish contact with the 53rd Brigade and close the gap in the line.

By 15:00 hours the line along the Mametz–Montauban Road had been consolidated. The 7th Queen's had secured their sector of the road establishing contact with the 8th East Surrey Regiment. The two platoons from the 7th Buffs had reinforced the 7th Queen's, who were preparing to link with the 53rd Brigade on their left flank. The 55th machine-gun Company had four guns positioned in the Carnoy Valley, six guns in the Pommiers Line and four guns positioned along the Mametz–Montauban Road. German machine-gunners still held Montauban Alley to the north. Their presence would make further consolidation of the Mametz–Montauban Road position extremely difficult. These enemy machine-gunners held out for a further two hours until, at 17:00 hours two Stokes mortars, under Lieutenant V. Hook of the 7th Queen's who was attached to the 55th Trench Mortar Battery, were brought up to the north end of Blind Alley and Montauban Orchard and they targeted the German machine-gunners.

Fifteen minutes later, at 17:15 hours, guns from the 51st Brigade Royal Field Artillery placed four rounds onto German position at Montauban Alley between Caterpillar Trench and 67 Trench. Lieutenant Hook's Stokes mortars also fired upon the same position. Immediately after this bombardment had stopped a party led by Lieutenant Tortiss and Company Sergeant Major King led a party from the 7th Queen's into this trench and captured the line. At the same time they established contact with the 7th Royal West Kent Regiment and a small party form the 8th Norfolk Regiment. It was not until 18:45 hours that contact with the 53rd Brigade had been established when they linked up with the main body of the 8th Norfolk.

The 55th Brigade spent the early part of the evening of the 1 July consolidating the positions that they had courageously contested and captured along Montauban Ridge. However, Montauban Ridge was not a safe place to be, because after spending the entire day fighting for this position, German forces were assembling to the north, preparing to recapture this ridge. German artillery began to bombard Montauban Ridge during the early evening. As well has being exhausted by the battle their numbers were reduced and it was doubtful that they would be able to resist a German attack.

German forces launched a counter-attack at 21:30 hours from a quarry located in Caterpillar Valley, north of Montauban, but this attack was repulsed. The 8th East Surrey Regiment was fortunate that the German counter-attack did not materialise on their sector. Its CO, Major Alfred Irwin, recalled:

> There were so few of us that there was very little we could do that night. But I posted the men as well as I could, and we were not attacked. We were heavily shelled that night – but not attacked. So we got away with it, and the next day we were relieved. We'd come down from about eight hundred to under two hundred in that attack. It seemed to me a dreadful waste of life.[11]

Montauban had been captured but the village and the surrounding area had been obliterated by the awesome ferocity of the British artillery. Captain William Bloor, from 'C' Battery, 149th Brigade Royal Field Artillery (30th Division), recorded in his diary on 3 July:

> I received orders to go up to the captured village of Montauban and relieve Gowland, who has been having an awful time there since we took it. I started at 8.30 am with four signallers, taking food and water for two days. It took us two hours to walk over the captured trenches, and the spectacle presented was truly horrible. Every inch of the ground was strewn with equipment, rifles, hats, etc; dead men, both British and Germans, lay about all over the place – some of them had been terribly knocked about, and the whole place was a succession of shell craters. On the way I was appalled by the sight of what artillery fire can do to a place. Nothing of what I had ever seen or even imagined comes near to the destruction which has been wrought here.[12]

The battalions of the 55th Brigade suffered heavy casualties. The 8th East Surrey Regiment had eight officers and 140 men killed, three officers and 272 men wounded, and twenty missing. The 7th Queen's suffered 532 casualties; seven officers and 174 men were killed, whilst nine officers and 284 men wounded.[13] According to the Official History the 7th Queen's lost fifteen officers and 463 men.[14]

The 55th Brigade's assault upon German lines on 1 July 1916 was greatly hindered by the presence of superior numbers holding the Carnoy Craters. The strength of the garrison (some 300 men supported by machine-guns which had not been knocked out by the British barrage) had been underestimated. To send just two platoons to attack such a position was a poor decision. They had a vast area to secure as well as a powerful enemy to overcome. If the Craters formed part of the centre of the assault as opposed to the flanks then it might have been easier to secure the position instead of relying upon a small force on the flanks. The inability to quickly capture the position meant that there was a gap between the 53rd and 55th Brigades which gave German defenders the chance to hold on to their positions. Some units were able to push forward whilst in many places others were held up. The infantry that were assisted by the use of the two Livens Flame Projectors, deployed west of the Carnoy Craters, were helped by these formidable weapons, but this was only on a small section of the front that was being attacked.

Chapter 23

Livens Flame Projectors at Breslau Trench

The Livens Flame Projector was one of the most horrific weapons of the war, instilling terror and amongst those that faced it. It was deployed along the sector held by the 55th Brigade opposite Breslau Trench. Invented by Captain William Livens from the Royal Engineers these weapons were meant to shake the confidence of and terrorise the enemy. The aim was to keep German troops below the parapets long enough to enable British infantry to cross No Man's Land and get into their trenches without being fired upon. Livens was in command of a secret unit known as Z Section, Royal Engineers, which focused its energies on designing long-range flamethrowers.

The Livens Flame Projector required seven men to operate and these devices were buried underground in shallow tunnels – Russian saps – where they would project burning oil from a nozzle a distance of 300 feet across No Man's Land into the German trenches. At fifty-six feet in length and weighing two-and-a-half tons it was a logistical challenge getting this device in positions underground within shallow confines of these Russian saps. The weapon was powered by air pressure. Once the pressure had reached a certain level the nozzle attached to the tanks was pushed through the ground above the surface and then the diesel and kerosene mixture was ignited, shooting flame towards the enemy like a mechanical dragon. It took 300 men to assemble this weapon, then once underground the tanks had to be filled with oil. These horrific killing machines had to be assembled in secret to preserve the element of surprise for the moment they were unleashed on the enemy.

Z Section, Royal Engineers left Southampton in two troopships at 18:00 hours on 24 June 1916, bound for Le Havre. Lieutenant Bansal with another officer and sixty-six men accompanied four Livens Flame Projectors aboard SS *Hunslet*, while Captain Livens with nine officers and 153 men sailed on SS *Copenhagen*. After an overnight crossing of the English Channel they reached Le Havre at 09:00 hours on 25 June and spent the day transferring the weapons and equipment from these troopships to nearby trains that would take them to the Somme sector.

They reached Corbie the following day and then they had to make their way to the frontline where the weapons would be deployed. Under the supervision of Lieutenant Bansall the four Projectors were loaded onto three-ton lorries at Bronfay Farm, near Bray, on 27 June, together with large supplies of oil and compressed gas. They arrived at Ludgate Circus close to Mametz at 22.00 hours that night where they were met by a 200-strong party from the Devonshire Regiment which was detailed to assist them in carrying this equipment to the front line.

This process was delayed when at 02:00 hours on 28 June as they were moving through a communications trench named 71 Street German artillery opened up a strong barrage on this trench. Parts of the Livens Flame Projectors that was designated for use at Sap 14, positioned between Bois Français and Mansell Copse, were dropped as the Royal Engineers and Devons took shelter. When the bombardment stopped at 05:30 hours they collected parts of the flamethrower and assembled them in Sap 14. Thirty minutes later the German guns resumed their bombardment and a shell burst directly above Sap 14, burying parts of the Projector beyond recovery.[1]

Three other Livens Flame Projectors were taken from Bronfay Farm and taken to the Montauban sector where they were to be installed in Sap 7, 10 and 13 dug by 183rd Tunnelling Company. The Projector intended for use at Casino Point from No 13 Sap was installed but was then damaged by enemy shellfire and was used for spare parts for the remaining two operational projectors.

These two remaining Projectors were to be used on the 55th Brigade's sector in between the Carnoy Crater and east of the Carnoy–Montauban Road. They were positioned close to each other and would engulf Mine Trench with deadly flames of burning oil. The device could only be fired three times emitting projections of burning oil for ten seconds.

At 07:15 hours, fifteen minutes before Zero Hour, the Projectors at Saps 7 and 10 discharged their deadly rain of burning oil across No Man's Land into the German frontline Mine Trench held by soldiers from the 6th Bavarian Reserve Regiment, who had recently been transferred here from Verdun for a rest. The Royal Engineers, Special Section War Diary reported:

> One shot was fired from each gun in No 7 and No 10 saps; the flames reached well over the enemy's trenches in each case. The moral effect on the enemy undoubtedly was very pronounced, for whom the infantry attack took place, the casualties were very much less in the width of front covered by the flame than in the flanks.[2]

Clouds of black smoke and flame rose a hundred feet into the sky before descending upon the unfortunate Bavarians. It was a horrific death for those German sentries in Mine Trench who were incinerated by these jets of burning oil. Their charred remains were later found.[3]

2nd Lieutenant R.W. Stewart, Royal Engineers, reported that soon after the Livens Flame Projector (here using the German term for these weapons) was deployed, fifty German soldiers immediately surrendered:

> The large flammenwerfer on the west of the craters proved a great success and very little resistance was met on that side. Had there been another flammenwerfer on the East, possibly the assaulting party would have been able to get in equally easily.[4]

The Livens Projector was used again in Belgium during 1917, but the weapon proved too cumbersome to use. It required large resources of labour in bringing the weapon to the front line and assembling it underground. There was also a great risk that it would be damaged by shellfire or buried underground before it could be used. Loading it with kerosene and diesel underground was dangerous and after all the effort of installing this weapon, it could only be used three times before being emptied. The use of this projector was abandoned and Livens and his team diverted their attention to the creation of the Livens Gas Projectors which was used in large numbers later in the war.

Chapter 24

Montauban

The 30th Division, commanded by Major-General J.S.M. Shea, was on the extreme eastern flank of the British assault with orders to capture Montauban, comprising of 274 houses and positioned along Montauban Ridge. The village and surrounding region were defended by the 6th Bavarian RIR, of the 10th Bavarian Division, which had relieved the 12th (Prussian) Division at Montauban two weeks earlier. During the intervening two weeks the men had worked hard on the defences, and by 1 July, they were exhausted. The 30th Division sector was separated from the 18th Division on their left flank by a long line of trees known as Talus Boisé and a railway track that dissected the Silesia–Faviere Trench on the first German line, Alt Trench and a newly-dug German defensive line named Dublin Trench.

The 30th Division had to take these trenches as well as capturing the Glatz Redoubt before they could enter the village of Montauban. Glatz Redoubt consisted of a labyrinth of trenches and hedgerows where German snipers and machine-gunners could conceal themselves. The village of Montauban, commonly known to the British soldier as 'Montybong', was defended by a trench that stretched along most of its perimeter. Behind the village, along the northern slope of the ridge, ran a communication trench named Montauban Alley, which connected to Pommiers Redoubt and Mametz. The Briqueterie, positioned southeast of Montauban, was another German fortified position that stretched across the road that linked Maricourt and Bernafay Wood.

The 89th Brigade was ordered to secure German trenches southeast of Montauban including the Briqueterie which stood astride the Bernafay Wood–Maricourt Road. The 21st Brigade was tasked with the capture of Silesia and Alt Trenches and then Glatz Redoubt. The capture of Glatz Redoubt was essential in order to allow the 90th Brigade to sweep through and assault and capture Montauban itself.

The British artillery in this sector had good views over the German lines from Peronne Ridge, which enabled it to target strongpoints to effectively cut the enemy wire defences.[1] The report of Oberstleutnant Bedall confirmed that as well as cutting the wire the shelling destroyed surrounding villages and billets. Bedall also went on to reveal the devastating affect the barrage had upon the soldiers who were holding the village:

> The troops who had so far held the lines south of Mametz and south of Montauban (Prussians among them) had sustained severe losses from the intense enemy bombardment which had been maintained for many days without a pause, and for the most part were already shot to pieces.[2]

Six Russian saps were driven into No Man's Land by 183rd Tunnelling Company. The tunnellers used push-picks to excavate through the hard chalk without being heard. As they dug closer to the German lines they resorted to using carpenters' augers to bore holes into the chalk. Vinegar was poured into these holes to soften the chalk, which could be scrapped out with minimal noise. In one instance a tunneller accidently bored into a German officer's dugout, but this error was unnoticed by its occupants. At 07:27 hours a Russian sap on the 30th Division's right flank was blown with the intention of extending the length of an approach trench. This resulted in a crater four feet deep, eighteen feet wide and 210 feet long. From this crater sixteen machine-guns fired into the German lines provided covering fire for the 30th Division's infantry.

89th BRIGADE SECTOR

The 89th Brigade, commanded by Brigadier-General the Honourable F.C. Stanley, was to assault on the extreme southern sector of the British attack, adjacent to the French line of advance. The 17th King's (Liverpool Regiment) – the 1st Liverpool Pals – on the right flank and the 20th King's (Liverpool Regiment) – the 4th Liverpool Pals – on the left, were ordered to capture the first German trench line known as Faviere Trench and then capture the second line Alt Trench. They were then to capture Dublin Trench including Glatz Redoubt and Dublin Redoubt and then to send a company to go on to secure the final objective the ruins of the Briqueterie, which was a strongly fortified German position southeast of Montauban. The Briqueterie comprised a chimney, which was used by German observers as an observation post, and two large buildings either side of the Longueval–Maricourt Road. German engineers had excavated beneath this position and installed iron girders and concrete rooms and tunnels creating an underground fortress. The ruins of the buildings above helped to conceal this strongpoint. Machine-guns nestled amongst the ruins had commanding views across the valley between Maricourt and Montauban.

When the whistles blew signalling the start of the attack at 07:30 hours the 89th Brigade advanced from four lines of assembly trenches. The 1st and 2nd Liverpool Pals were supported by the 2nd Bedfordshire Regiment with the 19th King's (Liverpool Regiment), the 3rd Liverpool Pals, held in reserve at Maricourt Chateau.

The 1st Liverpool Pals, commanded by Lieutenant-Colonel Bryan Fairfax, advanced between the Maricourt–Bernafay Wood Road and an isolated wood known as German's Wood. The French 153e Regiment d'Infanterie, 39th Division, XX Corps commanded by Commandant Lepetit, advanced on its right flank. This French unit had distinguished itself at Verdun and were known as 'Le Corps de Fer', translated as 'The Iron Corps'. The British and French units were on good terms with each other and both Fairfax and Lepetit left their trenches together and crossed No Man's Land with the second infantry wave.

The 4th Liverpool Pals, commanded by Lieutenant-Colonel H.W. Cobham, carried the left flank and had to advance west of German's Wood. Instead of ambling across No Man's Land at walking pace in accordance with their orders the 1st Liverpool Pals charged through the gaps in the wire towards the German trenches. A Liverpool Pal recalled: 'Our boys in the "Pals" went for the trenches in finest style. It was wonderful, no hesitation. No hesitation in face of sweeping fire, machine-gun, shrapnel and shells, they went on until they approached the village of Montauban.'[3] They encountered little resistance as they rushed through the broken wire, reaching the German lines before the enemy could leave their deep dugouts.

The 1st and 4th Liverpool Pals took the first German line, with Fairfax and Lepetit entering this trench together. From here the two battalions advanced towards Alt Trench. The 2nd Bedfordshire Regiment followed behind them in support and mopped up pockets of resistance. German's Wood was secured by the 1st Pals where a party of thirty Germans surrendered. The German defence of Alt Trench collapsed soon afterwards. The momentum of the attack was aided by the success on their right flank with the capture of Dublin Redoubt by the 153e Regiment d'Infanterie at 07:50 hours.

By 08:00 hours the 1st Liverpool Pals had secured Casement Trench, where they had to wait while British and French barrages bombarded Dublin Trench, their principle objective. The barrage lifted and the 1st and 4th Liverpool Pals advanced towards Dublin Trench where they found that the majority of its occupiers from 6th Bavarian RIR had retreated. Those that remained were eager to throw up their hands and surrender. By 08:30 hours the 1st and 4th Liverpool Pals had captured Dublin Trench with few casualties according to the scheduled time in the orders. The 4th Liverpool Pals continued westwards along Dublin Trench where they established contact with the 18th King's (Liverpool Regiment), and 19th Manchester Regiment from the 90th Brigade which had captured Glatz Redoubt.

German artillery fire was very soon directed upon Dublin Trench for they had the exact range. The 1st Liverpool Pals had to dig a new trench line north of Dublin Trench in order to avoid this shell fire. By 09:18 hours the 11th and 39th French Division's had secured all their objectives on the right flank. By 10:00 hours the headquarters of both the 1st and 4th Liverpool Pals moved forward. Fairfax set up his HQ in Faviere Support Trench while that of the 4th Liverpool Pals was established at the junction of Glatz Alley and Casement Trench.

The 2nd Bedfordshire Regiment was brought forward and ordered to dig a trench between a small trench running east from German's Wood to a German communication trench that ran east of the Maricourt–Bernafay Wood Road. A number of prisoners were being escorted towards Maricourt, as Oberleutnant Beddall later wrote:

> The position became even more critical, because afterwards it came out that the 6th Bavarian Reserve Regiment which on the morning of 1 July was thrown into Montauban, had been completely destroyed. Of the 3,500 men only 500 survivors remain, and these are for most part men who had not taken part in the battle, plus 2 regimental officers and a few stragglers who turned up on the following day. All the rest are dead, wounded or missing; only a small fraction fell into the enemy's hands as prisoners. (The Regimental Staff and the Battalions staff have all been captured in their dug outs). The 6th Bavarian Reserve is said to have surrendered owing to the complete shortage of ammunition, which had all been expended, but maintained a heroic resistance until the last moment. These dirty English are said to have slain these brave people without mercy, although the lack of ammunition rendered them all defenceless, and although by signals they showed their readiness to surrender.[4]

German artillery barrages were proving ineffective up until 11:00 hours. Although the 89th Brigade had captured German trenches, the German guns were still focusing their shells upon the British front line trenches which were empty. By 11:10 hours, however, Fairfax reported that his position in Faviere Support trench was being heavily shelled.

Lieutenant-Colonel Cobham established the 4th Liverpool Pals HQ in the north-western corner of Germans Wood, where, at 11:50 hours Cobham received orders from 89th Brigade HQ to begin the second phase of the assault which involved the capture of the Briqueterie. A briefing prior to the attack was carried out in German's Wood. At midday British artillery pounded the Briqueterie for thirty minutes. A Liverpool Pal recalled:

> In a wood just outside the village they saw for themselves the devastation of our artillery fire. The wood had been practically destroyed and the ground was ploughed in deep furrows. Few trees remained.

> Beyond the village, around half-a mile to the east, were large brickyards and buildings known as 'La Briqueterie', which had been converted by the Germans into a post of great strength.
>
> Our artillery had done its work well and those of the German garrison left were taken prisoners. The 'Pals' played an important part in capturing these strongholds.[5]

At 12:34 hours Captain E.C. Orford led No. 4 Company to attack the Briqueterie from Dublin Trench. A section of bombers led by 2nd Lieutenant Baker was sent from Glatz Redoubt up Nord Alley and along Chimney Trench to prevent German reinforcements reaching the Briqueterie. The only opposition encountered by Orford and his men was from a strongpoint which they overwhelmed by a bombing party resulting in the capture of a Colonel and adjutant of the 62nd Infantry Regiment, three other officers, thirty-four men and two machine-guns, some useful maps, together with a regimental staff officer and a party of German artillery observers. They also recovered a wounded soldier from the 2nd Bedfordshire Regiment who had been captured during a patrol on 28/29 June. Within five minutes, the Briqueterie was in British hands. Orford's party immediately set in motion the process of consolidation and a party of Royal Engineers was brought forward to assist them. The British artillery had carried out an effective bombardment and pulverised the trenches that surrounded the Briqueterie. The 4th Liverpool's War Diary recorded:

> Steps were immediately taken for consolidating the ground won, which, owing to the destruction wrought by our 'Heavies' was a matter of great difficulty, what had been trenches being almost unrecognisable as such, and the earth so pulverised that cover could only be made by aid of sandbags.[6]

Cobham moved the 4th Liverpool Pals Battalion HQ from German's Wood to the junction of Glatz Redoubt, Casement Trench and Dublin Trench. Although they had secured their objectives, the 1st and 4th Liverpool Pals came under considerable German artillery fire throughout the afternoon and night.

The 30th Division had captured all its objectives, including Montauban, by early afternoon on 1 July. RFC aerial reconnaissance reports received at 12:45 hours indicated that German reinforcements were moving from Longueval in a south-westerly direction towards Montauban. By 14:30 hours they were observed between Bernafay and Trones Wood. With the knowledge that German forces were closing in upon Montauban and a counter-attack was imminent, the relief of the 89th Brigade was postponed.

With German reinforcements converging upon Montauban, the 89th Brigade moved quickly in consolidating the positions that it had captured. The men were able to fortify their positions without being shelled by

German artillery from 14:00 hours until 16:00 hours, after which time German guns bombarded Dublin Trench and the remains of the Briqueterie.

By late afternoon the 1st Liverpool Pals had two companies in Dublin Trench and Casement Trench. The 4th Liverpool Pals had deployed one company in the Briqueterie, one-and-a-half companies in Dublin Trench and another one-and-a-half companies dug-in 100 yards behind Dublin Trench. One company from the 2nd Bedfordshire occupied Glatz Trench and Alt Trench, another company was holding Silesia Support, with two platoons in Casement Trench, two platoons in new trench and one company in Faviere Support. The 3rd Liverpool Pals were holding the original front line.

Montauban was heavily shelled by German artillery at 17:15 hours. The 90th Brigade HQ was fearful that a German counter-attack would be launched from the northeast of East and consequently reinforcements from the 4th Liverpool Pals King's went to the Briqueterie to support the company holding that position to bolster its defences.

SOS flares were fired from Montauban between 22.00 and 23:30 hours as German shells descended upon the village but a German counter-attack failed. German forces were reported to be occupying Bernafay Wood and British howitzers shelled the wood soon later. At 03:30 hours on 2 July the German guns opened up with a barrage upon the Briqueterie, Dublin and Casement Trenches. Twenty minutes later German infantry launched a counter-attack upon the Briqueterie and Montauban. This was repelled by a company of the 4th Liverpool Pals supported by two Vickers machine-guns and two German machine-guns which had been captured during the previous day.

German infantry entered the northwestern sector of Montauban, but the battalions from the 90th Brigade fought them off and regained control around 18:00 hours. Another counter-attack was repulsed at 07:00 hours and six German officers and 125 men were captured. Throughout the rest of the morning the 89th Brigade was able to continue consolidating Montauban and the Briqueterie.

Many German soldiers were relieved to have been captured by their British foe. They had spent the past week underground, with little food, unable to sleep or wash and their nerves shattered by the shellfire. Private Francis Woods in one of the Liverpool Pals' mopping up parties that followed behind the advancing waves, recalled:

> Our work was to follow up the other companies and to clear out the trenches. We bombed and searched dug outs, cleared the trenches of prisoners and dead, and held on. The prisoners seemed rather pleased than otherwise to fall into our hands, as for eight days during the bombardment they said they had hardly any food to eat, and that the shelling by the British had been terrific. They were in a fearfully unkempt condition with days of growth on their faces and some of

them looked to be quite fifty-nine years of age. In fact one man was fifty-nine. This prisoner said the war would last sometime yet, as the Germans have got plenty of men.[7]

The 4th Liverpool Pals had two officers killed and three wounded, with seventy-five casualties amongst the men. The 1st Liverpool Pals casualties were slight in comparison to battalions north of Montauban. Captain E.C. Torrey and 2nd Lieutenant P.L. Wright were wounded, Lieutenant D.H. Scott died from wounds and 100 men were lost. The Germans lost heavily at Montauban. The 109th RIR lost forty-two officers and 2,105men. The 6th Bavarian RIR losing thirty-five officers and 1,775 men.

21st BRIGADE SECTOR

The 21st Brigade, which advanced on the left flank of the 89th Brigade, experienced similar success on its sector. It was ordered to secure Silesia Trench, Silesia Support Trench, Alt Trench and Glatz Redoubt. The successful capture of Montauban was dependent upon the capture of Glatz Redoubt.

18th King's (Liverpool Regiment), the 2nd Liverpool Pals, commanded by Lieutenant-Colonel E.H. Trotter, DSO, advanced on the left flank and was ordered to secure positions east and north of Glatz Redoubt to prevent reinforcements reached the strongpoint, while the 19th Manchester Regiment, the 4th Manchester Pals, commanded by Lieutenant-Colonel Sir Henry Hill, carried the right flank being tasked with a direct assault upon the Redoubt,. The 2nd Wiltshire Regiment followed in support and 2nd Yorkshire Regiment (The Green Howards) were held in reserve.

The 6th Bavarian RIR defending the line had suffered a tragic setback when a British shell struck their command post at Glatz Redoubt and wiped out most of the regimental staff. This impacted upon the German defence of Montauban as, with the staff officers dead or wounded, no orders were issued and the defenders left in a state of confusion.

Private Albert Andrews, 4th Manchester Pals, recalled the moments before going over the top:

> The orders came down: 'Half an hour to go.' 'Quarter of an hour to go.' 'Ten minutes to go,' 'Three minutes to go.' I lit a cigarette and up the ladder I went. There was a section to a ladder and you waited until the others got up in line. Each company formed a wave, so a Battalion formed four waves, each of about 250 men in line about one yard apart.[8]

At 07:30 hours, the 4th Manchester Pals and the 2nd Liverpool Pals advanced through cut wire towards Silesia Trench, the first German line. These two battalions advanced east of the line of trees called Talus Boisé. Anyone walking the battlefield of Montauban today can see that this line of trees still exist. 'C' Company of the Manchester Pals suffered forty casualties from machine-gun fire from their left flank before they reached Silesia Trench. 2nd Lieutenant Atkinson and several of the NCOs fell but despite losing their leaders the men pushed forward towards Silesia Trench.

As the barrage moved forward German machine-gunners left their dugouts and into their firing positions and were able to cause some casualties amongst the advancing British waves. The 3rd Liverpool Pals, the 4th Manchester Pals and 2nd Wiltshire Regiment also came under heavy fire as they crossed the shell-cratered No Man's Land.[9]

Lieutenant-Colonel Trotter, of the 3rd Liverpool Pals reported: 'In many places our men could leave the trenches without being seen from the enemy's front line trenches. This was on the Fleche side, and to deal with them the enemy had, on the 18th Division front, well back, machine-guns in the open which it was impossible to locate before the action commenced. The hedge running in front of Montauban, which was the apparent place, was under the barrage from our artillery. These machine-guns dealt with men, unseen, leaving the parapet. On the right, where the men were more on the high ground, there was a machine-gun firing directly on our men advancing from the front line trench.'[10]

This machine-gun fire caused considerable casualties and Trotter immediately dispatched Private Sidney Steele to assess the situation and report back to him. Steele saw the devastating impact that this machine-gun had upon the battalion:

> I was with the Colonel, the adjutant and the signaller officer. I was the signal officer's batman ... Colonel asked me to see what has happened. I was only nineteen ... I went along the trench and got up on top I see a bottle with rum on the parapet. They was lucky the lads would be glad of that. They would not give them the rum ration when they went over they said they would be too excited ... so I took it with me. The first thing I saw on the top was all the dead, this some two, three or four dead high one mass of dead men. Jerries trenches were three hundred yards away and in front of us there had been ten machine-guns. There were six trees there and a Jerry machine-gun was chained to them and right in front of us there was a pillar box with a long slit and a machine-gun firing from the right and one from the left but they never used the one in front of us. When they opened up they wiped the battalion out.[11]

Private Albert Andrews recalled the journey of the 4th Manchester Pals across No Man's Land on the right flank:

> At 7.30 am on a beautiful sunny morning off we started, about 50 yards between each wave. I was carrying my rifle by the sling on my shoulder with the bayonet parallel to my ear and had not gone many yards, when

> whizz! – I felt as if someone had pulled at the top. However, I took no notice as we were at a quick march and it was taking us all our time to keep going. Like nearly every other fellow was smoking. No Man's Land was one mass of shell holes, the soil was loose and we had 400 yards of this to go to the first trench.
>
> Fritz let us have it with shrapnel, machine-guns and rifles. As we travelled along our lads kept falling killed and wounded, and about half way across the second wave catches us with the first to fill these gaps up. About 100 yards from the German trench, our officer turned and said, 'Up a bit on the left,' then pitched forwards. That was the last order he ever gave.[12]

The Germans in Silesia Trench welcomed them with hand grenades. 2nd Lieutenant Eric Fitzbrown from the 2nd Liverpool Pals was the first officer from the battalion to reach Silesia Trench where a battle for the German front line erupted. Fitzbrown emptied his revolver during this struggle and as more of his company arrived the Germans began withdrawing in haste to rear lines. Lieutenant-Colonel Trotter reported:

> The first line seems to have been taken with a certain amount of opposition, and one officer and some men surrendered, but previous to this on our advance men were seen to leave the back trenches and retreat towards Montauban. A certain amount of bombing took place in the second line trench and thirty men surrendered after being forced into dug outs by our advancing parties.[13]

As Private Sidney Steele crossed No Man's Land to assess the situation on behalf of Colonel Trotter he came across wounded officers from the battalion.[14] This included the battalion medical officer:

> I spotted the doctor with Burt Meakin attending the wounded. He shouted 'What are you doing there, get out of here we have enough casualties'. I said 'I have got to go there'. He said 'You will never get there'.[15]

Undaunted by the hostile fire Steele linked up with a small party led by Lieutenant Smith in the German line which was about to resist a German counter-attack. Smith's party fought off this enemy assault. When Steele reported to Smith that most of the battalion had been wiped out, Smith was disbelieving:

> I walked amongst all the dead towards the German front line and when I got near it a machine-gun opened fire, so I dropped down waited a bit, then run a bit, then dropped down until I got up to the trench and then

> I found about thirty of our men with one lieutenant. His name was Lieutenant Smith, he was the only survivor of the officers from Number 1 Company; all the others killed. Just then Jerry made a counter-attack. 'Go on get up there with them' said Smith. So I went on to the firing step. Jerry did not come he had enough. The fellas gave him some rapid fire and they went back. I said to Smith I had to go back with a message. He said aye you want to get back. I said no I stay and give you a hand, but we all volunteered but the colonel would not let us. There have been too many casualties. Have you looked over the top? [Smith] said no. They did not know what had happened. Their minds had been concentrated in getting in the Jerry trench. We were in the German front line. I have got to go back but he wants to know how things are. Tell him we want reinforcements. There are only thirty men here ...this is as far as I know all that is left. The rest is lying on top. [Smith] looked at me 'what do you mean?' I said they had been wiped out, the battalion has been practically wiped out there must be around 350 lying on top out there. He just walked away, he did not believe me.[16]

When Steele returned to Battalion HQ, and reported that the battalion had been annihilated to Lieutenant-Colonel Trotter, he also could not believe the news and sent another officer to verify the report.

> So I went back reported to the Colonel. You could see he was upset. He said to me 'are you sure?' I said 'yes sir, I would not come back with a story and make something like that up'. He turned round to signal officer Lieutenant Stacey you have got to go and check and see what you can find out.'[17]

Stacey also doubted the report and commented to Steele as they went forward 'You better not have made it up'.[18] Stacey saw the harsh reality with his own eyes confirming that they had sustained heavy casualties. As they went forward Stacey found Lieutenant Willey. Steel recalled:

> We got over the top and took him to a captain where he was lying. You would not think he was dead. We walked further along and we found Lieutenant Willey … we could not see where he was hit, but I think he was killed by shell fire, little tin box lying by him, full of capsules, little tubes, and one of them was missing, he had poisoned himself, he couldn't face it, he was a nice fellas.[19]

The 4th Manchester Pals on the right flank also reached Silesia Trench and were greeted by determined Germans with hand grenades as well as some coming forward with their hands in the air wanting to surrender. Private Albert Andrews recalled:

> I jumped into the German trench, what was left of it, just near a dug out door. In the doorway there was a big barrel. As soon as I jumped in, a German leapt from behind the barrel but I was already on guard and I had my bayonet on his chest. He was trembling and looked half mad with his hands above his head, saying something to me which I did not understand. All I could make out was that he did not want me to kill him! It was here I noticed my bayonet was broken and I couldn't have stuck him with it. Of course, I had 'one up the chimney' as we called it – that is, a bullet in the breech, so that you only have to pull the trigger. I pointed to his belt and bayonet. He took these off, and his hat and water bottle as well, emptied his pockets and offered the lot to me. Just then one of my mates was coming up the trench. 'Get out of the way, Albert. Leave him to me, I'll give him one to himself' – he meant he would throw a bomb at him, which would have blown him to pieces, 'Come here,' I said. He was on his knees in front of me now, fairly pleading. I said 'He's an old man' – he looked sixty. At the finish I pointed my thumb towards our lines, calling out all the time. He was trembling from head to foot and frightened to death. I honestly believe he could have done me as I jumped into the trench if he had not been so afraid. This was the only German I ever let off and I have never regretted it because I believe he could have done me quite easily.[20]

Private Albert Andrews demonstrated compassion for the old German soldier as he let him surrender, but as he went through Silesia Trench he showed no mercy for others who wanted to give themselves up:

> We both bombed the dug out and turned round to go along the trench, when three Germans came running towards us with their hands up. They would be about 20 yards away. We both fired and two fell, my mate saying as he let go. 'That's for my brother in the Dardanelles,' and, as he fired again a third German fell. 'That's for my winter in the trenches.' We walked up to them and one moved. My mate kicked him and pushed his bayonet into him. That finished him.[21]

The 4th Manchester Pals and 3rd Liverpool continued towards Silesia Support Trench and Alt Trench. A platoon from the Manchester Pals 'C' Company, was slowed down by a party of six German bombers but they were overwhelmed. When both battalions were yards from Alt Trench they caught up with the British artillery battery they were following. Once the barrage lifted at 07:45 hours they continued to advance upon Alt Trench. 'C' Company encountered some German bombers in its sector of Alt Trench, but they withdrew towards Glatz Redoubt. 'A' Company then joined in the fight for the redoubt.

The 3rd Liverpool Pals on the left lost heavily to machine-gun fire from the west side of Railway Valley. The machine-gun crew fired until the last moment. When they tried to surrender they were killed. The 2nd Yorkshire Regiment (The Green Howards) followed behind in support but were cut down by a German machine-gun position in the Warren preventing them from crossing No Man's Land. Only one corporal and thirty men from this battalion reached Silesia Trench.

The 2nd Liverpool Pals continued to advance without faltering along Train Alley and into Alt Trench. A German machine-gun on its left flank in Alt Trench close to the junction with Alt Alley opened fire upon them. This German position was defended by bombers and snipers who were concealed behind a hedgerow and they were protected by comrades providing covering fire from Train Alley which followed the railway track beyond Alt Trench and Dublin Trench towards Montauban. This machine-gun position was thought to be solely responsible for all the casualties suffered by the 2nd Liverpool. The entire advance upon Montauban was in jeopardy if this machine-gun and nearby snipers were not dealt with. Captain Arthur de Bels Adam MC, made a spirited attempt to subdue this position from Silesia Support Line with a bombing party but he and much of the party were immediately hit by sniper fire coming behind the hedge. He continued to advance towards the hedge but received another wound thirty yards from the hedge. His runner, Private F. Haslam, rushed to dress his wounds as waves of Liverpool bombers advanced towards the hedge. They were repulsed by the snipers and stick grenades. 2nd Lieutenant George Herdman came forward to offer support but was killed by a German grenade. 2nd Lieutenant Eric Fitzbrown who was the first man to enter the German front line also made an attempt to overwhelm this German strongpoint. With two bombs in his hands he tried to bomb Train Alley and the hedge where the snipers were positioned. Fitzbrown was also killed, shot through the head by a sniper. Private Sidney Steele discovered Fitzbrown's body and reported: 'Fitzbrown got a bomb in his face, it blew his head off by one of these potato mashers, you pull the string and throw.'[22]

Captain Adam, despite being seriously wounded, was able to co-ordinate the assault upon the German machine-gun emplacement, ordering a bombing party to conduct a reconnaissance of this troublesome position, but he was soon killed by an exploding stick grenade, thrown from behind the German occupied hedge, also wounding Private Haslam for a second time. Lieutenant H.C. Watkins leading a bombing party took control of the situation. As they made their way forward towards the hedge his party threw their own Mills grenades into the German strongpoint. This caused the German defence to collapse and they were able to bomb their way along Alt Trench and Train Alley. Lieutenant-Colonel Trotter reported:

> Lieut. Watkins attempted to go down and found the body of Second Lieut. Herdman, and threw a bomb which failed to reach the enemy bombing guard. Lieut. Watkins acted as one of Capt. Adam's subalterns would act, and grasping the situation immediately, he told off his longest throwers, who, with the greatest luck, threw a bomb into the German bombing guard, killing two and pushing the rest back into Train Alley, thus making the advance possible, and the bombing of Lieut. Watkins' party drove the enemy into their dug outs; many, including an officer, were shot in the hedge by riflemen, and thirty, including a medical officer surrendered to Lieut. Watkins on their dug outs being bombed; but the bombs do not appear to have done much damage to the dugouts.[23]

The success of Lieutenant Watkins' party enabled the 2nd Liverpool Pals to capture Glatz Redoubt at 08:35 hours where they established contact with the 4th Manchester Pals who fought their way into this stronghold from an easterly direction. Private Albert Andrews remembered British artillery bombarding Glatz Redoubt before the assault.

> Then we waited outside Glatz Redoubt, all our guns being turned on this ring of trenches, which was right on top of the ridge. We got the order 'Charge!' and away we went at the double, killing all that stayed there. A good many retreated towards Montauban and we opened rapid fire upon them.[24]

In Glatz Redoubt they found the bodies of dead German soldiers lying around amid the debris and deserted equipment. Some of those bodies were on fire or smouldering and some of the trenches had been blown in and were exposed. As Private Albert Andrews took part in the consolidation of the Redoubt he was told to take cover because German snipers were lurking in the vicinity:

> Then I was sent clearing dug outs. I know I was going over a bit of loose ground where the trench was blown down, when I heard someone call out, 'Get down!' Of course, I did not want telling twice, then they called me to go there on my stomach as there was a sniper there. I crawled over and looked down at the bottom of this bit of a hill and then saw it was a timely warning, there being several of our fellows dead there at the bottom that this sniper had caught.[25]

As the 2nd Liverpool Pals consolidated Glatz Redoubt some of its men began searching for souvenirs. One of these chaps found a sought-after pickelhaube spiked helmet, but as he wore it while joking around a soldier from the 4th Manchester Pals who was mopping-up mistook him for a

German soldier and shot him dead. Thirty German prisoners were secured in the redoubt.

Red flares were fired into the sky to signify that the redoubt had been captured at 08:30 hours. Each soldier carried a smoke candle and as soon as the line between Glatz Redoubt and Dublin Trench was in British hands they were lit in an effort to conceal the advance of the 90th Brigade as it passed through the redoubt towards Montauban.

At 09:00 hours twelve 4in Stokes mortars were brought forward to Glatz Redoubt by two subsections from No 5 Battalion, Special Brigade, Royal Engineers, led by Lieutenant Rathbone with the help from a carrying party from the 2nd Wiltshire Regiment. Here they were able to raise a thick smoke screen on their right flank in order to conceal the advancing infantry from German observers positioned in the Briqueterie. The smoke was so dense in Montauban and over the ridge in Caterpillar Valley that visibility was reduced to between two and three yards. The ruse succeeded because the focus of German artillery fire was directed upon this smoke and not on the British infantry, as an anonymous platoon sergeant reported:

> We had carried the first two lines, and on getting into the third, we saw the Germans coming up from the two exits of a deep dugout, and pairing off down the trench. Our platoon commander got into the trench and picked the Huns off as they came out. He had the mouth of the dugout on either side of him, say fifteen yards away. A German would rush out from No. 1 exit – over he went. Then one would come out from No 2 exit, and over he went. Our officer was as cool as a cucumber – he simply turned from left to right and fired just as if he was in a shooting saloon. It was the best bit of fancy shooting I've seen – all prizes, no blanks. After we'd finished that bit of business – it only took about a minute – off we went again, and I got shot in the shoulder, but I saw our officer and the rest of the boys going forward as if they were off to a picnic.[26]

The process of consolidation began immediately. Nord Alley, a communication trench that led from Glatz Redoubt to the eastern extremity of Montauban was blocked. Barbed-wire defences were hastily erected and two 'T' sap heads were dug and two Lewis Gun crews temporary installed in these positions until two Vickers machine-guns could be brought up with supplies of water and munitions.

The Liverpool and Manchester Pals success in capturing Glatz Redoubt enabled 90th Brigade to pass through their lines and capture Montauban. They paid a price for that success. The 2nd Liverpool Pals lost two-thirds of its strength in their assault upon Montauban and the 4th Manchester Pals had one officer and forty-one men killed, with one officer and eleven men missing. One officer and 136 men were wounded.

90th BRIGADE SECTOR

The 90th Brigade, commanded by Brigadier-General C.J. Stevenson, comprising the 2nd Royal Scots Fusiliers, the 16th, 17th and 18th Manchester Regiment (1st, 2nd and 3rd Manchester Pals) were ordered to sweep through lines captured by the 21st Brigade and take Montauban.

The entire brigade had assembled in Cambridge Copse, positioned south of the Carnoy–Maricourt Road during the night 30 June / 1 July. They occupied specially-dug trenches that were prepared in the Carnoy–Maricourt Valley. The 30th Division War Diary commented:

> The assembly involved the march by night of the whole 90th Brigade, right through the narrow front allotted to the division … Fortunately the enemy had not observed the march, nor did he appear to have observed the assembly trenches; it was an agreeable surprise that the 90th Brigade were hardly shelled at all prior to their advance.[27]

The 1st Manchester Pals' objective was to capture the western portion of Montauban and secure Montauban Alley which was 200 yards behind the village on the reverse slope of Montauban Ridge. On the right flank the 2nd Manchester Pals was to take the eastern section of the village. The 2nd Royal Scots Fusiliers followed behind in support while the 3rd Manchester Pals was held back as battalion reserve.

While the 21st Brigade were fighting for control of Glatz Redoubt the battalions from 90th Brigade assembled in British front line. In order to get there they advanced along a track sheltered by the woods of Talus Boisé.

It was a tense time for the battalions of the 90th Brigade. They had to wait an hour before they could advance, witnessing their comrades from the 21st Brigade go over the top. Private Watkin Wilson, 1st Manchester Pals recalled:

> When the mist rose the weather was beautifully sunny, just like a midsummer's day in 'old blighty.' During this time our artillery was bombarding with terrific force, and it gave all the boys confidence. As the bombardment got more and more terrible until nearly all the occupants of the trench were nigh deaf, bottles of rum (the soldier's friend in winter) appeared on the scene, and every man knew that this was the first sign to be ready for the day. Word came down the trench for us to get on the top, and we mounted up the ladders used for the occasion and then our casualties began, but the boys were not downhearted and after each had received a tot of rum they were ready to meet the devil and all the horrors of war; but it was easy to see who was going to win, From our position we could see unwavering lines of khaki figures a good distance to our left, and their bayonets were

> glistening like diamonds in the hot sun. Shells were bursting in their thousands, and the air was full of clouds of coloured smoke that made one feel like being poisoned. Then we received the news that certain villages along the lines had been taken by our troops.[28]

The 1st and 2nd Manchester Pals advanced from their starting positions at 08:30 hours, followed by the 2nd Royal Scots Fusiliers in support. Although the 21st Brigade had entered the German lines, pockets of resistance were able to pour machine-gun fire upon the British lines and cause significant casualties as the two Pals battalions left their trenches and advanced across No Man's Land. As they left the shelter of Talus Boisé they came under heavy German machine-gun fire from the position known as the Warren, which was close to where Breslau Alley connected with Train Alley. This machine-gun crew had accounted for a lot of casualties amongst battalions from the 18th Division who were attacking Pommiers Redoubt in the west. Now they turned their weapon to the east on the 90th Brigade. Private Albert Hurst of the 2nd Manchester Pals recalled the moment when they were about to go over the top:

> There was no whistle blown, the officer looked at his watch, and said 'Now!' We just got up there where there were a lot of ladders to get us over the top, and it was a scramble to get up with all the gear. By that time the advance units had occupied a German redoubt and German front line at Montauban we still came under a lot of fire and machine-gun fire as we went over. It must have been coming from Montauban from the German second line possibly.[29]

An artillery barrage upon this German machine-gun position at the Warren was not called because there were parties of the 8th East Surrey Regiment close by. The German machine-gun continued to cause havoc amongst the ranks of the two Pals battalions. Carrying lots of cumbersome equipment and tools slowed down their advance making easy targets for the German machine-gunner. Albert Hurst described the equipment that he carried across No Man's Land.

> We had two extra bandoliers of rifle ammunition, we had two Mills bomb each, on the back of the packs were a yellow dot to signify us as being Manchesters and a bright metal plate to reflect the light so aeroplanes could see how far we had gone in our advance. We also carried a full sized pick axe and Lewis Gun ammunitions carried in water buckets.
>
> This impeded our movement very much so. It weighed us down and slowed our movements. It was impossible to run. We could just about walk. We left nothing behind. Men were carrying barbed wire

> and posts for barbed wire to go on. Every man had some extra load. We had to put up barbed wire and dig ourselves in when we got there.[30]

The attack formation used by the 2nd Manchester Pals caused the men to bunch up in groups of ten as they sauntered towards the German lines, allowing the German machine-gunner to sweep their line of advance with little effort.

> We advance in block formation, about two of us, five pairs in file which was vulnerable to artillery fire.
>
> Over the top of the first wave who – I later found out – had captured the first line of the German trenches. The whole battalion moved forward in block formation – ten men keeping close together in files of five. We did not practise this in the attack. It was daft, it made us very vulnerable, but I did not have an impression of people falling around me. The British wire had been cut for us, and we had no problem getting through. Then we endeavoured to recognise the points that we were making for.
>
> The fire got heavier as we went across No Man's Land. I could hear the bullets whistling in the air. There was no cover. I was exposed, I was frightened and I got a bullet through my water bottle. We were suffering casualties, but I didn't know it at the time. Of our platoon, perhaps a dozen out of fifty men were casualties.[31]

The 1st Manchester Pals suffered a similar experience. Private Samuel Rigby related the experience of advancing across No Man's Land towards Montauban:

> At last the signal went for the start and with a loud cheer our lads were over the top and making for the village. As soon as we were over their machine-guns and rifles opened fire on us. It was awful, the poor lads dropping right and left. I heard a chap shouting 'Sam' just as we rested and I crawled across and saw a young chap out of my platoon and who works at our place, had been hit. I made him as comfortable as possible and we shook hands, and he just said 'Good luck and God bless you, Sam,' and then he fainted. I had to leave him as our line was going on, but I heard after that he had been picked up and I was glad.[32]

Lieutenant-Colonel H.A. Johnson, commanding the 2nd Manchester Pals, was hit and Major C.L. Macdonald, his adjutant, assumed command of the battalion. German shrapnel also posed a problem as it exploded above their advancing ranks. The 1st Manchester Pals suffered heavily. Sergeant James Payne was among the wounded:

> We were all knocked out. Their machine-guns were waiting for us. We didn't get through. None of us. There was a big shell hole full of dead and dying and blinded. Tall men got it through the jaw, shorter men through the eyes, there was a lot of blinded men there. I was five foot ten and shot through the cheek. I was walking along enfilade fire, and a bullet blew all my teeth out. I fell forward and spat all my teeth out and breathed. I collapsed and about four o'clock, I came round. My left eye was closed. I couldn't talk. I could breath. That was all. I got my field dressing out and wound it round my face and my left eye. I could see through my right eye and I saw one of my corporals (Corporal Bill Brock) who'd been shot through the foot. I took his boot off, bandaged it up, put his boot on again and gave him his rifle to use as a crutch and together we went back. There was no medics around, just the dead.[33]

The two Pals battalions, with the 2nd Royal Scots Fusiliers in support, passed over Alt Trench at 09:10 hours and were then able to join their comrades from the 21st Brigade who had captured Glatz Redoubt and laid down the smoke screen that confused the German gunners.

The 2nd Royal Scots Fusiliers, led by Lieutenant-Colonel R.K. Walsh, was a battalion of regulars assigned to stiffen the 90th Brigade and its three Pals battalions. The Scots were keen to make their mark in this assault and they caught up with their New Army counterparts. Their presence in the final surge for Montauban was extremely important because most of the officers and NCOs from the 1st and 2nd Manchester Pals had become casualties. The 2nd Royal Scots Fusiliers not only had combat experience, but they had officers and NCOs who could guide the remnants of the other battalions, who until the 1 July had never been in battle.

At 10:00 hours these three battalions advanced up the gradual slope towards Montauban. They did so under German machine-gun and shell fire and had to find gaps in the wire in front of Southern Trench which was the final line of defence that needed to be breached in order to gain entrance into the village. Private Richard Boardman who had advanced with the 1st Manchester Pals was hit just fifty yards from Montauban: 'We advanced over a mile, under shot and shell, which was terrible, but we kept plodding on'.[34]

The British barrage lifted from the south of the village to the north and they entered Montauban before the remaining German soldiers could come out of their dugouts. Montauban had been reduced to rubble and it was difficult for the Manchester battalions to identify positions in what was left of the village. One anonymous sergeant recalled the scene as they entered Montauban:

> We went over in grand style, and found nothing much in the way until we got into Montauban. Here the place was an awful mess. Most of the houses had been knocked head over heels – the only ones I saw standing were a couple of cafes. As we came on, we saw lots of

> Germans running out of the back of the village, but when we got into the streets there were plenty of them monkeying about the ruins. We had divided the company up into groups of six, but as we neared the village we all joined up again. My five pals were five of the best, and we kept well together. We saw some Huns in a ground-floor room so we dropped a Mill's bomb through the window, and didn't wait for an answer. As we turned the corner we saw a German lying round the end of the wall. He'd got a machine-gun and had made a little displacement with bricks. He turned this damned thing on me, and got me in the foot. It didn't stop me, though, and when I was getting near him I felt two kicks over the heart. I didn't wait to see what had happened, but simply went at him and bayoneted him.
>
> I couldn't go on much further, so I sat down to see what was the damage. My foot was pretty bad, but when I looked at my left hand breast pocket I saw two holes in it. I opened my pocket, and found that two bullets had gone through my metal shaving mirror, through my pocket-case, and had nosed their way into a book I was carrying. Funnily enough earlier in the morning my officer gave me the book, and said I could read it when I got into the German trenches, so I put it in my pocket little thinking that I should be able to read a bit of it on hospital ship coming back.
>
> I saw three Germans come up to two of our fellows and throw down their rifles. So our lads chucked down theirs too, and went for them with their fists, and they didn't half give 'em a dusting. The Germans seemed to be of all ages from 16 to 50, I should say. Some of them came up crying out that they had no food to eat for five days. One of our boys did wonders with the bayonet. He was chasing three Germans. He caught them up, and bayoneted two, and as he swung round he hit the third man down with the butt of his rifle.
>
> As we were going into Montauban we saw a German machine-gunner up a tree. He'd got the neatest little platform you ever saw, painted so that it was invisible. We shot him down, but he didn't fall clear. The last we saw of him was that he was hanging by his boots from the branches.[35]

The Germans defending this village pulled back so when the Manchesters arrived they found the village deserted. They pursued the German forces as they pulled back in large numbers. The 2nd Manchester Pals advancing on the right flank entered the south-eastern sector of Montauban by 10:35 hours. Five minutes later the 1st Manchester Pals had reached Southern Trench and within a couple of minutes they too were inside the village, as Private Albert Hurst recalled:

> We went on to the village of Montauban, which seemed to be flattened. The only thing left intact was a figure of Christ on the Cross, at the

> corner of the Peronne Road. We didn't see any Germans in Montauban and we took up a position on the right hand side, facing Bernafay Wood where we fixed up the machine-gun. There were no casualties amongst our team. It took about an hour to get across No Man's Land to position facing Bernafay Wood.[36]

Those Germans who remained in the village were too stunned, exhausted and concussed to offer any resistance and many surrendered. Once in the village the 1st Manchester Pals was confronted by a mass of Germans wanting to surrender. Private Samuel Rigby wrote:

> We arrived at the village and the first thing we saw was batches of Germans giving themselves up, others running about with their hands up and shouting "Mercy Comrade." I saw two running towards my section with their hands up wanting to be made prisoners, so we pushed them with the others. Others ran towards their other trenches, but we captured the village, or what was left of it.[37]

Together with the 2nd Royal Scots Fusiliers the Manchester battalions consolidated Montauban. The 201st Field Company Royal Engineers accompanied them into the village which had been reduced to rubble. Their commander, Lieutenant-Colonel H. Hall commented:

> Their job was to put the village in a state of defence. Of course there was no village when they got there; they went up immediately behind the support battalion, got thoroughly mixed up with the infantry could effect nothing really useful and suffered approximately 30 per cent casualties including 1 officer killed.[38]

The 30th Division pushed northwards beyond the village to capture Montauban Alley which ran along the reverse slope of Montauban Ridge. By 11:00 hours the division had captured Montauban Alley and its designated objectives including the village. The 1st Manchester Pals stumbled across a German battery, manned by the 21st Feldartillerie-Regiment located on the other side of the ridge in Caterpillar Valley, north of Spur Point and captured three 77mm field guns. These were the first German field guns captured during the battle. Due to heavy German artillery fire descending upon this slope they were unable to remove these artillery pieces for several days. Private Watkin Wilson, 1st Manchester Pals, recalled the efforts made to consolidate Montauban Alley:

> The roll of spectators did not last long, and we were ordered to advance through heavy artillery fire from the Boches. Our destination, which was a trench on the far side, a distance of 4,000 yards, was reached by

part of our battalion, who suffered very heavily from enfilade machine-gunners, but the Boches did not wait for us, and I can honestly say, without fear of contradiction that they can run! We had to work very hard for hours to make this newly captured German trench into something like a fire or front line trench. Soon we had a machine-gun and fire strips ready for the expected counter-attack. That really did take place at dawn, the 2nd July. They bombed us out of our bay, after we had done considerable damage with the gun, and the Boches who entered the trench were made prisoners later in the day. We were relieved after holding our new position for 36 hours, and we welcomed our relief with open arms.[39]

Although the 90th Brigade occupied Montauban it was unable to move above ground freely because the men were exposed to German shell fire and machine-guns from the north. The 30th Division War Diary reported:

During the afternoon of the 1st and the night 1st/2nd, affairs in Montauban were not comfortable. The village had been reduced to a pulp and very little cellar accommodation could be discovered. The slightest movement in the open was greeted with accurate machine-gun fire from Caterpillar Wood, the N. slopes of the ravine and Bernafay Wood. Shell fire not only never stopped after 1.45 pm, but became constantly worse.[40]

One brave sapper of 201st Field Company RE was wounded as he made a spirited attempt to lay barbed wire in front of Montauban. Lieutenant-Colonel Hall reported:

When the Boche were forming up on their counter-attack one detached sapper was asked by a C.O. what he could do to stop it. He went out with a roll of barbed wire and ran it amongst the trees in full view of both sides. He got a bullet through the neck and a MM on the recommendation of the C.O.[41]

The 2nd Manchester Pals fought off a German counter-attack from the north at 09:20 hours. Supported by a British barrage the attack soon collapsed.

During the early hours of 2 July, German artillery began to shell Montauban once again. Desperate to regain control of the village and the Briqueterie a counter-attack was launched by two German battalions between 03:15 and 04:00 hours. A small party from the 2nd Manchester Pals held Triangle Point northeast of Montauban and fought until the last man, when they were overwhelmed. The rest of this German initiative failed due to an accurate British barrage and those that got through this maelstrom of exploding shells were cut down by the machine-guns from the 4th Liverpool Pals in the Briqueterie.

The 1st Manchester Pals suffered heavy casualties during the day and had to resist German attempts to recapture the trenches that they were holding during the night, as Private Samuel Rigby recalled:

> We had a bit of peace for about two hours and then they started to shell us heavily and we had to lie or crouch down for an hour or so at a time. This was kept up all night, and in the early hours of the morning they started a counter-attack and they came across in mass, but our lads gave them socks. They managed to get in at one or two weak points. Bombers were told off to go and clear a trench where some of them had got in. We ran a long way and then we came to the trench where they were, so we had to go steady. We had not gone far when we spotted them. I saw one of them with a big camp board on his shoulder. I was the first bayonet man, but I was too far off to rush him, so I just dropped on one knee and shot at him. I could have shouted out when I saw him fall, but the others started to throw bombs at us from two points. We had to get back a little way and we were able to stop them from coming any further. A little later we got relieved by others so were able to go back. All this time we were being heavily shelled.[42]

The 1st Manchester Pals was relieved by the 2nd Wiltshire Regiment at 05:00 hours on 2 July. The 2nd Royal Scots Fusiliers and the 3rd Manchester Pals held onto Montauban until relieved by 27th Brigade, 9th Division, during the night of 2/3 July.

The capture of Montauban was one of the success-stories of 1 July. Accurate shelling of German wire and strongpoints by British and French artillery, together with effective communication and the ability to bring forward reinforcements, extra munitions, and equipment for consolidating the captured positions were contributing factors to this success. The 30th Division War Diary recorded:

> Communications worked well. The buried lines were never cut. Lines taken across by advancing troops were not satisfactory, but those laid after the objective had been reached worked well.
>
> The pigeon service was excellent – some messages taking only 23 minutes from Montauban via the Etinehem loft to Divisional Headquarters.
>
> Visual communications proved invaluable and well repaid the trouble devoted to its preparation. The Advanced Divisional Signalling Station at Peronne Road was constantly in use.
>
> The light French Lamp was better than the heavier Flying Corps Lamp. Flares, discs and patches all proved useful.[43]

The destruction of 6th Bavarian RIR's command post at Glatz Redoubt by a British shell had caused a significant setback disabling most of the regimental staff and their command structure. The troops that remained were too exhausted by the weeks of heavy labour in preparing the defences of Montauban and were in no fit state to defend this sector.

It is important to note that 30th Division's three Pals battalions from Kitchener's New Army had played a prominent part in the successful capture of Montauban and proved themselves to be effective fighting soldiers.

Part 8

Aftermath and Assessment

Chapter 25

Aftermath

Many of the soldiers who survived 1 July 1916 would regard it as possibly the worst experience they would ever encounter and would be haunted by the horrors of that traumatic day for the rest of their lives. Sergeant Holley, of the 1st Somerset Light Infantry wrote: 'I shall never forget the morning of the 1st the longest day I live. It was hell upon earth. I have been through the lot, but I think that is the worst game any of us have been in.'[1]

At first, both Haig and Rawlinson were unaware of the enormity of the disaster that had befallen the army on 1 July 1916. That evening they were oblivious to the fact that the British Army had suffered 57,470 casualties, the heaviest losses suffered by the British Army in one single morning. Rawlinson had watched the initial advance from a specially built platform close to Albert during the morning of 1 July and at 08:00 hours he returned to Fourth Army Headquarters at Château de Querrieu to wait for operational reports from his corps commanders. There was an extensive communications network that connected Rawlinson by telephone with his five corps commanders, Gough's Army Reserve, the Royal Flying Corps HQ and the Sixth French Army HQ. The corps commanders were in touch with their divisional HQs, artillery, Royal Flying Corps sections and kite balloon observers. The line of communications extended from division to each brigade and their respective battalion HQs. It was at the front line where communications broke down. Observers in the front line were unable to accurately assess the progress of the infantry advances, many of which failed in No Man's Land. In many instances they relayed contradictory information of successes and failures in the same areas.

The pilots of the RFC reported accurately occupied trenches, but in several cases on 25th Division sector at Ovillers-la-Boisselle some trenches were reported empty when in fact British troops were in them and were lying low and in some instances fearful of exposing their position to their opponents.[2]

Inaccurate information was further compounded by conflicting reports brought back from the wounded. In some cases there were stories of success, while in other cases reports of a disaster on an unprecedented scale were filtering through the long chain of communications.

Before Rawlinson left the observation platform at Albert, he had been told that VIII Corps had broken through the German lines. When he returned to Fourth Army HQ information was flowing frequently throughout the morning. He was under the impression that fresh assaults were progressing well during the morning. It was not until 09:00 hours that he was told that 29th Division had not reached the German first trench.

Rawlinson was placed in an extremely difficult position. Despite receiving 160 telegrams from Corps commanders, it was difficult for him to know which reports were accurate and which were not. A second attack was anticipated to take place later that day, but without reliable information and with conflicting reports of success and failure, it was difficult to implement any second assault. It was not until 14:45 hours that Rawlinson became aware that VIII Corps attack had completely failed on its sector when Hunter-Weston told Rawlinson that the remnants of 29th Division were back in the front line trenches. This was the first accurate information that Rawlinson had received, but it was too late to bring forward reserve divisions.

The overall scale of the losses the divisions had suffered was not realised until several days later. Rawlinson could not capitalise on the successes at Montauban because he was in command of too many divisions, lots of information were coming his way, and much of it unreliable. Reports from aerial reconnaissance contradicted reports from the ground. Unsure of what was happening Rawlinson could not take the risk of sending his reserves to exploit the success on those sectors where a breakthrough had been achieved for fear that other sectors would be vulnerable to counter-attack. There was also the possibility that if reserve units pushed further forward there was a danger they would become isolated and cut off from the British lines.

An example of the contradictory nature of the information available to Corps commanders can be seen in this note Haig made in his diary:

> North of the Ancre, the 8th Division (Hunter-Weston) said they began well, but as the day progressed their troops were forced back into the German front line, except two battalions which occupied Serre village, and were, it is said, cut off. I am inclined to believe from further reports that few of VIII Corps left their trenches![3]

So confusing was the situation the full impact of the tragedy was still not apparent to Haig the next day, recording the following in his diary on 2 July:

> The AG [Adjutant-General, Lieutenant-General George Fowke] reported today that the total casualties are estimated at over forty thousand to date. This cannot be considered severe in view of the numbers engaged, and the length of front attacked.'[4]

Haig had been involved in numerous operations with casualties totalling thousands of men during 1914 and 1915. To him 1 July was just another day, the opening of another campaign in this long bloody war and he did not seem perturbed that the underestimated figure of 40,000 casualties had been incurred on that single day. Approximately half a million British soldiers took part in the action on 1 July 1916, so this initial figure would be 4 per cent casualties which on paper looks small considering the amount of men involved. After two years of war the British command had seen horrendous casualties. Approximately 13,500 casualties were suffered at the Aisne in 1914 and losses at the First Battle of Ypres during October/November 1914 amounted to 58,000. The casualty rate continued during 1915 including 11,652 casualties at Neuve Chapelle, and 59,247 at Loos. Haig and Rawlinson would have become desensitised by the heavy casualties sustained and frustrated that they had lost so many officers and men without significant gains or any immediate of hope of ending the war. So on 1 July 1916 Haig thought that in view of the number of men deployed in the operation, however unpalatable it is to hear that the enormous amount of lives had been lost, he was expecting a higher casualty figure. Even at 40,000 casualties the Commander-in-Chief had no time to dwell on such figures for he had to continue to lead and orchestrate the campaign in the hope of breaking the stalemate of trench warfare and achieve ultimate victory over Germany on the Western Front. Initial figures sourced from war diaries stated the following combined casualties suffered by Fourth Army and VII Corps from Third Army which assaulted Gommecourt were 61,816 comprising:[5]

	Killed/Died of Wounds	Wounded	Missing	Total
Officers	721	1,531	339	2591
Other Ranks	7,449	34,357	17,419	59,225
Total	8,170	35,888	17,758	61,816

These figures were taken from roll calls that were taken immediately after that calamitous day and listed many missing personnel who were later accounted for. Even now it is difficult to confirm the exact number of casualties from 1 July 1916. Battalion unit histories and war diaries state different numbers than in Edmonds official history. Many men were wounded, but survived the war but would continue to suffer from wounds sustained on that day and eventually died decades after the war had finished. Other men who might not have been wounded physically were scarred mentally by the trauma of the first day of the Somme campaign. However, the official casualty figures listed in the Official History are as follows:[6]

	Killed/Died of Wounds	Wounded	Missing	Prisoners of War	Total
Officers	993	1,337	96	12	2,438
Other Ranks	18,247	34,156	2,056	573	55,032
Total	19,240	35,493	2,152	585	57,470

By the afternoon of 1 July 1916, No Man's Land on the Somme sector presented a horrifying sight. Thousands of dead bodies, rapidly decaying in the intense heat of the summer sun, lay scattered across the fields. Captain E.B. Lord, 10th Lancashire Regiment, described the ordeal that he and his men endured when trying to remove and bury their fallen comrades in the days that followed:

> Corpses lay everywhere, and the stench from the decaying bodies was very unpleasant. A blackened hand protruding from the ground was gruesome to say the least. One night I was detailed with a dozen men to bury some of our dead near our new front line. As some of them had been doing this the day before, they were feeling sick and groggy, so I ordered them to dig holes in the ground and make wooden crosses whilst I went with a Lewis Gunner to handle the corpses. It was a ghastly job in the dark feeling for their identity discs and effects, as most of them were bloated, having been killed some days earlier. We rolled them into adjacent shell-holes covering them with earth, and placing a cross at the head bearing their names. One man whom we had handled had lost both feet and the hand wearing his identity disc had been so badly smashed that the disc was mixed with putrefying flesh; after a vain attempt to recover it, we interred him as 'unknown'.[7]

Captain Lord's testimony highlights the difficulties of recovering the dead from the battlefield and partly explains why so many men were buried in unknown graves who were eventually listed on the Thiepval Memorial. The process of burying the dead proved problematic. There was not enough men to deal with the wounded let alone bury the vast number of corpses that were collected from the battlefield. Some corpses were transported to mass burial graves behind British lines using trams, but there were too many. In some cases the corpses of dead comrades were stacked, without dignity on top of each other immediately behind the lines in full view of other soldiers, as Major H.F. Dawes at 12th Brigade HQ opposite Redan Ridge recalled:

> Div orders stated that the trench tramway would be used and that all the bodies would be brought back and buried in communal graves which had been dug clear of the trenches. Anticipating heavy casualties, 12th Bdg asked for permission to bury on the spot, this was refused. As is known the casualties were enormous and whilst the removal of bodies from the battlefield to the tramway was carried out expeditiously, presumably, owing to the long carry to the graves and lack of men, the removal from the head of the tramway, outside the trench system, did not keep pace, and resulted in an enormous stack of corpses which was extremely bad for morale.[8]

Great difficulty was experienced in endeavouring to recover the dead during the night, but it was extremely dangerous to carry out burials during daylight hours through fear of being spotted by German observers who would direct artillery fire upon their position. The volunteers from the 8th East Surrey Regiment who had ventured into No Man's Land to recover their dead were denied the opportunity to attend their burial service on 3 July. All the survivors from the battalion wanted to attend, but they were forbidden, because they were too near to the front line and one German shell falling close by would wipe them all out. A small number of representatives from the battalion were permitted to attend their burial in Carnoy Valley. The battalion War Diary reported:

> At 2.00 pm the burial took place in Carnoy Valley of Captains Pearce, Plates and Nevill, Lieuts Soames and Musgrove, 2/Lieuts Kelly and Evans, this being attended by Major Irwin and Captain Grimson, RAMC and 6 representatives from each Company, as although the whole of Battalion wished to be present, it was thought inadvisable to have any large number of men together as the enemy were still occasionally shelling the valley.[9]

With so many losses for such small gains it was imperative that British commanders reassure the men under their command. VII Corps had suffered heavily and its commander, Lieutenant-General Sir Aylmer Hunter-Weston, distributed the following message in an effort to rally the morale within his Corps:

> By your splendid attack you held these enemy forces here in the north and so enabled our friends in the south, both British and French, to

achieve the brilliant success that they have. Therefore, though we did not do all we hoped to do, you have more than pulled your weight, and you and our even more glorious comrades who have preceded us across the Great Divide have nobly done your Duty.

We have got to stick it out and go on hammering. Next time we attack, if it please God, we will not only pull our weight but will pull off a big thing. (With such troops as you, who are determined to stick it out and do your duty, we are certain of winning through to a glorious victory.[10]

Although they had failed to take the Heidenkopf, Redan Ridge and Beaumont Hamel, he argued that the sacrifices made during the failed attacks on these positions enabled the British divisions in the south to achieve their objectives. Their losses had not been in vain.

Rawlinson also gave a positive view of the opening day of the Somme campaign in his Special Order of the Day dated 12 July 1916. He had to give a positive spin to the disastrous day, because there were more battles to fight:

On the main front of attack our troops have broken on a front of 12,000 yards right through systems of defence which the enemy has done his utmost for nearly two years to render impregnable. We have inflicted heavy losses on him, capturing 8,000 prisoners, and many guns, mortars, machine-guns and other war material.

The enemy has already used up most of his reserves and has very few available.

The defences which remain to be broken through are not nearly so deep, so strong or so well prepared as those already captured, and the enemy's troops exhausted and demoralised, are far less capable of defending them than they were ten days ago.

The battle is, in fact, already more than half won. What remains to be done is easier than what has been done already and is well within our power.

Let every attack be pushed home to its allotted objective with the same bravery and resolution as on 1st July 1916.

Let all objectives gained be held against all comers, as British soldiers have always known how to hold them.

There is no room for doubt that steady, determined, united, and unrelenting effort for a few days more will definitely turn the scale in our favour and open up the road. To further successes which will bring final and complete victory within sight.

H. Rawlinson General
Commanding 4th Army[11]

British generals had to use the minimal successes achieved on 1 July 1916 at Fricourt, Mametz and Montauban to present a positive view of the events on that day despite the enormous losses sustained and failure of other divisions to secure their objectives. They could not be pessimistic and offer messages of defeatism and dejection. They had to maintain morale and ensure that their units continued to fight the war, something which French generals were unable to do when the campaign on the Chemin des Dames broke down in 1917 and resulted in the French mutiny. However, optimistic words about the opening of the Somme battle and the war issued by commanders such as Rawlinson and Hunter-Weston could not console their soldiers. Those soldiers who had survived the first day of the Somme offensive would consider themselves lucky to be alive and think of their fallen comrades and their bereaved families back home. Private Arthur Hollings, a Leeds Pal wrote:

> Leeds will be mourning the loss of some of our best lads, and when one has lived, slept, eaten, worked and fought side by side with these lads, as I have, my heart goes out in sympathy to those dear to them at home.[12]

Survivors of that fateful day questioned the competencies of their commanders in sending them across No Man's Land in clear view of the guns. Private Fred Winn of the 3rd Liverpool Pals, who was wounded before the assault at Montauban, wrote:

> It seemed incredible, in this 20th Century of civilisation, that men could be induced to walk forward in face of all the modern machinery of war, but may it be recorded to their everlasting glory, they did it. British heroism truly reached its watermark [*sic*] on this day.[13]

News began to reach families of the bereaved from letters of condolence from comrades which were sent immediately after the battle. For some families this was the first news that they had lost a son, father or brother. In many cases these letters arrived before the official notification from the War Office were dispatched.

The effects of the disaster would resonate across the nation as news reached Britain of the heavy casualties. Communities within cities, towns and villages would learn that many of their menfolk would not be returning home. Numerous firms in Manchester who had actively encouraged their employees to enlist in 1914 would discover that many of their workforce were killed during that day. Messers William Delany & Co, a Manchester packing company lost four employees. Sergeant Mark Johnson, Private Arthur Johnson, and Private Robert Woolford, who served with the 2nd Manchester Pals, were lost on 1 July and their bodies never identified.

Some soldiers were so badly disabled on 1 July that they were unable to communicate with their relatives back home. Their anxious families would think the worst until they received letters from them written on their behalf. Private Sam Jackson from 7th Manchester Pals had his right hand blown off and lip injured during the advance on Montauban. The Reverend A.H. Belliene had to write home to his family from a military hospital in France to assure them that Jackson was still alive.

> Your son, Pte Jackson, 22nd Manchesters wishes me to send you a letter so that you may know where he is. He came here this morning wounded slightly on the upper lip, also with his right hand blown off by a shell. His condition is good, and he is making satisfactory progress. He will probably be sent across to England in a few days. He sends you his best love, and hopes that you will not worry about him. You may be certain that he is receiving every possible attention and care. You remember, I am sure to pray constantly for him, and to thank God for having him alive out of so many and great dangers.[14]

Private William Clarke had received a gunshot wound to the head while advancing with the 11th East Lancashire Regiment at Serre. Writing from his hospital bed a week later he considered the impact upon the community of Accrington and those families who had lost loved ones on the Somme during that fateful day.

> Here I am, a spared monument of God's mercy, I'm spared, but what of the Pals? We have paid a heavy price to get the thin end of the wedge in – the price of many brave men. Tell our people at home the boys marched into battle as though going on parade. What an Accrington there will be! God comfort the poor mothers and fathers and sisters and loved ones![15]

Thousands of men were missing. Their families had no communication from them, nor did they get any information from the War Office. With no official news, families at home started to speculate about their fate and as wounded men returned home or began to write home rumours about the whereabouts of the missing began to circulate within communities at home causing greater anxiety. The following notice appeared in the *Derry Standard* on 17 July 1916 in a forlorn attempt to alleviate the concerns of those families whose soldiers were missing.

> ULSTER DIVISION TROOPS
> IMPORTANT TO ANXIOUS RELATIVES
> Quite a number of relatives of men in the Ulster Division have received no word since the great offensive, and are naturally uneasy, but the

> following extracts from a letter written by Company Quartermaster Sergeant William Sinnott, of the Derry Volunteers to his mother should allay their anxiety. 'No one' he says 'should be uneasy but should await definite news. Tell any of the relatives of the men you know that the cause of the delay may be the fact that the men have not field cards, they are very difficult to get just now.'[16]

Sometimes word of a loved one's death was received by word of mouth from the wounded coming home, or via letters from comrades still in France. Many families were left in limbo, with no direct communication from their loved ones during the following weeks. Many communities anxiously awaited each day for the postmen to knock.

The Tyneside brigades were composed of miners from the collieries of Northumberland and County Durham, shipbuilders from the shipyards on the Rivers Tyne, Wear and Tees and workers from the iron and steel works. The losses incurred by these brigades on the 1 July 1916 were to have a devastating effect upon the Tyneside community, which touched every family, street, village and workplace. For example, fifteen men from the village of Graghead had enlisted in the 26th Northumberland Fusiliers (3rd Tyneside Irish). Only two were to survive the war. The majority of Tynesiders killed were never identified, because they wore their identity disks on their braces. This is where they wore them in their pre-war occupations as miners and continued the practice in the Army. As a result it would mean that burial parties would not find the disks around their necks, therefore they would be buried in graves where their headstones were inscribed with the words 'Known only to God'.

Private T. Wilson, 18th Battalion, Northumberland Fusiliers, wrote: 'When we were in the attack near Albert we lost a good few men, but nothing near as many as the Tyneside Irish and Scottish. The 27th Irish Battalion got all wiped out but about twenty of them. Just two days before we left the trenches we had to go to a certain place, lay them all side by side till we got a lot together before they buried them. I may tell you that both the smell and the sight was cruel to stand and see all the bodies all over.'[17]

Chapter 26

Assessment: Success and Failure

No one can ignore the appalling and unprecedented casualty figures of 57,470 suffered by the British Army on 1 July 1916. However, the opening day of the land assault of the Somme campaign was not the catastrophic defeat of which it has been portrayed. There were successes but these were overshadowed by the failure in most sectors to achieve the ambitious targets that had been set. This, though, was just one day at the beginning of a long campaign that would last until November. A true assessment of that day was not possible until after the German surrender more than two years later.

All divisions, irrespective of whether they were Regular, Territorial or Kitchener's New Army, had displayed the utmost determination and bravery in carrying out their orders, but resolve and courage were not enough to counter opponents armed with machine-guns and rifles firmly entrenched in formidable positions on high ground. British commanders placed great reliance upon their artillery destroying the German wire, the front line trenches and German artillery batteries. With the exception of Mametz and Montauban, this had not happened.

The attacks launched upon the northern sector of the British line were an unmitigated disaster except for 32nd Division's capture of Leipzig Redoubt. The 46th Division made no headway in penetrating the defences at Gommecourt as they were caught in the wire and their ranks decimated in No Man's Land.

The 56th Division, a Territorial division, succeeded in entering the German line and held onto the enemy's trenches throughout that day. Some parties managed to enter Gommecourt, but German reserves were brought forward and the enemy retook the position. The 56th Division were unable to hold onto their gains as they were worn out during the course of the day, German shell fire preventing British reinforcements and supplies of bombs and munitions from getting across No Man's Land to help sustain them. Before nightfall the remnants of the 56th Division had to withdraw and it was difficult to assess whether the diversionary assault upon Gommecourt had helped Fourth Army. The failure of the 46th Division to secure its objectives and the inability to get reinforcements and supplies of munitions to the captured German lines had a direct impact upon 56th Division sector which meant that they were unable to hold onto the trenches they had taken.

The 31st, 4th and 29th Divisions of Hunter-Weston's VIII Corps were severely mauled as they advanced towards Serre, the Heidenkopf and Beaumont Hamel. The explosion of Hawthorn Mine ten minutes before Zero Hour alerted the enemy, allowing them sufficient time to get into position. As a consequence the infantry was slaughtered in No Man's Land on these sectors. The men of the 31st Division, comprised entirely of battalions of Kitchener's New Army, were massacred as they left their trenches, only a small party got close to Serre. A breach in the Heidenkopf's defences was achieved by 4th Division, a Regular division, but it was unable to get reinforcements and supplies across No Man's Land to consolidate the captured ground and had to withdraw to British lines.

Further south, Lieutenant-General Morland's X Corps experienced some success because the wire on its front had been cut and the 36th (Ulster) Division, also from Kitchener's New Army, had charged through several German lines and succeeded in making the deepest penetration of the day into their opponents' ground. The foresight of their divisional commander in assembling his troops close to the Sunken Lane meant that they rapidly overwhelmed the Germans in the Schwaben Redoubt. When German Second Army HQ became aware of this major breach in its line reserves were brought forward and the position was shelled preventing the soldiers from Ulster receiving reinforcements or supplies. Worn down by attacks on all flanks they could not hold the salient that they had occupied and were compelled to retire. On their adjacent right flank, the 32nd Division formed of Pals battalions was unable to breakthrough into Thiepval, with the exception a small foothold in Leipzig Redoubt which had being fiercely contended and was the only captured position on the northern sector still in British hands by the end of 1 July.

III Corps achieved no significant breakthrough in the German lines. The 8th Division composed of Regulars was unable to secure Ovillers-la-Boisselle and the Pals battalions from 34th Division were cut down in No Man's Land before they could reach La Boisselle. The 8th Division had to cross some of the widest sections on No Man's Land in between two salients and suffered from enfilade fire from their left and right flanks. When all the battalions of the 34th Division were sent together across No Man's Land on a reverse slope, they were easily slaughtered by machine-gun fire from La Boisselle. With no one left in reserve the capture La Boisselle became impossible. Only a few isolated parties were able to hold onto small pockets of captured ground in between La Boisselle and Fricourt.

Lieutenant-General Horne's XV Corps achieved a partial success at Fricourt. By assembling in No Man's Land the men had only a short stretch of ground to cover when the assault was launched. Although by the evening the village had still not been taken, the 21st Division had secured ground north of Fricourt, while 7th Division had made significant gains to the south and was in a good position to compel the Germans to abandon the village the following day once they had realised that Mametz and Montauban had been captured.

XV Corps' capture of Mametz and XVIII Corps' capture at Montauban were the most significant successes achieved on 1 July. The German defences in these sectors were not as strong as sectors further north. This was especially the case at Mametz where there were few deep dugouts or support lines. Once the first line had been breached the German defenders, many of which were exhausted be heavy labour to build defences, found it difficult to hold the position and their defence collapsed.

At Montauban accurate British and French artillery bombardments, which cleared paths through the barbed-wire and pulverised German trenches and batteries, meant that the 18th and 30th Divisions of Lieutenant-General Congreve's XIII Corps were able capture the village with only light casualties. The 30th Division was made up of Pals battalions and they succeeded in securing a platform that would enable Rawlinson's Fourth Army to continue the offensive, wearing down the Germans for the next four-and-a-half-months

Such success meant little to the families who had lost loved ones on the Somme on 1 July 1916. Although commanders such as Haig and Rawlinson were accountable for those losses, no matter who was in charge overseeing this complex vast operation they would have had to deal with the same problems of breaking through the German lines with an army that mostly were inexperienced, supported by limited supplies of artillery shells. The strategies devised by British generals such as Haig and Rawlinson for the Somme campaign in 1916 were the best that could be conceived at that time given the resources available.

We must also remember that Haig was attacking at a date and location dictated by French High Command. He was obliged to co-operate with his French allies to ease pressure that was placed upon them at Verdun, to maintain the coalition and to keep France in the war. Haig would have preferred an offensive in Flanders to have taken place six weeks later when there was sufficient time to continue training his soldiers and ensure that there were ample artillery munitions and when the new British secret weapon, the Battle Tank, would be available for the first time.

If British artillery had succeeded in destroying all German strongpoints, trenches, artillery positions between Serre and Montauban and the British infantry had walked straight over No Man's Land and occupied the German lines without confrontation, Rawlinson's plan, sanctioned by Haig, would have been considered as a masterstroke of simplicity. The reliance of Haig and Rawlinson upon the artillery and the failure of the intensive British bombardment to knockout those positions was one of the decisive flaws in the plan.

The Somme was one of the strongest German-held positions along the Western Front. Its defenders had spent eighteen months strengthening the line and had established a line of redoubts and fortresses. German machine-guns placed in excellent positions on high ridges dominated the battlefield and were a key factor in holding back the British infantry waves. Although British forces had a numerical advantage of fifteen divisions against six German divisions, the strength and depth of the German positions, much of which overlooked the British line of advance was a key reason why the British failed to achieve their objectives north of the Albert–Bapaume Road. The British guns were unable to target the machine-gun positions and dugouts that sheltered German troops garrisoned in their front line. These dugouts were so deep it was impossible for any shell to destroy them. Private C. Whitehead, RAMC, would later confirm:

> We occupy the German trenches, and what a surprise their dugouts are. They are about 30 feet or more in depth, and are fitted with electric lights and bells. There are also proper beds, mirrors, tables, chairs and stoves, and practically impossible for shells to penetrate them.[1]

However, several heavy-calibre shells exploding successively upon one target did prove effective on some sectors, when they blocked the entrances burying alive the occupants. German commanders learnt valuable lessons from the 1 July and would redesign underground dugouts to include two entrances so that if one was blocked they could use the other to escape. In some sectors the British artillery barrage had succeeded in levelling trenches and blocking the entrances to the deep dugouts, as General Freiherr von Süsskind, commanding 2nd Guard Reserve Division, explained:

> The deep, tunnelled dugouts, with 5 or 6 metres of earth covering were only destroyed when they had been struck by several direct hits of the heaviest calibre. In many dug out entrances were blown in. It is recommended that several dugouts should be joined up by underground galleries.[2]

The British bombardment did succeed in shaking the morale of the Germans, keeping them underground, isolating them, and denying them food and water supplies. German prisoners belonging of the 109th RIR who had been captured close to Pommiers Redoubt, were psychologically shattered, malnourished and dehydrated. The 8th Suffolk's War Diary reported: 'German prisoners started to come down from the front. All looked pale and haggard and were apparently very hungry and thirsty. One prisoner stooped to drink from a cesspool.'[3]

The British artillery had succeeded in isolating German sections holding the front line. By targeting rear lines they were able to prevent supplies of food from being taken to the front. Private E.F.M. Lewis reported the condition of the German soldiers defending the front close to the Heidenkopf. 'We were told afterwards by some of the prisoners that they had been kept for four days without any supplies owing to the artillery fire, and they were practically starving.'[4] A 12in railway gun fired from behind Albert at Zero Hour on 1 July was able to fire shells into Bapaume thirteen miles away. This resulted in General von Stein ordering the evacuation of German XIV Corps Headquarters from Bapaume to a position three-and-a-half miles to the east at Beugny during the night of 1/2 July.[5]

Although the British artillery carried out a ferocious bombardment upon the German lines on unprecedented scale, there were not sufficient guns or munitions to provide a blanket concentration of German positions over such a wide front. The number of guns used in the preliminary bombardment of the Somme was significantly greater than that used at Loos during September 1915.[6]

Ammunition used allotted to Fourth Army at Loos 1915 and Somme 1916

Rounds	Loos 1915	Somme 1916
18-pounder	371,000	2,600,000
4.5in howitzer	56,400	260,000
6in howitzer	19,000	100,000

Although more munitions were available for the Somme campaign in comparison to Loos, there was still not enough to completely annihilate and destroy the enemy and his strong positions. Munition factories were increasing their productivity in an effort to meet the requirements of the generals in the field, but they were still unable to keep up with demand. There was also a considerable number of faulty shells being produced by inexperienced workers. The scale of the operation on the Somme was vast and there were simply not enough shells to maintain the intensity of bombardment the British generals wished for along a front that measured 25,000 yards, or approximately fourteen miles. During the successful Messines operation in June 1917 the front of attack had been reduced to 17,000 yards (9 miles) and, by that time, there was a greater number of guns and munitions. Twice as many rounds were fired at Messines in comparison to the preparatory bombardment on the Somme. The figures are startling. From 24 June to 1 July 1916, 1,732,873 rounds were fired. At Messines 3,258,000 rounds were fired during the period 3–10 June 1917. The following table shows that nearly twice as many guns were used at Messines.[7]

Artillery allotted for Somme 1916 vs Messines 1917

	Somme 1916	Messines 1917
Field Artillery		
18-pounder	808	1,314
4.5in howitzer	202	438
Heavy Guns		
4.7in	32	0*
60 pounder	128	198
6in	104	348
8in	64	108
9.2in	60	116
12in	11	20
15in	6	8

*The 4.7in Field Gun was obsolete by 1917 and not used during the Messines campaign.

The failure to knock out German batteries between La Boisselle and Gommecourt was one of the reasons why British units failed on that stretch of German front. By comparison, the success of the divisions which attacked Mametz and Montauban can be attributed, at least in part, to the British artillery's destruction of the German guns in Caterpillar Valley north of those villages. These guns and supplies of ammunition were completely wrecked during the preparatory bombardment.

The curtain of shellfire which preceded the advancing infantry was also not as effective as it was hoped. This was because the barrage moved at a predetermined pace but the following infantry were frequently held up by uncut wire or machine-gun positions that had not been knocked out. This meant that the wall of shellfire would race ahead of them, as Captain R.A. Wolfe-Murray reflected:

> Who can tell whether the lessons learnt on this day of bloody fighting will ever be of value again to the British Army but certainly these lessons were of the greatest value to those of us who lived to fight again. One learnt the hopelessness of the Infantry once having lost the protection of a barrage ever being able to catch it up again. To ensure that no such disaster should happen one can only trust to the junior officers and to the men themselves keeping as close to the line of bursting shells, which should be H.E. and not air burst shrapnel, as possible, crawling up to these on hands and knees. Some such signal, as

> a round of smoke shell fire from each gun, having been arranged between Infantry and Artillery, the second the barrage will lift, every sec. Comdr. will know exactly when to rush his men forward without having to depend on a watch. 50% of his casualties from our own barrage and a Battalion on its objective is to be preferred to the decimation caused by machine-guns which pop up the instant the barrage rolls by. Ever afterwards we worked for such an object and never without great success.[8]

Brigadier-General Hubert Rees believed that being unable to adjust the artillery barrages when things went wrong was one of the reasons why the attack failed at Serre:

> The result of the time table in this attack was that it was impossible to alter the artillery barrages before the artillery barrages had completed their programme, owing to the danger of firing on parties of our own troops, who might have got through and be holding portions of the German positions.[9]

Major V. Majendie, who took command of 1st Somerset Light Infantry after it suffered heavy losses on 1 July, concurred with Rees' view of the rigidity of the British artillery barrage:

> There is little more to add about this attack, which was a complete, but a glorious failure, and in many ways as creditable to those, who took part in it; as many subsequent successes. By the light of experience gained later, there is little doubt that the lack of a creeping barrage, which at the time had not been evolved, allowed the Germans to make use of their numerous machine-guns, and accounted to a great extent for our lack of success.[10]

Some Germans sought refuge in the shell holes and were missed as the British artillery barrage focused upon German trench lines. Lieutenant-Colonel C. Broad, III Corps BMRA, wrote:

> There is no doubt that we began the Battle of the Somme without really understanding the barrage. The barrage of the III Corps front was made to jump from one trench system to the next. We did not realise that the Germans would be driven out of their trenches and would occupy their shell holes with machine-guns and riflemen. It was this defence and combined with the concrete machine-gun emplacements, especially round Ovillers that caused the trouble on the first day owing mainly to the fact that the barrage jumped from one trench to another and did not touch the shell holes.[11]

Some waves of infantry advanced too slowly towards the German lines and did not keep pace with the artillery barrage. This meant that there was a gap in time which allowed the Germans to climb from their dugouts whilst the attackers were still in No Man's Land. Lieutenant-Colonel C. Broad, III Corps BMRA, wrote of this lack of co-ordination between artillery and infantry:

> We did not in the least realise how slowly attacking troops must move in fighting of this description ... it was about 100 yards in 2 minutes. I remember that some battalions were sent to penetrate between La Boisselle and Ovillers. This battalion disappeared and was never heard of again, owing to the fact that the barrage rushed away from it and left it unsupported. Our experiences thus led to the creeping barrage which was a development of the jumping barrage.'[12]

The creeping barrage was indeed developed and used for the first time during the assault upon Courcelette on 15 September 1916 later in the Somme campaign.

The Royal Flying Corps succeeded in disrupting German movements behind their lines. Bombing raids carried out by forty RFC bombers which attacked Germans troop concentrations, transport columns, ammunition dumps and headquarters in the Somme region during 1 July 1916. It was the intention to isolate the German Second Army by severing railway links into the region that would bring forward reserves and ammunition. Special raids were also conducted upon ammunition dumps at Mons, Namur and at the railway hubs at Cambrai, Busigny, Tergnier, St Quentin and St Sauveur Station at Lille, achieving limited success.

The 22nd Reserve Division had been ordered to proceed to the Somme sector to support the German Second Army which was resisting the British assault. Lieutenant Lawrence Wingfield in a BE2 C aeroplane flew above St Quentin railway station around 14:00 hours and dropped a bomb as the 1st Battalion 71st Reserve Regiment and 11th Reserve Jaeger Battalion were on platforms at the station preparing to board a train. There were 200 carriages loaded with ammunition, lined along an adjacent railway siding and when Wingfield's bomb exploded some of the carriages caught fire. Sixty of these carriages were destroyed in the fire, along with troop carriages and all the equipment that the 71st Reserve Regiment had loaded onto the train. With tremendous difficulty the remaining 140 ammunition carriages were saved, but Wingfield's direct hit caused 180 casualties amongst those German reserves. This bombing operation seriously hindered the German Army's ability to reinforce troops, and resupply ammunition on the Somme front. As a consequence of the raid upon St Quentin Railway Station the 71st Reserve Regiment could not take part in the battle on 1 July and had to return to its billets at Ham to be re-equipped.

Strategic surprise was seriously compromised by the increased traffic bringing troops, munitions and equipment to the region, which could be clearly seen by German observers from the heights which they held. The large numbers of captive observation balloons tethered to the ground close behind the British line and the constant presence of RFC reconnaissance aeroplanes over German trenches were strong indicators that something was about to happen on the Somme. German intelligence played an important role as they listened to British telephone conversations which gave clues to when the offensive would begin. The preliminary bombardment conducted during the week before the infantry assault was the greatest confirmation that an offensive was imminent. German soldiers knew that an attack was coming.

Haig was pushed into starting the battle before his troops were really ready. The men who enlisted in 1914 and formed Kitchener's New Army received basic training at home, which needed to be supplemented by further training when they reached France before they could go into action. The time needed to train was severely limited by the work that was needed to prepare for the offensive. With much of their time devoted to manual labour many soldiers were denied training and were left feeling exhausted. This lack of training was apparent to the Germans and, as a post-operational German report highlighted:

> The British Army ... in the battle of the Somme had not reached a sufficiently high tactical standard. The training of the infantry was clearly behind that of the German; the superficially trained British were particularly clumsy in movements of large masses. On the other hand, small bodies, such as machine-gun crews, bombers and trench blockers and special patrols, thanks to their native independence of character, fought very well. The strong, usually young, and well-armed British soldier followed his officers blindly, and the officers, active and personally brave, went ahead of their men in battle with great courage. But, owing to insufficient training, they were not skilful in action. They often failed to grasp the necessity for rapid, independent decision. They were in many cases unequal to dealing with sudden unexpected changes in the situation. Great attacks were carried out in thick, often irregular lines and with small columns following the heavy losses of the British in their attacks, although they were certainly made with the most conspicuous courage.[13]

Rapid changes in the course of a battle meant that officers and the men that they led must be flexible and know how to adapt and respond to those changing circumstances. When they got into the German lines they lacked the ability to consolidate those trenches and the experienced, well-trained Germans were able to quickly retake lost positions. The 1st, 2nd and 3rd

Manchester Pals battalions had contributed enormously to the assault upon Montauban, but they lost heavily, including many officers and NCOs, and it was left to the only battle-experienced regular battalion of the 90th Brigade, 2nd Royal Scots Fusiliers, to reorganise the remnants of those battalions and capture the village.

As a consequence of the heavy losses sustained by battalions on 1 July it was decided that more precise instructions were given to those who would be held back in reserve. In future operations the CO or second-in-command would be held back with a proportion of experienced junior officers and NCOs who would be able to reform the battalion with new reinforcements in the event of disaster. Major Majendie wrote:

> A few months later definite orders were very wisely issued defining exactly what officers and NCOs should be left out of a battle; included in these was the CO or second-in-command, two Company Commanders, and two Company Sergeant Majors. The result was that even after the heaviest casualties there would always be a nucleus on which to reform.[14]

Despite the preliminary bombardment and the large troop concentrations that had been observed, German commanders were not entirely convinced that a full-scale offensive would take place on the Somme. They thought the chances of the British launching an attack on a twenty mile front with insufficient reserves unlikely. A French attack on the Somme also appeared improbable, for after four months of heavy fighting at Verdun French resources and spirit would have been far too drained to contemplate such a venture. German commanders were in a sense dismissive of the Allies' ability to embark on a major offensive in the summer of 1916.

The attack on the Somme on 1 July 1916 immediately impacted upon the German offensive in Verdun. On that first day limits were placed on the use of ammunition at Verdun and Crown Prince Rupprecht was ordered to set aside the 4th and 21st Reserve Divisions, in readiness to be transferred to the Somme. On 2 July heavy artillery batteries were withdrawn from Verdun and moved to the Somme sector. The objective of diverting resources from Verdun in order to ease pressure upon the French had succeeded.

Despite the heavy losses sustained by the British Army, Haig's first phase of the Somme offensive had placed the German Army under severe pressure. Unable to fight two battles at the same time, General Falkenhayn was forced to close down the Verdun operation to prevent a British and French breakthrough on the Somme.[15]

Success was achieved by the French Sixth Army, commanded by General Émile Fayolle, as it attacked along both sides of the River Somme. Believing that the French were too heavily committed at Verdun to attack on the Somme, the Germans had distributed their troops thinly along that section of the line. By starting their offensive at 09:30 hours, two hours after the British launched their assault, the Germans on this sector were taken by surprise. A sufficient force of French guns for the length of front to be attacked, amply supplied with munitions, was able to knock out the opposing German batteries. The French also used gas which had a considerable effect on the Germans. They were able to punch a hole through the German lines and capture Frise, Dompierre, Fay and Bequincourt during the morning. These French soldiers also had more combat experience than their British counterparts. By the afternoon they had secured Herbécourt and Assevillers.

With a total of 57,470 casualties incurred in securing ground of just a mile deep and three and a half miles wide it was difficult at the time to see this action as a victory. The contrasting perceptions of that day are interesting to note. Private George Grunwell, of the 16th West Yorkshire Regiment who suffered a shrapnel wound to his hand at Serre was disheartened by the slaughter of his battalion commented 'I felt we had been sacrificed we eased the French line, purely and simply'.[16]

Major Alfred Irwin's 8th East Surrey Regiment lost heavy casualties during the assault upon Montauban Ridge and Irwin was scathing about the attack:

> After that, drafts came in, and it was no longer the 8th East Surreys in spirit. All my best chaps had gone. We buried eight young officers in one grave before we left. It was a terrible massacre. The attack should have been called off, until the wire was cut. They ought to have known through their intelligence officers the condition of the wire, before we ever got to 1 July.[17]

Other soldiers saw the opening phase of the Somme campaign in a different light. Some soldiers thought that the action on the 1 July 1916 was the beginning of an initiative to end the war. Private James Malkin, of the Border Regiment was positive and wrote on 5 July:

> On Saturday and Sunday we were very busy escorting German prisoners from the firing line down to a concentration camp a few miles away, and I can assure you we got a good haul … Our regiment has added more honours to its name for good work done in this week's battle. If things go on the same as they are doing at present I don't think the war will last much longer.[18]

Private Cleveland who advanced with the 8th Norfolk Regiment towards Montauban Alley also deemed the action on 1 July 1916 as a victorious success proclaiming, 'It was a most glorious victory. We won what we were supposed to win, and, what is more we held on to it.'[19]

In his diary, Sergeant John Wilson deemed the assault upon La Boisselle as 'a successful attack but heavy casualties'.[20] Some soldiers who had previously witnessed heavy casualties in past campaigns saw the losses suffered on the Somme as an acceptable reality of the war which would lead to a victory over Germany. Private Frank Smith of the 16th West Yorkshire Regiment who went over the top at Serre, wrote of the devastation of the 1st Bradford Pals but of the spirit that would continue throughout the Somme campaign and the war:

> Our battalion suffered very heavy losses and so did the other battalion: in fact there were few unscathed at the end of that fearful day, but this we can always say – we went forward without a flinch, just as if on manoeuvres, and not a man turned back or even stopped. Those who died like men and this spirit will win the war.[21]

Some bereaved families did not think that the losses were in vain. The family of thirty-six-year-old Lance Corporal George Robertson, 16th Highland Light Infantry, who died in the assault upon Leipzig Redoubt wanted the following words inscribed on his headstone at Lonsdale Cemetery. 'A NOT ENTIRELY WORTHLESS SACRIFICE'.

Private Downs, who advanced with the 10th Royal Inniskilling Fusiliers, perceived the assault upon the German lines at Thiepval as a success. In a letter home he commented:

> The 10th Battalion is very small in numbers now, but the Ulster Division has made a great name for itself, though they had to pay dearly for it ... We captured four lines of German trench and consolidated three – a great success, the Huns giving way before the pressure of steel.[22]

There were also many soldiers who questioned the capabilities and competences of their leaders. Some soldiers who survived the ordeal of the 1 July 1916 were scornful of General Sir Douglas Haig and his strategy of the 'Big Push'. Private Cyril Jose of the 2nd Devonshire Regiment had been wounded in the assault upon Ovillers-la-Boisselle and was scathing in his criticism of his Commander-in-Chief.

> Of course some 'big bug' thought it a great idea to go over in broad daylight instead of crawling up as near their parapet in the night under cover of the bombardment as possible as usual so that we could then dive in the trench with hardly any losses in going across. Of course Johnny wouldn't expect us then so much. I suppose they thought that as he wouldn't expect us he wouldn't see us. Certainly not! Result: Johnny spots us coming over the parapet and we have to go about 600 yards. What brains old Douglas must have. Made me laugh when I read his

> despatch yesterday 'I attacked' [Jose underlined the word 'I' five times to highlight his astonishment]. Old women in England picturing Sir Doug in front of British waves brandishing his sword [at] Johnny on trenches. I'll get a job like that in next war. Attack 'Johnny' from 100 miles back!![23]

Lance Corporal James Glenn, who had seen the first wave of the 12th York and Lancaster (Sheffield Pals) mown down at Serre, held a low opinion of Haig and Rawlinson. He considered them as 'Lousy. If they had them near they would have shot them. You read glossy books about Haig and Rawlinson how wonderful they were, perhaps we did not understand, just passing messages and going to champagne parties. That's what we thought of them'.[24]

Despite being regarded as an awful tragedy, the heaviest losses ever suffered by the British Army in a single day, many of the soldiers saw it as just another day in the war. They were oblivious to the newspaper reports at home which printed numerous pages devoted to the casualties suffered on that day. They were confident that they could eventually break the stalemate of trench warfare and force the Germans back into Germany.

With so many casualties suffered on the first day of the campaign it is remarkable that only one commander from the Third Army was held accountable and disciplined – Major-General Stuart-Wortley who was in temporary command of the VII Corps immediately before the assault while Corps Commander Lieutenant-General Snow was on leave. The 46th Division's failure to break through the German lines and establish contact with the 56th Division resulted in Snow severely criticising the 46th Division's 'lack of offensive spirit' and attributed their failure to Stuart-Wortley. Despite losing heavily in attacking the most heavily fortified position on the Western Front, a Court of Inquiry was held to assess the Division's performance at Gommecourt and the command abilities of Stuart-Wortley. The Court of Inquiry comprised of two Lieutenant-Colonels, one from the 46th Division, the other 56th Division, and one who did not participate in the action. The first sitting convened on 4 July and after listening to the testimonies from fourteen men from the 46th Division and two pilots from the RFC proceedings were adjourned until 6 July. However at 06:50 hours on 4 July, before any decision had been reached at the Inquiry, Stuart-Wortley was relieved of his command and ordered to return to England. The inquiry was reconvened and listened to a further twenty-five testimonies but nothing further was deciphered from these proceedings. One might be forgiven for wondering why Snow had been granted leave before the start of the BEF's largest operation to date and why Snow felt he had the right to question the conduct of the man he had left in charge at such a crucial time.

Haig and Rawlinson, of course, bore the overall responsibility for the failures and losses of that day, but as we could see in their planning both commanders had differing strategies, both trying to learn the lessons of past campaigns. Haig favoured an attack on a wider front, deep into enemy lines with a hurricane bombardment similar to that conducted at Neuve Chapelle, but at that time he had little understanding of the deficiencies in artillery, there was simply not enough quantities of munitions to launch such an intensive bombardment on a large front, nor was their quality in the munitions supplied for many were defective. Rawlinson preferred the 'bite and hold' of limited objectives with a bombardment over several days. Both commanders made compromises when agreeing to the final plan and both Haig and Rawlinson tried their best, given that they had limited supplies of munitions and were forced into committing their troops, many of which were inexperienced into a battle they were not ready to fight on ground that was not of their choosing.

There was no time to reflect on the heavy losses of 1 July 1916, Haig and Rawlinson had a war to fight. During that evening they were unaware of the enormity of those losses. By the time that more accurate figures became available and the sheer scale of those reached British newspapers, the campaign had moved on and their minds were focused on the next phase of the Somme campaign.

On the night of 1 July Rawlinson issued orders to take the German positions in the first and intermediate lines that had not been captured on the first day of the battle. He was aware that German reinforcements were being rushed to the Somme and he wanted to take these objectives before further reinforcements arrived. Haig did not agree with Rawlinson's plan to attempt to capture Thiepval, Beaumont Hamel and Serre in the north. He wanted Rawlinson to exploit the successes achieved in the south at Mametz and Montauban. However, Haig had realised that the vast twenty-mile frontage attacked was too much responsibility and pressure to place upon the shoulders of one commander. So, instead of using General Sir Hubert Gough's Fifth Army to charge through breaches made by Rawlinson in the German line, Haig decided to use his reserves to bolster the northern flank where they had failed to make any headway and sustained heavy casualties. At 20:00 hours on 1 July Haig transferred command of Hunter-Weston's VIII and Morland's X Corps which had been severely mauled losing over 20,000 casualties, to Gough, who immediately cancelled Rawlinson orders for another attack upon 2 July and set about reorganising the front. The wounded had to be recovered and evacuated from the battlefield and the sector had to be secured against the possibility of a German counter-account. While the situation was in disarray this sector was vulnerable and until the line was reorganised and strengthened there was no possibility of launching further initiatives to capture Thiepval, Beaumont Hamel and Serre.

Haig visited Fourth Army Headquarters at Querrieu on 2 July and told Rawlinson of his decision to relieve some of that stress by devolving command of VIII and X Corps to General Gough, so that he could press ahead with building on the successes gained in the south with III, XIII and XV Corps. Joffre was fearful that to continue attacks adjacent to the French sector might draw the French army into another war of attrition of equal proportions to Verdun, he therefore ordered Haig to attack on the northern sector. Haig realised that VIII and X Corps which had suffered horrendous losses on 1 July were in no position to continue the campaign. Resisting Joffre's request Haig ordered Rawlinson to continue the campaign in the south irrespective of whether the French were able to support the operation.

The Somme campaign continued for a further four months. The British were able to capture Thiepval on 26 September, this was a formidable objective targeted for capture on 1 July. On 1 October 1916 Gough's reserves were renamed the Fifth Army and on 13 November, aided by two tanks, they were able to secure Beaumont Hamel, another objective from 1 July. With the onset of winter, at a conference held at Compiègne, British and French generals agreed a cessation of operations on the Somme and the campaign was brought to an end.

Britain lost approximately 400,000 men, the French lost 200,000 but, significantly, the Germans suffered 680,000 casualties from 1 July to 13 November. 1916 marked the end of German hopes of winning the war in the West. During the course of four months fighting on the Somme their resolve had been irrevocably weakened and like their British and French counterparts the spirit of the army that existed in 1914 had gone. The German army had fought on occupied territory but increasingly they were fearful that if the Allies pushed them further back they would be fighting on their own German soil.

Despite the continuing losses, Haig persisted in pushing the advance forward and eventually the objectives set for 1 July were reached. It was only the onset of winter that forced Haig to cancel operations until the following spring. Ludendorff was concerned that if Haig was to adopt the same strategy in 1917, then Germany would not have the military resources or the capability to hold the Allies back. Ludendorff was aware that the Allies had seventy-five divisions on the Western Front compared to Germany's forty divisions. With the likelihood of further Allied offensives being undertaken and the impossibility of launching any offensives themselves, Ludendorff convinced the German High Command that a defensive policy was the way forward. The result was the withdrawal of German forces twenty-five miles across the Somme to newly established defensive positions. Since he appreciated the works of Wagner he named the defensive system the Seigfried Stellung after the principle protagonist from Wagner's opera 'The Ring'. This line of fortified trenches, deeply-excavated concrete dugouts, and gun emplacements protected by acres of high density barbed-wire entanglements would be known to the British as the 'Hindenburg Line'. Stretching for eighty-five miles it was built east of Arras and ran through Bullecourt to positions in the Champagne region near Soissons. By initiating a tactical withdrawal, Ludendorff shortened the front by twenty-seven miles and free ten infantry divisions to be deployed in reserve to counter any sections where the Allies broke through.

The true consequences of the Somme were summed up in the history of the 27th Wüttemberg Division:

> A culminating point was reached which was never again approached. What we experienced surpassed all previous conception. The enemy's fire never ceased for an hour. It fell night and day on the front line and tore fearful gaps in the ranks of the defenders. It fell on the approaches to the front line and made all movement towards the front hell. It fell on the rearward trenches and battery positions and smashed men and material in a manner never seen before or since. It repeatedly reached even the resting battalions behind the front and occasioned there terrible losses. Our artillery was powerless against it … in the Somme fighting of 1916 there was a spirit of heroism which was never again found in the division.'
>
> Other German regimental histories repeat the same theme: 'the tragedy of the Somme battle was that … the best soldiers, the stoutest-hearted men were lost; their numbers replaceable, their spiritual worth could never be.

Colonel Gudmund Schnitler, Norwegian military attaché to the armies of the Central Powers, wrote:

> If the battle of the Somme in the tactical and strategic sense had no direct importance, its consequences nevertheless were great, particularly from the moral aspect … The old steadfast highly-trained body of the German Army, particularly in the infantry, had for the most part also disappeared.

The last word is granted to Captain von Hentig of the General Staff Guard Reserve Division:

> The Somme was the muddy grave of the German field army, and of the faith in the infallibility of the German leading, dug by British industry and its shells … The most precious thing lost at the Somme was the good relationship between the leaders and the led. The German Supreme Command, which entered the war with enormous superiority, was defeated by the superior technique of its opponents. It had fallen behind in the application of destructive forces, and was compelled to throw division after division without protection against them into the cauldron of the battle of annihilation.'[25]

What the Battle of the Somme showed the Germans was that they were no longer fighting the British Army, they were now fighting the British nation.

Notes

CHAPTER 1: THE BRITISH ARMY 1914–1915

1 IWM Department of Sound, Ref 13082: Reel 1, Lance Corporal James Glenn.
2 IWM Department of Sound, Ref 9431: Reel 1, Private George Grunwell.
3 IWM Department of Sound, Ref 24549: Reel 1, Private Sidney Ralph Steele.
4 R.T. Grange interview, Somme Heritage Centre.

CHAPTER 2: THE PLAN FOR THE SOMME OFFENSIVE

1 TNA, WO 256/7: Haig's Diary.
2 ibid.
3 ibid.
4 ibid.
5 Charteris, *Field Marshal Earl Haig*.
6 ibid.
7 TNA, WO 256/8: Haig's Diary.
8 ibid.
9 ibid.
10 ibid.
11 TNA, WO 158/233: Fourth Army Operations, 27 February 1916 to 12 June 1916.
12 ibid.
13 ibid.
14 ibid.
15 ibid.
16 ibid.
17 ibid.
18 ibid.
19 ibid.
20 TNA, WO 256/9: Haig's Diary.
21 ibid.
22 ibid.
23 Prior and Wilson, *Command on the Western Front*.
24 TNA, WO 158/233: Fourth Army Operations, 27 February 1916 to 12 June 1916.
25 ibid.
26 ibid.
27 ibid.
28 TNA, WO 256/10: Haig's Diary.
29 GHQ to Rawlinson 16/5/16, Edmonds, *Military Operations: France and Belgium 1916*, Vol. 1, Appendix 11.
30 TNA, WO 158/233: Fourth Army Operations, 27 February 1916 to 12 June 1916.
31 TNA, WO 256/10: Haig's Diary.

32 ibid.
33 ibid.
34 ibid.
35 TNA, WO 158/233.
36 TNA, WO 256/10: Haig's Diary.
37 ibid.
38 IWM, Fourth Army Papers.
39 *Somme Nord 1 Zeil,* published Berlin 1927.

CHAPTER 3: WORKING OUT THE DETAILS

1 IWM Documents, Ref 1713: Papers of Major-General Sir John Laurie.
2 IWM Documents, Ref 7166: Papers of Brigadier-General H.C. Rees.
3 TNA, CAB 45/190: Brigadier-General Hubert Rees.
4 IWM Department of Sound, Ref 9954: Reel 3, Private James Snailham.
5 TNA, CAB 45/190.
6 IWM Documents, Ref 7166: Papers of Brigadier-General H.C. Rees.
7 The Gordon Highlanders Museum: Major R.A. Wolfe-Murray Diary.
8 IWM Department of Sound, Ref 9431: Reel 3, Private George Grunwell.
9 IWM Documents, Ref 1713: Papers of Major-General Sir John Laurie.
10 IWM Documents, Ref 4772: Papers of Chaplain Ernest Crosse.
11 Wyrall, *The History of the King's Regiment (Liverpool).*
12 IWM Department of Sound, Ref 9875: Reel 14, Corporal George Ashurst.
13 TNA, CAB 45/190.
14 ibid.
15 ibid.
16 TNA, CAB 45/190: Captain C.W. Martin.
17 ibid.

CHAPTER 4: PREPARATIONS

1 TNA, CAB 45/189: Major A.C. Girdwood.
2 IWM Department of Sound, Ref 9455: Reel 2, Private Maurice Symes.
3 The Gordon Highlanders Museum: Palithorpe, 'With the Highlanders'.
4 ibid.
5 Atkinson, *The Seventh Division 1914-1918.*
6 TNA, CAB 45/188: Staff Captain G.R. Codrington.
7 The Gordon Highlanders Museum: Major R.A. Wolfe-Murray Diary.
8 TNA, WO 95/2040: 8th Norfolk Regiment War Diary.
9 IWM Documents, Ref 7312: Papers of Private H. Russell.

CHAPTER 5: THE PRELIMINARY ARTILLERY BOMBARDMENT

1 TNA, WO 158/233: Fourth Army Operations, 27 February 1916 to 12 June 1916.
2 Ternan, *The Story of the Tyneside Scottish.*
3 TNA, WO 95/2280: 29th Division War Diary.
4 IWM Documents, Ref 7405: Papers of Leutnant F.L. Cassel.
5 ibid.
6 TNA, WO 95/2491: 36th (Ulster) Division War Diary.
7 IWM Documents, Ref 7405: Papers of Leutnant F.L. Cassel.
8 TNA, WO 95/1675: 8th Division War Diary.
9 TNA, WO 95/2280: 29th Division War Diary.
10 TNA, CAB 45/189: Captain Ian Grant.
11 *Ballymena Weekly Telegraph,* 29 July 1916.
12 IWM Documents, Ref 7405: Papers of Leutnant F.L. Cassel.
13 *Lowestoft Weekly Press,* 22 July 1916.
14 TNA, WO 95/2491: 36th (Ulster) Division War Diary.
15 IWM Department of Sound, Ref 13082: Reel 7, Lance Corporal James Glenn.
16 Edmonds, *op. cit.*

17 Prior and Wilson, p.173.
18 IWM Documents, Ref 7990: Lance Corporal Sidney Appleyard.
19 ibid.
20 Sheldon, *The German Army on the Somme*; Müller-Loebnitz, *Die Badener im Weltkrieg*.
21 ibid.
22 ibid.
23 IWM Documents, Ref 7990.
24 Henriques, *The War History of the 1st Battalion Queen's Westminster Rifles 1914-1918*.
25 IWM Documents, Ref 7990.
26 TNA, WO 256/10: Haig's Diary.
27 ibid.
28 ibid.

CHAPTER 6: THE DAY BEFORE – 30 JUNE 1916

1 *Londonderry Sentinel*, 18 July 1916.
2 IWM Department of Sound, Ref 13082: Reel 7, Lance Corporal James Glenn.
3 TNA, WO 95/2301: 2nd Royal Fusiliers War Diary.
4 IWM Department of Sound:, Ref 9875: Reel 14, Corporal George Ashurst.
5 ibid.
6 TNA, WO 256/10: Haig's Diary.
7 ibid.
8 Gardner, *The Big Push*.
9 IWM Documents, Ref 15087: Papers of Private W.J. Senescall.
10 Turner, *Accrington Pals*.
11 *Accrington Observer & Times*, 22 July 1916.
12 ibid.
13 *Essex County Telegraph*, 15 July 1916.
14 *The Robin Hoods 1/7th, 2/7th & 3/7th Battalions, Sherwood Foresters 1914-1918*, written by the officers of the Battalion.
15 Fusiliers Museum of Northumberland: Papers of Corporal Alfred Kettle.
16 *Sheffield Weekly Independent*, 22 July 1916.
17 IWM Department of Sound, Ref 11582: Private Albert Hurst.
18 Edmonds, *op. cit.*
19 ibid.
20 IWM Documents, Ref 15087: Papers of Private W.J. Senescall.

PART 2: VII CORPS SECTOR

1 Edmonds, *Military Operations: France and Belgium 1916*, Vol. 1.
2 ibid.
3 IWM Documents, Ref 4326: Papers of Private Arthur Schuman.
4 IWM Documents, Ref 7990: Lance Corporal Sidney Appleyard.

CHAPTER 7: GOMMECOURT: 46TH (NORTH MIDLAND) DIVISION

1 *The Robin Hoods 1/7th, 2/7th & 3/7th Battalions, Sherwood Foresters 1914-1918*.
2 TNA, WO 95/2663: 46th Division War Diary.
3 TNA, WO 95/2695: 1/5th Sherwood Foresters War Diary.
4 IWM Documents, Ref 4481: Papers of Private W.B Stevenson.
5 TNA, WO 95/2694: 1/6th Battalion Sherwood Foresters War Diary.
6 *The Derbyshire Times*, 8 July 1916.
7 TNA, WO 95/2663: 46th Division War Diary.

CHAPTER 8: GOMMECOURT: 56TH DIVISION

1 Lindsay, *The London Scottish in the Great War*.
2 TNA, WO 95/2944: 1/13th London Regiment (Kensington Battalion).

3 ibid.
4 Bailey and Hollier, *The Kensingtons, 13th London Regiment.*
5 TNA, WO 95/2944: 1/13th London Regiment (Kensington Battalion).
6 ibid.
7 Bailey and Hollier, *The Kensingtons, 13th London Regiment.*
8 ibid.
9 Lindsay, *The London Scottish in the Great War.*
10 Ibid.
11 IWM Documents, Ref 17166: Papers of Lieutenant-Colonel C. E. Moy.
12 IWM Documents, Ref 15064: Papers of Private F. Inglefield.
13 IWM Documents, Ref 4326: Papers of Private Arthur Schuman.
14 ibid.
15 ibid.
16 Maurice, *The History of the London Rifle Brigade 1859 – 1919.*
17 ibid.
18 ibid.
19 ibid.
20 IWM Documents, Ref 15064: Papers of Private F. Inglefield.
21 Henriques, *The War History of the 1st Battalion Queen's Westminster Rifles 1914-1918.*
22 ibid.
23 ibid.
24 Cuthbert Keeson, *History & Records of Queen Victoria's Rifles 1792-1922.*
25 Ibid.
26 Maurice, *The History of the London Rifle Brigade 1859 – 1919.*
27 TNA, WO 95/2693: 1/9th Queen Victoria's Rifles War Diary.
28 ibid.
29 IWM Documents, Ref 7990: Papers of Lance Corporal Sidney Appleyard.
30 Henriques, *The War History of the 1st Battalion Queen's Westminster Rifles 1914-1918.*
31 Maurice, *The History of the London Rifle Brigade 1859 – 1919.*
32 TNA, WO 95/2957: 169th Brigade War Diary.
33 Henriques, *The War History of the 1st Battalion Queen's Westminster Rifles 1914-1918.*
34 ibid.
35 Maurice, *The History of the London Rifle Brigade 1859 – 1919.*
36 IWM Documents, Ref 4326: Papers of Private Arthur Schuman.
37 Cuthbert Keeson, *History & Records of Queen Victoria's Rifles 1792-1922..*
38 ibid.
39 Maurice, *The History of the London Rifle Brigade 1859 – 1919.*
40 ibid.
41 ibid.
42 ibid.
43 Ibid.
44 IWM Documents, Ref 4326: Papers of Private Arthur Schuman.
45 IWM Documents, Ref 17166: Papers of Lieutenant-Colonel C. E. Moy.
46 TNA, W0 95/2955: 1/13th Kensington Battalion War Diary.
47 TNA, WO 95/2951: 168th Brigade War Diary.
48 Wheeler-Holohan and Wyatt, *The Rangers Historical Records From 1859 to the conclusion of the Great War.*
49 Maurice, *The History of the London Rifle Brigade 1859 – 1919.*
50 Sheldon, *The German Army on the Somme.*

CHAPTER 9: SERRE

1 IWM Documents.7166: Papers of Brigadier-General H.C. Rees.
2 TNA, WO 95/2365: 12th York & Lancaster Regiment War Diary.
3 TNA, WO 95/2363: 94th Brigade War Diary.
4 TNA, CAB 45/190: Brigadier-General Hubert Rees.
5 ibid.
6 IWM Documents, Ref 7166, Papers of Brigadier-General H.C. Rees.
7 IWM Department of Sound:, Ref 9954: Reel 3, Private James Snailham interview.

8 ibid.
9 ibid.
10 TNA, WO 95/2365: 12th York & Lancaster Regiment War Diary.
11 IWM Department of Sound, Ref 13082: Reel 7, Lance Corporal James Glenn.
12 *Accrington Observer & Times*, 22 July 1916.
13 *Accrington Gazette*, 22 July 1916.
14 Lais, *Die Schlacht an der Somme*.
15 *Accrington Gazette*, 22 July 1916.
16 *Accrington Observer & Times*, 15 July 1916.
17 IWM Department of Sound, Ref: 26877: Reel 2, Private Charles Swales.
18 ibid.
19 *Leeds Mercury*, 15 July 1916.
20 TNA, CAB 45/190: Lieutenant-Colonel R.B. Neill.
21 ibid.
22 ibid.
23 *Leeds Mercury*, 13 July 1916.
24 *Leeds Mercury*, 14 July 1916.
25 ibid.
26 IWM Documents, Ref 7166: Papers of Brigadier-General H.C. Rees.
27 TNA, CAB 45/190: Lieutenant-Colonel R.B. Neill.
28 TNA, WO 95/2366: 11th East Lancashire (Accrington Pals) War Diary.
29 *Accrington Observer & Times*, 15 July 1916.
30 TNA, WO 95/2341: 31st Division War Diary.
31 ibid.
32 ibid.
33 ibid.
34 ibid.
35 TNA, WO 95/2366: 11th East Lancashire (Accrington Pals) War Diary.
36 TNA, WO 95/2341: 31st Division War Diary.
37 TNA, CAB 45/190: Lieutenant-Colonel R.B. Neill.
38 TNA, WO 95/2341: 31st Division War Diary.
39 TNA, WO 95/2363: 94th Brigade War Diary,
40 ibid.
41 TNA, WO 95/2341: 31st Division War Diary.
42 ibid.
43 IWM Department of Sound, Ref 13082: Reel 7, Lance Corporal James Glenn.
44 IWM Documents, Ref 7166: Papers of Brigadier-General H.C. Rees.
45 IWM Department of Sound, Ref 13082: Reel 8, Lance Corporal James Glenn.
46 TNA, WO 95/2341: 31st Division War Diary.
47 ibid.
48 TNA, WO 95/2366: 11th East Lancashire (Accrington Pals) War Diary.
49 *Bradford Daily Telegraph*, 10 July 1916.
50 TNA, WO 95/2363: 94th Brigade War Diary.
51 Edmonds, *Military Operations: France & Belgium 1916*, Volume 1.
52 TNA, WO 95/2363: 94th Brigade War Diary.
53 IWM Department of Sound, Ref 9488: Private William Parry-Morris.
54 TNA, WO 95/2365: 12th York & Lancaster Regiment War Diary.
55 ibid.

CHAPTER 10: REDAN RIDGE AND THE HEIDENKOPF

1 *Accrington Observer & Times*, 22 July 1916.
2 TNA, CAB 45/188: Captain D.R. Adams.
3 TNA, CAB 45/190: Captain C.W. Martin.
4 TNA, WO 95/1496: 1st Rifle Brigade War Diary.
5 ibid.
6 TNA, CAB 45/190: Captain C.W. Martin.
7 *Accrington Observer & Times*, 22 July 1916.
8 ibid.

9 TNA, WO 95/1495:1st Hampshire Regiment War Diary.
10 *Somerset County Gazette*, 22 July 1916.
11 ibid.
12 ibid.
13 ibid.
14 ibid.
15 ibid.
16 TNA, CAB 45/188: Captain D.R. Adams.
17 TNA, WO 95/1481/4: 2nd Royal Dublin Fusiliers War Diary.
18 ibid.
19 IWM Documents, Ref 1713: Papers of Major-General Sir John Laurie.
20 *Halifax Courier*, 15 July 1916.
21 TNA, WO 95/1505: 2nd Essex Regiment War Diary.
22 TNA, WO 95/1445: 4th Division War Diary.
23 TNA, WO 95/1496: 1st Rifle Brigade War Diary.
24 TNA, CAB 45/190: Captain C.W. Martin.
25 TNA, WO 95/1496: 1st Rifle Brigade War Diary.
26 TNA, WO 95/1505: 2nd Essex Regiment War Diary.
27 IWM Documents, Ref 1713: Papers of Major-General Sir John Laurie.
28 TNA, WO 95/1483: 2nd Seaforth Highlanders War Diary.
29 IWM Documents, Ref 1713: Papers of Major-General Sir John Laurie.
30 TNA, CAB 45/190: Captain C.W. Martin.
31 Edmonds, *Military Operations: France & Belgium 1916*, Volume 1.
32 ibid.
33 TNA, WO 95/1496: 1st Rifle Brigade War Diary.

CHAPTER 11: BEAUMONT HAMEL

1 TNA, CAB 45/189: Major Rex Trowers.
2 TNA, CAB 45/191: Captain E.W. Sheppard, 1st Lancashire Fusiliers.
3 ibid.
4 TNA, WO 95/2298: 86th Brigade War Diary.
5 *Regimental History of Infantry-Regiment No.119*, published in 1920.
6 TNA, WO 95/2300: 1st Lancashire Fusiliers War Diary.
7 Edmonds, *Military Operations: France & Belgium 1916*, Volume 1.
8 Sheldon, *The German Army on the Somme*, and Whitehead, *The Other Side of the Wire*, Volume 2.
9 *Regimental History of Infantry-Regiment No.119*, published in 1920, translated by Robin Schäfer, Military Historian, Dinslaken.
10 Edmonds, *Military Operations: France & Belgium 1916*, Volume 1.
11 TNA, CAB 45/191: Captain E.W. Sheppard.
12 ibid.
13 IWM Department of Sound, Ref: 9875: Reel 15, Corporal George Ashurst.
14 ibid.
15 ibid.
16 TNA, CAB 45/191: Captain E.W. Sheppard.
17 TNA, WO 95/2300: 1st Lancashire Fusiliers War Diary.
18 TNA, CAB 45/189: Captain Ian Grant.
19 ibid.
20 TNA, CAB 45/190: Lieutenant-Colonel H. Nelson.
21 ibid.
22 TNA, CAB 45/188: Lieutenant-Colonel J. Hamilton Hall.
23 ibid.
24 ibid.
25 ibid.
26 TNA, CAB 45/191: Captain E.W. Sheppard.
27 IWM Department of Sound, Ref 9875: Reel 15, Corporal George Ashurst.
28 TNA, CAB 45/191: Captain E.W. Sheppard.
29 TNA, CAB 45/189: Major G.V. Goodliffe.
30 ibid.

31 TNA, WO 95/2298: 86th Brigade War Diary.
32 TNA, WO 45/191: Captain E.W. Sheppard.
33 IWM Department of Sound, Ref: 9875: Reel 16, Corporal George Ashurst.
34 TNA, CAB 45/188: Major G.F. Goodliffe.
35 TNA, WO 161/95/92: Captain Eric Hall, PoW Report.
36 TNA, CAB 45/189: Lieutenant-Colonel J. Hamilton Hall.
37 ibid.
38 TNA, CAB 45/189: Major G.V. Goodliffe.
39 Edmonds, *Military Operations: France & Belgium 1916*, Volume 1.

CHAPTER 12: BEAUMONT HAMEL: Y-RAVINE

1 TNA, CAB 45/189: Major Hardress-Lloyd.
2 TNA, WO 95/2280: 29th Division War Diary.
3 TNA, CAB 45/190: Major Wilfred Raikes.
4 *Western Mail*, 6 July 1916.
5 TNA, CAB 45/189: Lieutenant-Colonel John Going.
6 TNA, CAB 45/190: Major Wilfred Raikes.
7 ibid.
8 TNA, CAB 45/190: Captain G.E. Malcolm.
9 TNA, WO 95/2305: 1st Border Regiment War Diary.
10 TNA, WO 95/2308: 1st Newfoundland Regiment War Diary.
11 ibid.
12 TNA, CAB 45/190: Captain G.A.M. Paxton.
13 *Essex County Telegraph*, 22 July 1916.
14 Edmonds, *Military Operations: France & Belgium 1916*, Volume 1.
15 ibid.
16 Cramm, *The First Five Hundred*.

CHAPTER 13: SCHWABEN REDOUBT

1 TNA, WO 95/2505: 9th Royal Irish Fusiliers War Diary.
2 TNA, CAB 45/188: Major A.H. Burne DSO.
3 ibid.
4 TNA, WO 95/2504: 108th Brigade War Diary.
5 *Ballymena Weekly Telegraph*, 15 July 1916.
6 TNA, WO 95/2506: 12th Battalion, Royal Irish Rifles War Diary.
7 TNA, WO 95/2504: 108th Brigade War Diary.
8 *Ballymena Observer*, 21 July 1916.
9 Mitchell, *Three Cheers for the Derrys*.
10 Somme Heritage Centre: Private Thomas Ervine interview.
11 Somme Heritage Centre: Private Leslie Bell papers.
12 Mitchell, *Three Cheers for the Derrys*.
13 ibid.
14 Crozier, *The Men I Killed*.
15 ibid.
16 *Derry Standard*, 12 July 1916.
17 Somme Heritage Centre: Private Thomas Ervine interview.
18 ibid.
19 Somme Heritage Centre: Jack Christie interview.
20 *Derry Standard*, 12 July 1916.
21 TNA, WO 95/2510/4: 10th Royal Inniskilling Fusiliers War Diary.
22 Crozier, *A Brasshat in No Man's Land*.
23 *History of the 36th (Ulster) Division*, by Cyril Falls, published 1921.
24 TNA, CAB 45/188: Lieutenant-Colonel F.P. Crozier.
25 Crozier, *A Brasshat in No Man's Land*.
26 Crozier, *The Men I Killed*.
27 IWM Documents, Ref 6659: Papers of Private Davy Starrett.
28 ibid.

29 Crozier, *The Men I Killed*.
30 IWM Documents, Ref 6659: Papers of Private Davy Starrett.
31 TNA, CAB 45/188: Lieutenant-Colonel F.P. Crozier.
32 IWM Documents, Ref 6659: Papers of Davy Starrett.
33 TNA, WO 95/2507: 109th Brigade War Diary.
34 ibid.
35 TNA, WO 95/2505: 9th Royal Irish Fusiliers War Diary.
36 *Derry Standard*, 12 July 1916.
37 TNA, WO 95/2510/3: 9th Royal Inniskilling Fusiliers War Diary.
38 TNA, WO 95/2507: 109th Brigade War Diary.
39 ibid.
40 Sheldon, *The German Army on the Somme*.
41 ibid.
42 ibid.
43 TNA, WO 95/2491: 36th (Ulster) Division War Diary.
44 Crozier, *A Brasshat in No Man's Land*.
45 Somme Heritage Centre: Jack Christie interview.
46 *Londonderry Sentinel*, 8 July 1916.

CHAPTER 14: THIEPVAL

1 TNA, WO 95/2403: 16th Highland Light Infantry War Diary.
2 TNA, CAB 45/189: Brigadier-General C. Yatman.
3 *Eccles & Patricroft Journal*, 21 July 1916.
4 ibid.
5 IWM Documents, Ref 7405: Papers of Lieutenant F.L. Cassel.
6 Edmonds, *Military Operations: France & Belgium 1916*, Volume 1.
7 TNA, CAB 45/190: Historical Records of the 16th Northumberland Fusiliers.
8 TNA, WO 95/2398/1: 16th Northumberland Fusiliers War Diary.
9 Fusiliers Museum of Northumberland: Papers of Private Ernest Watson.
10 TNA, WO 95/2395: 96th Brigade War Diary.
11 IWM Documents, Ref 7405: Papers of Lieutenant F.L. Cassel.
12 Fusiliers Museum of Northumberland: Papers of Private Ernest Watson.
13 TNA, CAB 45/190: Historical Records of the 16th Northumberland Fusiliers.
14 *The Salford City Reporter*, 8 August 1916.
15 ibid.
16 ibid.
17 *Rochdale Observer*, 15 July 1916.
18 ibid.
19 TNA, WO 95/2397: 15th Battalion Lancashire Fusiliers War Diary.
20 Lancashire Fusiliers Museum: Papers of 2nd Lieutenant Charles Marriot.
21 ibid.
22 ibid.
23 *Eccles and Patricroft Journal*, 21 July 1916.
24 ibid.
25 TNA, WO 95/2368: 32nd Division War Diary.
26 TNA, WO 95/2397: 15th Battalion Lancashire Fusiliers War Diary.
27 *Eccles & Patricroft Journal*, 14 July 1916.
28 *Eccles & Patricroft Journal*, 21 July 1916.
29 *Rochdale Observer*, 15 July 1916.
30 TNA, CAB 45/189: Brigadier-General C. Yatman.

CHAPTER 15: LEIPZIG SALIENT

1 IWM Documents, Ref 7733; Papers of Lance Corporal J.L. Jack.
2 Arthur, *The 17th Highland Light Infantry*.
3 IWM Documents, Ref 7733: Papers of Lance Corporal J.L. Jack.
4 IWM Department of Sound, Ref 21195: Reel 1, Corporal Fred Francis interview.
5 TNA, WO 95/2403: 16th Highland Light Infantry War Diary.

6 TNA, CAB 45/189: Captain G. Hibbert.
7 Arthur, *The 17th Highland Light Infantry*.
8 ibid.
9 TNA, WO 95/2368: 32nd Division War Diary.
10 Arthur, *The 17th Highland Light Infantry*.
11 TNA, WO 95/2368: 32nd Division War Diary.
12 ibid.
13 Arthur, *The 17th Highland Light Infantry*.

CHAPTER 16: NORDWERK

1 TNA, WO 95/2188: 8th York & Lancaster Regiment War Diary.
2 ibid.
3 TNA, WO 95/2185: 70th Brigade War Diary.
4 Bond, *The King's Own (Yorkshire Light Infantry) in the Great War*.
5 TNA, WO 95/2188: 8th York & Lancaster Regiment War Diary.
6 ibid.
7 TNA, WO 95/2185: 70th Brigade War Diary.
8 ibid.
9 ibid.
10 ibid.
11 TNA, WO 95/2188: 8th York & Lancaster Regiment War Diary.
12 TNA, WO 95/2187/2: 8th King's Own (Yorkshire Light Infantry); Edmonds, *Military Operations: France & Belgium 1916*, Volume 1.
13 TNA, WO 95/2188: 8th York & Lancaster Regiment War Diary; Edmonds, *Military Operations: France & Belgium 1916*, Volume 1.
14 Edmonds, *Military Operations: France & Belgium 1916*, Volume 1.
15 ibid.

CHAPTER 17: OVILLERS-LA-BOISSELLE AND MASH VALLEY

1 Edmonds, *Military Operations: France & Belgium 1916*, Volume 1.
2 ibid.
3 ibid.
4 ibid.
5 TNA, WO 95/1712: 2nd Devonshire Regiment War Diary.
6 Keep Military Museum, Dorchester: Papers of Private Cyril Jose, 2nd Devonshire Regiment.
7 ibid.
8 Edmonds, *Military Operations: France & Belgium 1916*, Volume 1.
9 Keep Military Museum, Dorchester: Papers of Private Cyril Jose, 2nd Devonshire Regiment.
10 Atkinson, *The Devonshire Regiment 1914-1918*.
11 Edmonds, *Military Operations: France & Belgium 1916*, Volume 1.
12 TNA, WO 95/1712: 2nd Devonshire Regiment War Diary.
13 Keep Military Museum, Dorchester: Papers of Private Cyril Jose, 2nd Devonshire Regiment.
14 TNA, WO 95/1713: 2nd Middlesex Regiment War Diary.
15 Edmonds, *Military Operations: France & Belgium 1916*, Volume 1.
16 ibid.
17 ibid.
18 TNA, WO 95/1726: 25th Brigade War Diary.
19 ibid.
20 ibid.
21 Edmonds, *Military Operations: France & Belgium 1916*, Volume 1.
22 Ibid.
23 Ibid.
24 TNA, WO 95/1726: 25th Brigade War Diary.

CHAPTER 18: LA BOISSELLE

1 TNA, WO 95/244: 179th Tunnelling Company, Royal Engineers War Diary.
2 ibid.
3 ibid.
4 IWM Department of Sound, Ref 21195: Reel 1, Corporal Fred Francis interview.
5 ibid.
6 Ternan, *The Story of the Tyneside Scottish.*
7 Lewis, *Sagittarius Rising.*
8 TNA, WO 95/2342: 34th Division War Diary.
9 Simpson, *The History of the Lincolnshire Regiment 1914-1918.*
10 TNA, WO 95/2462/4: 20th Northumberland Fusiliers War Diary.
11 TNA, WO 95/2463/2: 23rd Northumberland Fusiliers (4th Tyneside Scottish) War Diary.
12 TNA, CAB 45/190: Major S.H. Mackintosh.
13 TNA, WO 95/2463/2: 23rd Battalion Northumberland Fusiliers (4th Tyneside Scottish) War Diary.
14 Stewart and Sheen, *Tyneside Scottish.*
15 TNA, WO 95/2463/2: 23rd Battalion Northumberland Fusiliers (4th Tyneside Scottish) War Diary.
16 The Gordon Highlanders Museum.
17 Shakespear, *The Northumberland Fusiliers 18th (Service) Battalion.*
18 TNA, WO 95/2463/3: 25th Northumberland Fusiliers War Diary.
19 *Londonderry Sentinel*, 15 July 1916.
20 ibid.
21 Ternan, *The Story of the Tyneside Scottish.*
22 ibid.
23 ibid.
24 ibid.
25 IWM Documents, Ref 6968: Papers of Major W.A. Vignoles DSO and Bar.
26 TNA, WO 95/2458: 11th Battalion Suffolk Regiment War Diary.
27 Murphy, *History of the Suffolk Regiment 1914-1927.*
28 Bryant, *Grimsby Chums.*
29 TNA, CAB 45/190: Lieutenant-Colonel E.A. Osborne.
30 TNA, WO 95/2458: 16th Royal Scots War Diary.
31 Fusiliers Museum of Northumberland: Corporal Robert Kennedy papers.
32 ibid.
33 ibid.
34 ibid.
35 TNA, WO 95/2455: 101st Brigade War Diary.
36 ibid.
37 TNA, WO 95/2458: 16th Royal Scots War Diary.
38 Ewing, *The Royal Scots 1914-1918.*
39 Edmonds, *Military Operations: France & Belgium 1916*, Volume 1.
40 Bryant, *Grimsby Chums.*

CHAPTER 19: FRICOURT

1 IWM of Sound, Ref 9752: Lieutenant Norman Musgrove Dillon.
2 TNA, WO 95/2159: 64th Brigade War Diary.
3 ibid.
4 ibid.
5 ibid.
6 TNA, WO 95/2162: 9th King's Own (Yorkshire Light Infantry) War Diary.
7 TNA, WO 95/2159: 64th Brigade War Diary.
8 Edmonds, *Military Operations: France & Belgium 1916*, Volume 1
9 TNA, CAB 45/188: Lieutenant-Colonel H.P.F. Bicknell.
10 TNA, WO 95/2158: Somerset Light Infantry War Diary.
11 IWM Department of Sound, Ref 9455: Reel 2, Private Maurice Symes.
12 TNA, WO 95/2158: 8th Somerset Light Infantry War Diary.

13 ibid.
14 TNA, WO 95/2158: 10th York & Lancaster Regiment War Diary.
15 TNA, WO 95/2158: 8th Lincolnshire Regiment War Diary.
16 TNA, CAB 45/188: Captain F. Brown.
17 ibid.
18 Wyrall, *The Die Hards in the Great War*; TNA, WO 95/2158: 8th Lincolnshire Regiment War Diary.
19 TNA, WO 95/2004/2: 7th Yorkshire Regiment War Diary.

CHAPTER 20: MAMETZ

1 *Ballymena Weekly Telegraph*, 29 July 1916.
2 TNA, WO 95/1670: 1st South Staffordshire War Diary.
3 TNA, WO 95/1670: 2nd Queen's (Royal West Surrey Regiment) War Diary.
4 ibid.
5 TNA, WO 95/1670: 1st South Staffordshire Regiment War Diary.
6 The Gordon Highlanders Museum: Major R.A. Wolfe-Murray Diary.
7 The Gordon Highlanders Museum: Palithorpe, 'With the Highlanders'.
8 TNA, CAB 45/188: Reverend Ernest Crosse.
9 *Rochdale Observer*, 15 July 1916.
10 TNA, WO 95/1653: 20th Brigade War Diary.
11 *Aberdeen Weekly Journal*, 7 July 1916.
12 The Gordon Highlanders Museum: Major R.A. Wolfe-Murray Diary.
13 *Ballymena Weekly Telegraph*, 29 July 1916.
14 The Gordon Highlanders Museum: Major R.A. Wolfe-Murray Diary.
15 TNA, WO 95/1656: 2nd Gordon Highlanders War Diary.
16 TNA, WO 95/1653: 20th Brigade War Diary.
17 TNA, WO 95/1656: 2nd Gordon Highlanders War Diary.
18 ibid.
19 ibid.
20 TNA, WO 95/1653: 20th Brigade War Diary.
21 *Aberdeen Weekly Journal*, 7 July 1916.
22 ibid.
23 *Burton Chronicle*, 18 July 1916.
24 ibid.
25 *Aberdeen Weekly Journal*, 7 July 1916.
26 ibid.
27 Atkinson, *The Devonshire Regiment 1914-1918*.
28 TNA, WO 95/1655: 8th Devonshire Regiment War Diary.
29 ibid.
30 TNA, WO 95/1656: 2nd Gordon Highlanders War Diary.
31 IWM Documents, Ref 4772: Papers of Chaplain Ernest Crosse.
32 Whitehead, *The Other Side of the Wire*, Volume 2.

CHAPTER 21: POMMIERS REDOUBT

1 TNA, CAB 45/188: Lieutenant-Colonel B.G. Clay.
2 O'Neill, *The Royal Fusiliers in the Great War*.
3 TNA, WO 95/2043: 7th Bedfordshire Regiment War Diary.
4 TNA, WO 95/2041: 54th Brigade War Diary.
5 TNA, WO 95/2043: 7th Bedfordshire Regiment War Diary.
6 *Londonderry Sentinel*, 13 July 1916.
7 TNA, WO 95/ 2044: 12th Middlesex Regiment War Diary.
8 O'Neill, *The Royal Fusiliers in the Great War*, published 1922.
9 Edmonds, *Military Operations: France & Belgium 1916*, Volume 1.
10 *Lowestoft Weekly Press*, 22 July 1916.
11 TNA, WO 95/2034: 18th Division War Diary.
12 IWM Documents, Ref 1502: Papers of Private Fred Henwood.
13 TNA, CAB 45/188: Lieutenant-Colonel B.G. Clay.

14 TNA, WO 94/2040: 8th Norfolk Regiment War Diary.
15 *Lowestoft Weekly Press*, 22 July 1916.
16 ibid.
17 ibid.
18 ibid.
19 ibid.
20 ibid.
21 ibid.
22 ibid.
23 ibid.
24 Edmonds, *Military Operations: France & Belgium 1916*, Volume 1.
25 TNA, WO 95/2037: 6th Royal Berkshire Regiment War Diary.

CHAPTER 22: MONTAUBAN RIDGE

1 TNA, WO 95/2059: 7th East Buff's War Diary.
2 TNA, CAB 45/189: Captain Arthur Kenchington.
3 IWM Department of Sound:, Ref 211: Reel 2, Major Alfred Irwin.
4 TNA, WO 95/2050: 8th East Surrey Regiment War Diary.
5 *Blackburn Times*, 22 July 1916.
6 IWM Documents, Ref 14390: 2nd Lieutenant Charles Alcock.
7 IWM Department of Sound:, Ref 211: Reel 2, Major Alfred Irwin.
8 TNA, WO 95/2059: 7th East Buff's War Diary.
9 TNA, CAB 45/189: Captain Arthur Kenchington.
10 TNA, WO 95/2059: 7th East Buff's War Diary.
11 IWM Department of Sound, Ref 211: Reel 2, Major Alfred Irwin.
12 IWM Document, Ref 8207: Papers of Captain William Henry Bloor.
13 Wylly, *History of the Queen's (Royal West Surrey Regiment) in the Great War*.
14 Edmonds, *Military Operations: France & Belgium 1916*, Volume 1.

CHAPTER 23: LIVENS FLAME PROJECTORS AT BRESLAU TRENCH

1 TNA, WO 94/122: Royal Engineers, Special Section War Diary.
2 ibid.
3 ibid.
4 TNA, WO 95/2046: 55th Brigade War Diary.

CHAPTER 24: MONTAUBAN

1 TNA, WO 95/2310: 30th Division War Diary.
2 TNA, CAB 45/190: Oberstleutnant Bedall.
3 *Birkenhead News*, 12 July 1916.
4 TNA, CAB 45/190: Oberstleutnant Bedall.
5 *Birkenhead News*, 12 July 1916.
6 TNA, WO 95/2335: 20th King's (Liverpool Regiment) War Diary.
7 *Wallasey & Wirral Chronicle*, 19 July 1916.
8 Richardson, *Orders Are Orders*.
9 IWM Department of Sound:, Ref 24549: Reel 1, Private Sidney Ralph Steele.
10 NA: WO 95/2330: 18th King's (Liverpool Regiment) War Diary.
11 IWM Department of Sound, Ref 24549: Reel 1, Private Sidney Ralph Steele.
12 Richardson, *Orders Are Orders*.
13 TNA, WO 95/2330: 18th King's (Liverpool Regiment) War Diary.
14 IWM Department of Sound, Ref 24549: Reel 1, Private Sidney Ralph Steele.
15 ibid.
16 ibid.
17 ibid.
18 ibid.
19 ibid.
20 Richardson, *Orders Are Orders*.

21 ibid.
22 IWM Department of Sound, Ref 24549: Reel 1, Private Sidney Ralph Steele.
23 TNA, WO 95/2330: 18th King's (Liverpool Regiment) War Diary.
24 Richardson, *Orders Are Orders*.
25 ibid.
26 *Cambrian*, 14 July 1916.
27 TNA, WO 95/2310: 30th Division War Diary.
28 *Ashton-under-Lyne Herald*, 19 August 1916.
29 IWM Department of Sound, Ref 11582: Private Albert Hurst.
30 ibid.
31 ibid.
32 *Ashton-under-Lyne Herald*, 22 August 1916.
33 IWM Department of Sound:, Ref 9894: Sergeant James Albert Payne.
34 *Eccles & Patricroft Journal*, 21 July 1916.
35 *Cambrian*, 14 July 1916.
36 IWM Department of Sound, Ref 11582: Private Albert Hurst.
37 *Ashton-under-Lyne Herald*, 22 August 1916.
38 TNA, CAB 45/189: Lieutenant-Colonel H. Hall.
39 *Ashton-under-Lyne Herald*, 19 August 1916.
40 TNA, WO 95/2310: 30th Division War Diary.
41 TNA, CAB 45/189: Lieutenant-Colonel H. Hall.
42 *Ashton-under-Lyne Herald*, 22 August 1916.
43 TNA, WO 95/2310: 30th Division War Diary.

CHAPTER 25: AFTERMATH

1 *Somerset County Gazette*, 22 July 1916.
2 TNA, CAB 45/188.
3 TNA, WO 256/11: Haig's Diary.
4 ibid.
5 Edmonds, *Military Operations: France & Belgium 1916*, Volume 1.
6 ibid.
7 IWM Documents, Ref 6559: Papers of Captain E.B. Lord.
8 TNA, CAB 45/188: Major H.F. Dawes.
9 TNA, WO 95/2050: 8th East Surrey Regiment War Diary.
10 *Essex County Standard*, 29 July 1916.
11 TNA, WO 95/2050: 8th East Surrey Regiment War Diary.
12 *Leeds Mercury*, 15 July 1916.
13 *Birkenhead News*, 22 July 1916.
14 *Ashton-under-Lyne Herald*, 22 August 1916.
15 *Accrington Observer & Times*, 15 July 1916.
16 *Derry Standard*, 17 July 1916.
17 Shakespear, *The Northumberland Fusiliers 18th (Service) Battalion*.

CHAPTER 26: ASSESSMENT: SUCCESS AND FAILURE

1 *Eccles & Patricroft Journal*, 28 July 1916.
2 Maurice, *The History of the London Rifle Brigade 1859 – 1919*.
3 TNA, WO 95/2039: 8th Suffolk Regiment War Diary.
4 *Somerset County Gazette*, 22 July 1916.
5 Edmonds, *Military Operations: France & Belgium 1916*, Volume 1.
6 ibid.
7 ibid.
8 The Gordon Highlanders Museum: Major R.A. Wolfe-Murray Diary.
9 IWM Documents, Ref 7166: Papers of Brigadier-General H.C. Rees.
10 Majendie, *A History of the 1 Battalion Somerset Light Infantry, 1 July 1916 to the end of the War*.
11 TNA, CAB 45/188: Lieutenant-Colonel C. Broad.
12 ibid.
13 Edmonds, *Military Operations: France & Belgium 1916*, Volume 1, quoting from *Somme Nord I*.

14 ibid.
15 Edmonds, *Military Operations: France & Belgium 1916*, Volume 1.
16 IWM Department of Sound, Ref 9431: Reel 3, Private George Grunwell.
17 IWM Department of Sound, Ref 211: Reel 2, Major Alfred Irwin.
18 *Wigan Examiner*, 11 July 1916.
19 *Lowestoft Weekly Press*, 22 July 1916.
20 Sergeant John Wilson's Diary, courtesy Katy Wilson.
21 *Bradford Daily Telegraph*, 10 July 1916.
22 *Derry Standard*, 12 July 1916.
23 Keep Military Museum, Dorchester: Papers of Private Cyril Jose, 2nd Battalion Devonshire Regiment.
24 IWM Department of Sound, Ref 24555: Reel 2, Lance Corporal James Glenn.
25 *Psycohologische Strategie des Grossen Krieges* by Captain von Hentig, and Edmonds, *Military Operations: France & Belgium 1916*, Volume 1.

Bibliography

LONDON GAZETTE
25 July 1916.
19 March 1919.

NATIONAL ARCHIVES
CAB 45/188: Captain D.R. Adams.
CAB 45/188: Major A.H. Burne.
CAB 45/188: Lieutenant-Colonel H.P.F. Bicknell.
CAB 45/188: Captain F. Brown.
CAB 45/188: Lieutenant-Colonel C. Broad.
CAB 45/188: Lieutenant-Colonel F.P. Crozier.
CAB 45/188: Staff Captain G.R. Codrington.
CAB 45/188: Reverend Ernest Crosse.
CAB 45/188: Major H.F. Dawes.
CAB 45/189: Major Austin Girdwood.
CAB 45/189: Major G.F. Goodliffe.
CAB 45/189: Captain Ian Grant.
CAB 45/189: Lieutenant-Colonel John Going.
CAB 45/189: Lieutenant-Colonel H. Hall.
CAB 45/189: Lieutenant-Colonel J. Hamilton Hall.
CAB 45/189: Major H.M. Hance.
CAB 45/189: Major Hardress-Lloyd.
CAB 45/189: Captain Arthur Kenchington.
CAB 45/189: Major Rex Trowers.
CAB 45/189: Major M. Kemp Welch.
CAB 45/189: Brigadier-General C. Yatman.
CAB 45/190: Major S.H. Mackintosh.
CAB 45/190: Captain G.E. Malcolm.
CAB 45/190: Lieutenant-Colonel R.B. Neill.
CAB 45/190: Lieutenant-Colonel H. Nelson.
CAB 45/190: Lieutenant-Colonel E.A. Osborne.
CAB 45/190: Oberstleutnant Bedall.
CAB 45/190: Captain G.A.M. Paxton.
CAB 45/190: Brigadier-General Hubert Rees.
CAB 45/190: Major Wilfred Raikes.
CAB 45/191: Captain E.W. Sheppard.
WO 94/122: Royal Engineers, Special Section War Diary.
WO 95/244: 179th Tunnelling Company, Royal Engineers War Diary.
WO 95/1445: 4th Division War Diary.
WO 95/1483: 2nd Seaforth Highlanders War Diary.
WO 95/1484: 1st Royal Warwickshire War Diary.

WO 95/1495: 1st Hampshire Regiment War Diary.
WO 95/1499: 1st Somerset Light Infantry War Diary.
WO 95/1505: 2nd Essex Regiment War Diary.
WO 95/1653: 20th Brigade War Diary.
WO 95/1655: 2nd Border Regiment War Diary.
WO 95/1655: 8th Devonshire Regiment War Diary.
WO 95/1656: 2nd Gordon Highlanders War Diary.
WO 95/1656: 9th Devonshire Regiment War Diary.
WO 95/1670: 1st South Staffordshire Regiment War Diary.
WO 95/1670: 2nd Queen's (Royal West Surrey Regiment) War Diary.
WO 95/1675: 8th Division War Diary.
WO 95/1712: 2nd Devonshire Regiment War Diary.
WO 95/1713: 2nd Middlesex Regiment War Diary.
WO 95/1726: 25th Brigade War Diary.
WO 95/2004/2: 7th Yorkshire Regiment War Diary.
WO 95/2034: 18th Division War Diary.
WO 95/2037: 6th Royal Berkshire Regiment War Diary
WO 95/2040: 8th Norfolk Regiment War Diary.
WO 95/2041: 54th Brigade War Diary.
WO 95/2043: 7th Bedfordshire Regiment War Diary.
WO 95/2046: 55th Brigade War Diary.
WO 95/2050: 8th East Surrey Regiment War Diary.
WO 95/2051: 7th Queen's (Royal West Surrey Regiment) War Diary.
WO 95/2158: 8th Somerset Light Infantry War Diary.
WO 95/2158: 10th York & Lancaster Regiment War Diary.
WO 95/2158: 8th Lincolnshire Regiment War Diary.
WO 95/2159: 64th Brigade War Diary.
WO 95/2162: 9th King's Own (Yorkshire Light Infantry) War Diary.
WO 95/2185: 70th Brigade War Diary.
WO 95/2187/2: 8th King's (Own Yorkshire Light) Infantry.
WO 95/2188: 8th York & Lancaster Regiment War Diary.
WO 95/2188: 8th King's (Own Yorkshire Light) Infantry War Diary.
WO 95/2298: 86th Brigade War Diary.
WO 95/2300: 1st Lancashire Fusiliers War Diary
WO 95/2301: 1st Royal Dublin Fusiliers War Diary.
WO 95/2305: 1st Border Regiment War Diary.
WO 95/2308: 1st Newfoundland Regiment War Diary.
WO 95/2310: 30th Division War Diary.
WO 95/2330: 18th Liverpool Regiment War Diary.
WO 95/2335: 20th King's (Liverpool Regiment) War Diary.
WO 95/2341: 31st Division War Diary.
WO 95/2363: 94th Brigade War Diary.
WO 95/2365: 12th York & Lancaster Regiment War Diary.
WO 95/2365: 14th York & Lancaster Regiment War Diary.
WO 95/2366: 11st East Lancashire Regiment (Accrington Pals) War Diary.
WO 95/2368: 32nd Division War Diary.
WO 95/2395: 96th Brigade War Diary.
WO 95/2397: 16th Northumberland Fusiliers (Newcastle Commercials) War Diary.
WO 95/2397: 2nd Royal Inniskilling Fusiliers War Diary.
WO 95/2397: 15th Lancashire Fusiliers (1 Salford Pals) War Diary.
WO 95/2397: 16th Lancashire Fusiliers (2 Salford Pals) War Diary.
WO 95/2398: 16th Northumberland Fusiliers (Newcastle Commercials) War Diary.
WO 95/2403: 16th Highland Light Infantry War Diary.
WO 95/2451/1: 18th Northumberland Fusiliers (Pioneers) War Diary.
WO 95/2455: 101st Brigade War Diary
WO 95/2457: 10th Lincolnshire Regiment War Diary.
WO 95/2457: 15th Royal Scots War Diary.
WO 95/2458: 11th Suffolk Regiment War Diary.
WO 95/2458: 16th Royal Scots War Diary.

WO 95/2462/4: 20th Northumberland Fusiliers (1st Tyneside Scottish) War Diary.
WO 95/2463/3: 25th Northumberland Fusiliers (2nd Tyneside Irish) War Diary.
WO 95/2491: 36th (Ulster) Division War Diary.
WO 95/2504: 108th Brigade War Diary.
WO 95/2505: 9th Royal Irish Fusiliers War Diary.
WO 95/2507: 109th Brigade War Diary.
WO 95/2510: 9th Royal Inniskilling Fusiliers War Diary.
WO 95/2510: 10th Royal Inniskilling Fusiliers War Diary.
WO 95/2663: 46th Division War Diary.
WO 95/2951: 168th Brigade War Diary.
WO 95/2957: 169th Brigade War Diary.
WO 95/2963: 1/16th London Regiment (Queen's Westminster Rifles War Diary.
WO 158/233: Fourth Army Operations 27 February 1916 to 12 June 1916.
WO 161/95/92: Captain Eric Hall Prisoner of War Report.
WO 256/5: WO 256/6: WO 256/7: WO 256/8: WO 256/9: WO 256/10: WO 256/11: Haig's Diary.

NEWSPAPERS

Aberdeen Weekly Journal, 7 July 1916.
Accrington Gazette, 22 July 1916.
Accrington Observer & Times, 15 and 22 July 1916.
Ashton-under-Lyne Herald, 22 July and 19 August 1916.
Ballymena Observer, 21 July 1916.
Ballymena Weekly Telegraph, 15 and 29 July 1916.
Birkenhead News, 12 and 22 July 1916.
Blackburn Times, 22 July 1916.
Bradford Daily Telegraph, 10 July 1916.
Burton Chronicle, 18 July 1916.
Cambrian, 14 July 1916.
Derbyshire Times, 8 July 1916.
Derry Journal, 18 July 1916.
Derry Standard, 12 and 17 July 1916.
Eccles & Patricroft Journal, 14, 21 and 28 July 1916.
Essex County Telegraph, 15 and 22 July 1916.
Halifax Courier, 15 July 1916.
Leeds Mercury, 10, 13, 14 and 15 July 1916.
Londonderry Sentinel, 8, 13, 15 and 18 July 1916.
Lowestoft Weekly Press, 22 July 1916.
Rochdale Observer, 15 July 1916.
Salford City Reporter, 8 August 1916.
Sheffield Weekly Independent, 22 July 1916.
Somerset County Gazette, 22 July 1916.
Wallasey & Wirral Chronicle, 19 July 1916.
Wigan Examiner, 11 July 1916.

FUSILIERS MUSEUM OF NORTHUMBERLAND

Papers of Private Ernest Watson, Corporal Alfred Kettle and Corporal Robert Kennedy.

THE GORDON HIGHLANDERS MUSEUM

Private Tom Easton Diary.
'With the Highlanders' by Major D.W. Palithorpe.
Captain R.A. Wolfe-Murray Diary.

IWM DEPARTMENT OF DOCUMENTS

IWM Documents.14390: 2nd Lieutenant Charles Alcock.
IWM Documents.7990: Lance Corporal Sidney Appleyard.
IMW Documents.8207: Captain William Henry Bloor.
IWM Documents.7405: Lieutenant F.L. Cassel.
IWM Documents.4772: Canon E.C. Crosse.

IWM Documents.1502: Private Fred Henwood.
IWM Dcuments.15064: Private F. Inglefield.
IWM Documents.7733: Lance Corporal J.L. Jack.
IWM Documents.1713: Captain John Laurie.
IWM Documents.6559: Captain E.B. Lord.
IWM Documents.17166: Lieutenant-Colonel C.E. Moy.
IWM Documents.7166: Brigadier-General H.C. Rees
IWM Documents.7312: H. Russell.
IWM Documents.4326: Private Arthur Schuman.
IWM Documents.15087: Private W.J. Senescall.
IWM Documents.6659: Private D. Starrett.
IWM Documents.4481: Private W.B. Stevenson.
IWM Documents.6968: Lieutenant-Colonel W.A. Vignoles DSO & Bar.

IWM DEPARTMENT OF SOUND

IMW Ref: 9875: Private George Ashurst.
IWM Ref: 9752: IWM Lieutenant Norman Musgrove Dillon.
IWM Ref: 21195: Corporal Fred Francis
IWM Ref: 13082: Lance Corporal James Glenn.
IWM Ref: 9431: Private George Grunwell.
IWM Ref: 11582: Private Albert Hurst.
IWM Ref: 211: Major Alfred Irwin.
IWM Ref: 4162: 2nd Lieutenant Cecil Lewis.
IWM Ref: 9488: Private William Parry-Morris.
IWM Ref: 9894: Sergeant Albert Payne.
IWM Ref: 9954: Private James Snailham.
IWM Ref: 24549: Private Sidney Steele.
IWM Ref: 26877: Private Charles Swales.
IWM Ref: 9455: Private Maurice Symes.

KEEP MILITARY MUSEUM, DORCHESTER

Papers of Private Cyril Jose.

SOMME HERITAGE CENTRE

Private Leslie Bell Papers.
Jack Christie: Interview 096.
Private Thomas Ervine interview.
R.T. Grange interview.

UNPUBLISHED SOURCES

Sergeant John Wilson's Diary, courtesy Katy Wilson.

PUBLISHED SOURCES

Arthur, John, *The 17th Highland Light Infantry* (J. Clark, Glasgow, 1920).
Atkinson, C.T., *The Seventh Division 1914-1918* (Naval & Military Press, 2006).
______, *The Devonshire Regiment 1914-1918* (Eland Brothers, 1926).
______, *The Queens Own Royal West Kent Regiment – 1914- 1919* (Simpkin, Marshall, Hamilton, Kent & Co. Ltd, 1924).
Bailey, Sergeant O.F., and Hollier, Sergeant H.M., *The Kensington's, 13th London Regiment* (Regimental Old Comrades Association 1935).
Banning, Jeremy & Barton, Peter, *The Somme: The Unseen Panoramas* (Constable, 2006).
Bond, Lieutenant-Colonel Reginald *The King's Own (Yorkshire Light Infantry) in the Great War* (Percy Lund, Humphries and Co. Ltd, 1929).
Bryant, Peter, *Grimsby Chums* (Hutton Press Limited, 1991).
Charteris, Brigadier-General John, *Field Marshal Earl Haig* (Cassell & Company Limited 1919).
Cramm, Richard, *The First Five Hundred* (C.F. Williams & Son, New York, 1921).
Crozier, F.P., *A Brasshat in No Man's Land* (Naval & Military Press, 2011).
______, *The Men I Killed* (Doubleday, 1938).

BIBLIOGRAPHY

Cuthbert Keeson, Major C.A., *History & Records of Queen Victoria's Rifles 1792-1922* (Constable & Company Limited 1923).
Edmonds, Brigadier-General Sir James, *History of the Great War, Military Operations, France & Belgium 1916* Volume 1 (Macmillan & Co., 1932).
Ewing MC, Major John, *The Royal Scots 1914-1918* (Oliver & Boyd, 1925).
Gardner, R.B., *The Big Push* (Cassell, 1961).
Gliddon, Gerald, *Somme 1916: A Battlefield Companion* (The History Press, 2009).
______, *VCs of the First World War – The Somme* (Sutton, 1995).
Grehan, John and Mace, Martin, *Slaughter on the Somme, 1 July 1916* (Pen & Sword, 2013).
Hammerton, J., and Wilson, H.W., *The Great War: The Standard History of the All -Europe Conflict, Volume 7* (The Amalgamated Press Ltd, 1916).
______, *The Great War: The Standard History of the All -Europe Conflict, Volume 8* (The Amalgamated Press Ltd, 1917).
Hart, Peter, *The Somme* (Weidenfeld & Nicolson, 2005).
Henriques, Major J.Q., *The War History of the 1st Battalion Queen's Westminster Rifles 1914-1918* (London Medici Society Limited, 1923).
Hentig, Captain von, *Psycohologische Strategie des Grossen Krieges* (C. Winter, Heidelberg, 1927).
Holmes, Richard, *The Western Front* (BBC Worldwide, 1999).
Lais, Otto, *Die Schlacht an der Somme* (G. Braun, 1935).
Lewis, Cecil, *Sagittarius Rising* (P Davies, London, 1936).
Lindsay, Lieutenant-Colonel J.H., *The London Scottish in the Great War* (Regimental Headquarters, London, 1926).
Majendie DSO, Major V., *A History of the 1 Battalion Somerset Light Infantry, 1 July 1916 to the end of the War* (Phoenix Press 1921).
Maurice, Major-General Sir Frederick, *The History of the London Rifle Brigade 1859 – 1919* (Constable and Co, 1921).
Middlebrook, Martin, *The First Day on the Somme* (Penguin, 1984).
Müller-Loebnitz, Wilhelm, *Die Badener im Weltkrieg* (G. Braun Verlag, 1935).
Murphy, Lieutenant-Colonel C., *The History of the Suffolk Regiment 1914-1927* (Hutchinson & Co., 1928).
Mitchell, Gardiner, *Three Cheers for the Derrys* (Yes Publications 2008).
O'Neill, H.C., *The Royal Fusiliers in the Great War* (Naval & Military Press, 2002).
Prior, Robin, and Wilson, Trevor, *Command on the Western Front, The Military Career of Sir Henry Rawlinson 1914-1918* (Pen & Sword, 2004).
Richardson, Neil, *Orders Are Orders: A Manchester Pal on the Somme* (Neil Richardson, 1987).
Shakespear, John, *The Northumberland Fusiliers 18 (Service) Battalion* (Newcastle and Gateshead Incorporated Chamber of Commerce, 1920).
Sheldon, Jack, *The German Army on the Somme 1914 – 1916* (Pen & Sword, 2006).
Simpson, Major-General C.R., *The History of the Lincolnshire Regiment 1914-1918* (Medici Society Ltd 1931).
Stewart, Graham, and Sheen, John, *Tyneside Scottish* (Pen & Sword, 1999).
Ternan, Trevor, *The Story of the Tyneside Scottish* (The Northumberland Press, 1919).
Turner, William, *'Accrington Pals'* (Pen & Sword, 1992).
Wheeler-Holohan, Captain A.V. & Wyatt Captain G.M.G., *The Rangers Historical Records From 1859 to the conclusion of the Great War* (Naval & Military Press, 2003).
Whithead, Ralph J, *The Other Side of the Wire, Volume 2* (Helion & Company, 2013).
Wylly, Colonel H.C., *History of the Queen's (Royal West Surrey Regiment) in the Great War* (A.C. Curtis & Co, 1917).
Wyrall, Everard, *The Die Hards in the Great War* (Harrison & Sons Ltd, 1926).
______, *The History of the King's Regiment (Liverpool) 1914 – 1919* (Edward Arnold & Co., 1928).

Index

PLACES

MILITARY UNITS